always up to date

The law changes, but Nolo is always on top of it! We offer several ways to make sure you and your Nolo products are always up to date:

1 **Nolo's Legal Updater**

We'll send you an email whenever a new edition of your book is published! Sign up at **www.nolo.com/legalupdater**.

2 **Updates @ Nolo.com**

Check **www.nolo.com/update** to find recent changes in the law that affect the current edition of your book.

3 **Nolo Customer Service**

To make sure that this edition of the book is the most recent one, call us at **800-728-3555** and ask one of our friendly customer service representatives. Or find out at **www.nolo.com**.

please note

We believe accurate and current legal information should help you solve many of your own legal problems on a cost-efficient basis. But this text is not a substitute for personalized advice from a knowledgeable lawyer. If you want the help of a trained professional, consult an attorney licensed to practice in your state.

3rd edition

Incorporate Your Business

by Attorney Anthony Mancuso

Third Edition	May 2005
Editor	Ilona Bray
Book Design	Susan Putney
Production	Margaret Livingston
Index	Ellen Sherron
Illustrator	Mari Stein
Cover Design	Toni Ihara
Proofreader	Bob Wells
Printing	Delta Printing Solutions, Inc.

Mancuso, Anthony.
  Incorporate your business : a legal guide to forming a corporation in your state / by
Anthony Mancuso.— 3rd ed.
    p. cm.
  Includes index.
  ISBN 1-4133-0185-1 (alk. paper)
   1. Incorporation—United States—Popular works. 2. Corporation law—United
States—Popular works. I. Title.

KF1420.Z9M36 2005
346.73'06622—dc22
                                                           2005040577

For information on bulk purchases or corporate premium sales, please contact the Special Sales department. For academic sales or textbook adoptions, ask for Academic Sales. Call 800-955-4775 or write to Nolo at 950 Parker Street, Berkeley, CA 94710.

Acknowledgments

Thanks to Shae Irving and Jake Warner for editing the first edition of this long-winded book, and to all the Noloids for their help in making this book a reality.

Table of Contents

Introduction

1 Choosing the Right Legal Structure for Your Business

2 How Corporations Work

3 Understanding Corporate Taxes

4 Seven Steps to Incorporation

5 After You Form Your Corporation

6 Lawyers and Accountants

Appendix A   State Sheets

Appendix B   2004 Federal Tax Act Update

Appendix C   How to Use the CD-ROM

Appendix D   Tear-Out Forms

Introduction

The start of the twenty-first century marks an exciting time for small business owners. With the downsizing of many larger, publicly held corporations and the rapid expansion of knowledge in a myriad of areas, small businesses have a key role to play in revitalizing and expanding the U.S. economy and, in the process, redefining the American workplace.

Whether you are beginning a brand-new business, expanding an existing enterprise, or simply planning to create a sideline business to supplement earnings from your salaried job, you need to consider how best to legally organize your undertaking. These days you have a number of choices, including organizing as a sole proprietorship, partnership, limited liability company, or corporation. (We review all these choices in detail in Chapter 1.) There are a few basic reasons why incorporating your business may the best way to go:

- **Limited liability.** One of the corporation's most appealing characteristics is the limited liability protection it provides to all business owners. That is, the owners, like the shareholders of a corporation, are not personally liable for the debts or liabilities of the business—their personal assets, such as homes and cars, are not at risk to satisfy business debts, losses, or legal liabilities, including lawsuits.

- **Corporate income splitting.** A corporation is a separate tax entity from its owners. This means you can use your corporation to shelter business income instead of having to pay individual income taxes on all business profits each year. (For most corporations, the IRS allows you to accumulate up to $250,000 of earnings in the business, no questions asked.) Of course, you have to pay corporate income taxes on money left in the corporation, but because initial corporate tax rates are lower than the individual tax rates most business owners pay, you may reap substantial overall tax savings.

- **Corporate capital incentives.** There is nothing better for attracting and motivating talented employees than sharing a piece of the ownership pie with them. The corporation easily accommodates employee capital participation through its ability to provide stock option, bonus, and purchase plans. Corporations are also the preferred vehicle for raising private and public startup and expansion capital through the sale of stock to investors.

- **Corporate activity structure.** The corporate form has a number of built-in ownership and activity layers—made up of shareholders, directors, and officers—that allow a number of people to sensibly participate in its operations. This built-in division of activity and authority becomes important as the corporation becomes larger and needs to look beyond the founders to find people to help manage and fund the enterprise. The corporate form is designed to allow you to set up and make changes to these activity layers with standard paperwork and procedures—by electing new members to the board, appointing new officers, and issuing stock to new investors.

A. How to Use This Book

This book contains a nuts-and-bolts approach to forming a corporation in each of the 50 states. Appendix A contains information on all 50 states organized by state; we call these packets of information "state sheets." Each state sheet lists the specific state offices you can contact to obtain the latest incorporation forms. We provide both Internet and standard contact information—if you are connected to the Web, it usually takes just a few minutes to get the latest forms and instructions. If a state does not provide a fill-in-the-blanks or sample incorporation form, we provide a form you can use that meets your state's statutory requirements. We also give you additional instructions to help you fill in each state form.

Each state sheet also provides the basic rules for operating your corporation under your state's specific corporate statutes. This information is important because it will help you fill in the bylaws included with this book. (Bylaws are an essential document that allows you to set up the practical rules for operating your corporation under your state's law.) The state sheets also contain state tax and securities law summaries and links to state websites where you can get additional information in these important areas.

Icons Used in This Book

 Tells you when you can skip information that doesn't apply in your situation.

 A caution that you need to slow down and consider potential problems.

 Alerts you to important tips.

 Tells you when we believe you need the advice of an expert—either an attorney or a tax adviser.

 Refers you to additional sources of information about the particular issue or topic discussed in the text.

 Shows you where in the book to turn for more information on a particular issue or topic discussed in the text.

 Points the way to forms and other materials included on the CD-ROM at the back of the book.

If you already know that you want to incorporate your business, you can skip ahead and follow the steps listed in Chapter 4, which explains how to use the state sheet information to prepare and file your Articles of Incorporation, prepare your bylaws, and issue shares of stock to your initial investors. However, if you are unsure whether incorporating is the best way to organize your business and you want to read more about alternative legal structures, start by reading Chapter 1.

Forms on CD-ROM. Included at the back of this book is a CD-ROM that contains the forms shown in Chapter 4. (These forms include Articles of Incorporation for states that do not provide an official form, ready-to-use bylaws, Minutes of First Board Meeting, and other forms.) For details on how to use the CD and install the files, see the instructions in Appendix C.

Another corporate resource from Nolo. This book covers the basics of how to set up your corporation. When you're ready for the next step, Nolo's *The Corporate Minutes Book*, by Anthony Mancuso, shows you how to prepare standard minutes of annual and special director and shareholder meetings for your corporation. It includes more than 80 board and shareholder resolutions to approve the various legal, tax, financial, and business transactions that commonly occur during the life of a small, closely held corporation. Forms are included as tear-outs and on CD-ROM. You can purchase the book in its entirety, or download just the parts you need from Nolo's website at www.nolo.com.

B. Using Professionals to Help You Incorporate

Lawyers may charge up to $2,000 or even more to incorporate your business. To allow you to save money and spend it more usefully elsewhere, this book shows you how to fill in your state's pre-printed incorporation form (or a standard form we provide), prepare corporate bylaws, and issue stock certificates. As you'll see, it's not hard to accomplish these routine tasks, and the investment of your time and energy will be modest.

Although not required by law (except in South Carolina, where a lawyer must sign your Articles of Incorporation), we think it makes sense to ask an attorney to look over your incorporation papers before you file them. This is particularly necessary if you have special questions or needs—for example, if you want to implement a complicated stock structure. And, of course, after reading the introductory tax material in this book, you may have additional questions concerning the tax implications of operating your business as a corporation, which you will want to discuss with a tax adviser. In Chapter 6, we tell you how to locate a good lawyer and tax adviser. ■

Choosing the Right Legal Structure for Your Business

If you know you want to incorporate your business. If you've already considered the different types of business structures available to you, and you are certain that you want to form a corporation, there's no need to read this chapter. Skip ahead to Chapter 2, *How Corporations Work.*

To make sure that forming a corporation is the best legal and tax approach for your business, this chapter compares the corporation to other small business legal structures, such as the sole proprietorship, the partnership, and the popular limited liability company. A corporation, like a limited liability company, protects your personal assets from business creditors. But the corporation stands apart from all other business forms due to its built-in organizational structure and unique access to investment sources and capital markets. It also uniquely answers a need felt by many business owners who are attracted to the formality of the corporate form, a quality not shared by the other business structures.

A. The Different Ways of Doing Business

There are a number of legal structures or legal forms under which a business can operate, including the sole proprietorship, partnership, limited liability company, and corporation. These basic structures have important legal and tax variants. For example, the partnership form has spawned the limited partnership and the registered limited liability partnership—two special types of partnership legal structures. And the corporation can be recognized, for tax purposes, as either a standard C corporation, in which the corporation and its owners are treated as separate taxpaying entities, or as an S corporation, in which business income passes through the corporate entity and is taxed only to its owners on their individual tax returns. Finally, the limited liability company can adopt corporate tax status if it wishes to obtain some of the tax benefits available to the C corporation. We know all of this may sound confusing. Take comfort: These legal and tax differences will become clear as you read through the material below.

Often, business owners start with the simplest, least expensive legal form (the sole proprietorship) then move on to a more complicated business structure as their business grows. Other business-people pick the legal structure they like best from the start, and let their business grow into it. Of course, you are not stuck with the legal entity with which you start out—you can change your legal and tax structure from one form to another during the life of your business whenever it makes sense to do so. In any case, choosing the initial legal structure for your business is one of the most important decisions when starting a business. The analysis we present here, which includes examples of businesses that choose each type of business structure, should help you make a good decision.

1. Sole Proprietorship

A sole proprietorship is the legal name for a one-owner business (spouses can help out in a sole proprietorship, too, as employees, but if they truly co-manage and run the business with their spouse, the business is a partnership). When people think of a "mom and pop" or a home-based business, they are usually thinking of a sole proprietorship. A sole proprietorship has the following general characteristics:

Ease of formation. The sole proprietorship is the easiest business form to establish, in the sense that it requires few formalities to get started. Just hang out your shingle or "Open for Business" sign, and you have established a sole proprietorship. Sure, there are other legal steps you may wish or be required to take—such as registering a fictitious business name if your business won't use your personal name, or registering for a business license or sales tax permit—but these steps are not necessary to legally establish your business.

Personal liability for business debts, liabilities, and taxes. In this simplest form of small business legal structures, the owner, who usually runs the business, is personally liable for its debts, taxes, and other liabilities. This means that personal assets—for example, cash in a bank account, equity in a home or car, or a personal stock portfolio—can be used to satisfy a court judgment entered against the business. Also, if the owner hires employees, the owner is personally responsible for legal claims—for example, an auto accident—made against these employees acting within the course and scope of their employment.

Simple tax treatment. All business profits and losses are reported on the personal income tax return of the owner each year (Schedule C, *Profit or Loss From Business*, filed with the owner's 1040 federal income tax return). And this remains true even if a portion of this money is invested back in the business—that is, even if the owner doesn't "pocket" business profits for personal use.

A corporate comparison. Earnings retained in a corporation are not taxed on the owner's individual income tax return. Instead, this money is taxed at separate corporate income tax rates. Since the corporate tax rates are sometimes lower than individual income tax rates, business owners who leave earnings in their business often save tax dollars by incorporating. We discuss this feature of corporations—called "income splitting"—in Section 4, below.

Legal life same as owner's. On the death of its owner, a sole proprietorship simply ends. The assets of the business normally pass under the terms of the deceased owner's will or trust, or by intestate succession (under the state's inheritance statutes) if there is no formal estate plan.

Don't let business assets get stuck in probate. Probate—the court process necessary to "prove" a will and distribute property—can take up to one year or more. In the meantime, it may be difficult for the inheritors to operate or sell the business or its assets. Often, the best way to avoid having a probate court involved in business operations is for the owners to transfer the assets of the business into a living trust during their lifetimes; this permits business assets to be transferred to inheritors promptly on the death of the business owner, free of probate. For detailed information on estate planning, including whether or not it makes sense to create a living trust, see *Plan Your Estate*, by Denis Clifford and Cora Jordan (Nolo), or Nolo's

Quicken WillMaker Plus 2005, software that allows you to prepare your own living trust.

Sole proprietorships in action. Many one-owner or spouse-owned businesses start small, with very little advance planning or procedural red tape. Celia Wong is a good example. Celia is a graphics artist with a full-time salaried job for a local book publishing company. In her spare time she takes on extra work using her home computer to produce audiocassette and CD jacket cover art for musicians. These jobs are usually commissioned on a handshake or over the phone. Without thinking much about it, Celia has started her own sole proprietorship business. Celia should include a Schedule C in her yearly federal 1040 individual tax return, showing the net profits (profits minus expenses) or losses of her sole proprietorship. Celia is responsible for paying income taxes on profits, plus self-employment (Social Security) taxes based on her sole proprietorship income. (IRS Form SE is used to compute self-employment taxes and is attached to her 1040 income tax return.) If Celia has any business debts (she usually owes on a charge account at a local art supply house), or a disgruntled client successfully sues her in small claims court if she fails to complete a job she has been paid for, Celia is personally liable for this money. In other words, she can't simply fold up Wong Designs and walk away from her debts, claiming that they were the legal responsibility of her business only.

Put some profits aside to buy business insurance. Once Celia begins to make enough money, she should consider taking out a commercial business insurance policy to cover legal claims against her business. While off-the-shelf insurance normally won't protect her from her own business mistakes—for example, failure to perform work properly or on time or to pay bills—it can cover many risks, including slip-and-fall lawsuits and damage to her or a client's property, as well as fire, theft, and other casualties that might occur in her home-based business.

Running her business as a sole proprietorship serves Celia's needs for the present. Assuming her small business succeeds, she will want to put it on a more formal footing by establishing a separate business checking account, possibly coming up with a fancier name and filing a fictitious business name statement with the county clerk, and, if she hires employees, obtaining a federal employer identification number (EIN) from the IRS. At some point, Celia may also feel ready to renovate her house to separate her office space from her living quarters. Besides the convenience this might offer, it can also help to convince the IRS that the portion of the mortgage or rent paid for the office is deductible as a business expense on her Schedule C.

Celia can quit her day job, expand her business, and still appropriately keep her sole proprietorship legal status. Unless her business grows significantly or she takes on work that puts her at a much higher risk of being sued—and therefore being held personally liable for business debts—it makes sense for her to continue to operate her business as a sole proprietorship.

More information about starting and running a sole proprietorship. A great source of practical information on how to start and operate a small sole proprietorship is *The Small Business Start-Up Kit*, by Peri H. Pakroo (Nolo). Also, see *Tax Savvy for Small Business*, by Frederick W. Daily (Nolo), a small business owner's guide to taxes that includes a full discussion of setting up a home-based business and deducting its expenses.

2. Partnership

A partnership is simply an enterprise in which two or more co-owners agree to share the profits. No written partnership agreement is necessary, though it's a good idea to make one. If two people go into business together, they automatically establish a "general partnership" under state law unless they incorporate, form a limited liability company, or file special paperwork with the state to establish a special type of partnership such as a limited partnership. (See "Limited Partnerships," below, for more on special partnerships.) A general partnership, simply stated, is one where each of the partnership owners is legally entitled to manage the partnership business.

General partnerships are governed by each state's partnership law. But since all states have adopted a version of the Uniform Partnership Act, general partnership laws are very similar throughout the United States. Mostly, these laws contain basic rules that provide for a division of profits and losses among partners and set out the partners' legal relationship with one another. These rules are not mandatory in most cases. You can (and should) spell out your own rules for dividing profits and losses and operating your partnership in a written partnership agreement. If you don't prepare your own partnership agreement, all provisions of state partnership law apply to your partnership.

A general partnership has the following characteristics:

Each partner has personal liability. Like the owner of a sole proprietorship, each partner is personally liable for the debts and taxes of the partnership. In other words, if the partnership assets and insurance are insufficient to satisfy a creditor's claim or legal judgment, the partners' personal assets are subject to attachment and liquidation to pay the debt.

The act or signature of each partner can bind the partnership. Each partner is an agent for the partnership and can individually hire employees, borrow money, sign contracts, and perform any act necessary to the operation of the business in which the partnership engages. All partners are personally liable for these debts and obligations. This rule makes it essential that the partners trust each other to act in the best interests of the partnership and each of the other partners.

Partners report and pay individual income taxes on profits. A partnership files a yearly IRS Form 1065—called *U.S. Partnership Return of Income*—that includes a schedule showing the allocation of profits, losses, and other tax items to all partners (Schedule K-1). The partnership must mail individual schedules (Schedule K-1s) to each partner at the end of each year, showing the items of income, loss, credits, and deductions allocated to each partner. When partners files an individual income tax return, the partners report their allocated share of partnership profits (taken from the partner's Schedule K-1) and pay individual income taxes on these profits. As with the sole proprietorship, partners are taxed on business profits even if the profits are plowed back into the business, unless the partners elect to have the partnership taxed as a corporation. In that case, the corporate entity is taxed separately. (See "Partnership Can Choose to Be Taxed Like Corporations," below.)

Partnerships Can Choose to Be Taxed Like Corporations

Unlike regular partnerships, where profits pass through the business and are taxed to the individual owners, corporations are taxed as separate entities. (This is explained in detail in Section 4, below.) If they choose, partners can elect to change the normal pass-through taxation their partnership receives and to have the IRS tax the business like a corporation. Specifically, the "check-the-box" federal tax rules, also followed in most states, let partnerships (and LLCs) elect to be treated as corporate tax entities by filing IRS Form 8832, *Entity Classification Election*. This election means that partnership income will be taxed at the entity level at corporate tax rates, and the partners pay individual income tax only on profits actually paid out to them (in the form of salaries, bonuses, and direct payouts of profits).

Most smaller partnerships will not wish to make this election, preferring instead to have profits divided among the partners and then taxed on their individual tax returns.

But this is not always true. For example, some partnerships—especially those that want to reinvest profits in expanding the business—may prefer to keep profits in the business and have them taxed to the business at the lower initial corporate tax rates. (For a discussion of corporate tax income splitting, see Section 4, below.) Your tax adviser can tell you if this tax strategy makes sense if you consider forming a partnership or LLC. We believe that any partnership seriously considering making a corporate tax election should also consider converting to a corporation (instead of filing a corporate tax election for the partnership) to get the additional capital benefits that a corporation provides. (See Section 4, below.)

Partnership dissolves when a partner leaves. Legally, when a partner ceases to be involved with the business of the partnership (when the partner withdraws or dies), the partnership is automatically dissolved as a legal entity. However, a properly written partnership agreement provides for these eventualities and allows the partnership to continue by permitting the remaining partners to buy out the interest of the departing or deceased partner (see "Why You Need a Written Partnership Agreement," below). Of course, if one person in a two-partner business leaves or dies, the partnership must end—you need at least two people to have a partnership.

Why You Need a Written Partnership Agreement

Although it's possible to start a partnership with a verbal agreement—or even with no stated agreement at all—there are drawbacks to taking this casual approach. The most obvious problem is that a verbal agreement may be remembered and interpreted differently by different partners. (And of course, having no stated agreement at all almost always means trouble.) Also, if you don't write out how you want to operate your partnership, you lose a great deal of flexibility. Instead of being able to make your own rules in a number of key areas—for example, how partnership profits and losses are divided among the partners—the lack of a written agreement means that, by default, state partnership law will come into play. These state-based rules may not be to your liking—for example, state law generally calls for an equal division of profits and losses, regardless of partners' capital contributions.

Another reason why it is usually a bad idea to do business without a written partnership agreement comes up when a partner wants to leave the business. Here are just a few of the difficult questions that can arise:

- If the remaining partners want to buy out the departing partner, how will the partner's ownership interest be valued?
- Assuming you agree on how much the departing partner's interest is worth, how will the departing partner be paid for that interest—in a lump sum, or in installments? If payment will be made in installments, how big will the down payment be, how many years will it take to pay the balance, and how much interest will be charged?
- What happens if none of the remaining partners wants to buy the departing partner's interest? Will your partnership dissolve? If so, can some of the partners form a new partnership to continue the partnership business? Who gets to use the dissolved partnership's name and client or customer list?

Partnership law, which is written in generalities, does not provide context-specific answers to these questions, meaning that in the absence of a written partnership agreement, you may face a long legal battle with a partner who decides to call it quits.

To avoid these and other problems, a basic partnership agreement should, at a minimum, spell out:

- each partner's interest in the partnership
- how profits and losses will be split up between or among the partners
- how any buyout or transfer of a partner's interest will be valued and handled, and
- how the former partners can continue the partnership's business if they want to.

A partnership resource. For a thorough look at the legal and tax characteristics of partnerships, and for a clause-by-clause approach to preparing a partnership agreement, see *The Partnership Book*, by Denis Clifford and Ralph Warner (Nolo).

Partnerships in action. George and Tamatha are good friends who have been working together in a rented warehouse space where they share a kiln used to make blown glass pieces. They recently collaborated on the design and production of a batch of hand-blown halogen light fixtures, which immediately become popular with local lighting vendors. Believing that they can streamline the production of these custom pieces, they plan to solicit and fill larger orders with retailers, and look into wholesale distribution. They shake hands on their new venture, which they name Halo Light Sculptures. Although they obtain a business license and file a fictitious name statement with the county clerk showing that they are working together as Halo Light Sculptures, they don't bother to write up a partnership agreement. Their only agreement is a verbal one to equally share in the work of making the glass pieces, splitting expenses and any profits that result.

This type of informal arrangement can sometimes be justified in the early exploratory days of a co-owned business where the owners, like George and Tamatha, have yet to decide whether to commit to the venture. However, for the reasons mentioned earlier, from the moment the business looks like it has long-term potential, the partners should prepare and sign a written partnership agreement. Furthermore, if either partner is worried about personal liability for business debts or the possibility of lawsuits by purchasers of the fixtures, then forming a limited liability company (LLC) or a corporation probably would be a better business choice.

Limited Partnerships

Most smaller partnerships are general partnerships, meaning that all owners agree to manage the partnership together, and each partner is personally liable for debts of the partnership. However, there are two other fairly common types of partnerships: limited partnerships and registered limited liability partnerships (RLLPs). Each of these is quite different from a general partnership.

The limited partnership. Owners use the limited partnership structure when one or more of the partners are passive investors (the "limited partners") and another partner runs the partnership (the "general partner"). You must file a Certificate of Limited Partnership with the secretary of state (or a similar state filing office) to form a limited partnership, and pay a filing fee. The advantage of a limited partnership is that, unlike a general partnership, where all partners are personally liable for business debts and liabilities, a limited partner is allowed to invest in a partnership without the risk of incurring personal liability. If the business fails, all that the limited partner can lose is a capital investment—that is, the amount of money or the property that partner paid for an interest in the business. However, in exchange for this big advantage, the limited partner normally is not allowed to participate in the management or control of the partnership. If the partner does, the partner can lose limited liability status and can be held personally liable for partnership debts, claims, and other obligations. This disadvantage has caused many business owners who might form a limited partnership to turn to the limited liability company (LLC). LLCs offer pass-through tax status, limited liability protection, *and* the ability to participate fully in the management of the business. We discuss LLCs in Section 3, just below.

Typically, a limited partnership has a number of limited partner investors and at least one general partner who is responsible for partnership management and is personally liable for its debts and other liabilities.

The registered limited liability partnership. The registered limited liability partnership (RLLP) is a special legal structure allowed in most states that is designed specifically for professionals (attorneys, accountants, architects, engineers, and other specially licensed businesspeople). An RLLP is formed by filing a Registration of Limited Liability Partnership form with the secretary of state (or other state agency that handles business filings). The point of an RLLP is to relieve professional partners from personal liability for claims against another partner for professional malpractice. However, professionals in an RLLP remain personally liable for their own professional malpractice.

Example: Martha and Veronica operate a two-person accounting partnership, registered as an RLLP. Each has her own clients. If Martha loses a malpractice lawsuit, and Veronica did not participate in providing services to the client who won the suit, Veronica should not be held personally liable for the judgment. If partnership insurance and assets are not sufficient to pay the judgment, Martha's personal assets, but not Veronica's, are subject to seizure to pay the money due. In a general partnership practice not registered as an RLLP, both Martha and Veronica could be held personally liable for either CPA's individual malpractice.

For more LP and RLLP information. To determine the forms and procedures necessary to set up a limited partnership or RLLP in your state, go to your state's business filing office website. We list the Web address of your state's business filing office in the "Corporate Filing Office" section of your state sheet, contained in Appendix A.

3. The Limited Liability Company (LLC)

The limited liability company (LLC) is the new kid on the block of business organizations. It has become popular with many small business owners, in part because it was custom-designed by state legislatures to overcome particular limitations of each of the other business forms, including, in some contexts, the corporation. Essentially, the LLC is a business ownership structure that allows owners to pay business taxes on their individual income tax returns like partners (or, for a one-person LLC, like a sole proprietorship), but that also gives the owners the legal protection of personal limited liability for business debts and judgments as if they had formed a corporation. Or, put another way, with an LLC you simultaneously achieve the twin goals of pass-through taxation of business profits and limited personal liability for business debts.

Here is a look at the most important LLC characteristics:

Limited liability. Under each state's LLC laws, the owners of an LLC are not personally liable for its debts and other liabilities. This personal legal liability protection is the same as that offered to shareholders of a corporation.

Pass-through taxation. Federal and state tax laws treat an LLC like a partnership—or, for a one-owner LLC, as a sole proprietorship. Again, this means that LLC income, loss, credits, and deductions are reported on the individual income tax returns of the LLC owners. The LLC entity itself does not pay income tax. However, as with partnerships, there are "check-the-box" tax rules that let LLCs elect corporate tax treatment if its owners wish to leave income in the business and have it taxed at separate corporate income tax rates. We explain how corporate tax treatment works in Chapter 3.

Finding your state's LLC tax rules. Some states impose an annual fee or tax on LLCs, in addition to individual income tax that owners pay on the LLC profits allocated to them each year. To find out whether your state imposes an LLC tax, go to your state's tax department website. We list the Web address of your state's tax office in the "State Tax Information" section of your state sheets, contained in Appendix A.

Because a co-owned LLC is taxed as a partnership, it files standard partnership tax returns (IRS Form 1065 and Schedules K-1) with the IRS and state, and the LLC owners pay taxes on their share of LLC profits on their individual income tax returns. (Each owner gets a Schedule K-1 from the LLC, which shows the owner's share of LLC profits and deductions. The owner attaches the K-1 to the owner's individual income tax return.) A sole-owned LLC is treated as a sole proprietorship for tax purposes. The owner includes profits or losses from LLC operations, as well as deductions and credits allowable to the business, on a Schedule C included with the owners' individual income tax returns. (In essence, for a sole LLC owner, the Schedule C works much like the K-1 schedule filed by the owners of a co-owned LLC.)

If a sole-owner or multiowner LLC elects corporate tax treatment, the LLC is treated and taxed as a corporation, not as a sole proprietorship or partnership. The LLC files corporate income tax returns, reporting and paying corporate income tax on any profits retained in the LLC. The LLC members report and pay individual income tax only on salaries paid to them or distributions of LLC profits or losses. However, as is true for partnerships, LLCs that may benefit from electing corporate tax treatment normally decide to go ahead and incorporate. By doing so, they get corporate tax treatment plus the other advantages the corporation provides, such as access to capital, capital sharing with employees, tax-deductible employee fringe benefits, and built-in management formalities. To learn more, see Section 4.

Ownership requirements. All states allow an LLC to be formed by one or more people. LLC members need not be residents of the state where they form their LLC, or even of the United States, for that matter, and other business entities, such as a corporation or another LLC, can be LLC owners.

Management flexibility. LLCs are normally managed by all the owners (also called members)—this is known as "member-management." But state law also allows for management by one or more specially appointed managers, who may be members or nonmembers. Not surprisingly (but somewhat awkwardly), this arrangement is known as "manager-management." In other words, an LLC can appoint one or more of its members, or one of its CEOs or even a person contracted from outside the LLC, to manage its affairs. This manager setup is somewhat atypical and normally only makes sense if one person wishes to assume full-time control of the LLC, with the other owners acting as "passive" investors in the enterprise.

Formation requirements. Like a corporation, an LLC requires paperwork to get going. You must file Articles of Organization with the state business filing office. And if the LLC is to maintain a business presence in another state, such as a branch office, you must also file registration or qualification papers with the other state's business filing office. LLC formation fees vary, but most are comparable to the fee each state charges for incorporation.

Like a partnership, an LLC should prepare an operating agreement to spell out how the LLC will be owned, how profits and losses will be divided, how departing or deceased members will be bought out, and other essential ownership details. If you don't prepare an operating agreement, the default provisions of the state's LLC Act will apply to the operation of your LLC. Since LLC owners will want to control exactly how profits and losses are apportioned among the members as well as other essential LLC operating rules, they need an LLC operating agreement.

For more information about LLCs. See Nolo's *LLC or Corporation?*, by Anthony Mancuso, for a comprehensive comparison of the legal and tax rules that apply to LLCs and corporations and to help you decide which form is best for your business. See *Form Your Own Limited Liability Company*, by Anthony Mancuso (Nolo), for instructions on how to form an LLC in each state, how to prepare an operating agreement, and how to handle all other LLC for-

mation requirements. If you prefer software, see *LLC Maker*, a Nolo Windows program, to learn about and form an LLC in any state. You can also learn more about LLC formation procedures and fees for your state by visiting your state's business filing office website. We list the Web address of your state's business filing office in the "Corporate Filing Office" section of your state sheets, contained in Appendix A.

LLCs in action. Barry and Sam jointly own and run a flower shop, Aunt Jessica's Floral Arrangements, which specializes in unique flower arrangements. (The name stems from the fact that Barry used to work for his Aunt Jessica, who taught him the ropes of floral design.) Lately, business has been particularly rosy, and the two men plan to sign a long-term contract with a flower importer to supply them with larger quantities of seasonal flowers. Once they receive the additional flowers, they will be able to create more floral pieces and wholesale them to a wider market. Both men are sensitive to the fact that they will encounter more risks as their business grows. Accordingly, they decide to protect their personal assets from business risks by converting their partnership to an LLC. They could accomplish the same result by incorporating, but they prefer the simplicity of paying taxes on their business income on their individual income tax returns—rather than splitting business income between themselves and their corporation and filing both corporate and individual income tax returns. They also realize that if they begin making more money than each needs to take home, they can convert their LLC to a corporation later to obtain lower corporate income tax rates on earnings kept in the business or, as an alternative, make an IRS election to have their LLC taxed as a corporation without having to change its legal structure at all.

4. The Corporation

A corporation is a statutory creature, created and regulated by state law. In short, if you want the "privilege"—that's what the courts call it—of turning your business enterprise into a corporation, you must follow the requirements of your state's Business Corporation Law or Business Corporation Act (BCA). What sets the corporation apart, in a theoretical sense, from all other types of businesses is that it is a legal and tax entity separate from any of the people who own, control, manage, or operate it. The state corporation and federal and state tax laws view the corporation as a legal "person." This means the corporation is capable of entering into contracts, incurring debts, and paying taxes separately from its owners.

a. Advantages of Incorporating

Let's start by looking at the advantages that flow from this separate entity treatment of the corporation. The first and foremost is built-in legal limited liability protection.

1. Limited Personal Liability

Like the owners of an LLC or the limited partners in a limited partnership, the owners (shareholders) of a corporation are not personally liable for business debts, claims, or other liabilities. Put another way, this means that people who invest in a corporation—shareholders—normally stand to lose only the amount of money or the value of the property that they have paid for its stock. As a result, if the corporation does not succeed and cannot pay its debts or other financial obligations, creditors cannot seize or sell the corporate investor's home, car, or other personal assets.

> **Example:** Rackafrax Dry Cleaners, Inc., a corporation, has several bad years in a row. When it finally files for bankruptcy it owes $50,000 to a number of suppliers and $80,000 as a result of a lawsuit for uninsured losses stemming from a fire. Stock in Rackafrax is owned by Harry Rack, Edith Frax, and John Quincy Taft. Fortunately, the personal assets of these people cannot be taken to pay the money Rackafrax owes.

Beware of Exceptions to the Rule of Limited Personal Liability

In some unusual situations, corporate directors, officers, and shareholders can be held responsible for paying money owed by their corporation. Here are a few of the most common exceptions to the rule of limited personal liability; these exceptions also apply to other limited liability business structures, such as the LLC.

Personal guarantees. Often when a bank or other lender lends money to a small corporation, particularly a newly formed one, it requires the principal corporate owners (shareholders) to agree to repay the loan from their personal assets if the corporation defaults. In some instances, shareholders may even have to pledge equity in a house or other personal assets as security for repayment of the debt.

Federal and state taxes. If a corporation fails to pay income, payroll, or other taxes, the IRS and the state tax agency are likely to attempt to recover the unpaid taxes from "responsible persons"— a category that often includes the principal directors, officers, and shareholders of a small corporation. The IRS and state sometimes succeed in these tax collection strategies. Therefore, paying taxes should be a top priority for all businesses.

Unlawful or unauthorized transactions. If you use the corporation as a means to defraud people, or if you intentionally make a reckless decision that results in physical harm to others or their property— for example, you fail to maintain premises or a worksite properly when you've been warned of the probability of imminent danger to others, or you deliberately manufacture unsafe products—a court may hold you individually liable for the monetary losses of the people you harm. Lawyers call this "piercing the corporate veil," meaning that the corporate entity is disregarded and the owners are treated just like the owners of an unincorporated business.

Fortunately, most of these problem areas can be avoided by following a few commonsense rules— rules you'll probably follow anyway:

- Don't do anything dishonest or illegal.
- Make sure your corporation does the same, by getting necessary permits, licenses, or clearances for its business operations.
- Pay employee wages, and withhold and pay corporate income and payroll taxes on time.
- Try not to become personally obligated for corporate debts unless you decide that the need for corporate funds is worth the personal risk.

2. Advantages of Corporate Tax Treatment

Unlike other business forms, a corporation is a separate tax entity, distinct from its owners. This means that the company itself is taxed on all profits that it cannot deduct as business expenses. This separate-entity tax treatment brings certain benefits to a corporation—for example, it permits income splitting between the corporation and its owners, and also allows the owners to be classified as "employees" of their own business, making them eligible to receive tax-deductible employee fringe benefits. (Employee benefits are introduced in Subsection 5, below.)

Income splitting. Because a corporation is a separate taxpayer, it has its own income tax rates and files its own tax returns, separate from the tax rates and tax returns of its owners. This double layer of taxation allows corporate profits to be kept in the business and taxed at corporate tax rates, which can be lower than those of the corporation's owners. (See Chapter 3, Section A, for tables setting out corporate and individual tax rates.) Such income splitting between the corporation and its owners can result in an overall tax savings for the owners, compared to the pass-through taxation that is standard for sole proprietorships, partnerships, and LLCs.

Example: Jeff and Sally own and work for their own two-person corporation, Hair Looms, Inc., a mail-order wig supply business that is starting to enjoy popularity with overseas purchasers. To keep pace with sprouting orders, they need to expand by investing a portion of their profits in the business. Since Hair Looms is incorporated, only the portion of the profits paid to Jeff and Sally as salary is reported and taxed to them on their individual tax returns—let's assume, at the top individual income tax rate of 35%. By contrast, the first $50,000 in profits left in the business for expansion is reported on Hair Looms's corporate income tax return and is taxed at the lowest corporate tax rate of only 15%, and the next $25,000 at 25%. Above $75,000, corporate income is taxed at 34% and higher.

LLCs and partnerships can elect corporate tax treatment. Income splitting is no longer a unique aspect of corporate life. As mentioned earlier in this chapter, partnerships and LLCs can elect to be taxed as corporations if they wish to keep money in the business to be taxed at corporate rates. (See the sidebar in Section A2, above.) However, partnerships and LLCs that can benefit from doing this normally decide to incorporate instead of electing corporate tax status for their unincorporated business. By changing to a corporate legal entity, they get corporate income tax splitting plus the other advantages the corporation provides, such as access to capital, capital sharing with employees, tax-deductible employee fringe benefits, and built-in management formalities. See below for more on these advantages.

How Small Corporations Avoid Double Taxation of Corporate Profits

What about the old bugaboo of corporate double taxation? Most people have heard that corporate income is taxed twice: once at the corporate level and again when it is paid out to shareholders in the form of dividends. In theory, the Internal Revenue Code says that most corporations are treated this way (except S corporations, whose profits automatically pass to shareholders each year; see below). In practice, however, double taxation seldom occurs in the context of the small business corporation. The reason is simple: Employee-owners don't pay themselves dividends. Instead, the shareholders, who usually work for their corporation, pay themselves salaries and bonuses, which are deducted from the profits of the corporate business as ordinary and necessary business expenses. The result is that profits paid out in salary and other forms of employee compensation to the owner-employees of a small corporation are taxed only once, at the individual level. In other words, as long as you work for your corporation, even in a part-time or consulting capacity, you can pay out business profits to yourself as reasonable compensation, and you avoid having your corporation pay taxes on these profits.

S corporation tax election. Just as partnerships and LLCs have the ability to elect corporate tax treatment, corporations can choose the type of pass-through taxation of business profits that normally applies to partnerships and LLCs. (But there are some technical differences that lend an advantage to partnerships and LLCs. See "A Comparison of LLC, Partnership, and S Corporation Tax Treatment," below.) You can do this by making an S corporation tax election with the IRS and your state tax authority.

If your corporation files an S corporation tax election, all profits, losses, credits, and deductions pass through to the shareholders, who report these items on their individual tax returns. Each S corporation shareholder is allocated a portion of profits and losses of the corporation according to that person's percentage of stock ownership in the corporation. For example, a 50% shareholder reports and pays individual income taxes on 50% of the corporation's annual profits. Note that these profits are allocated to the shareholders whether the profits are actually paid to them or kept in the corporation.

A Comparison of LLC, Partnership, and S Corporation Tax Treatment

You should know that S corporation tax status, though similar to the pass-through tax treatment given to LLC and partnership owners, is not quite as good. Specifically, LLC owners and partners are not required to allocate profits in proportion to ownership interests in the business. They can make what are known as "special allocations" of profits and losses under the federal tax code, but S corporation shareholders can't do this. Also, the amount of losses that can be passed through to an S corporation shareholder is limited to the total of the shareholder's "basis" in his stock (that is, the amount paid for stock plus and minus adjustments during the life of the corporation—plus amounts loaned personally by the shareholder to the corporation). Losses allocated to a shareholder that exceed these limits can be carried forward and deducted in future tax years if the shareholder qualifies to deduct the losses at that later time.

In contrast, LLC owners and partners may be able to personally deduct more business losses on their tax returns in a given year. The reason is that LLC members and partners get to count their pro rata share of all money borrowed by the business, not just loans personally made by the member or partner, when computing how much of any loss allocated to the member by the business can be deducted in a given year on an individual income tax return.

Given these differences, you might think that the owners of a regular corporation who wish to receive pass-through taxation of business income should dissolve the corporation and form an LLC or partnership, rather than electing S corporation tax treatment. But this is normally not the case. This type of conversion (from a corporation to an LLC or partnership) is expensive in terms of taxes and legal fees. In other words, it's normally best for an existing corporation to elect S corporation tax status if it wants pass-through tax treatment, even if the S corporation election does not provide full pass-through tax benefits. This is a complex tax issue; you should check with an expert tax adviser if you are considering S corporation status.

S corporation status can reduce self-employment taxes. There is one area where S corporations currently do better than LLCs or partnerships: self-employment taxes. Although the current federal tax rules are not specifically written for LLCs, tax experts generally advise their clients that LLC managing owners and managing partners must pay self-employment taxes on their share of business profits. The self-employment tax bite can be hefty: over 15% of taxable income. However, the owners of an S corporation pay self-employment taxes only on compensation (salaries and bonuses) paid to them, not on profits automatically allocated to them as a shareholder. To take advantage of this benefit, some corporate owners elect S corporation tax treatment, then pay themselves a low salary—this means that remaining S corporation profits (which are automatically allocated to the shareholders) are not subject to self-employment tax. This is an aggressive tax strategy, and the IRS may challenge S corporation owners who lower their salaries below a reasonable level simply to avoid self-employment taxes. Again, ask your tax adviser for guidance.

Why would a corporation want to elect S corporation status, given that the separate taxability of the corporation (which the S corporation eliminates) is normally a primary advantage of the corporation? The answer is that there may be times during the life of a corporation where pass-through taxation makes sense, for tax or other reasons. One example occurs when the incorporators expect start-up losses. In a regular corporation, these losses are normally locked into the business; they can be used only to offset future corporate profits. But if an S tax election is made, the losses may qualify to be used to offset other individual income earned by the owners from business activity outside the corporation—for example, salaried income they receive from another business.

As another example, if corporate shareholders who do not work in the business decide it's time for them to receive their share of corporate profits, but the corporation doesn't want to pay out nondeductible dividends, an S corporation election can be made to automatically allocate profits to shareholders—the S corporation itself pays no income tax on the passed-through allocated profits.

When Forming an S Corporation Doesn't Make Sense

S corporation tax status should be something you use only at particular times during the life of your corporation, rather than your corporation's permanent tax status. In other words, if you really want pass-through tax treatment throughout the life of your business (and you haven't yet formed your corporation), don't incorporate. Instead, form an LLC. You'll get pass-through taxation plus limited liability protection, just like an S corp—in fact, the pass-through benefits of an LLC are even better. (See "A Comparison of LLC, Partnership, and S Corporation Tax Treatment," above.)

A corporation must meet certain requirements to qualify for S corporation status. It must have 100 or fewer individual (not entity) shareholders who are U.S. citizens or residents (see Appendix B, Section 2C), and it must have only one class of stock. The shares may have different voting rights, but otherwise all corporate shares must have the same rights and restrictions. You can revoke an S corporation election to go back to regular C corporation tax treatment, but then you cannot reelect S corporation status for another five years. After you make an S corporation election with the IRS, you can make the election with your state tax agency as well. (Many states automatically recognize your federal S corporation election once it is filed.)

3.   Built-In Organizational Structure

A unique benefit of forming a corporation is the ability to separate management, executive decision making, and ownership into distinct areas of corporate activity. This separation is achieved automatically because of the unique legal roles that reside in the corporate form: the roles of directors (managers), officers (executives), and shareholders (owners). Unlike partnerships and LLCs, the corporate structure comes ready-made with a built-in separation of these three activity levels, each with its own legal authority, rules, and ability to share in corporate income and profits. To understand how this works, consider a couple of examples.

Example 1: Myra, Danielle, and Rocco form their own three-person corporation, Skate City, Incorporated, a skate and bike shop. Storefront access to a heavily used rollerblade, skating, and bike path makes it popular with local rollerbladers and cyclists. Needing more cash, the three approach relatives for investment capital. Rocco's brother, Tony, and Danielle's sister, Collette, chip in $30,000 each in return for shares in the business. Myra's Aunt Kate lends the corporation $50,000 in return for an interest-only promissory note, with the principal amount to be repaid at the end of five years.

Here's how the management, executive, and financial structure of this corporation breaks down:

Board of directors. The board manages the corporation, meeting once each quarter to analyze and project financial performance and to review store operations. The board consists of the three founders, Myra, Danielle, and Rocco, and one of the other three investors. Under the terms of Skate City's bylaws, the investor board position is a one-year rotating seat. This year Tony has the investor board seat, next year it goes to Collette, the third year to Aunt Kate—then the pattern repeats. Note that directors have one vote apiece, regardless of share ownership; this is a common approach for small corporations and one that is legally established in Skate City's bylaws. This means the founders can always get together to outvote the investor vote on the board, but it also makes sure that each of the investors periodically gets to hear board discussions and have a say on major management decisions.

Executive team. The officers of the corporation are charged with overseeing day-to-day business; supervising employees; keeping track of ordering, inventory, and sales activities; and generally putting into practice the goals set by the board. The officers are Myra (president) and Danielle (vice president). Rocco fills the remaining officer positions of secretary and treasurer of the corporation, but this is a part-time administrative task only. Rocco's real vocation—or avocation—is blading along the beach and training to be a professional, touring rollerblader with his own corporate sponsor (maybe Skate City if profits continue to roll in).

Participation in profits. Corporate profits, of course, are used to pay salaries, stock inventory, pay rent on the storefront, and pay all the other usual and customary expenses of doing business. The two full-time executives, Myra and Danielle, get a corporate salary, plus a year-end bonus when profits are good. Rocco gets a small stipend (hourly pay) for his part-time work. Otherwise, he and the investor shareholders are simply sitting on their shares. Skate City is not in a position yet to pay dividends—all excess profits of the corporation are used to expand the store's product lines and add a new service facility at the back of the store. Even if dividends are never paid, the shareholders know that their stock will be worth a good deal if the business is successful. They can cash in their shares when the business sells or when they decide to sell their shares back to the corporation—or, who knows, if Skate City goes public someday. Aunt Kate, the most conservative of the investment group, will look to ongoing interest payments as her share in corporate profits, getting her capital back when the principal amount of her loan is due.

As you can see from this example, the mechanisms used to put this custom-tailored management, executive, and investment structure into place are built into the Skate City corporation. To erect it, all that is needed is to fill in a few blanks on standard incorporation forms, including stock certificates, and prepare a standard promissory note. To duplicate this structure as a partnership or LLC would require a specially drafted partnership or LLC operating agreement with custom language and plenty of review by the founders and investment group—and, no doubt, their lawyers. The corporate form is designed to handle this division of management, day-to-day responsibilities, and investment with little or no extra time, trouble, or expense.

There is a potential downside to this division of corporate positions and participation in profits. Some businesspeople—particularly those who run a business by themselves or who prefer to run a co-owned business informally—feel that the extra activity levels of corporate operation and paperwork are a nuisance. That's why incorporating may be a bit of an overload for small startup companies. These may be better and more comfortably served by the less formal business structures of the sole proprietorship or partnership, or, if limited legal liability is an overriding concern, by the LLC legal structure.

Example 2: Leila runs a lunch counter business that provides her both a decent income and an escape from the cubicled office environment in which she was once unhappily ensconced. Business has been slow, but Leila has a new idea to give the business more appeal, as well as make it more fun for her. She changes the decor to reflect a tropical motif, installs a saltwater aquarium facing the lunch counter, adds coral reef (metal halide) lighting and light-reflective wall paneling, and renames the business The Tide Pool. The standard lunch counter fare is augmented with a special bouillabaisse soup entrée and a selection of organic salads and fruit juice drinks, and a seafood and sushi dinner menu is added to cater to the after-work crowd. Leila has her hands full, doing most of the remodeling work herself and preparing the expanded menu each day.

The new operation enjoys great success, and a major newspaper favorably reviews The Tide Pool in an article on trendy eating spots. Patronage increases, so Leila hires a cook and adds three waiters to help her.

A local entrepreneur, Sally, who represents an investment group, asks Leila if she would be interested in franchising other Tide Pools throughout the country. Sally says the investment group would help develop a franchise plan, plus fund the new operation. Leila would be asked to travel to help set up franchise operations for the first year, and she would receive a managerial role and a stake in the new venture.

Leila likes the idea. True, she'll have to get back into the work-a-day world, but on her own terms, and as a consultant and business owner. Besides, she's not feeling comfortable running the business side of The Tide Pool by herself, and it would be a relief to have the new venture take over. The investment group wants a managerial role in the franchise operation, plus a comprehensive set of financial controls. Leila and the investment group agree to incorporate the new venture as Tide Pool Franchising, Inc. The corporate business structure is a good fit. Leila will assume a managerial role as director of the new company, along with Sally and a member of the venture capital firm. The new firm hires two seasoned small business owners, one as president and one as treasurer, to run the new franchise operation. Business begins with the original Tide Pool as the first franchise, and Leila gets started working for a good salary, plus commission, setting up other franchise locations.

If the new venture makes a go of it, Leila and the investment group can either sell their shares back to the corporation at a healthy profit, or, if growth is substantial and consistent, take the company public in a few years. They will sell their stock in the corporation at a sizable profit, once a market has been established for the corporation's publicly held shares.

This example highlights the flexibility of the corporate form and its ability to provide an infrastructure to handle changes in corporate management and ownership. When you want to redesign your corporate mission and make management and capital changes, the built-in activity layers of the corporation are ready to meet your needs.

4. Raising Money—Corporate Access to Private, Venture, and Public Capital

Corporations offer a terrific structure for raising money from friends, family, and business associates. There is something special about stock ownership, even in a small business, that attracts others. The corporate structure is designed to accommodate various capital interests. For example, you can:

- issue common, voting shares to the initial owner-employees
- set up a special nonvoting class of shares to distribute to key employees as an incentive to remain loyal to the business, and
- issue a "preferred" class of stock to venture capitalists willing to help fund future expansion of your corporation. (Preferred stock puts investors at the front of the line when dividends are declared or when the corporation is sold.)

Corporate capital incentives also attract creditors who are more willing to help finance a promising corporate enterprise in return for an option to buy shares.

What's more, owners of a small corporation can set their sights someday on making a public offering of shares. Even if your corporation never grows large enough to interest a conventional stock underwriting company in selling your shares as part of a large public offering, you may be able to market your shares to your customers or to individual investors by placing your company's small offering prospectus on the Internet. This strategy has been approved by the federal Securities and Exchange Commission (SEC)). And the good news is that no matter how you market your shares, the possibility of handling your own small direct public offering (DPO) is much more available than it was even a few years ago. The reason is that federal and state securities laws have been liberalized to help smaller corporations raise from $1 million to $10 million annually by making a limited public offering of shares.

Of course, raising equity capital by selling stock is not the only way that corporations shine. Incorporated businesses also have an easier time in obtaining loans from banks and other capital invest-ment firms, assuming a corporation's balance sheet and cash flow statements look good. That's partially due to the increased structural formality of the corporation (discussed in the previous section). In addition, loans can be made part of a package where the bank or investment company obtains special rights to choose one or more board members or has special voting prerogatives in matters of corporate management or finance. For example, a lender may require veto power over expenditures exceeding a specified amount. The variety of capital arrangements possible, even for a small corporation, is almost limitless, giving the corporation its well-known knack for attracting outside investment.

> **Example:** Rara Avis Investment Group lends Eagle Eye Management Corporation $1 million under the terms of a standard commercial promissory note. However, an added kicker to the deal that helps Rara reach its decision to lend the funds is a warrant agreement (much like a stock option grant) that lets it buy future shares of Eagle at its current low share price of $1. Rara expects Eagle to use the funds wisely to increase corporate profitability and raise its share price well above the current $1 level. If so, Rara will exercise its warrant and buy shares at the $1 price, then sell them for a profit.

Employees often prefer to work for corporations. Don't forget that key employees are more likely to work for a business that offers them a chance to profit through the issuance of stock options and stock bonuses if future growth is strong—and that these financial incentives are built into the corporate form. See the next section for a brief discussion. (For more details, read Chapter 3, Section D, which covers the benefits and tax treatment of each of the main types of employee equity plans.)

5. Corporate Employee Benefits and Employee Incentives

Another advantage of the corporate structure is that business owners who actually work in the business become employees. This means that you, in your role as an employee, become eligible for reimburse-

ment for medical expenses and up to $50,000 of group term life insurance paid for by your business. These perks are not available to employees of unincorporated businesses. (For further information on standard employee fringe benefits, see Chapter 3, Section C.)

Owners can also establish tax-favored plans such as stock option, stock bonus, and stock purchase plans for nonowner employees. As a corporation grows, these employee equity-sharing plans motivate employees by giving them a piece of the corporate ownership pie—at a low cash cost to the business. (See Chapter 3, Section D, for detailed treatment of each of the most common types of corporate employee equity plans.)

> **Example:** Henry incorporates his sole proprietorship, Big Foot Shoes, Inc. He now works as a full-time corporate employee, and is entitled to tax-deductible corporate perks. He also attracts talented employees by setting up a qualified incentive stock option (ISO) plan. Under the plan, employees are granted stock options with a strike (purchase) price of $1 per share (their current fair value as determined by the board). Employees pay nothing for the options, and the corporation itself neither pays for nor deducts any money for the option grants. After the op-

tions vest, an employee may exercise the option and buy the shares. Then the employee can sell them for a gain—that is, for more than $1 per share—and get taxed at capital gains rates that are lower than normal individual income tax rates. (To do this, the employee must hold the stock options for one year after buying them, and other conditions must be met. See Chapter 3, Section D, for details.)

6. Perpetual Existence

A corporation is, in some senses, immortal. Unlike a sole proprietorship, partnership, or LLC, which may terminate on the death or withdrawal of an owner, a corporation has an independent legal existence that continues despite changeovers in management or ownership. Of course, like any business, a corporation can be terminated by the mutual consent of the owners for personal or economic reasons. In some cases, it is terminated involuntarily, as in corporate bankruptcy proceedings. Nevertheless, a corporation does not depend for its legal existence on the life or continual ownership interest of a particular individual. This encourages creditors, employees, and others to participate in the operations of the business, particularly as the business grows.

Does It Make Sense to Incorporate Out of State?

You have no doubt have heard about the possibility of incorporating in another state, most likely Delaware, where initial and ongoing fees are lower and regulations may be less restrictive than in other states. Does this make sense? For large, publicly held corporations looking for the most lenient statutes and courts to help them fend off corporate raiders, perhaps yes. But for a small, privately held corporation pursuing an active business, our answer is no—it is usually a very poor idea to incorporate out of state.

The big reason is that you will have to qualify to do business in your home state anyway, and this process takes about as much time and costs as much money as filing incorporation papers in your home state in the first place. You'll also need to appoint a corporate agent to receive official corporate notices in the state where you incorporate—another pain in the neck and the corporate bank account.

It is also important to realize that incorporating in another state with a lower corporate income tax isn't likely to save you any money. That's because if your business makes money from operations in your home state, even if it is incorporated in another state, you still must pay home-state income taxes on this income.

Example: Best Greeting Card, Inc., plans to open a Massachusetts facility to design and market holiday greeting cards throughout the country. If it incorporates in Delaware, it must qualify to do business in Massachusetts, and pay Massachusetts corporate income tax on its Massachusetts operations. It also must hire a registered agent to act on its behalf in Delaware. It decides to incorporate in Massachusetts.

Unless you plan to open up a business with offices and operations in more than one state and, therefore, have a real reason to compare corporate domiciles, you should stay where you are and incorporate in your home state.

b. Downsides of Incorporating

Just about everything, including the advantages of incorporating, comes at a price. Let's look at two of the primary disadvantages.

1. Fees and Paperwork

The answer to the question "How much does it cost?" is an important factor to weigh when considering whether to incorporate your business. For starters, a corporation, unlike a sole proprietorship or general partnership, requires the filing of formation papers—Articles of Incorporation—with the state business filing office. Incorporation fees are modest in most states—typically, $50 to $100—and fees are commonly based on the number of shares authorized for issuance in your articles. By the way, incorporation, limited partnership, and LLC fees and paperwork are about the same in terms of cost and complexity in most states.

Incorporation fee information. See the "Articles Instructions" section of your state sheets in Appendix A for the incorporation fee charged in your state.

The ongoing paperwork that is necessary to keep your corporation legally current is generally not burdensome. But, unlike other business forms, you must pay particular attention to holding and documenting annual meetings of shareholders and directors, and keeping minutes of important corporate meetings. Creating this paper trail is a good way to show the IRS (in case of an audit) or the courts (in case of a lawsuit) that you have respected the corporate form and are entitled to hide behind its insulating layer of limited personal liability.

2. Tax Consequences of Corporate Dissolution

A significant downside to forming a corporation is the tax burden that may result from a dissolution or sale of the business. The general rule is that when a corporation is sold or dissolved, both the corporation and its shareholders are subject to the payment of income taxes on assets held by the corporation. Generally, here's how it works.

When a corporation dissolves, the corporation pays tax on the difference between the market value of a corporate asset and its tax basis in the asset. The corporation's basis in the asset is generally what it paid for the asset, minus any depreciation it has deducted on the asset during ownership. Corporations pay taxes on this spread—the difference between market value and the corporation's basis—according to the corporate tax rate schedule.

Example: If your corporation buys a building for $400,000 and deducts $100,000 in depreciation during five years of ownership, it has a $300,000 basis in the property. When the company liquidates and sells the building for $500,000, it pays corporate income taxes on the difference between the basis and the sale price—in this case, $200,000.

Now, here's the second part: When the corporation liquidates its assets—that is, converts them to cash to distribute to shareholders—technically, it is buying back its shares of stock from the shareholders. As you probably know, any sale of property by an individual is subject to income tax, and this "stock sale" is no exception. This means that, in the example above, a portion of the $500,000 sales proceeds is taxed again to the shareholders when the corporation distributes cash to them. (Shareholders may qualify for lower capital gains tax rates, rather than individual tax rates, if they held their shares for more than one year. See Chapter 3, Section D.) The taxable amount for each shareholder is determined according to the shareholder's individual basis in that person's shares.

Example: Let's continue the previous example by assuming that Sharon was the sole shareholder of the dissolving corporation. Let's also assume she paid $100,000 into her corporation at the beginning to capitalize it. This amount represents her basis in her shares—that is, is the amount she paid for her corporate stock. When Sharon receives $500,000 from the sale of the building, she must pay individual income tax on $400,000 (the $500,000 her corporation distributes to her for her shares, minus her $100,000 basis). Because Sharon owned her

shares for more than one year (her corporation existed for five years), she qualifies for capital gains tax rates when she computes how much she pays on the $400,000 taxable amount. (In fact, she probably qualifies for special small business stock rates, as explained in Chapter 3, Section E.)

If a business owner incorporates by transferring to the corporation tangible property—such as equipment, land, or a building—the owner gets a basis in stock equal to the owner's existing basis in the transferred assets, instead of cash. (This is governed by Internal Revenue Code Section 351, which applies to the incorporation of most small businesses. See Chapter 3, Section F.)

Example: Continuing with our original example, assume Sharon transfers a building to her corporation (instead of cash) for her stock. She paid $100,000 for the building, but it is worth $400,000 when she transfers it to her corporation. Her individual basis in her shares is $100,000—the amount she paid for the building—even though she transfers it to her corporation for its current $400,000 market value. When her corporation liquidates and sells the building for $500,000, Sharon pays tax on the $400,000 difference between the $500,000 distributed to her and her $100,000 basis in her shares. What's more, the corporation pays corporate income taxes on $400,000, too. When Sharon transferred the building at the time of incorporation, it received her $100,000 basis in the property as its basis. So when the corporation liquidates the building at the time of dissolution, it pays corporate income tax on $500,000 minus its $100,000 basis in the property ($400,000).

You do not have to master these rules—your tax adviser does. But now you know enough to notice the following: Sharon probably should not have transferred the building to the corporation when she incorporated. Why not? Because, when the building is sold, she pays taxes on $400,000 twice: She pays once as a shareholder, and her corporation pays a second time. Each follows slightly different rules to compute taxable amounts, and each pays at different rates, but each pays tax on the same transaction.

Here are two general points to keep in mind if you think your corporation will own significant assets that are likely to appreciate or otherwise be sold for more than their income tax basis:

- If your business plans to own significant assets that will appreciate, you may save yourself a lot of tax when the business is sold by doing business in an unincorporated form—for example, as an LLC, which also provides limited liability protection.

- If the nontax benefits, such as the corporate capital and employee incentives discussed above, make incorporation a top priority, your tax adviser can help you conduct your incorporation so that existing assets that are likely to appreciate are not transferred to the corporation. For example, you may decide to sell business assets prior to incorporation, then use cash to capitalize the corporation. You will pay tax on the sale of property, but you will avoid the double tax consequences that follow from having your corporation own it. Or you may decide to lease the property to the corporation.

 Ask your tax adviser before you incorporate about the tax consequences of dissolving your corporation. Ask your tax adviser up front whether a major tax cost is likely when you sell or transfer shares in your corporation or sell its assets later. One of the most important preincorporation services your tax adviser can provide is to make sure that the possible dissolution or sale of your corporation will not result in an unexpectedly hefty tax bill for you or the business. If a huge bill looks unavoidable, your adviser will probably steer you away from incorporating and advise the formation of an LLC instead.

B. Comparing Business Entities at a Glance

In the table that follows, we highlight and compare general and specific legal and tax traits of each type of business entity. Should any of the additional points of comparison seem relevant to your business, we encourage you to talk them over with a legal or tax professional.

Business Entity Comparison Tables—Legal, Financial, and Tax Characteristics

	Sole Proprietorship	General Partnership	Limited Partnership	C Corporation	S Corporation	LLC
Who owns business?	sole proprietor	general partners	general and limited partners	shareholders	same as C corporation	members
Personal liability business debts	sole proprietor personally liable	general partners personally liable	only general partner(s) personally liable	no personal liability for shareholders	same as C corporation	no personal for liability for members
Restrictions on kind of business	may engage in any lawful business	may engage in any lawful business	same as general partnership	can't be formed for banking or trust business and other special business	same as C corporation— but excessive passive income (such as from rents, royalties, interest) can jeopardize S tax status	same as C corporation (in a few states, like California, certain professionals cannot form an LLC)
Restrictions on number of owners	only one sole proprietor (a spouse may own an interest under marital property laws)	minimum two general partners	minimum one general partner and one limited partner	one-shareholder corporation allowed in all states	same as C corporation, but no more than 100 shareholders permitted, who must be US citizens or residents	all states allow the formation of one-member LLCs
Who makes management decisions?	sole proprietor	general partners	general partner(s) only, not limited partners	board of directors	same as C corporation	ordinarily members, or managers if LLC elects manager-management
Who may legally obligate business?	sole proprietor	any general partner	any general partner, not limited partners	directors and officers	same as C corporation	any member if member-managed or any manager if manager-managed
Effect on business if an owner dies or departs	dissolves automatically	dissolves automatically unless otherwise stated in partnership agreement	same as general partnership	no effect	same as C corporation	some LLC agreements (and some default provisions of state law) say that LLC dissolves unless remaining members vote to continue business; otherwise LLC automatically continues
Limits on transfer of ownership interests	free transferability	consent of all general partners usually required under partnership agreement	same as general partnership	transfer of stock may be limited under securities laws	same as C corporation— but transfers to nonqualified shareholders terminate S tax status	most LLC agreements require membership consent to admit new member (absent such consent, transferee gets economic, not voting, rights in the transferor's membership)

Business Entity Comparison Tables—Legal, Financial, and Tax Characteristics, Continued

	Sole Proprietorship	General Partnership	Limited Partnership	C Corporation	S Corporation	LLC
Amount of organizational paperwork and ongoing legal formalities	minimal	minimal required, but partnership agreement recommended	start-up filing required, partnership agreement recommended	start-up filing required; bylaws recommended; annual meetings of directors and shareholders recommended	same as C corporation	start-up filing required, operating agreement recommended
Source of start-up funds	sole proprietor	general partners	general and limited partners	initial shareholders; in some states, share-holders cannot buy shares by promising to to perform future services or promising to pay for shares later (promissory notes)	same as C corporation— but cannot issue shares of different classes of stock with different dividend or liquidation rights	members
How business usually obtains additional capital	sole proprietor's contributions; working capital loans backed by personal assets of sole proprietor	capital contributions from general partners; business loans from banks backed by partnership and personal assets of partners	investment capital from limited partners; bank loans guaranteed by general partners	flexible; issuance of new shares to investors, banks loans (backed by personal assets of major shareholders if necessary)	generally same as C corporation—but can't have foreign or entity shareholders and cannot issue special classes of shares to investors (differences in voting rights are allowed)	capital contributions from members; bank loans backed by members' personal assets if necessary
Ease of conversion to another type of business	may change form at will to partnership (if a new owner is added), corpor-ation, or LLC	may change form to limited partnership, corporation, or LLC	may change to corporation or LLC	may change to S corporation by filing simple tax election; change to LLC can involve tax cost	generally same as C corporation—may terminate S tax status to become C corpora-tion, but cannot reelect S status for five years	may change to general or limited partner-ship or to corporation
Is establishment or sale of ownership interests subject to federal and state securities laws?	generally, no	generally, no	yes	yes	yes	generally, no, if all members are active in the business
Who generally finds this the best way to do business?	sole owner who wants minimum red tape and maximum autonomy	joint owners who are not concerned with personal liability for business debts	joint owners with passive investors who want limited liability protection and pass-through tax status (and prefer not to form an LLC); some real estate syndicates prefer to set up LPs rather than LLCs because they are accustomed to the LP form	owners who want the limited liability, formal structure, and capital incentives of the corporate form and the ability to split business income to reduce overall income taxes	owners who want the formal structure of the corporation form but want pass-through taxation of business profits (note: owners who wish limited liability protection plus pass-through taxation should usually set up an LLC instead of an S corporation); some owners form an S corporation simply to minimize the owner's self-employment taxes	owners who want limited liability legal protection and pass-through taxation of business profits

Business Entity Comparison Tables—Legal, Financial, and Tax Characteristicss, Continued

	Sole Proprietorship	General Partnership	Limited Partnership	C Corporation	S Corporation	LLC
How business profits are taxed	individual tax rates of sole proprietor	individual tax rates of general partners (unless partnership elects corporate tax treatment)	individual tax rates of general and limited partners (unless partnership elects corporate tax treatment)	profits are split up and taxed at corporate rates and individual tax rates of employee-shareholders	individual tax rates of shareholders	individual tax rates of members
Tax-deductible employee benefits available to owners who work in the business?	generally, no, but owner may deduct medical insurance premiums and establish IRA or Keogh retirement plan	same as sole proprietorship (unless partner-ship elects corporate tax treatment)	same as sole proprietorship (unless partner-ship elects corporate tax treatment)	tax-deductible fringe benefits, including corporate retirement and profit-sharing plan as well as tax-favored stock option and bonus plan for employee-shareholders; may reimburse employees' actual medical expenses; group term life insurance also deductible within limits	same as sole proprietorship	same as sole proprietorship (unless LLC elects corporate tax treatment)
Automatic tax status	yes	yes; can elect corporate tax status by filing IRS Form 8832	yes, on filing certificate of limited partnership with state filing office; can elect corporate tax status by filing IRS Form 8832	yes, on filing Articles of Incorpor-ation with state filing office	no; must meet requirements and file tax election form (IRS Form 2553)	yes; sole owner LLC automatically treated as sole proprietorship, co-owned LLC as partnership; can elect corporate tax status by filing IRS Form 8832
Deductibility of business losses	generally, owner may deduct losses from active business income on individual tax return	partners active in the business may deduct losses from active business income on individual tax returns	limited partners not active in the business cannot use losses to offset active business income, but may be able to use them to offset other investment income; limited partners normally get the benefit only of nonrecourse debts —those for which general partners are not at risk; check with your tax adviser	corporation, not individual shareholders, deducts business losses; shareholders who sell their stock for a loss may be able to deduct part of the loss from ordinary income	shareholders receive pro rata amount of corporate loss to deduct on their individual income tax returns, subject to special loss limitation rules	generally, same as general partnership, but subject to special rules—see your tax adviser
Tax level when business is sold	personal tax level of owner	personal tax levels of individual general partners	personal tax levels of individual general and limited partners	two levels: shareholders and corporation are subject to tax on liquidation	normally taxed at personal tax levels of individual shareholders, but corporate-level tax sometimes due if S corporation formerly was a C corporation	personal tax levels of individual members

C. Nolo's Small Business Resources

Nolo offers plenty of guidance for small business owners who want to set up a new venture and keep it running smoothly. The best place to start is Nolo's website at www.nolo.com. There, you'll find dozens of free articles to help you do everything from picking a good location to paying taxes. In addition, here's a partial list of Nolo's most popular small business publications.

1. Starting and Running Your Business

The Small Business Start-Up Kit, by Peri H. Pakroo (national and California editions), helps you launch a business quickly, easily, and with confidence. Among other topics, the book shows you how to write an effective business plan, file for necessary permits and licenses, and acquire and keep good accounting and bookkeeping habits.

Legal Guide for Starting & Running a Small Business, by Fred S. Steingold, is a comprehensive business owner's guide that provides in-depth coverage of topics ranging from raising start-up money and negotiating a lease to adopting the best customer policies, hiring workers, and avoiding legal problems.

Buy-Sell Agreement Handbook: Plan Ahead for Changes in the Ownership of Your Business, by Anthony Mancuso and Bethany K. Laurence, helps you ensure a smooth transition following the departure of a business partner by writing a buy-sell agreement at the start of your business relationship. The book carefully explains each step of the process, providing all the tax and legal information you need to draft your own agreement.

Tax Savvy for Small Business, by Frederick W. Daily, lays out year-round tax saving strategies for business owners that show you how to claim all legitimate deductions, maximize fringe benefits, and keep accurate records to avoid trouble with the IRS.

The Employer's Legal Handbook, by Fred S. Steingold, is a complete, plain-English guide to employee benefits, wage laws, workplace safety, and more.

Nondisclosure Agreements: Protect Your Trade Secrets & More, by Richard Stim and Stephen Fishman, is a downloadable eFormKit from the Nolo website (www.nolo.com) that explains what trade secrets are and shows you how to protect them from future competitors.

2. Partnerships

The Partnership Book: How to Write a Partnership Agreement, by Denis Clifford and Ralph Warner, thoroughly explains the legal and practical issues involved in forming a partnership and shows you how to write a comprehensive partnership agreement.

3. LLCs

LLC or Corporation? How to Choose the Right Form for Your Business, by Anthony Mancuso. This book explains the different legal and tax rules that apply to each entity and provides examples showing when it makes the most sense to form an LLC or to incorporate instead. The book isn't only relevant at the formation stage—it includes comprehensive treatment of the legal and tax effects of converting from one form of business to another as your business grows.

Nolo's Quick LLC: All You Need to Know About Limited Liability Companies, by Anthony Mancuso, teaches you the basics of limited liability companies and helps you figure out whether forming an LLC is the right thing to do.

LLC Maker, by Anthony Mancuso, is a powerful software program for Windows that allows you to create a limited liability company in your state and keep it running right. If you prefer a book to a software program, *Form Your Own Limited Liability Company*, by Anthony Mancuso, contains the forms and instructions you need to set up your LLC.

Your Limited Liability Company: An Operating Manual, by Anthony Mancuso, shows you how to maintain the legal validity of your LLC. The book explains how to prepare minutes of meetings; record important legal, tax, and business decisions; handle formal recordkeeping; and set up an LLC Records Book.

4. Nonprofit Corporations

How to Form a Nonprofit Corporation, by Anthony Mancuso, shows you step by step how to form and operate a tax-exempt corporation in all 50 states. (California readers should see *How to Form a Nonprofit Corporation in California*, which gives more detailed advice to nonprofiteers in the Golden State.) Both books include step-by-step instructions on how to prepare the completely revised IRS Form 1023 tax-exemption application that must be filed after April 30, 2005.

Starting & Building a Nonprofit, by Peri Pakroo, offers nuts-and-bolts advice on issues like finding people to run your organization, holding board meetings, bookkeeping, marketing, and more.

Effective Fundraising for Nonprofits: Real-World Strategies That Work, by Ilona Bray, is a comprehensive guide to fundraising planning and methods, including proposal writing, individual and major donor cultivation, special events, Internet outreach, earned income strategies, planned giving, and more.

5. Running a Corporation

The Corporate Minutes Book, by Anthony Mancuso, shows you how to establish the essential paper trail of your corporation's legal life: corporate meeting minutes. The book contains forms (both tear-out and on CD-ROM) to help you call and document meetings, including more than 80 individual resolutions that you can customize and include in your minutes when appropriate. ■

How Corporations Work

This chapter introduces you to the structures, procedures, and legal rules you need to know to form a profit-making corporation and keep it running.

To help you understand where a business corporation fits in the corporate landscape, we begin by briefly describing other types of corporations, including nonprofit, professional, and close corporations. Then we cover the basic legal paperwork and procedures that you must undertake to form and operate a business corporation, including the issuance of shares to your initial shareholders. This background information will help you follow the specific instructions we provide in the later chapters for preparing corporate articles, bylaws, and minutes, and making your first stock issuance. This chapter also helps you understand the specific corporate and securities rules contained in your state sheet in Appendix A and any corporate or securities statutes you may wish to browse in your state's Business Corporation Act or Securities Act.

Understanding and paying corporate taxes is covered in the next chapter, Chapter 3.

A. Kinds of Corporations

State law classifies and regulates different types of corporations. This book shows you how to form a business corporation (a few states call it a "profit corporation"). Essentially, a business corporation is one that engages in any lawful business that is not specially regulated under state law (such as the insurance, banking, or trust business).

Before discussing the rules that apply to business corporations—the type most readers of this book will want to form—let's look at a few other types of corporations that are set up and operated under special state rules. You must follow unique procedures to form one of these types of corporations, which are not covered in this book.

Domestic Versus Foreign Corporations

When browsing your state's corporate statutes, you may run into the terms "domestic corporation" and "foreign corporation." A domestic corporation is one that is formed under the laws of your state by filing Articles of Incorporation with the state's corporate filing office. A corporation that is formed in another state, even though it may be physically present and doing business in your state, is classified as a "foreign corporation" in your state's corporation statutes. In this context, "foreign" means out of state, not out of the country.

1. Nonprofit Corporations

A nonprofit corporation (in some states called a "not-for-profit" corporation) is formed under a state's Nonprofit Corporation Act for nonprofit purposes. In other words, its primary purpose is not to make money for its founders, but to do good work—for example, to establish childcare centers, shelters for the homeless, community health care clinics, museums, hospitals, churches, schools, or performing arts groups. Most nonprofits are formed for purposes recognized as tax-exempt under federal and state income tax laws. This means that the nonprofit doesn't have to pay corporate income tax on its revenues, that it is eligible to receive tax-deductible contributions from the public, and that it qualifies to receive grant funds from other tax-exempt public and private agencies.

State law as well as federal tax-exemption requirements typically prohibit a nonprofit corporation from paying out profits to nonprofit members, except in the form of reasonable salaries to those who work for it. When a nonprofit dissolves, the members are normally not allowed to share in a distribution of the nonprofit's assets. Instead, any assets remaining after the nonprofit dissolves must be distributed to another tax-exempt organization. Special types of nonprofits may be recognized under state law that do allow people to own, in one fashion or another, corporate assets, so they can receive a portion of these assets when the nonprofit dissolves. For example, a nonprofit homeowners' association or nonprofit trade group may give each member a proprietary interest in the assets of the nonprofit. But these special nonprofits do not enjoy the same benefits as a qualified tax-exempt nonprofit. They may be eligible for an income tax exemption, but they normally do not qualify to receive tax-deductible contributions or public or private grant funds.

Nonprofit corporations, like regular business corporations, have directors who manage the business of the corporation. Instead of shares of stock, membership interests can be issued for a purchase price that is paid by the members when they join. The nonprofit corporation may also collect enrollment fees, dues, or similar amounts from members. Like regular corporations, a nonprofit corporation may sue or be sued; pay salaries; provide various types of employee fringe benefits; incur debts and obligations; acquire and hold property; and engage, generally, in any lawful activity not inconsistent with its nonprofit purposes and tax-exempt status. It also provides its directors and members with limited liability for the debts and liabilities of the corporation and continues perpetually unless steps are taken to dissolve it.

There are key differences between forming and operating a nonprofit and a regular business corporation:

- To form a nonprofit, in most states you must file special Nonprofit Articles of Incorporation. These are normally available for downloading from your state corporate filing office website. (See your state sheet for contact information.)
- Nonprofit bylaws typically contain provisions similar to those of business corporations. However, nonprofits typically set up a number of special committees to handle nonprofit operations, and nonprofits routinely schedule more frequent meetings of directors than their commercial counterparts. Also, nonprofits replace shareholder provisions with member provisions, which specify the rules for membership meetings and the qualifications, responsibilities, and rights of members. Of course, nonprofit bylaws do not contain provisions relating payouts of profits (payment of dividends). The state Nonprofit Corporation Act typically follows or is in close proximity to the state Business Corporation Act in the corporate statutes. So you can usually use the citation to your state's Business Corporation Act to help you locate the Nonprofit Corporation Act. (A few states include nonprofit as well as business corporation statutes in a consolidated General Corporation Act.) See your state sheet in Appendix A for information about locating corporate laws.

- A critical part of forming and operating a nonprofit is obtaining a federal and state income tax exemption and making sure to operate the nonprofit in a way that meets the tax exemption requirements. The requirements for obtaining a state income tax exemption should be posted on your state tax agency website. (See the "State Tax Information" section of your state sheet in Appendix A.)

For more information about nonprofit corporations. For all the forms and instructions you need to organize a nonprofit corporation in your state, including step-by-step instructions on preparing nonprofit articles and bylaws and applying for and obtaining your federal 501(c)(3) nonprofit tax exemption, see *How to Form a Nonprofit Corporation*, by Anthony Mancuso (Nolo). (California readers should see Nolo's *How to Form a Nonprofit Corporation in California*, also by Anthony Mancuso.)

2. Professional Corporations

Most states have special requirements for forming a corporation whose owners will provide state-licensed professional services. The list of particular professions to which these rules apply varies from state to state, but typically lawyers, doctors, other health care professionals, accountants, engineers, and architects must follow these special rules when they incorporate. Other professionals ranging from acupuncturists to massage therapists may also be included.

Professionals That May Have to Incorporate Under Special Rules

Here is a typical list of professions that must incorporate as professional corporations, rather than as regular business corporations, in many states:

Accountant
Acupuncturist
Architect
Attorney
Audiologist
Clinical social worker
Dentist
Doctor (all medical doctors including surgeons)
Marriage, family, and child counselor
Nurse
Optometrist
Osteopath (physician or surgeon)
Pharmacist
Physical therapist
Physician's assistant
Podiatrist
Psychologist
Shorthand reporter
Speech pathologist
Veterinarian

How to find out whether you must form a professional corporation. If you plan to form a corporation to render professional services, check your state's corporate filing office website (see your state sheet) to see what professions must incorporate as professional corporations. If this information is not posted, send the office an email asking if your profession must incorporate as a professional corporation. If your profession is not on the state's professional corporation list, you can establish a regular business corporation—the type this book shows you how to form.

If your profession is on the professional corporation list in your state, you must file special Professional Corporation Articles of Incorporation to form your corporation, not the standard articles for a business corporation discussed in this book. In many states, Professional Corporation Articles are available for downloading from the corporate filing office website. (See your state sheet for contact information.)

In addition to the rules set out in this book that apply to business corporations, the following rules and requirements typically also apply to the formation and operation of professional corporations:

- The name of a professional corporation normally must include a special designator such as "Professional Corporation," "P.C.," or the like, and must meet any additional professional business name requirements imposed by the state licensing board that oversees the profession.

- In addition to Professional Corporation Articles, you may be required to file a certification from the state licensing board showing that all shareholders hold current professional state licenses.

- Generally, the corporation must be formed to render only one professional service, but some professions are allowed to form a corporation to render more than one professional service in related fields. For example, a licensed surgeon may be allowed to incorporate a professional corporation together with a licensed orthopedist.

- The corporation must render professional services only through licensed members, managers, officers, agents, and employees.

- Each licensed professional must carry the amount of liability insurance specified under the rules that apply to the profession.

- Generally, licensed shareholder/employees of professional corporations remain personally liable for their own negligent or wrongful acts, or acts of those under the professional's direct supervision or control, when performing professional services on behalf of the corporation. The limited liability shield of the corporation does, however, normally protect professionals from personal liability for the negligent acts of other professionals in the incorporated professional practice. (And, as for other corporations, the liability shield protects professional shareholders from personal liability for the regular commercial debts and other business liabilities of the corporation.)

The Registered Limited Liability Partnership (RLLP): An Alternate Choice for Professionals

All states allow certain professionals to form a Registered Limited Liability Partnership (RLLP). The RLLP is similar to a regular general partnership, legally and for tax purposes, but it also provides each RLLP partner with the limited liability protection of a professional corporation. Specifically, like a professional corporation, the RLLP gives its partners immunity from personal liability for the malpractice of other partners in the firm—though each professional partner remains personally liable for that partner's own negligence. The RLLP also may protect its owners from personal liability for the regular commercial debts and other liabilities of the business, depending on state law. Owners of an RLLP are taxed individually on business profits (like sole proprietors or nonprofessional partners), while a corporation is a separate taxable entity. If you are considering incorporating a professional practice but may prefer pass-through taxation of business profits, give the RLLP your consideration (and consult your tax adviser). Forms and instructions for creating an RLLP should be available from your state's corporate filing office website. (See your state sheet in Appendix A.)

Flat corporate income tax rate for certain professionals. Whether you form a regular business corporation or a professional corporation to render professional services, an important IRS tax provision may apply to you. Specifically, Internal Revenue Code §§ 11(b)(2) and 448(d)(2) provide that professionals engaged in the fields of health, law, engineering, architecture, accounting, actuarial science, or consulting are subject to a flat 35% federal corporate income tax rate. This rate is applied to any taxable income left in the corporation—that is, income not paid out as salary or fringe benefits to the professionals and other employees of the corporation—at the end of the corporation's tax year. In other words, these professionals, unlike the owners of regular business corporations, do not enjoy the benefit of keeping taxable income in the corporation at the lower corporate income tax brackets of 15% to 25%. (See Chapter 3.) For this reason, professionals who expect to retain income in their corporation often prefer to organize themselves as an RLLP to obtain limited liability protection and avoid the flat 35% corporate tax. Income earned in an RLLP, as in a partnership, passes through the entity and is taxed at regular individual income tax rates of the owners, which may be lower than the flat 35% professional tax rate.

3. The Close Corporation

Many states have enacted laws, usually as part of their Business Corporation Act, that allow for the organization of a special type of business corporation, called a "close corporation" or "statutory close corporation." These laws permit corporations with a small number of shareholders—usually no more than 35—to operate without a board of directors according to the terms of a specially prepared shareholders' agreement. In other words, the owners of a close corporation can dispense with normal corporate formalities and operate their corporation under a shareholders' agreement, similar to the way in which owners of a partnership operate their business under the terms of a partnership agreement.

Close vs. Closely Held Corporations: Confusing Legal Jargon Made Simple

Don't confuse the legal term "close corporation," discussed in this section, with the term "closely held corporation." The latter is a loosely used business term, not found in corporate statutes, that is usually used to describe any small privately held corporation owned and operated by a closely knit group of founders, such as a family or small group of business associates. Put another way, a closely held corporation is simply an incorporated small business, not one that has adopted special rules allowing shareholders to proceed without corporate formalities. However, the term "closely held corporation" does have a special tax meaning. Under Internal Revenue Code §§ 469(j)(1), 465(a)(1)(B), and 542(a)(2), a "closely held corporation" is defined as one where more than 50% of the value of the corporation's stock is owned by five or fewer individuals during the last half of the corporation's tax year. This special tax classification has no connection to state corporate statutes.

Operating a close corporation under a shareholders' agreement can provide business owners with a great deal of flexibility. For example, the shareholders' agreement can dispense with the the need for annual director or shareholder meetings, corporate officers, or even for the board of directors itself, allowing shareholders to manage and carry out the business of the corporation without having to put on their director or shareholder hats. And, as in a partnership, profits can be distributed without regard to capital contributions (stock ownership); thus a 10% shareholder could, for example, receive 25% of the profits (dividends). Special tax rules apply to this sort of special allocation of business profits; your tax adviser can fill you in on the details if you want to know more.

Despite the benefits of informality and flexibility, most incorporators don't want to form close corpo-

rations. Indeed, it is estimated that less than 2% of all business corporations are formed as close corporations. Why hasn't the close corporation business form caught on in the states that allow it? There are a number of reasons.

To begin with, most incorporators do not want to operate their corporation under informal or non-standard close corporation shareholder agreement rules and procedures. In fact, many incorporators form a corporation to rely on the traditional corporation and tax statutes that apply to regular business corporations. (By doing so, they know what is expected of directors, officers, and shareholders—for example, they can simply follow the rules set out in their state BCA to call and hold meetings of directors and shareholders without having to design their own procedures.) Second, shares of stock in a close corporation normally contain built-in restrictions on transferability, and most incorporators do not want their shares to be restricted in this way. Third, it is costly and time-consuming to prepare a shareholders' agreement. It's much simpler and less expensive to adopt standard corporate bylaws.

For more information about close corporations. Your state corporate filing office website, listed in your state sheet in Appendix A, should tell you whether you can form a close corporation in your state and, if so, how to do it. Typically, you must add special provisions to your Articles of Incorporation to elect close corporation status, prepare and adopt a special shareholders' agreement that follows the requirements set out in your state's Business Corporation Act, and prepare special stock certificates that contain language that limits the transfer of the shares represented by the certificate.

4. The Business Corporation

This is the type of corporation that this book shows you how to form. In the remainder of this chapter we'll review the statutes (laws), required documents, state offices, and other features on the legal landscape you'll encounter on your way to forming your own business corporation.

B. Corporate Statutes

Each state has many laws that regulate the organization and operation of a business corporation. The portion that governs most areas of corporate operation is the state's Business Corporation Act (BCA). Your state sheet, contained in Appendix A, provides the specific BCA provisions for major areas of corporate organization and operation. This section simply provides a summary of how the state BCA and other business laws will affect your corporate life and tells you how to locate the laws if you need to look something up.

1. Business Corporation Act

Most of the laws that govern corporations are contained in your state's business corporation statutes, usually titled the "Business Corporation Act" (BCA) or "Business Corporation Law." The BCA spells out the essential rules for forming and operating a corporation. For example, the BCA explains the requirements for preparing and filing Articles of Incorporation to form the corporation, the rules for preparing and changing corporate bylaws, and the basic rights and responsibilities of corporate directors, officers, and shareholders. The BCA explains when and how directors and shareholders meet to approve corporate decisions, and how much leeway a corporation has in setting its own rules that vary from the BCA requirements. We cover BCA director, officer, and shareholder rules in more detail in the remaining sections of this chapter.

The Model Business Corporation Act

The basic corporate statutes of many states contain the same, or quite similar, rules for organizing and operating business corporations. The reason for this uniformity is that a number of states have adopted some, most, or all of the provisions of a standard law: the Model Business Corporation Act. The Act undergoes periodic changes, which states are free to enact.

The following states have adopted most, or a substantial portion, of the provisions of the Revised Model Business Corporation Act:

Arkansas	Mississippi	Tennessee
Florida	Montana	Virginia
Georgia	North Carolina	Washington
Indiana	Oregon	Wisconsin
Iowa	South Carolina	Wyoming
Kentucky		

In the "Corporation Law Online" section of your state sheet in Appendix A, we list the name of your state's Business Corporation Act and tell you where you can browse it online. (Only one state, Pennsylvania, currently does not post its BCA online; your state sheet shows you how to order a printed copy of the Pennsylvania BCA.) If you do not have an Internet connection, you will need to find a BCA book or pamphlet to browse the law. Your state filing office may offer a free pamphlet that contains the state's BCA; call the office to see if one is available. (Some states charge a small fee for this material.) If your state filing office does not provide a printed version of the BCA, ask if they have the telephone number of a commercial publisher who does. Expect to pay about $30 for a printed commercial version. If you're willing to do a bit more legwork, your local law library is the best place to go to research the state BCA free of charge. Just ask a reference librarian to point you toward the right series of books. The business section of a local public library is another likely place to find your BCA.

2. Other Laws

In addition to the Business Corporation Act, other state laws regulate special areas of corporate activity. These include the following.

Securities act or blue sky law. This law contains each state's rules and procedures for offering, issuing, selling, and transferring shares of corporate stock and other securities within the state. The term "blue sky law" is derived from the sometimes underhanded, and often colorful, practices of corporate con artists who, in return for an investment in their latest get-rich-quick undertaking, would promise the "blue sky" to unsuspecting investors. The securities laws of each state attempt, through registration and disclosure requirements, to tone down the picture painted by stock promoters to a more realistic hue.

The "State Securities Information" section of your state sheet provides basic information on the securities laws and procedures that apply to issuing your initial shares to the founders of your corporation. This information includes the Web address of your state's securities law office, where you can usually find a link to your state's securities law. If the state securities office website does not provide this link, we give you the Web address where you can find your state's securities law online. If you do not have an Internet connection, call your state securities office; often it provides a free pamphlet that contains your state's securities act. (The telephone number for your state securities office is also listed in your state sheet.)

For more information on securities laws and procedures, see Section I, below.

State Tax or Revenue Code. All states except Nevada and South Dakota impose corporate income or franchise taxes that are based on the amount of taxable income earned in the state by a corporation. Your corporation pays these taxes in addition to federal IRS income taxes. Each state's Tax or Revenue Code typically contains the state's income or franchise tax rules.

Tax statutes are even more off-putting than legal statutes. We think you'll get the most useful information directly from your state's tax publications, forms, and other instructions posted on your state's tax agency website. The "State Tax Information" section of your state sheet provides the website and other contact information for this office, along with information about the type and rate of any corporate income or franchise tax imposed by your state. If you don't have an Internet connection, call the state tax office telephone number listed in the "State Tax Information" section of your state sheet and ask for corporate publications and forms by mail.

Other state and local laws. Other state laws affect the operations of all businesses, whether or not they are incorporated. For example, state and local building codes, professional and occupation licensing, environmental laws, local ordinances, zoning laws, and other laws and regulations may apply to your business and its operations.

Laws that apply when forming a business. For an excellent resource on the various state laws and regulations that apply to forming all types of businesses, corporate and noncorporate, see *The Small Business Start-Up Kit*, by Peri H. Pakroo (Nolo), available in both national and California editions.

C. Corporate Filing Offices

Each state has a corporate filing office with which you file paperwork (and pay fees) to create or dissolve a corporation. Typically, this filing office handles all state business filings, including limited partnership and limited liability company (LLC) filings as well as business corporation and nonprofit corporate filings. Throughout this book, we refer to the office that accepts corporate filings as *the corporate filing office*. Typically, the official name of this office is the Corporations Division of the Secretary (or Department) of State. The main corporate filing office is located in each state's capitol city. Some states maintain branch offices in secondary cities as well.

The "Corporate Filing Office" section of your state sheet contains the name, address, telephone number, and website of your state's corporate filing office. Generally, the best way to obtain the latest corporate filing and fee information and the latest corporate filing forms is to visit your state's corporate filing office website. Most state corporate filing office websites provide corporate statutory forms such as Articles of Incorporation, Amendment of Articles, Change of Registered Agent, or Registered Office Address, and the like. (Your state sheet lists the corporate forms available on each site.) Many state websites also contain links to the state's corporate tax office and state employment, licensing, and other agencies.

For a faster response, contact the filing office via email. Corporate filing offices typically respond to email inquiries much faster than they respond to snail mail or telephone messages. (It's not uncommon to have to wait a day or more to get a telephone call through to a busy state filing office.) In short, if your question is not answered on the filing office website, send the office an email inquiry. (You will find the email address on the state filing office website.)

D. Corporate Documents

The primary corporate legal documents are Articles of Incorporation, bylaws, stock certificates, and minutes of meetings. This section introduces you to each in turn.

1. Articles of Incorporation

The key corporate organizing document is the Articles of Incorporation. In some states, the articles go by a different name, such as the Corporate Charter or Certificate of Incorporation. A corporation comes into existence when its Articles of Incorporation are filed with the state corporate filing office. *The filing of articles is the only legal filing necessary to create a corporate entity.* However, you'll want to follow up after filing articles by preparing and adopting bylaws, holding a first meeting of directors, and issuing stock to your initial shareholders. These additional steps are necessary to make sure the legal organization of your corporation is complete.

The articles normally contain basic structural information, such as the name of the corporation, the names and addresses of its directors, its registered agent and registered office address, and the corporation's capital stock structure. The information that must be included is typically established by a section of the state Business Corporation Act titled "Contents of Articles of Incorporation." Standard state articles forms (and the custom articles forms that this book provides for Iowa and Nebraska—the two states that do not offer an official form) contain all required provisions. State articles statutes also normally list optional provisions that you can include in your articles, such as provisions to implement a complex stock structure with different classes or series of shares. (We discuss adding optional provisions to articles in Chapter 4, Step 2A.)

> **Example:** The Equine Equity Investors Corporation adds an optional provision to its articles that sets up a multiclass stock structure consisting of Class A Voting shares and Class B Nonvoting shares. Another optional provision is added that requires a vote of two-thirds of each class of stock for the approval of amendments (changes) to the corporation's articles or bylaws.

Most corporate filing office websites provide a downloadable, ready-to-use Articles of Incorporation form that you can use to establish your business corporation. This book provides an articles form for use in Iowa and Nebraska, the only states that do not offer a standard articles form. For all states, we provide specific instructions in the "Articles Instructions" section of the state sheet to help you obtain and complete your articles so that they are acceptable for filing with the corporate filing office.

2. Bylaws

After Articles of Incorporation, a corporation's bylaws are its second-most important document. You do not file bylaws with the state. They are an internal document that contains rules for holding corporate meetings and carrying out other formalities according to state corporate laws. Bylaws typically specify how often the corporation must hold regular meetings of directors and shareholders, as well as the call, notice, quorum, and voting rules for these meetings. Also, bylaws usually contain the rules for setting up and delegating authority to special committees of the board of directors, the rights of directors and shareholders to inspect corporate records and books, the rights of directors and officers to insurance coverage or indemnification (reimbursement by the corporation for legal fees and judgments) in the event of lawsuits, plus a number of other standard legal provisions.

Many of the procedures set out in corporate bylaws are controlled by statutes in your state's Business Corporation Act. For example, most states require corporations to hold an annual meeting of shareholders to elect or reelect the board of directors to a one-year term of office. In your bylaws, you set the date of this annual meeting. Similarly, most states require written notice of shareholders' meetings to be delivered to each shareholder no less than ten nor more than 60 days prior to the date of the meeting. In your bylaws, you can specify the exact number of days required for providing notice of shareholders' meetings. If you do, your notice period must fall within this ten-to-60 day range.

This book provides fill-in-the-blank bylaws (both tear-outs and on CD-ROM) that you can use for your corporation. In Chapter 4, we explain how to use your state sheet information to complete your bylaws.

Use Bylaws Instead of Articles for Corporate Operating Rules

Some states let corporations choose whether to place corporate operating rules and procedures in the Articles of Incorporation or bylaws. It's always best to use the bylaws because you can change them easily—without the need for filing your changes with the state. For example, many states allow you to place super-majority quorum or voting rules for directors' or shareholders' meetings in either document. If you use the bylaws for this purpose, you can change these provisions by amending your bylaws at a directors' or shareholders' meeting. But if you put these provisions in your articles, after the directors or shareholders approve the changes, you must file a formal amendment to the articles with your state's corporate filing office.

---

3. Stock Certificates

A new corporation issues stock to its founders and initial investors. Stock ownership is usually documented by stock certificates given to each shareholder. Today, many states do not require the actual completion and delivery of paper stock certificates to shareholders, but we think it continues to make sense to issue certificates. A stock certificate is tangible evidence of a person's ownership rights in your corporation, and most founders and investors expect to receive one after buying shares in a new corporation.

State law sets out the very basic content requirements for stock certificates. Normally, the minimum information necessary is the name of the corporation, the state where the corporation was formed, the name and number of shares issued to the shareholder, and the signature of two corporate officers. We provide ten tear-out stock certificates in Appendix D. We provide your state's stock certificate requirements in the "Share Issuance Rules" section of your state sheet. Blank certificates that comply with your state's requirements may be available in local stationery stores. If you want custom-printed certificates, a local legal printer will prepare your certificates for a higher cost. We provide specific information on how to issue the initial shares of your corporation in Section H, below.

4. Minutes of the First Directors Meeting

After filing articles and preparing bylaws, the initial board of directors meets to formally approve the bylaws, approve the issuance of stock to initial shareholders, appoint corporate officers, and handle other essential corporate startup tasks. If the initial members of the board are not named in the articles, the incorporator—the person who signed and filed your articles—prepares a written "Incorporator Statement" in which the incorporator appoints the initial board members prior to its first meeting. Once the board has been named—either in the filed articles or the Incorporator Statement—the board of directors can hold its first meeting. The actions taken by the board at its first meeting should be documented by written minutes that are filed in the corporate records book.

Chapter 4 of this book shows you how to prepare an Incorporator Statement (if you need one) and minutes of your first board meeting. (This book contains forms you can use for both purposes.)

For help with corporate minutes. For simple forms that you can use to record subsequent board and shareholders meetings, together with more than 80 resolutions you can adopt to handle the approval of standard legal, business, and tax decisions reached at these meetings, see Nolo's *The Corporate Minutes Book*, by Anthony Mancuso.

E. Corporate Powers

Each state's Business Corporation Act gives business corporations carte blanche to engage in any lawful business activity. In legalese, "lawful" doesn't just mean noncriminal; it means not otherwise prohibited by law. Generally this means that a corporation can do anything that a natural person can do. However, in most states, it is not lawful for a regular business corporation to engage in the banking, trust, or insurance business. If you want to set up one of these special financial corporations, you will need to follow special procedures—for example, obtain the written approval of your state's Banking or Insurance Commission, and prepare and file special Articles of Incorporation with the state.

Here's a partial list of things that a business corporation may do. These powers do not need to be listed in your articles and bylaws:

- Engage in any lawful business.
- Adopt, amend, and repeal bylaws.
- Qualify to do business in any other state, territory, dependency, or foreign country.
- Issue, purchase, redeem, receive, or otherwise acquire, own, hold, sell, lend, exchange, transfer, or otherwise dispose of, pledge, use, and otherwise deal in and with its own shares, bonds, and other securities.

- Assume obligations, enter into contracts, incur liabilities, borrow and lend money, or otherwise use its credit, and secure any of its obligations, contracts, or liabilities by mortgage, pledge, or other encumbrance of all or any part of its property, franchises, and income.
- Make donations for the public welfare or for community fund, hospital, charitable, educational, scientific, or civic or similar purposes. (Like individuals, business corporations are allowed to make charitable donations.)
- Establish and carry out pension, profit-sharing, stock bonus, share pension, share option, savings, thrift, and other employee retirement, incentive, and benefit plans.
- Participate with others in any partnership, joint venture, or other association, transaction or arrangement of any kind, whether or not such participation involves the sharing or delegation of control with, or to, others.
- Adopt, use, and alter a corporate seal. (A corporate seal is simply a stamped or embossed design showing the name of the corporation and its state of formation.) Although state law does not require the use of a corporate seal, some corporations use the seal on formal corporate documents, such as stock certificates, to signify formal approval of the document by the corporation.

Your corporation can engage in more than one line of business. Although state BCAs don't specifically say so, it is clear that a business corporation can engage in as many lines of business as management sees fit. You do not need to set up a separate corporation for each line of business.

F. Corporate People

While a corporation is considered a legal "person," capable of making contracts, paying taxes, and otherwise enjoying the legal rights and responsibilities of a natural person, of course it needs real people to carry out its business. State BCAs classify corporate people in the following ways:

- incorporators
- directors
- officers
- shareholders.

As we explain below, state statutes—and occasionally courts—give each of these corporate people different rights and responsibilities.

In a Small Corporation, One Person Often Wears Several Corporate Hats

In all states, one person may simultaneously serve in more than one of the corporate capacities listed above. For example, if you form your own one-person corporation (most states allow you to do this), you necessarily will be your corporation's only incorporator, director, and shareholder, and you will fill all the required corporate officer positions.

In all states, a business corporation may have just one director and just one shareholder, but in some states the number of directors cannot be less than the number of shareholders if the corporation has three or fewer shareholders. In these states, if your corporation has three or more shareholders, it must have at least three directors; if it has two shareholders, it needs two directors; if it has just one shareholder, it may have just one director. The "Director and Officer Rules" section of your state sheet tells you how many directors and officers are required by your state.

1. Incorporators

Your incorporator is the person who signs your Articles of Incorporation and files them with state corporate filing office. The incorporator is not required to be an initial director, officer, or shareholder of the corporation—nor must the incorporator be a resident of the state. The only legal requirement for incorporators is that, in many states, the incorporator must be at least 18 years old. (If your state imposes an age requirement for incorporators, we list it in the "Articles Instructions" section of your state sheet.)

Even though it is not required, we recommend that you pick one of your initial board members as your incorporator. This helps to ensure that the entire board of directors, which must pick up the reins of management immediately after the corporation is formed, is in the corporate formation loop right from the start. It also means that any correspondence between your new corporation and the state corporate filing office will reach at least one director.

Don't Start Business Until You File Articles

If you act as an incorporator for your corporation and do not limit your activities to preparing and filing articles, be careful. State courts usually say that a corporation is not bound by the incorporator's contracts with third parties prior to actual formation of the corporation, unless the contracts are later ratified by the board of directors or the corporation accepts the benefits of a contract—for example, uses office space under a preincorporation lease signed by an incorporator. Worse, the incorporator may be personally liable on these preincorporation contracts unless the incorporator signs the contract in the name of the corporation only and clearly informs the third party that the corporation does not yet exist, may never come into existence, and, even if it does, may not ratify the contract.

So, a suggestion: If you must arrange for office space, hire employees, or borrow money before you form the corporation, make it clear that any commitments you make are for and in the name of a proposed corporation and are subject to ratification by the corporation when, and if, it comes into existence.

The other party may, of course, refuse to do business with you under these conditions and tell you to come back after the corporation is formed. Again, this is usually the best approach to preincorporation business, anyway—namely, to postpone business until after your articles have been filed and approved by the state. Once this happens, all contracts should be signed in the name of the corporation by a corporate director, officer, or employee. (See "How to Sign Corporate Documents From Now On" at the end of Chapter 4.)

2. Directors

Under each state's Business Corporation Act, directors are given the authority and responsibility for managing the corporation. Let's look at some of the common features of state law that apply to directors.

a. Director Qualifications

State law does not impose residency or stock ownership requirements on directors. Your directors can come from any state and need not be shareholders. The only director requirement in some states is an age requirement—in these states, directors usually must be at least 18 years old.

The directors meet and make decisions collectively as the board of directors. In all states, the board may consist of one or more individuals. Many state BCAs specifically say that a director must be a natural (real) person, as opposed to another corporation or limited liability company (LLC). Even if your state's BCA doesn't say this, it is understood in all states that only real people may be elected as board members.

The "Director and Officer Rules" section of your state sheet lists any director requirements found in your state's BCA.

b. Director Meetings

In most states, directors must meet at least once each year. One reason for this requirement is that most state BCAs specify that directors must be elected (or reelected) for a one-year term at an annual meeting of shareholders. (See Section 4, below.) Once the board is voted in or continued in office at the annual shareholders' meeting, the newly elected or reelected board holds its annual meeting. At this meeting, board members accept their election to the board, then transact any business planned for the meeting.

The date, time, and place of the annual directors' meeting is normally specified in the bylaws. State BCAs usually allow the annual meeting to be held without having to give each director prior written notice of the meeting, but we think it's a good idea to provide written notice of all meetings, including annual board meetings. Directors, particularly newly elected ones, may not note or remember the annual director meeting date specified in the bylaws. Of course, boards often meet more frequently than once per year, particularly in larger corporations with multimember boards. (See "When Do Directors Meet?," below.)

Additional meetings are called "special meetings." State law typically requires that directors receive written notice of the date, place, and purpose of all special meetings of directors.

The "Director Meeting Rules" section of your state sheet in Appendix A lists your state's specific requirements for annual and special directors' meetings, including calling and giving notice of meetings, as well as setting a quorum and voting rights. This language indicates whether or not you can vary the statutory rules. (If you can, the language will say "except as otherwise provided in the articles or bylaws," which means that you are permitted to specify your own rule in your articles or bylaws.)

When Do Directors Meet?

In a small, closely held corporation, the directors meet mostly to satisfy the state BCA's minimal meeting requirements. This normally means an annual meeting at which the newly elected or re-elected board members accept their positions for the upcoming year and approve appropriate business objectives or strategies for the upcoming year. Many small boards also call special meetings during the year to conduct business in a formal setting, or when board approval must be sought under the BCA to make legal decisions, such as amendments to corporation articles or by-laws, issuance of corporate shares, declarations of dividends, appointments of officers, and the like. Other items of business necessary to run the corporation from day to day are normally handled by board members outside the boardroom in their capacities as corporate officers or in other supervisory corporate capacities. The holding of a minimal number of board meetings is the rule in sole-owner or family-managed corporations.

In larger corporations the board typically meets more frequently to review corporate performance and goals, not just to satisfy state BCA legal requirements. For example, the board of a larger corporation may meet quarterly or even monthly to discuss corporate policies and objectives and to establish and hear back from board committees. Since members of larger boards often come from outside corporations and financial institutions that have invested in the corporation, frequent meetings of the board help the corporations keep these investor representatives informed on current corporate performance.

c. Director Voting

Under state law, board members are given one vote each when making board decisions at directors' meetings. The BCA in most states normally sets the quorum requirement for board meetings—that is, the number of directors who must be present to hold a board meeting—at a majority of the full board. However, in most states, your bylaws can change this default rule and specify a greater- or less-than majority quorum rule for directors' meetings. State law also typically provides a majority-voting rule for the approval of board decisions at a meeting. This means that the board approves decisions at a meeting by the "yes" vote of at least a majority of the directors present at the meeting. Again, this majority rule is usually a default state rule; you are normally allowed to specify a different director approval rule in your bylaws.

> **Example:** Tie-Dyed RetroFitters, Inc., is a retro clothing store owned and managed by its four founders. The corporate bylaws establish a four-person board, with a quorum for board meetings specified as a majority of the authorized number of directors. Therefore, to hold a directors' meeting, three of the four directors must attend. A majority of those present at a meeting must approve a decision—remember, at a minimum, a quorum must be present. If all four board members attend a meeting, three directors must approve a decision proposed at the meeting. If a minimum quorum of three attends, then two of the three must approve a decision proposed at the meeting.

Some states set a minimum quorum requirement for directors. In many states, your bylaws cannot establish a quorum of directors that is less than one-third the number of the full board. We tell you if your state imposes this sort of minimum quorum rule for directors in the "Director and Officer Rules" section of your state sheet in Appendix A.

In addition to approving decisions at meetings, directors can also take action by written consent. Under state BCAs, this written "voting" procedure is allowed for all types of director action—that is, any type of action that directors can approve by voting in person at a real meeting. This means that the directors can individually or collectively date and sign a form that says they approve a particular item of business, without the need to hold a face-to-face meeting. State BCAs normally require the signature of *all* directors on a written consent form of this sort—obtaining the signed consent of a simple majority of directors is not sufficient under most state statutes. Look in your state BCA for a section with the title "Directors' Action by Written Consent" or "Directors' Action Without a Meeting" to see how many directors must sign a written consent form in your state.

d.   Board Committees

In smaller corporations, the owners who also run the corporation as officers or other supervisory personnel make up the full board of directors. In larger corporations, the board may include individuals who are not involved with day-to-day corporate operations. These outside directors, who may be representatives of venture capital groups or financial institutions that have provided capital or financing to the corporation, rely heavily on reports of board committees to get the information necessary to make good decisions. For example, the compensation committee of a larger corporation may report regularly to the board to propose the granting of salary increases, bonuses, and stock options to deserving corporate employees. Similarly, a special finance committee may be established by the board to review corporate performance in one or more lines of its business.

State BCAs recognize the need for these committees to help the board get its work done. Here is a typical statute:

> *In performing the duties of a director, a director shall be entitled to rely on information, opinions reports, or statements, including financial statements, prepared or presented by a committee of the board, as to matters within its designated au-*

thority, which committee the director believes to merit confidence.

The above statute is typical in that it allows directors to rely on committees *if* the director is satisfied that a committee report merits confidence. State BCAs also allow a board to delegate its managerial authority to special types of committees, called "executive committees of the board." These are committees made up of two or more board members, and often other corporate personnel such as officers, that take responsibility for one or more areas of board decision making. Larger corporations may set up one or more committees of this sort to handle ongoing areas of corporate management. The full board may meet less frequently to review overall corporate policy, while the committees of the board meet regularly to handle their assigned areas of responsibility.

State law limits the types of authority that can be delegated to an executive committee of the board. Typically, an executive committee cannot, without full board concurrence, amend the articles or bylaws, approve a corporate dividend, or take other specified major corporate actions. Here is a typical BCA statute covering executive committees:

> *Executive Committees of the Board: The board may, by resolution adopted by a majority of the authorized number of directors, designate one or more committees, each consisting of two or more directors, to serve at the pleasure of the board. Any such committee, to the extent provided in the resolution of the board or in the bylaws, shall have all the authority of the board except with respect to: 1) the approval of any action which also requires the approval of shareholders; 2) the filling of vacancies on the board; 3) the fixing of compensation of directors for serving on the board or any committee of the board; 4) a distribution by the corporation [typically, this is defined elsewhere in the Act as a dividend or other payment out of the profits and earnings of the corporation to shareholders]; and 5) the establishment of other committees of the board or appointment of members to these other committees.*

Despite the restrictions, executive committees are permitted to handle a variety of corporate decision-making matters, including hiring and payroll decisions, corporate projects and operations, and a variety of management and overview tasks that would otherwise be handled by the full board.

Appointing an Executive Committee to Handle Employee Compensation

Designating a special executive committee of the board to handle employment compensation and payroll tax decisions can have a collateral tax benefit: It helps insulate directors who do not serve on the committee from personal liability for any unpaid corporate payroll taxes. We've already mentioned that potential personal liability for tax debts is one of the exceptions to corporate limited liability. (See Chapter 1, Section A4.) Here's how this exception works.

Federal tax law permits the IRS and state income and payroll tax agencies to aggressively seek to collect unpaid corporate payroll taxes from "responsible persons" in a corporation. In its collection efforts, the IRS commonly maintains that board members who approve the payment of compensation to corporate employees, or specifically approve the payment of taxes to the IRS or state, are personally responsible for income or payroll taxes not paid by the corporation. Sometimes the IRS wins these arguments; sometimes it doesn't, depending on the overall facts and the extent of a director's involvement in running the corporation. In a small, closely held corporation, it's difficult for a board member who also serves as a principal corporate officer to deny being a responsible person—after all, the board member probably has the power to make the corporation pay its taxes if it has the funds to do so. But in a larger corporation with outside directors on its board, outside directors are less likely to be viewed as "responsible persons," if compensation and tax decisions are delegated to a special compensation or finance committee consisting of the more active board members. This helps them avoid personal liability in case of a payroll tax deficiency or dispute.

---

e. Directors' Duties

Directors are required under state BCA statutes to exercise care in making management decisions and act in the best interests of the corporation. If a court decides that a director has violated these duties, the director may be held personally liable for any resulting financial loss to the corporation or its shareholders.

1. Duty of Care

The first and foremost duty owed by a director to a corporation is the statutory "duty of care." Here is a typical state BCA statute that defines, in general terms, a director's duty of care:

> *A director must act in good faith, in a manner the director believes to be in the best interests of the corporation and its shareholders and with such care, including reasonable inquiry, as an ordinarily prudent person in a like position would use under similar conditions.*

This is a very broad standard. Courts interpret it to mean that a director is allowed to make mistakes that lead to financial loss for the corporation and its shareholders without fear of personal legal liability, as long as the director had good reason for making the decisions. And, as discussed in Subsection d, above, one good reason may be that the director relied on the apparently reliable reports of a board committee.

The duty of care is normally easy to fulfill. The standard for the directors' duty of care is fairly lenient. A director has to be negligent (careless), almost to the point of flagrant inattention or fraudulent disregard of the financial implications of board decisions, to violate the statutory standards. And in small corporations, even if the standard is violated, personal liability problems are rare. This is because the people who have legal standing to seek damages for a director's violation of the duty of care are those whose have been harmed financially by a director's bad decision making—namely, its shareholders. In a closely held corporation where all board members also are the corporation's only shareholders, it is unlikely that one director will sue another. But it's not unheard of, particularly if one or more directors officially disagreed with a corporate decision they felt was too risky and wrong-headed—and the value of their shares was diminished significantly because of it. But even if the disgruntled director-shareholders do bring suit against the other directors on behalf of the corporation, they will win only if they can convince a court that the directors had little or no business reason for their decision or that they made it simply to further their own personal financial interests, not those of the corporation.

In larger corporations with shareholders who are not members of the board of directors, chances increase that a disgruntled shareholder who has no voice in management may decide that the directors acted wrongly and should be held accountable for a major loss of share value. Even so, shareholder suits that seek to impose personal liability on a director are infrequent. They most often arise when a corporation is on the auction block—that is, when it is being sold or merged with another corporation. For example, courts have held the board personally liable to the shareholders for agreeing to a sale favored by a leading board member if the board did not adequately investigate the current market value of the corporation and seek counteroffers to the proposed sale.

How to avoid trouble. As a director, a court is more likely to find you in violation of your duty of care if you do not bother to attend and participate in board meetings, obtain information about the likely financial consequences of a board decision, or check alternative courses of action before going forward with an action that can affect share value. In other words, don't miss board meetings or simply attend and rubber-stamp proposals brought up by other board members for consideration, particularly if the decision involves a major commitment of corporate funds or resources. Another way of saying all of this is that it's okay for you to approve board decisions that put corporate capital or share values at risk as long as you are reasonably aware of the nature of these risks and decide they are worth taking to achieve a valid corporate business objective.

Many state BCAs underline the importance of a director paying full attention to corporate decision making, rather than merely sitting back and letting others muscle their pet projects past the board. Under many BCAs, a director present at a meeting during which an action is approved is legally considered to have approved all decisions reached at the meeting unless the director speaks up and votes "no" to the decision or specifically requests that his or her dissent or abstention be entered in the minutes (or hands the chairperson a written abstention to the proposal).

Here's a typical statute that stresses the importance of taking an active stance as a director:

> *A director who is present at a meeting of the board of directors when corporate action is taken is deemed to have assented to all action taken at the meeting unless:*
>
> *(a) The director objects at the beginning of the meeting, or promptly upon his or her arrival, to holding the meeting or transacting business at the meeting and does not thereafter vote for or assent to any action taken at the meeting;*
>
> *(b) The director contemporaneously requests that his or her dissent or abstention as to any specific action taken be entered in the minutes of the meeting; or*
>
> *(c) The director causes written notice of his or her dissent or abstention as to any specific action to be received by the presiding officer of the meeting before adjournment of the meeting or by the corporation promptly after adjournment of the meeting.*

Example: A trustee in bankruptcy sued to recover from the estate of a corporate director a large sum paid as "loans" to the director's sons, who also sat on the board of a successful banking and insurance business. The court agreed that even though the director had not personally received the funds, she should not have deferred to the decisions of her sons without making her own inquiries. She had a duty to question any payouts made by the corporation, to examine financial statements, and to learn the requirements of corporate and insurance law that limited the making of the excessive insider loans. The court held the director's estate liable for payback of the loans, saying that "ornamental" or so-called "dummy" directors have the same responsibility to actively and attentively protect corporate assets as all active board members. *Francis v. New Jersey Bank*, 87 N.J. 15, 432 A.2d 814 (1981).

Some state statutes provide extra protection from shareholder suits. In recognition of the increased willingness of shareholders and their attorneys to sue directors—particularly when share values fall following action by the board—many state legislatures have added special director immunity provisions to their BCAs to help directors avoid personal liability when shareholders launch legal challenges to corporate management. This additional help comes in the form of special BCA provisions that let a corporation place language in its articles that limits or eliminates all personal liability of the board to the corporation or shareholders except in a few special cases. Typically, immunity cannot be provided where the board has acted unlawfully or where it can be shown the director purposefully acted against the best interests of the corporation or otherwise in flagrant disregard of the director's statutory duty of care.

If a state's BCA contains a provision of this sort, you'll likely find it in the section that specifies the optional provisions that may be included in your Articles of Incorporation. Here's a typical provision, extracted from California's "Articles of Incorporation—Optional Provisions" statute (California General Corporation Law, § 204(a)(10)):

The Articles of Incorporation may set forth provisions eliminating or limiting the personal liability of a director for monetary damages in an action brought by or for or in the right of the corporation for breach of a director's duties to the corporation and its shareholders, provided, however, that such a provision may not eliminate or limit the liability of directors (1) for acts or omissions that involve intentional misconduct or a knowing violation of law, (2) for acts or omissions that a

director believes to be contrary to the best interests of the corporation or its shareholders or that involve the absence of good faith on the part of the director, (3) for any transaction for which the director derived an improper personal benefit, (4) for acts or omissions that show a reckless disregard for the director's duty to the corporation or its shareholders in circumstances in which the director was aware, or should have been aware, in the ordinary course of performing a director's duties, of a risk of serious injury to the corporation or its shareholders, or (5) for acts or omissions that constitute an unexcused pattern of inattention that amounts to an abdication of the director's duty to the corporation or its shareholders.

Again, it is probably unnecessary for a small business corporation where all shareholders will serve on the board of directors to adopt this type of provision. However, if you are worried about shareholder suits against your board—perhaps because you plan to have outside shareholders who may question risky policies the board must implement to achieve success in a competitive market—you may wish to look at your state BCA for this sort of director immunity provision. Adding this type of provision to your articles also makes sense if you want to reassure outsiders who serve on your board that they have the maximum legal protection possible. If you find an immunity statute in your state BCA, you can add the required language to your articles. A lawyer familiar with your state's BCA can help you get the job done right. (See Chapter 6.)

2. Duty of Loyalty

In addition to a director's statutory duty of care, state courts also say that a director has a duty of loyalty to the corporation. This duty of loyalty means a director must give the corporation a right of first refusal as to business opportunities the director becomes aware of while serving the corporation. If the corporation fails to take advantage of the opportunity after the board member discloses it, or if the corporation clearly would not be interested in it, the director can pursue it.

The duty of loyalty is simply a matter of fair dealing and common sense. No one wants a board member to take personal commercial advantage of an opportunity that arises within the corporate context unless the corporation itself is given first shot at it. If a board member violates the duty of loyalty, he or she can be held personally liable for the value of the commercial opportunity lost by the corporation.

> **Example:** A corporate director, who also works as an officer, is researching sites for new corporate headquarters when he discovers land being offered at a ridiculously low price. He buys the land for himself to launch his own sideline business without first reporting back to the full board and letting it decide whether to make an offer on the property. A court finds the director personally liable to the corporation for the value of the bargain the director appropriated for himself—that is, the difference between the bargain sales price and the higher prevailing market price the corporation ended up paying.

The duty of loyalty issue rarely presents a problem in a small corporation context where all directors are actively involved in the destiny of the corporation on a full-time basis; they don't have outside business interests that conflict with their corporation But in larger corporations with outside board members who have separate commercial interests, conflicts may more easily arise. For example, a board member with an outside business may discover a business opportunity that presents itself at a board meeting or as part of the reports or information the director reviews. This opportunity may provide a possible advantage to the director's outside business, as well as the corporation's. In this situation, board members can't blithely go ahead and use the opportunity for their outside business without first telling the board that they are interested in doing so and seeking the board's permission.

f. Conflicts of Interest

If you browse your state BCA, you'll probably find a law under the "Directors" heading that deals with board approval of transactions in which a director has a financial interest—for example, approval by the board of a lease of commercial real estate owned by a director. The title of this section may be "Directors' Conflict of Interests," "Board Approval of Self-Interested Transaction," or a similar title.

Throughout the states, these conflict of interest statutes share common provisions and features. In most states, the statute says that the full board is allowed to approve corporate business decisions that financially benefit one or more directors, as long as certain formalities are carried out. Typically, one way to approve such transactions is by the affirmative votes of a sufficient number of disinterested directors (those who will not benefit from the deal) after disclosure of the personal benefit to the interested director. The number of required votes is usually defined by statute as a majority of the full board without counting the vote of the interested director. (Most states allow you to count the interested director for purposes of obtaining a quorum for the meeting, but not to approve the deal.) Of course, in a small corporation it may not be possible to find a sufficient number of disinterested directors. For example, if two members of a three-person board financially benefit from a deal, the vote of the remaining one director will not constitute a majority of the full board.

Most states also allow the shareholders to approve a transaction that benefits a director. After full disclosure of the benefit to the director is made at a shareholders' meeting, a majority of shareholders must approve the transaction, not counting the votes of any shareholders who may benefit from the transaction. Again, in a small corporation, it may be difficult to obtain a sufficient number of disinterested shareholder votes, since the benefited directors may own most of the corporation's shares. Fortunately, most state statutes provide a third way to validate the decision. This alternative simply requires that the deal be fair to the corporation at the time it was approved by the board, even if it was approved in part by directors (or shareholders) who stand to benefit financially from the transaction.

Here are a few points to keep in mind when considering rules relating to conflicts of interest:

- These rules normally come into play only if a board decision is later challenged in court by a disgruntled shareholder who sues the benefited director on behalf of the corporation. Typically, the suit will demand the benefited director pay back the amount of the undeserved benefit to the corporation—plus interest, legal fees, court costs, and possibly punitive damages. If your small corporation does not have outside shareholders, you do not need to worry about shareholder suits, provided all your director-shareholders agree to the decision.

- If your deal is fair to the corporation—that is, if the benefit that accrues to a director is the same financial benefit that would accrue to anyone doing business with the corporation in a similar deal—it should withstand challenge, regardless of how it was approved. Another way of saying this is that a director, just like any other person or company, is entitled to do business with your corporation as long as the deal is fair and commercially reasonable. In fact, executives from other businesses, such as bank managers, investment advisers, and CEOs from other companies, sit on the boards of promising small corporations, not just to give expert advice and guidance but to help facilitate business between their corporations. Again, as long as the corporation doesn't put together sweetheart deals that favor these outside board interests at the expense of the corporation and its shareholders, the deals should be considered fair.

Boards Can Approve Their Own Compensation

Most state BCAs specifically allow the board to set its own compensation. In other words, no matter what the state's director conflict of interest statute says, it's okay for the board to vote to pay itself fair compensation for doing its work. Normally, board members are simply paid a reasonable per diem amount for attending meetings, plus travel and lodging expenses if appropriate. Board members also get stock options—a way to buy shares at current prices to give them an incentive to manage the corporation successfully and raise its share value.

g. Director Approval of Shareholder Distributions

State BCAs impose limits on the payout of corporate profits and earnings to shareholders and other corporate insiders. Typically, these payouts are made in the form of dividends to shareholders. In small, closely held corporations, dividends are rarely paid, since they are subject to double taxation (even though under current federal tax rules, dividends are subject to low individual tax rates—see Appendix B).

However, other types of distributions that are subject to these BCA restrictions can occur—for example, the buy-back of shares by a director/shareholder or the payback of a shareholder loan made by a corporate insider. If the board approves a shareholder distribution in violation of state BCA requirements, each director can be held personally liable for the amount not allowed under the state's BCA.

State requirements for shareholder distributions vary. Most apply what is called a solvency test, which requires that the corporation be able to meet its expected financial obligations after the distribution—that is, be able to pay its bills as they become due after the payout of funds to shareholders. Some states also add an "assets test," which requires that corporate assets exceed liabilities by a specified amount or ratio. In states that use a par value scheme in the corporate statutes, additional limitations are placed on paying out funds from the corporation's stated capital account. (This is the financial account that holds all par value amounts paid in by shareholders; see Section H2, below.)

To find your state's shareholder distribution requirements, browse your state BCA's Shareholder section, looking for a statute with the title "Dividends," "Distributions to Shareholders," or "Payments From Stated Capital."

⚠ It doesn't pay to bankrupt your own corporation. As a matter of practice, any payment approved by the board—whether to shareholders or to other corporate insiders, such as directors or officers—is likely to be subject to legal attack if it leaves a corporation insolvent. The reason: This type of overspending is likely to be challenged later on as a violation of the director's duty of care to the corporation. Court cases in this area show that even shareholders in small corporations can personally recover money from directors who approve a generous payout to corporate insiders—for example, a buy-back of the founder's shares or repayment of a founder loan—when it leaves the corporation without sufficient funds to stay in business. And even though general corporate creditors don't normally have legal standing to sue directors for breach of their statutory duty of care to the corporation, in extreme cases state courts have found ways to let creditors recover money from directors personally. For example, when directors close down their corporation by raiding its remaining cash reserves to buy back their shares without first paying off creditors, state courts have required the directors to personally pay the creditors.

h.   Personal Liability to Outsiders

So far, we've focused on a director's personal liability to insiders—that is, to corporate shareholders—for causing financial harm to a corporation by:

- breaching the duty of care or loyalty to the corporation

- entering into a preferential personal business deal with the corporation without full disclosure and approval by the other board members or shareholders, or
- approving an unlawful distribution of corporate funds.

But what about a director's liability to outsiders, such as banks, vendors, or suppliers? As you already know, the basic limited liability rule is that board members are not personally liable for corporate debts and liabilities owed to or claimed by outsiders. This means that if an outsider successfully sues a corporation for unpaid bills or for failure to pay or perform under a corporate contract, the directors are immune from personal liability arising from the dispute. However, as is almost always true in law, there are a few exceptions to this standard rule:

- **Personally signed loans and contracts.** In the early phase of corporate operations, a bank may ask corporate founders to cosign a corporate loan and personally guarantee repayment if the corporation defaults. It may also ask the founders to pledge their own personal assets—such as home equity—as security for the cosigned loan. If a director signs a bank loan or any other type of corporate contract in the director's own name, that director will be personally liable in the event of a default under the loan or contract—and any personal assets pledged as security are subject to seizure and liquidation.
- **Unpaid taxes.** If the corporation fails to pay corporate income or payroll taxes, the IRS and state tax agency can seek to hold any "responsible person," including a board member, personally liable for taxes plus interest and penalties. (See "Appointing an Executive Committee to Handle Employee Compensation" in Subsection d, above.)
- **Personal liability statutes.** State and federal law may hold corporate directors personally liable for violations of special statutes—for example, repeated or flagrant violations of environmental or toxic cleanup laws, or intentional violations of securities statutes. As a director, your best defense against this sort of personal li-

ability is to stay informed of any special legal rules that apply to your corporation, and to vote "no" if a board decision may give rise to a legal penalty.

- **Personal injuries.** Directors are personally liable for injuries and other damage they personally inflict on others. The legal way of saying this is that directors are personally liable for their own legal "torts." In other words, if you, as a corporate director, hold a press conference and unlawfully libel and cause harm to a competitor's business, don't expect the shield of corporate limited liability to protect you. You are personally liable for any damage you cause to other people, other companies, and their property.

- **Corporate raiding.** As mentioned in Subsection g, above, if you raid your corporate cookie jar—by approving an overly generous buy-out of your shares or some other self-interested business deal that leaves your corporation unable to pay its bills—you may face a creditor lawsuit. In some states, a court will make you return the money to your corporation so the creditors can get paid—plus order you to pay lawsuit-related costs and attorney's fees.

i. Director Indemnification and Insurance

As we've said, the directors of smaller, closely held corporations normally do not need to lose sleep worrying over whether they have met their statutory duty of care to their corporation. That's because corporate management and shareholders are normally the same people or, at the very least, are in close touch. Since directors and shareholders have the same information, even if corporate resources are used to implement risky corporate strategies that have lackluster financial results, shareholder lawsuits rarely follow.

But as a business grows and outside shareholders invest in the corporation's future, shareholder disputes can more easily arise. Outside shareholders are usually not aware of the nuances of board decisions. Even regular shareholder mailings and meetings may not be enough to educate shareholders about the wisdom of aggressive decisions made by the board to keep the corporation competitive. If the corporation loses money, one or more shareholders may file suit, seeking personal judgments from corporate directors for a failure to exercise their statutory duty of due care.

Fortunately, the laws of all states contain indemnification and insurance provisions that help a corporation protect its board members from having to pay money out of their own pockets, even if a shareholder suit succeeds or is settled on terms favorable to the shareholder. These statutes also help with other costs that must be paid even if the directors win, such as lawyers' fees and court costs (deposition costs and filing fees). Here's a brief rundown of how they work.

1. Indemnification

State BCAs contain indemnification statutes that cover some out-of-pocket lawsuit and settlement amounts a director may be asked to personally pay. "Indemnification" means that someone else promises to pay money to cover certain costs. BCA indemnification statutes specify the circumstances under which a corporation can agree to directly pay or reimburse a director for amounts that the director must pay because of an act—or failure to act—as a director.

If you browse your state's BCA, you'll find a corporate indemnification statute, titled "Indemnification," "Indemnification of Directors and Officers," or a similar title. These statutes tend to contain very similar provisions from state to state. Here's a summary of the provisions you're likely to find in your state's BCA:

- **If director wins.** Generally, if a director wins a lawsuit, corporations may indemnify—pay the director—legal costs incurred by the director, such as attorneys' fees and court costs. In many statutes, the corporation *must* pay these costs if the director succeeds in court.

- **If director loses or settles.** If a director loses a lawsuit or agrees to a settlement, the BCA normally allows the corporation to indemnify the director for legal judgments, settlements, attorneys' fees, and other costs if the director acted in good faith and in the best interests of the corporation. Typically, this determination must be made by a majority of the nonindemnified directors, by a majority of shareholders (not counting shares owned by the indemnified director), or by a court.

- **Limits on indemnity.** If the director loses a lawsuit or settles a controversy involving (1) the director's breach of the duty of care or loyalty; (2) the receipt of an improper personal benefit by the director; or (3) the payment of unlawful distributions to shareholders, the statutes normally prohibit any indemnification. These prohibitions make sense. In each of these situations, the director has unlawfully caused financial harm to the corporation. If the director pays the corporation for its loss and then the corporation reimburses the director for this payment, the corporation has won nothing at all—it is left in a losing position and the director is off the hook financially. Here's another way of saying this: A corporation cannot indemnify a director for unauthorized financial harm the director causes to the corporation; the director has to personally pay these amounts.

This is a very general summary. If indemnification is important to you, make a point to look at your BCA indemnification statute. Each state's law is different, and even small differences in wording can make a huge financial difference to your corporation and its directors if they are sued.

2. Insurance

Most state BCAs specifically allow a corporation to purchase insurance to pay for directors' personal lawsuit and settlement costs, including judgments, settlements, legal fees, and court costs. State statutes normally place no limit on what these policies may cover. Typically, they can cover all kinds of losses, whether or not the losses are eligible for indemnification under the state's BCA.

Commercial insurance companies call director and officer liability policies "D & O liability policies." As with any insurance policy, premium payments vary according to the deductible amount and total liability ceiling selected for the policy. Depending on the policy, insurance companies may make payouts to reimburse a corporation for indemnification it has paid a director, to advance or reimburse legal costs, or to cover settlements or judgments. And, since insurance can cover amounts that can't be indemnified under state law—such as personal liability for a director's breach of duty to the corporation—payouts also can go right to the directors to cover legal costs, settlements, and judgments not indemnified by their corporation.

Of course, D & O policies contain exclusions from coverage—most won't pay if a director knowingly violates the law or commits fraud.

3. Officers

State BCAs specify the officer positions that a corporation must fill. These are known as the corporation's "statutory officers" and usually include a president, vice president, secretary, and treasurer. You list the names and addresses of your statutory officers in the annual filing you must make each year with your state corporate filing office. (This filing is a formality, and the fee to file your annual statement is normally small.) Except in Alaska and West Virginia, which require a separate person to hold the offices of president and secretary, state law allows one person to hold all the required corporate officer positions.

We list the required statutory officer positions and related state law provisions applicable to officers in the "Director and Officer Rules" section of your state sheet in Appendix A.

State law normally does not impose specific requirements on what statutory officers must do, except to say that one officer—typically the corporate secretary—must be appointed to keep corporate records, including meeting minutes. Often, the boards of small business corporations fill the statutory officer positions as a formality to comply with state requirements, while the people who supervise and run the corporation day to day are given titles other than those required by law.

Example: DD Huge and Max MC form their own rap music publishing and artist representation company, Phat & Phunky Pheatures, Inc. To meet the statutory requirements, DD is appointed as the president and Max as the treasurer of the corporation. No salaries are paid for filling these statutory officer positions. DD is paid a corporate salary for acting as the Chief Rap Rep and Max is paid a salary as Caliph of Phinances. People are paid for what they do; not for their title.

In practice, the title given the top corporate officer is usually Chief Executive Officer (CEO) and the top finance officer is usually called the Chief Financial Officer (CFO). (A COO is a Chief Operating Officer.) Even the title "vice president" is outdated. Most corporations instead refer to second-tier corporate officers as associates, managers, or directors of a particular corporate department—such as marketing associate, sales director, publicity manager, or director of online operations—rather than using a vice president title.

The statutory officer position of secretary normally has no real-life counterpart in the everyday world of the corporation. In other words, the position of corporate secretary is one created to accommodate state BCA legal requirements, not the entrepreneurial needs of the corporation. However, the person appointed as secretary does have real work to do. As mentioned above, the secretary must keep the legal records of the corporation, preparing minutes of board and shareholder meetings. And banks and other financial institutions often require the signature or certification of the corporate secretary to attest that the board has approved items of business, such as a formal board resolution to approve a bank loan or line of credit. The secretary also normally handles all requests from the board or shareholders for copies of corporate legal documents—such as corporate articles, bylaws, or minutes of meetings, or records of stock ownership in the corporation. Common practice is to delegate many of the duties of corporate secretary to another salaried officer—commonly the chief corporate financial or administrative officer.

Whatever you call corporate officers—and whatever tasks you delegate to them—keep the following points in mind:

- Officers can bind the corporation legally to a contract or other business relationship unless the party they do business with knows the officer does not have authority to transact the particular business—an exception that rarely occurs.

- Officers, like all corporate employees, are generally not personally liable for their acts while working for the corporation. However, like other employees (as well as directors), they are personally liable for any harm (personal injuries or "torts") they cause to another person. (The corporation can be liable, too, if it was negligent in hiring the officer.)

⚠ **Officers should sign contracts in their corporate capacity.** No matter what their title, officers should sign contracts and transact business in the name of the corporation, showing the officer's title next to their signature. If the officer signs a contract without affixing a title after or under the signature, and the corporation defaults on the deal, the officer may be held personally liable for any loss caused by the corporation's default, if the other party can show it was reasonable to believe the officer was transacting business on the officer's own behalf.

4. Shareholders

Shareholders invest in a corporation and elect its board of directors. They are not personally liable for corporate debts or other obligations. A shareholder's basic financial rights in the corporation are:

- participation in corporate dividends, and
- a stake in corporate assets (the shareholders' equity as shown on the corporate balance sheet).

In practice, shareholders of small corporations normally do not receive dividends. Rather, they wait until the corporation's overall value increases, then sell their shares. In a small, closely held corporation, the only market for these shares is another share-holder or the corporation itself. If the corporation has a good chance for success, the shareholder waits until the corporation is sold to another business that cashes out the existing shareholders or converts their shares to marketable shares in the acquiring business. And, of course, the corporation may go public and create a market for its own shares.

State BCAs contain various provisions that regu-late and define shareholder responsibilities and rights. In this section, we look at the most common shareholder meeting provisions and stock issuance rules.

a.   Annual Shareholder Meetings

Most state BCAs require shareholders to meet annu-ally to elect (or reelect) the board of directors to a one-year term. Even in a small corporation, share-holders must receive written notice of annual meet-ings. Typically, this notice must be mailed or deliv-ered within ten to 60 days before the meeting.

At a shareholder's meeting, a quorum must be present before the meeting begins. Most state BCAs require the presence, in person or by written proxy, of at least a majority of all the voting shares. The corporate secretary is normally required to bring an alphabetically ordered list of current voting share-holders and their share interests to the meeting, and to have it available for inspection by anyone who wants to see it.

Once a quorum is counted and the annual meet-ing begins, the names of directors are placed in nomination by those present, and the shareholder votes are taken. The standard voting rule is that each share gets one vote, and the nominees to the board who receive the highest number of votes (up to the number of directors to be elected) are desig-nated as directors for the next one-year term.

Example: Widgetless Web Works, Inc., has a three-person board of directors and ten share-holders who own a total of 50,000 shares. At the annual meeting, five shareholders attend who collectively own 40,000 shares (8,000 each) and vote on four nominees to the board. The results of the voting are as follows:

Nominee	Votes	
Jane	40,000	(all five shareholders voted for her)
George	40,000	(all five shareholders voted for him)
Bill	24,000	(three shareholders voted Bill as their third choice)
Sally	16,000	(two shareholders voted Sally as their third choice)

Jane, George, and Bill are the three new board members.

In addition to standard voting practices, most states allow shareholders to use special cumulative voting procedures to elect directors. Under cumula-tive voting rules, a shareholder gets a number of votes to cast in an election that equals the number of shares owned multiplied by the number of direc-tors to be elected. This total number of votes can be cumulated and voted for just one director, or split up and voted for more than one nominee.

Cumulative voting procedures vary from state to state. Some statutes say that shareholders can use cumulative voting unless it is prohibited in the ar-ticles. Some say that the articles must specifically au-thorize cumulative voting before it can be used. Even if cumulative voting is authorized by state law or the articles, the normal rule is that a shareholder must specifically request to use it at a shareholder's meeting to elect directors. If so, then all sharehold-ers must cumulatively vote their shares for the elec-tion of directors.

Example: Building on the previous example but using cumulative voting in place of normal one-vote-per-share voting, each shareholder gets 24,000 votes (8,000 shares times three nominees to be elected). If the two shareholders who voted for Sally decide to cumulate and vote 24,000 votes each for Sally, letting the other shareholders have total control over the election of the other board members, and each of the other three shareholders cast 12,000 votes each for Jane, 8,000 for George, and 4,000 for Bill, the cumulative vote tally looks like this:

Nominee	Votes
Jane	36,000
George	24,000
Sally	48,000
Bill	12,000

This time, the Sally shareholders have enough voting clout to get her elected; they let the other directors decide the other two slots with their Jane and George votes, but they didn't allow the others to get Bill on the board. Cumulative voting was designed to allow minority shareholders to achieve exactly this kind of result—namely, getting someone elected to the board even though they own a minority of the total shareholder voting power.

We list your state's requirements for annual and special shareholder meetings in the "Shareholder Meeting Rules" section your state sheet. To read the full BCA provisions, see the "Shareholders" or "Shareholders' Meetings" section of your state's BCA. For cumulative voting provisions, look for a section called "Cumulative Voting" or "Election of Directors" under the "Shareholders" heading. Also look in the "Articles of Incorporation—Required Provisions" section of the BCA to see whether you must place provisions to authorize or prohibit cumulative voting in your articles.

Special Staggered Board Election Rules

Most states allow you to split up your board and elect just a portion of its directors each year. Larger corporations with bigger boards may prefer to elect directors this way, rather than electing a larger board en masse each year. Boards split up in this manner are referred to as "classified boards" or "staggered boards" in state BCAs. This jargon derives from the fact that using this scheme, shareholders elect only one class (or portion) of directors each year. For example, the shareholders of a corporation with a nine-person board can be asked to elect just three board members annually. This means that each group of three directors serves for three years before their time comes for reelection. If you are interested in authorizing the election of your board by shareholders under these staggered board rules, look for a statute titled "Staggered Board of Directors" or "Classified Board of Directors" in the "Directors" section of your state BCA. If you do decide to follow these rules, you will need to add your staggered election board procedure to your bylaws.

b. Special Shareholder Meetings

The board calls special shareholder meetings during the year whenever it needs shareholder approval for an important item of corporate business. In most states, the board must ask shareholders to approve:

- amendments (changes) to the corporation's articles
- the sale of substantially all corporate assets
- the merger of the corporation with another business, or
- other structural changes that affect existing shareholders.

For example, the board may wish to attract investment capital by creating a new class of preferred shares of stock that provide a liquidation preference to investors—that is, that guarantee the preferred shareholder a return of two times the purchase price of their shares when they are sold back to the corporation or when it liquidates or is merged. (Regular shares do not contain this sort of preference.) State BCAs normally require the approval of at least a majority of all the existing shares of the corporation to create a new class of shares that has preferences not enjoyed by the existing shareholders.

The shareholders, themselves, can decide to call a special meeting of shareholders to exercise authority granted under the state BCA—for example, to fill a vacancy on the board or replace a director, to amend the articles or bylaws, or even to vote to dissolve the corporation. State law normally sets a low ownership threshold for calling shareholders' meeting—typically, 10% or less of the corporation's shares.

A standard state corporate law requirement is that only the business described in the notice of a special shareholder's meeting can be approved at a special shareholder's meeting. If new business comes up during the meeting, another special shareholders' meeting must be called and held to take care of it. Again, we list your state's BCA rules for the calling of shareholder meetings in the "Shareholder Meeting Rules" section of your state sheet.

G. Capitalization of the Corporation

A corporation needs people and money to get started. The money or dollar value of assets used to set up a corporation is called its "capital," and the process of obtaining these start-up funds and property is called "capitalizing" the corporation. Most states have no minimum capitalization requirements. South Dakota is an exception: It says that a minimum of $1,000 in cash or property must be paid into the corporation by its initial shareholders before the corporation can begin doing business. (These requirements are explained in the "Articles Instructions" section of the South Dakota state sheet in Appendix A.)

While it may be tempting to start a business on a shoestring and earn as you learn, the idea of starting a corporation with little money or assets is usually impractical. Business corporations are in business to make money, and you normally need at least a rea-

sonable amount of cash and assets to begin corporate operations. To give your corporation the best chance of succeeding, we recommend that you fund your corporation with enough money and other assets to begin doing business and to cover short-range expenses, taxes, and debts. Of course, if your business will be based in your home, or otherwise get off to a low-key start, your initial investment or capitalization can be appropriately modest. In short, the important thing is not the amount you contribute, but that your start-up capital is large enough to meet initial business needs.

There are various ways to capitalize a new corporation. Here are the most common:

- **Incorporating an existing business.** The existing owners transfer the assets of an unincorporated business to the corporation in exchange for shares. Each owner of the previous business (who now becomes a corporate shareholder) receives a percentage of stock ownership equal to their ownership percentage in the prior business. This book provides a bill of sale form that unincorporated business owners can use to document the transfer of the assets from their unincorporated business to a new corporation in return for shares. (See Chapter 4, Step 7B, for the form and for a discussion of legal and tax issues that may arise when you incorporate an existing business.)

- **Incorporating a new business.** The founders pay cash and transfer property to the corporation in exchange for shares. If state law allows, some founders receive shares in return for a promise to provide services to the corporation or by promising to pay for the shares later. We discuss the specifics of stock issuance in Section H, below.

- **Personal loans.** Whether incorporating a new or existing business, some owners may decide to make a personal loan to the corporation in addition to buying shares. The corporation normally repays these loan funds within a few years, often with the corporation making interest-only payments during the loan term and paying off the principal at the end of the loan period.

Keep loan transactions reasonable. If shareholders will lend money to the corporation, it's best not to overdo it. Some tax advisers think it's dicey to have a debt-to-equity ratio of more than 3-1, while some are more aggressive and balk if the ratio gets close to 10-1. During a subsequent corporate tax audit, the IRS may become suspicious of a corporation with a high ratio of debt to equity or with very loose shareholder loan arrangements. The IRS may treat shareholder loans as contributions of capital if (1) all or most shareholders contribute very little equity capital to buy shares, and lend money to their corporation in relative amounts that reflect their share ownership percentages; and/or (2) the loans are not backed up with written promissory notes or don't contain a commercially reasonable rate of interest. This means that the corporation cannot deduct interest payments it makes under the loans and that all payouts made by the corporation—both interest and principal repayments—will be taxed to the shareholder as a taxable dividend.

For promissory notes and other corporate forms. Nolo's *The Corporate Minutes Book*, by Anthony Mancuso, provides several types of shareholder and corporate promissory note forms on CD-ROM with instructions, plus many useful corporate minute forms and resolutions for approving and implementing standard items of ongoing corporate business.

Courts Sometimes "Pierce the Corporate Veil"

What if you don't follow most of the basic rules for organizing and running your corporation outlined in this chapter? That is, if you don't contribute adequate capital to your corporation, adopt bylaws, appoint officers, issue stock, hold annual shareholder and director meetings, keep corporate records, or generally pay much attention to the director/officer/shareholder distinctions set up by your state's BCA? The answer is that if you end up in a court, a judge may decide that your corporation is not a real legal entity worthy of respect, but simply a bogus legal device you are using to cloak yourself in the mantle of corporate limited liability. If that happens, the court can hold you personally liable for corporate debts or claims. This dire result is called "piercing the corporate veil."

Veil piercing is the exception, not the rule. It happens mostly in cases where the corporation's founders have not only ignored all or most corporate formalities, but have also engaged in devious or underhanded business practices. Nonetheless, it's wise to take your corporation seriously to avoid even a remote chance of having your corporation's limited liability protection disregarded by a court. Just follow the standard corporate organizational and operational formalities discussed in this and the following chapters, and you should be safe from legal attack.

H. Sale and Issuance of Stock

Under state law, several things must happen before your corporation can issue stock to its shareholders:

- Your articles must authorize the number and type of shares you wish to issue. (See Sections 1 and 2, below.)
- Your corporation must actually receive cash or property in exchange for the stock be received by your corporation—or written shareholder promises to provide services or pay cash if your state allows it. (See Section 3, below.)
- Your board must approve the value of non-cash payments for stock. (Your Minutes of First Meeting of Directors, covered in Chapter 5, let you do this.)
- You must meet the requirements of state and federal securities laws. (See Section I, below.)

1. How Many Shares Should You Authorize in Your Articles?

Since many states charge an incorporation fee based on the number of shares authorized in the Articles of Incorporation, many small business incorporators sensibly authorize the maximum number of shares they can for the smallest incorporation fee. In some states, more shares that have a nominal or "par" value can be issued than shares without par value to obtain the smallest filing fee, so this also is a consideration. (For a full explanation of the par value concept, see Section 2, below.)

In the "Articles Instructions" section of your state sheet, we tell you whether your state charges an incorporation fee based on the number of shares authorized in your articles. We also tell you how many shares you can authorize (with or without par value) for the minimum fee.

In states where your incorporation fee is not based on the number or type of shares authorized in your articles, you can authorize as many shares as you wish, including shares for later issuance to shareholders. In all cases, keep the following points in mind:

- The shares authorized in your articles place an upper limit on the number and type of shares you can sell to your shareholders. If you want to issue more shares than the number authorized in your articles or wish issue a new type not mentioned in your articles, you must amend the articles and file the amendment with the state corporate filing office prior to issuing the new shares.
- The actual number of shares you authorize in your articles and later issue to your shareholders is arbitrary. It is the relative stock ownership percentages that have real meaning to shareholders when it comes time to pay dividends, buy back shares, or sell your corporation.

  Example: Bob and Charlie form their own corporation and contribute equal amounts of cash to buy its initial shares. Each should get one-half of the shares issued by the corporation, so that each ends up with half of the total shareholder voting power, each participates equally in any payouts of corporate profits, and each receives equal net sales proceeds when the corporation is sold. To accomplish this, the corporation could issue Bob and Charlie each one share, one million shares, or any number in between, as long as each gets the same number of shares.

- You set the value of your shares when you form a corporation. You can choose whatever price you wish, as long as it is set the same for all of your initial shareholders. If you set a low share price, you issue more shares to each shareholder than you would if you set a higher share price.

  Example: Let's say Bob and Charlie from the previous example each paid $10,000 into the corporation to buy its initial shares. If you set a share price of $10,000 per share, each is issued one share. If you set a share price of one cent per share, each receives one million shares (1,000,000 x $.01 = $10,000).

In some states, the maximum number of shares that can be authorized in the articles for the smallest fee is small—perhaps just 100 shares. But this isn't a problem, for the reasons set out above. If you have ten shareholders and issue each five shares (for a total of 50 shares), each gets a one-tenth ownership interest in the corporation, even though each holds only ten shares. And you have 50 shares left to issue to future shareholders.

2. Is Your State a Par Value State?

Skip ahead if your state doesn't use the concept of par value. The following states use par value in their state BCA: Arkansas, Delaware, District of Columbia, Illinois, Kansas, Louisiana, Maryland, Massachusetts, Missouri, Nebraska, Nevada, New York, North Dakota, Ohio, Oklahoma, Rhode Island, South Dakota, Texas, and West Virginia. If your state is not in included in this list, you do not need to master the legal and financial technicalities associated with par value shares, and you can skip to Section 3.

Par value is a nominal dollar amount given to corporate shares—it is not their real value, just a stated value that has legal significance under the laws of the states listed above. These "par value states" employ the concept of par value to regulate both the issuance of corporate shares and how the corporation uses the funds it receives for their issuance, as explained below. In par value states, shares of stock are authorized in the articles with either:

- a statement of their designated monetary par value, such as "100,000 shares with a par value of $1.00 per share," or
- a statement that the shares are without par value, such as "100 shares without par value" (these are referred to as "no-par" shares in some states).

Despite its continued use in some state BCAs, par value is not given much weight in the commercial marketplace. Instead, under modern financial reporting procedures, the value of shares is a floating figure, based on a corporation's current net asset value—that is, the amount by which corporate assets exceed corporate liabilities (also called "stockhold-ers' equity"). In other words, it's outdated to assign a fixed or par value to shares.

There are a number of legal and financial consequences to consider if you are incorporating in a par value state. Here are the main ones:

- Shares within each class must have the same par value or must all be designated "without par value." We assume your corporation will authorize just one class of stock—called "common stock"—in which each share has the same voting, dividend, and liquidation rights.
- The incorporation fee in many par value states is based on the total par value of the shares authorized in the articles; if you authorize shares without par value, the shares are nevertheless assigned an assumed par value per share for purposes of computing the incorporation fee. (If you are incorporating in a par value state, we tell you in the "Articles Instructions" section of your state sheet whether it makes sense to authorize par value shares to obtain the lowest incorporation fee.)
- Par value shares must be sold to shareholders for at least their par value. In most cases, as explained below, par value amounts are set at a low, nominal amount, so typically par value shares are sold for more—usually much more—than their stated par value. In par value states, there is no lower limit on the price for which you can sell shares without par value.
- The corporation's "stated capital account" must reflect the amount received by a corporation for the sale of par value shares, as well as the total amount received by the corporation for the sale of shares without par value. The stated capital account is a standard account used in corporate financial accounting. Any amount received by the corporation for par value shares in excess of par value is reflected in the "paid-in surplus" financial account—another standard account. Note that the board is allowed to allocate a portion—even most, but not all—of the amounts paid for shares without par value to this paid-in surplus account, rather than having it all sit in

the stated capital account. (This allocation, typically, must be made within 60 days of the sale of shares without par value.)

By the way, there is another capital account: "the earned surplus account." It contains the corporation's retained earnings, and it is from this account that the corporation may pay dividends to shareholders. We summarize these allocation rules and some of the important par value rules that apply to your shares in the "Stock Issuance Rules" in your state sheet.

Find an accountant who has experience with small corporations. At first encounter, some of this accounting information may appear daunting. Fortunately, the terms are often more complicated than the underlying concepts. If you don't have experience in this area, find an experienced small business accountant who does. A good accountant will make sure your financial record keeping system is properly designed to accommodate the par value rules in your state.

- In par value states, the BCA restricts any transfers of funds or allocations made on the books from the stated capital account to other accounts. The historical legal premise here is that the stated capital account is meant to serve as a cushion for creditors, and its balance cannot normally be lowered except in special, technical situations described in the state's BCA. This is true, even though the protection that a stated capital account is supposed to provide creditors is outmoded. Today, corporate creditors look at the entire financial picture of the corporation, not simply its stated capital account, to decide the

corporation's creditworthiness. Besides, corporations sidestep many of the par value restrictions by (1) placing a nominal par value on shares so that the lion's share of the funds received for par value shares is reflected in the paid-in surplus account, not the restricted stated capital account, or (2) issuing shares without par value, then making sure the board allocates most of the funds received for these shares to the paid-in surplus account.

3. Payments for Shares

In all states, a corporation may sell shares for cash and both tangible and intangible property, such as equipment, machinery, computers, patent rights, copyrights, or trademarks. A corporation can also issue stock in return for the cancellation of a debt owed by the corporation to the shareholder. Normally, this occurs when a corporation issues shares as a payback for money owed to a shareholder who helped start the corporation.

Issuance of Shares for Notes and Future Services May Be Prohibited

In some states, a corporation cannot issue stock in return for a promise by a shareholder to perform future services for the corporation (a written promise of this sort is normally made in an employment contract) or a promise to pay cash later (a written promise to pay cash later is normally memorialized by a promissory note). In the "Stock Issuance Rules" section of your state sheet, we summarize your state's requirements for the types of payment—legally called the "consideration"—that can be made for shares.

> **Example:** Thomas and Richard decide to form a hang-gliding tour service. They're sure someone with expertise can modify a standard solo hang glider to accommodate a workable tour seat outfitted with a short-range wireless intercom headset (to listen to scripted commentary on the shifting landscape below) as well as other amenities. In fact, they know someone who might be willing to strap himself in as their pilot: Harold, a local hang-gliding enthusiast, who can be seen most weekends soaring above the windswept hills that surround their city. After deciding to join Tom and Dick, Harry agrees to accept one-third of the corporation's shares in return for entering into an employment contract with the enterprise. The three toast the deal and their new corporate name, Go Fly a Kite, Inc. The next day, Tom browses the state BCA and discovers that it does not allow shares to be issued in return for future services. Harold suggests an alternative: The corporation can issue its shares to him in return for a long-term note; he'll be happy to pay for them after he's survived a few test flights in the dual glider. Tom explains that their state's BCA also prohibits the issuance of shares for a promissory note. Harold decides to pay (actually, borrow from the other founders) enough cash to purchase his shares outright.

Issuing stock certificates. The issuance of stock signifies the formal acceptance of payment for the shares and recording of a shareholder's interest in the corporate records. Technically, you do not have to issue paper stock certificates under most states' laws (recording the transaction on the corporate books is enough). But following tradition, most incorporators do issue certificates. For more information, see Section D3, above.

4. Stock Issuance and Taxes

Let's look at the basic tax treatment of the most common stock issuance scenarios: stock for cash, stock for services, and stock for property. This is a general guide. For more technical information, consult your tax adviser—and check the small business tax information on the IRS Small Business and Self-Employed Web page at www.irs.gov/businesses/small/index.html.

State tax law normally follows federal law. The very basic tax rules discussed here come from the federal Internal Revenue Code. Fortunately, state tax rules normally follow these federal rules.

a. Stock for Cash

The issuance of stock for cash is normally not taxed. The tax consequences of the investment are usually deferred until shareholders sell their shares. At that time, buyers report on their individual income tax return any gain or loss on the sale, paying capital gains tax on any gain. (The capital gains rates are usually lower than the individual income tax rate that would otherwise apply to income earned by the individual if the shares are held for at least one year.)

b. Stock for Services

The issuance of stock for services is normally taxable. The person who provides the services must pay income tax on the value of the stock received—just as if the corporation paid the person for performing work or promising to perform work for the corporation.

c. Stock for Property

The issuance of stock for property is normally taxable—the person transferring the property pays taxes on the difference between the value of the shares and the person's income tax basis in the property. The person's basis in the property is normally the amount paid for it, less depreciation and other adjustments to the basis that were or could have been claimed by the person on his or her individual income tax return.

Fortunately, there is one big exception to the rule that the issuance of shares in return for property is taxable. Specifically, Section 351 of the Internal Revenue Code says that a property transfer in exchange for shares is tax-free—just as if you bought corporate shares with cash—if all the shareholders buying shares with cash and property at the same time end up with at least an 80% ownership stake in the corporation. There are two basic ways to use Section 351 to qualify under this tax-free property exchange rule:

- **You transfer property to your corporation for shares.** If you, together with the other shareholders of your new corporation who pay cash and/or property for their shares, will own at least 80% of your corporation's voting shares, each of you qualifies for tax-free treatment for your exchange of shares for property (the cash transfers are already tax-free).
- **You and your co-owners incorporate an existing business.** If you and the other co-owners of the unincorporated business will own at least 80% of the voting shares of the new corporation, your transfer of business assets in return for shares will be tax-free under Section 351.

In addition, there are many rules under IRC 351 that cover special situations—such as the purchase of shares by someone who contributes both services and property. We discuss the special IRC 351 rules that apply when incorporating an existing business in Chapter 3, Section F. Again, your tax adviser and the IRS small business website (www.irs.gov/businesses/small/index.html) can help you further understand these technical tax rules.

I. Stock Issuance and the Securities Laws

A share of stock in your corporation is classified as a "security" under state and federal securities laws. These laws regulate the offer and sale of stock by small and large corporations alike. Federal securities law is contained in the federal Securities Act. We discuss its basic application to the sale of your initial stock to the founders of your corporation in Section I2, below. First, let's look at how your state regulates the sale of initial shares in your corporation.

1. State Securities Law

Each state enacts and enforces its own securities law. This law applies to the offer and sale of stock within the state. If you offer or sell shares outside your state, the securities law of the outside state applies to your out-of-state transactions.

a. Overview

The securities acts in each state are quite different, but they share the following five features:

- voluntary compliance
- disclosure requirements
- registration of nonexempt issues of stock
- agency approval of nonexempt issues of stock, and
- penalties for noncompliance.

Voluntary compliance. State securities agencies do not automatically track private sales of shares by corporations. You are expected to learn the rules and voluntarily comply with state law to protect your corporation and its investors.

Disclosure requirements. The basic rule for sales of stock in each state can be summarized simply: disclose, disclose, disclose. To comply with state law, you have a duty to disclose to investors all material financial and business information concerning the sale of shares. (This is called "material disclosure"; see "What Does 'Material Disclosure' Mean?," below.) If you don't follow this rule, an investor can sue your corporation—and in some cases, your founders personally—to get their money back. And in some situations, investors may be able to collect punitive damages to punish dishonest sellers of stock for their underhanded business practices. So, the best way to comply with this basic disclosure rule is to honestly, and in advance of any stock sales, discuss the risks inherent in purchasing stock in your corporation, and to provide full financial disclosure to potential investors. Doing this will minimize your chances of being sued later by a disgruntled investor—or, if you do get sued, of losing. In short, if you can show a court that an investor knew the risks of investing in your corporation before buying your corporation's shares, the investor, not your corporation or you, should have to assume any financial losses that result from the investment.

What Does "Material Disclosure" Mean?

Unfortunately, "material disclosure" is not specifically defined in securities statutes. Essentially, it means all the information and known risks associated with an investment that an investor would want to consider.

Think of it this way: If someone sells you something but fails to mention a fact that, had you known it, would have made you consider the investment slightly differently, then that fact is material information. If knowing the information would not have mattered in the slightest to you, then it is immaterial information.

Material facts related to an investment usually include all the basic financial information on past and expected financial performance you have on hand: profit and loss statements, cash flow statements, and balance sheets, plus the context and risks of the investment (for example, competing business pressures, how much more work your corporation needs to do to launch a product or service, and the other factors that will affect the success of your enterprise).

Registration. All states implement a securities registration system, which requires corporations that sell shares—called "issuers" under the securities laws—to file registration materials with the state prior to a sale of stock, unless the stock issuance is exempt from the registration requirements. Fortunately for new corporations, state securities laws contain exemptions that excuse you from registering your corporation's initial stock issuance. The idea behind these exemptions is to allow small corporations to obtain modest amounts of capital from well-informed insiders without having to bother with full-blown registration paperwork and fees. Most states provide more than one exemption that may apply to your new corporation. We discuss the most common exemptions in Subsection c, below.

Agency approval of nonexempt issues of stock. If your stock issuance is not exempt, you must wait for your registration application to be approved by the state securities agency. If it is, your corporation receives a permit from the state to issue its shares. Most states implement a "disclosure" registration system that requires the issuer to file paperwork with the state containing all the financial, legal, and business details of the stock sale, as well as the risks associated with the investment. Potential buyers of the stock normally must receive a copy of these disclosures in a prospectus provided by the issuer before the sale. You will probably need to hire a lawyer and an accountant to help you prepare both your registration application and your stock prospectus.

Other states implement what is called a "merit" system of registration. In these states, you must provide the state and potential investors with all necessary registration information, just as in a disclosure state. Then, you must satisfy the state securities agency that your sale of stock is fair. Essentially, they scrutinize your registration application, then ask questions. To assure fairness, the office may impose restrictions on the securities offering—for example, it may set a share price or limit the people to whom you may sell shares. The securities agency may place a limit on the sales price for shares, the number and types of shares you may sell, the types of people who may buy your shares, and how much each can invest.

Penalties for noncompliance. If you are required to register your stock issuance and you fail to do so, your corporation and you, personally, can be required to pay noncompliance penalties to the state.

In extreme cases, you may face criminal charges authorized under state securities laws; but these are rarely brought to bear unless you really rip off your investors—for example, by depositing their funds in your personal account instead of letting the money work to get your corporation off the ground.

To read your state's Securities Act and Regulations. In the "State Securities Information" section of your state sheet in Appendix A, we provide contact information, including a website, for your state's securities office. Securities office websites often contain a direct link to the state's Securities Act and Regulations. (If your state agency's website does not post or link to these statutes, we tell you how to find them elsewhere online.) Many securities office websites also provide general information on how to qualify for exemptions to registration requirements.

Further, most states encourage you to call the state securities office to learn more about available state securities exemptions—they want incorporators to know the rules and how to meet them. You do not need to be a lawyer to call the securities office. In fact, you'll probably find the securities staff more helpful if you aren't an attorney. Many state securities offices have a stated policy of wanting to help business entrepreneurs tackle the technicalities of the securities laws in order to encourage new business formations in their state. Below, we discuss strategies that will help you use your state securities office website information in a sensible way.

b. Determining Your Securities Law Comfort Level

Before we describe the types of securities act exemptions you are likely to learn about on your state's securities office website, it's important to place this information in the context of forming a small corporation. Once you see the big picture, you can narrow your focus to the details of your state's specific exemption requirements. To do this, we recommend that you assess your securities law comfort level. This means asking yourself two questions:

How eager are you to learn the legal and technical requirements of securities act exemptions? If the whole idea of learning about securities law exemption requirements is unappealing or too technical for your tastes, it makes sense to pay a business lawyer to help you learn the rules.

Are your investors sophisticated businesspeople who are involved in running the corporation? If you're forming a small corporation with a close-knit group of business-savvy people who know each other well and will work together to manage and run the corporation, no one stands in a superior position to any of the others. You all know the risks of the enterprise, and each of you will stay equally informed as you try to make it a success. If things go badly, it is unlikely that one investor will sue the others for damages under the securities laws.

However, if any of your founders are unsophisticated or if you sell shares to outside investors who will not actively manage and run the corporation, the securities laws take on added significance. After all, the laws are designed precisely to protect people who pay money to others with the expectation of making a profit from the business activities of those who get the money. In other words, if your corporation fails, an unsophisticated or outside investor is more likely to ask a lawyer to sue to recover their investment from your corporation and its managers—and that lawyer will, no doubt, look to see if the founders were in full compliance with the securities statutes when they asked for and received the investor's funds. If they weren't, the disgruntled investor may succeed in obtaining a court judgment for full repayment with interest to their clients plus attorney's fees, court costs, and perhaps punitive damages—without having to show that their clients were treated unfairly.

Example 1: Barry and Beth incorporate their existing co-owned partnership to insulate themselves from personal liability, take advantage of corporate income tax splitting (see Chapter 4), and set up a stock option plan to motivate their employees. Each will receive one-half of the new corporation's shares in return for a transfer of their one-half interest in the partnership's assets to their new corporation. They both have a very high securities law comfort level: (1) after checking the securities laws, they know an exemption is available for the issuance of their initial shares, and (2) each knows what to expect from the other and the risks associated with their existing business. Neither is very worried about their investment of partnership assets in the new corporation—both understand that they will have to continue working hard to continue making a profit. With full disclosure of all business prospects and risks, neither is likely to sue the other over securities laws issues.

Example 2: After establishing that the securities law provides an applicable exemption, Beth asks her parents if they'd like to invest in Beth and Barry's reorganized business by buying shares in the new corporation. Her parents are fairly familiar with the business, accustomed to receiving a blow-by-blow description of its ups and downs from their daughter in her phone calls home. They say they'd be happy to invest a little to help give Beth's business a corporate facelift. Beth's securities law comfort level is high—she believes her parents, who are reasonably experienced investors, understand the pros and cons of investing in her corporation. But Barry is more cautious. Knowing that Beth's parents may not fully appreciate the difficulties of making money in his and Beth's line of work, he insists on making a full disclosure of all material facts relating to their investment in a formal way. This consists of giving Beth's parents copies of current and past financial statements prepared for the partnership and a proposed business plan for the corporation's first year of operation. In addition, he insists on sitting down with both of them to explain the risks of their investment to them.

Example 3: Beth and Barry decide to use their incorporation as a means to obtain additional capital from unrelated outside investors. They plan on calling a number of their friends and acquaintances to see if any are interested in investing in their new company. This time, since they will be dealing with outside investors who won't know the business intimately, Beth's and Barry's security law comfort level is fairly low. Barry and Beth hire their own business lawyer to help them obtain a securities exemption for their stock issuance. They have browsed the securities laws and know they probably qualify for an exemption, but they want to make sure they dot all the i's and cross all the t's before selling any shares to outsiders. In addition, they recommend in writing that each investor have their own personal lawyer review the transaction.

As you consider your own situation, you may find that your comfort level is high. And that's fine. After reviewing your exemption choices, you'll probably go right ahead and issue your shares. But if the rules that apply to your situation look complex or your comfort level is lower than you'd like for other reasons, ask a business lawyer for help. (See Chapter 6.)

c. State Securities Law Exemptions

State securities laws contain different types of exemptions:

- **Exempt issuer transactions.** These exemptions apply to your corporation's initial sale of shares. Your corporation is the "issuer."
- **Exempt nonissuer transactions.** These apply to sales of shares owned by your shareholders. You need not be concerned about these exemptions now, but your shareholders may want to rely on a nonissuer exemption later when deciding to sell their shares.
- **Exempt securities.** These exemptions apply to special types of securities, whether sold by an issuer or shareholder. State law often exempts securities of banks and other financial institutions, pension plans, stock option shares, and the like. In most cases, these security exemptions do not apply to the average business corporation wishing to sell initial shares to its investors.

- **Broker or dealer exemptions.** States not only regulate the sale of securities, but also the people and businesses who sell them. State securities law requires those who sell shares to meet licensing requirements and register as brokers, dealers, and salespeople. Fortunately, since your corporation does not expect to engage in the regular sale of securities as a business, it should qualify for an exemption from registration as a broker, dealer, or salesperson. But to be absolutely sure your state's broker-dealer rules do not apply to your initial issuance of shares, make a quick call to your state's securities office.

The remainder of this section discusses state exemptions from security transactions for issuers. This is the category of state law that helps most smaller corporations offer and sell their initial shares, without having to obtain a registration permit from the state securities agency.

Your state's securities act may contain one or more of the following common exemptions in a section on exempt issuer transactions.

Incorporation exemption. Many states provide a straightforward exemption from registration for the initial issuance of shares to ten or fewer shareholders by a newly formed corporation. If your state offers this exemption, it is normally "self-executing." This means that you don't have to file a form or pay a fee to take advantage of the exemption.

Small offering exemption. Many states allow a corporation, whether new or existing, to issue shares to a relatively small number of individuals without registration—typically ten to 35—within a 12-month period. Some small offering exemptions require that: (1) you can't issue shares to more than ten in-state people within a 12-month period; and (2) the total number of in- and out-of-state shareholders during the 12-month period, counting all new and existing shareholders, cannot exceed 35. Pay particular attention to how the small offering exemption is worded. It can make a difference in how you count your shareholders. For example, you may not have to include certain shareholders in your count.

Limited offering exemption. Many states allow you to make a limited offering to 35 or fewer investors. Typically, you must offer and sell your shares privately, without advertisement. And you can't pay anyone a commission—a percentage of the stock sale proceeds—for helping to sell the shares. A limit may be placed on the total amount of money the corporation receives for the shares, and a time frame may be specified—for example, you must count all sales made within a 12-month period. Some states require you to file a notice and pay a fee to rely on the state limited offering exemption.

Most states make this exemption easier to use by saying you do not need to count "accredited investors" against the investor limit. (Spouses and relatives who share the same residence with an accredited investor normally do not need to be counted, either.) "Accredited investor" is a term borrowed from the federal Regulation D securities rules (see Subsection 2, below). Such investors often include corporate principals such as directors and executive officers, and sophisticated investors who meet specific net worth or annual income standards. Under most limited offering exemptions, you can sell shares to as many accredited investors as you like, as long as you meet the other exemption requirements.

Regulation D filings. Many states automatically exempt your issuance if you comply with one of the federal Regulation D stock issuance rules (see Subsection 2, below). Typically, you must file a copy of Form D, originally filed with the federal Securities and Exchange Commission, with the state, and pay a state filing fee.

If You Want to Make a Modest Public Offering

A common feature of all the exemptions listed above is the requirement that the issuer—your corporation—must offer and sell its shares privately, without advertising to the public. Since the great majority of small corporations are funded by friends and family, this normally causes no problem. But if you want to make an offering to the public, you must usually obtain a registration permit for your shares.

Some states let you make a public offering through a streamlined registration process, promulgated by the North American Securities Administrators Association (NASAA), called the Small Company Offering Registration, or SCOR, process. This standardized procedure allows you to raise up to $1 million from the public in the 45 states that have approved it. It utilizes a simple 50-item question-and-answer prospectus form and is less costly in terms of accounting and legal fees than a full-blown registration. Many states also let you use the SCOR prospectus to "test the waters" and raise $100,000 in capital from the public at the start of the SCOR offering. Some states also allow you to provide your prospectus to potential investors online. State rules for Internet solicitations for the sale of stock vary. Call your state securities office for more information. To learn more about SCOR, go to the NASAA site at www.nasaa.org.

Most state securities acts are arranged in a predictable way. One section of the act lays out the dealer registration requirements and exemptions. Another section contains the issuer registration rules and exemptions. A third section typically contains the non-issuer exemptions. You'll first want to go to the "Issuer" section to look for a law titled "Exemptions" or "Exemptions From Registration." This topic is normally broken down into (a) and (b) sections. The (a) section often contains the exemptions for specific types of securities, and is usually titled "Exempt Securities." The (b) section, usually titled "Exempt Transactions," is the one you are interested in. It should contain a list of specific exemptions from registration that apply to the offer and sale of securities by an issuer, including one or more of the exemptions discussed above.

d. Summing Up

Although state securities laws are highly technical, most states provide exemptions that small corporations can use easily, efficiently, and safely to offer their initial shares privately to founders and a limited group of family and/or sophisticated investors, without much red tape or fee expense. The "State Securities Information" section of your state sheet summarizes the most notable exemptions found in your state and shows you how to learn more by browsing your state's security office website and state securities act.

But the quickest way to find out whether your initial stock sale qualifies for a state securities exemption is to email or call the securities office and ask them if they have an exemption that applies in your circumstances. Just tell them what you plan to do—how many shareholders you'll have and what their connection is to your corporation—and they may be able to give you the green light over the phone or send you a form to file to get the job done. If your state office isn't helpful—most are, but there are exceptions—you may wish to dig into the information provided on your state website, or hand the task over to a lawyer. And again, let your comfort level be your guide. It is one of the best indicators of how much to do yourself, and how much you may decide to pass along to a lawyer to do for you.

2. Federal Securities Laws

Federal securities laws apply to the issuance of corporate shares in all states. The reason the feds have a say in your stock issuance is that, one way or another, you will use the telephone, the mail, the Internet, or some other form of interstate commerce to carry out offers and sales of shares. This means that you can't ignore the federal rules when issuing corporate shares.

Federal securities law regulations parallel the state model discussed just above. You must register your initial offering of stock with the federal Securities and Exchange Commission (SEC) unless you qualify for an exemption. Failure to register, if you're required to do so, can result in financial penalties under the act and liability for your corporation and its founders. A disgruntled shareholder can seek rescission of the stock sale and collect interest on the money plus, perhaps, punitive damages. As discussed in the previous section, your best approach is to know your shareholders, make full disclosure to your investors, and pay close attention to your comfort level.

There are several federal exemptions available. Most small corporations that are eligible for a state exemption from securities registration should qualify under at least one of them. We present the most commonly used federal exemptions in the remainder of this section, in their normal order of applicability and usefulness. The first two do not require you to file any forms or pay fees, so look to them first. The third choice—the Regulation D exemption scheme—requires the filing of a form (but no fees). You probably will find that the initial sale of your new corporation's stock qualifies under more than one of the exemptions listed below. You should pick the one that's most convenient for you to use.

For more federal exemption information. The SEC website has a small business information page with links to helpful information on each of the federal exemption rules covered here, plus information on streamlined small business registration procedures if you decide someday to make a public offering of shares to obtain higher levels of capital. Go to www.sec.gov/info/smallbus/shtml.

a. Intrastate Exemption

Section 3(a)(11) of the Securities and Exchange Act contains the intrastate offering exemption for a sale of shares "which is a part of an issue offered and sold only to persons resident within a single State or Territory, where the issuer of such security is a person resident and doing business within . . . such State or Territory." It is available for issuances of shares by a corporation to shareholders who reside in the state where the corporation was formed and where it carries out most of its business. This exemption is self-executing—meaning that there is no form to file or fee to pay, and no limit is placed on the number of shareholders or the amount of money they can pay for their shares.

The intrastate exemption comes in handy for most newly formed, locally based corporations that simply issue their shares privately to a local group of shareholders. If your company owns out of state assets or does a substantial amount of business out of state, it may not qualify for the exemption. Federal Rule 147 (see "Intrastate Offering Regulations," below) provides a "safe harbor" set of rules for meeting the generally expressed requirements of the exemption. That is, it shows one way to be sure you are making a qualified intrastate issuance of shares. In part, it says that your corporation should qualify for the intrastate exemption if your corporation:

- has at least 80% of its assets, and earns 80% of its revenue, in your state
- has its principal office in your state
- makes offers and sales only to people who reside in your state, and
- intends to use 80% of the proceeds for business operations in your state.

You can make reliance on the intrastate offering exemption safer by getting each shareholder to sign a statement affirming that they are a resident of your corporation's state of formation and agreeing not to sell the shares to an out-of-state resident for a period of at least nine months after the initial issuance of the shares by your corporation.

You also make reliance safer if you place language on the face of your stock certificates—this language is called a "legend"—that says the shares have not been registered with the SEC and that they are subject to restrictions on resale. You also should place a notation in your corporation's stock records that the corporation should not transfer any stock certificates within nine months to out-of-state shareholders.

To download Rule 147. Rule 147 is not currently posted on the SEC website (www.sec.gov), but it may be available soon. In the meantime, you can download it from the Center for Corporate Law's website at www.law.uc.edu/CCL/33ActRls/rule147.html.

Intrastate Offering Regulations

We've just summarized the intrastate offering exemption requirements, above, but here are the actual regulations if you want to look at the details. Be warned that they are full of legalese and not easy to follow. We provide them simply as an additional resource to help you assess your federal securities law comfort level. If you question your corporation's qualification for this exemption, and none of the other federal exemptions seems to apply to your initial stock issuance, you'll probably need a lawyer's help to sift through the regulations and find an applicable exemption.

Rule 147 — "Part of an Issue," "Person Resident," and "Doing Business Within" for Purposes of Section 3(a)(11)

Preliminary Notes

1. This rule shall not raise any presumption that the exemption provided by Section 3(a)(11) of the Act is not available for transactions by an issuer which do not satisfy all of the provisions of the rule.

2. Nothing in this rule obviates the need for compliance with any state law relating to the offer and sale of the securities.

3. Section 5 of the Act requires that all securities offered by the use of the mails or by any means or instruments of transportation or communication in interstate commerce be registered with the Commission. Congress, however, provided certain exemptions in the Act from such registration provisions where there was no practical need for registration or where the benefits of registration were too remote. Among those exemptions is that provided by Section 3(a)(11) of the Act for transactions in "any security which is a part of an issue offered and sold only to persons resident within a single State or Territory, where the issuer of such security is a person resident and doing business within . . . such State or Territory." The legislative history of that Section suggests that the exemption was intended to apply only to issues genuinely local in character, which in reality represent local financing by local industries, carried out through local investment. Rule 147 is intended to provide more objective standards upon which responsible local businessmen intending to raise capital from local sources may rely in claiming the Section 3(a)(11) exemption.

All of the terms and conditions of the rule must be satisfied in order for the rule to be available. These are:

i. that the issuer be a resident of and doing business within the state or territory in which all offers and sales are made; and

ii. that no part of the issue be offered or sold to nonresidents within the period of time specified in the rule. For purposes of the rule the definition of "issuer" in Section 2(4) of the Act shall apply.

All offers, offers to sell, offers for sale, and sales which are part of the same issue must meet all of the conditions of Rule 147 for the rule to be available. The determination whether offers, offers to sell, offers for sale, and sales of securities are part of the same issue (i.e., are deemed to be "integrated") will continue to be a question of fact and will depend on the particular circumstances. See Securities Act of 1933 Release No. 4434 (December 6, 1961). Release 33-4434 indicates that in determining whether offers and sales should be regarded as part of the same issue and thus should be integrated any one or more of the following factors may be determinative:

i.   Are the offerings part of a single plan of financing;

ii. Do the offerings involve issuance of the same class of securities;

iii. Are the offerings made at or about the same time;

iv. Is the same type of consideration to be received; and

v.   Are the offerings made for the same general purpose.

Subparagraph (b)(2) of the rule, however, is designed to provide certainty to the extent feasible by identifying certain types of offers and sales of securities which will be deemed not part of an issue, for purposes of the rule only.

Persons claiming the availability of the rule have the burden of proving that they have satisfied all of its provisions. However, the rule does not establish exclusive standards for complying with the Section 3(a)(11) exemption. The exemption would also be available if the issuer satisfied the standards set forth in relevant administrative and judicial interpretations at the time of the offering but the issuer would have the burden of proving the availability of the exemption. Rule 147 relates to transactions exempted from the registration requirements of Section 5 of the Act by Section 3(a)(11). Neither the rule nor Section 3(a)(11) provides an exemption from the registration requirements of Section 12(g) of the Securities Exchange Act of 1934, the anti-fraud provisions of the federal securities laws, the civil liability provisions of Section 12(2) of the Act, or other provisions of the federal securities laws.

Finally, in view of the objectives of the rule and the purposes and policies underlying the Act, the rule shall not be available to any person with respect to any offering which, although in technical compliance with the rule, is part of a plan or scheme by such person to make interstate offers or sales of securities. In such cases registration pursuant to the Act is required.

4. The rule provides an exemption for offers and sales by the issuer only. It is not available for offers or sales of securities by other persons. Section 3(a)(11) of the Act has been interpreted to permit offers and sales by persons controlling the issuer, if the exemption provided by that Section would have been available to the issuer at the time of the offering. See Securities Act Release No. 4434 (December 6, 1961). Controlling persons who want to offer or sell securities pursuant to Section 3(a)(11) may continue to do so in accordance with applicable judicial and administrative interpretations.

a. Transactions Covered.

Offers, offers to sell, offers for sale, and sales by an issuer of its securities made in accordance with all of the terms and conditions of this rule shall be deemed to be part of an issue offered and sold only to persons resident and doing business within such state or territory, within the meaning of Section 3(a)(11) of the Act.

b. Part of an Issue.

1. For purposes of this rule, all securities of the issuer which are part of an issue shall be offered, offered for sale, or sold in accordance with all of the terms and conditions of this rule.

2. For purposes of this rule only, an issue shall be deemed not to include offers, offers to sell, offers for sale, or sales of securities of the issuer pursuant to the exemptions provided by Section 3 or Section 4(2) of the Act or pursuant to a registration statement filed under the Act, that take place prior to the six month period immediately preceding or after the six month period immediately following any offers, offers for sale or sales pursuant to this rule, Provided, That, there are during either of said six month periods no offers, offers for sale, or sales of securities by or for the issuer of the same or similar class as those offered, offered for sale or sold pursuant to the rule.

Note: In the event that securities of the same or similar class as those offered pursuant to the rule are offered, offered for sale, or sold less than six months prior to or subsequent to any offer, offer for sale or sale pursuant to this rule, see Preliminary Note 3 hereof, as to which offers, offers to sell, offers for sale, or sales are part of an issue.

c. Nature of the Issuer.

The issuer of the securities shall at the time of any offers and the sales be a person resident and doing business within the state or territory in which all of the offers, offers to sell, offers for sale, and sales are made.

1. The issuer shall be deemed to be a resident of the state or territory in which:

   i.   it is incorporated or organized, if a corporation, limited partnership, trust, or other form of business organization that is organized under state or territorial law;

   ii. its principal office is located, if a general partnership or other form of business organization that is not organized under any state or territorial law;

   iii. his principal residence is located, if an individual.

2. The issuer shall be deemed to be doing business within a state or territory if:

   i.   the issuer derived at least 80 percent of its gross revenues and those of its subsidiaries on a consolidated basis

      A. for its most recent fiscal year, if the first offer of any part of the issue is made during the first six months of the issuer's current fiscal year; or

      B. for the first six months of its current fiscal year or during the twelve month fiscal period ending with such six month period, if the first offer of any part of the issue is made during the last six months of the issuer's current fiscal year from the operation of a business or of real property located in or from the rendering of services within such state or territory; provided, however, that this provision does not apply to any issuer which has not had gross revenues in excess of $5,000 from the sale of products or services or other conduct of its business for its most recent twelve month fiscal period;

   ii. the issuer had at the end of its most recent semi-annual fiscal period prior to the first offer of any part of the issue, at least 80 percent of its assets and those of its subsidiaries on a consolidated basis located within such state or territory;

   iii. the issuer intends to use and uses at least 80 percent of the proceeds to the issuer from sales made pursuant to this rule in connection with the operation of a business or of real property, the purchase of real property located in, or the rendering of services within such state or territory; and

   iv. the principal office of the issuer is located within such state or territory.

d. Offerees and Purchasers; Person Resident.

Offers, offers to sell, offers for sale, and sales of securities that are part of an issue shall be made only to persons resident within the state or territory of which the issuer is a resident. For purposes of determining the residence of offerees and purchasers:

1. A corporation, partnership, trust, or other form of business organization shall be deemed to be a resident of a state or territory if, at the time of the offer and sale to it, it has its principal office within such state or territory.

2. An individual shall be deemed to be a resident of a state or territory if such individual has, at the time of the offer and sale to him, his principal residence in the state or territory.

3. A corporation, partnership, trust, or other form of business organization which is organized for the specific purpose of acquiring part of an issue offered pursuant to this rule shall be deemed not to be a resident of a state or territory unless all of the beneficial owners of such organization are residents of such state or territory.

e. Limitation of Resales.

During the period in which securities that are part of an issue are being offered and sold by the issuer, and for a period of nine months from the date of the last sale by the issuer of such securities, all resales of any part of the issue, by any person, shall be made only to persons resident within such state or territory.

Notes:

1. In the case of convertible securities resales of either the convertible security, or if it is converted, the underlying security, could be made during the period described in paragraph (e) only to persons resident within such state or territory. For purposes of this rule a conversion in reliance on Section 3(a)(9) of the Act does not begin a new period.

2. Dealers must satisfy the requirements of Rule 15c2-11 under the Securities Exchange Act of 1934 prior to publishing any quotation for a security, or submitting any quotation for publication, in any quotation medium.

f. Precautions Against Interstate Offers and Sales.

1. The issuer shall, in connection with any securities sold by it pursuant to this rule:

    i. Place a legend on the certificate or other document evidencing the security stating that the securities have not been registered under the Act and setting forth the limitations on resale contained in paragraph (e);

    ii. Issue stop transfer instructions to the issuer's transfer agent, if any, with respect to the securities, or, if the issuer transfers its own securities, make a notation in the appropriate records of the issuer; and

    iii. Obtain a written representation from each purchaser as to his residence.

2. The issuer shall, in connection with the issuance of new certificates for any of the securities that are part of the same issue that are presented for transfer during the time period specified in paragraph (e), take the steps required by subsections (f)(1)(i) and (ii).

3. The issuer shall, in connection with any offers, offers to sell, offers for sale, or sales by it pursuant to this rule, disclose, in writing, the limitations on resale contained in paragraph (e) and the provisions of subsections (f)(1)(i) and (ii) and subparagraph (f)(2).

b. Private Offering Exemption

Another exemption available under the Securities and Exchange Act is the private offering exemption. (It's actually called the "nonpublic offering" exemption, but we prefer to characterize it positively.) It is a one-line exemption contained in Section 4(2) of the Act for "transactions by an issuer not involving any public offering." It is a very generally stated exemption. Mostly, it applies to the private issuance of shares by a corporation to a small number of people closely connected with the business of the corporation. These individuals buy shares understanding the risk of their investment and knowing there is no market for the shares—that is, they do not expect to sell the shares to another person. This is another self-executing exemption—there are no forms to file or fees to pay.

The courts have discussed the basic elements that should be present when relying on this exemption (a leading case is *SEC v. Ralston Purina Co.*, 346 U.S. 119 (1953)):

* The purchasers are able to fend for themselves due to their previous financial or business experience, because of their relationship to the issuer (the corporation, or its directors or officers), and/or because they have significant personal net worth.

- The transaction is truly a nonpublic offering involving no general advertising or solicitation.
- The shares are purchased by the shareholders for their own account and not for resale to others.
- The people to whom shares are offered are limited in number.
- The people to whom shares are offered have access to or are given information relevant to the stock transaction in order to evaluate the pros and cons of the investment—for example, financial statements, a business plan, and information about risks.

In order to better understand the factors that should, and should not, be present when relying on the private offering exemption, the SEC issued Release No. 33-4552. This document contains several statements and examples regarding the private offering exemption. (See the text of the release itself, below.) For the most part, the release restates the factors listed above. It does provide additional guidance, however, to make reliance on the private offering exemption more certain. The guidelines are "safe harbor" rules, meant to show you a safe way to issue shares in a qualified private offering. You do not have to follow them, but we suggest you do to increase your chances of qualifying for the exemption.

Here are a few of these additional points (we've paraphrased and lowered the legal content a notch or two to make the material more digestible):

- The sale of stock to promoters who take the initiative in founding or organizing the business falls within the exemption. Sales of shares to people who will constitute the executive level of the corporation—for example, directors and principal executive officers, such as the president, vice president, and chief financial officer—also qualify. However, if stock is sold to uninformed friends, neighbors, and associates with no connection to the inner workings of corporate management, the stock sale doesn't qualify.

- If you go out and ask everyone who will listen to buy shares in your new corporation, you are making a public, not a private, offering, and you do not qualify for this exemption. This is true even if you end up selling shares only to insiders.
- Size matters. If you sell a significant dollar amount of shares—even if you sell them to insiders, privately—you are making a non-qualified public offering. The release doesn't provide numbers, just this general admonition not to get greedy.
- Don't sell shares to day-traders or other high-rollers. Selling shares to people with a penchant for stock flipping—buying it one day, selling it the next—will taint your private offering and make it look more like a public sale of stock.
- Your corporation should make an effort to control resales of stock issued under the exemption. The release suggests getting each shareholder to sign a statement that says the shareholder is buying the shares for investment, not for resale. Another suggestion is to place language on each issued stock certificate (called a "legend") that says the shares have not been registered under the federal securities laws, have been purchased for investment, and can't be resold by the shareholder unless the resale transaction, itself, is registered under the federal securities laws or is exempt from these laws. Note that these procedural steps are offered in the release as suggestions. You don't have to follow them, but doing so helps your stock sale look even more like a private offering.

Federal Private Offering Exemption Regulations

Here is the text of the federal private offering exemptions regulations: Release No. 33-4552. It doesn't make for easy reading, but you can refer to it for more information and to help you assess how comfortable you feel about relying on this private offering exemption.

Nonpublic Offering Exemption—Release No. 33-4552

The Commission today announced the issuance of a statement regarding the availability of the exemption from the registration requirements of section 5 of the Securities Act of 1933 afforded by the second clause of section 4(1)1 of the Act for "transactions by an issuer not involving any public offering," the so-called "private offering exemption." Traditionally, the second clause of section 4(1)1 has been regarded as providing an exemption from registration for bank loans, private placements of securities with institutions, and the promotion of a business venture by a few closely related persons. However, an increasing tendency to rely upon the exemption for offerings of speculative issues to unrelated and uninformed persons prompts this statement to point out the limitations on its availability.

Whether a transaction is one not involving any public offering is essentially a question of fact and necessitates a consideration of all surrounding circumstances, including such factors as the relationship between the offerees and the issuer, the nature, scope, size, type and manner of the offering.

The Supreme Court in S.E.C. v. Ralston Purina Co., 346 U.S. 119, 124, 125 (1953), noted that the exemption must be interpreted in the light of the statutory purpose to "protect investors by promoting full disclosure of information thought necessary to informed investment decisions" and held that "the applicability of section 4(1) should turn on whether the particular class of persons affected need the protection of the Act." The court stated that the number of offers is not conclusive as to the availability of the exemption, since the statute seems to apply to an offering "whether to few or many." However, the court indicated that "nothing prevents the Commission, in enforcing the statute, from using some kind of numerical test in deciding when to investigate particular exemption claims." It should be emphasized, therefore, that the number of persons to whom the offering is extended is relevant only to the question whether they have the requisite association with and knowledge of the issuer which make the exemption available.

Consideration must be given not only to the identity of the actual purchasers but also to the offerees. Negotiations or conversations with or general solicitations of an unrestricted and unrelated group of prospective purchasers for the purpose of ascertaining who would be willing to accept an offer of securities is inconsistent with a claim that the transaction does not involve a public offering even though ultimately there may only be a few knowledgeable purchasers.[3]

A question frequently arises in the context of an offering to an issuer's employees. Limitation of an offering to certain employees designated as key employees may not be a sufficient showing to qualify for the exemptions. As the Supreme Court stated in the Ralston Purina case: "The exemption as we construe it, does not deprive corporate employees, as a class, of the safeguards of the Act. We agree that some employee offerings may come within section 4(a), e.g., one made to executive personnel who because of their position have access to the same kind of information that the Act would make available in the form of a registration statement. Absent such a showing of special circumstances, employees are just as much members of the investing "public" as any of their neighbors in the community." The Court's concept is that the exemption is necessarily narrow. The exemption does not become available simply because offerees are voluntarily furnished information about the issuer. Such a construction would give each issuer the choice of registering or making its own voluntary disclosures without regard to the standards and sanctions of the Act.

The sale of stock to promoters who take the initiative in founding or organizing the business would come within the exemption. On the other hand, the transaction tends to become public when the promoters begin to bring in a diverse group of uninformed friends, neighbors and associates.

The size of the offering may also raise questions as to the probability that the offering will be completed within the strict confines of the exemption. An offering of millions of dollars to non-institutional and non-affiliated investors or one divided, or convertible, into many units would suggest that a public offering may be involved.

When the services of an investment banker, or other facility through which public distributions are normally effected, are used to place the securities, special care must be taken to avoid a public offering. If the investment banker places the securities with discretionary accounts and other customers without regard to the ability of such customers to meet the tests implicit in the Ralston Purina case, the exemption may be lost. Public advertising of the offerings would, of course, be incompatible with a claim of a private offering. Similarly, the use of the facilities of a securities exchange to place the securities necessarily involves an offering to the public.

An important factor to be considered is whether the securities offered have come to rest in the hands of the initial informed group or whether the purchasers are merely conduits for a wider distribution. Persons who act in this capacity, whether or not engaged in the securities business, are deemed to be "underwriters" within the meaning of section 2(11) of the Act. If the purchasers do in fact acquire the securities with a view to public distribution, the seller assumes the risk of possible violation of the registration requirements of the Act and consequent civil liabilities.[4] This has led to the practice whereby the issuer secures from the initial purchasers representations that they have acquired the securities for investment. Sometimes a legend to this effect is placed on the stock certificates and stop-transfer instructions issued to the transfer agent. However, a statement by the initial purchaser, at the time of his acquisition, that the securities are taken for investment and not for distribution is necessarily self-serving and not conclusive as to his actual intent. Mere acceptance at face value of such assurances will not provide a basis for reliance on the exemption when inquiry would suggest to a reasonable person that these assurances are formal rather than real. The additional precautions of placing a legend on the securities and issuing stop-transfer orders have proved in many cases to be an effective means of preventing illegal distributions. Nevertheless, these are only precautions and are not to be regarded as a basis for Federal Private Offering Exemption regulations exemption from registration. The nature of the purchaser's past investment and trading practices or the character and scope of his business may be inconsistent with the purchase of large blocks of securities for investment. In particular, purchases by persons engaged in the business of buying and selling securities require careful scrutiny for the purpose of determining whether such person may be acting as an underwriter for the issuer.

The view is occasionally expressed that, solely by reason of continued holding of a security for the six month capital-gain period specified in the income-tax laws, or for a year from the date of purchase, the security may be sold without registration. There is no statutory basis for such assumption. Of course, the longer the period of retention, the more persuasive would be the argument that the resale is not at variance with an original investment intent, but the length of time between acquisition and resale is merely one evidentiary fact to be considered. The weight to be accorded this evidentiary fact must, of necessity, vary with the circumstances of each case. Further, a limitation upon resale for a stated period of time or under certain circumstances would tend to raise a question as to original intent even though such limitation might otherwise recommend itself as a policing device. There is no legal justification for the assumption that holding a security in an "investment account" rather than a "trading account," holding for a deferred sale, for a market rise, for sale if the market does not rise, or for a statutory escrow period, without more, establishes a valid basis for an exemption from registration under the Securities Act.5

An unforeseen change of circumstances since the date of purchase may be a basis for an opinion that the proposed resale is not inconsistent with an investment representation. However, such claim must be considered in the light of all of the relevant facts. Thus, an advance or decline in market price or a change in the issuer's operating results are normal investment risks and do not usually provide an acceptable basis for such claim of changed circumstances. Possible inability of the purchaser to pay off loans incurred in connection with the purchase of the stock would ordinarily not be deemed an unforeseeable change of circumstances. Further, in the case of securities pledged for a loan, the pledgee should not assume that he is free to distribute without registration. The Congressional mandate of disclosure to investors is not to be avoided to permit a public distribution of unregistered securities because the pledgee took the securities from a purchaser, subsequently delinquent.6

The view is sometimes expressed that investment companies and other institutional investors are not subject to any restrictions regarding disposition of securities stated to be taken for investment and that any securities so acquired may be sold by them whenever the investment decision to sell is made, no matter how brief the holding period. Institutional investors are, however, subject to the same restrictions on sale of securities acquired from an issuer or a person in a control relationship with an issuer insofar as compliance with the registration requirements of the Securities Act is concerned.

Integration of Offerings

A determination whether an offering is public or private would also include a consideration of the question whether it should be regarded as a part of a larger offering made or to be made. The following factors are relevant to such question of integration: whether (1) the different offerings are part of a single plan of financing, (2) the offerings involve issuance of the same class of security, (3) the offerings are made at or about the same time, (4) the same type of consideration is to be received, (5) the offerings are made for the general purpose.

What may appear to be a separate offering to a properly limited group will not be so considered if it is one of a related series of offerings. A person may not separate parts of a series of related transactions, the sum total of which is really one offering, and claim that a particular part is a nonpublic transaction. Thus, in the case of offerings of fractional undivided interests in separate oil or gas properties where the promoters must constantly find new participants for each new venture, it would appear to be appropriate to consider the entire series of offerings to determine the scope of this solicitation.

As has been emphasized in other releases discussing exemptions from the registration and prospectus requirements of the Securities Act, the terms of an exemption are to be strictly construed against the claimant who also has the burden of proving its availability.7 Moreover, persons receiving advice from the staff of the Commission that no action will be recommended if they proceed without registration in reliance upon the exemption should do so only with full realization that the tests so applied may not be proof against claims by purchasers of the security that registration should have been effected. Finally, sections 12(2) and 17 of the Act, which provide civil liabilities and criminal sanctions for fraud in the sale of a security, are applicable to the transactions notwithstanding the availability of an exemption from registration.

Footnotes

1 Second clause of section 4(1) is now section 4(2), as amended August 20, 1964.

2 See, also, *Gilligan, Will & Co. v. S.E.C.*, 267 F.2d 461, 467 (C.A. 2, 1959), cert. denied, 361 U.S. 896 (1960).

3 Reference is made to the so-called "investment clubs" which have been organized under claim of an exemption from the registration provisions of the Securities Act of 1933 as well as the Investment Company Act of 1940. It should not be assumed that so long as the investment club, which is an investment company within the meaning of the later Act, does not obtain more than 100 members, a public offering of its securities, namely the memberships, will not be involved. An investment company may be exempt from the provisions of the Investment Company Act if its securities are owned by no more than 100 persons and it is not making and does not presently propose to make a public offering of its securities (section 3(c)(1)). Both elements must be considered in determining whether the exemption is available.

4 See Release No. 33-4445.

5 See Release No. 33-3825 re The Crowell-Collier Publishing Company.

6 *S.E.C. v. Guild Films Company, Inc. et al.*, 279 F.2d 485 (C.A. 2, 1960), cert. denied sub nom. Santa Monica Bank v. S.E.C., 364 U.S. 819 (1960).

7 *S.E.C. v. Sunbeam Gold Mining Co.*, 95 F.2d 699, 701 (C.A. 9, 1938); *Gilligan, Will & Co. v. S.E.C.*, 267 F.2d 461, 466 (C.A. 2, 1959); *S.E.C. v. Ralston Purina Co.*, 346 U.S. 119, 126 (1953); *S.E.C. v. Culpepper et al.*, 270 F.2d 241, 246 (C.A. 2, 1959).

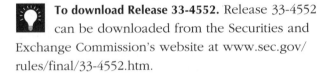 **To download Release 33-4552.** Release 33-4552 can be downloaded from the Securities and Exchange Commission's website at www.sec.gov/rules/final/33-4552.htm.

c. Regulation D Exemption Rules

Regulation D of the federal securities laws was enacted to make the sale of stock under the federal exemption rules more certain and to help smaller companies raise private capital. Regulation D contains three rules—504, 505, and 506—each of which is a separate exemption for the issuances of shares. The three rules have similarities, and each requires the filing of federal Form D with the SEC. There is no filing fee.

The amount of money your corporation may receive for shares, the number of purchasers, and the types of people to whom you can sell shares under each of the Regulation D rules vary. Each of the rules places importance on whether your shareholders are "accredited investors." This term includes the directors and executive officers of the corporation, and people with either a $1 million net worth or an annual income of at least $200,000. If you limit sales to accredited investors, you may be able to advertise the availability of your shares, issue shares to more

individuals, or have less stringent disclosure requirements. Following is a brief summary of the rules.

1. Rule 504

Rule 504 exempts offerings up to $1 million worth of shares in a 12-month period. In some cases, you can use Rule 504 to publicly advertise and sell your shares, depending on whether you registered your stock issuance with the state securities agency, delivered a disclosure document to your shareholders under your state's rules, or sell only to accredited investors. Many companies use Rule 504 together with their state's SCOR process (see the sidebar in Section 1c, above) to raise $1 million in capital in a limited public offering.

2. Rule 505

Rule 505 exempts private offerings up to $5 million. Generally there must be no more than 35 nonaccredited investors, no general advertising is permitted, and specific financial and business information must be disclosed to any nonaccredited investors included in the offering. Shareholders receive restricted stock: They must agree not to sell their shares for at least one year without registering the sale. And the stock certificates should contain language stating that the shares are unregistered and that they may not be resold, unless the resale is registered or exempt from registration under the securities laws.

3. Rule 506

Rule 506 contains an exemption for the private issuance of shares. Most smaller, closely held corporations turn to Regulation D to obtain their exemption for a private offering of shares if they are not comfortable issuing their shares informally (without a filing with the SEC) under the private offering exemption covered in Subsection b, above.

Unlike Rules 504 and 505, there is no limit on the amount of money you can raise under this rule, though advertising is prohibited. As with Rule 505, you can sell shares to an unlimited number of accredited investors, and to no more than 35 unaccredited people. However, all nonaccredited investors must be sophisticated. This means that they, or their lawyer or other adviser who they designate to represent them, must have enough knowledge and experience in financial and business matters to make them capable of evaluating the merits and risks of the prospective investment. The corporation must provide specific financial and business disclosures to all nonaccredited investors. You must also give each purchaser the opportunity to ask questions and receive answers concerning the terms and conditions of the offering and to obtain any additional information that the corporation possesses, or can acquire without unreasonable effort or expense, that is necessary to verify the accuracy of information already furnished to the prospective shareholders. Stock issued under this rule is restricted. A legend on the stock certificates should say that future resales must be registered or exempt from registration under the securities law.

Doing a Regulation D filing under any of the Regulation D exemption rules requires work and technical expertise. You'll probably need the help of a lawyer who knows the federal securities rules to pick the best rule to use, meet its requirements, and prepare Form D. Lawyers typically charge $3,000 or so to help you with this task.

d. Strategies for Dealing With the Federal Securities Rules

Please review our discussion of assessing your state securities law comfort level, above. It applies here as well. Then consider these suggestions for approaching the federal exemptions and your initial stock issuance:

- Start by determining whether you clearly fall within the intrastate or private offering exemption. Probably 80% or more of small corporations issue shares in their state to their founders and easily qualify for both.
- If you are fairly sure you qualify for one of the two basic exemptions, but you want to raise your comfort level a little, review Rule 147 and Release 33-4552. Each explains ways to make reliance on each exemption more certain. For example, after reading Rule 147, you may decide to have each shareholder sign a statement that they reside in your state and that they agree not to sell shares to an out-of-state shareholder for nine months. Similarly, Release 33-4552 may motivate you to place a legend on your share certificates indicating that the shares are being purchased for investment and not for resale, and cannot be resold without registration or a determination that an exemption is available.
- If you are not sure whether you qualify for one of the two basic federal exemptions or if you want to use Rule 147 or Release 33-4552 but need help, see a lawyer.
- If you decide that you'd just feel a whole lot better following the specific exemption guidelines of one of the Regulation D rules, see a lawyer to select and meet the requirements of the appropriate rule (most likely Rule 506) and file Form D with the SEC.

Again, let common sense and good business judgment guide you. Whatever you decide, one other point bears repeating: Remember to *disclose, disclose, disclose* all material information to all investors in your new corporation ■

3

Understanding Corporate Taxes

n this chapter we discuss the principal tax information and concerns associated with starting and operating a business corporation. We also describe the special tax treatment accorded corporate employee equity sharing plans, including stock option and stock purchase plans. These ownership sharing plans are part of the silver lining of the corporate form; they help you increase the profitability of your corporate enterprise by attracting and motivating key employees.

The tax information in this chapter is meant to introduce you to the most important areas of corporate taxation and to provide you with enough background to discuss the issues in greater depth with a tax expert. We focus on the federal rules found in both the Internal Revenue Code (IRC) and the federal income tax regulations, which are enforced by the IRS. Most states adopt and apply the federal rules to business corporations formed or operating in their state, though they apply their own corporate tax rates. In the "State Tax Information" section of your state sheet in Appendix A, we summarize the type and rate of tax applied to business corporations in your state. Your state tax section also lists the state tax office website where you can go to learn more and to download corporate tax publications and forms.

Keep up with changing tax laws. Though we've done our best to provide you with current information, tax laws, regulations, and rates do change. We've covered some of the most important recent federal tax law changes in Appendix B. To keep up to date, also see the most recent IRS and state tax publications, available from your state tax office website and from the IRS at www.irs.gov. Also, consult a tax adviser with small business experience on a regular basis to make sure you understand how to apply the latest tax rules to your corporation.

A. Federal Corporate Income Tax Treatment

In this section we look at federal corporate income tax rates and compare them to individual income tax rates. We also show you how to enjoy one of the best built-in benefits of forming a corporation: the ability to split income between the corporate and individual income tax brackets to achieve an overall income tax savings for the owners of the business.

1. Federal Corporate Income Tax Rates

Below are the federal corporate income tax brackets. These rates are imposed on corporate taxable income—that is, corporate net income computed by subtracting the cost of goods sold, depreciation of business assets, salaries, necessary business expenses, and other allowable credits, exclusions, and deductions from corporate gross income.

Federal Corporate Tax Payments and Rates	
Corporate Taxable Income	**Corporate Tax**
$0–$50,000	15% of taxable income
$50,001–$75,000	$7,500 + 25% of taxable income over $50,000
$75,001–$100,000	$13,750 + 34% of taxable income over $75,000
$100,001–$335,000	$22,250 + 39% of taxable income over $100,000
$335,001–$10,000,000	$113,900 + 34% of taxable income over $335,000
$10,000,001–$15,000,000	$3,400,000 + 35% of taxable income over $10,000,001
$15,000,001–$18,333,333	$5,150,000 + 38% of taxable income over $15,000,000
over $18,333,333	$6,416,667 + 35% of taxable income over $18,333,333

Notice that the first $50,000 of corporate taxable income is taxed at 15%, and the next $25,000 at 25%. Notice that corporate taxes go up to 39%, which is more than the current top individual income rate of 35%, for corporate taxable income between $100,000 and $335,000. The idea of the 39% rate is to make more profitable corporations pay back the benefits of the lower graduated tax rates of 15% and 25%. But note that even corporations subject to this 39% bracket still pay tax at an effective 34% rate when the lower brackets are averaged with the top 39% bracket. For highly profitable corporations, a 35% tax bracket is applied to taxable incomes over $10,000,000, with an additional 38% bubble set up to make corporations with taxable incomes over $15 million pay an overall tax rate of 35%. (The 38% bubble eliminates the advantage of the lower graduated tax brackets below 35%.)

Corporations don't have special capital gains tax rates like individuals. In fact, it's more difficult for corporations to generate capital gains than it is for individuals.

A Higher Corporate Tax Rate Applies to Corporations That Provide Personal Services

Under Internal Revenue Code §§ 11(b)(2) and 448(d)(2), certain incorporated professionals and others who provide personal services as a corporation, called "personal service corporations," pay a flat corporate tax of 35% on corporate taxable income. In other words, the lower 15%, 25%, and 34% federal corporate tax brackets do not apply.

This flat corporate tax rate is applied to corporations in which (1) substantially all the stock of the corporation is held by the employees performing professional services for the corporation, and (2) substantially all the activities of the corporation involve the performance of one of the following professions or activities:

- health
- law
- engineering
- architecture
- accounting
- actuarial science
- performing arts
- consulting.

Professionals who incorporate to protect themselves from personal liability for corporate commercial claims and the malpractice of others in their organization typically pay out corporate profits to themselves each year in the form of salaries and other corporate tax-deductible fringe benefits. (However, under state law, individual professionals are personally liable for their own malpractice.) These payouts leave little in the corporation to be taxed at the flat 35% corporate income tax rate.

2. Federal Individual Income Tax Rates

The owners of small corporations who work for their corporations, like all other employees, pay individual income tax on salaries and bonuses they receive from the business. The corporation can deduct these employee compensation payouts, so they are taxed just once, at the individual owner-employee level. Even better, some forms of employee fringe benefits paid to the owner-employees are deductible by the corporation and are not taxable to the employee, so no tax is paid. (More on corporate employee fringe benefits in Section C, below.)

Like employee compensation payouts, the payouts of corporate profits directly to the owners of a corporation in the form of dividends are taxed to the owner-employee. However, dividends are not deductible by the corporation. Therefore, owners of small corporations normally do not declare and pay dividends. Instead, to avoid the double tax, they pay out profits to the shareholders who work for the corporation as salaries, bonuses, or employee fringe benefits.

Currently, graduated federal individual tax rates climb to 35%, and individuals normally pay a 15% tax on dividends. (Individuals with low taxable incomes pay a 5% dividend rate, which is reduced to 0% in 2008.) For additional information on individual federal tax rates and rules, see Appendix B.

Be Aware of the Personal Holding Company Penalty

IRC Sections 541 through 547 impose a 15% surtax on the income of personal holding companies (PHCs). Generally, a corporation is a PHC if five or fewer shareholders own 50% or more of the corporation's stock, and if 60% or more of the corporation's gross income for the tax year is from "personal service contracts" (generally, contracts for personal services that name the person who must perform the services) or from passive sources such as dividends, interest, rents, or royalties. Generally, most small business corporations don't need to worry about being classified as a PHC and having to pay this tax even if they have five or fewer shareholders since: (1) a tax adviser can tell you how to use a corporate services contract that stays clear of being classified as a "personal services contract," and (2) most small corporations do not have significant passive income. Also, the PHC rules provide special exceptions for rental income and software royalties (this type of income is not counted to determine if a corporation is a PHC)—two of the categories of passive income most likely to be earned by small corporations. Further, if a corporation is found to be a PHC by the IRS and is assessed a PHC tax, the corporation is normally allowed to avoid the PHC surtax by making dividend payments (direct payments out of current earnings) and profits to shareholders. (Of course, these payouts will get hit with a dividends tax, usually equal to 15%, on each shareholder's income tax return.) In other words, you are allowed to pay out profits to your shareholders, not to the IRS in the form of a PHC tax.

See a tax adviser if your corporation may be classified as a PHC. The PHC rules are too complicated to fully explain here. Just realize that a corporation with five or fewer shareholders that performs services or earns passive income must check with a tax adviser to make sure it avoids the PHC surtax. Typically, tax advisers suggest the following: (1) corporate services contracts should allow the corporation, not the client, to designate the person who is to perform the services, and (2) the name of the individual who will be designated to perform the corporate services should not be specified in the contract.

3. Corporate Income and Tax Splitting

A corporation comes with the built-in advantage of allowing owner-employees to split business income between themselves and their corporation. This can result in real tax savings for owners who work for their corporation.

a. How Income Splitting Works

The way income splitting works is simple: Profits kept in the corporation are taxed at corporate tax rates, while profits paid out to the owners as salaries, bonuses, and other forms of employee compensation are deducted from corporate taxable income and taxed at the owner's individual tax rates. By splitting corporate income between yourself as an owner-employee and your corporation, you can keep corporate and individual income in the lowest possible corporate and individual income tax brackets to achieve an overall income tax savings.

> **Example:** Sally and Randolph are married and own their own incorporated lumber supply company called S & R Wood Supply, Inc. At the close of the third quarter, S & R's CFO reports that they are on course to make $75,000 in profits by the end of the tax year, after paying corporate salaries and other operating expenses. Sally and Randy already receive a generous salary from their corporation, which puts them in the top individual married filing jointly income tax bracket—any additional corporate salary paid to them will get taxed at this top individual tax rate. They decide to keep the profits in the business to fund expansion in the following tax year. This $75,000 of retained corporate income is taxed at the 15% and 25% corporate tax rates. By comparison, consider what would happen if S & R was a partnership or LLC. All profits would pass through the business, whether or not they were kept in the business bank account to fund expansion or actually paid out to the owners, and would be taxed at the owners' higher top individual tax rate. (Remember, unless a partnership or LLC elects corporate tax

treatment, all profits of an unincorporated business are allocated and taxed to the owners each year, whether or not they are actually paid out to them. Sole proprietors can't make this election.)

 Even corporations with sales over $1 million benefit from the 15% and 25% corporate tax rates. Even corporate gross receipts totaling millions of dollars can be reduced to a small taxable income amount and taxed at the lower corporate tax rates. Why? Because after the corporation subtracts the cost of goods sold, pays deductible corporate expenses (including employee salaries and other compensation), and takes other deductions from income (such as depreciation on business assets), net taxable income is reduced significantly—often below the $75,000 threshold, where only the 15% and 25% corporate tax rates apply.

b. How Much Money Can You Keep in or Pay out of Your Corporation?

With all the talk about corporate income splitting, it's natural to wonder just how much flexibility corporate owners have to shift business income between their corporation and themselves to save on income taxes. After all, the IRS knows about corporate income splitting, too, and you can be sure that it doesn't give you a completely free hand to do whatever you wish in an effort to keep business income in the lowest possible corporate and individual income tax brackets.

If the IRS had its druthers, it would probably like to see you keep all business income in the corporation, pay corporate taxes on it, and then pay out these after-tax corporate profits to the owners as dividends that will be taxed again—this time on the owners' individual income tax returns. Of course, you're not going to do this; small corporations rarely pay dividends to owners. Instead, as discussed above, they pay out pretax profits to the owners as salaries, bonuses, and employee fringe benefits, which are deducted from corporate income. This is what corporate income splitting is all about: being taxed only once, and at the lowest possible tax rates, on corporate profits. In this section, we discuss the basic rules that affect how far you can go under IRS rules when splitting corporate income.

1. Retaining Income to Cover Operating Expenses

So, how much income can you keep in your corporation to take advantage of the lowest corporate income tax brackets? The answer is simple: as much income as you need to do business. This is an obvious, practical rule, but the IRS also accepts it. IRS rules say that you can keep income in your corporation—that is, you do not have to pay it out as dividends that are taxable to your shareholders—as long as you have a business reason for retaining the income. Obviously this includes retaining income to meet normal operating expenses, such as rent, utilities, salaries (including the owners' salaries; we discuss this more below), working capital requirements, and other normal business expenses. A corporation can also retain income for nonrecurring costs, such as paying off debt, expanding the business, covering product liability losses, or acquiring a new business.

How Much Working Capital Do You Need?

The courts have adopted a formula that tells you how much working capital is normally necessary for one corporate business cycle. (One cycle includes the manufacture or procurement of inventory, its sale to consumers, and the eventual receipt of payment for the goods by the consumer.) This is called "the Bardahl formula," because it comes from a case called *Bardahl Mfg. Corp. v. United States* (29 A.F.T.R. 2d 72, 72-1 USTC 9158 (1971)). The IRS automatically signs off on this much working capital retention. The formula is complex, but your tax adviser can show you the math if you're interested in more information.

2. Retaining Additional Income: The Accumulated Earnings Credit

The basic rule for retaining income is simple enough, but things change when you want to retain income in your corporation that is not absolutely necessary for business. Let's look at an example to understand how.

Example: Nicole, who is the sole owner of Nicole's Soles, Inc., a shoe manufacturer, decides it would be nice to save tax dollars by keeping $200,000 in her corporation even though her corporate operating budget only requires $150,000. Here's where specific IRS rules kick in. Under Internal Revenue Code § 535(c), corporations automatically get what's called an "accumulated earnings credit" that allows them to keep a certain amount of money in the business whether or not it is needed for business purposes. The credit is $250,000 of earnings and profits (E & P) for most corporations. (Certain professional service corporations, such as health, law, accounting, architectural, engineering, actuarial, and consulting corporations, get a $150,000 credit.)

This credit seems simple enough, too. Nicole doesn't have to worry about keeping a $50,000 over-budget amount in her corporation because her automatic $250,000 credit covers the entire $200,000 of retained earnings. Of course, little is simple under the IRS rules, and the accumulated earnings credit is no exception. There are two technical points to keep in mind, each having to do with the fact that the automatic credit is a cumulative amount:

- The credit applies to the first $250,000 ($150,000 for certain professional service corporations) of retained corporate earnings, not just to the first $250,000 ($150,000 for certain PSCs) retained for nonbusiness purposes. In other words, if Nicole decides instead to keep $300,000 in her corporation—$150,000 to meet her budget plus $150,000 extra—her retained earnings credit covers the first $250,000—the remaining $50,000 isn't covered by the credit.

- You get one cumulative credit that applies to the ongoing balance in the corporation's earnings and profits account (a corporate financial account). In other words, you don't get a new credit that starts fresh at $0 each year. So, if Nicole starts the current year with a $100,000 balance in her corporation's E & P account, then accumulates $300,000 additional E & P during the current tax year, at year end her corporation's accumulated E & P exceed the automatic earnings credit by $150,000 ($400,000 cumulative E & P minus $250,000).

The upshot of all this is that if your corporation retains income—which it will unless all profits are paid out each year (highly unlikely)—and if the current running balance in the corporation's E & P account is equal to or less than your corporation's earnings and credit amount, you are fine. But if the E & P account exceeds the automatic credit amount, you should be able to show the IRS, if it audits your corporation's tax returns, that the amounts accumulated over the credit amount are for the business needs of your corporation. If you can show a business reason for excess accumulations of income, the IRS will leave you alone. If you can't, under IRC Section 531, the IRS can assess a 15% surtax on excess accumulations. This penalty tax is added to your regular corporate income tax liability for the tax year. In effect, the IRS is saying that you must either pay this money out to your shareholders (who normally pay a 15% dividend tax on the payout), or it will assume that you did and make the corporation pay an additional 15% tax on excess accumulations.

3. How Much Money Can a Corporation Pay Out?

Now that we've looked at the corporate side of the income splitting equation—namely, how much money a corporation can keep in the business— let's look at the other side. You'll want to understand how much money your corporation can pay out to its owner-employees in deductible salaries, bonuses, and fringe benefits. Fortunately, the answer is very straightforward: as much as it wants, as long as the owners earned it. In other words, a corporation can reduce its taxable income by paying out profits to owners, as long as the owners actually work in the business and are paid reasonably. We talk more about paying reasonable salaries in Section C1, below.

B. Corporate Accounting Period and Tax Year

Under IRS rules, a corporation's accounting period (the period for which it keeps its annual financial records) and its tax year (the period for which it files annual corporate income tax returns) must be the same. You will choose your corporation's tax year and accounting period when you file the first corporate tax return. The ending date of the accounting period for which the first tax return is filed becomes the ending date of the corporation's tax year.

Corporations can choose a calendar tax year ending on December 31—the same tax year used by most individuals. Or a corporation may choose a fiscal year instead, consisting of a 12-month period ending on the last day of any month other than December—for example, from July 1 to June 30. (Personal service corporations are an exception to this rule; see below.) In addition, a corporation may also choose a "52/53-week" year. This is a period that ends on a particular day closest to the end of a month—for example, "the last Friday in March" or "the Friday in March nearest to the end of the month." Most corporations choose either a calendar or a fiscal tax year.

The choice of tax year and accounting period is important. It determines how your books are kept and when corporate financial statements and tax returns must be prepared. Check with your tax adviser before making this decision.

Tax Year Rules for Personal Service Corporations

If your corporation is a "personal service corporation" as defined by the IRS, you must choose a calendar year for your corporate tax year (and your accounting period) unless the IRS approves your application to use a fiscal year. A personal service corporation is defined in the Internal Revenue Code as "a corporation the principal activity of which is the performance of personal services ... [if] such services are substantially performed by employee-owners." This means that if you are incorporating a service-only business or profession—for example, legal services, architecture, business consulting, or financial planning—you are required to adopt a calendar year as your corporate tax year, unless you qualify to apply for a fiscal tax year under a special IRS exception. If you want to adopt a fiscal tax year for your personal service corporation, your tax adviser can explain the requirements and application procedures.

C. Tax Treatment of Employee Compensation and Benefits

This section provides an overview of the tax treatment of corporate salaries and basic corporate employee fringe benefits. We'll start with the most basic tax issue: the tax treatment of employee salaries and bonuses.

For information about equity sharing plans. Section D, below, discusses the unique advantages of corporate employee equity sharing plans that allow employees to share a piece of the ownership pie, a particularly bright light in the constellation of corporate employee benefits.

1. Salaries and Bonuses

As mentioned earlier, a corporation may deduct amounts paid to employees as salaries (including bonuses) for corporate income tax purposes. Salaries and bonuses must be reasonable and must be paid for services actually performed by the employee. If the IRS thinks otherwise, it can disallow the deduction for the amount it decides is excessive. In practice, if your business is profitable enough to compensate its employees handsomely, you should be able to argue that they are worth top dollar, and therefore your salaries are reasonable.

Some payouts of employee compensation are more likely to attract the attention of the IRS, particularly in the context of a small corporation where the owners also manage and work for the corporation. For example, huge salary increases or large discretionary lump-sum bonuses paid to shareholder-employees of small corporations may be questioned by the IRS, because such compensation is sometimes used as a means of paying disguised dividends to the shareholders. That is, the compensation is a return of capital to the shareholder rather than a bona fide payment for services rendered by the employee.

In the unusual event that the IRS claims your salary unreasonable, it will treat the excess amount as a dividend. This will not have an adverse effect on you as a shareholder-employee, because you have to pay income tax on salaries as well as dividends. (In fact, the current dividend tax of 15% is no doubt less than your marginal tax rate, so you may save a little in individual tax if income is treated as a dividend.) However, it will prevent your corporation from deducting the disallowed portion of compensation as a business expense.

Don't worry too much about the IRS claiming that your corporation's salaries or bonuses are too high. In an age when top execs of publicly held corporations are often ludicrously overpaid, and when entertainment and sports figures earning $1,000,000 per season feel miserably underpaid, high levels of compensation should be considered reasonable, as long as your corporation remains profitable. If the IRS challenges you, you can argue that you are entitled to a high level of compensation. After all, in a small, closely held corporation, the efforts of the principal shareholder-executives are responsible for corporate profitability.

If you are fortunate enough to worry about paying yourself a salary and fringe benefit package so large it may attract the attention of the IRS (this is most likely to happen if you work for your corporation only part-time), ask your board of directors to adopt a resolution detailing your abilities, qualifications, and responsibilities, documenting why you are entitled to the wages and benefits that your corporation is paying you. (For board resolutions covering numerous legal and tax matters, including this one, see *The Corporate Minutes Book*, by Anthony Mancuso (Nolo).)

2. Corporate Retirement Plans

Corporations, like other businesses, may deduct payments made on behalf of employees to qualified retirement plans. Contributions and accumulated earnings under such plans are not taxed to the employee until the employee receives them. As you doubtless know, this is advantageous, because employees generally will be in a lower tax bracket at retirement age, and the funds, while they are held in trust, can be invested and allowed to accumulate with no tax due on investment income or gains prior to their distribution.

If your corporation decides to set up a retirement plan, you will need the help of a retirement plan specialist to establish, administer, and file reports for your plan. (See Subsection b, below.)

a. Types of Retirement Plans

There are two basic types of retirement plans: defined contribution and defined benefit plans. (Other plans are hybrids of these two basic types.) A defined contribution plan—the type used by many small corporations—specifies a yearly contribution amount or formula to use to compute contributions on behalf of each employee. A defined benefit plan guarantees a specified benefit on retirement, which can be as large as 100% of an employee's annual pay during the employee's highest-paid years. Defined benefit plans are more expensive to fund and administer, so smaller corporations usually opt for some type of defined contribution plan unless the founders are the only employees—for example, in an incorporated professional practice.

Today, the most common types of retirement plans are defined contribution plans. Here are the most popular:

- **401(k) plan.** Participating employees contribute a portion of their salary (before taxes) to their 401(k) account. The corporation may make contributions to each employee's account as well. The 401(k) plan has become the most widely used type of retirement plan. It is cost-effective for employers and typically allows employees to choose how they want to invest their funds.

- **SIMPLE plan.** A corporation with 100 or fewer employees can adopt this type of plan. The plan can take the form of an IRA established for each participant, or a cash or deferred 401(k) arrangement. The advantage of SIMPLE plans is that they are easier to set up and operate (less paperwork, fewer filing formalities, and simpler rules) than other qualified retirement plans. They also allow top executives to receive a greater level of contributions than those allowed under the nondiscrimination rules that apply to standard retirement plans.

- **SEP (Simplified Employee Pension) IRA.** This is another fairly simple type of retirement plan used by employers. Under a SEP, employers may contribute to their employees' IRAs. The employees maintain their accounts and can personally contribute to their IRAs also. Some SEP plans let employees receive cash payments instead of employer contributions (if so, employees pay tax on the payouts). Under a special type of salary reduction SEP, employees must receive cash payments instead of contributions.

- **Profit-sharing plan.** Unlike other plans, this plan contributes money to an employee's retirement account if the corporation turns a profit. If the corporation is profitable in a given year, a portion of company profits is allocated to each employee retirement account.

- **Money purchase plan.** Under this type of plan, the corporation contributes a percentage of each employee's salary to his or her retirement account.

- **Targeted benefit plan.** This is a hybrid defined contribution/defined benefit plan. Contributions are allocated to each employee's retirement account so that each employee can reach a targeted benefit amount at retirement.
- **Thrift or savings plan.** Employees can set aside a portion of their salary into a savings account. The corporation may make matching contributions.
- **Employee stock ownership plan (ESOP).** The corporation contributes shares of stock to each employee's account.

b. How to Set Up a Retirement Plan

Fortunately, you don't have to start from scratch with an accountant or tax attorney to adopt a retirement plan that meets your needs. Retirement plan sponsors, employee benefits firms, and even banks and insurance companies have plans from which you can choose. (These vendors can also provide you with one or more of the other types of employee benefit plans discussed below—such as a medical reimbursement or term life insurance plan.) Because the needs of many, if not most, small incorporated businesses are similar, you'll usually find happiness with a prepackaged plan.

All retirement plans have to be "qualified" (approved) by the IRS. The standard plans discussed above have already been accepted by the IRS. So what most financial advisers and employee benefits specialists do is let you adopt one of these master or prototype plans and then offer you options within it. To submit a custom plan—that is, a plan outside the established types—to the IRS for qualification takes a long time and costs money in consulting fees. Few smaller corporations think a custom plan is worth all the extra time and money.

When you pick a plan sponsor, keep in mind the difference between custodial and trustee retirement plans. Custodians such as banks and insurance companies often do not have as many options as trustees (who are usually private corporations) when it comes to offering diverse types of investments and flexibility in investment decision making. Thus, though a retirement plan offered by a bank or insur-

ance company is often sufficient and usually inexpensive, be sure that it allows you the freedom you may want to do things like change investments at any time, lend money to participants, allow voluntary contributions, and obtain preretirement death benefits.

For more information about retirement plans. To learn more about retirement plans, see the following IRS publications, available from the IRS website at www.irs.gov.

Publication 334: *Tax Guide for Small Business*
Publication 560: *Retirement Plans for Small Business*
Publication 575: *Pension and Annuity Income*
Publication 590: *Individual Retirement Arrangements*

Another helpful resource is *Creating Your Own Retirement Plan*, by Twila Slesnick and John C. Suttle (Nolo).

3. Medical Benefits

Tax-favored corporate medical benefits include deductible direct reimbursement plans and prepaid accident and health insurance. These benefits enjoy a double tax advantage: The corporation can deduct these employee perks from its taxable income, and the employee is not taxed on the benefit, either.

a. Accident and Health Insurance

A corporation may deduct premiums paid by the corporation for accident and health insurance coverage for employees, their spouses, and their dependents. And these premiums paid by the corporation are not included in the employee's income for tax purposes. In addition, insurance proceeds and benefits are not normally taxable. Coverage need not be part of a group plan. If you prefer, the employee may pick a policy, pay for it, and get reimbursement from the corporation.

Unincorporated business owners also can deduct premiums paid for themselves and their spouses for health insurance.

b. Medical Expense Reimbursement

A corporation may deduct amounts paid by the corporation to repay the medical expenses of employees, their spouses, and their dependents. These amounts are not included in the employee's income for tax purposes. Typically, a small corporation adopts a reimbursement plan to pay a portion of the medical expenses not covered by a corporate-sponsored health plan—for example, deductible amounts and medical expenses not picked up by the plan.

4. Term Life Insurance

A corporation can deduct a certain amount of the premiums paid on behalf of employees for group term life insurance, as long as the corporation is not the beneficiary. The employee is not taxed on the value of premium payments assumed by the corporation for up to $50,000 worth of insurance coverage. Death proceeds under such insurance are also generally not included in the employee's income for tax purposes. This corporate tax break is available only if the insurance plan does not discriminate in favor of key employees.

This corporate employee perk is not available to unincorporated business owners and their employees, who do not get to deduct life insurance premiums.

5. Disability Insurance

Another unique corporate perk is the ability to provide tax-deductible disability insurance for employees. Premiums paid by a corporation for employee disability insurance coverage are deductible by the corporation and not taxed to the employee. Benefits paid under a disability insurance policy are generally taxable to the employee unless the employee paid the premiums or suffers a permanent injury.

For more information about the tax treatment of employee benefits. IRS Publication 525, *Taxable and Nontaxable Income*, contains further information on the tax treatment of each of the fringe benefit plans and perks discussed in this section. You can browse or download this and other helpful publications from the IRS website at www.irs.gov.

D. Employee Equity Sharing Plans

One of the best aspects of the corporate form is its ability to motivate key employees by letting them share in corporate ownership. Giving employees a piece of the ownership pie through the issuance of corporate stock is a unique benefit built into the corporate legal structure and blessed with special tax benefits under the Internal Revenue Code. No other limited liability business form features this ready-made model for capital participation by employees. For example, in a limited partnership or LLC, attempting to give employees an ownership interest is legally complicated and expensive, as well as being uncertain from a tax perspective. The IRS equity sharing rules are meant to apply to corporate stock transactions, and they make an uneasy fit when applied to unincorporated businesses.

Equity sharing works for start-ups, too. One of the benefits of stock option and other forms of equity sharing plans is that your corporation does not have to be flush with cash or ready to go public to take advantage of them. In fact, equity sharing is one way many cash-challenged corporations provide perks to employees—letting them share in future profits instead of receiving payments from current cash reserves. And even if a small corporation never goes public to create an active trading market for its shares, its stock can be an extremely valuable asset that can be cashed in by employees. For example, once a company becomes profitable, another corporation may buy its shares in a merger or buyout transaction. As part of the merger or sales transaction, the employee stock and option holders get to join the founders of the corporation in cashing in their options and shares.

There are several types of stock participation plans set up by corporations to give employees a stake in corporate ownership. We briefly discuss the most common, below, providing down-to-earth examples to help you appreciate how these plans are used in the real world. Don't let the technicalities put you off; the underlying concepts are not difficult to grasp, and you can master the fine points later. And keep in mind that the main tax benefit all equity sharing plans seek to achieve is a simple one: to change the tax treatment of a person who receives stock for services from that of an employee (who pays individual income taxes on corporate compensation, including stock, when it is paid) into that of an investor (who pays lower capital gains taxes on stock later, when it is sold for a profit).

How to set up an equity sharing plan. When you are ready to consider implementing an equity sharing plan, ask your tax or legal adviser or an equity plan specialist for help. Many have a standard plan with alternative provisions you can select. If you want to try drafting your own plan to save legal and tax consulting fees, see *Model Equity Compensation Plans*, edited by Scott S. Rodrick (The National Center for Employee Ownership, www.nceo.org). It contains standard ISO, NSO, ESPP, and Phantom Stock plans (discussed below) that you can use as a first draft to customize when you consult a professional.

1. Stock Option Plans

Stock options come in two flavors: qualified incentive stock option (ISOs) and nonqualified stock option (NSOs). Typically, a corporation sets up a stock option plan that provides for the granting of both ISOs and NSOs to employees. Before discussing the difference between these two types of options, let's look at their similarities.

- Stock options can be granted in privately held or publicly traded corporations.
- Under the tax rules, stock options can be granted to selected employees. The normal employee benefit antidiscrimination rules that apply to retirement and profit-sharing plans do not apply to stock option plans.
- The board of directors or a special employee compensation committee set up by the board decides who gets options each year. The idea is to provide incentives for key employees to keep working for the company.
- An employee first receives a stock option grant, which is a future right to buy shares at

a set price (called a "strike price"). The strike price of options is critical to their value. The options become valuable to an employee only if the value of the stock rises above the option strike price. If the shares stay at or go below the option strike price, the options are valueless to the employee.

- The employee waits until the option "vests." This is the time, legally, when the employee can exercise the option and buy the shares specified in the option grant at the specified strike price. Vesting is not required under the tax rules—an option can vest as soon as it's granted—but many companies choose to have options vest over a few years. If an employee stays with the company, the options vest, and the employee can buy the shares. If the employee leaves before they vest, the options disappear and the employee loses the ability to buy shares at a low strike price. Option vesting can be made conditional on corporate performance criteria as well, such as the attainment of corporate profitability thresholds or R & D milestones. (Note that some companies use special reverse-vesting provisions in their option plan that provide for immediate vesting of options, but delayed vesting of the underlying stock. See Subsection c, below.)
- Once the employee exercises options and buys the underlying shares, the employee can either hold or sell them. In a privately held corporation, there is normally no market for the shares, so the employee waits until a market is created—for example, when the corporation goes public, or when the corporation is sold and the acquiring corporation purchases the shares as part of the buyout.

Now, let's look at the differences between ISOs and NSOs.

a. Incentive Stock Options (ISOs)

An incentive stock option qualifies for special tax treatment under the Internal Revenue Code. Employees normally pay lower capital gains taxes when they sell shares purchased under an ISO (more on how this works below). To qualify as ISOs, options must meet the rules set out in IRC § 422 and associated Income Tax Regulations. We don't cover all the requirements, but here are some of the most important:

- ISOs must be issued only to employees of the corporation. Independent contractors and others paid by the corporation for services but not classified as employees don't qualify.
- The ISO "strike" price—that is, the price at which an employee can exercise an ISO and buy the ISO shares—must be set at no less than the fair market value of the shares at the time the ISO grant is approved by the board.
- If an employee owns more than 10% of the voting stock of the company when the option is granted, the strike price must be set at no less than 110% of the stock's fair market value on the date of the grant.
- The maximum value of ISOs that can vest per employee per year is $100,000.
- Shares bought when an ISO is exercised cannot be sold by the employee until at least two years from the date the option was granted, and at least one year from the date of exercise.
- If any of the ISO rules are not met, the options become nonqualified stock options (NSOs), meaning that they get lesser tax benefits. (See Subsection b, below.)

Let's now look at the main benefits to employees conferred by the ISO tax rules—and the collateral tax consequences to the corporation.

First, an employee does not pay regular income taxes when an ISO is granted, when it vests, or when the employee exercises the ISO by buying the shares (but see discussion of alternative minimum tax, or AMT, below). Normally, employees are liable for income tax as soon as they have the legal right to receive or ask for a form of compensation. Avoiding this immediate income tax is the major tax benefit of ISOs.

Here's how the basic tax rules work: When an employee exercises an option by buying shares at their strike price, the employee gets an income tax basis in the shares that equals the strike price payment. This basis is used to collect tax from the employee later, when the employee sells the shares.

> **Example:** If Veronica exercises a vested ISO to buy 1,000 shares at $1, she pays no tax when she buys the shares for $1,000. Instead, she gets a tax basis of $1,000 in her shares. If the shares go up in value and she sells them two years later for $3,000, she pays tax on the difference between the $3,000 sales price and her $1,000 basis: $2,000. And, she pays tax at capital gains tax rates, which are lower than regular income tax rates if the stock has been held at least one year.

There is one tax wrinkle, however, that applies to ISOs. The employee is subject to paying an alternative minimum tax (AMT) when an ISO is exercised. This is a special federal tax system that imposes tax on special items of tax preference—that is, tax transactions in which taxpayers get a regular income tax break, such as the exercise of an incentive stock option. When an employee exercises an ISO, an AMT tax may be triggered, depending on the employee's total tax picture for the year and the amount of ISOs exercised during the year. Generally, if ISO shares have appreciated significantly since the date they were granted and an employee exercises a large number of ISOs, an AMT tax may be due. And, this AMT tax may be hefty—up to 26% or 28% of the difference between the current value of the stock and the lower stock purchase price the employee pays to buy the stock under the ISO.

Don't forget the AMT. It is important to investigate any AMT tax consequences before exercising an ISO under an employee stock option plan.

So far, our discussion applies to the way ISOs are taxed under normal rules. But, if an employee does not meet the ISO holding period requirements—that is, if the employee sells shares purchased under an ISO less than two years from the date of the initial grant and less than one year from the ISO exercise date—the ISO becomes an NSO. This means that the employee can't take advantage of the ISO tax rules.

Instead, the employee has to pay ordinary income taxes on the difference between the value of the shares on the ISO exercise date and the option strike price. (This is how NSOs are treated; see the discussion and example in Subsection b, below.)

Sales of ISO stock that violate these holding period requirements are called "disqualifying dispositions." They come up a lot in the ISO world because employees often sell their ISO shares before meeting the holding requirements. *In fact, many ISO holders buy and sell their options on the same date in a cashless exercise.* We talk about these real-world ISO transactions in Subsection c, below.

Now that you understand how employees do or don't get taxed on ISO transactions, let's look at the corporation itself. The corporation does not get to take an employee compensation deduction when an ISO option is granted, vests, or is exercised by an employee. This is the price the IRC charges a corporation for the tax benefits bestowed on ISO employees. Even though an employee is allowed to buy ISO shares at a strike price that is less than the current value of the shares, the corporation cannot deduct the cost of providing this benefit (the reduced payment for shares) to the employee.

b. Nonqualified Stock Options (NSOs)

A nonqualified stock option (NSO) is an option that does not meet the ISO rules described above. NSOs can be issued to employees or to nonemployees—such as independent contractors, corporate board members, attorneys, accountants, or even corporate suppliers. (Of course, outsiders often prefer to be paid hard cash, but the tax law lets a corporation issue NSOs as payment for services to outsiders, whereas ISOs can only go to corporate employees.)

NSOs do not get the same capital gains tax benefit as ISOs; they are subject to ordinary income tax when they are exercised, but this treatment is still better than other forms of employee compensation for two reasons: (1) NSOs are not taxed when they are granted, and (2) an employee pays capital gains rates on appreciation of shares that occurs after the NSO exercise date.

Where to go for NSO details. We explain the basics of NSO taxation in this section, but you'll find the details in Income Tax Regulation 1.83-7. You can browse this and other federal income tax regulations at www.taxsites.com.

If the options (as distinct from the underlying stock) have a readily ascertainable market value, NSOs are taxed to the employee at the time of the grant—and the corporation gets an equivalent employee compensation deduction. Options have a recognized value if they are publicly traded on an options exchange. Most options are not traded on an options market, so NSOs aren't normally taxed when granted.

NSOs without a marketable option value are not taxed when granted. Instead, they are taxed when the option holder exercises them and buys the underlying shares. At that time, the option holder pays ordinary income tax on the difference between the strike price paid for the shares and their value on the exercise date. The AMT tax does not apply.

> **Example:** Veronica exercises a vested NSO option to buy 1,000 shares with a strike price of $1. The shares have a market value of $3,000 on the date that she exercises the option. She owes tax on $2,000: the spread between the stock's $3,000 market value less her $1,000 payment. This is the tax value of the benefit she receives from the NSO grant. Veronica also gets a $3,000 tax basis in her shares (the market value of the shares at the time she purchases them). If she sells the shares later, she pays capital gains taxes on the difference between the selling price and her basis. For instance, if she sells them for $7,000, she pays capital gains taxes on the $4,000 difference.

NSO rules can apply to ISOs, too. As discussed in Section 1a, above, the ISO automatically becomes an NSO if an ISO holder exercises options by buying the shares but sells the shares earlier than two years from the ISO grant date or one year from the stock purchase date, or if the ISO becomes disqualified for any other reason. This means that the seller must pay regular income tax on the difference between the value of the shares on the exercise date and the lower strike price paid for them. (In other words, the seller is taxed just as in the previous example.) The rest of the stock sales proceeds are taxed at capital gains rates.

What are the NSO tax effects to the corporation? When an NSO is exercised, the corporation gets an employee compensation tax deduction equal to the amount that is taxed to the NSO holder (not the tax amount, but the larger amount subject to tax). In the previous example, Veronica's corporation gets to deduct $2,000—this is the amount of the transaction that was taxable to Veronica (the value of the stock she did not have to pay for).

c. ISOs and NSOs in the Real World

Some of the tax rules and consequences associated with options may seem unworkable at first sight. For example, why would a corporation want to grant ISOs if they can't deduct them from corporate taxable income? And how does an employee raise the cash to exercise an option and buy the underlying shares at their strike price? Here are some of the special considerations and workarounds that show how and why stock options are popular with small and large, start-up and established corporations alike. Let's first look at special stock option considerations from the corporation's perspective.

1. Corporate Considerations

Many fast-growing companies start out spending more than they earn and don't care about the non-deductibility of ISOs as an employee expense. They don't have profits to reduce anyway or, if they do, they want to keep profits on the books to impress investors. They like ISOs because they don't cost the company cash and they help attract key employees who will work hard to raise share value. ISOs are a perfect fit for them.

Moreover, even profitable corporations seeking ways to reduce corporate taxes on income are attracted to ISOs. They provide a strong incentive to employees and don't cost hard cash—except, of course, for the legal and tax help to set up the plan and the administrative costs to implement it. In addition, they know that most employees will not buy shares with their own money or keep them long enough to meet the ISO stock holding period requirements. Instead, they expect employees to make a cashless exercise of their options when the company makes a market for its shares by going public or merging with another company. At that time, the ISOs get converted to NSOs, and the corporation gets an employee compensation deduction to reduce its taxable income.

Now, what about successful companies with shares that already have a high market value? How do they get shares into their employees' hands without asking employees to pay a relatively high strike price? (Remember, an ISO strike price must be set at market value on the ISO grant date.) These companies usually prefer NSOs, which can be granted at a strike price that is below the current value of the shares. This lets key employees own a fistful of corporate equity without having to pay a lot for it. For example, a corporation whose shares have a current value of $10 may grant NSOs for $2 per share.

Don't go overboard when underpricing NSOs. There are some risks in aggressively underpricing NSOs. For example, the IRS may decide during an audit that the low-priced NSO grants are nothing more than a disguised payment of corporate shares in return for services—in other words, a stock bonus of discounted shares to deserving employees on the option grant date, not a bona fide option to buy shares. If this happens, the "options" are subject to tax on their grant, not exercise, date.

Tax advisers normally caution against setting a strike price that is too far below 50% of the shares' current value (30% may be okay, but 10% or less is definitely dicey). Also note that the issuance of cheap stock within two years of an IPO can cause problems: If your corporation did not fully "book" (take an expense on its financial statements for) the expense of the cheap stock prior to the IPO, the SEC or accounting firm preparing your financials probably will make you go back and restate prior year income (lower it by taking the below-market issuances of stock against past corporate earnings) before the IPO is allowed to go forward.

Here's another real-world option strategy for corporations: Companies that expect to have quickly rising stock prices try to lessen the tax cost of options granted to their employees by letting them exercise their options as soon as possible. This keeps the taxable spread between the market value of the stock and the exercise price small, reducing ISO AMT or NSO regular income taxes.

Of course, these companies don't want the employees to walk away from the corporation on the early option exercise date, either; they want their workers to stick around to help increase the corporation's share value. Here's what these companies do to achieve both goals: (1) they allow options to vest immediately upon their grant date, but (2) the stock, itself, does not vest until the employee has been with the company for a specified period after the option grant date. (This exercise-before-vesting technique is sometimes called "reverse vesting.") The unvested shares can be voted and are eligible to participate in dividends just like other shares of corporate stock, but they do not become the legal property of the shareholder until the end of the stock vesting period set up under the plan. If the employee leaves the company before the shares vest, the company can buy the shares back from the employee at the exercise price paid by the employee.

Note that options plans set up to issue this type of restricted stock work fine if the employee actually buys the shares early on before the stock appreciates. If the employee waits to buy the shares until after they have appreciated, any AMT or regular income tax savings have been lost.

Employees must file a tax election to avoid restricted stock taxes. The employee must file an IRS 83(b) tax election within 30 days of buying the unvested shares. (We discuss the 83(b) election procedure below.) This election allows unvested shares to be taxed for AMT and regular income taxes on the date of exercise, not later when the shares vest. If the employee gets taxed later when the shares vest, the spread between the market value and exercise price in a successful company will be higher, defeating the purpose of the reverse vesting strategy.

2. Employee Considerations

Now let's look at how employees use the stock options rules in real life. To start with, employees often don't have to pay cash to exercise their options—or don't really want to risk cash to invest in their corporation, no matter how rosy its balance sheet looks. Here are some strategies employees use to get around paying cash up front to buy option shares:

- Some plans allow employees to borrow cash from the company to buy their ISO or NSO shares.
- If there is a market for the shares, some plans permit employees to make a cashless exercise of some options (see below) to buy the remaining shares.

- Some plans let employees trade their options for the cash value of the stock appreciation rights (SARs) that have accrued on the underlying shares since the initial grant date. (See the discussion of SARs in "Other Equity Sharing Plans," below.)

⚠️ **Option loans can bite.** Employees should think twice before signing a promissory note to exercise options. If the value of the shares goes below the strike price paid for them, the shareholder will walk away with no cash after selling the shares and repaying the loan. Even worse, the employee will have to dip into personal funds to repay the portion of the loan not covered by the sale.

There is one additional strategy often used by stock option employees: ISO and NSO holders often do nothing. They simply hold onto their options until the company makes a move—that is, merges with another company or goes public. At that date, assuming share value has increased over the option strike price, they exercise their options, then immediately sell the shares.

Exercising options, then immediately turning around and selling them, is often accomplished in a "cashless exercise." The stockbroker (for publicly traded shares) or acquiring company "lends" the option holder the strike price value of the shares, uses this money to buy the shares from the corporation, sells the shares to the public, or transfers them to the acquiring company and gets repaid the strike price (plus commission if the buyer is a broker). The option holder gets what's left: the value of the shares less the strike price and any commissions paid. Note that a cashless exercise converts all ISOs automatically to NSOs because the one-year holding requirement from date of exercise to sale of stock is not met. Everyone—ISO and NSO holders alike—pays regular income taxes on the net conversion proceeds in a cashless exercise.

2. Employee Stock Purchase Plans (ESPPs)

Another equity sharing perk with tax advantages is the qualified employee stock purchase plan (ESPP) allowed under Internal Revenue Code (IRC) § 423. An ESPP is usually adopted as a component of a broad corporate equity plan that also provides for employee stock options. The plan allows a corporate employee to buy additional shares of corporate stock each year, in addition to shares the employee may be able to buy under the corporate ISO and/or NSO plans.

Unlike an option to purchase ISO or NSO shares under a stock option plan, ESPP stock normally must be bought each year by an employee—usually out of the employee's own pocket (employees don't get an option they can exercise in a later year). One of the advantages of an ESPP is that corporations can let employees buy ESPP shares at a discount of up to 15% of the stock's current value. (In comparison, ISOs must be granted at 100% of the value of the underlying shares.)

a. The Primary Features of an ESPP

Here are the main features of an ESPP:

- An ESPP, like an ISO, can cover only employees, not independent contractors or others not classified as employees.
- Generally, all corporate employees must be included in the ESPP, although some part-time workers, highly compensated employees, and others may be excluded from ESPP coverage; also, employees who own 5% or more of the corporation's voting stock *cannot* be included.
- Under an ESPP, an employee can purchase up to $25,000 worth of corporate stock each year at a price of not less than 85% of the stock's value—this means 85% of its value at the time of the ESPP grant or at time of its exercise, whichever is less. (Since the price of ISO stock must be set at 100% of value at the time

of the option grant, the stock discount is one of the advantages of ESPP stock from the employee's point of view.)

- An ESPP may link the purchase of stock to a specified percentage of employee income—for example, employees may be allowed to purchase discounted ESPP stock worth up to 10% of their annual salary, subject to the overall yearly purchase limit of $25,000.
- ESPP shares are subject to the same holding period rules that apply to ISO shares. That is, employees cannot sell ESPP shares within two years from the grant date and one year from the date they purchased their shares.

b. Tax Treatment of ESPPs

Now let's look at how the IRS treats ESPPs. To start, employees pay no tax when they buy the shares. But assuming the employee sells the ESPP shares at a gain later—and assuming the holding period rules

are met—ordinary income tax is due on the difference between the discounted price paid by the employee for the shares and the value of the shares on the date they were granted or purchased, whichever is less. (The corporation gets an employee compensation deduction for same amount.) The rest of an employee's ESPP stock sales profits are subject to capital gains taxes.

> **Example:** George buys 100 ESPP shares worth $100 per share at a discounted $85 per share price. He pays no tax when he buys the shares. George sells the shares two years later for a market value of $200 per share. For the year of sale, he pays regular income tax on the $15 per share purchase discount, and capital gains taxes on the remaining $100 per share profit.

If the holding period rules are not met when the employee sells ESPP shares, additional ordinary income tax may be due if the shares appreciate between the date of the ESPP grant and the date the employee buys the shares. In this case, the employee pays income tax on the difference between the value of the shares on the date of purchase, minus the discounted purchase price. (If the holding period rules had been met, the employee could pick the *lesser* of the grant date value and the purchase date value as the measure of how much tax the employee owes.) This tax is due even if the employee sells the shares at a loss.

> **Example:** Bob buys 100 ESPP shares worth $100 each for $85 each. He sells them two months later, owing taxes on the $15 per share discount, even if he sells the shares for $50 each.

Again, there is no need to master these ESPP tax rules. For now, just realize that an ESPP can be a valuable component of a larger employee equity sharing plan—one that lets employees buy discounted shares for favorable tax benefits if the shares go up in value.

Other Equity Sharing Plans

In this section, we've discussed the most popular corporate equity sharing plans—ISO, NSO, and ESPP plans—and their general tax treatment. But there are other equity sharing plans in common use by small and large corporations. Here are just a few.

Stock bonus plans. These plans award discretionary shares of restricted stock to key corporate employees. The employee must agree to transfer the shares back to the corporation if the employee does not continue working for the corporation for a specified period, or if specified profit or other corporate performance goals are not met. The employee makes an election under Section 83(b) of the Internal Revenue Code to include the current value of the shares in income. Future appreciation on the shares qualifies for lower capital gains tax treatment when the shares vest and the employer sells the shares. (See Section 3, below.)

Stock appreciation rights (SARs). Instead of issuing shares, a corporation may wish to let employees participate in an increase in corporate share value without granting them stock rights, such as the right to vote or participate in dividends or corporate sales proceeds. SARs let an employee receive cash for any increase in value of the corporation's stock that occurs from the vesting of the SAR. SARs are also used in conjunction with stock option plans. For example, under some plans, an employee can turn in a vested option and receive a stock appreciation rights payment equal to the current value of the shares underlying the option, minus the option exercise price. In effect, the SAR pays the option holder the appreciation value that has accrued on the shares underlying the option from the option grant date. SARs are also a handy way for a privately held corporation to make a market for its own shares: The corporation can cash out the employee option holder instead of waiting for a public market to develop for the shares.

Phantom stock plans. Like SARs, a phantom stock plan gives employees stock rights, but not the stock itself. A phantom stock plan can provide employees with a cash payment that tracks appreciation of the corporation's stock (like SARs) plus other stock-related rights, such as increases to the employee's phantom stock account when dividends are paid to the corporation's shareholders. Again, the employee gets treated like a shareholder without forcing the corporation to dilute the stock ownership percentages of its current shareholders.

Deferred compensation plans. DCPs are not equity plans per se, but because they often include payment in shares of corporate stock we mention them here. Under these plans, a corporation agrees to pay key employees cash or other benefits in the future. The compensation payments are spread out over time, which minimizes the tax bite to the employee—the employee isn't taxed on the payments until they are received. Deferred compensation plans may be tied to corporate profits or may simply specify amounts of stock or sums of money to be paid to an important employee—for example a signing bonus paid to a key exec, which will be paid and taxed in installments.

Tax, legal, and financial advisers who help set up ISO and NSO plans usually handle these additional plans as well. (See "How to set up an equity sharing plan" in the introduction to Section D, above.)

3. Restricted Stock Compensation

Restricted stock is often used to compensate corporate employees. This type of stock, described below, may be issued separately or as part of an employee equity sharing plan. However issued, restricted stock is such a regular and important feature of employee compensation that we want to discuss it here.

To begin with, the basic tax rule is that stock issued to a corporate employee is normally included in the employee's taxable compensation when it is issued, and its full value is subject to ordinary income tax. We have already looked at a few rules that carve out exceptions to this standard rule and bestow favorable income tax deferral and capital gains tax treatment for employee stock issued under ISOs, NSOs, and ESPPs. Here we briefly look at another category of stock that gets special treatment under IRS rules: restricted stock that is eligible for a special tax election under Section 83(b) of the Internal Revenue Code. This sounds more technical than it really is; the basic rules involved are straightforward.

Essentially, restricted stock that qualifies under Section 83(b) doesn't get taxed at the time that it is issued to an employee or other corporate service provider. Instead, the stock is taxed later when the restrictions are removed from the stock. This delayed taxation puts off the payment of tax by an employee—a good thing, because the employee gets to use his or her hard-earned dollars longer. And there's another tax break possible under Section 83(b) if the employee makes a special tax election when the employee gets restricted stock. It lets the employee pay capital gains, not regular income tax at higher rates, on the shares if the employee sells them later for more than the amount the stock was worth when it was issued to the employee. We explain these tax rules in Subsection b, below. But first, let's look at what types of stock qualify for special treatment under Section 83(b).

a. Does Section 83(b) Apply?

Section 83(b) of the Internal Revenue Code applies to restricted stock (or other restricted property) is-sued by a corporation to a person in exchange for the performance of services, either as an employee or as an independent contractor. Restricted stock is simply stock that has one or more legal limitations associated with it—for example, stock that is subject to being bought back by the corporation if the employee stops working for the corporation.

> **Example 1:** Bert's Cafe, Inc., has been going gangbusters for well over one year, due to the round-the-clock service provided by Bert's hard-working waiters. Bert rewards his cafe crew by issuing 1,000 shares of common stock to each worker. The stock has the following restriction typed on the back of each share certificate: "If the shareholder stops providing services for Bert's cafe during the one-year period following the stock issuance date, the shareholder agrees to transfer the shares back to Bert's Cafe for no consideration."

Section 83(b) provides tax deferral benefits (discussed in Subsection b, below) only for restricted stock with temporary restrictions. If the restrictions will never lapse, Section 83(b) does not apply, and the employee must follow the regular tax rules and pay income tax on the current value of the shares when they are issued. Of course, permanent restrictions of this sort may lower the value of the shares, so less income tax will be due. Here is an example of permanent restrictions to which Section 83(b) does not apply.

> **Example 2:** Bert wants his employees to get shares right away for all their hard work without having to wait one year before the shares are fully theirs, so he puts the following statement on the shares instead: "These shares are subject to a right of repurchase by the corporation. If the shareholder wishes to transfer the shares other than to a spouse or to the shareholder's beneficiaries upon the shareholder's death, Bert's cafe has a right of first refusal to purchase the shares from the shareholder at their book value. For a definition of book value and other provisions associated with this right

of first refusal, see the provisions of the Bert's Cafe buy-sell agreement on file with the Secretary of Bert's Cafe at its principal office."

Bert also drafts a buy-sell agreement that each shareholder is required to sign prior to receiving the shares. The agreement specifies the mechanics of how the buyback works and defines book value. (Normally, "book value" is the value of the corporate assets minus liabilities of the corporation divided by the number of shares outstanding.) The main point is that this right of first refusal restriction on the shares is a permanent restriction that never lapses, so Section 83(b) does not apply. Each employee must pay ordinary income taxes on the value of the shares when they are issued.

Of course, the value of shares with a restriction of this sort is probably less than the unrestricted common shares that Bert owns, so each shareholder pays lower taxes on these shares than would be the case if each received unrestricted common shares. And, as always, once employees pay ordinary income tax on their shares, future appreciation on the shares that the employees get when they sell them is taxed at capital gains rates if the shares are held for the minimum capital gains holding period. (See Example 5, below.)

b. Tax Treatment of Restricted Shares Under Section 83(b)

Section 83(b) provides two main tax advantages: The first is a tax deferral benefit, touched on above—namely, the person receiving stock that qualifies as restricted stock under Section 83(b) does not have to pay income tax on the value of the stock when it is issued, only when the temporary stock restrictions lapse. Let's go back to and build on Example 1, above, where Bert's Cafe issues stock with a temporary restriction that qualifies under Section 83(b).

Example 3: Assume that Bert's restricted shares are worth $1 each when issued. Bert's staff does not pay income tax on the shares when they are issued, only when the restrictions on the shares lapse one year from the issuance date. At that time they are included in the worker's income (at their current value) and taxed at the worker's regular individual income tax rates. Bert's Cafe gets a corresponding corporate income tax deduction at that time. After regular income taxes are paid on the shares, any future appreciation of the shares that the employee realizes on a sale of the stock is taxed at capital gains rates (assuming the capital gains holding period rules are met; see Example 5, below).

There is a second feature of Section 83(b) that delivers more good news. Here's how it works: Even though Section 83(b) says an employee must normally wait until the stock restrictions lapse to pay income taxes on the stock under 83(b), it allows the employee to change this income tax deferral tax treatment by electing within 30 days of receiving restricted stock to pay regular income taxes on the shares at the time they are issued. This election is made by mailing a simple 83(b) election form to the IRS. (The IRS doesn't provide a ready-made form to use; you or your tax adviser must prepare an election according to the 83(b) requirements.) If the employee makes this election, the employee is taxed right away on the current value of the shares. And future appreciation on the shares is taxed at capital gains tax rates when the shares are sold, as long as the shares are held for the minimum capitals gains holding period. (See Example 5, below.)

Why is this election a possible tax benefit in some situations? Let's go back to Example 1 again. The shares that Bert issues to employees contain restrictions that will lapse in one year, so the first rule of Section 83(b) says that the shares will be taxed at that time. This may be fine for shareholders who believe that Bert's Cafe is not on track to earn enough money to increase the value of its shares significantly. These shareholders will prefer to wait to pay income taxes on their shares when the restrictions lapse. But what if a shareholder believes that Bert's Cafe will continue to do well and its shares will be worth twice as much one year down the road? That's where the 83(b) election comes in. It allows a shareholder to pay income taxes on the current value of the shares instead of waiting to pay tax on the value of the shares when the restrictions lapse. If this election is made, the shareholder pays tax on the current $1 share value (from Example 3). If the shares are worth $2 one year later when the restrictions lapse, this increase in value is not taxed to the employee at regular income tax rates. Instead, the employee pays capital gains taxes on this increase in value when the employee sells the shares (assuming the employee holds the shares for the capital gains holding period as explained in Example 5, below). Another example is in order.

> **Example 4:** Katherine is the only Bert's employee who is concerned about the eventual income tax bite on Bert's Cafe shares when the restrictions lapse. She is the only employee who files an 83(b) election within 30 days of the issuance of the shares. She includes the $1,000 value of her 1,000 shares in her taxable income on her tax return and pays ordinary income tax on them at her current tax rates. One year later the restrictions lapse, and the value has increased to $5 per share. (Bert's Cafe had continued to do well and this is the price Bert charges his nephew Stan to buy shares in the cafe that following year.) Katherine pays no additional income tax when the restrictions lapse, but the other employees do. They must include $5,000 of income on their individual tax returns and pay regular income tax on it. When Katherine sells her shares, any amount she receives that exceeds $1,000 will be taxed at lower capital gains rates (if she owns the shares for the minimum capital gains holding period, discussed in the next example).

A final example will help illustrate the capital gains tax treatment of the shares.

> **Example 5:** Picking up where Example 4 left off, assume that Bert makes an offer six months after the restrictions lapse to buy the shares back from employees at $7 per share. If Katherine agrees, she has a capital gain of $6,000 ($7,000

minus the $1,000 value of the shares she paid income tax on when she filed her 83(b) election; this $1,000 is called her "basis" in her shares). Because Katherine filed the 83(b) election, her capital gains holding period started on the date she was issued the shares (this is another advantage of making the election). And because she held her shares for longer than one year, she pays lower capital gains tax on the $6,000. If another employee, Jeff, sells his shares back to Bert, Jeff's capital gain is $2,000 ($7,000 minus their $5,000 basis, the value of the shares Jeff paid tax on when the restrictions lapsed). But Jeff doesn't qualify for long-term capital gains rates yet. Because he didn't make an 83(b) election when the shares were issued, Jeff's capital gains holding period started on the date the share restrictions lapsed. He will probably want to wait until one year from this date to take Bert up on his offer.

The main point of the previous examples is that restricted stock provides tax advantages to an employee. It gives a shareholder flexibility to decide when to pay income tax on the restricted stock.

c. Other Tax Advantages of Restricted Stock

There are numerous other ways corporations take advantage of the tax flexibility of restricted stock to provide an advantage to corporate employees as well as the corporation. Here are just a few.

Discounted shares. A corporation can allow key employees to buy restricted shares at a low price—for example, one-half the current value of the corporation's regular common stock. These shares can be bought back by the corporation (for the amount paid by the employee) if the employee leaves or the corporation fails to meet performance goals during a specified period. The employee makes an 83(b) election and pays ordinary income tax on the sales price discount—in our example, the one-half of current value the employee did not have to pay—locking in future appreciation of the shares at capital gains rates.

Initial corporate shares issued for services. When a corporation is formed, a shareholder who receives shares of stock for services normally must pay income tax on the value of the shares. (See Chapter 2, Section H4.) However, if a person receives shares in return for the promise to provide future services and the shares are restricted (reverting to the corporation if the shareholder fails to perform the services), they are not taxed to the shareholder until the restrictions lapse—that is, until the shareholder performs the promised services. In other words, issuing restricted shares to a person who invests personal services in your corporation can delay the tax bite associated with this type of stock issuance transaction. Further, if the shareholder makes an 83(b) election at the time of issuance and pays income tax on the shares at their initial incorporation value, the shareholder does not pay tax when the restrictions lapse, even though the corporation's share value may have increased by then. Instead, the shareholder pays capital gains tax on the shares when sold, just like any other shareholder who invests in your corporation.

NSO plans. If restricted, unvested stock is bought by an employee as part of an NSO plan and the employee files an 83(b) election, the employee pays income tax on the current spread between market value and the exercise price, not the higher spread that may exist when the shares vest. (See the discussion of reverse vesting in Section 1c, above.)

Estate tax savings. The largest asset in the estate of a deceased business owner may be shares in the owner's corporation. If the shares are restricted—for example, if they are subject to the terms of a buy-sell agreement among the shareholders that requires the purchase of the shares from the estate at a price lower than the value of the shares an outsider might pay for them—the estate tax on the shares can be lowered significantly. If properly crafted as part of a buy-sell agreement, restricted stock conditions can work to dramatically lower the estate tax due on a deceased owner's shares. For more information on drafting a corporate buy-sell agreement, see *Buy-Sell Agreement Handbook: Plan Ahead for Changes in the Ownership of Your Business*, by Anthony Mancuso and Bethany K. Laurence (Nolo).

4. Other Equity Sharing Plan Issues

There are nontax issues that need to be considered when you adopt a corporate employee equity sharing plan. In this section, we discuss a few of the most important.

a. Financial Accounting Treatment

"Generally accepted accounting principles"(GAAP) are used by accountants and auditors to prepare corporate financial statements. They include special rules to reflect the cost of equity plans on a corporation's balance sheet. The GAAP rules are often different from the tax rules, and they have an enormous effect on how corporate insiders and outsiders judge the financial performance and value of a corporation. For example, even though the IRC may not allow a corporation to deduct the value of an ISO, NSO, ESPP, or other equity plan award to a corporate employee, GAAP may require the corporation to "book" (include) a portion or all of the employee equity benefit as an expense on the corporation's financial statements. This reduces reported corporate earnings.

Like tax rules, GAAP rules are complex. Generally, however, GAAP requires the corporation to book as an expense the grant of any employee award, whether an ISO, NSO, ESPP, or otherwise, unless it is issued for full value. Corporations intent on maximizing their reported earnings to satisfy investors and attract additional capital often choose an equity plan that has the fewest hits to earnings on the corporate financial statements. In other words they either issue employee equity at full value—ISO, NSO, and ESPP stock at 100% of current value—or else they make sure the current value of the equity is low by adding vesting restrictions to the ISO, NSO, or ESPP shares. (The corporation books the employee equity expense over time as the restrictions lapse.) Your tax adviser or equity plan specialist can clue you in on the GAAP rules to make sure you consider their impact when adopting an employee equity sharing plan.

b. ERISA

The federal Employment Retirement Income Security Act (ERISA) is a tangle of constantly changing rules that apply to employee benefit plans. ERISA imposes minimum mandatory vesting, coverage, distribution, and reporting rules. These rules apply to corporate pension and profit sharing plans (discussed in Section C2, above), but they can also apply to employee equity plans, unless a plan is specifically exempt from ERISA or is worded carefully to avoid the application of ERISA. In the absence of clear language in an equity plan, even large corporations can be surprised by a court decision that says ERISA requires the corporation to allow all employees and independent contractors to participate in the plan, even though this result was not intended when the plan was prepared.

Most corporations do not want ERISA to apply to their ISO, NSO, ESPP, or stock bonus plan. These plans are usually meant to motivate key employees whose work has a significant impact on corporate profitability, not to provide a pension or profit-sharing arrangement for the entire corporate workforce. Plan specialists that track the latest ERISA rulings and court decisions can help you make sure that your equity plan covers those workers you intend to cover.

c. Securities Laws

Equity interests in a corporation, such as options or shares of stock, are securities. They give option holders and other equity plan participants the chance to share in the profit-making potential of your corporation. As such, equity interests are regulated by state and federal securities laws. Fortunately, these laws contain exemptions that allow you to set up and issue equity plan options and stock with a minimum of red tape. Before setting up a plan, you will want to make sure to comply with the exemption rules. For example, you may need to file a notice with your state securities office prior to the award of any options under your corporation's ISO, NSO, or ESPP. The plan specialist or lawyer who helps you set up your equity sharing plan can help you meet these security law requirements.

E. Tax Concerns When Stock Is Sold

There are numerous tax concerns when selling shares of corporate stock. This section discusses two special provisions that apply to owners of small corporations when their corporation or its shares are sold. (Normally, both occur as part of the same transaction, but one owner may decide to sell shares separately to the corporation, its remaining shareholders, or an outsider.) The first part of this section covers the gloomier situation of an owner selling shares for less than their original purchase price—that is, for less than the amount paid by the owner for the shares when the corporation was founded. The second part is more optimistic, covering the pleasant prospect of selling shares of a small corporation at a profit (as well as the less-pleasant side effect of a profitable sale—paying taxes on the stock profits).

1. Section 1244 Tax Treatment for Stock Losses

We know you don't plan to sell your corporation or its stock at a loss—that is, for less than you paid for your shares. But if this happens, the sting will be ameliorated to some extent if your stock qualifies for what is called Section 1244 treatment. Although this sounds technical, the concept is simple: Under Section 1244 of the Internal Revenue Code, many corporations can provide shareholders with the benefit of treating losses from the sale, exchange, or worthlessness of their stock as "ordinary" rather than "capital" losses on their individual federal tax returns, up to a maximum of $50,000 ($100,000 for a husband and wife filing a joint return) in each tax year. This is an advantage, since ordinary losses are fully deductible against individual income, whereas capital losses are only partially deductible. (Normally they can be used only to offset up to $3,000 of individual income in a given tax year.)

To qualify for Section 1244 stock treatment, your loss on the sale of stock must meet the following requirements:

- You must be the original owner of the shares. For example, if you sell your shares to another shareholder, you give your shares to a family member, or the shares pass according to your will to heirs or living trust to beneficiaries at your death, the transferees, heirs, and beneficiaries are not entitled to claim a Section 1244 loss.

- You must have paid money or property (other than corporate securities) for your shares.
- More than 50% of the corporation's gross receipts during the five tax years preceding the year in which the loss occurred must have been derived from sources other than royalties, dividends, interest, rents, annuities, or gains from sales or exchanges of securities or stock. If the corporation has not been in existence for five tax years, the five-year period is replaced by the number of tax years the corporation existed prior to the loss.
- The total amount of money or the value of property received by the corporation for stock, as a contribution to capital and as paid-in surplus, cannot exceed $1 million.
- At the time of loss, you must submit a timely statement to the IRS electing to take an ordinary loss under Section 1244. There is no special form to use for this purpose; your tax adviser can draft a statement that contains the required information.

2. Section 1202 Capital Gains Tax Exclusion

People who own shares that qualify as "small business stock" receive the benefit of lower capital gains taxes when they report profits from the sale or other disposition of their corporate shares. Section 1202(a) of the Internal Revenue Code lets an individual shareholder exclude from taxation 50% of the gain on sales of "small business stock," subject to a maximum exclusion of $10 million or ten times the shareholder's basis in the stock.

Example: Bob and Ken are 50-50 owners of Grass Roots Turf Supplies, Inc. Each founder paid $20,000 for his initial shares. Bob decides six years later to move on to greener pastures and agrees to sell his shares to Ken for $50,000.

Bob's capital gain on the sale of his shares is $30,000. If Bob's stock qualifies as small business stock, he pays capital gains tax on only $15,000 of his capital gain; the other $15,000 is excluded on his income tax return.

For stock to qualify as small business stock, it must meet a number of requirements:

- You must hold the shares for at least five years. However, if you are given shares or inherit them during the five-year period, you can add on the amount of time the shares were held by the giver or deceased shareholder. Also, if you have held the shares for six months, 100% of the gain from a sale can be deferred from taxation if you reinvest the sales proceeds into another small business corporation within 60 days. (The taxes on the gain from the first sale are deferred until the sale of the second corporation's shares.)
- You must have purchased the stock with money or property (other than stock), or you must have received it as employee compensation.
- The corporation must have gross assets of $50 million or less on the date the shares are issued to you.
- The corporation must be engaged in the operation of an active business (not making money exclusively from investments, rents, and the like). However, the practice of an incorporated profession such as a medical, accounting, or engineering practice and several other types of businesses, such as hotels, farming, and mining, do not qualify under this tax provision.

One more point about this special tax provision: A shareholder who sells Section 1202 small business stock after holding it for at least five years gets to exclude 50% of the resulting gain from taxation, but the remaining half is taxed at a special Section 1202 capital gains tax rate of 28%. This rate is higher than the standard 15% capital gains rate that most taxpayers currently pay. However, since the special 28% rate apples to only one-half the gain in a sale of small business stock, you still get a small tax break:

You end up paying a 14% capital gains rate on the total gain from sale (1/2 x 28%), which is 1% less than the standard 15% capital gains rate.

The IRS 1040 tax return is used to report and pay taxes on Section 1202 stock gains. To learn more about how to do this, see the IRS instructions that accompany Form 1040 or ask your tax adviser.

F. Tax Treatment When Incorporating an Existing Business

In this section, we focus on the tax consequences of incorporating an existing unincorporated business, such as a sole proprietorship, partnership, or LLC. This transaction involves the transfer of the assets (and any liabilities) of the unincorporated business in exchange for shares of your new corporation. The mechanics of this type of transaction are simple: The assets and liabilities of the unincorporated business are transferred together to the new corporation, which issues stock to the prior business owners in proportion to each owner's interest in the unincorporated business. We provide instructions and forms for this in Chapter 4. (See particularly the Bill of Sale in Chapter 4, Step 7.)

Skip ahead if you are incorporating a new business. If you are not incorporating an existing business, you can skip this section and move on to the next chapter.

1. Tax-Free Exchange Treatment Under IRC Section 351

When you incorporate an existing unincorporated business, you transfer its assets and liabilities to the new corporation in return for shares of stock. Under the normal federal income tax rules, this sort of transfer of assets would be a sale. And, as you know, when you sell an asset you normally are liable for the payment of taxes on the profit you make from the transaction. In tax terms, the profit is the difference between the selling price and your *tax basis* in the property. Essentially, your tax basis

in the property is the amount you paid for it, minus depreciation, plus capital improvements.

> **Example:** Assume that your business purchased a building at a cost of $180,000. In the years since the purchase, the business has taken $90,000 depreciation on the property and made $20,000 in capital improvements to the property. This means the adjusted basis of the property is now $110,000 (cost of $180,000 – $90,000 depreciation + $20,000 improvements). If the property is sold for $210,000, the taxable gain (profit) is $100,000 ($210,000 – $110,000 adjusted basis). To keep things simple, we are ignoring the cost, sales price, and basis of the land on which the building is located (land is not depreciable). We are also ignoring special rules that make you "recapture" and pay ordinary income tax on a portion of the depreciation already claimed on the building.

Naturally, most incorporators of an existing business prefer not to pay taxes on the sale of property to their corporation in return for shares of stock. Fortunately, this is where IRC § 351 comes to the rescue, allowing incorporators (and others) to transfer property to a corporation in return for stock in a tax-free exchange without recognizing any present gain or loss on the transfer. Instead, payment of tax on the gain is deferred until the shares, themselves, are sold. To qualify for Section 351 tax-free exchange treatment, you must meet certain rules:

- **The transferors must transfer property to the corporation.** For purposes of Section 351, "property" includes cash and tangible property, such as tools, equipment, real estate, and the like, as well as intangible property, such as patents, copyrights, or stock in another corporation. The property can come from the assets of an existing business or from separate items of property paid in by shareholders who don't own a stake in the prior unincorporated business. "Property" does not include services, so stock issued to someone in return for work performed for the corporation does not qualify under Section 351 (more on this below). Also, stock issued in return for the cancellation of corporate indebtedness owed to a shareholder—for example, when a corporation issues shares to a founder instead of repaying money it owes to the founder—doesn't count under Section 351.

- **The transferors, as a group, must own at least 80%** of the total combined voting power of all classes of issued stock entitled to vote ("voting stock") after all the transfers are completed.
- **The transferors must also own at least 80%** of any other issued classes of stock of the corporation after the transfers are completed. (Most small corporations start out with just one class of voting stock and do need to worry about this rule.)

Most small corporations' initial stock issuances will meet these tests and therefore will be eligible for tax-free exchange treatment. This includes those who are incorporating an existing business. After all, in this situation, the same person or small group who owns the unincorporated business normally owns 100% of the new corporation's shares after the business assets are transferred.

Example 1: Frank and Francis, the owners of an existing partnership, decide to form a corporation. The corporation's initial stock issuance consists of 400 shares of stock at a price of $100 per share. The corporation has just one class of voting stock. Frank and Francis will receive 200 shares apiece for their equal interests in the assets of their partnership valued at $40,000. The transaction qualifies for Section 351 tax-free exchange treatment because at least 80% (in this case, 100%) of all shares in the corporation will be owned after the transfer by the transferors of money and property.

Section 351 also lets the incorporators of an existing business bring in additional investors when they incorporate.

Example 2: Frank and Francis decide to let their friend Harvey invest in the new corporation, too. He'll get 100 shares for the payment of $10,000 cash. The initial stock issuance in this situation is 500 shares: 200 to each of the prior business owners and 100 to Harvey. Cash counts as property under Section 351, so it is still true that 100% of the corporation's shares are issued for property. In fact, even if Harvey bought his shares in return for promising to perform future services for the corporation, the transaction qualifies under Section 351. Frank and Francis own 80% (400 of the 500 shares equals 80% of all voting shares and 80% of all classes, which happen to be the same in this example), and they transferred property that qualifies under Section 351. Harvey will have to pay income tax on his shares because of another tax rule (explained in Section 2a, below), but the entire transaction qualifies under Section 351, so Frank and Francis still get their shares tax-free.

Of course, very little is really free under tax statutes and regulations. A tax-free Section 351 exchange simply defers the payment of taxes until you sell your shares or your corporation is sold or liquidated. At that time, your shares will have the same basis as the property you originally transferred to the corporation, plus or minus any adjustments made to your shares while you held them and any adjustments made after you incorporate.

Example: You transfer property with a fair market value of $200,000 and an adjusted basis of $100,000 to the corporation in a Section 351 tax-free exchange for shares worth $200,000. Your shares will then have a basis of $100,000. If you sell the shares for $300,000, your taxable gain will be $200,000 ($300,000 selling price – $100,000 basis). Note also that the corporation's basis in the property received in a tax-free exchange will also generally be the same as the adjusted basis of the transferred property. In this example, the corporation's basis in the property will be $100,000.

Even in a tax-free transaction, the shareholders must pay tax on any money or property they receive in addition to stock. For example, if you transfer a truck worth $50,000 in a tax-free exchange to the corporation in return for $40,000 worth of shares and a $10,000 cash payment by the corporation, you will have to report the $10,000 as taxable income.

The IRS Requires Information About Section 351 Transactions

Federal income tax regulations require the corporation and each shareholder to file statements with their income tax returns listing specific information about any tax-free exchange under Section 351. The corporation and shareholders must also keep permanent records containing the information listed in these tax statements.

2. Potential Problems With IRC Section 351 Tax-Free Exchanges

There are, of course, complexities that may arise when you attempt to exchange property for stock in your corporation under Section 351. Let's look at a few of the most common problem areas. As we do, realize that seemingly simple tax rules can often mask many hidden technicalities and exceptions and that this is particularly true in this area. It follows that if you will be transferring property and possibly services to your new corporation in return for shares of stock (and, possibly, promissory notes or other evidence of debt to be repaid by the corporation), you will need to check with an accountant to ensure favorable tax results under IRC Section 351.

a. Issuing Shares in Return for the Performance of Services

The performance of services is not considered "property" for purposes of Section 351. (Remember, stock must be issued in return for cash or property to qualify for tax-free treatment.) What this means is that you cannot count shares issued to shareholders in exchange for services or the promise to perform services when calculating the 80% control require-

ment under Section 351. Even if you are able to meet the 80% control test (not counting the stock issued for services), keep in mind that any shareholder who receives stock for services will have to report the value of the shares as taxable income.

Example: Your corporation plans to issue $50,000 worth of shares on its incorporation to you and the cofounder of your corporation, Fred. You will transfer property previously used in your sole proprietorship—a copyright in software, reasonably worth $35,000—for $35,000 in shares. Fred will receive $15,000 in shares in return for work valued at $15,000 that he has already performed organizing the corporation. The transfer will be taxable to both you and Fred, since the basic 80% post-issuance control test of Section 351 is not met. You are the only person who will transfer property that qualifies under Section 351 in return for stock, and you will only own 70% of the shares of the corporation.

If we change the facts in this example so that you receive 80% of the stock in exchange for property—for example if you transfer $40,000 worth of property and Fred contributes $10,000 in services—the transfer will be tax-free under Section 351, but Fred will have to report his $10,000 in shares as taxable income.

 How shareholders who contribute services can receive shares that qualify under Section 351. There are ways to issue shares to a service provider and still have your stock issuance transaction qualify under Section 351. Section 351 says that if a shareholder contributes both services and cash or property, all the shares issued to the shareholder can be counted under the Section 351 requirements, including the shares issued for services, provided the value of the cash and property is not just a token amount compared to the value of the services. (Income Tax Regulation 1.351-1(a)(1)(ii).) Tax advisers generally say that the property contributed by a service provider must be equal to at least 10% of the value of the services to pass muster under this regulation.

Intangible Property Qualifies Under Section 351

Unlike services, intangible property, such as the goodwill of a business or patents and copyrights, is considered property for purposes of Section 351. Thus, if you, as a prior business owner, contribute a valuable copyright, trademark, or patent to a new corporation, it qualifies as property under Section 351, and the shares you are issued can be counted in determining whether your incorporation meets the 80% control requirement of Section 351.

b. Issuing Nonqualified Preferred Shares

Section 351 tax-free exchange treatment applies only to the issuance of stock in exchange for cash or property. Most corporations issue common stock that gives each shareholder a proportionate right to vote and receive any dividends paid by the corporation, as well as an equal right to receive assets and sales proceeds when the corporation is liquidated or sold. However, corporations do sometimes issue preferred shares of stock that give certain shareholders extra rights—such as the right to convert their shares into a specified number of common shares, a preferential right to receive dividends, or a special right to get paid more for their shares if the corporation is liquidated.

You probably will not issue preferred shares as part of your initial stock issuance but, if you plan to, keep the following point in mind: IRS rules say that certain types of preferred stock do not qualify as "stock" under Section 351. Preferred shares that have a dividend rate that fluctuates with interest rates, or preferred shares that a shareholder can force the corporation to buy back (that is, shares redeemable at the option of the shareholder), and other special types of preferred shares are nonqualified under Section 351.

If you receive nonqualified preferred shares in exchange for property you transfer to the corporation, you are treated as though you were paid cash.

The entire transaction and the other shareholders may still qualify for Section 351 tax-free exchange treatment, but you will have to pay tax on the value of your nonqualified shares. The lesson is this: If you plan to issue preferred shares as part of your initial stock issuance, see a tax adviser to find out how they affect your eligibility for Section 351 tax treatment.

c. Issuing Stock and a Promissory Note in Return for the Transfer of Business Assets

Section 351 tax treatment applies to the transfer of property to a corporation in exchange for stock, not corporate promissory notes or other debt instruments. For example, if you transfer $100,000 worth of business assets to your new corporation in return for (1) $75,000 in shares, which represents 80% or more of your corporation's initial shares, and (2) a $25,000 promissory note from your corporation (it promises to pay $25,000 cash plus interest to you over a few years), the transaction still generally qualifies under Section 351. However, you will owe tax on the $25,000 face amount of the note. The IRS treats the note portion of the transaction as though you sold property to the corporation and received cash back equal to the face amount of the note—in other words, just as though you sold a piece of property to your corporation that was not part of Section 351 property for stock swap.

Check with your tax adviser. Consult your tax adviser if you plan to incorporate an existing business and wish to receive a promissory note in addition to shares of stock from your corporation.

d. Agreeing to Pay Liabilities Associated With the Transferred Property

Here is another potential hitch contained in the Section 351 rules: Shareholders may have to pay taxes if the liabilities assumed by the corporation exceed the basis of the business assets transferred to the corporation. These liabilities may be those of a prior business that the corporation agrees to assume, or liabilities attached to a specific item of property, such as a mortgage on real estate transferred to the corporation.

Skim this material. Again, these Section 351 rules are technical, and you don't need to master them. We provide this information to give you a sense of how the rules and their exceptions may apply to you. If any of the issues discussed here raise a red flag or provide an exception that may affect your incorporation, ask you tax adviser to take a closer look at Section 351.

Example 1: If you transfer business assets with a basis of $40,000 to your corporation, but your corporation also assumes $60,000 worth of your unincorporated business's debts, the difference of $20,000 is generally taxable to you. Another consequence is that the full amount of the assumed debt (in this case, $60,000) minus the amount of taxable gain recognized (in this case, $20,000) is subtracted from your basis in the stock you receive. This means you pay more tax when the shares are eventually sold. (This reduction of stock basis happens in most situations when a shareholder transfers property along with debts to a corporation in return for shares, not just when the debts exceed the value of the assets transferred.)

Fortunately, shareholders who transfer business assets along with liabilities to their new corporation do not owe any immediate tax, even though the liabilities assumed by the corporation exceed the value of the assets transferred to it. This is because the tax law contains an exception for some transactions when a cash-basis taxpayer (one who uses the cash method of accounting) transfers assets and liabilities to a corporation. (IRC § 357(c).) Since the majority of unincorporated businesses use the "cash method" of accounting—income is reported when received, and expenses are deducted when paid—this exception often applies to the incorporation of a business. Because "accounts receivable" (money owed to a business—an asset) have a zero basis for a cash method business, and since the assets of a business normally have a low basis due to depreciation taken on them, it's easy for the liabilities of an unincorporated business to exceed the basis of its assets.

In other words, this exception can be very useful when an existing business is being incorporated.

Example 2: Felicia incorporates her dog-walking service, Canine Companions. Her assets consist of $3,000 cash, a computer system, furniture, phones, and other miscellaneous items that originally cost $20,000 but now have a depreciated basis of $7,000. Her accounts receivable are $30,000, but they have a zero basis since Felicia's sole proprietorship uses the cash method of accounting. The business has accounts payable—money owed to others—of $25,000. The liabilities of the business ($25,000 accounts payable) exceed the basis of the business assets ($3,000 cash plus $7,000 of depreciated assets) by $18,000. Under the standard 351 rules, Felicia would pay tax on this $18,000 taxable "gain" at the time of her incorporation, and her shares would have a basis of $3,000 ($10,000 basis in assets plus the $18,000 taxable gain minus the full amount of liabilities transferred of $25,000). However, because of the special exception for cash method businesses, she can ignore the accounts payable in her calculations, and her basis in assets ($10,000) will exceed liabilities (zero), so there will be no tax due when she incorporates. Further, her basis in her stock will be higher (she pays less tax later when she sells her shares), since she can ignore the accounts payable in her stock basis calculations. Her stock basis is $10,000 (the basis of the assets transferred, with no adjustment for liabilities assumed by the corporation).

3. Is a Section 351 Tax-Free Exchange Desirable?

As discussed above, most incorporators want to qualify for a Section 351 tax-free exchange. But this isn't always true. Some incorporators may wish to avoid Section 351 exchange treatment and recognize a gain or loss on the transfer of property to a corporation. If this is what you want, you may have to do some advance planning—for example, by making sure that *less* than 80% of your shareholders receive shares for qualified property under Section 351 or by transferring property to your corporation for cash or promissory notes, not stock.

Here are some reasons why an incorporator might wish to avoid tax-free exchange treatment under IRC Section 351:

- Some incorporators may wish to recognize a *gain* on the transfer of business assets. For example, incorporators may already have capital losses for the tax year. If they recognizes a capital gain on a transfer of property to his corporation, their capital losses can be used to offset the gain, and they still pay no taxes. Without a capital gain, the amount of capital losses an individual can deduct against taxable income is limited (currently, $3,000 per year).

- Some incorporators wish to avoid Section 351 to increase the corporation's basis in the transferred property. In a tax-free exchange, the corporation gets the transferor's basis in the assets; in a taxable exchange it gets a basis in the property equal to its full market value.

Example: Assume that you plan to transfer assets with a fair market value of $50,000 to your corporation. Your basis in these assets is $30,000. If you transfer these assets to the corporation for $50,000 worth of stock in a qualified Section 351 exchange, the corporation's basis in the assets is $30,000 (your preincorporation basis in the assets). But if the exchange is taxable—let's say you sell it to the corporation for cash or in a property-for-stock exchange that does not meet the 351 control requirements—the corporation uses the fair market value of the assets as its basis, or $50,000. You, as the shareholder, have a $20,000 capital gain—the difference the $50,000 sales price and your $30,000 basis in the property.

- Incorporators might want their corporation to have a higher basis in property because a higher basis allows the corporation to take higher depreciation deductions on the property, which reduces the corporation's

taxable income. The corporation also may end up with a higher basis in the property when the property is sold, which means the corporation pays less tax on the sale.

- Some incorporators may wish to recognize a *loss* on the transfer of assets to their corporation, to offset capital gains they have recognized from other property sales during the year. If you transfer assets to your corporation in a qualified Section 351 exchange for stock, you cannot recognize a loss on the transfer—you have to wait until your corporation is sold or liquidated or you sell your shares to take the loss on your individual tax return.

Example: You paid $70,000 for a business asset. Your depreciated basis in the asset is $50,000 and its current market value is $40,000. You will need to transfer the asset to the corporation for $40,000 cash or in a property-for-stock exchange that does not qualify under Section 351 in order to recognize a $10,000 loss ($40,000 sales price minus $50,000 basis) for tax purposes.

Major shareholders can't sell property to the corporation at a loss. Even if you can avoid Section 351 exchange treatment, you still may not be able to transfer depreciated property to your corporation and claim a loss on your individual income tax return. The reason is that another section of the Internal Revenue Code, IRC § 267, does not let a shareholder who owns more than 50% of a corporation's stock sell property to it at a loss. (These restrictions are meant to hinder self-serving tax-avoidance schemes between related people and entities they control.)

4. Additional Tax Considerations When Incorporating an Existing Business

Let's look at some additional tax and business issues associated with the incorporation of an existing business, starting with the best time to switch from an unincorporated business to a corporation.

a. When Is the Best Time to Incorporate an Existing Business?

Most incorporators have some wiggle room when deciding when to form a corporation—that is, there are no pressing legal reasons for incorporating at a particular time. But the timing of your incorporation may make a difference in terms of taxes.

Example: If you anticipate a loss this year and a healthy profit next year, you may wish to remain unincorporated now and take a loss on your individual tax return. (Remember, profits and losses of unincorporated businesses are reported on owners' personal income tax returns; corporate losses can be taken only on the corporation's income tax return.) Next year you can incorporate and split your business income between yourself and your corporation to reduce your overall tax liability. (See Section A3, above, for more on the tax savings that can be achieved by income splitting.)

b. Should You Transfer All Assets and Liabilities to the New Corporation?

When an existing business is incorporated, all assets and liabilities are usually transferred to the corporation in a tax-free exchange under Section 351. But this may not always be the case. In special circumstances, incorporators may not wish to transfer all assets or liabilities of the prior business to the corporation.

1. Retaining Some of the Assets of the Prior Business

In some instances, the prior business owners may not wish to transfer some of the assets of the prior business to their new corporation. Here are a couple of reasons:

- You need to retain sufficient cash in the old business to pay liabilities not assumed by the corporation, such as payroll and other taxes.
- You want to continue to own some of the assets of the prior business. For example, you may wish to continue to own a building in

your name and lease it to your corporation. By doing this, you can continue to personally deduct depreciation, mortgage interest payments, and other expenses associated with the property on your individual tax return. And, of course, your corporation can deduct rent payments made under the lease. (A rent comparable to the amounts that similar commercial space rents for in your geographical area should pass IRS muster.)

2. Retaining Some of the Liabilities of the Prior Business

You may not wish to transfer—that is, have your corporation assume—all of the liabilities of the existing business. Here are two reasons for this:

- Assuming the liabilities of the prior business sometimes results in the payment of tax, even in a Section 351 qualified exchange. (Shareholders must pay tax on the amount by which the liabilities exceed the basis of the transferred assets. See Section 2d, above.)
- Payment of expenses by the prior business owners, rather than by the corporation, allows the owners to deduct these expenses on their individual tax returns, which reduces their individual taxable incomes.

5. Liability for the Debts of the Unincorporated Business

Another consideration when incorporating an existing business is whether the owners of the unincorporated business remain personally liable for its debts after it is incorporated. Although this is technically a legal, not a tax, issue, it is closely tied to the transfer of assets and liabilities to the corporation, so we include it here.

These rules normally have little practical significance for most incorporators who, as a matter of course and good-faith business practice, will promptly pay all the debts and liabilities passed on to the new corporation. But, in case a debt is contested or for some other reason you wish to extend the time for payment, here are the basics of legal liability:

- Whether or not the corporation assumes the debts and liabilities of the prior business, the prior owners remain personally liable for these debts and liabilities unless the creditor signs a release that lets the business owners off the hook personally.
- The new corporation is not liable for the debts and liabilities of the prior business unless it specifically agrees to assume them. If it does assume them, both the corporation and the prior owners are liable.
- If a transfer of assets to the corporation is fraudulent (done with the intent to cheat or deceive creditors), the creditors of the prior business can file legal papers to seize the transferred business assets. Similarly, if the corporation does not, in fact, pay the assumed liabilities of the prior business, the creditors of the prior business may be allowed to seize the transferred assets.

- If transferred assets are subject to recorded liens—for example, a mortgage on real estate or a recorded security interest on personal property—these liens will survive the transfer and the assets will continue to be subject to them.
- The former business owners can be personally liable for postincorporation debts if credit is extended to the corporation by creditors who in good faith reasonably think that they are still dealing with the prior business—for example, a creditor who has not been notified of the incorporation. (See Chapter 5, Section A, for the steps to take to notify creditors when you incorporate.)
- In many states, the corporation may be liable for delinquent sales, employment, or other taxes owed by the unincorporated business. (This type of liability is called "successor liability," and you may see this term used in materials you receive from your state's business or employment tax department.) ∎

Seven Steps to Incorporation

This chapter shows you how to take the steps necessary to form a corporation in your state. Most important, this means preparing and filing your Articles of Incorporation. After that, you will prepare your corporate bylaws and the minutes of your organizational meeting. Finally, you'll issue your initial shares of corporate stock. You may be surprised how easy all this is—the basic forms are so easy to understand you can often complete them in less than an hour. Although we point out areas where you may wish to take a little more time to customize the forms to suit special needs, in most cases the basic forms will work just fine to start your small corporation.

After you file your articles, your corporation is an official legal entity. The other steps explained in this chapter are necessary for sound practical reasons. The bylaws contain the essential rules needed to operate your corporation. And the first (organizational) meeting of your directors is necessary to transact the initial business of your corporation by issuing shares of stock in return for investors' capital contributions.

Forms on CD-ROM. Included at the back of this book is a CD-ROM that contains all the forms shown in this chapter. (These forms include Articles of Incorporation for states that do not provide an official form, ready-to-use bylaws, Minutes of First Board Meeting, and others.) For details on how to use the CD and install the files, see the instructions in Appendix C. If you do not use a computer, Appendix D contains tear-out versions of all incorporation forms on the CD-ROM.

Step 1. Choose a Corporate Name

The first step in organizing your corporation is selecting and reserving a corporate name. To do this, there are a number of hurdles and hoops you must jump over and through. We take you through them in order of importance, below. But before we do, here's something to keep in mind: There are many existing businesses names already on file with the secretary of state, associated with existing business products and services, and in use as domain names online. You will see that your name must be as distinct as possible from these existing names. Plus, you will want to pick a name that you like and that adds the right spark to your corporation's identity. It isn't easy to satisfy these criteria, particularly in a crowded marketplace. Our best advice is to be patient and to choose a few alternate names you're willing to settle for in case your first choices are unavailable; you may need to compromise a bit. If you're willing to do so, you'll avoid future legal squabbles with existing business name owners, and have a workable name you can use throughout the life of your corporation.

A. Meet State Corporate Name Requirements

Your first task when choosing a corporate name is to make sure you meet your state's corporate name requirements. In most states, the most basic requirement is that you include a corporate designator in your corporate name such as "Corporation," "Incorporated," "Limited," or an abbreviation of one of these words—"Corp.," "Inc.," or "Ltd." (We list your state's specifics in the "Articles Instructions" section of your state sheet in Appendix A.) Even if not required, most incorporators use one of these designators at the end of their corporate name precisely because they want others to know that their business is incorporated.

The second basic corporate name requirement is that, in most states, a business corporation cannot use words that connote the formation of a certain type of business, such as a bank or insurance company. Therefore, you should normally avoid words like "bank, "trust," or "insurance" in a corporate name unless, of course, you will obtain the additional state or federal permits necessary to operate in one of these fields.

In addition, most states have special corporate name requirements for professional corporations—that is, corporations formed to practice a state-licensed profession in the medical, legal, accounting, engineering, or architectural fields.

B. Pick a Likeable, Workable Name

It is extremely important to choose a good name for your corporation. First of all, you have to live with it. Second, everyone you do business with, including your customers, clients, other merchants, vendors, independent contractors, lenders, and the business community generally, will identify your business primarily by these few words. And you certainly want to get it right the first time, since making a change later will often mean printing new stationery, changing advertising copy, creating new logos, and ordering new signs. You will also need to amend your corporate articles if you wish to change your original corporate name.

Of course, if you are incorporating an existing business, you'll likely want to use your current name as your corporate name if it has become associated with your products and services. Many businesses do this by simply adding an "Inc." after their old name—for example, Really Good Widgets may incorporate as Really Good Widgets, Inc. Using your old name is not required, however, and if you have been hankering after a new one, this is your chance to claim it.

Here are a few guidelines to help you in your search for the right corporate name.

Make your name memorable. A creative, distinctive name will not only be entitled to a high level of legal protection; it will stick in the minds of your customers. Forgettable names are those of people (like O'Brien Web Design), those that include geographic terms (like Westside Health Foods), and names that literally describe a product or service (like Appliance Sales and Repair, Inc.). Remember, you want to distinguish yourself from your competitors.

Your name should be appealing and easy to use. Choose a name that's easy to spell and pronounce, and that is appealing to both eye and ear. Try to pick a catchy name that people will like to repeat. Make sure that any images or associations it evokes will suit your customer base.

Avoid geographical names. Besides being easy to forget, and difficult to protect under trademark law, a geographical name may no longer fit if your business expands its sales or service area. If you open Berkeley Aquariums & Fish, for instance, will it be a problem if you want to open a second store in San Francisco? Especially if you plan to sell products on the Internet, you should think twice about giving your business a geographic identifier.

Don't limit expanded product lines. Similarly, don't choose a name that might not be representative of future product or service lines. For instance, if you start a business selling and installing canvas awnings using the name Sturdy Canvas Awnings, your name might be a burden if you decide to also start making other products such as canvas signs or vinyl awnings.

Get feedback. Before you settle on a name, get some feedback from potential customers, suppliers, and others in your support network. They may come up with a downside to a potential name or suggest an improvement you haven't thought of.

C. Check With the State Filing Office to See If Your Proposed Name Is Available

This is the first procedural hurdle on the way to securing a corporate name. When you file your Articles of Incorporation with the state, you will include your proposed corporate name. The filing office will not accept your corporate name—and will, therefore, reject your Articles of Incorporation—unless the name is sufficiently different from other corporate names it has already registered. Each state corporate filing office maintains a list of names that are already taken, including existing in-state corporations, out-of-state corporations qualified to do business in the state, names that have been registered with the state by other out-of-state corporations, and names that have been reserved for use by other corporations in the formation stage. If your proposed name is the same as or "confusingly similar" to any of these, the state will reject it.

We can't give you an exact definition of the phrase "confusingly similar," but for practical purposes, this restriction simply means that the wording of your proposed name cannot be so close to that of a name already on file with the state that it might result in public confusion. Each state has its own guidelines for determining whether a proposed name is sufficiently different from other registered names. (Some state filing offices publish their name comparison rules on their website.)

As a general rule, a state will disregard differences between corporate name endings, common connectives, prepositions, and the like, as well as descriptive terms. For example, if you want to set up a wholesale house for computer equipment under the name "Compusell, Inc.," and a corporation is already on file with the name "Compusel International, Inc.," your name will most likely be rejected as too similar.

There is one big exception to this rule: Most states let you use personal names in a corporate name, even if the resulting corporate name is similar to a name that's already on file with the state. Thus, while there could be only one Greenal Corp., there could be two corporations called Allworth & Green, Inc. However, if you use a personal name, your state will usually insist that you include a corporate designator, even if a corporate designator normally is not required for a corporate name in your state. For example, "Biff Baxter" normally would be considered an invalid corporate name, but "Biff Baxter, Inc.," would be acceptable in most states.

Because your Articles of Incorporation will be rejected if the name you've chosen is too similar to the name of a corporation already on file with the state filing office, we strongly recommend that you check your proposed name's availability before filing your articles with the state. If it turns out that your name is available and it will take you a few days or more to get your articles on file, we encourage you to reserve the name in advance. (See Section F, below.)

Many states let you check name availability by visiting the state filing office website and comparing your proposed name with names already entered in the state corporate database. Doing this is a good way to see if someone else is already using your proposed name. If you discover another name that is close to, but not the same as, your proposed

name, you should call the state filing office to see if your name is too close to the similar name. The office will search for similar names and tell you whether your proposed name is too close to them.

Whether or not you visit the state's website first, most states let you call and check name availability for one to three proposed names, free of charge. Call the main phone number for the state filing office and select the option to check name availability. (We list your state filing office telephone number in the "Corporate Filing Office" section of your state sheet in Appendix A.)

If the name you want is unavailable, you need to select a new name for your corporation. We recommend picking a new name, even though it is possible in most states to use an unavailable name if you get the signed consent of the corporation using it. It's normally not practical to do this; the other company either will refuse to consent or will charge you a bundle to use a name that is similar to theirs.

Filing Your Corporate Name With the Secretary of State Does Not Guarantee Your Right to Use It

When you file Articles of Incorporation, the state corporate filing office formally approves your corporate name after making sure it meets state law requirements and is not the same or very similar to a name already on file. But of course the state filing office list does not contain all business names and trademarks in use everywhere. In many states, the state filing office list just shows corporate names already registered for use in the state, not the names of unincorporated businesses in the state or even registered state trademarks. In other words, having your name approved by the state corporate filing office does not guarantee that you have the absolute right to use it. You must do some additional research to be relatively sure that no one else has a prior claim to your proposed corporate name. In Section E, "Perform Your Own Trademark Search," below, we discuss some self-help measures you may wish to take before you decide on a corporate name.

Here's one more point to consider when checking name availability with the state filing office: Most states allow corporations, as well as other types of business, to use an "assumed name" (called a "fictitious business name" in some states). For a corporation, an assumed name is defined as a name that is different from the formal corporate name contained in the articles. Assumed or fictitious business names are registered by filing an assumed or fictitious business name statement either at the state level (usually with the corporate filing office) or at the county level (typically with the local county clerk's or recorder's office). Sometimes the filing must be made at both the state and county levels. Your state corporate filing office website should be able to tell you how to register a fictitious or assumed name for your corporation. Many websites even provide a downloadable form for this purpose. (Your state's filing office website is listed in the "Corporate Filing Office" section of your state sheet.)

But even though you may be permitted to use an assumed name, it's not wise to latch onto one as a way of skirting name availability problems. For example, assume you want to incorporate your business as Creativity Systems, Inc., but the state filing office already has a Creativity Systems Corp. on file and tells you that your corporate name choice is unavailable. You decide to pick another corporate name that is available for use in your Articles, but hope to register and use your preferred name, Creativity Systems, as an assumed corporate name. Is this a good idea? Probably not. First of all, you'll probably get a lawyer letter from Creativity Systems Corp. demanding that you stop using your assumed name. Second, this double-name strategy is too complicated. Most corporations have a hard enough time establishing a sound corporate identity for one name, let alone two. We suggest you do your best to find one available name for your corporation, then use it in your articles and for all business purposes. In short, don't bother picking a second name and registering it as your assumed or fictitious corporate name.

D. Choose a Name You Can Use as an Internet Domain Name

Now for your next hurdle. Besides picking a name that's available with the state, you should choose a name that is also available for use as an Internet domain name—that is, your corporation's website address or URL (for example, "mycorporatename .com"). Here's why: If your corporation is a success, you will probably want to promote it on the Internet by setting up a corporate website. And in most cases you will want your Internet domain name to be the same as or very close to your corporate name. For example, if your corporate name is Unipode, Inc., no doubt you will want to register and use the domain name unipode.com for your website. Even if you are not itching to launch a corporate website right away, you may want to do so later. So pick a corporate name, if you can, that is available as a domain name, and register your domain name immediately.

You can go to Network Solutions (www .networksolutions.com) to do a domain name search and register your name. If someone else is already using your proposed corporate name as a domain name, we suggest you choose another name for your corporation. Also, we recommend that you register all major variants of your domain name to avoid anyone else grabbing them later. For instance, the founders of Unipode, Inc., should register unipode.com as well as unipode.org, unipode.net, unipode.tv, and unipode.cc. We know this adds expense to your organizational costs (and your annual budget, because you will want to renew your domain registrations every year), but it is worth it to avoid the much more expensive proposition of changing your name later or fighting with someone else who comes along and grabs one of these domain name variants before you do.

Beware of domain name selection tools. If you use a name selection tool—such as Name Fetcher on the Network Solutions website—to help find an available domain name, do so carefully. These tools find available names by adding words and special characters to the beginning, middle, and end of names—for example, a name finding tool may suggest myunipode.com if unipode.com is already taken. We think this just leads to trouble: You want your domain name to be as close as possible to your corporate name and as far away as possible from other registered domain names. Simply adding extra letters to an unavailable name is not the best way to select a domain name. Again, if your proposed corporate name is already taken as a domain name, try to choose a distinctly different corporate name that is available as a domain name.

Even if you find that your corporate name is available for use as a domain name, we suggest that you do a wider Internet search to make sure someone else is not using a similar name as a domain name or as the name of their business or product linked to a website. Obviously, this is a large chore, and you probably can't discover all Internet-related names. But here are two basic and easy suggestions to help you uncover similar Internet names:

- When you do your domain name search, also search for slightly different names—for example, the incorporators of Unipode can search for unipodecorp.com, unipodeinc.com, and other variants. Domain name registration engines search for exact matches, so you have to spell out all variations for which you want to search.
- Go to yahoo.com, altavista.com, excite.com, google.com, and other major Internet search engines to hunt for any links to your proposed corporate name. Type your proposed corporate name in the search box without the ending corporate designator. For example, Unipode's incorporators would type "unipode" and see what links come up for the name. Try all major search engines; this will give you a good idea of all major competing names currently linked to the Internet.

If you discover a business or individual already using your proposed name or one similar to it as a domain name, a business name, or the name of a product or service, we suggest you pick another corporate name rather than risk tangling with the owner of the competing name.

For more information about domain names. For information on choosing and registering domain names and avoiding domain name conflicts, see Nolo's articles on Internet law at www.nolo.com.

E. Perform Your Own Trademark Search

Here's another hoop we suggest you jump through in your corporate name selection process. It adds work to the task, but we think it is worth it to avoid legal hassles later. As mentioned, acceptance of your name by the corporate filing office simply means that your name does not conflict with that of another corporation already on file—it doesn't necessarily mean that you have the legal right to use your name. That's because another business (corporate or noncorporate) may already be using the same or a similar name as their tradename (the name of their business), or as a federal or state trademark or service mark used to identify their goods or services.

Without providing a long-winded analysis of the intricacies of federal and state trademark and trade name law, the basic rule is that the ultimate right to use a particular trademark or business name is usually decided on the basis of who was first to actually use the name in connection with a particular trade, business activity, service, or product. For example, if the Beacon Lock Co. has sold padlocks for 50 years, you do not have the legal right to use the same name to sell locks. This remains true even if you have formed a corporation with the name Beacon Lock, Inc., registered Beacon Lock as an assumed or fictitious name with the state or county, or registered beaconlock.com as your domain name on the Internet.

Even if two companies produce different products—let's say there are two Beacon, Inc.s, one in Maine, one in Iowa, each producing different products—trademark law can allow the company that used the name first to stop the other company from using Beacon in its name, if the court decides that use by the second company is diluting the value of the first company's trademark. Although trademark law traditionally placed importance on the geographical proximity of the two businesses—for example, by looking to see if the two Beacon, Inc.s, market their products in the same geographical region—the Internet has pretty much made this consideration moot. With the predominance of the Web as a relatively cheap and easy place for companies to market their products, it's safe to assume you will someday be marketing your company and products to the same world market served by all other Internet-linked companies.

For more information about business names and trademark law. Nolo's website offers plenty of free information on business names, trademarks, and other useful legal information for businesses. See the following areas of Nolo's free legal encyclopedia at www.nolo.com: Small Business, Trademark and Copyright, and Internet Law. For more details, you may want to see Nolo's *Trademark: Legal Care for Your Business & Product Name*, by Stephen Elias, which provides detailed information about trademarks and business names and instructions on how to search for, pick, and register a trademark.

The upshot of this discussion is that you should do your best to make sure that your proposed corporate name does not conflict with existing names used by other enterprises to identify their business, services, or products. In Section D, above, we discussed how you can use the Internet to search for other companies that use your desired name in connection with their business. Here are some additional suggestions:

- **Call your state's trademark registration office.** Ask whether your proposed corporate name is already registered with them for another company's use. (When you file articles or call

to ask the filing office to perform a corporate name availability search, most states do not automatically compare your proposed corporate name to registered state trademarks and service marks. You usually need to do this yourself.) The telephone number of the state trademark office should be listed on your state corporate filing office website—look under "related links" or simply email the corporate filing office and ask for the telephone number.

- **If your state has a centralized fictitious or assumed name office,** call it to ask if your name, without the "Inc." or other corporate designator, is already in use by another business. (Your state's fictitious or assumed business name office, if there is one, should be listed on the corporate filing office website under "related links.") In states where fictitious names are registered at the county level, check with the counties where you plan to do business. Most county clerks require you to come in and check the files yourself—but it takes just a few minutes to do this.

- **Check with the United States Patent and Trademark Office (PTO)** for trademarks and service marks registered at the federal level. You can perform a free search from the PTO website at www.uspto.gov. If your name, or one similar to it, is registered as a federal trademark, you need to think carefully about using your proposed name. In most cases, it's safest simply to pick a new name rather than risk the possibility of getting tangled up in a trademark lawsuit because your corporate name comes too close to a registered trademark.

- **Check other resources.** To search for trade names that have not yet arrived on the Internet, check major metropolitan phone book listings, business and trade directories, and other business listings, such as the Dun & Bradstreet business listing. Larger public libraries have phone directories for many major cities within and outside of your state.

If you want to check further or don't want to do all the work yourself, you can pay a private records search company to check federal and state trademarks and service marks as well as local and state-wide business listings. These firms can check your proposed name against the sources we've listed above plus many other sources.

Alternatively, or in conjunction with your own efforts, you can pay a trademark lawyer to oversee or undertake these searches for you. They will take the responsibility of hiring a private search company. In addition, they may provide a legal opinion on the relative legal safety of your proposed corporate name. Normally, this opinion isn't necessary, but it can be valuable if your own search discovers several similar, but not identical, names.

Obviously, the amount of checking and consulting you can do is limited only by the amount of effort or money you are willing to devote to the task and by how safe you need to feel about your choice of a corporate name. If your company is growing fast or will compete with many other businesses over the Internet, you may want to do a fair amount of name checking. If your business will be based locally and compete only with others located in your immediate vicinity, then a more modest amount of name searching may make more sense.

Pick the best level search for you. Use your own business judgment and your individual comfort level to tell you how many of the self-help measures listed above make sense for you, and whether to pay someone else, like a name search service or a trademark lawyer, to do additional name checking for you.

F. Reserve Your Corporate Name

After you have completed the above steps and feel satisfied that your corporate name is available and safe to use, it normally makes sense to reserve the name with the state corporate filing office. Doing this means that you have the exclusive right to include the name in your articles (which you will prepare and file to form your corporation as part of Step 2, below) for a specified period of time—usually 60 days, though some states give you a longer reservation period. (We list your state's corporate name reservation fee and period in the "Corporate Name Information" section of your state sheet.)

Reserving your name ensures that your name will not be rejected because someone else has grabbed it between the time you check its availability and the date your articles are actually received by the state. If you cannot file your articles within the reservation period, most states let you extend the reservation for another period. (A few states say you must wait at least one business day between consecutive reservations to let others jump in and grab the name by submitting their own reservation during this one-day interval.)

In most states, you can download an Application for Reservation of Corporate Name from your state's corporate filing office website. A few states even allow you to complete the application form and submit it online. If your state does not provide an online form, rather than call the state office and wait for it to mail you a form, it's speedier simply to prepare and mail the reservation of name letter shown below. (You can find this form in Appendix D and on the CD-ROM included with this book.)

If your name is available when your reservation request is received, the state will mail back a reservation certificate or receipt, showing your corporate reservation date and/or number. Keep the certificate or receipt handy. You will need this reservation information when your file your articles. (See Step 2, below.)

The person who applies for your corporate name reservation should be the same person who prepares and files your corporation's articles. When you file your Articles of Incorporation, the state filing office will look to make sure the person who submits the articles (the incorporator) is the same person who reserved the name. If not, it will ask you to obtain the written consent of the person who reserved the name before it will accept your articles. Avoid this delay by having the same person—usually one of the corporation's initial directors—perform both tasks. Following is a sample of the corporate name reservation form contained in Appendix D and on the CD-ROM (filename: NAMERES). Again, prepare and mail this form if your state does not provide a ready-to-use Application for Reservation of Corporate Name on its site.

Request for Reservation of Corporate Name

[date]

[your name]
[your address]
[your telephone number]

[name of state filing office]
[address of state filing office]   ❶

Re: Request for Reservation of Corporate Name

Corporate Filing Office:

Please reserve the first available corporate name from the list below for my use.
My proposed corporate names, listed in order of preference, are as follows:

_____

_____

_____   ❷

I enclose a check for the required reservation fee.   ❸

Sincerely,

[your signature]
[your typed name]

Instructions

❶ Insert the name and address of your state's corporate filing office. This information is contained in the "Corporate Filing Office" section of your state sheet in Appendix A.

❷ Many states let you list alternative names in case your first choice for a corporate name is taken. If you have chosen one or two backup names that you are sure you will wish to use in case your first choice is unavailable, list them here. Don't list more than a total of three names—most states won't look at more than three choices.

❸ The reservation fee is shown in the "Articles Instructions" section of your state sheet. Confirm that this fee information is current by taking a quick look at the corporate fee page on your state filing office website.

Step 2. Prepare and File Articles of Incorporation

After you've chosen a name for your corporation, it's time to prepare and file Articles of Incorporation. (A few states call this form a Certificate of For-

---

Sample Articles of Incorporation

Pursuant to the __[name of state]__ Business Corporation Act, the undersigned incorporator submits the following Articles of Incorporation:

1.The name of the corporation is __[name of corporation]__ . ❶

2.The corporation is authorized to issue one class of common shares. The total number of such shares it is authorized to issue is __[number]__ . ❷

3.The street address of the corporation's initial registered office is __[address of registered office]__ , and the name of its initial registered agent at this address is __[name of agent]__ . ❸

4.The name and address of the incorporator is __[name and address of incorporator, who dates and signs, below]__ . ❹

Date: _____

Signature of Incorporator: _____

---

mation, Certification of Organization or Charter; your state sheet tells you the name of the form in your state.) You will file your articles with the state corporate filing office. When they are accepted, your corporation is a legal entity. Although the content of the articles form varies from state to state, it's similar enough throughout the country that we can sensibly guide you through it here.

A. Sample Articles Form

To get a better understanding of what articles are—what they contain and what the form looks like—glance at the following generic articles form and read the accompanying instructions. The next section will show you how to obtain and file your state's articles form.

Instructions

❶ Your proposed corporate name must be shown in your articles. If the name is available for your use, your articles will be filed; if it isn't, your articles will be returned to you. As discussed in Step 1, above, it makes sense to check name availability in advance and, if possible, reserve the name you want. If you have reserved your corporate name, the name you specify must exactly match your reserved name.

❷ In Chapter 2, Section H1, we explain the basic considerations to take into account when deciding how many shares to authorize in your articles. As you probably know, this authorized number of shares is the number that can be issued to shareholders after your articles are filed. The key point here is that you are not required to issue all of your authorized shares. In fact, most incorporators don't; they want to have a reserve in case they want to issue additional shares later. Generally, if your state bases its filing fee on the number of shares you authorize, you will want to authorize the maximum number of shares for the smallest filing fee. However, if you are located in a state where there is no relationship between the amount of the filing fee and the number of shares, you can authorize as many shares as you wish. (The "Articles Instructions" section of your state sheet tells you how to compute your filing fee and authorize the greatest number of shares for the smallest filing fee.) In some states, you must also specify whether or not your shares will have a dollar or par value amount. As discussed in detail in Chapter 2, Section H2, unless the state charges a smaller fee for par value shares, most incorporators opt for shares without a specified par value, since the par value concept is a holdover from the nineteenth century and no longer has practical meaning.

❸ The registered agent is the person authorized under state law to receive legal papers on behalf of your corporation. The agent need not be a corporate director, officer, employee, or shareholder. The registered office is the agent's business address for purposes of receiving legal papers. The registered office must be located within your state. In practice, incorporators typically name an initial director or officer as agent and specify the address of the corporation as the registered office address.

❹ The incorporator (in some states called the "organizer") is the person who prepares and files your articles. You need just one. Typically, an initial director of the corporation acts as incorporator. In most states, the incorporator must sign the Articles at the bottom of the form.

Optional Article Provisions

State-provided articles forms (or our form if your state does not provide one) contain the minimum information and provisions legally required under each state's Business Corporation Act. For example, most simply allow you to authorize one class of common shares—that is, shares that have equal voting power and proportional rights. (A 10% shareholder, for instance, gets 10% of total voting power and a has right to receive 10% of any dividends or corporate assets that remain after the corporation is dissolved.)

However, state law allows you to add other provisions to your articles to implement more involved management and ownership rights and procedures. Optional provisions vary from state to state, but typically include the following:

- **Delayed effective date for articles.** Many incorporators add a provision that says the articles are effective on a date later than the date the articles are filed. This allows the legal existence of the corporation to start on a day chosen by the incorporator—for example, on the first or last day of a month, rather than on the unknown date the articles will be processed and filed by the state filing office. The BCA of most states allows the articles to contain this sort of delayed effective date provision, as long as the date specified is within a certain period after the actual filing date, most often 90 days. (This period is set out in the "Articles Instructions" section of your state sheet.) Your state's articles form may include a blank line where you can specify a delayed date; if not, you can add an article in the "Other Provisions" portion of the form that simply says, "The effective date of these Articles is [*insert the delayed date*]." Before adding this extra article, check your state corporate filing office website or call your state filing office to make sure your delayed date falls within the period allowed under your state BCA.

- **Authorizing more than one class of shares.** Some incorporators set up different classes of stock for different types of investors. Establishing different classes or series of stock—for example, one voting class and one nonvoting class, or one common class and one preferred class entitled to a greater proportionate share of corporate assets if the corporation dissolves—is a common addition to basic articles. For additional information on authorizing more than one class of shares in your articles, see the "Articles In-

structions" summary in the introduction to the state sheets in Appendix A.

- **Election of directors.** Some incorporators wish to give one or more individuals or shareholders special rights to elect one or more directors. For example, a corporation may give a major investor the right to appoint a board member or let a class of preferred shareholders separately elect their own director.

- **Liability of directors.** If appropriate, you can add provisions that immunize directors from personal liability in suits brought against them by the corporation or the shareholders. As explained in Chapter 2, Section F2e, these provisions can help directors in larger, publicly held corporations avoid personal liability to shareholders.

- **Antidilution provisions.** Some incorporators include preemptive rights that allow existing shareholders a right of first refusal to buy stock issued in the future by the corporation. Or, conversely, they include restrictions that prohibit shareholders from having such preemptive rights. Adding preemptive rights to articles can help ensure that current shareholders get a chance to maintain their current percentage of share ownership when new shares are issued.

- **Cumulative voting.** Your articles can include rights of shareholders to cumulate their votes when voting to elect directors. (See Chapter 2, Section F4.) Some state BCAs require the articles to either allow or prohibit cumulative voting. The "Shareholder Meeting Rules" section of your state sheet provides your state's default cumulative voting rule and tells you, if applicable, how you can change it in your articles. Most smaller corporations will not be concerned with cumulative voting procedures nor want to change the state's default cumulative voting rule in their articles. Cumulative voting is helpful mostly in larger corporations to let minority shareholders seat one or more board members.

If you want to customize your articles, browse your state BCA with your Web browser by going to the link shown in the "Corporation Law Online" section of your state sheet. Look for a section in the BCA titled "Contents of Articles—Optional Provisions." If any catch your eye, you can add them to your articles. If you need help drafting a provision, ask a business lawyer for help. (See Chapter 6.)

B. Get and Prepare Your State's Articles

Below we explain how to get and prepare your state's articles form.

→ If you don't use the Internet. If you don't want to obtain your state's articles form using the Internet, skip ahead to Section 2.

1. If You Have an Internet Connection

Follow these steps to prepare your articles if you have a Web connection:

- Go to your state's corporate filing office website. (Type the Web address shown in the "Corporate Filing Office" section of your state sheet into the browser address bar, then press Enter.)
- Explore the corporate forms page on your state website to find your state's Articles of Incorporation form for business (profit) corporations. In some states, an additional form must be filed with the articles (such as a Consent to Appointment as Registered Agent). Any additional form can also be downloaded from the site. (The "State Corporate Forms" section of your state sheet tells you what your state's articles form is called and whether there are additional forms you need to file with your articles.)

⚠ Note for Iowa and Nebraska incorporators. At the time of this edition, these states do not provide a sample articles form, either online or off. Therefore, we provide a ready-to-use articles form in the "Articles" section of Appendix D and on the CD-ROM. (See the IAARTS and NEARTS files in the "Articles" folder.) But first check the state's website or call the state office to see if an articles form has been made available. If not, use the form we provide, following the directions in the "Articles Instructions" section of the state sheet.

⚠ Note for professional corporations. If you are forming a professional corporation to provide services in the fields of health, law, accounting, engineering, architecture, and the like (see Chapter 2, Section A), look for special Articles for Professional Corporations. (The state filing office website should list the licensed professions that must use special professional articles to incorporate.)

- Some states allow you to prepare your articles online. Depending on the state, there are different ways to do this:
  - A number of states provide a "fill-inable" (that's what they call it) PDF version of the articles that you can complete online, without having to download and print the PDF file. If your state offers this option, you will probably wish to use it. After filling in the form, print it from your browser, then mail it with the required fee to the state filing office as explained in the instructions that accompany the form. (See Section C, below.)
  - Other states go a step farther and let you fill in *and file* your articles online, either paying online via your credit card or making telephone arrangements to pay your filing fee.
- In states that don't offer online form completion services, you will need to download the articles form to your computer, then open it from your desktop. All states that provide articles offer them in Adobe Acrobat Reader (PDF) format. (If you don't have the Adobe Acrobat Reader program, you can download the latest version free of charge from www .adobe.com.) You must print out the PDF forms since they can't be edited with the Reader program. Use black ink to fill in the blanks; many states require it. Some states also provide their articles in alternate word processing file formats, such as Microsoft Word or Corel WordPerfect, which you can fill in prior to printing if you have the appropriate word processor installed on your computer.

For more information about online forms. For additional information on using online forms, see "State Corporate Forms" in the introduction to the state sheets in Appendix A.

No matter how you obtain your articles form, we provide specific instructions for completing it in the "Articles Instructions" section of your state sheet. Follow the instructions for your state as you fill in the form.

2. If You Don't Have an Internet Connection

If you are forming a corporation and don't have a Web connection, simply call the state filing office (see the "Corporate Filing Office" section of your state sheet) and ask for a copy of their articles form for a business (profit) corporation. Once you receive it, use our instructions to fill it in before mailing it back to the filing office with the required filing fee.

C. Prepare Your Articles Cover Letter

Most incorporators file their articles by mailing them to the state corporate filing office—unless their state provides an online filing service or the filing office is located close by so the incorporators can easily file their articles in person. (See "Filing your articles in person," in Section D, below.) If you will file your articles by mail, you should include a cover letter like the one that follows. (We provide this letter as a tear-out form in Appendix D and as a file on the CD-ROM (filename: COVERLET).)

Sample Cover Letter for Filing Articles

  [date]

  [your name]
  [your address]
  [your telephone number]

  [name of state filing office]
  [address of state filing office]

Corporate Filing Office:

I enclose an original and ___*[number]* ❶ copy/copies of the *[insert name of document: in most states, "Articles of Incorporation"]* ❷ of ___*[name of corporation]*___ . Please file the original document and return any file-stamped copies to me, at the above address.❸

This corporate name was reserved by the undersigned incorporator on *[date of reservation and reservation number, if applicable]* ❹.

I enclose payment of required filing fees. ❺

Sincerely,

  [incorporator's signature]   ❻
  [incorporator's typed name]

Instructions

❶ Insert the number of copies (in addition to the original) you are including, according to the "Articles Instructions" section of your state sheet. Some states require just the original—in this case, insert "0" in the blank. Many states require the original and just one copy. In most states, you can simply photocopy the signed original of the articles when making copies; in a few others, the incorporator must manually sign each copy. In most states, after the filing office approves your articles, one copy will be file-stamped and/or certified (stamped with a seal or statement that the copy has been compared to the original) for no charge. But in a few states, you must pay to have a copy certified. After checking the rules in your state sheet, you may want to go online to your state corporate filing office website or call the office to confirm that the information provided in your state sheet is current.

Don't pay for what you don't need. You will want to receive at least one file-stamped copy of your articles for your records. Then you can make additional copies yourself, without paying the state for them. There is no need to include extra payment for a certified copy unless this is required by your state—a file stamp is enough proof that your articles are valid and have been accepted by the state.

❷ Insert the name of the corporate organizational document. In most states, it is "Articles of Incorporation." But some states use other names. For example, the document is called a "Certificate of Incorporation" in Connecticut, New York, and Oklahoma; "Articles of Organization" in Louisiana and Massachusetts; and a "Certificate of Formation" in Washington. In Tennessee, the document is called the "Charter," while in New Jersey, you file "Business Registration Forms." Check your state sheet for the proper terminology.

❸ If you have any special instructions for the state filing office, include them at the end of the first paragraph. For example, if you are paying extra for expedited filing, insert an appropriate reference to this. If you added a delayed effective date provision to your articles (see "Optional Articles Provisions" in Section A, above), it's a good idea to flag it here in your cover letter. Just add a sentence that says: "Note that the Articles request a delayed effective date of [insert delayed date]."

❹ If you reserved your corporate name (see Step 1, Section F, above), fill in the blank with the date of your name reservation. This date should be stamped on the application or request for name reservation you received from the state filing office. If the reservation was assigned a number by the office, include that number in this blank as well. If you did not reserve your corporate name prior to filing your articles, just insert "N/A" in the blank. Remember that the person who signs your articles and this cover letter should be the same person who reserved the name. (Again, see Section F, above.)

Include a copy of your name reservation. If you received a written name reservation form or receipt, include a copy with your cover letter and articles.

❺ Include the required filing fee as explained in the "Articles Instructions" of your state sheet. All states take personal checks. (In New York, however, you must include a certified check if your fees exceed $500.) Remember to double check the filing fee information in your state sheet by going to your state filing office website or by calling the office just prior to writing your check.

❻ Your incorporator—the same person who signed your articles—should sign your cover letter. Type the incorporator's name under the signature line.

D. File Your Articles

Filing your articles is a formality. The corporate filing office will accept your papers if they conform to law and you pay the proper fees. The time it takes to have your articles processed and filed varies from state to state and depends on the office's current workload. In most states you can expect to receive your file-stamped copy or copies back from the office in one or two weeks, but in some states at busy times of the year, it can take longer. To avoid this delay, you may wish to send your articles to the state filing office by express mail. (Make sure you send them to the street address specified on your state filing office website for express mailings; it may be different from the main address.) To get even quicker service in many states, you can pay extra for expedited filing; this usually ensures that your articles will be processed within one or two days of receipt by the office. (Again, expedited filing procedures, if available, and related fees are posted on your state's corporate filing office website.)

Filing your articles online. Some states let you prepare and file articles online. This is the quick and easy way to do it, and we recommend you file online if your state lets you. Go to your state's corporate filing office online (see your state sheet in Appendix A) to see if your state provides an online filing service.

Filing your articles in person. If you want to file your articles immediately and you are located reasonably close to a corporate filing office, you may usually file them in person, though you may be charged an additional handling fee for this. Check your state corporate filing office website or call the office to obtain guidelines for over-the-counter filing.

If You Create Your Own Articles or Attachment Pages

Most states allow you to prepare and submit your own articles form, even if the state provides an official form, as long as your form contains the minimum information required under your state's BCA. (In Iowa and Nebraska you must create your own form, since the state does not provide an official version; this book provides a form for articles in these states.) Most states will not accept fully hand-printed articles. States do allow you to fill in blanks on a typewritten or computer-generated form, as long as you print legibly. If you prepare your own Articles form, we assume you will either type your articles or generate them with a computer. Most likely you will use a computer word processor and printer.

Even if you use a state-provided articles form (as will most incorporators), you may need to prepare an attachment page to the state form if the space for a response on the official articles form cannot accommodate a response—for example, if you need to list five initial directors and your state form only provides space for three. Again, don't hand-print the attachment: use a computer or a typewriter.

If you do create your own articles or include an attachment page with the official state form, make sure to follow any requirements noted in the "Ar-

ticles Instructions" section of your state sheet. Even if not required, we suggest any articles or attachment pages you create conform to the following guidelines. These are standard format rules preferred by most corporate filing offices unless otherwise noted in your state sheet:

- the printout must be legible, with good contrast
- use black ink
- use letter-size paper (8-1/2" x 11")
- print or type on only one side of the page
- use at least one-inch top and side margins
- place the title of your document—for example, "Articles of Incorporation" or "Certificate of Organization"—at the top of any attachment pages, and note the article number associated with any text on the page. For example, if you include an attachment page in response to Article III, title the text "Continuation to Article III." If the attachment page contains additional articles that pick up where the articles on the state-provided form stop, simply list the article number before any text—for instance, "Article 10. [*your text*]," "Article 11. [*your text*]."

Step 3. Set Up a Corporate Records Book

Establishing a corporate records book is an essential part of forming your corporation. Your records book will help you keep important corporate papers in good order, including your articles, bylaws, minutes of your first board meeting and ongoing director and shareholder meetings, stock certificates, and stock certificate stubs. Keep your corporate records book at the principal office of your corporation.

A. Create a Records Book or Order a Corporate Kit

You can set up a funky, but perfectly effective, corporate records book in any three-ring binder. Or if you prefer, you can order a special corporate records kit (for example, from Blumberg/Excelsior at www.blumberg.com) that will look a bit nicer in your bookcase.

B. Corporate Seals

A corporate seal is not a flippered mascot—it is simply a metal or rubber stamp that embosses (with raised letters) or prints the corporate name on documents. A corporation is not legally required to have or use a corporate seal, but many find it handy to do so. A corporate seal is a formal way of indicating that a given document is the duly authorized act of the corporation. It is not normally used on everyday business papers (invoices, purchase orders, and the like) but is commonly employed for more formal documents such as stock certificates, leases, deeds of trust, and certifications of board resolutions. Embossed and stamped seals are also available separately through legal stationers. Most seals are circular in form and contain the name of the corporation, the state, and the year of incorporation. A corporate seal is available as an option when ordering the corporate kits advertised at the back of this book.

People love seals. Believe it or not, we have been told over and over how much fun it is to pull out a corporate seal and imprint an impor-

tant document. Having done it ourselves here at Nolo, we know that "master of the universe" feeling. As one person remarked, if you order the leather car seats, you'll definitely want the seal; if you prefer the cloth, forget it.

C. Stock Certificates

This book provides you with ten black-and-white certificates printed on book-quality paper. (See the tear-out certificates in Appendix D.) Just like a homemade corporate records binder, these are perfectly legal. By contrast, corporate kits may contain 20 lithographed green certificates with your corporate name and state of incorporation preprinted on each. If you think you will need more, you can order additional certificates at the time you order a corporate kit or later, as a separate order.

Wait before ordering stock certificates or a seal. We suggest you wait until you have received file-stamped articles from the corporate filing office before you order a corporate kit, printed certificates, or a seal. This way, you'll be sure that you really have set up a corporation before you pay for these materials. However, if you are committed to forming your corporation and you have already reserved your corporate name, it's probably safe to order these corporate materials before you file your articles.

Step 4. Prepare Your Bylaws

After you have received file-stamped articles from the corporate filing office and set up your records book, your next incorporation task is to prepare bylaws. Bylaws are an internal corporate document that set out the basic ground rules for operating your corporation. They are not filed with the state. We provide a bylaws form that you can use in Appendix D and on the CD-ROM (filename: BYLAWS).

A. The Importance of Bylaws

Bylaws are a basic corporate management document that should always be prepared as part of the incorporation process. This is true even though in most states no law specifically requires you to adopt bylaws. Bylaws are important because they let directors, officers, and shareholders know when and how meetings can be held, or, in the absence of meetings, how decisions can be reached and recorded by mutual written consent. In addition, they cover many other essential operating rules, such as notice, quorum, and voting requirements for meetings; the basic titles and responsibilities of corporate officers; rights of directors and shareholders to inspect corporate records; and the requirements for providing annual financial information to shareholders.

Adopting bylaws also shows that your corporation takes its corporate identity seriously. It's a simple fact that shareholders, other businesses, banks, creditors, the IRS, and a court (should your corporation become involved in a lawsuit) will expect your corporation to have bylaws. It's fairly common for a bank, a creditor, or the IRS to ask to see a copy. Even the smallest one-person corporation absolutely needs to adopt bylaws, if for no other reason than to look legitimate to the outside world.

Having said all of this, we should not overstate the legal significance of your bylaws. While they provide many key details for day-to-day corporate housekeeping, the real source of legal authority—and the place you should look whenever you want to make sure your corporation is acting lawfully—is your state's Business Corporation Act. This is why we include the basic state rules for operating your corporation in your state sheet, together with the citation for the statute in your state's BCA where you can find the entire text of the law. (You can do this by going to the website shown in your state sheet for your state's online BCA; see "How to Find Your State's Current Corporate Rules Online," below.)

Example: Let's say that your corporation decides to amend its previously filed articles to authorize a new class of preferred shares to investors. The first thing to do is look at your bylaws to see if it tells you the required procedures for amending your articles. Your bylaws cover the process generally, but you want to make sure you have the latest, most complete rules before you approve this important amendment. You go online to your state's BCA and find a section called "Amendment of Articles." You see that the amendment must be approved by directors and by a majority of all the outstanding shareholders (your bylaws got this right). You also see that the notice of the meetings held to approve the amendment must state the purpose of the meeting—that is, the meeting notice must state that the purpose of the meeting is to amend the articles to add a new class of shares (your bylaws didn't mention this requirement). You also double check your bylaw meeting provisions against the BCA meeting rules to make sure your rules for calling and providing notice of, and quorum rules for, directors' and shareholders' meetings are completely current, too.

Many corporations, particularly those formed with the help of a lawyer, adopt lengthy bylaws that go on for pages repeating the provisions of the state BCA. Having loads of statutory rules repeated in the bylaws may look impressive, but it's counterproductive: Your state BCA will change frequently, meaning the more of it you restate in your bylaws, the more often you'll need to update them or pay a lawyer to do it.

The bylaws included in this book are designed to sensibly accommodate the need to provide procedural specifics without unnecessarily restating areas of the law that can just as easily be found in your BCA. Our bylaws provide commonsense procedures (valid in all states) for holding director and shareholder meetings. For example, the bylaws provide for an annual shareholders' meeting, and this procedure works in all states. But our bylaws do not specifically list the rules for calling special meetings during the year, because each state has different rules for doing this. Instead, the bylaws simply authorize the people who are allowed under your state's BCA to call a special meeting to do so. When you wish to call a special meeting, this bylaw provision alerts you to check your state BCA (it only takes a few minutes when you follow the procedure explained below) to find out who can call a special meeting under your state's BCA rules. This method makes sure you follow the current law.

We also provide bylaws that deal with other areas of interest to corporate directors, officers, and shareholders, such as the rights of directors and shareholders to inspect corporate records, corporate indemnification and insurance, executive committees of the board, and the like. Again, we either provide a bylaw provision that will work in every state, or we use language that makes reference to your state's specific statutory requirements so you can look them up and follow the latest rule when the need arises.

It is also possible to customize your bylaws by adding your own provisions to our standard form. Below, we explain common items you may wish to cover in your bylaws, and how to find your state's specific rule to implement them. But recognize that in our complicated world there are always additional things you can add. For small business corporations, the most common addition is what are called "buy-sell provisions" that spell out what happens if one co-owner decides to sell shares or leave the corporation. (See Chapter 5, Section A7.) These provisions are complex and require a great deal of thought, so we cover them in detail in another book, *Buy-Sell Agreement Handbook: Plan Ahead for Changes in the Ownership of Your Business*, by Anthony Mancuso and Bethany K. Laurence (Nolo).

How to Find Your State's Current Corporate Rules Online

In each of the corporate rules sections of your state sheet—for example, "Director Meeting Rules" and "Shareholder Meeting Rules"—we provide the basic text of the most important rules regarding an area of corporate operation. For instance, we include the rules for calling, giving notice of, and voting at director and shareholder meetings. These are the current rules at the time of this edition. We also provide the code (law) number where you can find the rule in your state's BCA. To check the current language of the full statute, go to your state's BCA by following the instructions in the "Corporation Law Online" section of your state sheet, then scroll or drill down through the headings of the BCA until you find the section number of interest. This method keeps you as well informed and up to date as the most active business attorney. (See the "Corporation Law Online" instructions in the introduction to the state sheets for additional general information on how to use your online BCA.)

B. How to Prepare Your Bylaws

Preparing your bylaws is as simple as filling in a few blanks. Use the tear-out bylaws in Appendix D or the file on the CD-ROM (filename: BYLAWS) as you follow the sample below. We include bracketed instructions within the sample to help you fill in the blanks and understand the purpose and effect of our bylaw provisions.

Bylaws
of
[Name of Corporation]

ARTICLE 1. OFFICES

SECTION 1. PRINCIPAL OFFICE

The location of the principal office of the corporation will be within the state of __[insert the name of your state]__ at an address fixed by the board of directors. The secretary of this corporation will keep a copy of the corporation's Articles of Incorporation (or similar incorporating document), these bylaws, minutes of directors' and shareholders' meetings, stock certificates and stubs, a register of the names and interests of the corporation's shareholders, and other corporate records and documents at the principal office. **[State law allows a corporation to have offices both within and outside the state. But since most smaller corporations also designate the principal office as their corporation's registered office (this designation is made in the articles) and that office must be in the state, the bylaws specify that the principal office will be within the state.]**

SECTION 2. OTHER OFFICES

The corporation may have offices at other locations as decided by its board of directors or as its business may require.

ARTICLE 2. SHAREHOLDERS' MEETINGS

SECTION 1. PLACE OF MEETINGS

Meetings of shareholders shall be held at the principal office of the corporation or at other locations as may be decided by the board of directors.

SECTION 2. ANNUAL MEETINGS

The annual meeting of the shareholders will be held each year on and at the following date and time: __[insert the time and date of your annual shareholders' meeting]__. At the annual shareholders' meeting, shareholders will elect a board of directors and transact any other proper business. If this date falls on a legal holiday, then the meeting shall be held on the following business day at the same time. **[Most states require an annual meeting for the election of directors (see "Shareholder Meeting Rules" in your state sheet) unless the corporation elects a staggered board. (See Chapter 2, Section F4.) Staggered boards are normally only of interest to larger corporations, and we assume you will wish to elect directors annually.]**

SECTION 3. SPECIAL MEETINGS

Special meetings of the shareholders may be called by the individuals authorized to do so under the state's corporation statutes. **[Special meetings are infrequently called between annual meetings to seek shareholder approval of special business, such as amending the corporate articles or bylaws. See the "Shareholder Meeting Rules" in your state sheet to find out who may call a special shareholders' meeting in your state.]**

SECTION 4. NOTICES OF MEETINGS

Notices of meetings, annual or special, must be given in writing to shareholders entitled to vote at the meeting by the secretary or an assistant secretary or, if there is no such officer, by any director or shareholder. **[Written notice of both annual and special shareholder meetings is normally required under state law. See the "Shareholder Meeting Rules" in your state sheet.]**

Notices of shareholders' meetings must be given either personally or by first-class mail or other means of written communication, addressed to the shareholder at the address of the shareholder appearing on the stock register of the corporation or given by the shareholder to the corporation for the purpose of notice. Notice of a shareholders' meeting must be given to each shareholder no less than 30 days prior to the meeting. **[Most state BCAs require notice to be mailed no fewer than ten days nor more than 60 days before the meeting (see the "Shareholder Meeting Rules" in your state sheet). In practice, 30 days' notice of a shareholder's meeting works fine for smaller corporations.]**

This notice will state the place, date, and hour of the meeting and the general nature of the business to be transacted. The notice of an annual meeting and any special meeting at which directors are to be elected will include the names of the nominees that, at the time of the notice, the board of directors intends to present for election. **[Under most state BCAs, the notice of a special meeting must describe, in general terms, the purpose of the meeting, and only matters included in the notice can be decided at the special meeting. In contrast, most states don't require similar specificity in the notice of annual shareholder meetings—by law, directors can be elected at an annual meeting and any other business can be considered at them without prior notice to shareholders. We think this is a poor idea, so our bylaws require that shareholders be told what to expect at both annual and special meetings.]**

SECTION 5. WAIVER OF NOTICE

The transactions of any meeting of shareholders, however called and noticed, and wherever held, are as valid as though undertaken at a meeting duly held after regular call and notice, if a quorum is present, whether in person or by proxy, and if, either before or after the meeting, each of the persons entitled to vote, not present in person or by proxy, signs a written waiver of notice or a consent to the holding of the meeting or an approval of the minutes thereof. If the waiver does not include an approval of the minutes of the meeting, it must state the general nature of the business of the meeting. All such waivers, consents, and approvals will be filed with the corporate records or made a part of the minutes of the meeting. **[Most states specifically allow shareholders who do not attend a meeting to waive notice before as well as after a shareholders' meeting. This is necessary when you call a quick meeting to deal with an emergency and don't have time to notify everyone 30 or more days in advance, as required by these bylaws. In some states, the waiver need not include a description of the nature of the business brought up at the meeting except for special decisions. However, for obvious reasons, we believe the waiver should contain such a description, unless a shareholder approves minutes of the meeting that set forth the decisions reached at the meeting. That's why our language, above, requires this.]**

SECTION 6. LIST OF SHAREHOLDERS

Prior to any meeting of shareholders, the secretary of the corporation will prepare an alphabetical list of shareholders entitled to vote at the meeting that shows the address of each shareholder and number of shares entitled to vote at the meeting. This list will be available for inspection at the principal office of the corporation by any shareholder within a reasonable period prior to each meeting and be made available for inspection at the meeting on request of any shareholder at the meeting. **[Most states require the corporation to maintain an alphabetical list of shareholders and have it available for inspection at the meeting. Some states require the list to be available for inspection a specified number of days prior to the meeting. Our bylaws include a "reasonable period" premeeting inspection requirement that should suffice. If you wish to read the exact language of your state's shareholder list inspection rule, see the "List of Shareholders" statute (or a similarly titled section) under the "Shareholder Meeting" heading in your state BCA.]**

SECTION 7. QUORUM AND VOTING

Every shareholder entitled to vote is entitled to one vote for each share held, except as otherwise provided by law. A shareholder entitled to vote may vote part of his or her shares in favor of a proposal and refrain from voting the remaining shares or vote them against the proposal. If a shareholder fails to specify the number of shares he or she is affirmatively voting, it will be conclusively presumed that the shareholder's approving vote is with respect to all shares the shareholder is entitled to vote. **[One-vote-per-voting-share is the normal shareholder voting rule under state BCAs. Some states allow shareholders to receive fractional shares (for example, 1.5 shares) with fractional**

voting power (say 1.5 votes), but we assume you will not wish to issue shares of this sort nor issue special shares that have disproportionate voting power, such as two votes per share.]

A majority of the shares entitled to vote, represented in person or by proxy, will constitute a quorum at a meeting of shareholders. If a quorum is present, the affirmative vote of the majority of shareholders represented at the meeting and entitled to vote on any matter will be the act of the shareholders, unless the vote of a greater number is required by law. **[This section restates the standard shareholder meeting quorum and voting rules found in most state BCAs. (See Chapter 2 for a discussion of the issue.) If you wish to change either of these rules, check the language of your state's shareholder quorum and voting rules, contained in the "Shareholder Meeting Rules" section of your state sheet. This section of the bylaws recognizes that state law may require a greater vote requirement in special cases—for example, the approval of a majority of all shares, not just those present at a meeting, may be required to amend your articles or change stock rights. Again, it's best to check your state BCA before taking major shareholder action of this sort.]**

The shareholders present at a duly called or held meeting at which a quorum is present may continue to transact business until adjournment notwithstanding the withdrawal of enough shareholders to leave less than a quorum, if any action is approved by at least a majority of the shares required to constitute a quorum. **[This is a standard state BCA rule enacted to defeat "quorum busting" tactics at shareholder meetings. It lets the remaining shareholders vote even if one or more shareholders leaves the meeting and the remaining number of shareholder votes is less than a quorum.]**

Notwithstanding other provisions of this section of the bylaws, if permitted by law and not prohibited by provision of the corporation's Articles of Incorporation (or similar incorporating document), shareholders may cumulate votes for the election of directors as provided in this paragraph. If permitted to cumulate votes in an election, a shareholder must state his or her intention to cumulate votes after the candidates' names have been placed in nomination at the meeting and before the commencement of voting for the election of directors. Once a shareholder has stated his or her intention to cumulate votes, all shareholders entitled to vote must cumulate their votes in the election for directors. A shareholder cumulates votes by giving one candidate a number of votes equal to the number of directors to be elected multiplied by the number of his or her shares or by distributing these votes on the same principle among any number of candidates as he or she decides. The candidates receiving the highest number of votes, up to the number of directors to be elected, are elected. Votes cast against a candidate or which are withheld will have no effect in the cumulative voting results. **[We explain how cumulative voting works in Chapter 2. Cumulative voting is not normally used in smaller corporations, only in larger companies with a significant number of shareholders. This bylaw provision is included just in case you want to use cumulative voting in your elections for directors and (1) state law automatically allows it, or (2) you specifically completed a provision in your articles to allow cumulative voting (the official articles form in a few states allows you to do so). If cumulative voting is allowed under law or in your articles, this bylaw lets your shareholders cumulate their votes if at least one shareholder asks to cumulate votes after names have been placed in nomination and before the voting starts at a meeting held to elect directors.]**

In any election for directors at a shareholders' meeting, on the request of any shareholder made before the voting begins, the election of directors will be by ballot rather than by voice vote. **[This is a sensible provision; state BCAs either specifically provide for this or are silent on the subject. Note that this and the preceding paragraph are the only two rules we provide on shareholder election of directors. Many state BCAs cover other election procedures, such as appointing neutral inspectors who oversee the nomination and mailing of notices to shareholders of an upcoming election of directors, or creating special proxy solicitation and candidate nomination rules. We don't think smaller corporations, which commonly have ten or fewer shareholders, benefit from these extra provisions, so we don't include them in these bylaws. Of course, you are free to follow any election procedures allowed under state law, even though they are not included in your bylaws. If you want to learn about additional options you can use when electing your board, scan your state BCA for statutes that deal with technical provisions for the election of directors.]**

SECTION 8. PROXIES

Every person entitled to vote shares may authorize another person or persons to act by proxy with respect to those shares by filing a proxy with the secretary of the corporation. For purposes of these bylaws, a "proxy" is a written authorization signed by a shareholder or the shareholder's attorney-in-fact giving another person or persons power to vote with respect to the shares of the shareholder. Every proxy continues in full force and effect until the expiration of any period specified in the proxy or until revoked by the person executing it, except as otherwise provided by law. **[As discussed in Chapter 2, state law allows shareholders to appoint another person as a proxy to vote shares at a meeting. Typically, state law limits the effectiveness of a proxy to specified period—11 months is common—unless it specifically says it will last longer. To find your state's proxy rule, look for a statute titled "Proxies" in the "Shareholder Meeting" section of your state BCA.]**

SECTION 9. ACTION WITHOUT MEETING

Any action that may be taken at any annual or special meeting of shareholders, except for the election of directors, may be taken without a meeting and without prior notice if a consent, in writing, setting forth the action so taken, is signed by all the holders of outstanding shares entitled to vote on the action. **[This provision lets shareholders reach a decision by signing a written consent instead of voting at a meeting. Notice that we exclude the election of directors from those actions that may be approved by unanimous written shareholder consent. Many states don't allow election of directors by written consent. We also think shareholders should meet to elect directors to allow the candidates to be discussed and so that names not previously presented by management can be placed in nomination by the shareholders. And we believe a unanimous written consent rule is wisest. If one or more shareholders disagrees with a decision, its best to air these differences at a face-to-face shareholders' meeting. Your state BCA may be more lenient. (See "Action by Written Consent" or a similarly titled section in the "Shareholder Meeting" part of your state BCA.)]**

ARTICLE 3. DIRECTORS

SECTION 1. POWERS

The business and affairs of the corporation will be managed by, or under the direction of, its board of directors.

SECTION 2. NUMBER

The authorized number of directors is __[number]__. **[All states allow a corporation to have one or more directors, but a few states have a restriction on appointing just one or two directors. Specifically, California, Hawaii, Maine, Maryland, Massachusetts, Ohio, Utah, and Vermont say the following: A corporation can have one director only if it has just one shareholder; if the corporation has two shareholders, it must have at least two directors; and if the corporation has three or more shareholders, it must have at least three directors. (See the "Director and Officer Rules" section of your state sheet.) Missouri is a special case: A corporation must have at least three directors unless the articles specifically say it will have just one or two directors. (The official Missouri Articles form lets you specify that your corporation will have just one or two directors.) Many states let you set up a variable board—that is, one that has a certain minimum or maximum number of directors (within the allowable lower limits in the states just mentioned). Most smaller corporations prefer to set up a fixed board, so we do not allow for establishing a variable board in these bylaws. If you want to authorize a variable board, read the relevant rules in your state's BCA. (Look for the "Board of Directors" or "Variable Board" statute.)]**

SECTION 3. ELECTION AND TENURE OF OFFICE

The directors are elected at the annual meeting of the shareholders and hold office until the next annual meeting and until their successors have been elected and qualified. **[Most states specify a one-year term for directors and require their election (or reelection) by shareholders each year. Even if your state allows a longer term, we think annual elections make sense to confirm management by the current directors or the election of new directors if the shareholders desire a change. Most states allow you to set up a staggered system of director election (see Chapter**

2, Section F4) that appoints a portion of the board each year, which obviously also means that each director serves for more than one year. Most small corporations with modest-sized boards do not need to stagger elections. But if you are interested in adopting a staggered board system to replace this bylaw provision, see the "Staggered Board of Directors" or "Classified Board of Directors" (a "classified" board is the legal term used in some states to describe a staggered board) statute in your state BCA.]

SECTION 4. RESIGNATION AND VACANCIES

Any director may resign, effective on giving written notice to the chairperson of the board of directors, the president, the secretary, or the board of directors, unless the notice specifies a later time for the effectiveness of the resignation. If the resignation is effective at a later time, a successor may be elected to take office when the resignation becomes effective. [This provision simply lets a director resign at any time. There is no point in trying to be more restrictive, since you really can't stop a person from leaving if he or she wishes to do so.]

A vacancy on the board of directors exists in the case of death, resignation, or removal of any director or in case the authorized number of directors is increased, or in case the shareholders fail to elect the full authorized number of directors at any annual or special meeting of the shareholders at which directors are elected. The board of directors may declare vacant the office of a director who has been declared of unsound mind by an order of court or who has been convicted of a felony. [State law may contain special requirements for approving an increase in the authorized number of directors or the removal of a director by other directors or shareholders. In the highly unlikely event you'll ever need to remove a director, check your state BCA prior to taking action. This bylaw simply notes that these and other acts result in the creation of a vacancy on the board.]

Vacancies on the board may be filled by the remaining board members unless a vacancy is required by law to be filled by approval of the shareholders. Each director approved to fill a vacancy on the board holds that office until the next annual meeting of the shareholders and until his or her successor has been elected and qualified. [This provision refers you to your state BCA before filling a vacancy. In most cases, state law will let the directors (even if less than a quorum) appoint a temporary director to a board seat until the next annual election of directors by shareholders. State law may require that a vacancy caused by the removal of a director be filled by the shareholders, and may give shareholders the right to fill any vacancy on the board not filled by the remaining directors.]

SECTION 5. PLACE OF MEETINGS

Meetings of the board of directors may be held at any place, within or without the state, that has been designated in the notice of the meeting or, if not stated in the notice or if there is no notice, at the principal office of the corporation or as may be designated from time to time by resolution of the board of directors. Meetings of the board may be held through use of conference telephone, computer, electronic video screen communication, or other communications equipment, so long as all of the following apply:

(a) Each member participating in the meeting can communicate with all members concurrently.

(b) Each member is provided the means of participating in all matters before the board, including the capacity to propose, or to interpose, an objection to a specific action to be taken by the corporation.

(c) The corporation adopts and implements some means of verifying both of the following:

(1) A person communicating by telephone, computer, electronic video screen, or other communications equipment is a director entitled to participate in the board meeting.

(2) All statements, questions, actions, or votes were made by that director and not by another person.

[This section recognizes that directors of corporations may not always be able to meet in person, and sometimes may need or prefer to hold a meeting through a conference call, computer chat on the corporation's intranet, or a video conference-call hookup. Only a few technology-savvy states specifically mention virtual meetings of this sort in their statutes; the few that do make provisions similar to those above to require some means of ensuring that the directors can simultaneously "talk" to one another and that the corporation is able to verify that each person involved in the discussion is, in fact, who they claim to be.]

SECTION 6. ANNUAL AND REGULAR MEETINGS

An annual meeting of the board of directors will be held immediately after and at the same place as the annual meeting of the shareholders. [**This provision reflects the standard practice of holding the annual meeting of directors on the same date and just after the annual shareholders' meeting. The newly elected or reelected board members accept their election to the board, then discuss and approve any items of business specified in the notice of the annual board meeting. You can change this provision to schedule the annual directors' meeting on whatever date you decide best meets the needs of your corporation and its directors.**]

Other regular meetings of the board of directors will be held at the times and places fixed from time to time by the board of directors. [**This provision simply lets the board decide when to hold other regular meetings—that is, meetings held at regular times throughout the year in addition to the annual meeting scheduled in the previous paragraph. If you know when you will hold regular board meetings, you can specify their dates in this provision. Often, bylaws make it unnecessary to notify directors of annual and regular board meetings. Since we think it's a good idea to remind directors of every meeting, our bylaws require all director meetings to be noticed. (See Section 8 of this article, below.)**]

SECTION 7. SPECIAL MEETINGS

Special meetings of the directors may be called by the individuals authorized to do so under the state's corporation statutes. [**Directors may want to call special meetings during the year to discuss management issues, to review corporate goals and performance, to set up and hear from special committees of the board, and to transact special corporate business such as authorizing the signing of a lease or bank loan. (See Chapter 2, Section F2.) The "Director Meeting Rules" section of your state sheet shows who may call a special directors' meeting under your state's BCA.**]

SECTION 8. NOTICES OF MEETINGS

Notices of directors' meetings, whether annual, regular, or special, will be given in writing to directors by the secretary or an assistant secretary or, if there be no such officer, by any director. [**Notice of both annual and regular directors' meetings is normally not required under state law but, as we say above, we think you should give notice to make sure each director knows to attend. State BCAs normally require notice of special directors' meetings and, of course, we require that, too. (To see your state's requirements for notice of directors meetings, see the "Director Meeting Rules" in your state sheet.) Remember that, if you are pressed for time, an alternative to holding a special meeting is to obtain the written consent of directors to an action. (See Section 11 of this Article, below.)**]

Notices of directors' meetings will be given either personally or by first-class mail or other means of written communication, addressed to the director at the address of the director appearing on the records of the corporation or given by the director to the corporation for the purpose of notice. Notice of a directors' meeting will be given to each director at least two weeks prior to the meeting, unless a greater period is required under the state corporation statutes for giving notice of a meeting. [**Most states require notice of special directors' meetings to be given a specified number of days before the meeting. Two days is typical; some states require more, sometimes up to ten days. Again, no notice is normally required for other director meetings. We think two weeks' prior notice is appropriate for all meetings. Our notice rule applies unless your state BCA requires more. (See the "Director Meeting Rules" in your state sheet for the notice rules in your state.)**]

This notice will state the place, date, and hour of the meeting, and the general nature of the business to be transacted. [**Under most state statutes, the notice of a directors' meeting does not need to describe the purpose of the meeting. However, we think it makes good sense to state the purpose of a meeting, so our bylaws require it. (For your state's director meeting notice requirements, see the "Director Meeting Rules" section of your state sheet.)**]

SECTION 9. WAIVER OF NOTICE

The transactions of any meeting of the board, however called and noticed or wherever held, are as valid as though undertaken at a meeting duly held after regular call and notice if a quorum is present and if, either before or after the meeting, each of the directors not present signs a written waiver of notice, a consent to holding the meeting, or an approval of the minutes of that meeting. If the waiver does not include an approval of the minutes of the meeting, it will state the general nature of the business of the meeting. All such waivers, consents, and approvals will be filed with the corporate records or made a part of the minutes of the meeting. [**As noted just above, most states specifically allow directors who do not attend a meeting to waive notice before as well as after a directors' meeting (those who attend obviously received notice of the meeting). Your state's waiver of notice rule should be contained in the "Directors' Meeting" section of the BCA. We don't include it in the state sheet because most states' waiver rules are the same as, or very similar to, our rule. Having nonattending directors sign a written waiver makes sense when you need to act quickly and don't have time to formally call or notice a directors' meeting as required under your bylaws. In many states, the waiver need not include a description of the nature of the business brought up at the meeting, except for special decisions. However, we think waivers should contain this sort of description, unless a director is approving minutes of the meeting that describe decisions reached at the meeting. Our bylaws specify this. For a written waiver form you can use at both shareholder and director meetings, see** *The Corporate Minutes Book* **(Nolo).]**

SECTION 10. QUORUM AND VOTING

A quorum for all meetings of the board of directors consists of a majority of the authorized number of directors. [**This is the standard rule in most states. Within limits, you can change this quorum requirement if you wish. In most states, you can't lower your quorum far below a majority of the full board. But you can usually raise it to whatever level you wish. (To find your state's director meeting quorum rules, see the "Director Meeting" section of your state sheet.)]**

Except as otherwise required under state corporate statutes, every act or decision done or made by a majority of the directors present at a meeting duly held at which a quorum is present is the act of the board. [**This is the standard vote approval rule under state BCA statutes. (For more information on how directors vote at meetings, see Chapter 2, Section F2.) Your state's law is contained in the "Director Meeting" section of your state sheet. Your state BCA may have special director voting rules for certain types of decisions, such as the approval of business that personally benefits one or more directors. You must follow the state rules if they are different from the basic majority-vote rule stated here. That's why we always suggest checking your BCA before taking major corporate action.]**

SECTION 11. ACTION WITHOUT MEETING

Any action required or permitted to be taken by the board may be taken without a meeting, if all members of the board individually or collectively consent in writing to that action. Such written consents will be filed with the minutes of the proceedings of the board. Such action by written consent has the same force and effect as a unanimous vote of the directors. [**This provision lets directors approve a decision by unanimous written action or consent. The written document should describe the transaction or matter to be approved, and it should be signed by all directors. This requirement of unanimous signed approval of directors is found in most states. (If you want to look up the rule in your state, look for "Action Without Meeting" or "Written Consent by Directors" under the "Director Meeting" heading in your state BCA.)]**

SECTION 12. COMPENSATION

No salary will be paid directors, as such, for their services but, by resolution, the board of directors may allow a reasonable fixed sum and expenses to be paid for attendance at regular or special meetings. Nothing contained in these bylaws prevents a director from serving the corporation in any other capacity and receiving compensation for it. Members of special or standing committees may also be allowed compensation for attendance at meetings. [**This provision states the generally accepted practice of not paying salaries to directors, but permitting directors to be compensated per diem, per meeting, and/or for travel expenses and other costs associated with attending a meeting. It also makes it clear that directors may be paid for working for the corporation in a nondirector capacity. (This is the normal practice in small corporations where owner-directors also work as officers or in other salaried supervisory capacities.)]**

ARTICLE 4. OFFICERS

SECTION 1. OFFICERS

The officers of the corporation include a president, a secretary, and a treasurer, or officers with different titles that perform the duties of these offices as described in Sections 2 though 4 of this Article. Except as otherwise provided under state corporate statutes, any number of these offices may be held by the same person. The corporation may also appoint other officers with such titles and duties as determined by the board of directors. **[Your state's officer rules are contained in the "Directors and Officers Rules" section of your state sheet. They are all pretty much the same. Most states allow one or more (or all) of any required officer positions to be held by the same person, but Alaska and West Virginia say that different individuals must serve as president and secretary. Notice that the first sentence of this bylaw has been worded to allow you to call your president, secretary, and treasurer whatever you want, as long as someone is appointed to perform the duties associated with these positions, which we list in Sections 2 through 4 of this Article. This means that, if you prefer, you can call your president the Chief Executive Officer (CEO) and your treasurer the Chief Financial Officer (CFO). There is no common alternative title for corporate secretary, but you are free to make one up (Chief Corporate Record Keeper or CCR, perhaps).]**

SECTION 2. PRESIDENT

The president (or chief executive officer or alternately titled chief corporate officer designated by the board of directors) has general supervision, direction, and control of the day-to-day business and affairs of the corporation, subject to the direction and control of the board of directors. He or she presides at all meetings of the shareholders and directors and is an ex officio member of all the standing committees, including any executive committee of the board, and has the general powers and duties of management usually vested in the office of president or chief executive officer of a corporation and other powers and duties as may from time to time be prescribed by the board of directors or these bylaws. **[State law normally does not specify what a president must do. This bylaw tries to fill in the gaps in a general way. It lists the generally accepted duties of a corporate president, and it indicates that the president chairs all director and shareholder meetings and is a member of all board committees. This is standard corporate procedure. Also, the president generally runs the corporation as its chief officer on a day-to-day basis. But because state law is silent in this area, you can change or add any provisions you wish when defining the role of your CEO. We believe, however, that this is normally unnecessary, since a general statement of the sort provided here is sufficient to allow you maximum flexibility to define the role of CEO without being hemmed in by a more specific bylaw provision.]**

SECTION 3. SECRETARY

The corporate secretary (or other corporate officer designated by the board of directors to maintain and keep corporate records) will keep, or cause to be kept, at the principal office of the corporation, a book of minutes of all meetings of directors and shareholders. The minutes will state the time and place of holding of all meetings; whether regular or special, and if special, how called or authorized; the notice given or the waivers of notice received; the names of those present at directors' meetings; the number of shares present or represented at shareholders' meetings; and an account of the proceedings.

He or she will keep, or cause to be kept, at the principal office of the corporation, or at the office of the corporation's transfer agent, a share register, showing the names of the shareholders and their addresses, the number and classes of shares held by each, the number and date of certificates issued for shares, and the number and date of cancellation of every certificate surrendered for cancellation.

He or she will keep, or cause to be kept, at the principal office of the corporation, the original or a copy of the bylaws of the corporation, as amended or otherwise altered to date, certified by him or her.

He or she will give, or cause to be given, notice of all meetings of shareholders and directors required to be given by law or by the provisions of these bylaws. He or she will prepare, or cause to be prepared, an alphabetical listing of shareholders for inspection prior to and at meetings of shareholders as required by Article 2, Section 6, of these by-laws.

He or she has charge of the seal of the corporation and has such other powers and may perform such other duties as may from time to time be prescribed by the board or these bylaws. [**A corporation may delegate the duties of the corporate secretary to another officer or high-level corporate employee, such as the corporate treasurer or CFO, who is paid primarily for performing other more active corporate duties. Remember, though, that in Alaska and West Virginia you can't appoint your president as secretary.**]

SECTION 4. TREASURER

The treasurer (or other officer designated by the board of directors to serve as chief financial officer of the corporation) will keep and maintain, or cause to be kept and maintained, adequate and correct books and records of accounts of the properties and business transactions of the corporation.

He or she will deposit monies and other valuables in the name and to the credit of the corporation with the depositories designated by the board of directors. He or she will disburse the funds of the corporation in payment of the just demands against the corporation; will render to the president and directors, whenever they request it, an account of all his or her transactions as chief financial officer and of the financial condition of the corporation; and will have such other powers and perform such other duties as may from time to time be prescribed by the board of directors. [**Your corporation, of course, needs a chief financial officer. The duties listed here are general and comprise the basic responsibilities of this office. You can add to the list of duties and responsibilities if you wish, but there is normally no need to do so.**]

SECTION 5. APPOINTMENT, REMOVAL AND RESIGNATION

All officers of the corporation will be approved by, and serve at the pleasure of, the board of directors. An officer may be removed at any time, either with or without cause, by written notification of removal by the board. An officer may resign at any time on written notice to the corporation given to the board, the president, or the secretary of the corporation. Any resignation takes effect at the date of receipt of the notice or at any other time specified in it. The removal or resignation of an officer is without prejudice to the rights, if any, of the officer or the corporation under any contract of employment to which the officer is a party. [**This provision recognizes that the board approves officers and can decide to dismiss and replace them, subject, of course, to the general precepts of employment law and any employment contract officers may have with the corporation. Officers, too, must abide by the terms of any contract when deciding to leave the corporation—for example, by providing sufficient notice to the board and abiding by the terms of any noncompete provisions in their contract.**]

ARTICLE 5. EXECUTIVE COMMITTEES

SECTION 1. REGULAR AND EXECUTIVE COMMITTEES OF THE BOARD

The board may designate one or more regular committees to report to the board on any area of corporate operation and performance.

To the extent allowed under state corporate statutes, the board also may designate and delegate specific decision making authority to one or more executive committees, each consisting of two or more directors, that will have the authority of the board to approve corporate decisions in the specific areas designated by the board. [**This provision allows the board to set up regular committees that report to the board. For example, corporations with larger boards may want to set up finance, personnel, and perhaps other committees. In addition, this section allows the board to establish one or more executive committees, consisting of at least two directors, that can take over decision making authority on specific matters delegated to them by the full board. (For a discussion of regular and executive committees of the board, see Chapter 2, Section F2.) Most state statutes allow you to establish executive committees of this sort, but do not allow the committees to approve a few types of major corporate decisions such as distributions to shareholders, and the amendment of articles or bylaws. In practice, most small business corpora-**

tions with relatively small boards made up of owners who participate in the business will not set up decision-making committees, preferring instead to reserve management power to the full board. To find your state's executive committee requirements, look for a section in your state BCA titled "Executive Committees of the Board" under the "Directors" heading of your BCA.]

ARTICLE 6. CORPORATE RECORDS AND REPORTS

SECTION 1. INSPECTION BY SHAREHOLDERS AND DIRECTORS

The corporate secretary will make available within a reasonable period after a request for inspection or copying made by a director or shareholder or a director's or shareholder's legal representative the Articles of Incorporation (or similar organizing document) as amended to date; these bylaws as amended to date; minutes of proceedings of the shareholders and the board and committees of the board; the share register of the corporation, and its accounting books and records; and any other corporate records and reports. The requested records will be made available for inspection and copying at the principal office of the corporation within business hours. Any copying costs incurred by the corporation necessary to comply with a request for copies of records may be collected by the secretary from a requesting shareholder; the corporation assumes the cost of copies made for a requesting director. **[This general and permissive provision allows directors and shareholders complete access to all corporate records within a reasonable time after a request is made. Copying costs may be charged to a shareholder, but directors always get free copies—after all, they volunteer their time and make requests for inspection and copying to carry out their official director duties. Your state BCA may not require such generous inspection and copying rights—for example, it may only require inspection and copying by shareholders for a purpose reasonably related to a shareholder's interest in the corporation, or it may allow the corporation an extended period to comply with an inspection request. (Directors are normally given complete access to all corporate records under state BCA rules.) We don't think most corporations should worry about the reasons for requests or decide to limit access to any corporate records. However, if you wish to give shareholders only the specific inspection and copying rights mandated by your state BCA, look for a section titled "Inspection of Records" under the "Records and Reports" heading toward the end of the BCA. You can use your state's language to craft a more limited provision in place of ours.]**

SECTION 2. ANNUAL REPORTS TO SHAREHOLDERS

The secretary will mail a copy of any annual financial or other report to shareholders on the secretary's own initiative or on request made by one or more shareholders as may be required by state corporate statutes. **[This is a general section that reminds the corporate secretary to comply with any annual financial disclosure requirements contained in your state BCA. (We list your state's annual financial report requirement in the "Financial Disclosure Rules" section of your state sheet.) If you wish, you can substitute your state's specific disclosure requirements in this provision.]**

ARTICLE 7. INDEMNIFICATION AND INSURANCE OF DIRECTORS AND OFFICERS

SECTION 1. INDEMNIFICATION

The directors and officers of the corporation will be indemnified by the corporation to the fullest extent permitted under law. **[This provision means that the corporation will reimburse the directors and officers for any legal expenses, settlements, fines, and judgments permitted under the state's BCA indemnification statute. (See Chapter 2, Section F2, for a discussion of corporate indemnification.) If you want to learn your state's specific indemnification rules, look for a section in your state BCA titled "Indemnification." Most states require indemnification of legal expenses for a director or officer who is successful in a lawsuit or proceeding. In other situations, indemnification of expenses and other amounts may be allowed if the director or officer is found by the corporation to have acted in good faith and in the best interests of the corporation. If you want to be certain that your directors and officers get as much indemnification as possible under your state's law, see a lawyer to find out whether it's possible to create** a separate agreement that will be signed by each director and officer of the corporation. Another (easier) approach is to purchase a directors' and officers' liability insurance policy. (See Chapter 2, Section F2.)]

SECTION 2. INSURANCE

The corporation has the power to purchase and maintain insurance on behalf of any director or officer against any liability asserted against or incurred by the agent in that capacity or arising out of the agent's status as such, whether or not the corporation has the power to indemnify the agent against that liability under law. [This is an enabling provision that lets the corporation obtain director and officer liability (D & O) insurance on behalf of directors and officers. For information on this type of insurance, see Chapter 2, Section F2.]

ARTICLE 8. SHARES

SECTION 1. CERTIFICATES

The corporation will issue certificates for its shares when fully paid. Certificates of stock will be issued in numerical order, and will state the name of the record holder of the shares represented by each certificate; the number, designation, if any, and class or series of shares represented by the certificate; and other information, including any statement or summary required by any applicable provision of state corporate statutes. Each certificate will be signed by the corporate officers empowered under state law to sign the certificates, and may be sealed with the seal of the corporation. [Although issuing stock certificates to each shareholder is not specifically required under most state BCAs, we assume you will want to follow this traditional practice. (See Chapter 2, Section D3.) This bylaw lists the general contents of each certificate and also requires any additional information required by state law to be placed on the certificate. For a list of the specific requirements for stock certificates imposed by your state BCA, see the "Share Issuance Rules" section of your state sheet. The state sheet also indicates who is required to sign stock certificates in your state. (If not specified, it is common to have certificates signed by the corporate president and secretary.) Note that state law also requires you to place additional language—called a legend—on stock certificates that summarizes or states in full any special restrictions and rights associated with classes of shares. Since we assume you will issue just one class of common shares, your certificates will not require a legend. But realize that you must place a legend of this sort on any special class of shares you issue in the future. Also, if, as is common, you impose special transfer restrictions on your shares, should an owner die or want to sell out, you will need to mention these restrictions in a legend on your certificates. To see the specific types of legends that must be added to stock certificates in your state, look for a section titled "Contents of Stock Certificates" or "Restrictions on Stock Certificates" under the "Shares of Stock" heading of your BCA.]

SECTION 2. TRANSFER OF SHARES

On surrender to the secretary or transfer agent of the corporation of a certificate for shares duly endorsed or accompanied by proper evidence of succession, assignment, or authority to transfer, it is the duty of the secretary of the corporation to issue a new certificate to the person entitled to it, to cancel the old certificate, and to record the transaction on the share register of the corporation. [This basic provision is self-explanatory. Typically, the transferring shareholder completes the transfer section of the certificate (usually on the reverse side), then gives the certificate to the secretary. The secretary then cancels the old certificate and issues a new one to the person to whom the shares are transferred, being sure to record the transaction in the corporation's share register.]

SECTION 3. RECORD DATE

The board of directors may fix a time in the future as a record date for the determination of the shareholders entitled to notice of and to vote at any meeting of shareholders or entitled to receive payment of any dividend or distribution, or any allotment of rights, or to exercise rights in respect to any other lawful action. The record date so fixed will conform to the requirements of state law. When a record date is so fixed, only shareholders of record on that date are entitled to notice of and to vote at the meeting, or to receive the dividend, distribution, or allotment of rights, or to exercise their rights, notwithstanding any transfer of any shares on the books of the corporation after the record date.

[This record date provision is simply a reminder that the board of directors may establish a date for determining who is a shareholder of record on the corporation's books for purposes of notice of shareholders' meetings, shareholder voting, and payment of dividends and other distributions to shareholders. In a small corporation, the board normally does not set record dates, since shares rarely change hands. Similarly, in the somewhat rare event that the corporation declares a dividend (for tax reasons, it is more common to hand out profits in other ways; see Chapter 3, Section A), the shareholders of record on the dividend declaration date are presumed to be the shareholders entitled to receive the dividend. These practices are generally in line with state BCAs. To see your state's rules for declaring a record date and for determining shareholders of record when no date has been set by the board, go to the "Shareholders" section of your BCA, then look for a "Record Date for Shareholders" statute. In many states, any record date set by the board must be no more than 60 nor less than ten days before the upcoming meeting or transaction to which the record date applies.]

ARTICLE 9. AMENDMENT OF BYLAWS

SECTION 1. BY SHAREHOLDERS

Except as otherwise provided by law, these bylaws may be adopted, amended, or repealed by the affirmative vote at a meeting of holders of a majority of the outstanding shares of the corporation entitled to vote. [This bylaw allows a majority of the outstanding voting shares (not just a majority in attendance at a meeting) to amend bylaws, except where the state BCA requires a greater vote. In many states, a lesser vote may be allowed—such as a majority of shareholders present at a meeting—but we think our stricter voting requirement makes sense to ensure sufficient shareholder consensus to a bylaw change. State BCAs sometimes limit the right to amend certain bylaws, such as the ability to lower the quorum requirements for meetings below a certain threshold. To find your state's rules for amending bylaws, look for a "Bylaws" or "Amendment of Bylaws" statute in your BCA.]

SECTION 2. BY DIRECTORS

Except as otherwise provided by law, the directors may adopt, amend, or repeal these bylaws. [This provision also allows the directors to amend the bylaws. They can do so under normal director voting rules—that is, by a majority of the directors in attendance at a meeting. This is standard practice under most state BCAs. But it is important to understand that state law may limit the ability of directors to change certain bylaws. For example, directors may not be allowed to lower the authorized number of directors below a certain point without also obtaining shareholder approval. Look for a "Bylaws" or "Amendment of Bylaws" statute in your BCA to see any special rules that apply in your state.]

CERTIFICATE

This certifies that the foregoing is a true and correct copy of the bylaws of the corporation named in the title and that these bylaws were duly adopted by the board of directors of the corporation on the date set forth below. [After you prepare the minutes of your first board meeting, your corporate secretary should date and sign below. (See Step 6.)]

Dated: _____

Signature: _____, Secretary

Incorporator's Statement

The undersigned, the incorporator of *[name of corporation]* , who signed and filed its Articles of Incorporation or similar organizing document with the state, appoints the following individuals to serve as the initial directors of the corporation, who will serve as directors until the first meeting of shareholders for the election of directors and until their successors are elected and agree to serve on the board: ❶

_____

_____

_____

_____

_____

Date: _____

Signature: _____, Incorporator ❷

Step 5. Appoint Initial Corporate Directors

➡ **If you named initial directors in your Articles of Incorporation.** If your initial board is listed in your articles, as is required in some states, you have already completed this step. Skip ahead to Step 6.

Your next step is to have your incorporator appoint initial corporate directors if they are not all named in your articles. This is an extremely simple step. The incorporator—the person who signed your articles—fills in an "Incorporator's Statement" to show the names and addresses of the initial directors who will serve on the board until the first annual meeting of shareholders (when the board members who will serve for the next term are elected by the shareholders). The incorporator signs the statement and places a copy in the corporate records book.

To complete this step, have your incorporator complete the Incorporator's Statement included in Appendix D or on the CD-ROM (filename:

INCORPST), following the sample form and instructions below.

Instructions

❶ Article 3, Section 2, of your bylaws (prepared in Step 4, above) shows the full number of members on your board. The incorporator should appoint this number of board members if possible. If you must leave a seat open because you have not yet found all the right people to serve on your board, that's okay. Just make sure that you appoint enough directors to meet your bylaws' quorum requirement. Article 3, Section 10, defines a quorum as a majority of the authorized number of directors. So, if your bylaws authorize a four-person board but you only appoint three initial directors, all three of your initial directors must attend board meetings. If less than three attend, you don't have a quorum and the meeting can't be held.

❷ Have the incorporator date and sign the form, then place a copy in the corporate records book.

Step 6. Prepare Minutes of the First Board Meeting

Now that you've filed articles, prepared bylaws, and appointed your initial board of directors, it's time to transact the first important business of your new corporation: You must prepare minutes for your first meeting of the board. This book provides a simple minutes form for you to fill in. Your incorporator or any of the initial directors can prepare the document then ask all the directors to sign it, as explained in the instructions below. Although in theory your board is expected to discuss and complete the minutes together, this is often impractical, since it may take two or more weeks to conclude all the business reflected in the document—such as ordering stock certificates, selecting an accounting period, selecting a corporate bank, settling on the details of your initial stock issuance, and other matters. In other words, it usually works better to prepare your minutes over a period of a couple of weeks, then pass the minutes around to all directors for their approval once the document is complete.

A. Fill In the Minutes Form

The purpose of your minutes is to document essential organizational actions approved by your initial board of directors, including:

- specifying the street location of the corporation's principal office
- adopting the bylaws
- electing officers
- selecting the corporation's accounting period
- choosing a bank for corporate accounts
- authorizing the issuance of the initial shares of stock of the corporation, and
- making initial tax elections and decisions.

Complete the minutes form contained in Appendix D or on the CD-ROM (filename: MINUTES), following the sample form and instructions below.

Waiver of Notice and Consent to Hold
First Meeting of Board of Directors

We, the undersigned, being all the directors of _[name of corporation]_ , hereby waive notice of the first meeting of the board of directors of the corporation and consent to the holding of the meeting at _[street address of corporation's principal office]_ on _[date of meeting; this can be any date after the preparation of your bylaws and on or before the same date shown below (the date the waiver is signed)]_ at _[time of meeting]_ and consent to the transaction of any and all business at the meeting including, without limitation, the adoption of bylaws, the election of officers, the selection of the corporation's accounting period, the designation of the location of the principal office of the corporation, the selection of the place where the corporation's bank accounts will be maintained, and the authorization of the sale and issuance of the initial shares of stock of the corporation.

DATE: _____ **❶**

Signatures:

_____ , Director **❽**

_____ , Director

_____ , Director

_____ , Director

_____ , Director

Minutes of First Meeting of the Board of Directors

The board of directors of ___[name of corporation]___ held its first meeting at ___[street address of corporation's principal office]___ on ___[date of meeting]___ , at ___[time of meeting]___ . ❷

The following directors, marked as present next to their names, were in attendance at the meeting and constituted a quorum of the board: ❸

___[name of director]___	[ ] Present [ ] Absent
___[name of director]___	[ ] Present [ ] Absent
___[name of director]___	[ ] Present [ ] Absent
___[name of director]___	[ ] Present [ ] Absent
___[name of director]___	[ ] Present [ ] Absent

On motion and by unanimous vote, ___[name of director]___ was appointed chairperson and then presided over the meeting. ___[name of director]___ was elected secretary of the meeting. ❹

The meeting was held pursuant to written waiver of notice and consent to holding of the meeting signed by each of the directors. On a motion duly made, seconded, and unanimously carried, it was resolved that the written waiver of notice and consent to holding of the meeting be made a part of and constitute the first page of the minutes of this meeting.

ARTICLES OF INCORPORATION

The chairperson announced that the Articles of Incorporation or similar organizing document of the corporation were filed with the state corporate filing office on ___[insert the date that the articles were file-stamped or the date shown on your filing receipt (if you requested a delayed effective date for your articles, show the delayed date instead)]___ . The corporate secretary was asked to place a file-stamped copy of the articles or filing receipt showing this filing in the corporation's records book. ❺

BYLAWS

A proposed set of bylaws of the corporation was presented for adoption. On motion duly made and seconded, it was unanimously:

RESOLVED, that the bylaws presented to this meeting are adopted as the bylaws of this corporation;

RESOLVED FURTHER, that the secretary of this corporation is asked to execute a Certificate of Adoption of the bylaws, and to place the bylaws as so certified with the corporation's records at its principal office. ❻

PRINCIPAL EXECUTIVE OFFICE

On motion duly made and seconded, it was:

RESOLVED, that the principal office of this corporation be located at ___[insert the street address of the principal corporation office, including city, state, and zip code]___ . ❼

APPOINTMENT OF OFFICERS

On motion, the following persons were unanimously appointed to the following offices: ❽

President (CEO):   _[name of officer]_

Treasurer (CFO):   _[name of officer]_

Secretary: _[name of officer]_

CORPORATE SEAL

On motion duly made and seconded, it was:

RESOLVED, that the corporate seal impressed directly below this resolution is adopted as the corporate seal of this corporation. The secretary of the corporation is directed to place the seal with the corporate records at the principal office of the corporation, and to use the seal on corporate stock certificates and other appropriate corporate documents as the secretary sees fit. ❾

STOCK CERTIFICATE

On motion duly made and seconded, it was:

RESOLVED, that the form of stock certificate attached to these minutes is adopted for use by this corporation for the issuance of its initial shares.❿

CORPORATE BANK ACCOUNTS

On motion duly made and seconded, it was

RESOLVED, that the funds of this corporation be deposited with the following bank at the following branch office: ___*[name of bank and branch name or number]*___ located at ___*[address]*___ . **⓫**

RESOLVED FURTHER, that the treasurer of this corporation is authorized and asked to establish one or more accounts with this bank and to deposit the funds of this corporation in these accounts.

RESOLVED FURTHER, that any officer, employee, or agent of this corporation is authorized to endorse checks, drafts, or other evidences of indebtedness made payable to this corporation, but only for the purpose of deposit.

RESOLVED FURTHER, that all checks, drafts, and other instruments obligating this corporation to pay money be signed on behalf of this corporation by any ___*[number]*___ of the following: **⓬**

___*[name and title of person authorized to sign checks]*___

___*[name and title of person authorized to sign checks]*___

___*[name and title of person authorized to sign checks]*___

RESOLVED FURTHER, that the bank is hereby authorized to honor and pay any and all checks and drafts of this corporation signed in this manner.

RESOLVED FURTHER, that the authority hereby conferred remain in force until revoked by the board of directors of this corporation and until written notice of revocation has been received by the bank.

RESOLVED FURTHER, that the secretary of this corporation is authorized to certify as to the continuing authority of these resolutions and to complete on behalf of the corporation the bank's standard form of resolution, provided that the form does not vary materially from the terms of the foregoing resolutions.

ACCOUNTING PERIOD

After discussion and on motion duly made and seconded, it was:

RESOLVED, that the accounting period of this corporation ends on ___*[ending date of the accounting period of the corporation]*___ of each year. **⓭**

PAYMENT, DEDUCTION, AND AMORTIZATION OF START-UP AND ORGANIZATIONAL EXPENSES

On motion duly made, seconded, and unanimously approved, it was:

RESOLVED, that the treasurer of this corporation is authorized and empowered to pay all reasonable and proper expenses incurred in connection with the start-up and organization of the corporation, including, among others, expenses prior to the start of business necessary to investigate and create the business, as well as organization costs necessary to form the corporation and to reimburse any persons making such disbursements for the corporation.

RESOLVED FURTHER, that the treasurer is authorized to elect to deduct and amortize appropriate start-up and organization expenditures pursuant to and as permitted under Sections 195 and 248 of the Internal Revenue Code and as permitted under similar state tax provisions. ⓮

AUTHORIZATION OF ISSUANCE OF SHARES

On motion duly made and seconded, it was unanimously:

RESOLVED, that the corporation sell and issue the following number of its authorized common shares to the following persons, in the amounts and for the consideration set forth next to their names, below. The board also determined that the fair value to the corporation of any consideration for such shares issued other than for money is as stated below: ⓑ

Name	Number of Shares	Consideration
_____	_____	_____
_____	_____	_____
_____	_____	_____
_____	_____	_____
_____	_____	_____

RESOLVED FURTHER, that the amount of consideration received by the corporation for each and any of the above shares issued without par value that is to be allocated to capital surplus is $___. ⓰

RESOLVED FURTHER, that the appropriate officers of this corporation are hereby authorized and directed to take such actions and execute such documents as they deem necessary or appropriate to effectuate the sale and issuance of shares for the consideration listed above.

Since there was no further business to come before the meeting, on motion duly made and seconded, the meeting was adjourned.

_____, Secretary **⑰**

Instructions

Waiver of Notice

❶ The waiver of notice form dispenses with formal notice requirements that apply to board meetings under our bylaws. Insert the name and street address of the corporation (its principal office location). Date the form at the bottom of the page and obtain each director's signature after you finish preparing the minutes. (See Instruction 18, below.) This form is effective only if all directors sign it.

Title Page—Minutes of First Meeting of the Board of Directors

❷ The next page of the minutes contains the title of the document. The first paragraph repeats the name of your corporation and the address, date, and time of the meeting given on the waiver of notice.

❸ List the names of each initial director, and check the box that indicates whether each director is present or absent. Normally, you will show each director as present, since we assume that each initial director will approve and sign the minutes. However, if you hold a real meeting for which required notices have been sent and a director does not attend, check the box indicating that the director is absent.

❹ Insert the name of any director as chairperson of this first meeting, and one as secretary (you have not yet appointed officers to serve in these capacities for coming year). You can insert the name of one director in both blanks if you have only one director.

Articles of Incorporation Resolution

❺ Insert the date your articles (or other organizing document) were filed with the state. If you asked for a delayed effective date in your articles, insert the delayed date instead. Include a file-stamped copy of the articles or the filing receipt returned to you by the state with your completed minutes.

Bylaws Resolution

❻ This resolution shows the formal adoption of your bylaws (prepared in Step 4, above) by the directors. As explained below, after you prepare these minutes, the corporate secretary will fill out the "Certificate" section at the end of the bylaws, which certifies that they have been formally adopted by your board of directors. Our bylaws (and state law) require you to keep copies of minutes and your bylaws at the principal office of the corporation. The best way to do this is to place all your corporate paperwork in a corporate records book, and keep this book at the principal office. (See Step 3, above.)

Principal Office Resolution

❼ Insert the official address of your corporation, which normally is the same as your main place of business. It is also normally the same as your corporation's registered office, as stated in your articles, which is the location where legal papers can be served on your corporation.

Appointment of Officers Resolution

❽ Here you formally appoint the officers whose positions are listed in your bylaws. (See Article 4, Section 1, of the bylaws.) These three positions are normally the minimum required under state law, as well as those that you will need to operate your corporation. As discussed earlier, you can change the titles of the officers listed in this resolution to reflect any alternate titles you will give your CEO, CFO, or secretary. Remember, in most states, you can appoint the same person to fill more than one or all of these three basic officer positions. (Alaska and West Virginia require different individuals to serve as president and secretary.)

Corporate Seal Resolution

❾ Use of a corporate seal is optional in all states. (See Step 3, above.) If you ordered one, impress the seal in the space provided below the resolution. (You can make this impression after you prepare the minutes if you have not yet received your seal.) If you did not order a seal, leave the space blank. The secretary should keep the seal with the corporate records at the principal corporate office.

Stock Certificate Resolution

❿ Here you formally adopt the type of stock certificate you will use. Normally this is the bare-bones certificate included in Appendix D of this book or the fancier certificates that you have purchased on your own. (Again, certificates can be purchased separately, for example at www .blumberg.com.) Attach a copy of your approved stock certificate, marked "SAMPLE" across its face, to the minutes of your meeting.

Bank Account Resolution

⓫ This resolution authorizes the opening of one or more accounts with a specified bank. Fill in the blanks to show the bank name and branch office name (or number) and the address where the accounts will be located.

⓬ Specify how many signatures will be required on corporate checks, then list the names and titles of individuals authorized to sign these checks. Generally, you will list the name of one or more officers or key employees (such as your salaried in-house bookkeeper) as individuals authorized to sign checks. You may wish to change this provision to say that one person can sign checks up to a certain amount, but that two signatures must be obtained for checks exceeding the stated amount.

> **Example:** The following language can be substituted for our standard check-writing resolution: "RESOLVED FURTHER, that all checks, drafts, and other instruments obligating this corporation to pay money in an amount less than $ _[specify threshold amount]_ be signed on behalf of this corporation by any one of the following; that all checks, drafts, and other instruments obligating this corporation to pay money in an amount greater than the amount just stated be signed on behalf of this corporation by any two of the following: _[specify at least two names with titles]_."

Typically, to open a corporate account, the treasurer must fill out, and impress the corporate seal on, a separate bank account authorization form provided by your bank. But before opening an account, your bank will require your corporation to have a federal employer identification number (EIN). This number is obtained by filing form SS-4 with the IRS. All corporations will also need to register as an employer with the state and make deposits of state and federal withholding and employment taxes with an authorized bank. All of this is explained more fully in Chapter 5.

Accounting Period Resolution

⓭ This resolution reminds you to check with your tax adviser to select an accounting period for your corporation. (For general information on corporate accounting periods and tax years, see Chapter 5.) Insert the expected ending date of the accounting period in the blank—for example, "December 31" or "June 30." Realize that this resolution simply reflects your intention to adopt this accounting period. Your accounting period, which must match your corporate tax year, is officially determined when you file your first corporate income tax returns and specify your tax year. Pay attention to this decision. You must occasionally seek IRS approval if you wish to change your tax year (and accounting period) after you file your first tax returns. If you meet certain conditions, your corporation can change its tax year once every ten years without seeking IRS approval.

Payment, Deduction, and Amortization of Organizational and Start-Up Expenses Resolution

⓮ As explained in Appendix C, the federal American Jobs Creation Act allows a corporation to deduct up to $5,000 of organizational plus up to $5,000 of start-up expenses in the first corporate tax year. You can amortize and deduct remaining organizational and start-up expenses over the next 15 years. Start-up costs are those incurred before the start of business to investigate or create the business, such as market surveys and analysis, advertisements related to opening the business, and other necessary pre-opening costs such as travel and employee training. Organizational costs are those paid to actually form the corporation, such as state filing fees, lawyer and tax adviser fees, and the cost of this book.

This resolution authorizes the treasurer to reimburse incorporators for out-of-pocket payments of start-up and organizational costs. It also authorizes the treasurer to make the appropriate elections on the corporation's income tax returns (under IRC Sections 195 and 248 and, if applicable, state corporate income tax law provisions) to deduct and amortize start-up and organizational expenses. The approval of this resolution does not result in the making of these elections. It simply reminds you to cover this matter later—by consulting your tax adviser and having your adviser prepare and include the election statements and necessary information with your first and subsequent income tax returns. Check with your tax adviser for help in deciding whether to use this resolution and for help in preparing your tax returns and statements to send to the IRS to make sure you deduct and amortize these expenses properly.

Authorization of Issuance of Shares Resolution

⓯ Here you authorize your corporation to issue its initial shares to your shareholders after the meeting of your board. Throughout the book, we refer to this resolution as your "stock issuance resolution." This resolution does not result in the actual issuance of shares—it simply authorizes the appropriate corporate officers to issue shares to the shareholders after the meeting. You will issue shares as part of Step 7, below.

Insert the name of each shareholder, the number of shares the shareholder will receive, and the shareholder's payment for shares. For any noncash payment, such as services or property, state the fair value of the property as a dollar amount. You may need more than one line per shareholder to describe property or services paid as consideration, but be as brief as possible. Before you fill in your resolution, make sure to review the stock issuance considerations discussed in Chapter 2, Section H.

Issuing Shares: A Quick Review

We discuss stock issuance rules in Chapter 2, Section H. Here's a recap:

- Make sure that the total number of shares that you will issue to all shareholders is not greater than the number of shares authorized in your Articles of Incorporation. (The authorized number of shares stated in your articles places an upper limit on the number of shares that you can actually issue; see Chapter 2, Section H1, and Step 2, Section A, above.) Also, you cannot issue a class of shares other than those authorized in your articles. We assume you will authorize and issue only common shares with equal voting and liquidation rights, so our stock issuance resolution refers to "common shares."

- If your articles authorize par value shares, most states require each shareholder to pay at least the par value amount for her shares. (See Chapter 2, Section H2.) In most cases, par value is set at a low or nominal amount in the articles, and shareholders pay much more than the par value to buy their shares from the corporation.

- In some states, you cannot issue shares in return for the performance of future services by a shareholder or for promissory notes—that is, a promise by the shareholder to pay for the shares later. (See Chapter 2, Section H3.)

- As a matter of common sense, and to avoid charges of unfairness or fraud, you should charge the same price per share for all the shares you issue to initial shareholders. Place a fair value on the assets, property, or services received in return for the shares. Be realistic in your determination of fair value of all noncash payments for shares, particularly if you will be issuing shares in return for speculative or intangible property such as the goodwill of a business, copyrights, patents, and the like. You don't want to "shortchange" other shareholders who have put up cash or tangible property of easily determined value. Tax advisers are good source of information on how to place a fair value on business assets.

- We assume you will issue shares in compliance with state and federal securities laws. In most cases, this means making sure you qualify for both a state and a federal securities law exemption before you issue your shares. (See Chapter 2, Section I.)

Stock Issuance Examples

Here are some examples to help you fill in the blanks on your stock issuance resolution.

Issuance of shares for cash. If shareholders will pay cash for shares, simply state the dollar amount followed by "cash" in the consideration column—for example, "Sarah Bennet—100— $1,000 cash."

Issuance of shares for specific items of property. If a shareholder will purchase shares by transferring specific items of property to the corporation (we are referring to discrete items of property, such as a computer system, a truck, a patent, or copyright; not the complete assets of a business—the latter situation is covered by the next example), be as specific as you can when entering the consideration. Show the fair market value of the property as its dollar value—for example, "$9,000, 1998 Ford Truck, Vehicle ID# VIN555-555-5555."

 It's okay for a shareholder to pay different types of property for shares. A shareholder may pay for shares by contributing two or more types of property for shares—for example, $10,000 in tangible property and $5,000 in cash, for $15,000 worth of shares. If so, show the total number of shares the shareholder is buying in the "number of shares" column, then combine the different payments in the value column—for instance, the description may read "$5,000 cash; $10,000 _[description of property]_ ."

Issuance of shares for assets of a prior business. If you are incorporating an existing business, and one or more shareholders will transfer their part, or full, interest in it to the corporation in return for shares, describe the interest in the prior business that will be transferred by each owner.

Example: If two business owners incorporate their preexisting partnership, Just Bagels, the following simple description in the payment blank would be appropriate for each shareholder (each prior business owner), assuming the entire business was worth $100,000: "$50,000, one-half interest in assets of the partnership 'Just Bagels,' as more fully described in a bill of sale to be prepared and attached to these minutes." (See below for more information about preparing the bill of sale.)

Issuance of shares for a shareholder's cancellation of indebtedness owed by the corporation. This type of transaction is unusual, since a newly formed corporation will not normally owe shareholders any amounts except, perhaps, by way of small advances made to help meet organizational costs that will be directly reimbursed by the corporation. (See "Payment and Deduction of Start-Up and Organizational Expenses Resolution," above.) But if shares will be issued for the cancellation of a debt owed by the corporation to a shareholder, a description of the debt should be given as the consideration for the shares—for example, "cancellation of $4,500 owed on promissory note dated March 31, 2003." The dollar value of the payment to be made by this shareholder is the dollar amount of the remaining unpaid principal amount due on the debt, plus any unpaid accrued interest. If possible, attach a copy of the note or other written evidence of the debt to the minutes, marked as "cancelled on ___*[date]*___, ___*[signature of shareholder]*___."

Issuance of shares for past services. If you will issue shares to a shareholder in return for past services performed for the corporation (perhaps organizational work for which the person will receive shares), indicate the period of performance of the services and their fair value—for example, "$5,000 in

services performed by Bob Beamer, January 5 to February 15, 2004." A bill from the shareholder to the corporation showing the amount due for these services should be attached to your minutes, particularly if you have other shareholders—the bill helps document the amount and value of the services.

Issuance of shares for future services. If you will issue shares in return for a promise by a shareholder to perform future services, describe the nature of the work to be performed, the period for performance, and the cash value of the services. Alternatively, you can prepare a simple contract for the performance of the services and refer to it in your resolution. (We provide a contract you can use for this purpose in Step 7, Section B2, below.) If you do prepare a contract, you can fill out the description of consideration as follows: "$_____ in services to be performed as described in a contract for future services dated _____, attached to these minutes."

⚠ **State and federal law can complicate or prevent the issuance of shares for services.** Before issuing shares in exchange for services, check to see that your state permits it. (See Chapter 2, Section H3, and the "Share Issuance Rules" section of your state sheet for the types of payment that can be made for shares in your state.) Also, remember that a shareholder who receives shares for services normally must pay income tax on the value of the shares received (which are worth the value of the services paid for them). Finally, if you will issue a significant amount of shares for services, you may cause the entire stock issuance transaction—not just the shares for services portion—to be taxable. Check Chapter 3, Section F2, to be sure you avoid this unfavorable result.

Issuance of shares for promissory notes. If your state allows you to issue shares for promissory notes (again, see Chapter 2, Section H3, and the "Share Issuance Rules" section of your state sheet for the types of payment that can be made for shares in your state), you may decide to let a shareholder sign a note agreeing to pay for the shares later. If so, prepare the promissory note (we explain how to prepare one in Step 7, below), and refer to it in the consideration column—for example: "$10,000 promissory note, plus interest, payable on the terms described in the promissory note dated September 15, 2004, attached to these Minutes."

⓰ This paragraph applies to you only if you form a corporation in a par value state (see Chapter 2, Section H2) and you authorize shares without par value. If you are not in this situation, insert "N/A" in the blank and go on to prepare the next Minutes resolution. If this paragraph does apply to you, understand that most states allow you to allocate a portion of the payments received for shares without par value to capital surplus (we list any BCA allocation-to-surplus rules in the "Share Issuance Rules" section of your state sheet). As explained in more detail in Chapter 2, Section H2, it's normally a good thing to make this allocation between the stated capital account (the amount needed to cover the total par value of all the shares you issue) and the capital surplus account (the value of all additional contributions). Without the allocation, the amounts received for no-par shares in a par value state will stay in your corporation's more restricted stated capital account, which reduces your ability to use payments received from shareholders to conduct corporate business. To repeat the main point, if you are in a par value state and your initial stock issuance consists of "shares without par value" or "no-par shares," you will probably want to allocate some, or even, most of the payments you receive for the shares to capital surplus. You should ask your tax adviser just how much of the dollar amount received for each no-par share you should allocate to surplus. Once you get this number, insert it in this blank, and you're done.

Signature of Secretary

⓱ Have your corporate secretary sign at the bottom of the last page of the minutes.

Signatures of Directors

⓲ After you fill in the minutes, present them to each of your initial directors for approval. Have each director sign at the bottom of the waiver of notice.

B. Consolidate Your Minutes

After preparing and printing your minutes of the first directors' meeting, make sure to do the following before going on to Step 7, below:

1. Have the corporate secretary date and sign the certificate section at the end of your bylaws.
2. Set up a corporate records book containing at least the following four sections (see Step 3, above):
   • Articles of Incorporation
   • bylaws
   • minutes of meetings
   • stock certificates.
3. Place your minutes and attachments (file-stamped articles, bylaws, a sample stock certificate, and any other papers referred to in your minutes resolutions) in your corporate records book.
4. Keep your corporate records book at the corporation's principal office.

Remember that it's important to properly keep your corporate records. Be sure to document future corporate transactions by preparing standard minutes of annual and special director and shareholder meetings and placing copies of the minutes and other documents in your corporate records book. (Nolo publishes *The Corporate Minutes Book,* by Anthony Mancuso, which explains in more detail how to prepare minutes of future meetings; see Chapter 5, Section C.)

You have now completed the minutes of your first meeting. Next, we explain how to accomplish your last major organizational task: the issuance of stock to your initial shareholders. Stay with us, you're just a step away from completing your incorporation.

Step 7. Issue Shares of Stock

The final step in your incorporation process is issuing stock to your initial shareholders and recording your actions in the corporate records. Before you do this, however, glance at "Issuing Shares: A Quick Review," above. And remember: You must issue shares in compliance with state and federal securities laws. In most cases, this means making sure you qualify for a state and federal securities law exemption. (See Chapter 2, Section I.)

A. Fill Out Your Stock Certificates

Ten blank, ready-to-use stock certificates are included in Appendix D at the back of this book. Or you can order more professional looking ones, as explained in Step 3, above. In either case, fill in the blanks on the tear-out stock certificates contained in Appendix D (or on the fancier ones you may have ordered), following the sample stock certificate and instructions, below.

Each stock certificate should represent the total number of shares the corporation is issuing to a particular individual—or two people, such as spouses, if they are buying the shares together.

Certificate Number _____ ❶

for _____ Shares
(number of shares)

Issued to:
_____
(name of shareholder)
_____
(address of shareholder)

Dated _____, 20 ___
(date of issuance)

Received Certificate Number _____ ❶

for _____ Shares
(number of shares)

This _____ Day of _____, 20 ___
(date of issuance)

_____
(signature of shareholder)
SIGNATURE

From Whom Transferred ❽

Dated _____, 20 ___

No. Original Shares	No. Original Certificate	No. of Shares Transferred

Number _____ ❶

Shares _____ ❷

[Name of Corporation]

Incorporated Under the Laws of   [State of Formation]

[include capitalization statement if required under state BCA] ❸

This Certifies that _[name of shareholder]_ ❹ is the owner of _[number of shares]_ ❺ full paid and assessable
[class and par value designation of shares] ❻ of the above Corporation transferable only on the books of the
Corporation by the holder in person or by duly authorized Attorney on surrender of this Certificate, properly
endorsed.

In Witness Whereof, the Corporation has caused this certificate to be signed by its duly authorized officers and to
be sealed with the Seal of the Corporation.

Dated: _[date of issuance]_ ❼

[signature of officer] , _[title]_ , _[signature of officer]_ , _[title]_ ❼

❾

Instructions

❶ Complete the left and right portions of the stub as indicated on the sample. The date of issuance and shareholder signature lines on the stubs will be filled out when you actually distribute your stock certificates. (See Step 7, Section C, below.)

Number each certificate and its associated stub. (If you've ordered a corporate kit, these stub pages are already numbered.) Each shareholder gets one certificate no matter how many shares the shareholder purchases (joint owners of shares, too, get just one certificate for their jointly owned shares). The stock certificates issued by the corporation should be consecutively numbered and issued in order. This is important, since it helps the corporation to keep track of who owns its shares.

> **Example:** Let's say you establish the price of your shares at $50 per share. If you plan to issue stock to four people (no matter how many shares each person will receive), you should first number the certificates 1 through 4. Then, if Jack pays $10,000, Sam $5,000, and Julie $2,500, and Ted transfers a computer with a fair market value of $1,000, Jack receives a certificate for 200 shares, Sam receives one for 100 shares, Julie gets one for 50 shares, and Ted gets a certificate for 20 shares.

Remember, as discussed in Chapter 2, Section H1, fixing your share price is arbitrary. In the above example, it would be just as easy and sensible to establish a share price of $25, with each shareholder receiving a stock certificate representing twice as many shares. But you obviously want to choose a value that avoids a shareholder receiving fractional shares. For example, you wouldn't want to set a share price of $30 per share in the previous example, since the result would be that your shareholders would get fractional shares. Jack, who pays $10,000, would be entitled to 333-1/3 shares. (Actu-

ally, for the math-minded reader, Jack is entitled to receive an irrational number of shares with an infinitely trailing sequence of 333s to the right of the decimal: 333.3333333 … and so on. This is not very workable in real life or in the mathematical domain.)

❷ Type in the number of shares that each certificate represents. The number of shares each person is entitled to receive is indicated in the stock issuance resolution of your organization minutes. (See Step 6, above.)

❸ In the first blank of the stock certificate heading, enter the name of the corporation exactly as it appears in your Articles of Incorporation. Then enter the state where you formed your corporation in the second blank. (Both of these items will be preprinted in any specially ordered certificates.) Adding text on the third line of the heading is optional. The old-fashioned practice is to specify the total capitalization of your corporation on this line—that is, the total number and type of authorized shares specified in your articles (for example: "Authorized Shares: 300,000 Common Shares Without Par Value"). We suggest, as is common today, that you omit this item, since authorized capital information isn't really useful to shareholders. After all, if you amend your articles to authorize a second class of shares or to increase the authorized number of your original class of shares, any information you provide on this line of your certificate will be out of date. Besides, most shareholders just want to know how many shares they are getting, not what your articles say.

❹ Type the name of the shareholder. If the stock certificate will be held by two people, such as spouses, include both names and the form of co-ownership here—for example, "Carolyn Kimura and Sally Sullivan, as joint tenants" or "Mai Chang and Lee Chang, as community property." (For more information, see "How to Take Title (Ownership) to Stock," below.)

How to Take Title (Ownership) to Stock

Taking title to stock, essentially, means putting the owner's name on the ownership line of the stock certificate. For purposes of this book and state corporate statutes, the name or names you put on the ownership line of your stock certificate are important because they specify the record holder of the shares. These are the people who, under state BCAs:

- are entitled to notice of shareholder meetings
- get to vote at these meetings, and
- are entitled to any distributions made by the corporation, such as dividends and distributions of assets when the corporation liquidates.

Many married shareholders take title to stock jointly—that is, in the names of both spouses—to show that they own shares together. Doing this does not make much difference for corporate purposes. Each share still has one vote attached to it and the same proportionate interest in corporate distributions. But joint ownership can make a difference for other legal purposes and for tax reasons. For example, if married people take title to shares in joint tenancy—a common form of co-ownership—the shares normally do not go through state probate if one of the co-owners dies. In a community property state—Alaska (by written agreement between the spouses), Arizona, California, Idaho, Louisiana, Nevada, New Mexico, Texas, Washington, and Wisconsin—spouses can take title to property "as community property" and sometimes achieve a better tax result when one of the spouses dies.

Since it's impractical for this book to deal with all the estate and tax planning issues surrounding the different forms of co-ownership of shares, we recommend that you check to make sure you take title to your shares in a way that provides the best overall legal and tax implications for you. Ask a financial or tax adviser, or check out one of Nolo's helpful resources, including *8 Ways to Avoid Probate*, by Mary Randolph, and *Plan Your Estate*, by Denis Clifford and Cora Jordan.

❺ Enter the same number that you indicated in Instruction 2, above.

❻ State BCAs normally require stock certificates to show the name of the class of shares being issued and, in par value states, the stated par value of the shares or a statement that they are without par value. We list your state's stock certificate requirements in the "Share Issuance Rules" section of your state sheet. Place the required information in this blank on your certificate. Here's an easy way to fill in this blank in all states.

Start by entering "Common Shares" in this blank. We assume you specified only one class of shares in your articles that were either (1) called "common shares" or (2) did not have a name associated with them—for example, you simply authorized "100,000 shares." For many incorporators, that's all you need to do. But if your articles also say (1) that the shares you are issuing have a par value or (2) are "no-par" shares or shares "without par value," you must also add this description in this blank. Here are a few examples.

Example 1: Your articles authorize 100,000 shares of common stock. In this line, describe your shares simply as "Common Shares." (By the way, capitalization does not matter, but most people use title case—that is, first-letter capitalization—to describe the type of shares being issued.)

Example 2: Your articles authorize 1,000 shares with par value of $1 per share. Describe your shares as "Common Shares, par value $1.00."

Example 3: Your articles authorize 1,000 common shares without par value. Describe your shares as "Common Shares without par value."

Example 4: Your articles authorize 1,000 common no-par shares. Fill in this blank to read "Common Shares without par value." In these last two examples, you could say "Common Shares, no-par" instead.

⚠ **If you will issue more than one class of stock.** Very few small corporations issue more than one class of stock. But there are sometimes good reasons to do this—for example, to authorize different voting rights or liquidation preferences. If you authorized more than one class of shares in your articles, you must type the name of the class you are issuing to your shareholders on this line of your stock certificate—for instance, "Class A Preferred Shares."

❼ Enter the date of issuance of the shares, and obtain the signature of your corporate officers when you distribute your certificate as explained in Step 7, Section C, below.

❽ Do not fill in the transfer sections on the stub or on the back of each certificate. These sections should be used only if and when the original shareholders later transfer the stock certificates. If you've ordered a corporate kit, this applies to the transfer sections on the separate stub pages and on the back of the printed stock certificates. The kit should also contain instructions on preparing the transfer information if the stock is resold.

❾ If you have a corporate seal, you should impress it on each certificate. The stock is valid without it, but many private corporations formalize their certificates by impressing them with their corporate seal.

After filling out the stock certificates and stubs, place the completed stubs in consecutive order in the stock certificate section of your corporate records book. (If you use the certificates in this book, you'll need to neatly cut the stub away from the top of the stock certificate along the dotted line. It's easier to do this if you first tear out the entire page.) These stubs represent your corporation's share register.

B. Prepare Receipts for Your Shareholders

After filling out your stock certificates, you may wish to issue receipts to your shareholders for the cash or property they paid for their shares. Similarly, if you are incorporating a prior business, you may also want to prepare a bill of sale for your shareholders. You are not legally required to prepare these forms, but we think it's a sensible precaution that will avoid confusion about who paid what for stock in your corporation. This paperwork allows both the corporation and its shareholders to have written statements of the details of each shareholder's stock issuance transaction.

A tear-out Bill of Sale and separate receipt forms are contained in Appendix D and on the CD-ROM that accompanies this book. (The Bill of Sale is contained in the BILLSALE file on the CD-ROM; all other receipts are included in the RECEIPT file on the CD-ROM.) Make copies of the appropriate forms and prepare them according to the sample forms and instructions below.

1. Preparing a Bill of Sale for the Assets of a Prior Business

If you are transferring the assets of an unincorporated business to your corporation in return for the issuance of shares to the prior owners, here is information on how to prepare a Bill of Sale. Below is a sample of the Bill of Sale form. (As mentioned, you can find the blank form in Appendix D and on the CD-ROM, file BILLSALE.) Fill out the form, following the instructions below. If you have any questions, your tax adviser can help you choose among the options offered by this form. Your adviser can also help you prepare the balance sheet to attach to the Bill of Sale, as explained in the instructions that follow.

Extra Steps Are Required to Transfer Real Estate or Leases to the Corporation

Real estate transfers. Prepare any new corporate ownership papers, such as deeds and mortgages, and record them with the county recorder or similar local office. If the property being transferred is mortgaged, then you will most likely need the permission of the lender to transfer the property. If your real estate promissory note contains a "due on sale or transfer" clause (which means that if the underlying property is sold or transferred, the entire principal amount of the note becomes due), you may even be required to refinance your deed of trust (mortgage) if rates have gone up substantially since the existing deed of trust was executed. This, of course, may be so undesirable that you decide not to transfer the real estate to the corporation, preferring to keep it in the name of the original owner and lease it to the corporation.

Also, don't forget that the transfer of real estate to your corporation may not be the best way to go for tax purposes. Remember that any prior appreciation in the property gets passed along to and locked into the corporation—and this appreciation probably will be taxed to the corporation and to the shareholders (a double tax) when the corporation liquidates. (See Chapter 1, Section A4.) Also, remember to check the tax consequences of incorporating a prior business with your tax adviser.

Transfers of leases. If you are transferring a lease from a prior business to your new corporation, you should talk to the landlord about having a new lease prepared showing the corporation as the new tenant. An alternative is to have the prior tenants assign the lease to the corporation; however, read your lease carefully before trying to do this, as many leases are not assignable without the landlord's permission. You should prepare and sign new lease documents before you give the prior leaseholders their shares.

Sample Bill of Sale for Assets of a Business

This is an agreement between:

 [name of prior business owner]

 [name of prior business owner]

 [name of prior business owner] , ❶

transferor(s), and [name of corporation)] , ❷ a corporation.

In return for the issuance of [number of shares] ❸ shares of stock of the corporation, transferor(s) hereby sell(s), assign(s), and transfer(s) to the corporation all right, title, and interest in the following property:

All the tangible assets listed on the balance sheet attached to this Bill of Sale and all stock in trade, goodwill, leasehold interests, trade names, and other intangible assets [except [list any nontransferred assets here]] ❹ of [name of unincorporated business] ❺, located at [address of unincorporated business] . ❻

In return for the transfer of the above property to it, the corporation hereby agrees to assume, pay, and discharge all debts, duties, and obligations listed on the balance sheet attached to this Bill of Sale [except [list any unassumed liabilities here]]. ❼ The corporation agrees to indemnify and hold the transferor(s) and their property free from any liability for any such debt, duty, or obligation and from any suits, actions, or legal proceedings brought to enforce or collect any such debt, duty, or obligation.

The transferor(s) hereby appoint(s) the corporation as representative to demand, receive, and collect for itself any and all debts and obligations now owing to [name of unincorporated business] . The transferor(s) further authorize(s) the corporation to do all things allowed by law to recover and collect these debts and obligations and to use the transferor's(s') name(s) as it considers necessary for the collection and recovery of these debts and obligations, provided, however, without cost, expense, or damage to the transferor(s). ❽

Date: _____

 [signature of unincorporated business owner] , Transferor

 [signature of unincorporated business owner] , Transferor

 [signature of unincorporated business owner] , Transferor

Date: _____

 [name of corporation] , Corporation ❾

By:

 [signature of president or CEO] , President

 [signature of treasurer or CFO] , Treasurer

Instructions

❶ Insert the names of the unincorporated business owners.

❷ Insert the name of your corporation.

❸ Enter the total number of shares to be issued to all unincorporated owners of the business in return for the transfer of the business to the corporation.

> **Example:** If Patricia and Kathleen will each receive 2,000 shares in return for their respective half-interests in their preexisting partnership (which they are now incorporating), they would indicate 4,000 shares here.

❹ Use this line to show any assets of the prior business that are not being transferred to the corporation. For example, you may wish to continue to personally own real property associated with your business and lease it to your new corporation. If you will transfer all prior business assets to the corporation, insert "No Exceptions" here. As indicated in this (and the next) paragraph of the bill of sale, attach a current balance sheet showing the assets and liabilities of the business transferred to the corporation.

❺ Indicate the name of the unincorporated business being transferred to the corporation. For sole proprietorships and partnerships not operating under a fictitious business name, the name(s) of the prior owners may simply be given here—for example, "Heather Langsley and Chester Dodd."

❻ Show the address of the prior business.

❼ This paragraph says that your corporation will assume the liabilities of the prior business that appear on the balance sheet discussed above. Here, list any liabilities of the prior business that will not be assumed by the corporation. If your corporation will assume all liabilities of the prior business, indicate "No Exceptions" here.

❽ This paragraph is included in the Bill of Sale form to indicate that your corporation is appointed to collect for itself any debts and obligations (accounts receivable) owed to the prior business which are being transferred to the corporation.

❾ Type the name of the corporation on the line indicated. Don't fill out the date and signature lines yet. You will do this when you distribute the stock certificates to the prior business owners, as explained in Section C, below.

2. Preparing Receipts

You may wish to prepare one or more receipts for your shareholders. You can find receipt forms in Appendix D and in the RECEIPTS file on the CD-ROM. These forms allow you to document the following types of payment made by a shareholder:

- cash
- specific items of property
- past and future services
- promissory notes
- cancellation of a debt.

Let's look at each of these transactions and the relevant receipt form below. If you'll need several of a certain type of receipt—for example, separate receipts for three shareholders who contribute cash—make copies.

 Don't sign receipts until you receive payment and distribute stock certificates. Don't fill in the date or signature lines on your receipts until you successfully distribute your stock certificates in return for the payments made by each of your shareholders. (See Section C, below.)

(To prepare a bill of sale for the assets of a prior business, see the previous section.)

Receipts for Joint Shareholders and Joint Payments

If you will issue shares to joint owners, it's best to show the names of both joint owners on the receipt. Of course, if two shareholders jointly contribute an item of property but prefer to receive two separate blocks of individually owned shares, you should prepare a separate receipt for each shareholder.

Example 1: Teresa and Vernon Miller will pay $1,000 for 1,000 shares that they will own jointly. You make out a receipt in the name of both shareholders.

Example 2: Mike and his brother, Burt, transfer a jointly owned lathe with a value of $5,000. Each will receive 250 shares in exchange for his half-interest in the lathe. You make out a separate receipt for each brother, showing the transfer of a one-half interest in the lathe in return for the issuance of 250 shares.

a. Receipt for Cash Payment

If your corporation issues shares for cash, the shareholder normally pays by check and the shareholder's cancelled check serves as additional proof of payment. Here is a sample of the tear-out cash receipt form.

Sample Receipt for Cash Payment

Receipt of $ _[amount of cash payment]_ from _[name of shareholder]_ representing payment in full for ___[number of shares]___ shares of the stock of this corporation is hereby acknowledged.

Date: _[date of payment]_ ❶

Name of Corporation: _[name of corporation]_

By: _[signature of treasurer]_ , Treasurer❶

Instructions

❶ After receiving payment from the shareholder (see Section C, below), your treasurer should date and sign the receipt.

b. Receipt for Specific Items of Property

If a shareholder is transferring specific items of property to the corporation (other than the assets of an existing business; in which case see Section B1,

above), you may wish to prepare a receipt (bill of sale) for the property before issuing shares to the shareholder. Make sure that the property has first been delivered to the corporation and that any ownership document—such as the title slip for a vehicle—has been signed over to the corporation. If you are transferring real estate interests to your corporation, see the sidebar about transferring real estate in Section B1, above.

Below is a sample of the bill of sale for property.

Sample Bill of Sale for Items of Property

In consideration of the issuance of _[number of shares]_ shares of stock in and by _[name of corporation]_, _[name of shareholder]_ hereby sells, assigns, conveys, transfers, and delivers to the corporation all right, title, and interest in and to the following property:

[description of property] ❶

Date: _____ ❷

[signature of shareholder]

Instructions

❶ Provide a short description of the property that the shareholder is transferring to the corporation. This description should be brief but specific—for example, the make, model, and serial numbers of property, or vehicle identification number for vehicles.

❷ Complete this date line and have the shareholder sign the bill of sale when you distribute your shares as described in Section C, below.

c.   Receipt for Past Services

If you are transferring shares in return for past services performed by a shareholder for the corporation, you may wish to prepare the receipt form as explained, shown below. Have the shareholder submit a signed invoice for these services, marked "Paid in Full," showing the date of payment by the corporation. (This is the date you distribute the shares in return for these services; see Section C, below.)

Some states don't allow the issuances of shares for services. Before issuing shares for services performed by a shareholder, make sure your state allows it. (See the "Share Issuance Rules" in your state sheet in Appendix A.) Even if your state permits it, the issuance of shares for performed services is not a common type of stock issuance transaction for newly formed corporations because of practical considerations. First, most work done for the corporation will occur after your stock issuance. Second, most contractors or other professionals who have performed services will want cash (not shares of stock) as payment for their services. However, if one of the principals of your closely held corporation has performed services for the corporation prior to your stock issuance, this type of stock issuance transaction may make sense—after you, the corporation, and the shareholders check the tax consequences. (See Chapter 3, Section F2.) To avoid unfairness to your other stockholders, be sure that the shareholder charges no more than the prevailing rate for the services performed.

Sample Receipt for Services Rendered

In consideration of the performance of the following services actually rendered to _[name of corporation]_ , _[name of shareholder]_ , the provider of such services, hereby acknowledges the receipt of _[number of shares]_ shares of stock in _[name of corporation]_ as payment in full for these services, described as follows:

 [description of past services] ❶

Date: _____ ❷

 [signature of shareholder]

Instructions

❶ Provide a short description of the services performed by the shareholder—for example, the dates, description, and value of (amount billed for) the work. As an alternative, simply refer to the attached bill for services, which should contain this information. (You can insert "see attached bill for services" in this blank on the receipt.)

❷ When you distribute the shares in return for the services (see Section C, below), provide the date of issuance of the shares and have the shareholder sign the receipt.

d. Contract for Future Services

If you are issuing shares in return for a promise by a shareholder to perform future services (assuming your state allows this form of payment for shares; see Chapter 2, Section H3, and the "Share Issuance Rules" section of your state sheet), you can prepare a short contract for future services to document the transaction. The following form, contained in the tear-out receipts section of Appendix D and in the RECEIPTS file on the CD-ROM, can be used for this purpose. Of course, you may also wish to prepare a complete employment or independent contractor agreement to more fully describe the services and terms associated with the promised work that the shareholder will perform.

Sample Contract for Future Services

In return for the issuance of _[number of shares]_ shares of _[name of corporation]_ , _[name of shareholder]_ hereby agrees to furnish the following services to the corporation:

[description and schedule of services to be performed]

It is understood that the corporation may place the shares in escrow or make other arrangements to restrict the transfer of shares until the above services are performed in accordance with the above schedule. ❶

Date: _____ ❷

[signature of shareholder]

Name of Corporation: _[name of corporation]_

By:_ [signature of treasurer]_ , Treasurer

Instructions

❶ Many states that allow shares to be issued for future services specifically allow corporations to place these shares in an escrow account until the shareholder completes performance of the promised services. On completion, the corporation releases the shares to the shareholder. We list your state's BCA rules for issuing shares for future services, including any share escrow provisions, in the "Share Issuance" section of your state sheet. If your state allows the issuance of shares for future services but is silent on whether the corporation can place these shares in escrow pending the completion of the services, it should be fine to do so as long as the shareholder agrees to the escrow condition (as in the contract for future services, above).

❷ Have the shareholder and corporate treasurer sign the contract now, prior to any distribution of shares.

e.   Issuance for Promissory Notes

If you are issuing shares in return for a promise of a shareholder to pay for the shares in the future, prepare the promissory note form provided in Appendix D or on the CD-ROM (filename: PROMNOTE), following the sample form and instructions below. Remember,

your state must allow the issuance of shares for promissory notes. (See Chapter 2, Section H3, and the "Share Issuance Rules" section of your state sheet.)

Our promissory note requires payment of equal monthly installments of principal and interest. You will have to consult a loan amortization chart (available from banks, real estate offices, and bookstores, as well as online sources such as www.nolo.com) to figure the amount of monthly payments: Just plug in the term of the loan, the principal amount, and the interest rate, and the chart tells you the total amount of the monthly payment. Our form can be used as is, or you can modify it to reflect your own repayment terms. For example, you may wish to require interest-only payments during the term of the loan, with a payment of the entire principal amount of the loan plus any accrued and unpaid interest at the end of the term. Or you may decide to eliminate monthly payments altogether, and simply require one complete payment at the end of the loan term. If you need help figuring the payment amounts or writing your own note terms, see *The Corporate Minutes Book* (Nolo), by Anthony Mancuso; it contains various shareholder promissory note forms that include a range of repayment options.

Sample Promissory Note

In consideration of the issuance of _[number of shares]_ shares of _[name of corporation]_ , _[name of share-holder]_ promises to pay to _[name of corporation]_ the principal amount of $_[dollar amount of loan extended to the shareholder to buy the shares]_ together with interest at a rate of _[rate of interest]_ ❶ rate per annum. Payments are to be made in _[number of monthly installments]_ ❷ equal monthly installments of $_[amount of monthly payment]_ , ❸ each payable on the _[day of the month when payments are due, for example "1st" or "15th"]_ day of each month, with the first installment due on _[date of first installment payment]_.

Date: _____ ❹

[signature of shareholder]

Instructions

❶ Specify a reasonable commercial rate. For example, the current prime rate plus two points might be what lenders are charging commercial clients. Check with your bank to see what it currently charges creditworthy customers.

❷ Normally, the number of monthly payments is the yearly term of the loan multiplied by 12, for example, 60 payments for a five-year note.

❸ Again, use a loan amortization chart to figure the amount of monthly principal plus interest payments.

❹ The shareholder should date and sign the note on the date when you distribute your stock certificates. (See Section C, below.)

f.   Receipt for Cancelling a Debt

If you issue shares in return for cancelling a debt owed by the corporation to a shareholder, you can prepare the receipt form shown below to document the transaction.

Sample Form for Cancellation of Debt

The receipt of _[number of shares]_ shares of this corporation to _[name of shareholder]_ for the cancellation by _[name of shareholder]_ of a current loan outstanding to this corporation, dated _[date of loan]_ , with a remaining unpaid principal amount and unpaid accrued interest, if any, totaling $ _[loan balance]_ , ❶ is hereby acknowledged.

Date: _____ ❷

 [signature of shareholder]

Instructions

❶ Show the total of the outstanding principal amount and accrued and unpaid interest (if any) owed on the loan. If you have a copy of the loan or other debt instrument (such as a promissory note), attach it to the receipt.

❷ When you distribute your stock certificates (see the next section), date the receipt and have the shareholder sign it.

C. Distribute Your Stock Certificates

Now it's time to distribute stock certificates to your initial shareholders. To complete this step, do the following:

- Have each shareholder (or both shareholders if the stock certificate is to be held jointly) sign his or her stock certificate stub. Indicate the date of stock issuance on each stub.
- Date each stock certificate and have your officers sign each one. Some states specify the officers who are required to sign certificates—normally, the president and secretary sign, but many states allow any two corporate officers to sign. (See the "Share Issuance Rules" in your state sheet.)
- Impress your corporate seal in the seal space provided on the certificate. Remember, you are not legally required to seal your certifi-

cates, but many incorporators prefer to use the seal to make the certificates look official.

- Write the date of issuance for each shareholder in the stock transfer ledger (share register).
- Complete the date and signature lines on your receipts as explained in Section B, above. Give each shareholder a copy of his or her receipt(s).
- Make sure to place all your completed stock stubs and completed copies of all receipts and any attachments—such as the closing balance sheet for a prior business, cancelled notes, or a paid-in-full bill for services—in your corporate records book.

How to Sign Corporate Documents From Now On

Now that your incorporation is almost complete, there is one last point we wish to make that is central to the operation of your newly formed corporation. One of the reasons you decided to form a corporation was to limit your personal liability in business affairs. So, from now on, whenever you sign a document on behalf of the corporation, be certain to do so in the following manner:

[name of corporation]
By: _[signature of corporate officer]_
 [typed name of officer] , _[title of officer]_

If you fail to sign documents this way—that is, on behalf of the corporation in your capacity as a corporate officer or director—you may be leaving yourself open to personal liability for corporate obligations. This is but one example designed to illustrate a basic premise of corporate life: From now on, it is extremely important for you to maintain the distinction between the corporation and those of you who are principals of the corporation. As we've said, the corporation is a separate legal "person," and you want to make sure that other people, businesses, the IRS, and the courts respect this distinction. (See "Courts Sometimes 'Pierce the Corporate Veil'," in Chapter 2, Section G, for a short discussion of this point.)

CONGRATULATIONS!

You have completed your last incorporation step. Please glance through the postincorporation procedures contained in Chapter 5 to see how they may apply to your corporation. ■

After You Form Your Corporation

Successfully organizing your corporation is just the first step in establishing and protecting its legal integrity. In this chapter, we briefly discuss the important steps you should take *after* forming your corporation. And we also explain the many good reasons why most jointly owned corporations should adopt a buy-sell shareholder agreement to help control what happens to the business if one owner dies or decides to leave. Due to the individual nature of each corporation and its business, as well as the wide diversity of employment and tax procedures in each state, it's not possible to discuss every possible ongoing tax or legal formality you will encounter. Rather, this discussion is intended to be a general guide to routine formalities and tax obligations that most corporations face. You can get most of the tax information and forms we discuss below from the IRS and your state tax and business registration agency websites.

A. Postincorporation Tasks

There are a few formalities that you should take care of shortly after you organize your corporation. Some apply to all incorporators; others are optional or may not apply to you at all. We tell you the circumstances under which each step must be taken.

1. File a Corporate Annual Report

Shortly after you file your Articles of Incorporation, you are normally required to file your first corporate report form with the state corporate filing office. In most states, this report must be filed each year. It's usually a cinch to complete an annual report form. Typically, the form will simply list and ask you to update the corporation's principal office and the names and addresses of its registered agent, directors, and officers. There will be a small filing fee.

Normally, the filing office will mail a report form to the principal office of your corporation in advance of the filing date. To plan ahead and to be sure you meet your state's filing requirements, you can to go your state corporate filing office website

(listed in the "Corporate Filing Office" section of your state sheet in Appendix A), where you should find your state's annual report filing requirements, plus a downloadable form to use for your initial and ongoing report filings.

Watch out for penalties if you don't file reports. If you fail to file a report on time, state law typically says that your corporation can be assessed penalties. If reports are not filed for several years or more, your corporate charter can even be suspended until you make the required annual reports and pay any penalties. Among other things, if your corporation is suspended, it usually can't use the courts to sue or defend itself in a lawsuit. In short, make sure you comply with this required formality.

2. Register an Assumed or Fictitious Business Name

If your corporation will do business under a name other than the exact corporate name contained in your Articles of Incorporation, it makes sense in most states to register it as an assumed business name. Depending on the state, this second name will be called your "doing business as (dba)," "assumed," or "fictitious business" name. (See Chapter 4, Step 1, for more on corporate names.) Most states let you register an assumed name for your corporation.

> **Example:** If the name stated in your Articles is "Acme Business Computers, Inc.," and you plan to do business under the acronym "ABC, Inc.," you may register "ABC, Inc." as the assumed or fictitious business name of your corporation.

However, we don't recommend that you adopt an assumed name in addition to your formal corporate name (see Chapter 4, Step 1), primarily because you need to establish a solid business identity for your real corporate name in most cases. Adding a second name dilutes your real corporate name, rather than strengthening it.

That said, registering your existing corporate name—the one stated in your articles—as an assumed or fictitious business name might be sensible. Why? Because registering an assumed name is one of many important ways to put others on notice that your business exists, and that they should not try to do business under a similar name.

If you do decide to register your corporate name as an assumed name, you will want to drop the corporate designator ("Inc." or "Corp.") because, under the assumed and fictitious business name statutes, your assumed name must be different from your formal corporate name.

> **Example:** Righteous Ron's Realty, Inc., could register "Righteous Ron's Realty" as an assumed corporate name.

⚠️ **Business name rules are complicated.** Realize that registering an assumed name simply gives you a legal presumption that your corporation is the rightful owner of an assumed name. Even if you are first to register an assumed name for your corporation, if another business in your field can prove in court that it was the first to use the name, it will probably be awarded the right to use the name and to stop you from using the name as well. Another way of saying this is that other state and federal laws governing trade names and trademarks often have more force than the assumed name laws. (For a brief discussion of trade name and trademark laws, see Chapter 4, Step 1.)

State procedures for registering an assumed or fictitious business name vary. Your state's corporate filing office website (see the "Corporate Filing Office" section of your state sheet) should explain your state's registration procedure. In some states, you will register your assumed name with the state corporate filing office. In others, you will make your filing with the clerk of the county where the corporation has its principal office. In some states, you must file at both the state and county levels.

The registration process normally consists of three steps:

(1) File an assumed or fictitious business name statement with the state and/or county, de-claring the formal name of the corporation, the corporation's address, and the assumed or fictitious name.

(2) Publish a notice of intent to use an assumed or fictitious business name in the county of the corporation's principal office. This publication normally must be made in the local newspaper for several consecutive weeks.

(3) File an affidavit of publication of the newspaper notice with the office where you made the assumed name filing.

The total cost to register an assumed name is modest: Filing and publication fees should total approximately $50.

3. File Final Papers on a Prior Business

If you have incorporated a prior business (transferred the assets of a business to the corporation in return for shares), the prior business owners should file all papers needed to terminate their prior business, including final sales tax and employment tax returns, if appropriate. Of course, you should close your previous business bank accounts and open the corporate bank accounts indicated in the bank account resolution of your organizational minutes. (See Chapter 4, Step 6.) In addition, if the old business holds any licenses or permits, you may need to cancel these and obtain new licenses or permits in the name of the corporation. (See Section 6, below.)

4. Notify Creditors and Others of the Incorporation of a Prior Business

If you have incorporated a prior business, it is important to notify the creditors of the prior business and other interested parties—for example, suppliers, vendors, banks, and businesses with whom you have open lines of credit—of the incorporation of the prior business. You will want to do this in writing.

If you keep your business accounts current—that is, you pay bills and other debts as they become due—your creditors should not care that you are now doing business as a corporation. But if your prior unincorporated business owed significant debts when you incorporated—particularly if any of these debts were overdue—you can expect the creditor to call you and ask about the status of these debts after you send out notification of your incorporation. If, as we assume, your corporation will pay the debts of the unincorporated business, just tell the creditor so. If, on the other hand, you incorporated to duck one or more debts of the prior business, watch out—the owners of the prior business will probably continue to be personally liable for the prior business debts. (See Chapter 3, Section F5.) If you intend to dispute any debts of the prior unincorporated business, you will need the help of a lawyer. (See Chapter 6.)

Prepare a short letter along the lines of the sample below. Your goal is to notify creditors that you have dissolved the prior business and that you are now doing business as a corporation. State the old name and address of the business and the new corporate name and address. Add whatever friendly remarks you feel appropriate to the closing of your letter ("We're still here, ready to serve you"). Place a copy of each mailed letter in your corporate records book.

Sample Notification Letter

[date]

[name and address of your corporation]

Re: Incorporation of *[name of prior business]*

Dear *[name of company or individual]* :

I'm writing to let you know that our unincorporated business, *[name of prior business]*, was incorporated in *[state]* on *[date your articles were filed]* as *[name of corporation]* . This is a formal change that will help the business pursue its mission and the attainment of its goals with increased structure and efficiency.

We have enjoyed doing business with you in the past and look forward to continuing to do so in the future. Please call me at the telephone number shown below if you need additional information to update our records or accounts.

Sincerely,

 [signature of officer] , *[title]* ❶
 [printed name of officer]
 [officer's corporate telephone number]

Instructions

❶ Normally, the corporate treasurer prepares and signs the letter, but any corporate officer may do so.

5. Investigate Private Insurance Coverage

An item of business that should be near the top of your "to do" list after you incorporate is to check out the availability and cost of commercial liability insurance for your corporation. Corporations, like other businesses, should carry the usual kinds of commercial insurance to cover financial loss in the event of an accident, fire, theft, or other potential liability. Although the corporate form normally insulates shareholders from personal liability for business debts and judgments, it obviously won't prevent corporate assets from being jeopardized by these events. And since many entrepreneurs have much of their net worth tied up in their businesses, it will be no fun to have business assets taken to pay claims that could have been covered by insurance.

Your commercial policy should include coverage for business vehicles, inventory, and personal injuries on the premises. Additional coverage for product liability, or directors' and officers' liability (see Chapter 2, Section F2), and other specialized types of insurance, may also be appropriate. To keep premiums down, many smaller companies purchase policies with reasonably large deductibles. (For a detailed discussion about business insurance, see Nolo's *Legal Guide for Starting & Running a Small Business*, by Fred S. Steingold.)

6. Obtain Corporate Licenses and Permits

Many businesses, whether or not they are incorporated, are required to obtain state or local licenses or permits before commencing business. This includes businesses that sell food or drink, provide professional services, emit toxic substances, and so on. You may need to pay fees and take out a bond to cover losses or injuries to the public. Of course, a license to practice a state-regulated profession requires meeting state education requirements and the passage of a state-administered test. The state agency that regulates your profession can explain any special licensing rules that apply to providing licensed services as a corporation.

An excellent resource for state licensing and permit rules is *The Small Business Start-Up Kit*, by Peri Pakroo (Nolo). It lists federal, state, and local start-up requirements that apply to all types of businesses.

7. Adopt a Shareholders' Buy-Sell Agreement

By now you're surely tired of incorporation paperwork and are ready to get down to business. Not so fast—there is one more postincorporation formality we want you to seriously consider. It involves the adoption of a shareholder agreement (commonly called a buy-sell agreement) to control who can own shares in your corporation in the future and how much people or the corporation must pay for them. In a nutshell, here's the problem.

When a shareholder in a closely held corporation dies, sells shares, gives shares away, or (in some cases) gets a divorce, there is the risk of bringing an outsider into the shareholder ranks. Think about it: Do you really want to be forced to deal with another shareholder's spoiled son or hostile ex-husband? Remember, not only does a shareholder in a small corporation get to vote at annual meetings for the election of the board, that person has a say in all major decisions brought before the shareholders for a vote. These decisions may include significant structural changes to the corporation, such as amending the Articles of Incorporation or the corporate bylaws. But that isn't the worst part. A shareholder in a small corporation also may be able to attain a board position through an election. This is true because in most smaller corporations, a plurality—not a majority—shareholder vote is all that is needed to elect someone to the board. If an outsider is elected to the board, that newcomer will get a management vote equal to all other board members (each board member has one vote), thereby getting to participate in all major corporate decisions. (Even if you outvote the new board member, you'll still have to listen to him.)

You may be wondering why you should worry about these issues while your corporation is in the start-up phase. The answer is simple: You have a golden opportunity to deal with potentially explosive issues now, when everyone is in a good mood. By contrast, if you wait until an ownership change occurs or is imminent, you risk ending up in a dispute—and perhaps even a lawsuit.

Some Corporations Don't Need to Adopt a Buy-Sell Agreement

If you own 100% of your corporation, there is no need to prepare a buy-sell agreement. Similarly, if you and your spouse own the business together and you agree there is virtually no possibility that you will divorce, you may conclude that there is little reason to go to the trouble of creating a buy-sell agreement. After all, if one of you dies while you still own the business, chances are excellent that the other person will inherit the deceased spouse's shares—or that the shares will be left to a child or children according to a mutually agreeable estate plan.

A buy-sell agreement may also be unnecessary if shares are all owned by parents and their children in a very close knit family, where all agree that the children will eventually be given or inherit the parents' interests.

The great utility of a shareholder buy-sell agreement is that it spells out whether the corporation and/or remaining shareholders get a chance, or are required, to buy the shares of a shareholder who stops working for the corporation, dies, divorces, or, under provisions in some agreements, becomes disabled. It also addresses the important issue of setting a price (or a procedure to place a price) on the shares when the corporation or shareholders buy shares under the agreement. This valuation issue is crucial, because one of the most potentially contentious issues involved in any share buy-back is how much the business is worth. In the absence of an agreed-on formula, the chances of a lawsuit are significant. If you doubt this even for a moment, consider how much an angry ex-spouse who receives shares in your corporation as part of a divorce may claim they are worth.

Issues Covered in Shareholder Buy-Sell Agreements

Here are some of the basic issues normally addressed by corporate buy-sell agreements, and typical ways they are handled:

- **Buy-back price or formula.** Agreements specify a default price or procedure that will be used to value shares for purposes of any buy-out covered in the agreement.

- **Buy-back payment method.** Agreements set out the terms for payment of the buy-back price. Typically, agreements provide for the payment of the buy-out price in stages, with part cash paid at the time of buy-back, and the balance, plus interest, payable by the corporation in monthly installments.

- **Shareholder death.** Some agreements give the corporation or remaining shareholders a right to purchase the shares from a deceased shareholder's estate within a specified number of days from the date of the shareholder's death. Other agreements require the corporation, if financially able, to buy back the shares from the estate or heirs of a deceased shareholder on request by the representative of the estate or an heir.

- **Life insurance funding of buy-back.** Often, the corporation and/or shareholders are required to take out and pay for life insurance policies on each shareholder. If a shareholder dies, the cash proceeds from these policies are used to purchase the deceased shareholder's shares.

- **Shareholder tries to sell to an outside buyer.** Agreements often provide that either the corporation or the other shareholders have a right to buy the shares before an outside shareholder gets a chance.

- **Shareholder wants to give or transfer shares to relatives.** Some agreements restrict all gifts or other transfers of shares. Others allow gifts to family members, as long as certain conditions are met (for example, less than one-half of a shareholder's stock may be gifted to relatives).

- **Shareholder leaves the corporation.** Many agreements adopted by closely held corporations require the corporation to buy back shares held by a shareholder who quits the corporation. Other agreements simply give the corporation an option to demand such a buy-back, or let ex-shareholders demand a buy-back if they wish to sell the shares.

- **Current shareholder asks to be cashed out.** Some agreements let shareholders request a buy-out of their shares, even if the shareholder remains an employee of the corporation.

- **Shareholder divorces.** Agreements often provide that if a shareholder divorces, and shares are transferred to the shareholder's ex-spouse by court order as part of a marital settlement agreement, the corporation can demand a buy-back of the shares from the ex-spouse. (Typically, spouses of shareholders also sign shareholder buy-sell agreements when they are adopted.)

- **Shareholder becomes disabled.** Some agreements require or permit the corporation to buy out the shares of a disabled shareholder, if one or two doctors sign a written statement of disability.

- **Shareholder has debt problems.** If a shareholder files for personal bankruptcy, many agreements require the corporation, if financially able, to buy the shares back from the bankruptcy trustee.

Fortunately, armed with good information and forms, you can prepare a sound buy-sell agreement for your corporation. But this means doing the reading necessary to climb a reasonably steep learning curve. A good source of up-to-date information on this subject, designed for use by self-help incorporators, is Nolo's *Buy-Sell Agreement Handbook: Plan Ahead for Changes in the Ownership of Your Business*, by Bethany K. Laurence and Tony Mancuso. This book takes you step by step through the process of adopting buy-sell provisions for your small corporation, limited liability company, or partnership, paying particular attention to the concerns and issues of the small, closely held business. Ready-to-use agreements are included as tear-outs and on a CD-ROM to help you accomplish the task efficiently.

Of course, you may find other sources for a buy-sell agreement, including information designed for use by attorneys, at a business or law library. But no matter how you prepare your agreement, the range of legal and tax considerations involved means that it often makes sense to have a legal or tax adviser review your document before you adopt it.

B. Tax and Employer Registration Requirements

As you know, another basic corporate formality is reporting and paying ongoing income and employment taxes. To get the latest and complete business and tax reporting rules and forms, go to the following websites:

- For state corporate income or franchise tax filing requirements and forms, go to your state's corporate tax office website listed in the "State Tax Information" section of your state sheet.
- To find your state's business registration requirements and employment tax procedures and forms, go to your state's business registration and employment tax office. (Both of these areas are normally covered by one agency or office, often a subdivision of the main state tax agency.) You can probably find a link to the office on both your state's tax agency site (again, listed in the "State Tax Information" section of your state sheet) and your state's corporate filing office site (listed in the "Corporate Filing Office" section of your state sheet).
- To obtain federal corporate income tax publications and forms, as well as federal employment registration and employment tax information and forms, go to the IRS website at www.irs.gov. We suggest all corporations obtain IRS Publication 509, *Tax Calendars*, prior to the beginning of each year. This pamphlet contains tax calendars showing the dates for federal corporate and employer filings during the year. Other particularly helpful publications include IRS Publication 15, *Circular E, Employer's Tax Guide*, and the *Publication 15 Supplement*. Further federal corporate income tax information can be found in IRS Publication 542, *Corporations*, and Publication 334, *Tax Guide for Small Business*.
- An excellent small business resource for finding your state's other business and tax requirements is *The Small Business Start-Up Kit*, by Peri Pakroo (Nolo). Its appendix lists state business registration addresses and websites as well as business resource centers located in each state.

C. Ongoing Corporate Meetings

After forming your corporation, you should plan ahead for holding regular corporate meetings. We discuss the basic legal rules for holding annual and special meetings of directors and shareholders in Chapter 2, Sections F2 and F4. Your state sheet lists the specific call, notice, quorum, and voting rules for annual and special director and shareholder meetings (see the "Director Meeting Rules" and "Shareholder Meeting Rules"). In this section, we discuss when and how to hold ongoing directors' and shareholders' meetings, and provide a basic form you can use to prepare minutes for these meetings.

1. When to Hold Formal Corporate Meetings

You will wish to hold the following formal corporate meetings, remembering to prepare minutes and record them in your corporate records book:

- **An annual shareholders' meeting** should be held each year to elect or reelect your board of directors. The date, place, and time of this meeting is scheduled in your organizational minutes. (See Chapter 4, Step 6.)

- **An annual directors' meeting** is normally held just after the annual shareholders' meeting, when the directors accept their positions on the board for the upcoming year and discuss past corporate performance and upcoming business. You will also want to hold any additional directors' meetings scheduled in your organizational minutes, in addition to the annual directors' meeting. (Some corporations may schedule twice a year, quarterly, or even monthly directors' meetings in their organizational minutes; see Chapter 4, Step 6.)

- **Special directors' and shareholders' meetings** may be called during the year to formally discuss and approve legal, tax, and business matters. You don't need to hold a formal corporate meeting to discuss routine business decisions, just those that you want to document with formal corporate minutes. Such decisions may include:
  —amending corporate Articles of Incorporation or bylaws
  —declaring dividends
  —authorizing the issuance of additional shares of stock
  —approving real estate construction, lease, purchase, or sale
  —appointing key corporate officers and departmental managers and setting corporate salaries
  —approving the terms of the loan of money to or from shareholders, directors, officers, and banks or other outsiders

  —the commitment of substantial corporate resources
  —the adoption of new corporate strategies or goals, or
  —an immediate discussion and review of corporate performance.

Of course, many of these matters can be handled at annual or regular directors' meetings, but one or more of these decisions may come up during the year between regular meetings. If so, a special directors' meeting needs to be called. Special shareholders' meetings normally need to be called only when state law requires the ratification by shareholders of a director decision made during the year, such as the amendment of corporate articles or bylaws, or a change in stock rights or restrictions. Your state BCA lists any special shareholder ratification rules that apply in your state. (See the "Corporation Law Online" section of your state sheet to find your state BCA online.)

2. How to Document a Formal Corporate Meeting

You will want to call and provide notice of all directors' and shareholders' meetings as required in your bylaws and current state law. (Again, the BCA meeting rules are contained in your state sheet.) At the meeting the chairperson calls the meeting to order, then items of business are discussed and voted on (usually by voice vote at meetings held by small corporations). At or shortly after the meeting, you should prepare formal minutes to record the matters discussed and approved at the meeting, showing the number of votes cast for and against each matter brought to a vote together with a description of the action taken or rejected by the meeting participants. State law does not specify how minutes should be prepared—you can simply draft your own to suit your needs. Below is a sample standard minutes form that you can follow to prepare minutes for any annual or special directors' or shareholders' meeting. (Use the tear-out minutes form in Appendix D or the "GENMIN" file on the CD-ROM.)

Sample General Minutes of Meeting

Minutes of ___*[type of meeting, such as "SPECIAL DIRECTORS"]*___ Meeting
of
___*[name of corporation]*___

A ___*[insert type of meeting]*___ meeting of the corporation was held on ___*[date, time, and place]*___ for the purpose(s) of ___*[purpose of meeting stated in the notice of the meeting]*___ .

___*[name of corporate officer, usually the president]*___ acted as chairperson, and ___*[name of corporate officer, usually the secretary]*___ acted as secretary of the meeting.

The chairperson called the meeting to order.

The secretary announced that the meeting was called by ___*[if applicable, name of person who called the meeting]*___ .

The secretary announced that the meeting was held pursuant to notice as required under the bylaws of this corporation.

The secretary announced that the following ___*["directors" or "shareholders"]*___ were present at the meeting, representing a quorum: ___*[names of directors or names and shareholdings of shareholders present]*___ .

The secretary announced that the next item of business was the consideration of one or more formal resolutions for approval by the board. After introduction and discussion, and on motion duly made and carried by the affirmative vote of ___*["a majority" or other vote requirement (or list names of those voting for and against the proposal and, if a shareholders' meeting, each person's shareholdings)]*___ of ___*["directors" or "shareholders"]*___ at the meeting, the following resolutions were adopted by directors entitled to vote at the meeting: *[describe one or more resolutions adopted at the meeting]* .

There being no further business to come before the meeting, it was adjourned on motion duly made and carried.

___*[signature of meeting secretary]*___ , Secretary

For more minutes help and ready-to-use forms. If you are concerned about preparing minutes for annual and special meetings (and we think you should be, of course, now that you've incorporated), you owe it to yourself to see *The Corporate Minutes Book,* by Anthony Mancuso (Nolo). It helps you schedule, organize, and prepare all ongoing corporate paperwork, with specialized minutes forms for directors' and shareholders' annual and special meetings, plus more than 80 ready-to-use resolutions to plug into the minutes to describe the approval of common corporate legal, tax, and business decisions. It also contains forms to waive notice of meetings and approve decisions by written consent (without a meeting) for those times when you are too busy to comply with all the meeting requirements specified in your bylaws or state BCA. ■

6

Lawyers and Accountants

A. Lawyers

If you form a straightforward corporation with just a few owners, one class of stock, and no special by-law provisions, you probably won't run into any problems that require expert legal help. But if you wish to form a more complicated corporation, getting legal help or advice may be necessary before you file your Articles of Incorporation.

Throughout this book we have flagged areas of potential complexity where a degree of customization may be warranted—for example, complying with unique requirements of your state's securities law, adding a second class of stock to your articles, or adding special provisions to your bylaws. If any of these loom large for you, review them with an experienced business lawyer before filing your articles. The lawyer should have experience in small business incorporations in your state; should be prepared to answer your specific, informed questions; and should review—not rewrite (unless absolutely necessary)—any forms you have prepared.

Even if you have all your incorporation paperwork covered, it's not too early to find a lawyer to use later for ongoing business consultations. Once enmeshed in a crisis, you may not have time to hire a lawyer at affordable rates. Chances are you'll wind up settling for the first person available—and that's almost a guarantee you'll pay too much for possibly poor service.

1. Using a Legal Coach

Most readers will not want a lawyer who is programmed to take over all legal decision making and form drafting—this just builds up billable hours that few can afford. Instead, we suggest you find someone we call a "legal coach": a professional who is willing to work with you, not just *for* you, when answering your particular questions and meeting your special corporate legal needs. Under this model, the lawyer helps you customize your legal paperwork—rather than writing on his or her own, from scratch—and is available to help you later if a complicated corporate legal issue comes up that you can't handle by yourself.

Not all lawyers are comfortable taking a legal coach role, so you may need to interview several lawyers before finding a compatible adviser. When you call a lawyer, announce your intentions in advance: Tell the lawyer that you are looking for someone who is willing to review and perhaps customize the corporate formation papers you have prepared, or to handle specific legal questions. Mention that you are looking for someone who is willing to be flexible, point you in the right direction as the need arises, serve as a legal adviser as circumstances dictate, and tackle particular legal problems if necessary. In exchange for this, let the lawyer know you are willing to pay promptly and fairly.

When you find a lawyer who agrees to the arrangement you've proposed, ask to meet with him or her for a half hour or so. Expect to pay for this initial consultation. At the in-person interview, re-emphasize that you are looking for a legal coach relationship. You'll also want to discuss other important issues in this meeting, such as the lawyer's customary charges for services, as explained further below. Pay particular attention to the rapport between you and your lawyer. Remember, you are looking for a legal adviser who will work with you. Trust your instincts and seek a lawyer whose personality and business sense are compatible with your own.

Using Different Levels of Legal Talent

There is a lawyer surplus these days, and many recently graduated lawyers are open to nontraditional business arrangements. In your quest for a lawyer, remember:

- **You don't need a big-time business lawyer.** Look for a lawyer with some small business experience, preferably in your field or area of operations. For the most part, you don't want a lawyer who works with big businesses (publicly held corporations, large limited partnerships, or investment pools, and the like). Not only will this person deal with issues that are far from your concerns, but he or she is almost sure to charge too much.

- **You don't need to start with a top echelon legal specialist.** Even if you have a very technical legal question, it's usually not necessary to seek out a legal specialist in an area such as insurance, banking, or securities law. Start by finding a good small business lawyer to act as your coach. Then rely on this person to suggest specialized materials or experts as the need arises. Again, finding a lawyer with corporate experience is essential, but specialized legal involvement in narrower realms of business practice can wait until you actually need advice on a particular legal issue or problem.

- **Look elsewhere for tax advice, unless your lawyer also specializes in corporate taxation.** When it comes to corporate tax questions, we think a tax adviser with corporate experience is the best person to ask for help. (See Section C, below.) For other tax and financial decisions, such as the best tax year, accounting period, or employee benefit plan for your corporation, you'll find that accountants, financial planners, retirement and employee benefit plan specialists, and bank officers often have a better grasp of the issues than lawyers. And an added bonus is that although tax advice doesn't come cheap, it often costs less than legal advice.

2. How to Find a Lawyer

When you're ready to look for a lawyer, one excellent way to find one is to talk to people in your community who own or operate businesses of comparable size and scope. If you talk to half a dozen businesspeople, chances are you'll come away with several good leads. People who provide services to small businesses—such as bankers, accountants, insurance agents, or commercial real estate brokers—may also be able to provide the names of lawyers they trust to help them with business matters. In short, try to get a personal recommendation from someone who is qualified to evaluate small business lawyers, which probably excludes your sister who just hired a lawyer to increase her child support.

3. Paying for Legal Help

When you hire a lawyer, get a clear understanding about how fees will be computed. For example, ask how you will be billed if you want to call the lawyer from time to time for general advice, to be steered to a good information source, or to have the lawyer review documents. Some lawyers bill a flat amount for a call or a conference; others bill to the nearest six-, ten-, or 20- minute interval. Whatever the lawyer's system, you need to understand it.

Particularly at the beginning of your relationship, when you bring a bigger job to a lawyer, ask specifically about what it will cost. If you feel it's too much, don't hesitate to negotiate; perhaps you can do some of the routine work yourself, thus reducing the fee for larger jobs.

Example: You decide to add buy-sell provisions to your bylaws (see Chapter 5, Section A7). You buy a self-help resource and prepare a draft of your buy-sell provisions. The area is complicated enough that you decide to have your provisions checked by a small business lawyer you know. You call and ask the hourly fee for this review of your work. The fee seems acceptable and competitive, and you schedule an appointment to have the lawyer look over and customize your work (after the lawyer explains the reasons for doing so, of course).

It's a good idea to get fee arrangements in writing. (In several states, this is mandatory where a fee of $1,000 or more is expected.)

How Lawyers Charge for Legal Services

You can expect your lawyer to bill you in one of these ways:

- **By the hour.** In most parts of the United States, you can get competent services for your small business for $150 to $250 an hour, and often less. Newer attorneys still in the process of building a practice may be available for paperwork review, legal research, and other types of legal work at lower rates.

- **Flat fee for a specific job.** Under this arrangement, you pay an agreed-on amount for a given project, regardless of how much or how little time the lawyer spends. Particularly when you begin working with a lawyer and are worried about hourly costs getting out of control, it can make sense to negotiate a flat fee for a specific job, such as doing a pre-filing review of your articles or a review of your bylaws. For example, the lawyer may review your articles and bylaws for $300.

- **Retainer.** Some businesses can afford to pay relatively modest amounts, perhaps $1,000 to $2,000 per year, to keep a business lawyer on retainer for ongoing phone or in-person consultations or routine business matters. Of course, your retainer won't cover a full-blown legal crisis, but it may take care of routine contract and other legal paperwork preparation and reviews.

- **Contingent fee based on settlement amounts or winnings.** This type of fee typically occurs in personal injury, products liability, fraud, and employment discrimination disputes, where a lawsuit will likely be filed, not in the corporate service area. Just so you know, however, the lawyer gets a percentage of the recovery (often 33% to 40%) if the client wins and nothing if the client loses. Even in the personal injury business, when a client gets sued, lawyers charge by the hour to defend a client, not a percentage of the money the lawyer saves the client if the defense is successful.

4. Resolving Problems With Lawyers

If you have any questions about a lawyer's bill or the quality of his or her services, speak up. Buying legal help should be just like purchasing any other consumer service. If you are dissatisfied, seek a reduction in your bill or make it clear that the work needs to be redone properly. For example, tell the lawyer that you need a more comprehensive lease or a better contract. If the lawyer you are dealing with runs a consumer-friendly business, he or she will promptly and positively deal with your concerns. If you don't get an acceptable response, find another lawyer pronto. If you switch lawyers, you are entitled to get your important documents back from the first lawyer.

Even if you fire your lawyer, you may still feel unjustly treated and overcharged. If you can't get satisfaction from the lawyer, write to the client grievance office of your state bar association (and send the lawyer a copy of your letter). Often, a phone call from this office to your lawyer will bring the desired results.

B. How to Look Up the Law Yourself

Many incorporators want to research legal information on their own. This book provides you with an easy way to do your own research by going to your state's online Business Corporation Act. In the various corporate rules sections of your state sheet, we give you the specific statutory citations (the actual BCA section numbers) of each important area of corporate law. It's a simple matter to look up any of these BCA sections in your online BCA to get more information and the latest state corporation rules that apply in your state. For general guidance about searching a state's BCA online, see the "Corporation Law Online" instructions in the introduction to the state sheets in Appendix A. To locate your state's BCA on the Web, go to the "Corporation Law Online" section of your state sheet.

Standard corporate forms and instructions used in your state to handle changes to your corporation's legal structure are provided online at your state's corporate filing office website. (See the "Corporate Filing Office" section of your state sheet.) Typically, this site offers forms for amending articles and changing your corporation's registered agent or office. You'll probably also find annual report forms (see Chapter 5, Section A1) and other routine corporate filing forms used in your state.

If you are not wired to the Internet, you can take advantage of a local law or business library to do your own legal research. County law libraries are open to the public (you will not be asked to produce a bar card before being helped), and they are not difficult to use once you understand how the information is categorized and stored. Libraries are an invaluable source of corporate and general business forms, corporate tax procedures and information, and the like. Research librarians will usually go out of their way to help you find the right statute, form, or background reading on any corporate or tax issue.

For more information about the laws that govern corporations and how to find them online or in the library, see Chapter 2, Section B.

An excellent legal research resource. If you are interested in doing self-help legal research, an excellent source of information on how to both find the law online and break the code of the law libraries is *Legal Research: How to Find & Understand the Law*, by Stephen R. Elias and Susan Levinkind (Nolo).

More help from Nolo. As mentioned throughout this book, Nolo offers resources of all kinds—both on the Web and off—to help you start your business and keep it healthy. See Chapter 1, Section C, for a detailed list of Nolo's most popular tools for small business owners, and remember to visit the Business and Human Resources area of Nolo's website at www.nolo.com.

C. Accountants and Tax Advisers

As you already know, organizing and operating a corporation involves a significant amount of financial and tax work, and you'll need to make many important decisions about these matters. Throughout this book we have flagged areas of special consideration involving financial planning and corporate tax issues.

Generally, although we tend to use the terms "tax adviser," "financial consultant," and "accountant" interchangeably, you may wish to refer your initial incorporation tax concerns to a certified public accountant (CPA) with corporate experience. For general assistance and advice, a qualified financial planner may also be very helpful.

Once your initial incorporation tax questions have been answered, your corporation set up, and your books established, you may want to have routine tax filings and bookkeeping tasks performed by corporate personnel or independent contractors who have been trained in corporate bookkeeping and tax matters. (In many instances your accountant may either train or recommend these individuals.) Most corporations have their accountant or other tax return preparer handle at least their annual corporate tax returns.

For future financial advice, you may wish to contact an officer in the corporate department of the bank where you keep your corporate accounts. Banks are an excellent source of financial advice, particularly if they are corporate creditors—after all, they have a stake in the success of your business. Further, the Small Business Administration (www.sba.gov) can be an ideal source of financial and tax information and resources (as well as financing in some cases).

Whatever your arrangement for financial or tax assistance, you may wish to order the IRS and state tax publications listed in Chapter 5, Section B, to familiarize yourself with some of the tax and bookkeeping aspects of operating a corporation.

When you select a tax adviser, the same considerations apply as when selecting a lawyer. Choose someone you know or someone who has been recommended by a friend with business experience. Be as specific as you can about the services you need, and find someone with experience in corporate taxation. Above all, find someone who will listen to and work with you, not simply charge high prices to give you one-sided, take-it-or-leave-it tax advice.

Find a compatible tax adviser. Tax issues, in particular, are often cloudy and subject to a range of interpretations and strategies, particularly in the corporate arena, so it is absolutely essential that you discuss and reach agreement about the level of tax-aggressiveness you expect from your adviser. Some incorporators like to live on the edge, saving every possible tax dollar. Others are content to forgo contestable tax strategies to gain an extra measure of peace of mind. Whatever your tax comfort level, make sure you find a tax adviser who feels the same way you do, or who is willing to defer to your more liberal or conservative tax tendencies. ∎

State Sheets

How to Use the State Sheets

The state sheets that follow provide you with the state-specific information on forming and operating a corporation under the laws of the state where you are incorporating. To use this information as you go through the incorporation steps in this book, locate the state sheet pages for your state, then tear out and refer to these pages as you follow your incorporation steps, starting with Chapter 4, Step 1, "Meet State Name Requirements."

Each state sheet is divided into twelve sections:

1. Corporate Filing Office

2. State Corporate Forms

3. Articles Instructions

4. Director and Officer Rules

5. Share Issuance Rules

6. Director Meeting Rules

7. Shareholder Meeting Rules

8. Financial Disclosure Rules

9. State Tax Information

10. Corporation Law Online

11. State Securities Information

12. Creating Your Own Articles Form.

The following is a summary of the information contained in each state sheet section.

How to Stay Current

The information in this appendix—from addresses to legal rules—changes often. Use the Internet to confirm that our entries are still current (and to learn what's changed).

- For information and the latest forms for filing Articles of Incorporation and other routine corporate filings, go to your state's corporate filing office website (we give you the link).
- To check for any changes in the legal rules described in this appendix, use the state corporate law link listed in your state sheet to go to your state's Business Corporation Act. Navigate your way to the relevant statute (we cite the statute number for each corporate law rule in brackets [ ]).
- To get the latest state tax and securities law information, go to the tax and securities office links listed for each state.

For the latest federal corporate tax forms and information, go to the IRS website at www.irs.gov.

1. Corporate Filing Office

This section provides the name, address, telephone number, and website of the office that handles corporate filings in your state. This is the office where you must file Articles of Incorporation to form your corporation. You can also contact this office to check the availability of your proposed corporate name and to reserve your name if you wish to do so. State filing office websites typically provide downloadable Articles of Incorporation, name reservation request forms, and the latest corporate filing information for your state.

2. State Corporate Forms

In this section, we indicate whether your state provides an official articles form that you can use to form your corporation (most states do). We also indicate whether you can download the official form from your state filing office website (in most states, you can). A few states do not provide an official articles form. For these states, we provide a sample articles form that meets your state's specific requirements.

Online filing. Some states provide both online preparation and filing of articles, and we expect this trend to continue. If your state offers an online filing service, you simply fill in the articles form from your Internet browser and select a method for paying the filing fees (by credit card or telephone call to the state filing office to receive an authorization code). Some states reduce the filing fee for people who file online. Your final step is to submit the form online.

Printing and mailing online forms. In states without an online filing service, forms are normally provided by the states in Adobe Reader (PDF) format. You must have the Adobe Acrobat Reader file installed on your computer to use the PDF form. If you don't already have Adobe Reader, you can download the latest version for free at www.adobe.com. An installable version of Adobe Reader is provided on the CD-ROM included with this book.

Standard PDF forms. You can use a standard PDF file in one of two ways. Either:

- click the name of the PDF file listed on the state website to open the file from your browser and print it from there (select "File," then "Print" from the browser menu), or

- right click the filename and select "Save Target As" to download the file to your computer; then exit the browser and double click on the PDF filename saved on your computer. This launches Adobe Reader. You can open and print the form with the Reader program by selecting "File," then "Print" from the Reader menu.

After printing your PDF form, fill in the blanks with a typewriter (if you can find one) or neatly print your responses in the blanks with a black ink pen. Mail the completed articles form together with a check for filing fees to the state filing office.

Fill-in PDF forms. Another type of PDF form is popular as a format for state-provided articles: PDFs that you can fill in with the Adobe reader program, called "fillinable" forms. With these forms, you fill in the blanks on the form before, not after, you print it. After you open a fillinable PDF within your browser or separately from the Reader program, use the Tab key to move from one blank to the next, typing your response in each blank. You can't normally save the filled-in PDF form unless you have purchased the Adobe Acrobat program, but you can print it from your browser or Adobe Reader program and send it to the state filing office. Note, however, that some states (and the IRS) now provide fillinable, saveable PDF forms. This means that if you use the most recent version of the Adobe Reader program, you can save the filled-in form on your computer. Your responses to the filled-in items will stay in the form and will be there waiting for you when you reopen the form.

Other file formats. In addition to PDF files, some states provide Microsoft Word and/or Corel WordPerfect versions of their articles. If you have the Word or WordPerfect program installed on your computer, you may prefer to use one of these formats instead of the PDF. The advantage of using one of these alternate file versions is that you can fill in, edit, and reformat the Word or WordPerfect form before you print it, and you can save the completed form on your computer. (Even with fillinable, saveable PDFs, you can type information only in the blanks; you can't change the surrounding text using the free Adobe Reader program.) This full editing capability allows you to make changes or additions to the standard articles form provided by your state if you wish to do so, without retyping the entire form.

 For more information. For additional instructions on completing PDF article forms, see Chapter 4, Step 2.

3. Articles Instructions

This section provides instructions to help you complete your state's Articles of Incorporation form—or to help you prepare your own form in one of the few states without an official form. We don't explain all the blanks in the form, just the ones that may require special help and that may not be fully explained in the state's official instructions to the state-provided articles form or in the instructions posted on the state's corporate filing office website.

Keep in mind the following general points when completing articles.

Corporate name. In all states, we list the rules for selecting a name for your corporation. We also tell you how to reserve a name prior to submitting your articles if you want to be sure your name is available when you file. We recommend you use the state's reservation of corporate name form if one is provided on your state's corporate filing office website. Use our generic reservation of name form, provided in Appendix D and on the CD-ROM, if your state does not provide a reservation of name form online.

Registered agent. In all states, you must designate a registered agent and registered office in your articles. In some states, this person goes by another title, such as the "agent for service of process." The agent is the person you designate to receive legal papers in any future lawsuit against your corporation. We assume you will designate an initial director, officer, or shareholder as your agent, to avoid having to pay a "registered agent" fee to another

person or company. We also assume you will show the principal address of the corporation as the location of your registered office. The person designated as your initial agent must be a resident of your state, and the registered office address must be located in your state.

Authorized shares. In all states, you authorize in your articles the number of shares of stock that you can later issue to shareholders. Generally, you should authorize the maximum number of shares you will issue to shareholders in the foreseeable future. If you don't do this, you will have to amend and refile your articles with the state if you later want to increase the number of shares. In some states, the initial filing fee or later annual fees are based on the number of shares authorized in the articles. In these states, we tell you the maximum number of shares you can authorize for the smallest fee.

Most states allow you to simply authorize a specific number of shares, but in some states you must also specify whether the shares have a stated "par value" or are without par value. States that make this distinction use the concept of par value in their corporations law. Par value is an outdated concept, and many states have eliminated it. Traditionally, it was used to provide a "cash cushion" in the corporation that creditors could look to for repayment of debts. Under modern financial accounting practices, the complete corporate financial picture, not just par value amounts, is used to assess the creditworthiness of a corporation. We tell you if your state still uses the concept of par value, and, if so, whether it is best to authorize par value shares or shares without par value in your articles. In par value states, the filing fee often depends on whether your shares have or do not have a par value. In these states, we help you select the type of shares that qualifies for the lowest filing fee and the most authorized shares.

 For more information. For more information on par value, see Chapter 2, Section H2.

For most smaller corporations, it is sufficient to authorize one class of common shares in the articles—that is, shares that have equal rights to vote and participate in corporate dividends and distributions. Most state articles forms are set up to provide for one class of common shares only, so you normally must retype your articles and add language if you want to create more than one class of shares—for example, if you want to authorize common shares, plus a special class of preferred shares that have special dividend, voting, or liquidation rights. We tell you where to include this additional information if you wish to authorize more than one class of common shares. Note that this book does not show you how to draft language to authorize a special class of common or preferred shares in your articles. You may find sample language in corporate practice manuals available at law libraries or online at law-related websites. In most cases, however, we recommend that you ask a business lawyer to help you draft language to authorize special classes of shares in your articles.

For more information. For more information on authorized shares, see Chapter 2, Section H1.

Incorporator. The incorporator is the person who signs and files your articles—or who submits your online form for filing with the state. In all states, the incorporator need not be associated with your corporation as a director, officer, shareholder, or otherwise, nor must the incorporator be a resident of your state. However, even though not required, it is typical for an initial director or shareholder of a small corporation to act as its incorporator. In some states, your incorporator must be at least 18 years old (a good idea whether or not your state requires it to make sure your incorporator has attained the age of legal consent). We tell you if there is an age requirement in your state. Only one state—South Carolina—requires that an attorney sign your articles. In all other states, it is not necessary for a lawyer to act as or with your incorporator. In all other states, you can prepare and file articles yourself.

Directors. Directors are normally not named in articles, though some states require it. Keep in mind that any initial directors you name in your articles can be reelected or replaced at the first annual meeting of shareholders. In other words, the directors named in your articles are simply your corporation's initial directors. In all states, directors are not required to be shareholders of your corporation or residents of your state. And in most states, your corporation needs just one director, but you can designate more. (In a few states, a corporation must have at least three directors unless the corporation has fewer than three shareholders. In these states, two directors are required if there are only two shareholders, and one director is allowed if the corporation has just one shareholder. We tell you if your state has these special director rules.)

Corporate purposes. Some states require a statement of corporate purposes in the articles. In many of these states, a general purposes clause is sufficient—for example, "to engage in any lawful business for which corporations may be formed under the state's Business Corporation Act." Your state sheet includes any general language approved by your state for use in the corporate purposes clause of the articles. In some states, you must provide a statement of specific business purposes—such as "to sell retail and wholesale merchandise." We tell you if this is the case in your state. Unless your state requires it, we recommend that you do not provide a statement of specific purposes in your articles. Filing your articles without a stated purpose avoids the implication that your corporation is formed for limited purposes and gives you the flexibility to engage in any type of business that seems appropriate (and profitable) at different stages in the life of your corporation.

Filing fees. We show you how to calculate your filing fees and give you the name of the office to which you should make your check payable. In some states, the incorporation filing fee is based on the number and type of shares of stock authorized in your articles. For these states, we explain how to do the math and pay the lowest filing fee.

Special requirements. We tell you if you must follow additional formalities when you file your articles or after filing. For example, some states require you to include an additional form with your articles, such as a consent form signed by your registered agent. If so, we tell you where to get it (usually from the state website) and how to fill in any unobvious information on the additional form. In some states, you must file a notice of publication after filing your articles. If so, we tell you how to do it.

4. Director and Officer Rules

This section, and the remaining sections covered below, provide the basic state-specific rules for organizing and operating your corporation that are contained in your state's Business Corporation Act (BCA). You will use this information to fill in the blanks in the bylaws included with this book. Each rule is followed by a citation to the corresponding section of the state BCA so you can find it in your state's laws if you wish to read the complete law on which the rule is based and to check for any recent changes. (We provide the website for your state's Business Corporation Act, in case you want to browse the statutes online; see Section 10, below.) Note that a citation to a section of the law in brackets [ ] may follow several paragraphs of information. This means that the preceding paragraphs are taken from the cited statute.

Directors. This section provides the basic rules that apply to the selection of directors. In most states, the only requirement is that you must select a specific number of directors—typically, just one director is required. We also tell you whether or not a term of office is stated in the BCA for your state. Normally, directors must be elected (or reelected) by the shareholders each year to serve one-year terms on the board.

Officers. Most states require you to appoint a corporate president, treasurer, and secretary. In many states, one person may simultaneously hold more than one, or all, officer positions. We tell you your state's rules for designating officers.

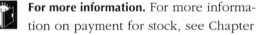 **For more information.** For more information on directors and officers, see Chapter 2, Sections F2 and F3.

5. Share Issuance Rules

This section sets out your state's basic rules for issuing shares of stock.

Payment for shares. Each state has rules on the forms of allowable payment for shares. (This payment is called the "consideration" paid for shares.) In some states, shares cannot be bought in exchange for a shareholder's promise to perform future services for the corporation, and/or for a promise to pay cash later—that is, in exchange for a promissory note. We tell you if either or both of these special restrictions applies in your state.

For more information. For more information on payment for stock, see Chapter 2, Section H3.

Form of stock certificate. In most states, stock may be issued to shareholders without providing a paper stock certificate. (These paperless shares are called "uncertificated shares.") However, it is still standard practice to issue stock certificates to shareholders as proof of their investment in the corporation. Each state has specific rules for the form of stock certificates. The rules cover the information that must be contained on the certificate and tell you who may sign it. We provide these rules to make sure you issue certificates in accordance with your state's statutes.

Par value rules. In some states, corporate statutes still recognize the concept of par value. (See the discussion in Section 3, above.) This means that the statutes include special rules about the payment for shares and how this payment is reflected on the corporation's financial records. If your state has par value rules, we list the most significant ones, but you should browse the BCA to read all the share rules in a par value state. Primarily, in a par value state, shares must be issued for at least their stated par value amount, but, typically, par value shares are sold for more than their nominal par value. If you issue shares without par value in a par value state, you may issue them for any amount.

The par value of par value shares and the entire amount of payment for shares without par value are reflected in the corporation's stated capital account on its books. However, the rules normally also allow the board to allocate a portion, but not all, of the payment made for shares without par value to a capital surplus account, which is not as restricted as the stated capital account. The board typically must make this allocation shortly after the payment for shares, usually within 60 days.

The stated capital account has a protected status under the statutory rules in par value states, and money cannot be paid out of or transferred from this account to another account unless specific statutory rules are met. The idea is that par value payments serve as a cash cushion for creditors of the corporation. These rules are complicated, and in a par value state you should ask your tax or legal adviser for help if you wish to transfer amounts out of the stated capital account after you incorporate.

For more information. For more information on par value and stated capital account rules, see Chapter 2, Section H2.

6. Director Meeting Rules

In this section, we list your state's specific rules for holding board of director meetings: how often the board must meet, how you must give notice of meetings, and the quorum and voting rules that apply. In most states, the board holds a regular meeting at least once each year, and special meetings are held when called by a board member, an officer, or a specified number of shareholders. Usually, you need not give notice for regular board meetings—that is, meetings provided for in the corporation's bylaws—but you must send notice of special board meetings to all directors a specified number of days prior to the special board meeting. Many of these rules are default rules that you may wish to alter in your bylaws. However, some rules, such as director quorum rules, cannot be lowered beyond a certain point in some states. We tell you which rules are mandatory or whether you are limited in how you may change them.

For more information. For more information on board of director meeting rules, see Chapter 2, Section F2.

7. Shareholder Meeting Rules

Your state sheet provides basic rules for holding shareholder meetings and electing directors.

Meetings. This section tells you how often the shareholders must meet, how you must give notice of shareholder meetings, and the quorum and voting rules that apply. In most states, shareholders must hold an annual meeting for the election of directors. Special meetings are held when called by a board member or a specified number of shareholders. Notice is required for all shareholder meetings—typically sent out at least ten and not more than 60 days prior to the meeting—and shareholders typically cannot decide any matter at a meeting not included in the notice of a special shareholders meeting. We tell you whether or not your bylaws can change your state's rules.

For more information. For more information on shareholder meeting rules, see Chapter 2, Section F4.

Election of directors. Most states have special rules called "cumulative voting" rules that you can use to cast votes at an annual shareholders' meeting. Cumulative voting allows a shareholder to cast a pool of votes in favor of one nominee to the board or to split up this pool of votes in favor of more than one nominee. The number of votes in the pool is equal to the number of shares the person owns multiplied by the number of directors to be elected at the meeting. This is different from the standard way a shareholder votes, by casting one vote for each share owned. Cumulative voting can allow a minority shareholder to help elect a board member. It is normally not important in the context of a smaller corporation, where each current director is routinely reelected by a plurality of votes using standard (noncumulative) voting rules. State law either automatically gives shareholders the right to cumulate votes in an election for directors, or allows them to do so only if cumulative voting is authorized in the articles. We provide your state's cumulative voting rules and tell you how a shareholder may exercise cumulative voting rights at a shareholders' meeting in your state, just in case you are interested in these special rules.

For more information. For more information on cumulative voting rules, see Chapter 2, Section F4.

8. Financial Disclosure Rules

In most states, even small corporations are required to make annual financial disclosures to shareholders, such as mailing or making available an annual corporate balance sheet and income statement shortly after the close of the corporation's fiscal year. We tell you what the financial disclosure rules are in your state.

9. State Tax Information

Most states collect an annual corporate income or franchise tax. Some states collect both. We list your state's corporate tax agency and describe the basic corporate tax scheme implemented in your state.

10. Corporation Law Online

This section shows you where to find and browse your state's Business Corporation Act online. (For most states, you can find the laws that pertain to

corporations by visiting Nolo's website at www.nolo.com/statute/state.cfm. Once you get to the Web page for your state's BCA, you will see either a search box that asks for a statute number, or a list of state BCA headings or statute numbers. If your state provides a search box, enter a specific statute number and click "Search" to go to the statute. We give you the specific state BCA statute section numbers in brackets [ ] of each basic rule discussed in the state sheet rules sections.) So, to search for the director meeting rule in your state, look for the bracketed section number we provide for your state's director meeting rule. If you are simply browsing through your state's BCA for a general subject, select the heading from the heading list in your BCA that seems most appropriate for the subject. For example, open the "Directors" heading to look for statutes about directors or directors' meeting requirements, then select the particular statute of interest listed under the heading.

BCAs normally are not extremely long, so it should not be difficult to search through heading or statute lists to find the subject areas you're seeking. With practice, you'll soon get to know how your BCA is organized, and future generalized searches should take less and less time.

11. State Securities Information

An important part of organizing a corporation is to making sure you issue initial shares in compliance with your state's securities laws. This is particularly true if you issue shares to investors who are not actively involved in organizing and operating your corporation, since they can complain to the state or start a lawsuit if the stock issuance was not performed in compliance with the statutes. We provide contact information for each state's securities agency, the name of the State Securities Act, and the website where you can browse the act online (if the act is not directly linked to the securities agency website). Most states provide an easy-to-use exemption from state securities registration for the initial issuance of shares by a small corporation to a limited number of investors.

We provide a brief summary of the sections of the act that are most likely to provide an exemption for the initial stock issuance of your corporation. When applicable, we also mention state securities rules developed under the act that help fill in the requirements for obtaining a state exemption. For the latest and most specific securities exemption information, we recommend that you call your state securities agency directly prior to your initial stock issuance. Most states are extremely helpful in guiding you through the state's securities regulations to make sure your initial stock issuance complies with state laws.

For more information. For more information about state and federal securities laws, see Chapter 2, Section F4.

12. Creating Your Own Articles Form

Most states allow you to create your own articles document—and, of course, the few states that do not provide an official form for you to use require you to create your own articles form. Normally, however, you will not wish to prepare your own form; it's easier to fill in an articles form provided by your state. In some cases, however, you may want to add provisions to your articles and prefer not to include them as attachments to the standard form in your state. If so, follow the instructions in this section to prepare your own form.

Many states specifically say that articles forms must be typed or printed in black ink. We expect you will use a computer printer or typewriter (if you're not interested in filing or able to file online in your state). And while it is okay to print out a form with blanks and fill in the blanks by hand (using a black ink pen), a state may not accept articles that are completely handwritten. If you want to handprint your entire articles document, call the state filing office to make sure they will accept it.

ALABAMA

Corporate Filing Office

Secretary of State
Corporations Division
Box 5616
Montgomery, AL 36103
334-242-5324
www.sos.state.al.us/business/corporations.cfm

State Corporate Forms

The Alabama Secretary of State provides fill-in-the-blanks Articles of Incorporation.

Internet Forms: Alabama Articles of Incorporation (Form SOSDF-1.PDF) and other statutory forms can be downloaded from the state website.

Articles Instructions

Article I: An Alabama corporate name must contain the word "corporation" or "incorporated," or an abbreviation of one of such words, or if a banking corporation the words "bank," "banking," or "bankers." [10-2B-4.01]

You must reserve your name with the state filing office before filing your articles. Name reservations cost $10 and are good for 120 days. Visit the state filing office website to search the corporate database for available names, or call the state filing office to ask whether your proposed corporate name is available. You can reserve an available name over the phone or by fax. After processing your request, the filing office will send you a Certificate of Name Reservation.

Article II: This article gives the corporation a perpetual duration, which is the standard practice. If you wish to limit the duration of your corporation, you can retype the articles and state a specific future date or period after which you want your corporation to dissolve.

Article III: State the purpose of your corporation. We recommend that you state the following general purpose: "the transaction of any or all lawful business for which corporations may be incorporated under the Alabama Business Corporation Act." This language allows your corporation to engage in as many types of business as your directors wish. If you want to limit the corporation's business to one or more specific businesses, insert your specific business purposes instead.

In Article IV, since Alabama law does not use the concept of par value, you only need to specify the number of shares you wish to authorize for later issuance to your shareholders. The filing fee is not based on how many shares you authorize, so you can authorize as many as you wish. The state-supplied form authorizes one class of common shares with equal voting, dividend, and liquidation rights. This is sufficient for most incorporators. If you wish to authorize one or more special classes of shares, you must prepare your own articles, stating the name of each class or series, the number of shares in each, and the rights and restrictions associated with each class or series.

Article VI: List the name and address of at least one initial director. This can be the same person who is listed as the incorporator (the person who signs the articles) in Article VII.

Submit an original plus two copies of signed articles and your name reservation certificate to the nearest county probate court judge (check local governmental telephone listings and call for address). The judge will record the original Articles of Incorporation and forward a copy with fees to the Secretary of State.

Filing Fee: $40, payable to the "Secretary of State," plus a separate check for $35 for the "Probate Court Judge," who receives and files the original articles (call the probate court to confirm the most current filing fee).

Director and Officer Rules

Only one director is required. [10-2B-8.02] Directors are elected annually to serve for one-year terms. [10-2B-8.03] The directors or the bylaws may designate and appoint the officers. The bylaws or the board of directors must delegate to an officer responsibility for preparing minutes of the directors' and shareholders' meetings and for authenticating records of the corporation. Unless the bylaws provide otherwise, the same individual may simultaneously hold more than one office in a corporation. [10-2B-8.40]

Share Issuance Rules

The board of directors may authorize shares to be issued for consideration consisting of money, labor done, or property actually received. [10-2B-6.21] Each share certificate must state on its face:

(1) the name of the issuing corporation and an assertion that it is organized under the law of Alabama

(2) the name of the person to whom the certificate is issued and

(3) the number and class of shares and the designation of the series, if any, the certificate represents.

Each share certificate: (1) must be signed (either manually or in facsimile) by two officers designated in the bylaws or by the board of directors, and (2) may bear the corporate seal or its facsimile. [10-2B-6.25]

Director Meeting Rules

Regular meetings of the board of directors may be held with or without notice as prescribed in the bylaws. Unless the Articles of Incorporation or bylaws provide for a longer or shorter period, special meetings of the board of directors must be preceded by at least two days' notice of the date, time, and place of the meeting. The notice need not describe the purpose of the special meeting unless required by the Articles of Incorporation or bylaws. [10-2B-8.22]

Unless the Articles of Incorporation or bylaws require a greater number, a quorum of a board of directors consists of: (1) a majority of the fixed number of directors if the corporation has a fixed board size, or (2) a majority of the fixed number of directors prescribed, or, if no number is prescribed, the number in office immediately before the meeting begins, if the corporation has a variable-range size board.

The Articles of Incorporation or bylaws may authorize a quorum of a board of directors to consist of no less than one-third of the fixed or prescribed number of directors.

If a quorum is present when a vote is taken, the affirmative vote of a majority of directors present is the act of the board of directors unless the Articles of Incorporation or bylaws require the vote of a greater number of directors. A director is, unless established to the contrary, presumed present for quorum purposes for the remainder of a meeting at which he or she has been present for any purpose. [10-2B-8.24]

Shareholder Meeting Rules

The corporation must hold a meeting of shareholders annually at a time stated or fixed in accordance with the bylaws. [10-2B-7.01]

The corporation must hold a special meeting of shareholders: (1) on call of its board of directors or the person or persons authorized to do so by the Articles of Incorporation or bylaws; or (2) if the holders of at least 10% of all the votes entitled to be cast on any issue proposed to be considered at the proposed special meeting sign, date, and deliver to the corporation's president or secretary one or more written demands for the meeting describing the purpose or purposes for which it is to be held, who shall, within 21 days of the receipt of such demand, cause notice to be given of the meeting to be held within the minimum time following the notice prescribed by Section 10-2B-7.05(a); or (3) on call of the holders of

at least 10% of the votes entitled to be cast at the proposed special meeting who signed a demand for a special meeting valid under Section 10-2B-7.02(a)(2), if: (i) notice of the special meeting was not given within 21 days after the date the demand was delivered to the corporation's president or secretary, or (ii) the special meeting was not held in accordance with the notice. Only business within the purpose or purposes described in the meeting notice may be conducted at a special shareholders' meeting. [10-2B-7.02]

The corporation, or, in the case of a special meeting called pursuant to Section 10-2B-7.02(a)(3), the persons calling the meeting, shall notify shareholders in writing of the date, time, and place of each annual and special shareholders' meeting no fewer than ten nor more than 60 days before the meeting date. Unless the Business Corporation Act or the Articles of Incorporation require otherwise, the corporation, or other persons calling the meeting, are required to give notice only to shareholders entitled to vote at the meeting. Notwithstanding the provisions of this section or any other provisions of the BCA, the stock or bonded indebtedness of a corporation shall not be increased at a meeting unless notice of such meeting shall have been given as may be required by Section 234 of the Constitution of Alabama of 1901 as the same may be amended from time to time. Unless the Business Corporation Act or the Articles of Incorporation require otherwise, notice of an annual meeting need not include a statement of the purpose or purposes for which the meeting is called. Notice of a special meeting must include a statement of the purpose or purposes for which the meeting is called. [10-2B-7.05]

The corporation shall prepare an alphabetical list of the names of all its shareholders who are entitled to notice of a shareholders' meeting. The list must be arranged by voting group (and within each voting group by class or series of shares) and show the address of and number of shares held by each shareholder. The shareholders' list must be available for inspection by any shareholder, beginning two business days after notice of the meeting is given for which the list was prepared and continuing through the meeting, at the corporation's principal office or, if the corporation's principal office is located outside the state of Alabama, at its registered office. A shareholder, the shareholder's agent or attorney, is entitled on written demand to inspect and, for a proper purpose, to copy the list, during regular business hours and at his or her expense, during the period it is available for inspection. The corporation shall make the shareholders' list available at the meeting, and any shareholder, the shareholder's agent or attorney, is entitled to inspect the list at any time during the meeting or any adjournment. [10-2B-7.20]

Unless otherwise provided in the Articles of Incorporation, directors are elected by a majority of the votes cast by the shares entitled to vote in the election at a meeting at which a quorum is present when the vote is taken. Shareholders do not have a right to cumulate their votes for directors unless the Articles of Incorporation so provide. [10-2B-7.28]

Shares entitled to vote as a separate voting group may take action on a matter at a meeting only if a quorum of those shares exists with respect to that matter. Unless the Articles of Incorporation or the Business Corporation Act provides otherwise, a majority of the votes entitled to be cast on the matter by the voting group constitutes a quorum of that voting group for action on that matter, but in no event shall a quorum consist of less than one-third of the votes entitled to be cast on the matter by the voting group. If a quorum is present when a vote is taken, action on a matter (other than the election of directors) by a voting group is approved if the votes cast within the voting group favoring the action exceed the votes cast opposing the action, unless the Constitution of Alabama of 1901 as the same may be amended from time to time, the Articles of Incorporation, or the Business Corporation Act requires a greater number of affirmative votes. [10-2B-7.25]

Financial Disclosure Rules

A corporation is required to mail annual financial statements to each shareholder within 120 days after the close of each fiscal year. [10-2B-16.20]

State Tax Information

Department of Revenue, Montgomery
334-242-1170
www.ador.state.al.us

Alabama assesses a business privilege tax, an annual tax on corporate shares based on net worth of the corporation. A state constitutional amendment has been proposed that would replace the shares tax with an annual corporate income tax (but, apparently, leave the business privilege tax in place).

Corporation Law Online

The Alabama Business Corporation Act is contained in Title 10, Chapter 2B, of the Alabama statutes. To find it, visit the legal research area of Nolo's website at www.nolo.com/statute/state.cfm. Click on "Alabama." From there, you can browse Title 10, Chapter 2B, of the statutes.

State Securities Information

Securities Commission
770 Washington Avenue
Suite 570
Montgomery, AL 36130-4700
334-242-2984 or 800-222-1253
http://asc.state.al.us

The Alabama Securities Act is contained in Title 8, Chapter 6, of the Alabama Statutes. You can find it by visiting the legal research area of Nolo's website at www.nolo.com/statute/state.cfm. Click on "Alabama." From there, choose Title 8.

Section 8-6-11 of the Act contains exemptions from registration. In particular, Section 8-6-11(9) contains an exemption for sales of securities to ten or fewer purchasers during any period of 12 consecutive months, subject to certain rules and restrictions. Call the Securities Commission for additional information on this and other available exemptions.

Creating Your Own Articles Form

You can create your own articles form.

ALASKA

Corporate Filing Office

Department of Commerce and Economic Development
Division of Banking, Securities and Corporations
Corporations Section
Box 110808
Juneau, AK 99811-0808
907-465-253
www.dced.state.ak.us/bsc/corps.htm

State Corporate Forms

Alaska provides fill-in-the-blanks Articles of Incorporation with instructions (Form 08-400). The state also offers an information booklet, "Establishing a Business in Alaska," that summarizes the requirements for organizing and operating an Alaska business, including a corporation. Be aware, however, that some of the information in the booklet may be outdated, particularly the discussions that compare the legal and tax characteristics of different types of business entities.

Internet Forms: You can download Alaska Articles and other corporate forms from the state website.

Articles Instructions

Article I: An Alaska corporate name must contain the word "corporation," "company," "incorporated," or "limited," or an abbreviation of one of these words. The corporate name may not contain the word "city," "borough," or "village," or otherwise imply that the corporation is a municipality. The name of a city, borough, or village may be used in the corporate name.

You can search for names already in use by visiting the state filing office website or by calling the state filing office. An available corporate name may be reserved for 120 days for $25. A proposed corporate name may be registered (kept on the rolls of the state filing office) by paying an annual fee of $25. Note that the Alaska statutes do not provide for the registration of fictitious or assumed business names.

Article II: This article states the purpose of your corporation. We recommend that you state the following general purpose: "the transaction of any lawful business allowed by the Alaska Corporation Code." This language allows your corporation to engage in as many types of business as your directors wish. If you want to limit the corporation's business to one or more specific activities, you can state your specific business purposes here instead.

Article III: Most incorporators simply state the number of shares they wish to authorize and leave the class, series, and par value items blank. This means your corporation will have common shares only, with equal dividend, liquidation, and voting rights and without special restrictions or a specified par value. Note that Alaska follows the modern trend of not designating shares as "par value" or "no par value" shares. If you have a special reason to specify a par value for your shares, insert the amount in the par value blank. And if you want to authorize a special class or series of shares, be sure to fill in the name of the class or series in the blanks and add additional language to your Articles that specifies the rights and restrictions associated with each class or series of shares.

Article V: In Article V, either you check the box that indicates that your corporation has no "alien affiliates," or you must provide their names and addresses. We assume you will not have any alien affiliates, and you that you will check the box. However, if you will have alien affiliates, provide the names and addresses in the table. The definitions of "alien" and "affiliate" are included in the Alaska Articles instructions available with the blank Articles form provided on the state corporate filing office website. Essentially, "alien" means a non-U.S. citizen or a person without permanent residence status. The term also includes legal entities such as corporations formed outside the U.S. or U.S. entities controlled by non-U.S. citizens. An "affiliate" includes corporate directors, officers, and shareholders and other persons or entities that control or are controlled by a corporate entity.

The Articles form provided by the state filing office contains a separate page for specifying the North American Industry Classification System (NAICS) Code Standard Industrial Code (SIC) that most clearly describes the initial activities of your corporation. The code number that best matches your corporation's activities can be obtained from the NAICS Code List included in the official instructions to the online Alaska articles form.

Filing Fee: $250 (includes $100 biennial license fee—due every two years), payable to the "State of Alaska."

Director and Officer Rules

Only one director is required. Directors are elected annually to serve for one-year terms. [10.06.453] A corporation shall have a president, a secretary, a treasurer, and other officers with titles and duties as stated in the bylaws of the corporation or determined by the board and as may be necessary to enable the corporation to sign instruments and share certificates. Any two or more offices may be held by the same person, except the offices of president and secretary. When all of the issued and out-standing stock of the corporation is owned by one person, the person may hold all or any combination of offices. [10.06.483]

Share Issuance Rules

Consideration for the issuance of shares may be paid, in whole or in part, in money; in other property, tangible or intangible; or in labor or services actually performed for the corporation. Unless otherwise provided in the articles of incorporation, when payment of the consideration for shares is received by the corporation, the shares are considered fully paid and nonassessable.

A promissory note or future service does not constitute payment or part payment for shares of a corporation. [10.06.338]

Share certificates must be signed by the president or vice president and the secretary or an assistant secretary of the corporation, and may be sealed with the seal of the corporation or a facsimile of the seal. [10.06.348] Each certificate representing shares shall state on its face (1) that the corporation is organized under the laws of the state; (2) the name of the person to whom issued; (3) the number and class of shares, and the designation of the series, if any, that the certificate represents. [10.06.350]

Director Meeting Rules

A majority of the number of directors fixed by the articles or bylaws of a corporation constitutes a quorum for the transaction of business unless a greater number is required by the articles or bylaws. The act of a majority of the directors present at a meeting at which a quorum is present is the act of the board, unless the act of a greater number is required by the articles or the bylaws. [10.06.473.]

A regular or special meeting of the board or a committee of the board may be called by the chairman of the board, the president, a vice president, the secretary, or a director and may be held at any place inside or outside the state of Alaska.

A regular meeting of the board or a committee designated by the board may be held without notice if the time and place of the meeting is fixed by the bylaws or the board. A special meeting of the board or a committee designated by the board shall be held as provided in the bylaws or, in the absence of bylaw provision, after either notice in writing sent ten days before the meeting or notice by electronic means, personal messenger, or comparable person-to-person communication given at least 72 hours before the meeting. Unless otherwise provided in

the bylaws, the notice of a special meeting shall include disclosure of the business to be transacted and the purpose of the meeting. [10.06.470]

Shareholder Meeting Rules

An annual meeting of the shareholders shall be held at the time as provided in the bylaws. If the annual meeting is not held within any 13-month period, the superior court may on the application of a shareholder summarily order a meeting to be held.

Special meetings of the shareholders may be called by the board, the chairman of the board, the president, the holders of not less than one-tenth of all the shares entitled to vote at the meeting, or other persons as may be authorized in the Articles of Incorporation or the bylaws. [10.06.405]

Written or printed notice of a meeting of shareholders stating the place, day, and hour of the meeting and, in the case of a special meeting, the purpose for which the meeting is called, shall be delivered not less than 20 or more than 60 days before the date of the meeting, either personally or by mail, by or at the direction of the president, the secretary, the officer, or the persons calling the meeting, to each shareholder of record entitled to vote at the meeting. [10.06.410]

Unless otherwise provided in the Articles of Incorporation, a majority of the shares entitled to vote, represented in person or by proxy, constitutes a quorum at a meeting of shareholders, but in no event may a quorum consist of less than one-third of the shares entitled to vote at the meeting. If a quorum is present, the affirmative vote of the majority of shares represented at the meeting and entitled to vote on the subject matter is the act of the shareholders, unless the vote of a greater number or voting by classes is required by the Business Corporation Act, the Articles of Incorporation, or the bylaws. [10.06.415]

Unless the Articles of Incorporation provide otherwise, at an election for directors each shareholder entitled to vote at the election may vote, in person or by proxy, the number of shares owned by the shareholder for as many persons as there are directors to be elected and for whose election the shareholder has a right to vote, or to cumulate votes by giving one candidate votes equal to the number of directors multiplied by the number of shares of the shareholder, or by distributing votes on the same principle among any number of candidates. [10.06.420(d)]

The board shall send an annual report to the shareholders not later than 180 days after the close of the fiscal year or the date on which notice of the annual meeting in the next fiscal year is sent under AS 10.06.410, whichever is first. A corporation with less than 100 holders of record of its shares, as determined under AS 10.06.408, is exempt from this annual requirement unless its articles or bylaws impose the requirement. [10.06.433]

Financial Disclosure Rules

A shareholder or shareholders holding at least 5% of the outstanding shares of a class of a corporation may make a written request to the corporation for an income statement of the corporation for the three-month, six-month, or nine-month period of the current fiscal year ended more than 30 days before the date of the request and a balance sheet of the corporation as of the end of the period and, in addition, if an annual report for the last fiscal year has not been sent to shareholders, the statements required by (a) of this section [requires corporations to send out annual financial statements if the corporation has 100 or more shareholders for the last fiscal year]. The statement shall be delivered or mailed to the person making the request within 30 days of the request. A copy of the statements shall be kept on file in the principal office of the corporation for 12 months and shall be exhibited at all reasonable times to a shareholder demanding an examination of the statements, or a copy of the statements shall be mailed to that shareholder. [10.06.433]

State Tax Information

Department of Revenue
Juneau 907-465-5887
Fairbanks 907-451-2830
Anchorage 907-269-6900.
www.revenue.state.ak.us

Alaska imposes a corporate income tax similar to the federal corporate income tax, based on graduated tax rates.

Corporation Law Online

The Alaska Business Corporation Act is contained in Title 10, Chapter 10.06, of the Alaska statutes, starting at Section 10.06.005. To find the Act, visit the legal research area of Nolo's website at www.nolo.com/statute/state.cfm. Click on "Alaska." From there, choose "Current Alaska Statutes." You will then be able to browse Title 10, Chapter 10.06.

State Securities Information

Alaska Department of Community and Economic Development
Division of Banking, Securities, and Corporations
P.O. Box 110807
Juneau, AK 99811-0807
907-465-2521
www.dced.state.ak.us/bsc/secur.htm

The Alaska Securities Act is contained in Title 45, Chapter 55, of the Alaska Statutes. You can browse the Act from a link to the Alaska statutes provided on the DBSC website. The Act contains four exemptions that allow small businesses to privately place their securities without registering them. Two of the exemptions are self-executing and do not require a filing, while the other two require you to file a notice with the DBSC prior to the sale and pay a $50 fee. See the DBSC website for more information.

Creating Your Own Articles Form

You can create your own articles form.

ARIZONA

Corporate Filing Office

Arizona Corporation Commission
Corporation Filing Section
1300 West Washington
Phoenix, AZ 85007-2929
800-345-5819 (in AZ only) or 602-542-3135
Tucson Branch Office: 520-628-6560 (accepts corporate filings)

www.cc.state.az.us/corp/index.htm

State Corporate Forms

Arizona provides fill-in-the-blanks Articles of Incorporation (CF0042), and a Cover Sheet (CFCVLR), which must be completed and included with the articles. A Certificate of Disclosure for Business Corporations (CF0022) is also provided, which must be signed by the incorporator and submitted with the articles. The Certificate of Disclosure asks for information regarding criminal convictions or civil fraud actions instituted against any of the corporation's founders, and about prior corporate bankruptcies, as well as the fiscal year end of the corporation.

Internet Forms: The latest Arizona corporate Articles of Incorporation with instructions, plus other Arizona corporate forms (Cover Sheet for Articles, Certificate of Disclosure, Application for Reservation of Name, and others) can be downloaded from the state filing office website. You can also download general instructions for forming an Arizona corporation.

Articles Instructions

Article 1: An Arizona corporate name must contain the word "corporation," "association," "company," "limited," or "incorporated," or an abbreviation of one of these words, or words or abbreviations of like import in another language. It cannot include the words "bank," "deposit," "trust," or "trust company" separately or in combination to indicate or convey the idea that the corporation is engaged in banking or trust business unless the corporation is to be and becomes actively and substantially engaged in the banking or trust business or the corporation is a holding company holding substantial interest in companies actively and substantially engaged in the banking or trust business. [10-401]

You can search for available corporate names online at the state filing office website. Due to budge constraints and increased filing activity, the state filing office no longer responds to name availability requests over the phone. An available corporate name may be reserved for 120 days for $10.

Article 2: Provide a specific statement of the type of business the corporations intends to pursue (for example, "retail sales" or "automotive repair)"

Article 3: Arizona law does not use the concept of par value, so you only need to specify the number of shares you wish to authorize for later issuance to your shareholders. The filing fee is not based on how many shares you authorize, so you can authorize as many as you wish. If you wish to authorize one or more special classes of shares, you must prepare your own your articles, stating the name of each class or series, the number of shares in each, and the rights and restrictions associated with each class or series.

Article 6: This article lists the names and addresses and number of the corporation's initial directors, who will serve on the board until the election or reelection of the board at the first annual meeting of shareholders. In Arizona, your corporation must have at least one director.

Articles 8 & 9: Article 8 requires indemnification (reimbursement) of legal expenses incurred by corporate directors, officers and agents in their official corporate capacities to the fullest extent permitted by law. Article 9 gives directors protection against personal liability in lawsuits brought by or in the name of the corporation (shareholder derivative lawsuits) to the maximum extent permitted by law.

File the original and one copy of your articles. Be sure to include a completed Cover Sheet and Certificate of Disclosure for Business Corporations form, signed by the same person who signs and files your articles. Note that if, within 60 days of filing the disclosure, you appoint a director or officer, or issue shares to a shareholder who already owns at least 10% of the corporation, and this person was not included on the initial disclosure form, you are required to submit a new disclosure form marked "amended."

Filing Fee: $60, payable to the "Arizona Corporation Commission."

Postfiling Formalities: Within 60 days after filing the articles, you must publish a copy of your file-stamped Articles of Incorporation in a newspaper of general circulation in the county of the corporation's place of business in Arizona. The publication must be made three consecutive times. Within 90 days after filing, an affidavit of publication must be filed with the state filing office. The newspaper should be able to prepare and file this affidavit as part of its publication service. A list of approved newspapers of general circulation can be viewed from the state filing office website.

Director and Officer Rules

A board of directors shall consist of one or more individuals, with the number specified in or fixed in accordance with the articles of incorporation or bylaws. Directors shall be elected at the first annual shareholders' meeting and at each annual meeting thereafter unless their terms are staggered under section 10-806. [10-803]

The terms of the initial directors of a corporation expire at the first shareholders' meeting at which directors are elected. The terms of all other directors expire at the annual shareholders' meeting following their election except in the case of directors whose terms are staggered under section 10-806. [10-805]

A corporation shall have the officers described in its bylaws or appointed by the board of directors in accordance with the bylaws. The bylaws or the board of directors must delegate to one of the officers responsibility for preparing minutes of the directors' and shareholders' meetings and for authenticating records of the corporation. The same individual may simultaneously hold more than one office in a corporation. [10-840]

Share Issuance Rules

The board of directors may authorize shares to be issued for consideration consisting of any tangible or intangible property or benefit to the corporation including cash, services performed, or other securities of the corporation, except that neither promissory notes nor future services constitute valid consideration. [10-621]

Each share certificate shall state on its face all of the following: 1) the name of the issuing corporation and that it is organized under the laws of this state; 2) the name of the person to whom issued; 3) the number and class of shares and the designation of the series, if any, the certificate represents. Each share certificate shall be signed either manually or in facsimile by one or more officers designated in the bylaws or by the board of directors, and may bear the corporate seal or its facsimile. [10-625]

Director Meeting Rules

Unless the Articles of Incorporation or bylaws provide otherwise, regular meetings of the board of directors may be held without notice of the date, time, place or purpose of the meeting.

Unless the Articles of Incorporation or bylaws provide otherwise, special meetings of the board of directors shall be preceded by at least two days' notice of the date, time, and place of the meeting. The notice need not describe the purpose of the special meeting unless required by the Articles of Incorporation or bylaws. [10-822]

Unless the Articles of Incorporation or bylaws require a different number, a quorum of board of directors consists of either:

- a majority of the fixed number of directors if the corporation has a fixed board size, or

- a majority of the number of directors prescribed, or if no number is prescribed, the number in office immediately before the meeting begins, if the corporation has a variable-range size board.

The Articles of Incorporation or bylaws may authorize a quorum of a board of directors to consist of at least one-third of the fixed or prescribed number of directors determined under Subsection A [above].

If a quorum is present when a vote is taken, the affirmative vote of a majority of directors present is the act of the board of directors unless the Articles of Incorporation or bylaws require the vote of a greater number of directors. [10-824]

Shareholder Meeting Rules

A corporation shall hold a meeting of shareholders annually at a time stated in or fixed in accordance with the bylaws. [10-701]

Except as provided in Section 10-2703 [corporate takeovers], a corporation shall hold a special meeting of shareholders either:

- on the call of its board of directors or the person or persons authorized to do so by the Articles of Incorporation or bylaws, or

- as provided in Section 10-810, Subsection D [filling vacancies on the board].

Only business within the purpose or purposes described in the meeting notice may be conducted at a special shareholders' meeting. [10-702]

A corporation shall notify shareholders of the date, time, and place of each annual and special shareholders' meeting at least ten but not more than 60 days before the meeting date. Unless Chapters 1 through 17 of the Business Corporation Act or the Articles of Incorporation require otherwise, the corporation is required to give notice only to shareholders entitled to vote at the meeting.

Unless Chapters 1 through 17 of the Business Corporation Act or the Articles of Incorporation require otherwise, notice of an annual meeting need not include a description of the purpose or purposes for which the meeting is called. [10-705]

Shares entitled to vote as a separate voting group may take action on a matter at a meeting only if the quorum of those shares exists with respect to that matter. Unless the Articles of Incorporation or Chapters 1 through 17 of the Business Corporation Act provide otherwise, a majority of the votes entitled to be cast on the matter by the voting group constitutes a quorum of that voting group for action on that matter.

If a quorum exists, action on a matter, other than the election of directors, by a voting group is approved if the votes cast within the voting group favoring the action exceed the votes cast opposing the action, unless the Articles of Incorporation or Chapters 1 through 17 of the Business Corporation Act require a greater number of affirmative votes.

The election of directors is governed by Section 10-728 of the Business Corporation Act. [10-725]

Unless otherwise provided in the Articles of Incorporation, directors are elected by a plurality of the votes cast by the shares entitled to vote in the election at a meeting at which a quorum is present.

At each election for directors, shareholders are entitled to cumulate their votes by multiplying the number of votes they are entitled to cast by the number of directors for whom they are entitled to vote and casting the product for a single candidate or distributing the product among two or more candidates. [10-728]

Financial Disclosure Rules

A corporation shall mail or transmit annual financial statements to each shareholder within 120 days after the close of each fiscal year. On written request from a shareholder the corporation shall mail or transmit that shareholder the latest annual financial statements. [10-1620]

State Tax Information

Department of Revenue, Phoenix
602-542-2076
www.revenue.state.az.us

Arizona imposes a corporate income tax, which is based on the corporation's federal taxable income.

Corporation Law Online

The Arizona Business Corporation Act is contained in Title 10 of the Arizona Statutes, starting with Article 4, Section 10-140. To find it, go to the legal research area of Nolo's website at www.nolo.com/statute/state/cfm. Click on "Arizona." Choose "Click here to view statutes organized by title." You can then browse Title 10, starting with Article 4.

State Securities Information

Securities Division
Arizona Corporation Commission
1300 W. Washington - Third Floor
Phoenix, AZ 85007
602-542-4242
www.ccsd.cc.state.az.us

The Arizona Securities Act is contained in Title 44, Chapter 12, of the Arizona statutes. You can browse the Act from a link provided on the Securities Division website. The Act includes exemptions from registration of securities for sales to ten or fewer individuals for $100,000 or less, nonpublic offerings to 35 or fewer individuals, and private offerings and sales to accredited investors. Note that filing for an exemption may require you to pay a fee. The Securities Act and related securities rules are contained in the *Securities Rules Handbook*, which you can order from the website.

Creating Your Own Articles Form

You can create your own articles form.

ARKANSAS

Corporate Filing Office

Arkansas Secretary of State
Corporations Division
State Capitol
Little Rock, AR 72201-1094
Telephone: 501-682-3409
www.sosweb.state.ar.us/corp_ucc.html

State Corporate Forms

Arkansas provides Articles of Incorporation (Form DN-01) with instructions (also see the Cover Letter from the Secretary of State, which contains additional corporate start-up contact information). In addition, the state provides a simple one-page Franchise Tax Registration form (Form FT-11) that you must complete and file with your articles.

Internet Forms: The latest Articles of Incorporation with instructions (Form DN-01), the Cover Letter from Secretary of State, and other Arkansas statutory forms (including the Application for Reservation of Corporate Name) can be downloaded from the state corporate filing office website.

Articles Instructions

First Article: An Arkansas corporate name must contain the word "corporation," "incorporated," "company," or "limited," or the abbreviation "corp.," "inc.," "co.," or "ltd.," or words or abbreviations of like import in another language. Call the state filing office to check name availability. You can reserve an Arkansas corporate name for 120 days for $25.

Second Article: Arkansas still uses the concept of par value. You must insert the total number of authorized shares and the par value per share in the first two blanks of this article. You can insert the par value of your shares in the designated blank—for example, $0.01 per share—or you can state that your shares are "without par value." (See the note below for information about how to compute the franchise tax, which is based on the stated value of your authorized shares.)

The second part of this article contains four columns for describing in more detail the type of shares you are issuing. The total number of all shares listed in this part should equal the total number of shares indicated in the very first blank of the article. If, like most incorporators, you wish to authorize only common shares that have equal voting, dividend, and liquidation rights and no spe-

cial restrictions, simply repeat the total number of shares in the leftmost column of the second part, leave the class and series columns blank, then repeat the par value or the fact that your shares are "without par value" in the rightmost column. If you want to authorize separate classes or series of shares with special rights or restrictions, you should insert the name of each class or series, the number of shares in each class or series, and whether or not they have a par value. Again, the total number of all classes and series should equal the number given in the first blank of the article. You must also add language to your articles that specifies the rights and restrictions associated with each class or series of shares; a lawyer can help you draft these provisions.

Note: Each year you must pay an annual state tax based on the total number of shares currently authorized in your Articles. The fee equals .0027 times the stated par value of all of your authorized shares. Shares without par value are valued at $25 per share for purposes of this tax. Currently, there is a minimum franchise tax payment of $50. And there is a maximum number of shares you can authorize in your articles for the minimum $50 franchise tax: approximately 740 shares without par value (740 x $25 = $18,500; $18,500 x .0027 = $49.95) or approximately 1,850,000 shares with a stated par value of $.01 (1,850,000 x $.01 = 18,500 x .0027 = $49.95). Adjust the numbers accordingly for different par values. For example, authorizing 18,500 shares with a stated par value of $1 yields the same $49.95 tax (18,500 x $1 = $18,500 x .0027 = $49.95), which means you still pay the minimum $50 franchise tax.

Fifth Article: Insert a short description of the primary business purpose of your corporation. This statement is provided for informational purposes only, and it does not limit the business or activities of your corporation.

Submit the original articles for filing. Remember to include a completed Corporate Franchise Tax Registration form (FT-11) with your articles. This form simply asks for the name of the corporation and the name, address, and telephone number of a contact person. The state Revenue Division uses this information to generate and mail future corporate franchise tax report forms to your corporation. (If you don't provide this contact information, future report forms will be mailed to the registered agent named in your articles.) After your articles are approved, the state filing office will mail a file-stamped copy of the articles to your incorporator.

Filing Fee: $50 fee, payable to the "Arkansas Secretary of State." The fee is reduced to $45 if you prepare and file the online Articles form provided on the state filing office website.

Online Filing: Arkansas provides an online Corporate Articles preparation and filing service. If you wish to use this form instead of preparing and filing paper articles, go to the state corporate filing office website, select Domestic Corporations, Articles of Incorporation, Form DN-01, then click the mouse icon to go to the online form preparation and filing page. Online form preparation and filing takes just a few minutes.

Director and Officer Rules

Except as provided in Subsection C of this section, each corporation must have a board of directors.

All corporate powers shall be exercised by or under the authority of, and the business and affairs of the corporation managed under the direction of, its board of directors, subject to any limitation set forth in the Articles of Incorporation.

A corporation having fifty (50) or fewer shareholders may dispense with or limit the authority of a board of directors by describing in its Articles of Incorporation who will perform some or all of the duties of a board of directors. [4-27-801]

A board of directors must consist of one (1) or more individuals, with the number specified in or fixed in accordance with the Articles of Incorporation or bylaws.

Directors are elected at the first annual shareholders' meeting and at each annual meeting thereafter unless their terms are staggered under § 4-27-806. [4-27-803]

The terms of the initial directors of a corporation expire at the first shareholders' meeting at which directors are elected.

The terms of all other directors expire at the next annual shareholders' meeting following their election unless their terms are staggered under § 4-27-806. [4-27-805]

A corporation has the officers described in its bylaws or appointed by the board of directors in accordance with the bylaws.

A duly appointed officer may appoint one (1) or more officers or assistant officers if authorized by the bylaws or the board of directors.

The bylaws or the board of directors shall delegate to one (1) of the officers responsibility for preparing minutes of the directors' and shareholders' meetings and for authenticating records of the corporation.

The same individual may simultaneously hold more than one (1) office in a corporation. [4-27-840]

Share Issuance Rules

Arkansas still uses the concept of par value in its Business Corporation Act. The Articles of Incorporation must prescribe the classes of shares, the number of shares of each class that the corporation is authorized to issue, and a statement of the par value of the shares of each class or a statement that the shares of a class are to be without par value. If more than one (1) class of shares is authorized, the Articles of Incorporation must prescribe a distinguishing designation for each class, and, prior to the issuance of shares of a class, the preferences, limitations, and relative rights of that class must be described in the Articles of Incorporation. All shares of a class must have preferences, limitations, and relative rights identical with those of other shares of the same class except to the extent otherwise permitted by § 4-27-602.

The Articles of Incorporation must authorize: (1) one (1) or more classes of shares that together have unlimited voting rights; and (2) one (1) or more classes of shares (which may be the same class or classes as those with voting rights) that together are entitled to receive the net assets of the corporation on dissolution. [4-27-601]

The board of directors may authorize shares to be issued for consideration consisting of money paid, labor done, or property actually received. Neither promissory notes nor the promise of future services shall constitute valid consideration for the issuance of shares.

Shares having a par value may not be issued for consideration less than the par value of such shares. [4-27-621]

At a minimum each share certificate must state on its face: 1 the name of the issuing corporation and that it is organized under the law of this state; 2 the name of the person to whom issued; 3 the number and class of shares and the designation of the series, if any, the certificate represents; and 4 the par value of the shares, or if the shares have no par value, a statement of such fact.

Each share certificate: (1) must be signed (either manually or in facsimile) by two (2) officers designated in the bylaws or by the board of directors, and (2) must bear the corporate seal or its facsimile. [4-27-625]

Director Meeting Rules

Unless the Articles of Incorporation or bylaws provide otherwise, regular meetings of the board of directors may be held without notice of the date, time, place, or purpose of the meeting.

Unless the Articles of Incorporation or bylaws provide for a longer or shorter period, a special meeting of the board of directors must be preceded by at least two days' notice of the date, time, and place of the meeting. The notice need not describe the purpose of the special meeting unless required by the Articles of Incorporation or bylaws. [4-27-822]

Unless the Articles of Incorporation or bylaws require a greater number, a quorum of a board of directors consists of: (1) a majority of the fixed number of directors if the corporation has a fixed board size; or (2) a majority of the number of directors prescribed, or if no number is prescribed, the number in office immediately before the meeting begins, if the corporation has a variable-range size board.

The Articles of Incorporation or bylaws may authorize a quorum of a board of directors to consist of no fewer than one-third of the fixed or prescribed number of directors determined under Subsection A of this section [quoted in the previous paragraph].

If a quorum is present when a vote is taken, the affirmative vote of a majority of directors present is the act of the board of directors unless the Articles of Incorporation or bylaws require the vote of a greater number of directors. [4-27-824]

Shareholder Meeting Rules

A corporation shall hold a meeting of shareholders annually at a time stated in or fixed in accordance with the bylaws.

Annual shareholders' meetings may be held in or out of the state of Arkansas at the place stated in or fixed in accordance with the bylaws. If no place is stated in or fixed in accordance with the bylaws, annual meetings shall be held at the corporation's principal office. [4-27-701]

A corporation shall hold a special meeting of shareholders: (1) on call of its board of directors or the person or persons authorized to do so by the Articles of Incorporation or bylaws; or (2) if the holders of at least 10% of all the votes entitled to be cast on any issue proposed to be considered at the proposed special meeting sign, date, and deliver to the corporation's secretary one or more written demands for the meeting describing the purpose or purposes for which it is to be held.

Only business within the purpose or purposes described in the meeting notice may be conducted at a special shareholders' meeting. [4-27-702]

A corporation shall notify shareholders of the date, time, and place of each annual and special shareholders' meeting no fewer than 60 nor more than 75 days before

the meeting date if a proposal to increase the authorized capital stock or bond indebtedness of the corporation is to be submitted, and no fewer than ten nor more than 60 days before the meeting date in all other cases. Unless the Business Corporation Act or the Articles of Incorporation require otherwise, the corporation is required to give notice only to shareholders entitled to vote at the meeting.

Unless the Business Corporation Act or the Articles of Incorporation require otherwise, notice of an annual meeting need not include a description of the purpose or purposes for which the meeting is called.

Notice of a special meeting must include a description of the purpose or purposes for which the meeting is called. For purposes of this section, an annual meeting at which a proposal to increase the authorized capital stock or bond indebtedness of the corporation is to be submitted shall be deemed a special meeting. [4-27-705]

Shares entitled to vote as a separate voting group may take action on a matter at a meeting only if a quorum of those shares exists with respect to that matter. Unless the Articles of Incorporation or the Business Corporation Act provides otherwise, a majority of the votes entitled to be cast on the matter by the voting group constitutes a quorum of that voting group for action on that matter.

If a quorum exists, action on a matter (other than the election of directors) by a voting group is approved if the votes cast within the voting group favoring the action exceed the votes cast opposing the action, unless the Articles of Incorporation or the Business Corporation Act requires a greater number of affirmative votes. [4-27-705]

Unless otherwise provided in the Articles of Incorporation, directors are elected by a plurality of the votes cast by the shares entitled to vote in the election at a meeting at which a quorum is present.

Shareholders do not have a right to cumulate their votes for directors unless the Articles of Incorporation so provide.

A statement included in the Articles of Incorporation that "[all] [a designated voting group of] shareholders are entitled to cumulate their votes for directors" (or words of similar import) means that the shareholders designated are entitled to multiply the number of votes they are entitled to cast by the number of directors for whom they are entitled to vote and cast the product for a single candidate or distribute the product among two or more candidates.

Shares otherwise entitled to vote cumulatively may not be voted cumulatively at a particular meeting unless: (1) the meeting notice or proxy statement accompanying the notice states conspicuously that cumulative voting is authorized; or (2) a shareholder who has the right to cumulate his votes gives notice to the corporation not less than 48 hours before the time set for the meeting of his intent to cumulate his votes during the meeting, and if one shareholder gives this notice all other shareholders in the same voting group participating in the election are entitled to cumulate their votes without giving further notice. [4-27-728]

Financial Disclosure Rules

A corporation shall furnish its shareholders with annual financial statements, which may be consolidated or combined statements of the corporation and one or more of its subsidiaries, as appropriate, that include a balance sheet as of the end of the fiscal year, an income statement for that year, and a statement of changes in shareholders' equity for the year unless that information appears elsewhere in the financial statements. If financial statements are prepared for the corporation on the basis of generally accepted accounting principles, the annual financial statements must also be prepared on that basis.

If the annual financial statements are reported on by a public accountant, his report must accompany them. If not, the statements must be accompanied by a statement of the president or the person responsible for the corporation's accounting records: (1) stating his reasonable belief whether the statements were prepared on the basis of generally accepted accounting principles and, if not, describing the basis of preparation; and (2) describing any respects in which the statements were not prepared on a basis of accounting consistent with the statements prepared for the preceding year.

A corporation shall mail the annual financial statements to each shareholder within 120 days after the close of each fiscal year. Thereafter, on written request from a shareholder who was not mailed the statements, the corporation shall mail him the latest financial statements. [4-27-1620]

State Tax Information

Department of Finance & Administration, Revenue Division, Little Rock
501-682-4775
www.ark.org/dfa

Arkansas imposes a corporate income tax. Note that an Arkansas corporation must also pay an annual franchise tax based on the number of shares authorized in its Articles to the secretary of State, Corporations Division.

Corporation Law Online

The Arkansas Business Corporation Act is located in Title 4 (Business and Commercial Law), Subtitle 3 (Corporations and Associations), Chapter 27, of the Arkansas Code, starting with Section 4-27-101. You can find the Act in the legal research area of Nolo's website at www.nolo.com/statute/state/cfm. Click on "Arkansas." Click through until you reach the Code's home page and then, under "Contents," click on the file "arcode." This will allow you to browse Title 4, Subtitle 3, Chapter 27.

State Securities Information

Arkansas Securities Department
Heritage West Building
Suite 300
201 E. Markham
Little Rock, AR 72201
501-324-9260
www.state.ar.us/arsec

The Arkansas Securities Act is contained in Title 23, Chapter 42, of the Arkansas Code. You can browse the Act from the Securities Department website by clicking "Acts" under Legal Issues, then choosing "Securities Act." Section 23-42-504(9) of the Arkansas Securities Act contains an exemption for sales to 35 or fewer investors provided certain requirements are met and a notice form is filed with the State Securities Commissioner. Other exemptions for securities and securities transactions are contained in the Act, including a small business offering exemption under 23-42-503(b), which requires the filing of a notice form signed by an attorney. Visit the Securities Department website for further information.

Creating Your Own Articles Form

You can create your own articles form.

CALIFORNIA

Corporate Filing Office

California Secretary of State
Corporations Unit
1500 11th Street
Sacramento, CA 95814
Telephone: 916-657-5448

www.ss.ca.gov/business/business.htm

Branch offices of the Secretary of State are located in Fresno, Los Angeles, San Diego, and San Francisco. Corporate forms may be filed in person at a branch office for an additional handling fee

State Corporate Forms

California provides a sample Articles of Incorporation form with instructions, plus other statutory forms.

Note for professionals: Certain licensed professionals, such as doctors and other licensed health care professionals, lawyers, accountants, and others must incorporate as professional corporations. To form a professional corporation, you must use a special articles form (you can download, sample professional corporation articles from the state filing office website). Contact your state licensing board to see if you have to form a professional corporation.

Internet Forms: You can download a sample articles form from the state filing office website. You must retype this form before filling it in—it has the word "Sample" printed across it and has printed instructions inserted in its blanks.

Articles Instructions

Article I: Insert the proposed name of your corporation. This name must be available for your use or reserved for your use prior to filing your Articles. The name of a California corporation may, but is not required to, contain a corporate designator such as "incorporated," "corporation," or "limited," or an abbreviation of one of these designators. If the name of the corporation is the name of an individual, a corporate designator must be added—for example, John Smythe, Inc. The name may not include the words "bank," "trust," or "trustee."

You can check name availability by sending a letter to the Sacramento filing office; the office will check up to three names for free. (You cannot check name availability by phone unless you set up a prepaid account.) The best way to check name availability and secure a name at the same time is to reserve the name by letter sent to the Sacramento or to go in person to any office of the Secretary of State. If you reserve your name by letter, list up to three proposed names in order of preference. You can reserve an available corporate name for 60 days for a $10 fee (the fee is $20 if you reserve a name in person at an office of the Secretary of State). Letters you can use to check name availability and reserve a corporate name are available online at the state filing office website.

Note that you can search the names of corporations, LLCs, and limited partnerships already registered with the Secretary of State by visiting the state filing office website (other types of entities are not in this name database). If your search turns up an active company that has a name similar to the one you want, you can still ask Secretary of State to check name availability for you. In this way, you can find out whether the Secretary believes the name is too similar, under the office's name regulations, to allow you to use your proposed name.

Article III: Insert the name and address of your corporation's initial agent for service of process. The agent is the person you designate to receive legal papers on behalf of your corporation. The person named as agent must be a California resident. Typically, one of the initial directors or officers of the corporation serves as initial agent. You can show the business or residence address of the agent, but be sure to use a California street address, not a P.O. Box.

Article IV: State the number of shares you wish to authorize for later issuance to your shareholders. The standard articles form creates only one class of common shares with equal dividend, liquidation, and voting rights and no special restrictions. You should authorize sufficient shares to cover your initial stock issuance plus additional shares to cover other foreseeable stock issuances (stock options, bonuses to employees, and the like). Note that if you decide to change the standard language to authorize one or more special classes or series of shares, you must specify the name of the class or series in your articles and summarize the rights and restrictions associated with each class or series of shares.

Any person may act as your incorporator by signing the articles; this person need not be a director, officer, or shareholder of your corporation. If you have previously reserved a corporate name, the person who reserved your corporate name should act as incorporator.

Mail the original Articles of Incorporation and two copies to the state filing office in Sacramento, to the attention of the Document Filing Support Unit. Include a check for the filing fee and a stamped, self-addressed envelope. To expedite processing, also include a short cover letter showing the proposed name of your corporation and the name, address, and telephone number of your incorporator, and if you reserved your corporate name, the number or date of the reservation certificate that you received from the Secretary of State. After your articles are approved, you will receive two file-stamped, certified copies from the filing office.

Filing Fee: $100, payable to the "Secretary of State."

It may take up to four weeks for your articles to be processed and filed by mail. You can file articles in person at any office of the Secretary of State for an additional $15. If you file in person at a branch office, submit two signed originals of your articles. Branch offices do not accept mailed filings.

Director and Officer Rules

A California corporation must have three directors with the following exceptions: (1) if the corporation has just two shareholders, it may have as few as two directors; and (2) if the corporation has just one shareholder, it may have just one director. [212]

Directors serve for one-year terms, until the next annual meeting of shareholders. [301]

A corporation must have a chairman of the board or a president or both, a secretary, a chief financial officer, and such other officers with such titles and duties as shall be stated in the bylaws or determined by the board and as may be necessary to enable it to sign instruments and share certificates. The president, or if there is no president the chairman of the board, is the general manager and chief executive officer of the corporation, unless otherwise provided in the articles or bylaws. Any number of offices may be held by the same person unless the articles or bylaws provide otherwise. [312]

Share Issuance Rules

Shares may be issued for consideration consisting of any or all of the following: money paid, labor done, services actually rendered to the corporation or for its benefit or in its formation or reorganization, debts or securities canceled, and tangible or intangible property actually received either by the issuing corporation or by a wholly owned subsidiary; but neither promissory notes of the purchaser (unless adequately secured by collateral other than the shares acquired or unless permitted by Section 408, which covers stock option or purchase plans) nor future services shall constitute payment or part payment for shares of the corporation. [409]

Every holder of shares in a corporation shall be entitled to have a certificate signed in the name of the corporation by the chairman or vice chairman of the board or the president or a vice president and by the chief financial officer or an assistant treasurer or the secretary or any assistant secretary, certifying the number of shares and the class or series of shares owned by the shareholder. [416]

Director Meeting Rules

Unless otherwise provided in the Articles or in the bylaws: (1) meetings of the board may be called by the chair of the board or the president or any vice president or the secretary or any two directors; (2) special meetings of the board shall be held on four days' notice by mail or 48 hours' notice; (3) the articles or bylaws may not dispense with notice of a special meeting; (4) a notice need not specify the purpose of any regular or special meeting of the board; (5) a majority of the authorized number of directors constitutes a quorum of the board for the transaction of business; (6) the Articles or bylaws may not provide that a quorum shall be less than one-third the authorized number of directors or less than two, whichever is larger, unless the authorized number of directors is one, in which case one director constitutes a quorum; (7) an act or decision done or made by a majority of the directors present at a meeting duly held at which a quorum is present is the act of the board, subject to the provisions of Section 310 [covering board decisions that personally benefit a director] and Subdivision (e) of Section 317 [covering the approval of indemnification of corporate directors and officers]; and (8) the articles or bylaws may not provide that a lesser vote than a majority of the directors present at a meeting is the act of the board. [307]

Shareholder Meeting Rules

An annual meeting of shareholders shall be held for the election of directors on a date and at a time stated in or fixed in accordance with the bylaws. Any other proper business may be transacted at the annual meeting. Special meetings of the shareholders may be called by the board, the chairman of the board, the president, or the holders of shares entitled to cast not less than 10% of the votes at the meeting or such additional persons as may be provided in the articles or bylaws.

Whenever shareholders are required or permitted to take any action at a meeting a written notice of the meeting shall be given not less than ten (or, if sent by third-class mail, 30) nor more than 60 days before the date of the meeting to each shareholder entitled to vote. The notice shall state the place, date, and hour of the meeting and (1) in the case of a special meeting, the general nature of the business to be transacted, and no other business may be transacted, or (2) in the case of the annual meeting, those matters which the board, at the time of the mailing of the notice, intends to present for action by the shareholders, but subject to the provisions of Subdivision (f) of this section [covering special votes by shareholders to approve indemnification, amendments to articles, and other major changes to the corporate structure] of this section any proper matter may be presented at the meeting for such action. The notice of any meeting at which directors are to be elected shall include the names of nominees intended at the time of the notice to be presented by the board for election. [601]

Unless otherwise provided in the articles, a majority of the shares entitled to vote, represented in person or by proxy, constitutes a quorum at a meeting of the shareholders, but in no event shall a quorum consist of less than one-third of the shares entitled to vote at the meeting or of more than a majority of the shares entitled to vote at the meeting. Except as provided in Subdivision (b) of this section [covering shareholder voting at a meeting when so many shareholders leave the meeting that a quorum is lost], the affirmative vote of a majority of the shares represented and voting at a duly held meeting at which a quorum is present (which shares voting affirmatively also constitute at least a majority of the required quorum) is the act of the shareholders, unless the vote of a greater number or voting by classes is required by this division or the articles. [602]

Except as provided in Section 301.5 [applicable to corporations listed on national securities exchanges], every shareholder complying with Subdivision (b) [quoted in the next paragraph] and entitled to vote at any election of directors may cumulate such shareholder's votes and give one candidate a number of votes equal to the number of directors to be elected multiplied by the number of votes to which the shareholder's shares are normally entitled, or distribute the shareholder's votes on the same principle among as many candidates as the shareholder thinks fit.

No shareholder shall be entitled to cumulate votes (that is, cast for any candidate a number of votes greater than the number of votes which such shareholder normally is entitled to cast) unless such candidate or candidates' names have been placed in nomination prior to the voting and the shareholder has given notice at the meeting prior to the voting of the shareholder's intention to cumulate the shareholder's votes. If any one shareholder has given such notice, all shareholders may cumulate their votes for candidates in nomination.

In any election of directors, the candidates receiving the highest number of affirmative votes of the shares entitled to be voted for them up to the number of directors to be elected by such shares are elected; votes against the director and votes withheld shall have no legal effect. Elections for directors need not be by ballot unless a shareholder demands election by ballot at the meeting and before the voting begins or unless the bylaws so require. [708]

Financial Disclosure Rules

The board must make sure that an annual report (consisting of financial statements) is sent to the shareholders not later than 120 days after the close of the fiscal year, unless—in the case of a corporation with less than 100 shareholders of record—this requirement is waived in the bylaws. [1501]

State Tax Information

Franchise Tax Board, Sacramento
800-852-5711
www.ftb.ca.gov

California imposes a corporate franchise tax, with a minimum annual payment of $800. The minimum annual payment is waived for the first tax year of a new California corporation. This means that for the first tax year, the corporation estimates and pays only what it owes based on the current corporate franchise tax rate.

Corporation Law Online

The California General Corporation Law is contained in Title 1, Division 1, of the California Corporations Code, starting with Section 100. To find it, visit the legal research area of Nolo's website at www.nolo.com/statute/state/cfm. Click on "California." Select "Corporations Code" to view the law.

State Securities Information

Department of Corporations
980 9th Street, Suite 500
Sacramento, CA 95814-2725
916-445-7205
www.corp.ca.gov

Branch offices are located in Los Angeles, San Diego, and San Francisco.

The California Corporate Securities Act is contained in Title 4, Division 1, of the California Corporations Code. (To find it, follow the instructions in "Corporation Law Online," above. Then select Title 4, Division 1, and begin browsing Section 25000.) California securities law contains a limited offering exemption under Section 25102(f) of the California Corporations Code, similar to the Fed-

eral Regulation D exemption, for private offers and sales of securities to 35 or fewer individuals or to accredited investors. A Notice of Issuance form under Section 25102(f) must be filed with the Department of Corporations. A small offering exemption is also available under Section 25102(h) for the incorporation of a new business for cash or the transfer of assets of an existing business being converted to a corporation by the prior owners. A shareholder limit of 35 applies. You must file a 25102(h) notice form with the department, which includes an opinion of counsel section that must be signed by an active California lawyer. The department website provides additional information and downloadable forms.

Creating Your Own Articles Form

You can create your own articles form.

COLORADO

Corporate Filing Office

Secretary of State
1560 Broadway, Suite 200
Denver, CO 80202
303-894-2200 (refers you to a 900 number for individual assistance)
www.sos.state.co.us/pubs/business/main.htm

State Corporate Forms

Colorado provides fill-in-the-blanks Articles of Incorporation. Instructions for preparing articles plus additional information on forming a Colorado corporation is contained in the Department Filing Manual.

Internet Forms: You can download Articles of Incorporation with instructions (Form 200), plus other Colorado statutory forms (Reservation of Name and others), from the state corporate filing office website. You can also browse or download the Department Filing Manual.

Articles Instructions

Corporation Name: The name of a Colorado corporation must contain the word "corporation," "incorporated," "limited," "company," or an abbreviation of one of these words ("corp.," "inc.," "ltd.," or "co.").

Go online to the state corporate filing office to perform a name availability search. You can reserve an available corporate name for 120 days for $10 (when filing a paper name-reservation form). To save money and time, we suggest you file the name-reservation request online rather than preparing and mailing a paper name-reservation form. The current online name-reservation fee is only $0.99. (This is an introductory offer, and the online fee may be increased.)

Stock Information: Colorado law does not require you to specify a par value for your shares. Also, the filing fee is not based on how many shares you authorize, so you can authorize as many as you wish. To authorize one class of common stock with equal voting, dividend, and liquidation rights and no special restrictions, insert the number of shares you wish to authorize in the "number" blank, then type "Common" in the "class" blank. The number authorized should be sufficient to cover your initial stock issuance, and, if you wish, foreseeable stock issuance needs—for example, you might want to authorize additional shares if you think you'll later want to implement an employee stock option or bonus plan. If you want to authorize special classes or series of shares, you must specify the name of each class, and attach a separate statement to your articles that specifies the rights and restrictions associated with each class. Most incorporators start by authorizing only common shares.

Delayed Effective Date: You may specify a delayed date on which your articles will be effective. (Your corporation's legal existence and its first tax year start on this date.) Your delayed date must be no more than 90 days after the date your articles are filed by the state filing office. If you want your articles to be effective on the date they are filed, insert "N/A" in this blank.

Incorporator: You need only one person to act as your incorporator. Insert this person's name and address in the blanks, and then have the person sign the form.

When you mail your articles, include an original and one copy of the completed, signed form, together with a stamped, self-addressed envelope. If you have reserved your name or specified a delayed effective date in your articles, we suggest that you include a cover letter that notes either or both of these items. After approving your articles, the Secretary of State will return a file-stamped copy to you.

Filing Fee: $50, payable to "Secretary of State."

Director and Officer Rules

A board of directors shall consist of one or more members, with the number specified in or fixed in accordance with the bylaws. Directors are elected at each annual meeting of the shareholders (to serve for one-year terms) except as provided in Section 7-108-106 [applies if the corporation staggers the election of directors]. [7-108-103]

A corporation shall have the officers designated in its bylaws or by the board of directors. An officer shall be a natural person who is 18 years of age or older. The bylaws or the board of directors shall delegate to one or more of the officers responsibility for the preparation and maintenance of minutes of the directors' and shareholders' meetings and other records and information required to be kept by the corporation under Section 7-116-101 and for authenticating records of the corporation. The same individual may simultaneously hold more than one office in the corporation. [7-108-301]

Share Issuance Rules

The articles may authorize shares with a stated par value, but this statement is optional. [7-102-102]

The board of directors may authorize the issuance of shares for consideration consisting of any tangible or intangible property or benefit to the corporation, including cash, promissory notes, services performed, and other securities of the corporation. The promissory note of a subscriber or an affiliate of the subscriber for shares shall not constitute consideration for the shares unless the note is negotiable and is secured by collateral, other than the shares, having a fair market value at least equal to the principal amount of the note. "Promissory note" means a negotiable instrument on which there is an obligation to pay independent of collateral and does not include a nonrecourse note. Unless otherwise expressly provided in the Articles of Incorporation or bylaws, shares having a par value may be issued for less than the par value. [7-106-202]

Each share certificate shall state on its face: (a) the name of the issuing corporation and that the corporation is incorporated under the laws of this state; (b) the name of the person to whom the certificate is issued; and (c) the number and class of shares and the designation of the series, if any, the certificate represents. Each share certificate: (a) shall be signed, either manually or in facsimile, by one or more officers designated in the bylaws or by the board of directors; (b) may bear the corporate seal or its facsimile; and (c) may contain such other information as the corporation deems necessary or appropriate. [7-106-206]

Director Meeting Rules

Unless otherwise provided in the bylaws, regular meetings of the board of directors may be held without notice of the date, time, place, or purpose of the meeting. Unless the bylaws provide for a longer or shorter period, special meetings of the board of directors shall be preceded by at least two days' notice of the date, time, and place of the meeting. The notice need not describe the purpose of the special meeting unless required by the bylaws. [7-108-203]

Unless a greater number is required by the bylaws, a quorum of a board of directors consists of: (a) a majority of the number of directors fixed if the corporation has a fixed board size; or (b) a majority of the number of directors fixed or, if no number is fixed, of the number in office immediately before the meeting begins, if a range for the size of the board is established pursuant to Section 7-108-103 (2) [governs variable-range boards]. The bylaws may authorize a quorum of a board of directors to consist of: (a) no fewer than a majority of the number of directors fixed if the corporation has a fixed board size; or (b) no fewer than a majority of the number of directors fixed or, if no number is fixed, of the number in office immediately before the meeting begins, if a range for the size of the board is established pursuant to Section 7-

108-103 (2) [governs variable-range boards]. If a quorum is present when a vote is taken, the affirmative vote of a majority of directors present is the act of the board of directors unless the vote of a greater number of directors is required by Articles 101 to 117 of the Business Corporation Act or the bylaws. [7-108-205]

Shareholder Meeting Rules

A corporation shall hold a meeting of shareholders annually at a time and date stated in or fixed in accordance with the bylaws, or, if not so stated or fixed, at a time and date stated in or fixed in accordance with a resolution of the board of directors.

A corporation shall hold a special meeting of shareholders: (a) on call of its board of directors or the person or persons authorized by the bylaws or resolution of the board of directors to call such a meeting; or (b) if the corporation receives one or more written demands for the meeting, stating the purpose or purposes for which it is to be held, signed and dated by the holders of shares representing at least 10% of all the votes entitled to be cast on any issue proposed to be considered at the meeting. Only business within the purpose or purposes described in the notice of the meeting may be conducted at a special shareholders' meeting. [7-107-102]

A corporation shall give notice to shareholders of the date, time, and place of each annual and special shareholders' meeting no fewer than ten nor more than 60 days before the date of the meeting; except that, if the number of authorized shares is to be increased, at least 30 days' notice shall be given. Unless Articles 101 to 117 of the Business Corporation Act or the Articles of Incorporation require otherwise, notice of an annual meeting need not include a description of the purpose or purposes for which the meeting is called. Notice of a special meeting shall include a description of the purpose or purposes for which the meeting is called. [7-107-105]

Shares entitled to vote as a separate voting group may take action on a matter at a meeting only if a quorum of those shares exists with respect to that matter. Unless otherwise provided in Articles 101 to 117 of the Business Corporation Act or in the Articles of Incorporation, a majority of the votes entitled to be cast on the matter by the voting group constitutes a quorum of that voting group for action on that matter, but a quorum shall not consist of fewer than one-third of the votes entitled to be cast on the matter by the voting group. If a quorum exists, action on a matter other than the election of directors by a voting group is approved if the votes cast within the voting group favoring the action exceed the votes cast within the voting group opposing the action, unless a greater number of affirmative votes is required by Articles 101 to 117 of the Business Corporation Act or the Articles of Incorporation. The election of directors is governed by Section 7-107-209. [7-107-206]

At each election for directors, every shareholder entitled to vote at such election has the right: (a) to vote, in person or by proxy, all of the shareholder's votes for as many persons as there are directors to be elected and for whose election the shareholder has a right to vote unless the Articles of Incorporation provide otherwise; or (b) if the articles permit cumulative voting, to cumulate votes by multiplying the number of votes the shareholder is entitled to cast by the number of directors for whom the shareholder is entitled to vote and casting the product for a single candidate or distributing the product among two or more candidates. In an election of directors, that number of candidates equaling the number of directors to be elected, having the highest number of votes cast in favor of their election, are elected to the board of directors. [7-107-209]

Financial Disclosure Rules

On the written request of any shareholder, a corporation shall mail to such shareholder its most recent annual financial statements, if any, and its most recently published financial statements, if any, showing in reasonable detail its assets and liabilities and results of its operations. [7-116-105]

State Tax Information

Department of Revenue, Denver
303-232-2414
www.revenue.state.co.us/main/home/asp
Colorado imposes a corporate income tax.

Corporation Law Online

The Colorado Business Corporation Act is contained in Title 7, Articles 101 through 117, of the Colorado Revised Statutes, starting with Section 7-101-101. You can browse it from the link below (select "Colorado Statutes" in the left pane, then select Title 7, then "Corporations and Associations" (ignore the first "Corporations" heading), then "Colorado Business Corporations," then select from the list of headings to browse sections of the BCA):

http://198.187.128.12/colorado/lpext.dll?f=templates&fn=fs-main.htm&2.0

State Securities Information

Colorado Division of Securities
1580 Lincoln, Suite 420
Denver, CO 80203
303-894-2320
www.dora.state.co.us/Securities

The Colorado Securities Act is contained in Title 11, Article 51, of the Colorado Statutes. To find it, follow the instructions in "Corporation Law Online," above, selecting Title 11, Article 51. The state website provides information on state securities law exemptions for private offerings of stock and other securities. Colorado has three private placement exemptions: one that parallels the federal Section 4(2) nonpublic offering exemption, one for sales to ten or fewer persons in Colorado, and one that requires you to pay a fee and file a notice form. See the Division of Securities website and call the Division office for more information.

Creating Your Own Articles Form

You can create your own articles form.

CONNECTICUT

Corporate Filing Office

Connecticut Secretary of State
30 Trinity Street
P.O. Box 150470
Hartford, CT 06115-0470
860-509-6002
www.sots.state.ct.us

State Corporate Forms

Connecticut provides a fill-in-the-blanks Certificate of Incorporation (Stock Corporation) with instructions.

Internet Forms: The latest Certificate of Incorporation (Stock Corporation) with instructions, plus other Connecticut corporate forms (Reservation of Name, Organization and First Report, and others) are available for downloading from the state website.

Articles Instructions

Article 1: The name of a Connecticut corporation must contain the word "corporation," "incorporated," "company," or "limited," or the abbreviation "corp.," "inc.," "co.," or "ltd." The Italianate corporate designator "Societa per Azioni" or its abbreviation "S.p.A." are also allowed.

You can check the availability of a corporate name by calling the state filing office (limited partnership names do not appear on the Secretary of State's list). You can reserve an available corporate name for 120 days for a $30 fee.

Article 2: Connecticut does not require you to specify a par value for your shares. Insert the total number of authorized shares. The maximum number of shares you can authorize for the lowest filing fee is 20,000. This results in payment of the minimum franchise tax of $150 when you file your articles (see below).

Most incorporators wish to authorize common shares with equal voting, dividend, and liquidation rights and no special restrictions. If you wish to authorize one or more special classes of shares, you must fill in the additional lines in Article 2, specifying the name of each class and the number of shares per class. If you do specify different classes in this section, the total number of shares of each class listed should equal the total number of authorized shares stated in the beginning of Article 2.

Article 3: Fill in Article 3 only if you have specified different classes of shares in Article 2. List the rights, preferences, and restrictions associated with each class or se-

ries. You may need a lawyer's help to draft the language for these rights and restrictions.

Article 4: Most incorporators specify an individual, who must be a Connecticut resident, as the registered agent in Section A. The agent must sign the line titled "Acceptance of Appointment" at the end of Article 4.

Send your original articles to the state filing office. After your articles are approved, the filing office will send you an "acknowledgment of filing" letter.

Filing Fee: $50 plus a minimum $150 franchise tax (see below), payable to the "Secretary of State." An Organization and First Report form, available from the state filing office website, must be filed within 30 days of the holding of the corporation's organizational meeting; this costs $75.

Compute your franchise tax as follows: One cent per share up to and including the first ten thousand authorized shares; one-half cent per share for each authorized share in excess of ten thousand shares up to and including one hundred thousand shares; one-quarter cent per share for each authorized share in excess of one hundred thousand shares up to and including one million shares; and one-fifth cent per share for each authorized share in excess of one million shares.

Under this formula, the maximum number of shares you can authorize for the minimum $150 franchise tax is 20,000 shares ($.01 x 10,000 = $100 plus .005 x 10,000 = $50).

Director and Officer Rules

A board of directors shall consist of one or more individuals, with the number specified in or fixed in accordance with the Certificate of Incorporation or bylaws. The number of directors may be increased or decreased from time to time by amendment to, or in the manner provided in, the Certificate of Incorporation or the bylaws.

Directors are elected at the first annual shareholders' meeting and at each annual meeting thereafter unless their terms are staggered under Section 33-740. [33-737]

A corporation has the officers described in its bylaws or appointed by the board of directors in accordance with the bylaws. A duly appointed officer may appoint one or more officers or assistant officers if authorized by the bylaws or the board of directors. The bylaws or the board of directors shall delegate to one of the officers responsibility for preparing minutes of the directors' and shareholders' meetings and for authenticating records of the corporation. The same individual may simultaneously hold more than one office in a corporation. [33-763]

Share Issuance Rules

The Certificate of Incorporation may authorize shares with a stated par value, but this statement is optional. [33-636]

The board of directors may authorize shares to be issued for consideration consisting of any tangible or intangible property or benefit to the corporation, including cash, promissory notes, services performed, contracts for services to be performed, or other securities of the corporation. The corporation may place in escrow shares issued for a contract for future services or benefits or a promissory note, or make other arrangements to restrict the transfer of the shares, and may credit distributions in respect of the shares against their purchase price, until the services are performed, the note is paid, or the benefits received. If the services are not performed, the note is not paid or the benefits are not received, the issuance of the shares are escrowed or restricted, and the distributions credited may be rescinded in whole or part. Shares whose issuance has been so rescinded shall return to being authorized but unissued. [33-672]

At a minimum each share certificate shall state on its face: (1) the name of the issuing corporation and that it is organized under the law of this state; (2) the name of the person to whom the certificate is issued; and (3) the number and class of shares and the designation of the series, if any, the certificate represents. If the issuing corporation is authorized to issue different classes of shares or different series within a class, the designations, relative rights, preferences and limitations applicable to each class and the variations in rights, preferences and limitations determined for each series, and authority of the board of directors to determine variations for future series shall be summarized on the front or back of each certificate. Alternatively, each certificate may state conspicuously on its front or back that the corporation will furnish the shareholder this information on request in writing and without charge. Each share certificate (1) shall be signed either manually or in facsimile by two officers designated in the bylaws or by the board of directors and (2) may bear the corporate seal or its facsimile. [33-676]

Director Meeting Rules

The board of directors may hold regular or special meetings in or out of the state of Connecticut.

Unless the Certificate of Incorporation or a bylaw provides otherwise, the board of directors may permit any or all directors to participate in a regular or special meeting by, or conduct the meeting through the use of, any means of communication by which all directors participating may simultaneously hear each other during the meeting. A director participating in a meeting by this means is deemed to be present in person at the meeting. [33-748]

Unless the Certificate of Incorporation or a bylaw provides otherwise, regular meetings of the board of directors may be held without notice of the date, time, place, or purpose of the meeting.

Unless the Certificate of Incorporation or a bylaw provides for a longer or shorter period, special meetings of the board of directors shall be preceded by at least two days' notice of the date, time, and place of the meeting. The notice need not describe the purpose of the special meeting unless required by the Certificate of Incorporation or bylaws. [33-750]

Unless the Certificate of Incorporation or a bylaw requires a greater number, a quorum of a board of directors consists of: (1) a majority of the fixed number of directors if the corporation has a fixed board size; or (2) a majority of the number of directors prescribed or, if no number is prescribed, the number in office immediately before the meeting begins, if the corporation has a variable-range size board. The Certificate of Incorporation or bylaws may authorize a quorum of a board of directors to consist of no fewer than one-third of the fixed or prescribed number of directors determined under the rules just described. If a quorum is present when a vote is taken, the affirmative vote of a majority of directors present is the act of the board of directors unless the Certificate of Incorporation or a bylaw requires the vote of a greater number of directors. [33-752]

Shareholder Meeting Rules

A corporation shall hold a meeting of shareholders annually at a time stated in or fixed in accordance with the bylaws. [33-695]

A corporation shall hold a special meeting of shareholders: (1) on call of its board of directors or the person or persons authorized to do so by the Certificate of Incorporation or bylaws; or (2) if the holders of at least 10% of all the votes entitled to be cast on any issue proposed to be considered at the proposed special meeting sign, date, and deliver to the corporation's secretary one or more written demands for the meeting describing the purpose or purposes for which it is to be held, except that if the corporation has a class of voting stock registered pursuant to Section 12 of the Securities Exchange Act of 1934, as amended from time to time, and no person held 10% or more of such votes on February 1, 1988, the corporation need not hold such meeting except on demand of the holders of not less than 35% of such votes. [33-696]

A corporation shall notify shareholders of the date, time, and place of each annual and special shareholders' meeting no fewer than ten nor more than 60 days before the meeting date. Unless Sections 33-600 to 33-998, inclusive, or the Certificate of Incorporation requires otherwise, the corporation is required to give notice only to shareholders entitled to vote at the meeting.

Unless Sections 33-600 to 33-998, inclusive, or the Certificate of Incorporation requires otherwise, notice of an annual meeting need not include a description of the purpose or purposes for which the meeting is called. Notice of a special shareholders' meeting shall include a description of the purpose or purposes for which the meeting is called. [33-699]

Shares entitled to vote as a separate voting group may take action on a matter at a meeting only if a quorum of those shares exists with respect to that matter. Unless the Certificate of Incorporation or Sections 33-600 to 33-998, inclusive, provide otherwise, a majority of the votes entitled to be cast on the matter by the voting group constitutes a quorum of that voting group for action on that matter. Once a share is represented for any purpose at a meeting, it is deemed present for quorum purposes for the remainder of the meeting and for any adjournment of that meeting unless a new record date is or must be set for that adjourned meeting. If a quorum exists, action on a matter, other than the election of directors, by a voting group is approved if the votes cast within the voting group favoring the action exceed the votes cast opposing the action, unless the Certificate of Incorporation or Sections 33-600 to 33-998, inclusive, require a greater number of affirmative votes. [33-709]

Unless otherwise provided in the Certificate of Incorporation, directors are elected by a plurality of the votes cast by the shares entitled to vote in the election at a meeting at which a quorum is present. Shareholders do not have a right to cumulate their votes for directors unless the Certificate of Incorporation so provides. A statement included in the Certificate of Incorporation that "all or a designated voting group of shareholders are entitled to cumulate their votes for directors," or words of similar import, means that the shareholders designated are entitled to multiply the number of votes they are entitled to cast by the number of directors for whom they are entitled to vote and cast the product for a single candidate or distribute the product among two or more candidates. Shares otherwise entitled to vote cumulatively may not be voted cumulatively at a particular meeting unless: (1) the meeting

notice or proxy statement accompanying the notice states conspicuously that cumulative voting is authorized; or (2) a shareholder who has the right to cumulate his votes gives notice to the corporation not less than 48 hours before the time set for the meeting of his intent to cumulate his votes during the meeting, and if one shareholder gives this notice all other shareholders in the same voting group participating in the election are entitled to cumulate their votes without giving further notice. [33-712]

Financial Disclosure Rules

A corporation, except a corporation required by law to file financial reports with the Commissioner of Banking, the Insurance Commissioner, or the Department of Public Utility Control, shall furnish its shareholders annual financial statements, which may be consolidated or combined statements of the corporation and one or more of its subsidiaries, as appropriate, that include a balance sheet as of the end of the fiscal year, an income statement for that year, and a statement of changes in shareholders' equity for the year unless that information appears elsewhere in the financial statements.

If financial statements are prepared for the corporation on the basis of generally accepted accounting principles, the annual financial statements must also be prepared on that basis. If the annual financial statements are reported on by a public accountant, his report must accompany them. If not, the statements must be accompanied by a statement of the president or the person responsible for the corporation's accounting records: (1) stating his reasonable belief whether the statements were prepared on the basis of generally accepted accounting principles and, if not, describing the basis of preparation; and (2) describing any respects in which the statements were not prepared on a basis of accounting consistent with the statements prepared for the preceding year.

A corporation shall mail required annual financial statements to each shareholder within 120 days after the close of each fiscal year. Thereafter, on written request from a shareholder who was not mailed the statements, the corporation shall mail him the latest financial statements. [33-951]

State Tax Information

Department of Revenue Services, Hartford
203-566-8520
www.ct.gov/drs/site/default.asp

Connecticut imposes a corporation business tax.

Corporation Law Online

The Connecticut Business Corporation Act is contained in Title 33, Chapter 601, of the Connecticut Statutes, starting with Section 33-600. To find the Act, visit the legal research area of Nolo's website at www.nolo.com/statute/state/cfm. Click on "Connecticut." At the Connecticut website, choose "Law and Legislation," then scroll down and select "Connecticut General Statutes." From there, select "Browse—One Chapter at a Time" and choose Title 33, Chapter 601.

State Securities Information

Connecticut Department of Banking
Securities and Business Investments Division
260 Constitution Plaza
Hartford, CT 06103-1800
800-831-7225
www.state.ct.us/dob

The Connecticut Uniform Securities Act is contained in Title 36b of the Connecticut Statutes, starting with Chapter 672a. To find the Act, follow the instructions in "Corporation Law Online" above, choosing to browse Title 36b, Chapter 672a. The Securities and Business Investment Division website provides a downloadable guide to raising capital under Connecticut's securities laws, called *Small Business: A Guide to Raising Capital*. It discusses the requirements and procedures for issuing shares of stock under exemptions to the state's securities laws, including a "de minimus" exemption for issuances to ten or fewer purchasers and a private placement exemption that parallels the Federal Regulation D exemption rules. The state also allows qualified corporations to offer shares under a Small Corporation Offering Registration (SCOR) procedure. For more information, view the guide and other information and forms—all available from the division's website.

Creating Your Own Articles Form

You can create your own articles form.

DELAWARE

Corporate Filing Office

Department of State
Division of Corporations
P.O. Box 898
Dover, DE 19903
302-739-3073
www.state.de.us/corp/default.shtml

State Corporate Forms

Delaware provides a corporate formation package. Included in this package is a fill-in-the-blanks Certificate of Incorporation for a Stock Corporation, with instructions.

Internet Forms: The latest Delaware Certificate of Incorporation for a Stock Corporation, plus other corporate forms (Reservation of Corporate Name and others), can be downloaded from the state website.

Articles Instructions

First Article: The name of a Delaware corporation must contain the word "association," "company," "corporation," "club," "foundation," "fund," "incorporated," "institute," "society," "union," "syndicate," or "limited" (or abbreviations of one of these words, with or without punctuation), or a word (or abbreviations of a word, with or without punctuation) of similar meaning of foreign countries or jurisdictions (provided it is written in roman characters or letters). The name requirements may be waived for corporations that certify that they have $10 million or more in total assets.

You can check name availability and reserve a name online from the state filing office website. A name reservation costs $10 and is effective for 30 days.

Fourth Article: Delaware still uses the concept of par value shares. You can authorize shares with a stated par value or without par value. To conform to modern practice and obtain the smallest filing fee, many incorporators simply authorize 1,500 shares without par value. (This results in payment of the minimum authorized shares filing fee, as explained below). You can also pay the minimum filing fee by authorizing par value shares whose total par value equals $75,000, such as 75,000 shares with a par value of $1.00 each or 750,000 shares with a par value of $.10 each. Note that authorizing 3,000 or fewer shares in the articles, whether par or no par, results in the payment of the minimum annual Delaware franchise tax each year of $30. State Tax Information, below.

Send the Department of State an original Certificate of Incorporation; you do not need to include a copy. The minimum filing fee is $74. Increase the fee amount if your authorized shares tax or county recording fee exceeds the minimum amounts (see filing fee information, below). If you wish to have a certified copy of your certificate returned to you, include an additional $20.

Filing Fee: Delaware has a complicated filing fee structure. The minimum filing fee is $74. This includes a minimum authorized shares tax of $15, a minimum county recording fee of $24, a flat receiving and indexing fee of $25, and a flat data fee of $10. If necessary, increase your filing fee by the rules that follow.

The county recording fee is $15 plus $9 per page. If your certificate is only one page (the standard length of the Delaware Certificate of Incorporation), you pay the minimum county recording fee of $24. If your certificate is more than one page, increase your county fee by $9 for each additional page.

The authorized shares portion of the filing fee (which we call the "authorized shares tax") is based on the number of authorized shares without par value and/or on the capital value of the authorized shares with par value. The minimum tax is $15. The capital value of par value shares is calculated by multiplying the number of each class of par value shares by their respective par value and then totaling the results of each multiplication. For the purpose of computing the tax on par value stock, each $100 of capital value is counted as one taxable share. The following tables give the rates for calculating the authorized shares tax:

STOCK WITH NO PAR VALUE

	Rate Per Share
Shares up to 20,000	$.01
Shares between 20,000 and 2,000,000	$.005
Shares over 2,000,000	$.004

STOCK WITH PAR VALUE

	Rate Per Taxable Share
Taxable shares up to 20,000	$.02
Taxable shares between 20,000 and 200,000	$.01
Taxable shares over 200,000	$.004

Examples:

For a corporation with 1,500 authorized shares without par value, the authorized shares tax is 1,500 x .01 =

$15, the minimum tax. Total filing fees, therefore, are $74 (all these examples assume the minimum county recording fee of $24).

For a corporation with 20,000 authorized shares without par value, the authorized shares tax is 20,000 x .01 = $200. The total filing is $259 ($200 + $25 receiving and index fee + $10 data fee + $24 minimum county recording fee). For a corporation with 20,000 authorized shares with a par value of $1, the capital value of the company is $20,000. The total capital is divided by 100 to obtain the number of taxable shares (200). The tax is 200 taxable shares x .02 = $4. While the calculated tax is $4, there is a minimum tax of $15. The total filing fee is the $74 minimum.

For a company with 75,000 authorized shares with a par value of $1, the total authorized capital is $75,000. This yields 750 taxable shares ($75,000/100 = 750). So the tax would be 750 taxable shares x .02 = $15, the minimum authorized shares tax. The total filing fee would be the $74 minimum.

Corporations having shares both with and without par value pay an authorized shares tax equal to the sum of the tax on the no-par shares plus the tax on the par value shares.

Delaware also charges an annual franchise tax, which is separate from the authorized shares tax. If you authorize 3,000 or fewer shares in your Articles, whether par or no par, you will have to pay the minimum annual franchise tax each year of $30—see State Tax Information, below.

Director and Officer Rules

The board of directors of a corporation shall consist of one or more members. The number of directors shall be fixed by, or in the manner provided in, the bylaws, unless the Certificate of Incorporation fixes the number of directors, in which case a change in the number of directors shall be made only by amendment of the certificate. Directors need not be stockholders unless so required by the Certificate of Incorporation or the bylaws. The Certificate of Incorporation or bylaws may prescribe other qualifications for directors. Each director shall hold office until such director's successor is elected and qualified or until such director's earlier resignation or removal. Any director may resign at any time on written notice to the corporation. [141] Every corporation organized under this chapter shall have such officers with such titles and duties as shall be stated in the bylaws or in a resolution of the board of directors which is not inconsistent with the bylaws and as may be necessary to enable it to sign instruments and stock certificates which comply with §§

103(a)(2) and 158 of this title. One of the officers shall have the duty to record the proceedings of the meetings of the stockholders and directors in a book to be kept for that purpose. Any number of offices may be held by the same person unless the Certificate of Incorporation or bylaws otherwise provide.

Officers shall be chosen in such manner and shall hold their offices for such terms as are prescribed by the bylaws or determined by the board of directors or other governing body. Each officer shall hold office until such officer's successor is elected and qualified or until such officer's earlier resignation or removal. Any officer may resign at any time on written notice to the corporation. [142]

Share Issuance Rules

Every corporation may issue one or more classes of stock or one or more series of stock within any class thereof, any or all of which classes may be of stock with par value or stock without par value [Delaware uses the concept of par value in its General Corporation Law] and which classes or series may have such voting powers, full or limited, or no voting powers; and such designations, preferences, and relative, participating, optional, or other special rights, and qualifications, limitations, or restrictions thereof; as shall be stated and expressed in the Certificate of Incorporation or of any amendment thereto, or in the resolution or resolutions providing for the issue of such stock adopted by the board of directors pursuant to authority expressly vested in it by the provisions of its Certificate of Incorporation. [151]

Shares of stock with par value may be issued for such consideration, having a value not less than the par value thereof, as determined from time to time by the board of directors, or by the stockholders if the Certificate of Incorporation so provides.

Shares of stock without par value may be issued for such consideration as is determined from time to time by the board of directors, or by the stockholders if the Certificate of Incorporation so provides. [153]

Any corporation may, by resolution of its board of directors, determine that only a part of the consideration which shall be received by the corporation for any of the shares of its capital stock which it shall issue from time to time shall be capital; but, in case any of the shares issued shall be shares having a par value, the amount of the part of such consideration so determined to be capital shall be in excess of the aggregate par value of the shares issued for such consideration having a par value, unless all the shares issued shall be shares having a par value, in which case the amount of the part of such consideration so determined to be capital need be only equal to the aggregate par value of such shares. In each such case the board of directors shall specify in dollars the part of such consideration which shall be capital. If the board of directors shall not have determined (1) at the time of issue of any shares of the capital stock of the corporation issued for cash or (2) within 60 days after the issue of any shares of the capital stock of the corporation issued for property other than cash what part of the consideration for such shares shall be capital, the capital of the corporation in respect of such shares shall be an amount equal to the aggregate par value of such shares having a par value, plus the amount of the consideration for such shares without par value. The amount of the consideration so determined to be capital in respect of any shares without par value shall be the stated capital of such shares. [154]

The shares of a corporation shall be represented by certificates, provided that the board of directors of the corporation may provide by resolution or resolutions that some or all of any or all classes or series of its stock shall be uncertificated shares. Any such resolution shall not apply to shares represented by a certificate until such certificate is surrendered to the corporation. Notwithstanding the adoption of such a resolution by the board of directors, every holder of stock represented by certificates and on request every holder of uncertificated shares shall be entitled to have a certificate signed by, or in the name of the corporation by the chairperson or vice chairperson of the board of directors, or the president or vice president, and by the treasurer or an assistant treasurer, or the secretary or an assistant secretary of such corporation representing the number of shares registered in certificate form. [158]

Director Meeting Rules

Unless otherwise restricted by the Certificate of Incorporation or bylaws, the board of directors of any corporation organized under the General Corporation Law may hold its meetings, and have an office or offices, outside of the state of Delaware.

A majority of the total number of directors shall constitute a quorum for the transaction of business unless the Certificate of Incorporation or the bylaws require a greater number. Unless the Certificate of Incorporation provides otherwise, the bylaws may provide that a number less than a majority shall constitute a quorum which in no case shall be less than 1/3 of the total number of directors except that when a board of one director is authorized under this section, then one director shall constitute

a quorum. The vote of the majority of the directors present at a meeting at which a quorum is present shall be the act of the board of directors unless the Certificate of Incorporation or the bylaws shall require a vote of a greater number. [141]

Shareholder Meeting Rules

Meetings of stockholders may be held at such place, either within or without the state of Delaware, as may be designated by or in the manner provided in the bylaws or, if not so designated, at the registered office of the corporation in the state of Delaware.

Unless directors are elected by written consent in lieu of an annual meeting as permitted by this subsection, an annual meeting of stockholders shall be held for the election of directors on a date and at a time designated by or in the manner provided in the bylaws. Stockholders may, unless the Certificate of Incorporation otherwise provides, act by written consent to elect directors; provided, however, that, if such consent is less than unanimous, such action by written consent may be in lieu of holding an annual meeting only if all of the directorships to which directors could be elected at an annual meeting held at the effective time of such action are vacant and are filled by such action. Any other proper business may be transacted at the annual meeting.

Special meetings of the stockholders may be called by the board of directors or by such person or persons as may be authorized by the Certificate of Incorporation or by the bylaws.

All elections of directors shall be by written ballot, unless otherwise provided in the Certificate of Incorporation. [211]

The Certificate of Incorporation of any corporation may provide that at all elections of directors of the corporation, or at elections held under specified circumstances, each holder of stock or of any class or classes or of a series or series thereof shall be entitled to as many votes as shall equal the number of votes which (except for such provision as to cumulative voting) such holder would be entitled to cast for the election of directors with respect to such holder's shares of stock multiplied by the number of directors to be elected by such holder, and that such holder may cast all of such votes for a single director or may distribute them among the number to be voted for, or for any two or more of them as such holder may see fit. [214]

Subject to the General Corporation Law in respect of the vote that shall be required for a specified action, the Certificate of Incorporation or bylaws of any corporation authorized to issue stock may specify the number of shares and/or the amount of other securities having voting power the holders of which shall be present or represented by proxy at any meeting in order to constitute a quorum for, and the votes that shall be necessary for, the transaction of any business, but in no event shall a quorum consist of less than one-third of the shares entitled to vote at the meeting, except that, where a separate vote by a class or series or classes or series is required, a quorum shall consist of no less than one-third of the shares of such class or series or classes or series. In the absence of such specification in the Certificate of Incorporation or bylaws of the corporation:

- A majority of the shares entitled to vote, present in person or represented by proxy, shall constitute a quorum at a meeting of stockholders.

- In all matters other than the election of directors, the affirmative vote of the majority of shares present in person or represented by proxy at the meeting and entitled to vote on the subject matter shall be the act of the stockholders.

- Directors shall be elected by a plurality of the votes of the shares present in person or represented by proxy at the meeting and entitled to vote on the election of directors.

- Where a separate vote by a class or series or classes or series is required, a majority of the outstanding shares of such class or series or classes or series, present in person or represented by proxy, shall constitute a quorum entitled to take action with respect to that vote on that matter, and the affirmative vote of the majority of shares of such class or series or classes or series present in person or represented by proxy at the meeting shall be the act of such class or series or classes or series. [216]

Whenever stockholders are required or permitted to take any action at a meeting, a written notice of the meeting shall be given which shall state the place, date, and hour of the meeting, and, in the case of a special meeting, the purpose or purposes for which the meeting is called.

Unless otherwise provided in the General Corporation Law, the written notice of any meeting shall be given not less than ten nor more than 60 days before the date of the meeting to each stockholder entitled to vote at such meeting. If mailed, notice is given when deposited in the United States mail, postage prepaid, directed to the stockholder at such stockholder's address as it appears on the records of the corporation. An affidavit of the secretary or an assistant secretary or of the transfer agent of

the corporation that the notice has been given shall, in the absence of fraud, be prima facie evidence of the facts stated therein. [222]

Financial Disclosure Rules

Any stockholder, in person or by attorney or other agent, shall, on written demand under oath stating the purpose thereof, have the right during the usual hours for business to inspect for any proper purpose the corporation's stock ledger, a list of its stockholders, and its other books and records, and to make copies or extracts therefrom. A proper purpose shall mean a purpose reasonably related to such person's interest as a stockholder. In every instance where an attorney or other agent shall be the person who seeks the right to inspection, the demand under oath shall be accompanied by a power of attorney or such other writing which authorizes the attorney or other agent to so act on behalf of the stockholder. The demand under oath shall be directed to the corporation at its registered office in the state of Delaware or at its principal place of business.

If the corporation, or an officer or agent thereof, refuses to permit an inspection sought by a stockholder or attorney or other agent acting for the stockholder pursuant to Subsection (b) [the previous paragraph] of this section or does not reply to the demand within five business days after the demand has been made, the stockholder may apply to the court of chancery for an order to compel such inspection. The court of chancery is vested with exclusive jurisdiction to determine whether or not the person seeking inspection is entitled to the inspection sought. The court may summarily order the corporation to permit the stockholder to inspect the corporation's stock ledger, an existing list of stockholders, and its other books and records, and to make copies or extracts therefrom; or the court may order the corporation to furnish to the stockholder a list of its stockholders as of a specific date on condition that the stockholder first pay to the corporation the reasonable cost of obtaining and furnishing such list and on such other conditions as the court deems appropriate.

Where the stockholder seeks to inspect the corporation's books and records, other than its stock ledger or list of stockholders, such stockholder shall first establish (1) that such stockholder has complied with the rules described in this section regarding the form and manner of making a demand to inspect such documents, and (2) that the inspection such stockholder seeks is for a proper purpose. Where the stockholder seeks to inspect the corporation's stock ledger or list of stockholders and such stockholder has complied with the rules for making a demand to inspect such documents, the burden of proof shall be on the corporation to establish that the inspection such stockholder seeks is for an improper purpose. The court may, in its discretion, prescribe any limitations or conditions with reference to the inspection, or award such other or further relief as the court may deem just and proper. The court may order books, documents, and records; pertinent extracts therefrom; or duly authenticated copies thereof to be brought within the state of Delaware and kept in the state of Delaware on such terms and conditions as the order may prescribe. [220]

State Tax Information

Department of Finance

Division of Revenue, Dover
302-577-8450
www.state.de.us/revenue/services/BusServices.shtml

Delaware corporations pay an annual corporate income tax to the Division of Revenue. Delaware corporations are also required to file an Annual Franchise Tax Report and pay an annual franchise tax. You must make these reports and payments directly to the Division of Corporations, Franchise Tax Office. The minimum annual franchise tax is $30; the maximum is $150,000. You can use either an authorized shares or assumed par value method to compute your annual franchise tax. The following schedule shows how to compute the annual franchise tax based on the authorized shares method:

3,000 shares or less (minimum tax)	$30
3,001 - 5,000 shares	$50
5,001 - 10,000 shares	$90
Each additional 10,000 shares or portion thereof	$50

Examples:

A corporation with 10,005 shares pays $140 ($90 + $50).

A corporation with 100,000 shares pays $540 ($90 + ($50 x 9)).

You can find information on calculating the franchise tax under both methods on the state corporate filing office website.

Corporation Law Online

The Delaware General Corporation Law is contained in Title 8, Chapter 1, of the Delaware Statutes, starting with Section 101. You can browse it from the following Web page:

www.state.de.us/corp/DElaw.htm

State Securities Information

Department of Justice
Division of Securities
820 N. French Street, 5th Floor
Wilmington, DE 19801
302-577-8424
www.state.de.us/securities

The Delaware Securities Act is contained in Title 6, Chapter 73, of the Delaware Code. You can browse the Act from the Securities Division website. It includes exemptions for the sales of securities to 25 or fewer investors; a limited offering exemption for offers and sales of securities made under Federal Regulation D, Rule 505; and an accredited investor exemption. You must file a Notice of Sale with the Division of Securities when relying on one or more of these exemptions. The Division's website provides downloadable notice forms.

Creating Your Own Articles Form

You may use your own articles form if you follow these guidelines:

- Documents must be submitted on 8.5" x 11" paper.

- Documents should have margins of 1" on sides, 2" at top, and 1.5" at bottom.

- Documents should be prepared using black ink. Also use black ink for signatures and any handwritten material.

- All documents must be clear enough to be legible when faxed, copied, scanned, or otherwise imaged.

- Any document that appoints a Registered Agent will not be accepted by the state unless the Registered Agent signs the form.

DISTRICT OF COLUMBIA

Corporate Filing Office

Department of Consumer & Regulatory Affairs
Business and Professional Licensing Administration
Corporations Division
941 North Capitol Street, NE
Washington, DC 20002
202-442-4432
http://dcra.dc.gov/cra/cwp/
view,a,1342,Q,600904,dcraNav,|33408|.asp

State Corporate Forms

The District of Columbia provides guidelines and a sample form for Articles of Incorporation. It also provides a separate instruction sheet to help you complete your articles.

Internet Forms: The latest D.C. Articles of Incorporation Guidelines, Articles of Incorporation Instruction Sheet, and other corporate forms are available for viewing and downloading at the filing office website. If you are forming a professional corporation, download the Professional Corporation Guidelines.

Articles Instructions

The Articles of Incorporation Guidelines provide instructions on the language you should use when completing your articles. In addition, you should be aware of the following rules and customs.

First Article: The name of a District of Columbia corporation must contain the word "corporation," "company," "incorporated," or "limited," or an abbreviation of one of these words.

You can check name availability by calling the filing office. An available corporate name can be reserved for 60 days for a $35 fee.

Second Article: Most incorporators give their corporation a "perpetual" duration.

Third Article: Insert the specific business purpose or purposes of your corporation. A general purpose, such as "any lawful purpose," is not acceptable in District of Columbia articles. You must indicate the nature of the corporation's actual business—for example, "to sell real estate" or "to operate a computer sales and service business."

Fourth Article: State whether your shares have a par value or whether they are without par value. You can authorize up to $100,000 of capitalization for the minimum filing fee (see the filing fee information, below). Most incorporators authorize only common shares with equal voting, dividend, and liquidation rights and no special restrictions. Assuming you want to authorize the maximum number of common shares without par value, you can complete Article 4 as follows: "The aggregate number of shares that the corporation is authorized to issue is 100,000, without par value." To authorize par value shares, say $100,000 at $1 par each, insert the following: "The aggregate number of shares that the corporation is authorized to issue is 100,000, with a par value of $1.00 each." If you wish to authorize one or more special classes of shares, you must state the name of each class or series; the number of shares in each; and the par value, if any, associated with each class or series, or you must state that the shares in each class or series are without par value.

Fifth Article: If you authorize separate classes or series of shares, insert the rights and restrictions associated with each class or series. If you do not use this article, renumber the succeeding articles accordingly.

Sixth Article: D.C. law requires that your corporation obtain at least $1,000 of capitalization before it starts doing business. Your financial records should show that this much cash or property was paid into your corporation by the initial shareholders.

Seventh Article: If you want to limit or deny your shareholders' preemptive rights (which give them the right to buy future shares before new shareholders can), include the limitation or denial language here. If this doesn't concern you now, you can simply state: "None."

Eighth Article: If you do not want to add additional provisions to the standard articles, state "None."

Ninth Article: Insert the street address of the registered office of the corporation, followed by the name of the initial agent at this address. Note that you must also separately state the principal business address of the agent in this article, as shown in the sample form. If you select one of your corporate directors as the initial agent, the address of the registered office and the agent's business address will be the same.

Tenth Article: Your corporation may have one or more directors. Insert the number of directors in the first paragraph. In the space after the paragraph, list the names and street addresses, with zip codes, of your initial directors.

Eleventh Article: List the name and street address of the person who signs your articles as incorporator. This person may be one of your initial directors, or anyone else who is 18 years of age or older. Make sure to have the incorporator date and sign the form at the bottom.

Submit two original, signed copies (sign each form), together with a signed Written Consent of Registered Agent. A Written Consent to Act as Registered Agent form is available for downloading from the state filing office website. The individual agent should complete only Section (A) of the form.

Filing Fee: $120 minimum incorporation fee, payable to the "D.C. Treasurer." This includes a $100 filing fee, plus a minimum $20 authorized stock fee. You may authorize up $100,000 of capitalization in your articles for this minimum $20 fee—for example, 100,000 shares with a par value of $1 each or 200,000 with a par value of $0.50 each. Shares without par value are given a $1 per share value for purposes of this fee, so you can authorize up to 100,000 shares without par value for the minimum $20 authorized stock fee. If you wish to authorize more than the minimum amount of capitalization, call the filing office to find out how much more to pay when you file your articles.

Director and Officer Rules

The number of directors of a corporation shall be one or more. The number of directors shall be fixed by the bylaws, except as to the number constituting the first board of directors, which number shall be fixed by the Articles of Incorporation. The number of directors may be increased or decreased from time to time by amendment to the bylaws. In the absence of a bylaw fixing the number of directors, the number shall be the same as that stated in the Articles of Incorporation. The names and addresses of the members of the first board of directors shall be stated in the Articles of Incorporation. The directors shall hold office until the first annual meeting of shareholders, or until their successors shall have been selected and qualified. At the first annual meeting of shareholders and at each annual meeting thereafter, the shareholders shall elect directors to hold office until the next succeeding annual meeting, except as hereinafter provided. Each director shall hold office for the term for which elected or until a successor shall have been elected and qualified. [29-101.33] A corporation shall have a president and other officers, if any, prescribed in its bylaws, each of whom shall be elected by the board of directors at a time and in a manner prescribed by the bylaws.

All officers and agents of the corporation, as between themselves and the corporation, shall have such authority and perform such duties in the management of the property and affairs of the corporation as may be provided in the bylaws, or as may be determined by resolution of the board of directors not inconsistent with the bylaws. [29-101.43]

Share Issuance Rules

Each corporation shall have power to create and issue the number of shares stated in its Articles of Incorporation. Such shares may be divided into 1 or more classes, any or all of which classes may consist of shares with par value or shares without par value, [D.C. uses the concept of par value] with such designations, preferences, voting powers, special or relative rights; and such limitations, restrictions, or qualifications thereof as shall be stated in the articles of incorporation. The Articles of Incorporation may limit or deny the voting power of the shares of any class. [29-101.13]

Shares having a par value may be issued for such consideration, not less than the par value thereof, as shall be fixed from time to time by the board of directors.

Shares without par value may be issued for such consideration as may be fixed from time to time by the board of directors unless the Articles of Incorporation reserve to the shareholders the right to fix the consideration. In the event that such right be reserved as to any shares, the shareholders shall, prior to the issuance of such shares, fix the consideration to be received for such shares, by a vote of the holders of a majority of all outstanding shares entitled to vote thereon. [29-101.16]

The consideration for the issuance of shares may be paid, in whole or in part, in money; in other property, tangible or intangible; or in labor or services actually performed for the corporation. When payment of the consideration for which shares are to be issued, which, in the case of shares having a par value, shall be not less than the par value thereof, shall have been received by the corporation, such shares shall be deemed to be full paid and nonassessable.

Neither promissory notes nor future services shall constitute payment or part payment for shares of a corporation. [29-101.17]

If the shares issued shall consist wholly of shares having a par value, then the stated capital represented by such shares shall be not less than the aggregate par value of the shares so issued.

In order to determine that only a part of the consideration for which shares without par value may be issued from time to time shall be stated capital, the board of directors shall adopt a resolution setting forth the part of such consideration allocated to stated capital and the part otherwise allocated, and expressing such allocation in dollars.

If the board of directors shall not have determined (1) at the time of the issuance of any shares issued for cash, or (2) within 60 days after the issuance of any shares issued for labor or services actually performed for the corporation or issued for property other than cash, that only a part of the consideration for shares so issued shall be stated capital, then the stated capital of the corporation represented by such shares shall be an amount equal to the aggregate par value of all such shares having a par value, plus the consideration received for all such shares without par value. [29-101.18]

The shares of a corporation shall be represented by certificates, provided that the board of directors of the corporation may provide by resolution that some or all classes or series of its stock shall be uncertificated shares. A resolution shall not apply to shares represented by a certificate until the certificate is surrendered to the corporation. Every holder of stock represented by certificates shall be entitled to have a certificate signed by the president or a vice president of the corporation. [29-101.20]

Director Meeting Rules

Meetings of the board of directors, regular or special, may be held at such place within or without the District of Columbia as may be provided in the bylaws or by resolution adopted by a majority of the board of directors. [29-101.38]

Except as provided in Section 29-101.134 [which allows waiver of notice], meetings of the board of directors shall be held on such notice as is prescribed in the bylaws. Attendance of a director at a meeting shall constitute a waiver of notice of such meeting, except where a director attends a meeting for the express purpose of objecting to the transaction of any business because the meeting is not lawfully called or convened. Neither the business to be transacted at, nor the purpose of, any regular or special meeting of the board of directors need be specified in the notice or waiver of notice of such meeting. [29-101.39]

A majority of the number of directors fixed by the bylaws or, in the absence of a bylaw fixing the number of directors, of the number stated in the Articles of Incorporation, shall constitute a quorum for the transaction of business unless a greater number is required by the Articles of Incorporation or the bylaws. The act of the majority of the directors present at a meeting at which a quorum is present shall be the act of the board of directors, unless the act of a greater number is required by the Articles of Incorporation or the bylaws. [29-101.36]

A corporation shall have a president and other officers, if any, prescribed in its bylaws, each of whom shall be elected by the board of directors at a time and in a manner prescribed by the bylaws.

All officers and agents of the corporation, as between themselves and the corporation, shall have such authority and perform such duties in the management of the property and affairs of the corporation as may be provided in the bylaws, or as may be determined by resolution of the board of directors not inconsistent with the bylaws. [29-101.43]

Shareholder Meeting Rules

Meetings of shareholders may be held at such place within or without the District of Columbia as may be provided in the bylaws. In the absence of any such provision, all meetings shall be held at the registered office of the corporation.

An annual meeting of the shareholders shall be held at such time as may be provided in the bylaws. Failure to hold the annual meeting at the designated time shall not work a forfeiture or dissolution of the corporation.

Special meetings of the shareholders may be called by the president, the secretary, the board of directors, the holders of not less than one-fifth of all the outstanding shares entitled to vote, or such other officers or persons as may be provided in the Articles of Incorporation or the bylaws. [29-101.25]

Except as provided in Section 29-101.134 [which provides for waiver of notice], written or printed notice stating the place, day, and hour of the meeting, and, in case of a special meeting, the purpose or purposes for which the meeting is called, shall, in the absence of a provision in the bylaws specifying a different period of notice, be delivered not less than 10 nor more than 50 days before the date of the meeting, either personally or by mail, by or at the direction of the president, the secretary, or the officer or person calling the meeting, to each shareholder of record entitled to vote at such meeting. [29-101.26]

Unless otherwise provided in the Articles of Incorporation, each outstanding share shall be entitled to one vote on each matter submitted to a vote at a meeting of shareholders.

The Articles of Incorporation may provide that in all elections for directors every shareholder entitled to vote shall have the right to vote, in person or by proxy, the number of shares owned by him, for as many persons as there are directors to be elected, or to cumulate said shares, and give one candidate as many votes as the number of such directors multiplied by the number of his shares shall equal, or to distribute such votes on the same principle among any number of such candidates. [29-101.27]

Unless otherwise provided in the Articles of Incorporation or bylaws, a majority of the outstanding shares having voting power, represented in person or by proxy, shall constitute a quorum at a meeting of shareholders; provided, that in no event shall a quorum consist of less than one-third of the outstanding shares having voting power.

If a quorum is present, the affirmative vote of the majority of the shares represented at the meeting and entitled to vote on the subject matter shall be the act of the shareholders, unless the vote of a greater number, or voting by classes, is required by the Business Corporation Act or the Articles of Incorporation, and except that in elections of directors, those receiving the greatest number of votes shall be deemed elected even though not receiving a majority. [29-101.31]

Financial Disclosure Rules

If any person or persons holding in the aggregate 5% or more of all of the outstanding shares of a corporation shall present to any officer, director, or registered agent of the corporation a written request stating the purpose thereof, for a statement of its affairs, it shall be his [the officer's, director's, or agent's] duty to make or procure such a statement sworn to by the president or a vice president or by the treasurer or an assistant treasurer, embracing a particular account of its assets and liabilities in detail, and to have the same ready and on file at the registered office of the corporation within 30 days after the presentation of such request. Such statement shall at all times during business hours be open to the inspection of any shareholder, and he shall be entitled to copy the same. [29-101.45]

State Tax Information

Office of Tax and Revenue
202-727-4TAX (4829)
http://cfo.dc.gov/otr/site/default.asp

D.C. imposes a corporate franchise tax based on net taxable income. Note that D.C. also imposes an unincorporated business tax on noncorporate businesses.

Corporation Law Online

The D.C. Business Corporation Act is contained in Division V, Title 29 (Corporations), Chapter 1 of the D.C. Code, starting with Section 29-101. You can browse it from the following web page (expand District of Columbia Code, Division 5, Title 29, then select Chapter 1 to begin browsing the Act):

http://198.187.12/dc/lpext.dll?f=templates&fn=fs-main.htm&2.0

State Securities Information

Department of Insurance and Securities Regulation
810 First Street, NE, Suite 701
Washington, DC 20002
202-727-8000
http://disr.dc.gov/disr/cwp/view,a,1299,q,577307,disrNav,|32810|.asp

The D.C. Securities Act is contained in Title 2, Chapter 26, of the D.C. Code. The securities law regulations and publications are available from the DISR (Department of Insurance and Securities Regulation) website. Section 2-2601(6)(E) of the Act provides a securities transaction exemption for sales of shares to 25 or fewer persons during a 12-month period if the investors are purchasing the shares for investment only. Subsection (H) of the same section provides a securities transaction exemption for sales of shares to corporate employees or directors if no commissions are paid as part of the stock sales transactions. See the DISR website and call the Securities Bureau of the DISR for additional information on these and other exemptions available under D.C. law.

Creating Your Own Articles Form

You must create your own articles using the D.C. Articles of Incorporation Guidelines, discussed above.

FLORIDA

Corporate Filing Office

Florida Department of State
Division of Corporations
Corporate Filings
P.O. Box 6327
Tallahassee, FL 32314
850-245-6052
www.dos.state.fl.us/doc/index.html

State Corporate Forms

Florida provides Articles of Incorporation for a Profit Corporation with instructions and a Transmittal Letter.

Internet Forms: You can fill out and file Articles of Incorporation online from the state corporate filing office website. If you wish to prepare paper articles to mail to the state filing office, the state filing office website provides a downloadable fill-in-the-blanks articles (Profit Articles of Incorporation) form with instructions, plus other statutory forms.

Articles Instructions

Article I: The name of a Florida corporation must contain the word "corporation," "company," or "incorporated," or the abbreviation "Corp.," "Inc.," or "Co."

Names for use by corporations (and other business entities) cannot be reserved. You can search for available corporate names (as well as Florida fictitious name filings) at the following website affiliated with the department: www.sunbiz.org, or you can call the state filing office. Once you have determined that a corporate name is available, submit your proposed articles for filing as soon as possible. If the name is not available at the time of filing, you will be notified by the filing office.

Article III: For your corporation's specific purposes, you can simply state: "to engage in any and all lawful business." You can also leave this article blank or omit it altogether. (Only professional corporations are required to state a specific purpose.)

Article IV: In Florida, you do not need to state a par value for your shares. The filing fee is not based on your authorized shares, so you can authorize as many as you wish. Most incorporators authorize common shares with equal voting, dividend, and liquidation rights and no special restrictions. To do this, simply state the number of shares you wish to authorize. If you want to authorize one or more special classes of shares, you must state the name of each class or series, the number of shares in

each, and the rights and restrictions associated with each class or series.

Article V: You can leave this article blank or omit it.

Article VI: State the name and Florida street address of your initial agent.

Make sure the person named as agent in Article VI and the incorporator named in Article VII each sign the appropriate signature line at the bottom of the articles. Provide a date for each signature.

Filing Fee: $35 for filing articles, plus $35 for Designation of Registered Agent (included in articles) for a total of $70, payable to the "Florida Department of State." Include an additional $8.75 if you want to receive a certified copy of your articles. Add $8.75 more for a Certificate of Status, if you want one (this document is not very helpful; it just says your corporation is active).

Submit an original and one copy of your articles, plus a Transmittal Letter (included with the downloadable articles available from the state filing office website). Make sure to check the correct box on the Transmittal Letter to indicate the amount of fees included with your mailing (most incorporators will simply pay the minimum filing fee of $70). After you file, the department will send you a letter of acknowledgment. If you want to receive a certified copy of your approved articles from the filing office, add $8.75 to your check. Add an additional $8.75 if you want a Certificate of Status (not very helpful; it says simply that your corporation is active).

Director and Officer Rules

Directors must be natural persons who are 18 years of age or older but need not be residents of this state or shareholders of the corporation unless the Articles of Incorporation or bylaws so require. [607.0802]

A board of directors must consist of one or more individuals, with the number specified in or fixed in accordance with the Articles of Incorporation or bylaws.

Directors are elected at the first annual shareholders' meeting and at each annual meeting thereafter unless their terms are staggered under Section 607.0806. [607.0803]

The terms of the initial directors of a corporation expire at the first shareholders' meeting at which directors are elected.

The terms of all other directors expire at the next annual shareholders' meeting following their election unless their terms are staggered under Section 607.0806. [607.0805]

A corporation shall have the officers described in its by-laws or appointed by the board of directors in accordance with the bylaws.

The bylaws or the board of directors shall delegate to one of the officers responsibility for preparing minutes of the directors' and shareholders' meetings and for authenticating records of the corporation.

The same individual may simultaneously hold more than one office in a corporation. [607.08401]

Share Issuance Rules

Florida law does not use the concept of par value.

The board of directors may authorize shares to be issued for consideration consisting of any tangible or intangible property or benefit to the corporation, including cash, promissory notes, services performed, promises to perform services evidenced by a written contract, or other securities of the corporation.

The corporation may place in escrow shares issued for a contract for future services or benefits or a promissory note, or make other arrangements to restrict the transfer of the shares, and may credit distributions in respect of the shares against their purchase price, until the services are performed, the note is paid, or the benefits received. If the services are not performed, the shares escrowed or restricted and the distributions credited may be canceled in whole or part. [607.0621]

Shares may but need not be represented by certificates. Unless this act or another statute expressly provides otherwise, the rights and obligations of shareholders are identical whether or not their shares are represented by certificates.

At a minimum, each share certificate must state on its face: (a) the name of the issuing corporation and that the corporation is organized under the laws of this state; (b) the name of the person to whom issued; and (c) the number and class of shares and the designation of the series, if any, the certificate represents.

Each share certificate: (a) must be signed (either manually or in facsimile) by an officer or officers designated in the bylaws or designated by the board of directors, and (b) may bear the corporate seal or its facsimile. [607.0625]

Director Meeting Rules

The board of directors may hold regular or special meetings in or out of the state of Florida.

Meetings of the board of directors may be called by the chair of the board or by the president unless otherwise provided in the Articles of Incorporation or the bylaws. [607.0820]

Unless the Articles of Incorporation or bylaws provide otherwise, regular meetings of the board of directors may be held without notice of the date, time, place, or purpose of the meeting.

Unless the Articles of Incorporation or bylaws provide for a longer or shorter period, special meetings of the board of directors must be preceded by at least two days' notice of the date, time, and place of the meeting. The notice need not describe the purpose of the special meeting unless required by the Articles of Incorporation or bylaws. [607.0822]

Unless the Articles of Incorporation or bylaws require a different number, a quorum of a board of directors consists of a majority of the number of directors prescribed by the Articles of Incorporation or the bylaws.

The Articles of Incorporation may authorize a quorum of a board of directors to consist of less than a majority but no fewer than one-third of the prescribed number of directors determined under the Articles of Incorporation or the bylaws.

If a quorum is present when a vote is taken, the affirmative vote of a majority of directors present is the act of the board of directors unless the Articles of Incorporation or bylaws require the vote of a greater number of directors. [607.0824]

Shareholder Meeting Rules

A corporation shall hold a meeting of shareholders annually, for the election of directors and for the transaction of any proper business, at a time stated in or fixed in accordance with the bylaws. [607.0701] Unless the Business Corporation Act or the Articles of Incorporation require otherwise, notice of an annual meeting need not include a description of the purpose or purposes for which the meeting is called. [607.0705]

A corporation shall hold a special meeting of shareholders: (a) on call of its board of directors or the person or persons authorized to do so by the Articles of Incorporation or bylaws; or (b) if the holders of not less than 10%, unless a greater percentage not to exceed 50% is required by the Articles of Incorporation, of all the votes entitled to be cast on any issue proposed to be considered at the proposed special meeting sign, date, and deliver to the corporation's secretary one or more written demands for the meeting describing the purpose or purposes for which it is to be held.

Only business within the purpose or purposes described in the special meeting notice may be conducted at a special shareholders' meeting. [607.0702]

A corporation shall notify shareholders of the date, time, and place of each annual and special shareholders' meeting no fewer than ten or more than 60 days before the meeting date. Unless the Business Corporation Act or the Articles of Incorporation require otherwise, the corporation is required to give notice only to shareholders entitled to vote at the meeting. Notice shall be given in the manner provided in Section 607.0141, by or at the direction of the president, the secretary, or the officer or persons calling the meeting. If the notice is mailed at least 30 days before the date of the meeting, it may be done by a class of United States mail other than first class. Notwithstanding Section 607.0141, if mailed, such notice shall be deemed to be delivered when deposited in the United States mail addressed to the shareholder at her or his address as it appears on the stock transfer books of the corporation, with postage thereon prepaid.

Notice of a special meeting must include a description of the purpose or purposes for which the meeting is called. [607.0705]

Except as provided in Subsections (2), (3), and (4) of this section [covering shares owned by corporations and other special types of legal entities] or unless the Articles of Incorporation or the Business Corporation Act provides otherwise, each outstanding share, regardless of class, is entitled to one vote on each matter submitted to a vote at a meeting of shareholders. Only shares are entitled to vote. If the Articles of Incorporation provide for more or less than one vote for any share on any matter, every reference in the Business Corporation Act to a majority or other proportion of shares shall refer to such a majority or other proportion of votes entitled to be cast. [607.0721]

Shares entitled to vote as a separate voting group may take action on a matter at a meeting only if a quorum of those shares exists with respect to that matter. Unless the Articles of Incorporation or the Business Corporation Act provides otherwise, a majority of the votes entitled to be cast on the matter by the voting group constitutes a quorum of that voting group for action on that matter.

If a quorum exists, action on a matter (other than the election of directors) by a voting group is approved if the votes cast within the voting group favoring the action exceed the votes cast opposing the action, unless the Ar-

ticles of Incorporation or the Business Corporation Act requires a greater number of affirmative votes.

The election of directors is governed by Section 607.0728. [607.0725]

Unless otherwise provided in the Articles of Incorporation, directors are elected by a plurality of the votes cast by the shares entitled to vote in the election at a meeting at which a quorum is present.

Each shareholder who is entitled to vote at an election of directors has the right to vote the number of shares owned by him or her for as many persons as there are directors to be elected and for whose election the shareholder has a right to vote. Shareholders do not have a right to cumulate their votes for directors unless the Articles of Incorporation so provide.

A statement included in the Articles of Incorporation that "all or a designated voting group of shareholders are entitled to cumulate their votes for directors," or words of similar import, means that the shareholders designated are entitled to multiply the number of votes they are entitled to cast by the number of directors for whom they are entitled to vote and cast the product for a single candidate or distribute the product among two or more candidates. [607.0728]

Financial Disclosure Rules

Unless modified by resolution of the shareholders within 120 days of the close of each fiscal year, a corporation shall furnish its shareholders annual financial statements which may be consolidated or combined statements of the corporation and one or more of its subsidiaries, as appropriate, that include a balance sheet as of the end of the fiscal year, an income statement for that year, and a statement of cash flows for that year. If financial statements are prepared for the corporation on the basis of generally accepted accounting principles, the annual financial statements must also be prepared on that basis.

If the annual financial statements are reported on by a public accountant, his or her report must accompany them. If not, the statements must be accompanied by a statement of the president or the person responsible for the corporation's accounting records: (a) stating his or her reasonable belief whether the statements were prepared on the basis of generally accepted accounting principles and, if not, describing the basis of preparation; and (b) describing any respects in which the statements were not prepared on a basis of accounting consistent with the statements prepared for the preceding year.

A corporation shall mail the annual financial statements to each shareholder within 120 days after the close of each fiscal year or within such additional time thereafter as is reasonably necessary to enable the corporation to prepare its financial statements if, for reasons beyond the corporation's control, it is unable to prepare its financial statements within the prescribed period. Thereafter, on written request from a shareholder who was not mailed the statements, the corporation shall mail him or her the latest annual financial statements.

If a corporation does not comply with the shareholder's request for annual financial statements pursuant to this section within 30 days of delivery of such request to the corporation, the circuit court in the county where the corporation's principal office (or, if none in this state, its registered office) is located may, on application of the shareholder, summarily order the corporation to furnish such financial statements. If the court orders the corporation to furnish the shareholder with the financial statements demanded, it shall also order the corporation to pay the shareholder's costs, including reasonable attorney's fees incurred to obtain the order and otherwise enforce its rights under this section. [607.1620]

State Tax Information

Department of Revenue, Tallahassee
800-352-3671
http://sun6.dms.state.fl.us/dor

Florida imposes a corporate income tax. The Department of Revenue also collects a documentary stamp tax, due on the original issuance of your shares. The state does not provide a form automatically. Download Form DR-228, "Documentary Stamp Tax Return for Nonregistered Taxpayers," from the Department of Revenue website, and pay the tax with the return. Stamps are no longer issued—you simply pay the tax and make a note in your stock register that you did so. The tax rate is $.35 per $100 (or portion thereof) of par value of all the shares issued to your shareholders as part of your initial stock issuance. If you issue shares without par value, the tax applies to the actual amount paid for all the shares issued to your initial shareholders.

Corporation Law Online

The Florida Business Corporation Act is contained in Title XXXVI (Business Organizations), Chapter 607, of the Florida Statutes, starting with Section 607.0101. To find the Act, visit the legal research area of Nolo's website at www.nolo.com/statute/state.cfm. Click on "Florida." From there, you can browse Title XXXVI of the Statutes.

State Securities Information

Florida Department of Banking and Finance
Division of Securities and Finance
101 E. Gaines Street
Tallahassee, FL 32399-0350
850-410-9805
www.dbf.state.fl.us/licensing/securitiesofferings.html

The DBF website provides the Florida Securities and Investor Protection Act (Title XXXIII, Chapter 517, of the Florida Statutes) and the rules for exemption from registration of securities and securities dealers. Various securities and securities transaction exemptions are available. For example, Section 517.061(11) of the Act exempts private offers and sales to 35 or fewer persons if (1) there is no advertisement of the offering, (2) there is full disclosure of pertinent information, (3) no commissions are paid in connection with the offering, and (4) a few other requirements are met. The site provides explanations of the requirements associated with this and other securities exemptions, as well as the forms you must to submit to qualify for certain exemptions. Or you can call the Division of Securities and Finance for more information.

Creating Your Own Articles Form

You can create your own articles form.

GEORGIA

Corporate Filing Office

Secretary of State
Corporations Division
Suite 315, West Tower
2 Martin Luther King, Jr., Drive
Atlanta, GA 30334
404-656-2817
Satellite Office: Tifton, Georgia 229-391-3732
www.sos.state.ga.us/corporations

State Corporate Forms

Georgia provides sample Articles of Incorporation, plus a transmittal form (Form BR227), which must be filed with the articles.

Internet Forms: Corporate forms, including sample articles, transmittal of articles form, and other corporate forms are available for downloading from the state filing office website.

Articles Instructions

Type articles on white 8-1/2" x 11" paper, following the sample form and instructions provided by the state filing office. Here are special instructions that correspond to the articles in the Georgia sample form:

Article 1: The name of a Georgia corporation must contain the word "corporation," "incorporated," "company," or "limited," or the abbreviation "corp.," "inc.," "co.," or "ltd."

A corporate name reservation for 30 days costs $25. You can check name availability and reserve an available corporate name from the corporate filing office website (click the "Online Requests for Name Reservations" link on the main filing office Web page). Once a name is reserved, the office will email a name reservation number to you. If you reserve a name, make sure this number is inserted on the Transmittal Form you include with your Articles (see below).

Article 2: Georgia law does not use the concept of par value, so you do not need to state a par value for your shares. The filing fee is not based on your authorized shares, so you can authorize as many as you wish. Most incorporators authorize common shares with equal voting, dividend, and liquidation rights and no special restrictions. To do this, simply state the number of shares you wish to authorize. If you want to authorize one or more special classes of shares, you must state the name of each class or series, the number of shares in each, and

the rights and restrictions associated with each class or series.

Article 4: Insert the name and street address of your incorporator. This person should sign your Articles. Make sure to show the person's title as "Incorporator" after the signature line at the bottom of the form. The incorporator should also sign the transmittal form.

Post-filing Publication: No later than one business day after your articles are filed, you must publish a Notice of Intent of Incorporation in a designated legal notice newspaper in the county where the initial registered office of your corporation is located. The charge is $40 for the required filing once per week for two consecutive weeks. A sample notice that you can fill in and send to the newspaper is provided in the incorporation instructions available online from the state filing office website. To determine the officially designated newspaper for your county, call the Clerk of the Superior Court listed in your telephone directory (or go online to www.sos.state.ga.us/elections/legalorgans.htm). You should mail or deliver your Notice of Intent to Incorporate to the designated newspaper on the same day you mail your articles to the state.

File the original and one copy of the Articles of Incorporation, plus the transmittal form. A Certificate of Incorporation will be mailed to you within five business days of filing.

Filing Fee: $100, payable to "Secretary of State." Attach the check to your completed transmittal form.

Director and Officer Rules

Directors shall be natural persons who are 18 years of age or older but need not be residents of this state nor shareholders of the corporation unless the articles of incorporation so require. The articles of incorporation or bylaws may prescribe additional qualifications for directors. [14-2-802]

A board of directors must consist of one or more individuals, with the number specified in or fixed in accordance with the articles of incorporation or bylaws.

After initial election or appointment pursuant to Code Section 14-2-205, directors are elected at each annual shareholders' meeting unless their terms are staggered under Code Section 14-2-806. [14-2-803]

The terms of the initial directors of a corporation expire at the first shareholders' meeting at which directors are elected.

The terms of all other directors expire at the next annual shareholders' meeting following their election unless their terms are staggered under Code Section 14-2-806. [14-2-805]

A corporation has the officers described in its bylaws or appointed by the board of directors in accordance with the bylaws.

The bylaws or the board of directors shall delegate to one of the officers responsibility for preparing minutes of the directors' and shareholders' meetings and for authenticating records of the corporation.

The same individual may simultaneously hold more than one office in a corporation. [14-2-840]

Share Issuance Rules

Georgia law does not use the concept of par value.

The board of directors may authorize shares to be issued for consideration consisting of any tangible or intangible property or benefit to the corporation, including cash, promissory notes, services performed, contracts for services to be performed, or other securities of the corporation.

The corporation may place in escrow shares issued for a contract for future services or benefits or a promissory note, or make other arrangements to restrict the transfer of the shares, and may credit distributions in respect of the shares against their purchase price, until the services are performed, the note is paid, or the benefits received. If the services are not performed, the note is not paid, or the benefits are not received, the shares escrowed or restricted and the distributions credited may be canceled in whole or in part. [14-2-621]

At a minimum each share certificate must state on its face: (1) the name of the issuing corporation and that it is organized under the law of this state; (2) the name of the person to whom the certificate is issued; and (3) the number and class of shares and the designation of the series, if any, the certificate represents.

Each share certificate: (1) must be signed, either manually or in facsimile, by one or more officers designated in the bylaws or by the board of directors; and (2) may bear the corporate seal or its facsimile. [14-2-625]

Director Meeting Rules

Unless the Articles of Incorporation or bylaws provide otherwise, regular meetings of the board of directors may be held without notice of the date, time, place, or purpose of the meeting.

Unless the Articles of Incorporation or bylaws provide for a longer or shorter period, special meetings of the board of directors must be preceded by at least two days' notice of the date, time, and place of the meeting. The notice need not describe the purpose of the special meeting unless required by the Articles of Incorporation or bylaws. [14-2-822]

Unless the Business Corporation Code, Articles of Incorporation, or bylaws require a greater number or unless otherwise specifically provided in the Business Corporation Code, a quorum of a board of directors consists of: (1) a majority of the fixed number of directors if the corporation has a fixed board size; or (2) a majority of the number of directors prescribed or, if no number is prescribed, the number in office immediately before the meeting begins, if the corporation has a variable-range size board.

The Articles of Incorporation or bylaws may authorize a quorum of a board of directors to consist of no fewer than one-third of the fixed or prescribed number of directors determined under Subsection (a) of this Code section [previous paragraph].

If a quorum is present when a vote is taken, the affirmative vote of a majority of directors present is the act of the board of directors unless the Business Corporation Code, Articles of Incorporation, or bylaws require the vote of a greater number of directors. [14-2-824]

Shareholder Meeting Rules

A corporation shall hold a meeting of shareholders annually at a time stated in or fixed in accordance with the bylaws. [14-2-701]

A corporation shall hold a special meeting of shareholders (1) on call of its board of directors or the person or persons authorized to do so by the Articles of Incorporation or bylaws; (2) [not quoted here; it applies to corporations with more than 100 shareholders] (3) in the case of a corporation having 100 or fewer shareholders of record, if the holders of at least 25%, or such lesser percentage as may be provided in the Articles of Incorporation or bylaws, of all the votes entitled to be cast on any issue to be considered at the proposed special meeting sign, date, and deliver to the corporation one or more written demands for the meeting describing the purpose or purposes for which it is to be held. [14-2-705]

A corporation shall notify shareholders of the date, time, and place of each annual and special shareholders' meeting no fewer than ten nor more than 60 days before the meeting date. Unless the Business Corporation Code or the Articles of Incorporation require otherwise, the corporation is required to give notice only to shareholders entitled to vote at the meeting.

Unless the Business Corporation Code or the Articles of Incorporation require otherwise, notice of an annual meeting need not include a description of the purpose or purposes for which the meeting is called.

Notice of a special meeting must include a description of the purpose or purposes for which the meeting is called. [14-2-705]

Only business within the purpose or purposes described in the meeting notice may be conducted at a special shareholders' meeting. [14-2-702]

Except as provided in Subsections (b) and (c) of this section [covering special shares of stock owned by a corporation], or unless the Articles of Incorporation provide otherwise, each outstanding share (other than shares of preferred stock issued or authorized before July 1, 1989), regardless of class, is entitled to one vote on each matter voted on at a shareholders' meeting. Only shares are entitled to vote. [14-2-721]

Shares entitled to vote as a separate voting group may take action on a matter at a meeting only if a quorum of those shares exists with respect to that matter. Unless the Articles of Incorporation or the Business Corporation Code provides otherwise, a majority of the votes entitled to be cast on the matter by the voting group constitutes a quorum of that voting group for action on that matter.

If a quorum exists, action on a matter (other than the election of directors) by a voting group is approved if the votes cast within the voting group favoring the action exceed the votes cast opposing the action, unless the Articles of Incorporation, a bylaw adopted by the shareholders under Section 14-2-1021, or the Business Corporation Act requires a greater number of affirmative votes.

The election of directors is governed by Code Section 14-2-728. [14-2-725]

The Articles of Incorporation or a bylaw adopted under Section 14-2-1021 may provide for a greater or lesser quorum (but not less than one-third of the votes entitled to be cast) or a greater voting requirement for shareholders (or voting groups of shareholders) than is provided for by the Business Corporation Code. [14-2-727]

Unless otherwise provided in the Articles of Incorporation, directors are elected by a plurality of the votes cast by the shares entitled to vote in the election at a meeting at which a quorum is present.

Shareholders do not have a right to cumulate their votes for directors unless the Articles of Incorporation so provide.

Shares otherwise entitled to vote cumulatively may not be voted cumulatively at a particular meeting unless: (1) the meeting notice or proxy statement accompanying the notice states that cumulative voting will be in effect; or (2) a shareholder who has the right to cumulate his votes gives notice to the corporation not less than 48 hours before the time set for the meeting of his intent to cumulate his votes during the meeting, and if one shareholder gives this notice all other shareholders in the same voting group participating in the election are entitled to cumulate their votes without giving further notice. [14-2-728]

Financial Disclosure Rules

Not later than four months after the close of each fiscal year and in any case prior to the annual meeting of shareholders, each corporation shall prepare (1) a balance sheet showing in reasonable detail the financial condition of the corporation as of the close of its fiscal year; and (2) a profit and loss statement showing the results of its operation during its fiscal year. On written request, the corporation promptly shall mail to any shareholder of record a copy of the most recent balance sheet and profit and loss statement. If prepared for other purposes, the corporation shall also furnish on written request a statement of sources and applications of funds and a statement of changes in shareholders' equity for the fiscal year.

If financial statements are prepared by the corporation on the basis of generally accepted accounting principles, the annual financial statements must also be prepared, and disclose that they are prepared, on that basis. If financial statements are prepared otherwise than on the basis of generally accepted accounting principles, they must so disclose and must be prepared on the same basis as other reports or statements prepared by the corporation for the use of others.

If the annual financial statements are reported on by a public accountant, his report must accompany them. If not, the statements must be accompanied by a statement of the president or the person responsible for the corporation's accounting records: (1) stating his reasonable belief whether the statements were prepared on the basis of generally accepted accounting principles and, if not, describing the basis of preparation; and (2) describing any respects in which the statements were not prepared on a basis of accounting consistent with the statements prepared for the preceding year. [14-2-1620]

State Tax Information

Department of Revenue, Atlanta
404-656-4071
www2.state.ga.us/departments/dor
Georgia imposes a corporate income tax.

Corporation Law Online

The Georgia Business Corporation Code begins with Section 14-2-101 of the Georgia Code. To find the Code, visit the legal research area of Nolo's website at www.nolo.com/statute/state.cfm. Click on "Georgia." Type 14-2-101 in the "Search by Code Number" box to start browsing the laws.

State Securities Information

Securities and Business Regulation Division
Suite 802, West Tower
2 Martin Luther King, Jr., Drive
Atlanta, GA 30334
404-656-2894
www.sos.state.ga.us/securities

The Georgia Securities Act is contained in Title 10, Chapter 5, of the Georgia Code. You can browse it from a link provided on the Securities Division website. It provides several securities exemptions, which may require you to file a notice form with the Division and pay a fee. For example, Section 10-5-9(13) of the Act contains an exemption for the private offer and sale of securities to 15 or fewer persons, provided that you meet certain requirements. In addition, a uniform limited offering exemption is provided under Rule 590-4-5-.01. This exemption parallels the Federal Regulation D securities exemption, allowing the sale of securities to no more than 35 unaccredited investors. For more information and forms, see the Division website.

Creating Your Own Articles Form

You must create your own articles following the Georgia sample form and the instructions provided in "Articles Instructions," above.

HAWAII

Corporate Filing Office

Department of Commerce and Consumer Affairs
Business Registration Division
P.O. Box 40
Honolulu, HI 96810
808-586-2744
Interisland toll-free telephone numbers are listed on the state filing office website.

www.businessregistrations.com

State Corporate Forms

Hawaii provides fill-in-the-blanks Articles of Incorporation.

Internet Forms: You can fill out and file Articles of Incorporation online from the state corporate filing office website. If you wish to prepare paper articles to mail to the state filing office, you can view and download a fill-in-the-blanks Corporate Articles form (Form DC-1), separate articles instructions, and other statutory forms from the state filing office website.

Articles Instructions

Articles must be printed and signed in black ink.

Article I: The name of a Hawaii corporation must contain the word "Corporation," "Incorporated," or "Limited" or the abbreviation "Corp.," "Inc.," or "Ltd."

You can check name availability by doing a business name search from www.ehawaiigov.org/main/html, which is linked to the state filing office website home page. An available corporate name may be reserved for 120 days for $20. Check the website to see whether it allows you to reserve a name online. (The online name reservation service was being modified when we checked the site prior to the publication of this edition.)

Article IV: Hawaii law does not use the concept of par value, so you do not need to state a par value for your shares. The filing fee is not based on your authorized shares, so you can authorize as many as you wish. Most incorporators authorize common shares with equal voting, dividend, and liquidation rights and no special restrictions. To do this, simply state the number of shares you wish to authorize. If you want to authorize one or more special classes of shares, you must state the name of each class or series, the number of shares in each, and the rights and restrictions associated with each class or series.

Article V: At least one person (typically, an initial director or officer) must sign as incorporator at the bottom of the form.

Submit one original and one copy of the completed articles. Include the name, address, and telephone number of the incorporator in a note or cover letter. After approving your articles, the Department will send you a file-stamped copy.

Filing Fee: $100, payable to the "Department of Commerce and Consumer Affairs." Expedited one-day filing costs an additional $50. If you want certified copies of your articles, submit the number of copies you desire, and make sure to request certification of the copies in a note or cover letter. The extra fee for each certified copy is $20 per copy.

Director and Officer Rules

If the corporation has only one shareholder, the corporation shall have one or more directors. If the corporation has two shareholders, the corporation shall have two or more directors. If the corporation has three or more shareholders, the corporation shall have three or more directors. The number of directors shall be fixed by, or in the manner provided in, the Articles of Incorporation or the bylaws, except as to the number constituting the initial board of directors, which number shall be fixed by the Articles of Incorporation. The number of directors may be increased or decreased from time to time by amendment to, or in the manner provided in, the Articles of Incorporation or the bylaws, but no decrease shall have the effect of shortening the term of any incumbent director. In the absence of a bylaw providing for the number of directors, the number shall be the same as that provided for in the Articles of Incorporation. The names and addresses of the members of the first board of directors shall be stated in the Articles of Incorporation. Such persons shall hold office until the first annual meeting of shareholders, and until their successors shall have been elected and qualified. At the first annual meeting of shareholders and at each annual meeting thereafter the shareholders shall elect directors to hold office until the next succeeding annual meeting, except in case of the classification of directors as permitted by this chapter. Each director shall hold office for the term for which the director is elected and until the director's successor shall have been elected and qualified. [415-36]

The officers of a corporation shall consist of a president, one or more vice presidents as may be prescribed by the bylaws, a secretary, and a treasurer, each of whom shall be elected or appointed by the board of directors at such time and in such manner as may be prescribed by the bylaws. Such other officers and assistant officers and agents as may be deemed necessary may be elected or appointed by the board of directors or chosen in such other manner as may be prescribed by the bylaws. Any two or more offices may be held by the same individual, provided that every corporation which has two or more directors shall have not less than two individuals as officers. [415-50]

Share Issuance Rules

Hawaii law, generally, does not use the concept of par value, but share certificates must state whether the shares have a stated par value or are without par value. Modern practice favors the issuance of shares without par value.

Subject to any restrictions in the articles of incorporation: (1) shares may be issued for such consideration as shall be authorized by the board of directors establishing a price (in money or other consideration) or a minimum price or general formula or method by which the price will be determined; and (2) on authorization by the board of directors, the corporation may issue its own shares in exchange for or in conversion of its outstanding shares, or distribute its own shares pro rata to its shareholders or the shareholders of one or more classes or series, to effectuate stock dividends or splits, and any such transaction shall not require consideration; provided that no such issuance of shares of any class or series shall be made to the holders of shares of any other class or series unless it is either expressly provided for in the Articles of Incorporation, or is authorized by an affirmative vote or the written consent of the holders of at least a majority of the outstanding shares of the class or series in which the distribution is to be made. [415-18]

The powers granted in this section to the board of directors may be reserved to the shareholders by the Articles of Incorporation.

The board of directors may authorize shares to be issued for consideration consisting of any tangible or intangible property or benefit to the corporation, including cash, promissory notes, services performed, contracts for services to be performed, or other securities of the corporation.

During the first two years after incorporation the corporation shall, and thereafter the corporation may, place in escrow shares issued for a contract for future services or benefits or a promissory note, or make other arrange-ments to restrict the transfer of the shares. The corporation may credit distributions in respect of the shares against their purchase price, until the services are performed, the note paid, or the benefits received. If the services are not performed, the note is not paid, or the benefits are not received, the shares escrowed or restricted and the distributions credited may be cancelled in whole or in part.

If a corporation issues or authorizes issuance of shares for promissory notes or for promises to render services in the future, the corporation shall report in writing to the shareholders the number of shares authorized or issued, and the consideration received by the corporation, with or before the notice of the next shareholders' meeting. [415-19]

The shares of a corporation shall be represented by certificates or shall be uncertificated shares. Certificates shall be signed by the chairperson or vice chairperson of the board of directors or the president or a vice president, and by the treasurer or an assistant treasurer, or the secretary or an assistant secretary of the corporation, and may be sealed with the seal of the corporation or a facsimile thereof. Any or all of the signatures on a certificate may be a facsimile. In case any officer, transfer agent, or registrar who has signed or whose facsimile signature has been placed on the certificate has ceased to be an officer, transfer agent, or registrar before the certificate is issued, the certificate may be issued by the corporation with the same effect as if the officer, transfer agent, or registrar were an officer, transfer agent, or registrar at the date of its issue.

Every certificate representing shares issued by a corporation which is authorized to issue shares of more than one class shall set forth on the face or back of the certificate, or shall state that the corporation will furnish to any shareholder on request and without charge, a full statement of the designations, preferences, limitations, and relative rights of the shares of each class authorized to be issued, and if the corporation is authorized to issue any preferred or special class in series, the variations in the relative rights and preferences between the shares of each such series so far as the same have been fixed and determined and the authority of the board of directors to fix and determine the relative rights and preferences of subsequent series.

Each certificate representing shares shall state on the face thereof: (1) that the corporation is organized under the laws of this State; (2) the name of the person to whom the certificate is issued; (3) the number and class of shares, and the designation of the series, if any, which the certificate represents; and (4) the par value of each share represented by the certificate, or a statement that the shares are without par value. [415-23]

Director Meeting Rules

Meetings of the board of directors, regular or special, may be held either within or without the state of Hawaii.

Regular meetings of the board of directors or any committee designated thereby may be held with or without notice as prescribed in the bylaws. Special meetings of the board of directors or any committee designated thereby shall be held on such notice as is prescribed in the bylaws. Attendance of a director at a meeting shall constitute a waiver of notice of the meeting, except where a director attends a meeting for the express purpose of objecting to the transaction of any business because the meeting is not lawfully called or convened. Neither the business to be transacted at, nor the purpose of, any regular or special meeting of the board of directors or any committee designated thereby need be specified in the notice or waiver of notice of the meeting unless required by the bylaws. [415-43]

A majority of the number of directors fixed by or in the manner provided in the bylaws or in the absence of a bylaw fixing or providing for the number of directors, then of the number stated in the Articles of Incorporation, shall constitute a quorum for the transaction of business unless a greater number is required by the Articles of Incorporation or the bylaws. The act of the majority of the directors present at a meeting at which a quorum is present shall be the act of the board of directors, unless the act of a greater number is required by the Articles of Incorporation or the bylaws. [415-40]

Shareholder Meeting Rules

An annual meeting of the shareholders shall be held at such time as may be stated in or fixed in accordance with the bylaws. If the annual meeting is not held within any 13-month period any circuit court may, on the application of any shareholder, summarily order a meeting to be held.

Special meetings of the shareholders may be called by the board of directors, the holders of not less than one-tenth of all the shares entitled to vote at the meeting, or such other persons as may be authorized in the Articles of Incorporation or the bylaws. [415-28]

Written notice stating the place, day, and hour of the meeting and, in the case of a special meeting, the purpose or purposes for which the meeting is called, shall be delivered not less than ten nor more than 75 days before the date of the meeting, either personally or by mail, by

or at the direction of the president, the secretary, or the officer or persons calling the meeting, to each shareholder of record entitled to vote at the meeting. If mailed, the notice shall be deemed to be delivered when deposited in the United States mail addressed to the shareholder at the shareholder's address as it appears on the stock transfer books of the corporation, with postage thereon prepaid. [415-29]

The officer or agent having charge of the stock transfer books for shares of a corporation shall make a complete record of the shareholders entitled to vote at the meeting or any adjournment thereof, arranged in alphabetical order, with the address of and the number of shares held by each shareholder. The record shall be produced and kept open at the time and place of the meeting and shall be subject to the inspection of any shareholder during the whole time of the meeting for the purposes thereof.

Failure to comply with the requirements of this section shall not affect the validity of any action taken at the meeting.

An officer or agent having charge of the stock transfer books who shall fail to prepare the record of shareholders, or produce and keep it open for inspection at the meeting, as provided in this section, shall be liable to any shareholder suffering damage on account of such failure, to the extent of such damage. [415-31]

Unless otherwise provided in the Articles of Incorporation, a majority of the shares entitled to vote, represented in person or by proxy, shall constitute a quorum at a meeting of shareholders, but in no event shall a quorum consist of less than one-third of the shares entitled to vote at the meeting. If a quorum is present, the affirmative vote of the majority of the shares represented at the meeting and entitled to vote on the subject matter shall be the act of the shareholders, unless the vote of a greater number or voting by classes is required by the Business Corporation Act or the Articles of Incorporation or bylaws. [415-32]

Each outstanding share, regardless of class, shall be entitled to one vote on each matter submitted to a vote at a meeting of shareholders, except as may be otherwise provided in the Articles of Incorporation. If the Articles of Incorporation provide for more or less than one vote for any share on any matter, every reference in the Business Corporation Act to a majority or other proportion of shares shall refer to such a majority or other proportion of votes entitled to be cast.

If, not less than 48 hours prior to the time fixed for any annual or special meeting, any shareholder or shareholders deliver to any officer of the corporation, a request that the election of directors to be elected at the meeting be by cumulative voting, then the directors to be elected at the meeting shall be chosen as follows: (1) each shareholder present in person or represented by proxy at the meeting shall have a number of votes equal to the number of shares of capital stock owned by the shareholder multiplied by the number of directors to be elected at the meeting; (2) each shareholder shall be entitled to cumulate the votes of said shareholder and give all thereof to one nominee or to distribute the votes of said shareholder in such manner as the shareholder determines among any or all of the nominees; and (3) the nominees receiving the highest number of votes on the foregoing basis, up to the total number of directors to be elected at the meeting, shall be the successful nominees. The right to have directors elected by cumulative voting as aforesaid shall exist notwithstanding that provision therefor is not included in the Articles of Incorporation or bylaws, and this right shall not be restricted or qualified by any provisions of the Articles of Incorporation or bylaws; provided that this right may be restricted, qualified, or eliminated by a provision of the Articles of Incorporation or bylaws of any corporation having a class of equity securities registered pursuant to the Securities Exchange Act of 1934, as amended, which are either listed on a national securities exchange or traded over the counter on the National Market of the National Association of Securities Dealers, Inc., Automated Quotation System. This section shall not prevent the filling of vacancies in the board of directors, which vacancies may be filled in such manner as may be provided in the Articles of Incorporation or bylaws. [415-33]

Financial Disclosure Rules

The Hawaii Business Corporation Act does not contain a specific law governing financial disclosures.

State Tax Information

Hawaii Department of Taxation, Honolulu (also Hawaii, Maui, and Kauai)
808-587-4242
www.state.hi.us/tax/tax.html

Hawaii imposes a corporate income tax.

Corporation Law Online

The Hawaii Revised Business Corporation, Chapter 414 of the Hawaii Statutes, starting with section 414-1, can be browsed from the web page shown below (select "Legal Info" at the bottom of the page, click "Statutes," then select "Hawaii Business Corporation Act Chapter 414"). If the statutes are not linked (we occasionally experience this problem), go to www.capitol.hawaii.gov, then click "Links," then "Hawaii Revised Statutes," then click "Browse the HRS sections" at the bottom of the page and select the volume that contains Chapter 414 of the Hawaii revised Statutes, which is shown as "hrs414".

www.businessregistrations.com

State Securities Information

Department of Commerce and Consumer Affairs
Business Registration Division
Securities Registration Section
P.O. Box 40
Honolulu, HI 96810
808-586-2722
www.state.hi.us/dcca/breg-seu/compliance.html

The Hawaii Uniform Securities Act is contained in Chapter 485 of the Hawaii Revised Statutes. Section 485-6(9) provides an exemption for offers of securities to 25 or fewer investors if all buyers represent that they are purchasing for investment and certain other conditions are met. Section 485-6(16) provides an exemption for offers and sales of securities to accredited investors as defined by Federal Regulation D. To qualify, you must file a notice with the Securities Section and meet other conditions. The Securities Section website currently provides necessary forms, but not links to the securities statutes or regulations. To view a specific section of the Act, you can visit the legal research area of Nolo's website at www.nolo.com. Click on "State Laws" and then on "Hawaii." In the "Hawaii Revised Code" search box at the bottom of the page, type in the specific Securities Act Code section you would like to see (such as "486-6," without the quotes). Contact the Securities Section for additional information on securities exemptions.

Creating Your Own Articles Form

Incorporators may create their own articles form. Articles of Incorporation must be typewritten or printed in black ink.

IDAHO

Corporate Filing Office

Idaho Secretary of State
Corporations Division
700 West Jefferson
P.O. Box 83720
Boise, ID 83720-0080
208-334-2301
www.idsos.state.id.us/corp/corindex.htm

State Corporate Forms

Idaho provides fill-in-the-blanks Articles of Incorporation for a general business corporation, with instructions.

Internet Forms: Corporate forms, including articles, are available for downloading from the state filing office website.

Articles Instructions

Article 1: The name of an Idaho corporation must contain the word "corporation," "incorporated," "company," or "limited," or the abbreviation "corp.," "inc.," "co.," or "ltd.," provided, however, that if the word "company" or its abbreviation is used, it cannot be immediately preceded by the word "and" or by an abbreviation of or symbol representing the word "and."

To check name availability, you can search the business entity name database from the state filing office website. It costs $20 to reserve a corporate name for four months.

Article 2: Idaho law does not use the concept of par value, so you do not need to state a par value for your shares. The filing fee is not based on your authorized shares, so you can authorize as many as you wish. Most incorporators authorize common shares with equal voting, dividend, and liquidation rights and no special restrictions. To do this, simply state the number of shares you wish to authorize. If you want to authorize one or more special classes of shares, you must retype the articles to state the name of each class or series, the number of shares in each, and the rights and restrictions associated with each class or series.

Submit your original Articles of Incorporation and one copy. Have the incorporator sign both the original and the copy at the bottom of each form on the line provided. The Customer Account Number box may be left blank.

Filing Fee: $100, payable to the "Idaho Secretary of State." If the articles are not typed or if attachments are included, the filing fee is $120.

Director and Officer Rules

A board of directors must consist of one (1) or more individuals, with the number specified in or fixed in accordance with the articles of incorporation or bylaws.

If a board of directors has power to fix or change the number of directors, the board may increase or decrease by thirty percent (30%) or less the number of directors last approved by the shareholders, but only the shareholders may increase or decrease by more than thirty percent (30%) the number of directors last approved by the shareholders.

Directors are elected at the first annual shareholders' meeting and at each annual meeting thereafter unless their terms are staggered under Section 30-1-806, Idaho Code. [30-1-803]

The terms of the initial directors of a corporation expire at the first shareholders' meeting at which directors are elected.

The terms of all other directors expire at the next annual shareholders' meeting following their election unless their terms are staggered under Section 30-1-806, Idaho Code. [30-1-805]

A corporation has the officers described in its bylaws or appointed by the board of directors in accordance with the bylaws.

The bylaws or the board of directors shall delegate to one (1) of the officers responsibility for preparing minutes of the directors' and shareholders' meetings and for authenticating records of the corporation.

The same individual may simultaneously hold more than one (1) office in a corporation. [30-1-840]

Share Issuance Rules

The board of directors may authorize shares to be issued for consideration consisting of any tangible or intangible property, including cash, promissory notes, services performed, or other securities of the corporation.

The corporation may place in escrow shares issued for a promissory note, or make other arrangements to restrict the transfer of the shares, and may credit distributions in respect of the shares against their purchase price, until the note is paid. If the note is not paid, the shares escrowed or restricted and the distributions credited may be cancelled in whole or part. [30-1-621]

At a minimum each share certificate must state on its face (a) the name of the issuing corporation and that it is organized under the law of this state; (b) the name of the person to whom issued; and (c) the number and class of shares and the designation of the series, if any, the certificate represents.

Each share certificate (a) must be signed, either manually or in facsimile, by two (2) officers designated in the bylaws or by the board of directors, and (b) may bear the corporate seal or its facsimile. [30-1-625]

Director Meeting Rules

Unless the Articles of Incorporation or bylaws provide otherwise, regular meetings of the board of directors may be held without notice of the date, time, place, or purpose of the meeting.

Unless the Articles of Incorporation or bylaws provide for a longer or shorter period, special meetings of the board of directors must be preceded by at least two days' notice of the date, time, and place of the meeting. The notice need not describe the purpose of the special meeting unless required by the Articles of Incorporation or bylaws. [30-1-822]

Unless the Articles of Incorporation or bylaws require a greater number or unless otherwise specifically provided in the Business Corporation Act, a quorum of a board of directors consists of (a) a majority of the fixed number of directors if the corporation has a fixed board size; or (b) a majority of the number of directors prescribed, or if no number is prescribed the number in office immediately before the meeting begins, if the corporation has a variable-range size board.

The Articles of Incorporation or bylaws may authorize a quorum of a board of directors to consist of no fewer than one-third of the fixed or prescribed number of directors determined under Subsection (1) of this section [previous paragraph].

If a quorum is present when a vote is taken, the affirmative vote of a majority of directors present is the act of the board of directors unless the Articles of Incorporation or bylaws require the vote of a greater number of directors.

A director who is present at a meeting of the board of directors or a committee of the board of directors when corporate action is taken is deemed to have assented to the action taken unless (a) he objects at the beginning of the meeting, or promptly on his arrival, to holding it or transacting business at the meeting; (b) his dissent or abstention from the action taken is entered in the minutes of the meeting; or (c) he delivers written notice of his dissent or abstention to the presiding officer of the meeting before its adjournment or to the corporation immediately after adjournment of the meeting. The right of dissent or abstention is not available to a director who votes in favor of the action taken. [30-1-824]

Shareholder Meeting Rules

A corporation shall hold a meeting of shareholders annually at a time stated in or fixed in accordance with the bylaws. [30-1-701]

A corporation shall hold a special meeting of shareholders (a) on call of its board of directors or the person or persons authorized to do so by the Articles of Incorporation or bylaws; or (b) if the holders of at least 20% of all the votes entitled to be cast on any issue proposed to be considered at the proposed special meeting sign, date, and deliver to the corporation's secretary one or more written demands for the meeting describing the purpose or purposes for which it is to be held.

A corporation shall notify shareholders of the date, time, and place of each annual and special shareholders' meeting no fewer than ten nor more than 60 days before the meeting date. Unless the Business Corporation Act or the Articles of Incorporation require otherwise, the corporation is required to give notice only to shareholders entitled to vote at the meeting.

Unless the Business Corporation Act or the Articles of Incorporation require otherwise, notice of an annual meeting need not include a description of the purpose or purposes for which the meeting is called.

Notice of a special meeting must include a description of the purpose or purposes for which the meeting is called. [30-1-705] Only business within the purpose or purposes described in the meeting notice may be conducted at a special shareholders' meeting. [30-1-702]

Shares entitled to vote as a separate voting group may take action on a matter at a meeting only if a quorum of those shares exists with respect to that matter. Unless the Articles of Incorporation or the Business Corporation Act provides otherwise, a majority of the votes entitled to be cast on the matter by the voting group constitutes a quorum of that voting group for action on that matter.

If a quorum exists, action on a matter, other than the election of directors, by a voting group is approved if the votes cast within the voting group favoring the action exceed the votes cast opposing the action, unless the Articles of Incorporation or the Business Corporation Act requires a greater number of affirmative votes.

The election of directors is governed by Section 30-1-728. [30-1-725]

Unless otherwise provided in the Articles of Incorporation, directors are elected by a plurality of the votes cast by the shares entitled to vote in the election at a meeting at which a quorum is present.

Shareholders do not have a right to cumulate their votes for directors unless the Articles of Incorporation so provide.

A statement included in the Articles of Incorporation that "[all] [a designated voting group of shareholders] are entitled to cumulate their votes for directors," or words of similar import, means that the shareholders designated are entitled to multiply the number of votes they are entitled to cast by the number of directors for whom they are entitled to vote and cast the product for a single candidate or distribute the product among two or more candidates. [30-1-728]

Financial Disclosure Rules

On written shareholder request, a corporation shall furnish its shareholders annual financial statements or, if annual financial statements are not available, other appropriate accounting records, which may be consolidated or combined statements of the corporation and one or more of its subsidiaries, as appropriate, that include a balance sheet as of the end of the fiscal year, an income statement for that year, and a statement of changes in shareholders' equity for the year unless that information appears elsewhere in the financial statements. If financial statements are prepared for the corporation on the basis of generally accepted accounting principles, the annual financial statements must also be prepared on that basis.

If any annual financial statements furnished pursuant to Subsection (1) of this section [previous paragraph] are reported on by a public accountant, his report must accompany them. If not, the statements must be accompanied by a statement of the president or the person responsible for the corporation's accounting records (a) stating his reasonable belief whether the statements were prepared on the basis of generally accepted accounting principles and, if not, describing the basis of preparation; and (b) describing any respects in which the statements were not prepared on a basis of accounting consistent with the statements prepared for the preceding year. [30-1-1620]

State Tax Information

State Tax Commission, Boise
800-972-7660
http://tax.idaho.gov
Idaho imposes a corporate income tax, with a minimum $20 payment.

Corporation Law Online

The Idaho Business Corporation Act is contained in Title 30 (Corporations), Chapter 1, of the Idaho Statutes, starting with Section 30-1-101. To find the Act, visit the legal research area of Nolo's website at www.nolo.com/statute/ state.cfm. Click on "Idaho." From there, you can browse Title 30, Chapter 1, of the Statutes.

State Securities Information

Idaho Securities Bureau
700 West State Street, 2nd Floor
P.O. Box 83720
Boise, ID 83720-0031
208-332-8004
http://finance.state.id.us/industry/securities.asp

The Securities Bureau website provides basic information on available state securities exemptions, plus downloadable forms to use to apply for certain exemptions. Here's an excerpt from "Raising Small Business Capital Through Securities," a publication available at the website:

Most offerings made by small businesses will be exempt from registration. A filing with the Department, however, may be necessary to obtain an exemption. For some exemptions, no filing is required. Where an exemption filing is required, the corporation usually must file a form and an offering document with the Department of Finance before beginning a securities offering and may have to adhere to certain limitations on the number of persons to whom offers and sales of securities may be made as well as certain other specific conditions. The consequences for not making a filing when required or exceeding these numerical limitations can be costly as well as embarrassing. A phone call or letter to the Department's Securities Bureau at (208) 332-8004 BEFORE YOU ACT is a low-cost way to obtain accurate information about your specific circumstance.

The Idaho Securities Act is contained in Title 30, Chapter 14, of the Idaho Statutes. You can browse the Act from a link provided on the Securities Bureau website. Section 30-1435(i) contains an exemption for offers and sales to ten or fewer individuals within a 12-month period provided other conditions are met. A limited offering exemption, which parallels Federal Regulation D, is also available. See Rule 270 of the Rules and Regulations issued under the Act for more information on the limited offering exemption. (The Securities Bureau website also provides a link to the Securities Rules.)

Creating Your Own Articles Form

You can create your own articles form.

ILLINOIS

Corporate Filing Office

Illinois Secretary of State
Department of Business Services
501 S. Second Street
Suite 328
Springfield, IL 62756
217-782-9522 or 9521 (Toll Free: 800-252-8980)
Chicago Branch Office (information only, not filings):
312-793-3380
www.sos.state.il.us/departments/business_services/
business.html

State Corporate Forms

Illinois provides fill-in-the-blanks Articles of Incorporation.

Internet Forms: The latest Illinois Articles of Incorporation (Form BCA-2.10), plus other Illinois corporate forms (Reservation of Corporate Name and others) can be downloaded from the state filing office website. You can also view and download the helpful "Guide to Organizing Domestic Corporations" on the website.

Articles Instructions

Article 1: An Illinois corporate name must contain the word "corporation," "company," "incorporated," or "limited," or an abbreviation of one of these words.

You can check corporate name availability online, by email or by calling the state filing office. It costs $25 to reserve an available corporate name for 90 days.

Article 3: For the purpose of your corporation, you may insert "the transaction of any or all lawful business for which corporations may be incorporated under the Illinois Business Corporation Act."

Article 4: Illinois law does not use the concept of par value, so simply state the number of shares you wish to authorize for later issuance to shareholders. The articles filing fee is not based on your authorized shares (although it is based on the amount paid for shares issued to your initial shareholders—see filing fee information, below). Most incorporators authorize only common shares with equal voting, dividend, and liquidation rights and no special restrictions. To do this, insert "Common" in the Class column, then insert the total number of shares authorized. In the next column, insert the number of shares you expect to issue. This number must be equal to or less than the total number of authorized shares. Finally, show the total amount (cash or value of property) you expect to receive from your initial shareholders as

payment for their shares in the rightmost column (and if you are issuing only one class of common shares as we assume, repeat this number in the Total blank at the bottom). The franchise tax portion of the filing fee is based on this number (see the filing fee information, below).

If you want to authorize one or more special classes of shares, you must provide information about each class on a separate line. Also, in Paragraph 2, you must describe the rights and restrictions associated with each class.

Articles 5, 6, & 7: These are optional articles. You can leave them blank if you wish.

IMPORTANT: If Article 6 is left blank, the state assumes that 100 percent of the corporation's paid-in capital (the amounts paid by shareholders for their initial shares) is located within Illinois. This is the typical situation for most small, newly formed corporations. This means that your corporation's state franchise tax will be computed on the basis of the entire paid-in capital of the corporation. Ask your tax adviser if you should fill in Article 6 to allocate property and business outside Illinois (and, thus, reduce your Illinois franchise tax).

Article 8: A person 18 years of age or older must sign, date, and provide a street address as your incorporator. Have the incorporator sign two copies of the articles in black ink.

Submit the signed original and one copy of the Articles of Incorporation form.

Filing Fee: $175 minimum fee, consisting of a $150 filing fee plus a minimum $25 tax fee. You must pay your fee by certified check, cashier's check, money order, or Illinois attorney's or CPA's check, made payable to the "Secretary of State." Personal checks are not accepted.

The franchise tax portion of the fee is computed at a rate of $1.50 per $1,000 of the corporation's paid-in capital, subject to a $25 minimum. Paid-in capital is the total amount of payment you expect to receive from your initial shareholders when you issue stock to them, minus any commissions or expenses you incur in connection with the issuance of shares. (This is the amount you must report in your articles.) Your corporation can have paid-in capital of up to $16,667 and pay the minimum franchise tax.

Examples:

If your articles authorize 100,000 shares, and you expect to issue 16,000 shares for $1 per share to your initial shareholders, your total paid-in capital is $16,000, and the computed franchise tax is $1.50 x 16 = $24. You must pay the minimum $25 franchise tax when filing your articles. Total fees, therefore, are $25 + $150 filing fee is $175.

If your articles authorize 10,000 shares, and you expect to sell 1,205 shares at $50 per share to your initial shareholders, total paid-in capital will be $60,250. The franchise tax is $1.50 x 60.25 = $90.38. The total fee to file articles is $240.38 ($90.38 franchise tax plus $150 filing fee).

Director and Officer Rules

The board of directors of a corporation shall consist of one or more members.

The terms of all directors expire at the next annual shareholders' meeting following their election unless their terms are staggered under subsection (e). [Sec. 8.10]

A corporation shall have such officers as shall be provided in the bylaws, each of whom shall be elected by the board of directors at such time and in such manner as may be prescribed by the bylaws. Officers and assistant officers and agents as may be deemed necessary may be elected or appointed by the board of directors or chosen in such other manner as may be prescribed by the bylaws. If the bylaws so provide, any two or more offices may be held by the same person. One officer, in this Act generally referred to as the secretary, shall have the authority to certify the bylaws, resolutions of the shareholders and board of directors and committees thereof, and other documents of the corporation as true and correct copies thereof. Sec. [8.50]

Share Issuance Rules

Illinois law does not use the concept of par value.

The consideration for the issuance of shares may be paid, in whole or in part, in money; in other property, tangible or intangible; or in labor or services actually performed for the corporation. [Sec. 6.30]

Certificates shall be signed by the appropriate corporate officers and may be sealed with the seal, or a facsimile of the seal, of the corporation, if the corporation uses a seal.

Each certificate representing shares shall also state: (a) that the corporation is organized under the laws of this state; (b) the name of the person to whom issued; (c) the number and class of shares, and the designation of the series, if any, which such certificate represents. [Sec. 6.35]

Director Meeting Rules

Meetings of the board of directors shall be held on such notice as the bylaws may prescribe. Attendance of a director at any meeting shall constitute a waiver of notice of such meeting except where a director attends a meeting for the express purpose of objecting to the transaction of any business because the meeting is not lawfully called or convened. Neither the business to be transacted at, nor the purpose of, any regular or special meeting of the board of directors need be specified in the notice or waiver of notice of such meeting. [8.25]

A majority of the number of directors fixed by the bylaws, or in the absence of a bylaw fixing the number of directors, the number stated in the Articles of Incorporation or named by the incorporators, shall constitute a quorum for the transaction of business unless a greater number is specified by the Articles of Incorporation or the bylaws.

The act of the majority of the directors present at a meeting at which a quorum is present shall be the act of the board of directors, unless the act of a greater number is required by the Articles of Incorporation or the bylaws. [8.15]

Shareholder Meeting Rules

An annual meeting of the shareholders shall be held at such time as may be provided in the bylaws or in a resolution of the board of directors pursuant to authority granted in the bylaws.

Special meetings of the shareholders may be called by the president, by the board of directors, by the holders of not less than one-fifth of all the outstanding shares entitled to vote on the matter for which the meeting is called or by such other officers or persons as may be provided in the Articles of Incorporation or the bylaws. [7.05]

Written notice stating the place, day, and hour of the meeting and, in the case of a special meeting, the purpose or purposes for which the meeting is called, shall be delivered not less than ten nor more than 60 days before the date of the meeting, or in the case of a merger, consolidation, share exchange, dissolution or sale, or lease or exchange of assets not less than 20 nor more than 60 days before the date of the meeting, either personally or by mail, by or at the direction of the president, or the secretary, or the officer or persons calling the meeting, to each shareholder of record entitled to vote at such meeting. [7.15]

Subject to Subsections (b), (c), and (d) of this Section 7.40 [covering special cumulative voting rules and super-majority voting rules a corporation can choose to adopt], each outstanding share, regardless of class, shall be entitled to one vote in each matter submitted to a vote at a meeting of shareholders, and except as specifically provided in Section 8.30 [covering the filling of vacancies on the board], in all elections for directors, every shareholder shall have the right to vote the number of shares owned by such shareholder for as many persons as there are directors to be elected, or to cumulate such votes and give one candidate as many votes as shall equal the number of directors multiplied by the number of such shares or to distribute such cumulative votes in any proportion among any number of candidates. [7.40]

Unless otherwise provided in the Articles of Incorporation, a majority of votes of the shares, entitled to vote on a matter, represented in person or by proxy, shall constitute a quorum for consideration of such matter at a meeting of shareholders, but in no event shall a quorum consist of less than one-third of the votes of the shares entitled so to vote. If a quorum is present, the affirmative vote of the majority of the votes of the shares represented at the meeting and entitled to vote on a matter shall be the act of the shareholders, unless a greater number of votes or voting by classes is required by the Business Corporation Act or the Articles of Incorporation. The Articles of Incorporation may require any number or percent greater than a majority of votes up to and including a requirement of unanimity to constitute a quorum. [7.60]

Financial Disclosure Rules

On the written request of any shareholder of a corporation, the corporation shall mail to such shareholder within 14 days after receipt of such request a balance sheet as of the close of its latest fiscal year and a profit and loss statement for such fiscal year; provided that if such request is received by the corporation before such financial statements are available, the corporation shall mail such financial statements within 14 days after they become available, but in any event within 120 days after the close of its latest fiscal year. [7.75]

State Tax Information

Department of Revenue, Springfield
217-524-4772 (business tax questions)
www.revenue.state.il.us

Illinois imposes a corporate income tax. Note that Illinois corporations also pay an annual franchise tax to the Department of Business Services. It is based on the current amount of paid-in capital—that is, stated capital plus paid-in surplus. The rate is $1.50 per $1,000 of paid-in capital, with a minimum annual franchise tax of $25. See the state corporate filing office website for annual franchise tax information.

Corporation Law Online

The Illinois Business Corporation Act is contained in Chapter 805 (Business Organizations), Title 5, of the Illinois Compiled Statutes, starting with Section 5/1.01. To find the Act, visit the legal research area of Nolo's website at www.nolo.com. Click on "State Laws" and then on "Illinois." From there, you can browse Chapter 805, Title 5, of the Statutes.

State Securities Information

Illinois Securities Department
17 North State Street
Suite 1100
Chicago, IL 60602
312-793-3384 (Springfield: 217-782-2256)
www.cyberdriveillinois.com/departments/securities/home.html

The Illinois Securities Law is contained in Chapter 815, Title 5, of the Illinois Statutes. You can browse it from a link on the Securities Department website. The Act contains a private placement exemption for the sale of stock to less than 35 persons or less than $1,000,000 in aggregate sales. There must be no general advertising or general solicitation, and no commission, discount, or other remuneration exceeding 20% of the sale price of the security may be paid. To qualify, you must file a Report of Sale on Illinois Form 4G or Form D (Rule 504) with the Secretary of State within 12 months of the first sale to an Illinois resident in reliance on the exemption. The filing fee is $100. The law also provides a uniform limited offering exemption that parallels the Federal Regulation D Rule 505 or 506 exemptions. You must file a Form D with the Secretary of State. See the Securities Department website for further information and forms related to these exemptions.

Creating Your Own Articles Form

You can create your own articles form.

INDIANA

Corporate Filing Office

Indiana Secretary of State
Corporations Division
302 W. Washington, Room E018
Indianapolis, IN 46204
317-232-6576
www.in.gov/sos/business/corporations.html

State Corporate Forms

Indiana provides fill-in-the-blanks Articles of Incorporation.

Internet Forms: You can find an Articles of Incorporation form (Form 4159) and other corporate forms on the state filing office website.

Articles Instructions

Top of Form: Check the box at the top-left of the articles form that says "Indiana Business Corporation Law." This means that you are preparing and filing articles for a standard Indiana business corporation. If you are forming a professional corporation, delete the "X" in the left box and insert an "X" in the right box. Professional corporations also must complete and file a Certificate of Registration (contact the state corporate filing office for information).

Article I: The name of an Indiana corporation must contain the word "corporation," "incorporated," "company," or "limited," or the abbreviation "corp.," "inc.," "co.," or "ltd."

You can check name availability online or by telephone. It costs $20 to reserve an available name for 120 days.

Article III: Indiana law does not use the concept of par value, so you do not need to state a par value for your shares. The filing fee is not based on your authorized shares, so you can authorize as many as you wish. Most incorporators authorize common shares with equal voting, dividend, and liquidation rights and no special restrictions. To do this, simply state the number of shares you wish to authorize. If you want to authorize one or more special classes or series of shares, you must attach a statement to your articles that lists the name of each class or series, the number of shares in each, and the rights and restrictions associated with each class or series.

Article IV: You must list one person as your incorporator. This person need not be a director, officer, or shareholder.

Bottom of Form: Include the incorporator's name and address as the preparer of the form. The incorporator must date and sign the Articles.

File the original and one copy of the Articles. The filing office will mail you a receipt.

Filing Fee: $90, payable to "Secretary of State."

Director and Officer Rules

A board of directors must consist of one (1) or more individuals, with the number specified in or fixed in accordance with the articles of incorporation or bylaws.

Directors are elected at the first annual shareholders' meeting and at each annual meeting thereafter unless their terms are staggered under section 6 of this chapter. [23-1-33-3]

A corporation has the officers described in its bylaws or elected or appointed by the board of directors in accordance with the bylaws or appointed by a duly elected or appointed officer in accordance with the bylaws. However, a corporation must have at least one (1) officer.

The bylaws or the board of directors shall delegate to one (1) of the officers responsibility for preparing minutes of the directors' and shareholders' meetings and for authenticating records of the corporation, and that officer is considered the secretary of the corporation for purposes of this article.

The same individual may simultaneously hold more than one (1) office in a corporation. [23-1-36-1]

Share Issuance Rules

The board of directors may authorize shares to be issued for consideration consisting of any tangible or intangible property or benefit to the corporation, including cash, promissory notes, services performed, contracts for services to be performed, or other securities of the corporation. If shares are authorized to be issued for promissory notes or for promises to render services in the future, the corporation must comply with IC 23-1-53-2(b).

The corporation may (but is not required to) place in escrow shares issued for a contract for future services or benefits or a promissory note, or make other arrangements to restrict the transfer of the shares, and may (but is not required to) credit distributions in respect of the shares against their purchase price, until the services are performed, the note is paid, or the benefits received. If the services are not performed, the note is not paid, or the benefits are not received, the shares escrowed or restricted and the distributions credited may be cancelled in whole or in part. [23-1-26-1]

If a corporation authorizes the issuance of shares for promissory notes or for promises to render services in the future, the corporation shall report in writing to the shareholders the number of shares authorized to be so issued with or before the notice of the next shareholders' meeting. However, a corporation that is subject to the Exchange Act (as defined in IC 23-1-43-9) satisfies the reporting requirement of this subsection by complying with the proxy disclosure provisions of the Exchange Act. [23-1-53-2]

At a minimum each share certificate must state on its face: (1) the name of the issuing corporation and that it is organized under the law of this state; (2) the name of the person to whom issued; and (3) the number and class of shares and the designation of the series, if any, the certificate represents.

Each share certificate: (1) must be signed (either manually or in facsimile) by at least two (2) officers (or the sole officer, if the corporation has only one (1) officer) designated in the bylaws or by the board of directors, and (2) may bear the corporate seal or its facsimile. [23-1-26-6]

Director Meeting Rules

Unless the Articles of Incorporation or bylaws require a greater number, a quorum of a board of directors consists of: (1) a majority of the fixed number of directors if the corporation has a fixed board size; or (2) a majority of the number of directors prescribed, or if no number is prescribed, the number in office immediately before the meeting begins, if the corporation has a variable-range size board.

Unless the Articles of Incorporation or bylaws provide otherwise, regular meetings of the board of directors may be held without notice of the date, time, place, or purpose of the meeting.

Unless the Articles of Incorporation or bylaws provide for a longer or shorter period, special meetings of the board of directors must be preceded by at least two days' notice of the date, time, and place of the meeting. The notice need not describe the purpose of the special meeting unless required by the Articles of Incorporation or bylaws. [23-1-34-3]

The Articles of Incorporation or bylaws may authorize a quorum of a board of directors to consist of no fewer than one-third of the fixed or prescribed number of directors determined under Subsection (a) [the first paragraph of this section, above].

If a quorum is present when a vote is taken, the affirmative vote of a majority of directors present is the act of the board of directors unless the Articles of Incorporation or bylaws provide otherwise. [23-1-34-5]

Shareholder Meeting Rules

A corporation must hold a meeting of the shareholders annually at a time stated in or fixed in accordance with the bylaws. [23-1-29-1]

A corporation with 50 or fewer shareholders must hold a special meeting of shareholders: (1) on call of its board of directors or the person or persons (including, but not limited to, shareholders or officers) specifically authorized to do so by the Articles of Incorporation or bylaws; or (2) if the holders of at least 25% of all the votes entitled to be cast on any issue proposed to be considered at the proposed special meeting sign, date, and deliver to such corporation's secretary one or more written demands for the meeting describing the purpose or purposes for which it is to be held.

A corporation shall notify shareholders of the date, time, and place of each annual and special shareholders' meeting no fewer than ten nor more than 60 days before the meeting date. Unless this article or the Articles of Incorporation require otherwise, the corporation is required to give notice only to shareholders entitled to vote at the meeting.

Unless this article or the Articles of Incorporation require otherwise, notice of an annual meeting need not include a description of the purpose or purposes for which the meeting is called.

Notice of a special meeting must include a description of the purpose or purposes for which the meeting is called. [23-1-29-5] Only business within the purpose or purposes described in the meeting notice may be conducted at a special shareholders' meeting. [23-1-29-2]

Except as provided in Subsections (b) and (c) of this section [covering the voting of shares held by a corporation or other types of nonindividual shareholders] or unless the Articles of Incorporation provide otherwise, each outstanding share, regardless of class, is entitled to one vote on each matter voted on at a shareholders' meeting. Only shares are entitled to vote. [23-1-30-2]

Shares entitled to vote as a separate voting group may take action on a matter at a meeting only if a quorum of those shares exists with respect to that matter. Unless the Articles of Incorporation or the Business Corporations Act provides otherwise, a majority of the votes entitled to be cast on the matter by the voting group constitutes a quorum of that voting group for action on that matter.

If a quorum exists, action on a matter (other than the election of directors) by a voting group is approved if the votes cast within the voting group favoring the action exceed the votes cast opposing the action, unless the Articles of Incorporation or the Business Corporation Act requires a greater number of affirmative votes.

The election of directors is governed by Section 9 of this chapter. [23-1-30-6]

Unless otherwise provided in the Articles of Incorporation, directors are elected by a plurality of the votes cast by the shares entitled to vote in the election at a meeting at which a quorum is present.

Shareholders do not have a right to cumulate their votes for directors unless the Articles of Incorporation so provide.

A statement included in the Articles of Incorporation that "(all) (a designated voting group of) shareholders are entitled to cumulate their votes for directors" (or words of similar import) means that the shareholders designated are entitled to multiply the number of votes they are entitled to cast by the number of directors for whom they are entitled to vote and cast the product for a single candidate or distribute the product among two or more candidates.

Shares otherwise entitled to vote cumulatively may not be voted cumulatively at a particular meeting unless: (1) the meeting notice or proxy statement accompanying the notice states conspicuously that cumulative voting is authorized; or (2) a shareholder who has the right to cumulate the shareholder's votes gives notice to the corporation not less than 48 hours before the time set for the meeting of the shareholder's intent to cumulate the shareholder's votes during the meeting, and if one shareholder gives this notice, all other shareholders in the same voting group participating in the election are entitled to cumulate their votes without giving further notice. [23-1-30-9]

Financial Disclosure Rules

On written request of any shareholder, a corporation shall prepare and mail to the shareholder annual financial statements, which may be consolidated or combined statements of the corporation and one or more of its subsidiaries, as appropriate, that include a balance sheet as of the end of the fiscal year most recently completed, an income statement for that year, and a statement of changes in shareholders' equity for that year unless that information appears elsewhere in the financial statements. If financial statements are prepared for the corporation on the basis of generally accepted accounting principles, the annual financial statements must also be prepared on that basis.

If the annual financial statements are reported on by a public accountant, the public accountant's report must accompany them. If not, the statements must be accompa-

nied by a statement of the president or the person responsible for the corporation's accounting records: (1) stating the person's reasonable belief whether the statements were prepared on the basis of generally accepted accounting principles and, if not, describing the basis of preparation; and (2) describing any respects in which the statements were not prepared on a basis of accounting consistent with the statements prepared for the preceding year. [23-1-53-1]

State Tax Information

Department of Revenue, Indianapolis
317-232-2189
www.state.in.us/dor

Indiana imposes a corporate income tax.

Corporation Law Online

The Indiana Business Corporation Act is contained in Title 23 (Business and Other Associations), Article 1, Chapters 17 through 54, of the Indiana Code, starting with Section 23-1-17. To find the Act, visit the legal research area of Nolo's website at www.nolo.com/statute/state.cfm. Click on "Indiana." From there, you can browse Title 23, Chapter 17.

State Securities Information

Securities Division
302 W. Washington Street
Room E-111
Indianapolis, IN 46204
317-232-6681
www.in.gov/sos/securities/index.html

The Securities Division website does not currently post information on securities law exemptions. But you can browse the Indiana Securities Act, contained in Title 23, Article 2, of the Indiana Code, by following the instructions in "Corporation Law Online," above. Section 23-2-1-2(b) contains exemptions from registration for various securities transactions. For example, Section 23-2-1-2(b)(9) contains an exemption for sales of stock to corporate directors and executive officers. Section 23-2-1-2(b)(10) contains an exemption for sales to 20 or fewer purchasers in Indiana (no more than 35 from all states). Additional requirements apply to these exemptions. For further information, call the Securities Division.

Creating Your Own Articles Form

You can create your own articles form.

IOWA

Corporate Filing Office

Iowa Secretary of State
Corporations Division
Lucas Building, 1st Floor
Des Moines, IA 50319
515-281-5204
www.sos.state.ia.us/business/index.html

State Corporate Forms

Iowa does not currently provide Articles of Incorporation.

Internet Forms: Articles of Incorporation are currently not available online (the corporate filing office website link to sample articles was under construction at the time of this edition). The Secretary of State provides other statutory forms, including an Application for Reservation of Name, which you may complete online. You can browse a tutorial on Iowa business organizations and formation procedures, plus links to various sections of the Iowa Business Corporation Act, from the site.

Articles Instructions

You must prepare Articles of Incorporation that meet the requirements of Section 490.202 of the Iowa Business Corporation Act. Your articles must contain the following:

1. A corporate name. The name of an Iowa corporation must contain the word "corporation," "incorporated," "company," or "limited," or the abbreviation "corp.," "inc.," "co.," or "ltd." You can search the corporate database online from the state filing office website to see if your proposed name is already in use by another active Iowa corporation. An available corporate name may be reserved for 120 days for $10.

2. The number of shares the corporation is authorized to issue. Iowa does not require a statement of par value. To create one class of common shares with equal rights and preferences, simply state the number of shares. The number of shares should at least be sufficient for initial stock issuance; you can authorize more if you wish because the filing fee is not based on the number of authorized shares. If you want to create special classes of shares, you must list them, together with the rights and restrictions associated with each.

3. The street address of the corporation's initial registered office and the name of its initial registered agent at that office. Use a street address, not a P.O. Box.

4. The name and address of each incorporator. Only one incorporator is required, who need not be a director, officer, or shareholder.

Below is a sample articles form you can use to create one class of common shares. The articles must be entirely typewritten or computer printed.

Articles of Incorporation

Pursuant to the Iowa Business Corporation Act, the undersigned incorporator submits the following Articles of Incorporation:

1. The name of the corporation is [insert name of corporation].

2. The corporation is authorized to issue one class of common shares. The total number of such shares it is authorized to issue is [insert number here] shares.

3. The street address of the corporation's initial registered office is [typically, the business address of the corporation is inserted here], and the name of its initial registered agent at this address is [typically, the name of an initial director or officer is inserted here].

4. The name and address of the incorporator is [insert name and address of incorporator, who dates and signs below].

Date: _____

Signature of Incorporator:

_____

Submit an original and one copy of your articles, together with an SASE.

Filing Fee: $50, payable to the "Iowa Secretary of State."

Director and Officer Rules

A board of directors must consist of one or more individuals, with the number specified in or fixed in accordance with the Articles of Incorporation or bylaws.

Directors are elected at the first annual shareholders' meeting and at each annual meeting thereafter unless their terms are staggered under Section 490.806. [490.803]

A corporation having 50 or fewer shareholders may dispense with or limit the authority of a board of directors by describing in its Articles of Incorporation who will perform some or all of the duties of a board of directors. [490.801]

A corporation has the officers described in its bylaws or appointed by the board of directors in accordance with the bylaws.

The bylaws or the board of directors shall delegate to one of the officers responsibility for preparing minutes of the directors' and shareholders' meetings and for authenticating records of the corporation. [490.840]

Share Issuance Rules

The board of directors may authorize shares to be issued for consideration consisting of any tangible or intangible property or benefit to the corporation, including cash, promissory notes, services performed, contracts for services to be performed, or other securities of the corporation.

The corporation may place in escrow shares issued for a contract for future services or benefits or a promissory note, or make other arrangements to restrict the transfer of the shares, and may credit distributions in respect of the shares against their purchase price, until the services are performed, the note is paid, or the benefits received. If the services are not performed, the note is not paid, or the benefits are not received, the shares escrowed or restricted and the distributions credited may be canceled in whole or in part. [490.621]

At a minimum each share certificate must state on its face all of the following: (a) the name of the issuing corporation and that it is organized under the law of this state; (b) the name of the person to whom issued; (c) the number and class of shares and the designation of the series, if any, the certificate represents.

Each share certificate: (a) must be signed either manually or in facsimile by two officers designated in the bylaws or by the board of directors; (b) may bear the corporate seal or its facsimile. [490.625]

Director Meeting Rules

Unless the Articles of Incorporation or bylaws provide otherwise, regular meetings of the board of directors may be held without notice of the date, time, place, or purpose of the meeting.

Unless the Articles of Incorporation or bylaws provide for a longer or shorter period, special meetings of the board of directors must be preceded by at least two days' notice of the date, time, and place of the meeting. The notice need not describe the purpose of the special meeting unless required by the Articles of Incorporation or bylaws. [490.822]

Unless the Articles of Incorporation or bylaws require a different number, a quorum of a board of directors consists of either: (a) a majority of the fixed number of directors if the corporation has a fixed board size; (b) a majority of the number of directors prescribed, or, if no number is prescribed the number in office immediately before the meeting begins, if the corporation has a variable-range size board.

The Articles of Incorporation or bylaws may authorize a quorum of a board of directors to consist of no fewer than one-third of the fixed or prescribed number of directors determined under Subsection 1 [the previous paragraph].

If a quorum is present when a vote is taken, the affirmative vote of a majority of directors present is the act of the board of directors unless the Articles of Incorporation or bylaws require the vote of a greater number of directors. [490.824]

Shareholder Meeting Rules

A corporation shall hold annually, at a time stated in or fixed in accordance with the bylaws, a meeting of shareholders. [490.701]

Except as provided in Subsection 5 [which applies if the corporation has more than 2,000 shareholders or has shares listed on a securities exchange], a corporation shall hold a special meeting of shareholders on the occurrence of either of the following: (a) on call of its board of directors or the person or persons authorized to call a special meeting by the Articles of Incorporation or bylaws; (b) if the holders of at least 10% of all the votes entitled to be cast on any issue proposed to be considered at the proposed special meeting sign, date, and deliver to the corporation's secretary one or more written demands for the meeting describing the purpose or purposes for which it is to be held.

A corporation shall notify shareholders of the date, time, and place of each annual and special shareholders' meeting no fewer than ten nor more than 60 days before the meeting date. Unless the Business Corporation Act or the Articles of Incorporation require otherwise, the corporation is required to give notice only to shareholders entitled to vote at the meeting.

Unless the Business Corporation Act or the Articles of Incorporation require otherwise, notice of an annual meeting need not include a description of the purpose or purposes for which the meeting is called.

Notice of a special meeting must include a description of the purpose or purposes for which the meeting is called. [490.705] Only business with the purpose or purposes described in the meeting notice may be conducted at a special shareholders' meeting. [490.702]

Shares entitled to vote as a separate voting group may take action on a matter at a meeting only if a quorum of those shares exists with respect to that matter. Unless the

Articles of Incorporation or the Business Corporation Act provides otherwise, a majority of the votes entitled to be cast on the matter by the voting group constitutes a quorum of that voting group for action on that matter.

If a quorum exists, action on a matter, other than the election of directors, by a voting group is approved if the votes cast within the voting group favoring the action exceed the votes cast opposing the action, unless the Articles of Incorporation or the Business Corporation Act requires a greater number of affirmative votes.

An amendment of Articles of Incorporation adding, changing, or deleting a quorum or voting requirement for a voting group greater than specified in Subsection 2 or 3 [Subsection 2 is quoted in the paragraph just above; Subsection 3 covers the quorum rule for adjourned meetings and is not quoted here] is governed by Section 490.727.

The election of directors is governed by Section 490.728. [490.725]

Unless otherwise provided in the Articles of Incorporation, directors are elected by a majority of the votes cast by the shares entitled to vote in the election at a meeting at which a quorum is present.

Shareholders do not have a right to cumulate their votes for directors unless the Articles of Incorporation so provide.

A statement included in the Articles of Incorporation that "(all) (a designated voting group of) shareholders are entitled to cumulate their votes for directors," or words of similar import, means that the shareholders designated are entitled to multiply the number of votes they are entitled to cast by the number of directors for whom they are entitled to vote and cast the product for a single candidate or distribute the product among two or more candidates. [490.728]

Financial Disclosure Rules

A corporation shall prepare annual financial statements, which may be consolidated or combined statements of the corporation and one or more of its subsidiaries, as appropriate, that include a balance sheet as of the end of the fiscal year and an income statement for that year. On written request from a shareholder, a corporation, at its expense, shall furnish to that shareholder the financial statements requested. If the annual financial statements are reported on by a public accountant, that report must accompany them. [490.1620]

State Tax Information

Department of Revenue & Finance, Des Moines
800-367-3388
www.state.ia.us/government/drf/index.html

Iowa imposes a corporate income tax.

Corporation Law Online

The Iowa Business Corporation Act is contained in Title XII (Business Entities), Chapter 490, of the Iowa Code, starting with Section 490.101. To find the Act, visit the legal research area of Nolo's website at www.nolo.com/statute/state.cfm. Click on "Iowa." From there, choose the most recent version of the Code and enter "490" in the "Chapter" box. You can then browse the law.

State Securities Information

Iowa Securities Bureau
340 E. Maple Street
Des Moines, IA 50319
515-281-4441
www.iid.state.ia.us/division/securities/default.asp

The Securities Bureau website does not provide specific information on Iowa securities laws and exemptions for small Iowa corporations. To browse the Iowa Uniform Securities Act, contained in Chapter 502 of the Iowa Code, follow the instructions in "Corporation Law Online," above, and enter "502" in the "Chapter" box.

Note that an exemption from registration of securities under the Act is contained in Section 502.203(9) for qualified sales within a 12-month period to less than 36 purchasers. Contact the Securities Bureau for additional information on this and other available exemptions.

Creating Your Own Articles Form

You must create your own articles following the Articles Instructions, above.

KANSAS

Corporate Filing Office

Kansas Secretary of State
Corporation Division
First Floor, Memorial Hall
120 SW 10th Avenue
Topeka, KS 66612-1240
785-296-4564
www.kssos.org/main.html

State Corporate Forms

Kansas provides fill-in-the-blanks Articles of Incorporation (Form CF), plus instructions. It also publishes the "Kansas Corporate Handbook," which contains comprehensive information on organizing a Kansas corporation.

Internet forms: You can download Kansas corporate Articles of Incorporation (Form CF), the Corporate Handbook, and other corporate forms from the corporate filing office website.

Kansas provides an online Articles of Incorporation preparation and filing service called KSBusinessCenter, at www.accesskansas.org/businesscenter/index.html. Online form preparation and filing takes just a few minutes and costs less than filing paper Articles. After you are a member, enter your user name and password at the bottom of the main Business Center Web page, then follow the instructions to prepare and file your online Articles.

Articles Instructions

Article One: A Kansas corporate name must contain the word "association," "church," "college," "company," "corporation," "club," "foundation," "fund," "incorporated," "institute," "society," "union," "syndicate," or "limited," or one of the abbreviations "co.," "corp.," "inc.," or "ltd."

You can check name availability by searching the corporate database online or by calling the corporate filing office. An available corporate name may be reserved for 120 days for $20 by preparing and filing a paper name reservation request. An online name reservation, which is much easier and quicker to do, costs $27. To check name availability and obtain an online name reservation, go to the KSBusinessCenter at www.accesskansas.org/businesscenter/index.html. Enter the name you wish to reserve in the "Name Available" box at the bottom of the page for filing Articles online, then press "Search." If the name is available, you can proceed by following the instructions.

Article Three: You may state your corporate purposes as follows: "to engage in any lawful act or activity for which corporations may be organized under the Kansas General Corporation Code." You do not need to state a specific business purpose, and most incorporators do not do so.

Article Four: You can authorize shares with a stated par value or without par value; modern practice is to issue shares without par value. The filing fee is not based on your authorized shares, so you can authorize as many as you wish. Most incorporators authorize common shares with equal voting, dividend, and liquidation rights and no special restrictions. For example, to authorize 100,000 shares without a stated par value, fill in either the third or fourth lines in Article Three (these are the no-par lines) as follows: "100,000 shares of Common stock, class _____, without nominal or par value." Note that the Class item is left blank; this blank is filled in only if you authorized different classes such as Class A, B, or C. As another example, to authorize 100,000 shares with a par value of $1 per share, fill out either the first or second lines (these are the par value lines) in Article Three as follows: "100,000 shares of Common stock, class _____, par value of $1 dollar each." Again, note that the Class item is left blank. If you do authorize special classes of stock, such as Class A, B, or C, you must insert the rights and restrictions associated with each class in the additional lines at the bottom of this article.

Article Five: Insert the name and address of one incorporator, who may be anyone you choose.

Article Six: If you know who will act as the initial directors of your corporation, insert their names and addresses here. If you do not yet know who will serve on your initial board, you can simply insert "N/A" in this article.

Article Seven: Check "Yes" to give your corporation an unlimited legal life. If you wish the legal existence of your corporation to terminate on a certain date, check "No" and insert the date. If you know the date when the tax year of your corporation will end each year, insert it in the blank after the words "Tax closing date, if known."

Have the incorporator sign on the signature line. The signature must be exactly the same as the name spelled out in Article Five.

Submit the original signed articles.

Filing Fee: $90 fee, payable to the "Kansas Secretary of State." Filing online Articles costs $84; Articles can be prepared and filed from the KSBusinessCenter as explained above.

Director and Officer Rules

The board of directors of a corporation shall consist of one or more members. The number of directors shall be fixed by, or in the manner provided in, the bylaws, unless the Articles of Incorporation establish the number of directors, in which case a change in the number of directors shall be made only by amendment of the articles. Directors need not be stockholders unless so required by the Articles of Incorporation or the bylaws. The Articles of Incorporation or bylaws may prescribe other qualifications for directors. Each director shall hold office until a successor is elected and qualified or until such director's earlier resignation or removal. Any director may resign at any time on written notice to the corporation. [17-6301]

Officers; Manner of Selection; Terms of Office; Resignation; Duties; Failure to Select; Vacancies: Every corporation organized under this act shall have such officers with such titles and duties as shall be stated in the bylaws or in a resolution of the board of directors which is not inconsistent with the bylaws and as may be necessary to enable it to sign instruments and stock certificates which comply with subsection (a)(2) of K.S.A. 17-6003 and K.S.A. 17-6408, and amendments thereto. One of the officers shall have the duty to record the proceedings of the meetings of the stockholders and directors in a book to be kept for that purpose. Any number of offices may be held by the same person unless the Articles of Incorporation or bylaws otherwise provide. [17-6302]

Share Issuance Rules

Every corporation, whether or not organized for profit, may issue one or more classes of stock or one or more series of stock within any class thereof, any or all of which classes may be of stock with par value or stock without par value and which classes or series may have such voting powers, full or limited, or no voting powers; and such designations, preferences, and relative, participating, optional, or other special rights, and qualifications, limitations; or restrictions thereof, as shall be stated and expressed in the Articles of Incorporation or of any amendment thereto, or in the resolution or resolutions providing for the issue of such stock adopted by the board of directors pursuant to authority expressly vested in it by the provisions of its Articles of Incorporation. [17-640]

The consideration, as determined pursuant to subsections (a) and (b) of K.S.A. 17-6403, and amendments thereto, for subscriptions to, or the purchase of, the capital stock to be issued by a corporation shall be paid in such form and in such manner as the board of directors shall determine. In the absence of actual fraud in the transaction, the judgment of the directors as to the value of such con-

sideration shall be conclusive. The capital stock so issued shall be deemed to be fully paid and nonassessable stock if: (a) the entire amount of such consideration has been received by the corporation in the form of cash, services rendered, personal property, real property, leases of real property, or a combination thereof; or (b) not less than the amount of the consideration determined to be capital pursuant to K.S.A. 17-6404, and amendments thereto, has been received by the corporation in such form and the corporation has received a binding obligation of the subscriber or purchaser to pay the balance of the subscription or purchase price; provided, however, nothing contained herein shall prevent the board of directors from issuing partly paid shares under K.S.A. 17-6406, and amendments thereto. [17-6402]

Shares of stock with par value may be issued for such consideration, having a value not less than the par value thereof, as is determined from time to time by the board of directors, or by the stockholders if the Articles of Incorporation so provide.

Shares of stock without par value may be issued for such consideration as is determined from time to time by the board of directors, or by the stockholders if the Articles of Incorporation so provide. [17-6403]

Any corporation, by resolution of its board of directors, may determine that only a part of the consideration which shall be received by the corporation for any of the shares of its capital stock which it shall issue from time to time shall be capital; but, in the event that any of the shares issued shall be shares having a par value, the amount of the part of such consideration so determined to be capital shall be in excess of the aggregate par value of the shares issued for such consideration having a par value, unless all the shares issued shall be shares having a par value, in which case the amount of the part of such consideration so determined to be capital need be only equal to the aggregate par value of such shares. In each such case, the board of directors shall specify in dollars the part of such consideration which shall be capital. If the board of directors shall not have determined what part of the consideration for such shares shall be capital (1) at the time of issue of any shares of the capital stock of the corporation issued for cash or (2) within 60 days after the issue of any shares of the capital stock of the corporation issued for property other than cash, the capital of the corporation in respect of such shares shall be an amount equal to the aggregate par value of such shares having a par value, plus the amount of the consideration for such shares without par value. The amount of the consideration so determined to be capital in respect of any shares without par value shall be the stated capital of such shares. The capital of the corporation may be increased from time to time by resolution of the board of directors, directing that a portion of the net assets of the corporation in excess of the amount so determined to be capital be transferred to the capital account. The board of directors may direct that the portion of such net assets so transferred shall be treated as capital in respect of any shares of the corporation of any designated class or classes. At any given time, the excess, if any, of the net assets of the corporation over the amount so determined to be capital shall be surplus. Net assets means the amount by which total assets exceed total liabilities, but capital and surplus are not liabilities for this purpose. [17-6404]

The shares of a corporation shall be represented by certificates, provided that the board of directors of the corporation may provide by resolution or resolutions that some or all of any or all classes or series of its stock shall be uncertificated shares. Any such resolution shall not apply to shares represented by a certificate until such certificate is surrendered to the corporation. Notwithstanding the adoption of such a resolution by the board of directors, every holder of stock represented by certificates and on request every holder of uncertificated shares shall be entitled to have a certificate signed by, or in the name of the corporation by the chairperson or vice chairperson of the board of directors, or the president or vice president, and by the treasurer or an assistant treasurer, or the secretary or assistant secretary of such corporation representing the number of shares registered in certificate form. Any or all of the signatures on the certificate may be a facsimile. In the event that any officer, transfer agent, or registrar who has signed or whose facsimile signature has been placed on a certificate has ceased to be such officer, transfer agent, or registrar before such certificate is issued, it may be issued by the corporation with the same effect as if the person were such officer, transfer agent, or registrar at the date of issue. [17-6408]

Director Meeting Rules

Unless otherwise restricted by the Articles of Incorporation or bylaws, the board of directors or governing body of any corporation organized under the General Corporation Code may hold its meetings, and have an office or offices, outside of the state of Kansas.

A majority of the total number of directors shall constitute a quorum for the transaction of business unless the Articles of Incorporation or the bylaws require a greater number. Unless the Articles of Incorporation provide otherwise, the bylaws may provide that a number less than a majority shall constitute a quorum which in no case shall be less than 1/3 of the total number of directors except

that, when a board of one director is authorized under the provisions of this section, one director shall constitute a quorum. The vote of the majority of the directors present at a meeting at which a quorum is present shall be the act of the board of directors, unless the Articles of Incorporation or the bylaws shall require a vote of a greater number. [17-6301]

Shareholder Meeting Rules

An annual meeting of stockholders shall be held for the election of directors on a date and at a time designated by or in the manner provided in the bylaws. Any other proper business may be transacted at the annual meeting.

Special meetings of the stockholders may be called by the board of directors or by such person or persons as may be authorized by the Articles of Incorporation or by the bylaws.

Unless otherwise provided in the Articles of Incorporation, all elections of directors shall be by written ballot. [17-6501]

Unless otherwise provided in the Articles of Incorporation and subject to the provisions of K.S.A. 17-6503, and amendments thereto [allows the board to set a record date to establish who has the right to vote shares], each stockholder shall be entitled to one vote for each share of capital stock held by such stockholder. [17-6502]

The Articles of Incorporation of any corporation may provide that at all elections of directors of the corporation, or at elections held under specified circumstances, each holder of stock or of any class or classes or of a series or series thereof shall be entitled to as many votes as shall equal the number of votes which, except for such provision as to cumulative voting, such holder would be entitled to cast for the election of directors with respect to such holder's shares of stock multiplied by the number of directors to be elected by each holder, and that such holder may cast all of such votes for a single director or may distribute them among the number to be voted for, or for any two or more of them as such holder may see fit, provided that the General Corporation Code shall not apply to a corporation organized prior to the effective date of the General Corporation Code unless the stockholders of such corporation shall amend its Articles of Incorporation to eliminate the requirements of cumulative voting in force at the time of its organization. [17-6504]

Subject to the provisions of the General Corporation Code with respect to the vote that shall be required for a specified action, the Articles of Incorporation or bylaws of any corporation may specify the number of shares or the amount of other securities conferring voting power, the holders of which shall be present or represented by proxy at any meeting in order to constitute a quorum for, and the votes that shall be necessary for, the transaction of any business, but in no event shall a quorum at the meeting consist of the holders of less than 1/3 of the shares conferring voting powers. In the absence of such specification in the Articles of Incorporation or bylaws of the corporation: (a) the holders of a majority of the shares conferring voting powers, present in person or represented by proxy, shall constitute a quorum at a meeting of stockholders; (b) in all matters other than the election of directors, the affirmative vote of the holders of a majority of shares who are present in person or represented by proxy at the meeting and entitled to vote on the subject matter shall be the act of the stockholders; (c) directors shall be elected by a plurality of the votes of the stockholders present in person or represented by proxy at the meeting and entitled to vote on the election of directors; and (d) where a separate vote by a class or classes of stockholders is required, the holders of a majority of the outstanding shares of such class or classes, present in person or represented by proxy, shall constitute a quorum entitled to take action with respect to that vote on that matter and the affirmative vote of the holders of a majority of shares of such class or classes who are present in person or represented by proxy at the meeting shall be the act of such class. [17-6506]

Whenever stockholders are required or permitted to take any action at a meeting, a written notice of the meeting shall be given which shall state the place, date, and hour of the meeting, and, in the case of a special meeting, the purpose or purposes for which the meeting is called.

Unless otherwise provided in the General Corporation Code, the written notice of any meeting shall be given not less than ten nor more than 60 days before the date of the meeting to each stockholder entitled to vote at such meeting. If mailed, notice is given when deposited in the United States mail, postage prepaid, directed to the stockholder at his address as it appears on the records of the corporation. An affidavit of the secretary or an assistant secretary or of the transfer agent of the corporation that the notice has been given shall be prima facie evidence of the facts stated therein in the absence of fraud. [17-6512]

Financial Disclosure Rules

Any stockholder, in person or by attorney or other agent, on written demand under oath stating the purpose thereof, shall have the right during the usual hours for business to inspect for any proper purpose the corporation's bylaws, its stock register, a list of its stockholders, its books of account, records of the proceedings of the stockholders and directors, and the corporation's other books and records, and to make copies or extracts therefrom. A proper purpose shall mean a purpose reasonably related to such person's interest as a stockholder. In every instance where an attorney or other agent shall be the person who seeks the right of inspection, the demand under oath shall be accompanied by a power of attorney or such other writing which authorizes the attorney or other agent to so act on behalf of the stockholder. The demand under oath shall be directed to the corporation at its registered office in the state of Kansas or at its principal place of business. [17-6510]

State Tax Information

Department of Revenue, Topeka
1-877-KANSREV
www.ksrevenue.org

Kansas imposes an annual franchise tax and a corporate income tax, plus a surtax on corporate taxable income over $50,000.

Corporation Law Online

The Kansas General Corporation Code is contained in Chapter 17 of the Kansas Statutes, Articles 60 through 75, starting with Section 17-6001. To find the Code, visit the legal research area of Nolo's website at www.nolo.com/statute/state.cfm. Click on "Kansas." In the section at the bottom of the page titled "Find a Statute Using the Statute Table of Contents," select Chapter 17, then select Article 60 to begin browsing the law.

State Securities Information

Kansas Securities Commissioner
618 S. Kansas Avenue
Topeka, KS 66603
785-296-3307
www.securities.state.ks.us

The Kansas Securities Act is contained in Chapter 17 of the Kansas Statutes, beginning with Article 12. You can browse the Act and information about exemptions from the Securities Commissioner website. Section 17-1262 contains exemptions from registration under the Act including an exemption under 17-1262(l) for private sales of securities to 20 or fewer people, provided other requirements are met. For further information on available exemptions, call the Office of the Securities Commissioner.

Creating Your Own Articles Form

You can create your own articles form.

KENTUCKY

Corporate Filing Office

Kentucky Secretary of State
Business Filings
P.O. Box 718
Frankfort, KY 40602
502-564-2848
www.kysos.com/BUSSER/BUSFIL/forms.asp

State Corporate Forms

The Kentucky Secretary of State provides a form for Articles of Incorporation, plus other statutory forms (Application for Reserved Name, Change of Registered Agent or Office, and more).

Internet Forms: You can find a fill-in-the-blanks Articles of Incorporation (Form SOS PAOI) and other corporate forms on the state corporate filing office website.

Articles Instructions

Article I: The name of a Kentucky corporation must contain the word "Corporation," "Incorporated," "Company," "Limited," "Corp.," "Inc.," "Co.," or "Ltd." You can conduct a search for available names online at the state filing office website or by calling the filing office. An available corporate name can be reserved for 120 days for $15.

Article II: Kentucky does not require a statement of par value. To create one class of common shares with equal rights and preferences, simply state the number of shares. Typically, incorporators authorize 1,000 shares to pay the minimum filing fee of $50 (see below for filing fee information). If you want to create special classes of shares, you must list them, together with the rights and restrictions associated with each.

Article III: Typically, an initial director or shareholder is named as initial registered agent (the person authorized to receive legal documents on behalf of the corporation). Most incorporators use the street address of the corporation as the registered office address (which must be the same as the business address of the registered agent). The registered agent must be a Kentucky resident and the registered office must be in Kentucky. Make sure to insert the name of the agent twice at the bottom of the articles form, and have the agent sign on the signature line provided.

Article V: Only one incorporator is required, who need not be a director, officer, or shareholder. The incorporator signs the articles on the line provided.

Mail an original plus TWO copies for filing. After the Secretary of State's office approves your articles, it will return two file-stamped copies to you. You must file one of the file-stamped copies of your articles with the county clerk of the county where your corporation's registered office is located.

Filing Fee: $40, plus an organization tax based on the number of shares authorized in the articles. The minimum organization tax for 1,000 or fewer authorized shares is $10, so the minimum total filing fee is $50. Increase the total fee amount according to the directions below if you authorize more than 1,000 shares in your articles. Make your check payable to the "Secretary of State."

Organization Tax:

$.01 per share up to 20,000 shares (minimum fee for 1,000 shares or less is $10)

$.005 per share for the next 180,000 shares

$.002 per share for any remaining shares.

Examples:

If you authorize 1,000 shares in your articles, the organization tax is $10 ($.01 x 1,000 = $10) plus $40 = a total filing fee of $50.

If you authorize 5,000 shares in your articles, the organization tax is $50 ($.01 x 5,000 = $50) plus $40 = a total filing fee of $90.

If you authorize 30,000 shares in your articles, the organization tax is $250 ($.01 x 20,000 = $200 plus $.005 x 10,000 = $50) plus $40 = a total filing fee of $290.

Director and Officer Rules

A board of directors shall consist of one (1) or more individuals, with the number specified in or fixed in accordance with the Articles of Incorporation or bylaws.

If a board of directors has power to fix or change the number of directors, the board may increase or decrease by thirty percent (30%) or less the number of directors last approved by the shareholders, but only the shareholders may increase or decrease by more than thirty percent (30%) the number of directors last approved by the shareholders.

Directors shall be elected at the first annual shareholders' meeting and at each annual meeting thereafter unless their terms are staggered under KRS 271B.8-060. [271B.8-030]

A corporation shall have the officers described in its bylaws or appointed by the board of directors in accordance with the bylaws.

The bylaws or the board of directors shall delegate to one (1) of the officers responsibility for preparing minutes of the directors' and shareholders' meetings and for authenticating records of the corporation.

The same individual may simultaneously hold more than one (1) office in a corporation. [271B.8-400]

Share Issuance Rules

The board of directors may authorize shares to be issued for consideration consisting only of an equivalent in money paid or labor done, or property actually received and applied to the purposes for which such corporation was created, and neither labor nor property shall be received in payment of consideration for the issuance of shares at a greater value than the market price at the time such labor was done or property delivered, and all fictitious increase of shares shall be void. [271B.6-210]

At a minimum each share certificate shall state on its face: (a) the name of the issuing corporation and that it is organized under the law of this state; (b) the name of the person to whom issued; and (c) the number and class of shares and the designation of the series, if any, the certificate represents.

Each share certificate: (a) must be signed (either manually or in facsimile) by two (2) officers designated in the bylaws or by the board of directors, and (b) may bear the corporate seal or its facsimile. [271B.6-250]

Director Meeting Rules

Unless the Articles of Incorporation or bylaws provide otherwise, regular meetings of the board of directors may be held without notice of the date, time, place, or purpose of the meeting.

Unless the Articles of Incorporation or bylaws provide for a longer or shorter period, special meetings of the board of directors shall be preceded by at least two days' notice of the date, time, and place of the meeting. Unless otherwise provided by the Articles of Incorporation or bylaws, the notice shall not be required to describe the purpose of the special meeting. [271B.8-220]

Unless the Articles of Incorporation or bylaws require a greater number, a quorum of a board of directors shall consist of: (a) a majority of the fixed number of directors if the corporation has a fixed board size, or (b) a majority of the number of directors prescribed, or if no number is prescribed the number in office immediately before the meeting begins, if the corporation has a variable-range size board

The Articles of Incorporation or bylaws may authorize a quorum of a board of directors to consist of no fewer

than one-third of the fixed or prescribed number of directors determined under Subsection (1) of this section [previous paragraph].

If a quorum is present when a vote is taken, the affirmative vote of a majority of directors present shall be the act of the board of directors, unless the Articles of Incorporation or bylaws require the vote of a greater number of directors. [271B.8-240]

Shareholder Meeting Rules

A corporation shall hold a meeting of shareholders annually at a time stated in or fixed in accordance with the bylaws. [271B.7-010]

A corporation shall hold a special meeting of shareholders: (a) on call of its board of directors or the person or persons authorized to do so by the Articles of Incorporation or bylaws; or (b) if the holders of at least 33-1/3% (or such higher or lower percentage as is contained in the Articles of Incorporation) of all the votes entitled to be cast on any issue proposed to be considered at the proposed special meeting sign, date, and deliver to the corporation's secretary one or more written demands for the meeting describing the purpose or purposes for which it is to be held.

A corporation shall notify shareholders of the date, time, and place of each annual and special shareholders' meeting no fewer than ten nor more than 60 days before the meeting date. Unless the Business Corporation Act or the Articles of Incorporation require otherwise, the corporation shall be required to give notice only to shareholders entitled to vote at the meeting.

Unless the Business Corporation Act or the Articles of Incorporation require otherwise, notice of an annual meeting shall not be required to include a description of the purpose or purposes for which the meeting is called.

Notice of a special meeting shall include a description of the purpose or purposes for which the meeting is called. [271B.7-059] Only business within the purpose or purposes described in the meeting notice may be conducted at a special shareholders' meeting. [271B.7-020]

Shares entitled to vote as a separate voting group may take action on a matter at a meeting only if a quorum of those shares exists with respect to that matter. Unless the Articles of Incorporation or the Business Corporation Act provides otherwise, a majority of the votes entitled to be cast on the matter by the voting group shall constitute a quorum of that voting group for action on that matter.

If a quorum exists, action on a matter (other than the election of directors) by a voting group shall be approved if the votes cast within the voting group favoring the action exceed the votes cast opposing the action, unless the Articles of Incorporation or the Business Corporation Act requires a greater number of affirmative votes.

The election of directors shall be governed by KRS 271B.7-280. [271B.7-250]

At each election for directors each shareholder entitled to vote at such election shall have the right to cast, in person or by proxy, as many votes in the aggregate as he shall be entitled to vote under the corporation's Articles of Incorporation, multiplied by the number of directors to be elected at such election; and each shareholder may cast the whole number of votes for one candidate, or distribute such votes among two or more candidates. Such directors shall not be elected in any other manner. [271B.7-280]

Financial Disclosure Rules

On the written request of any shareholder or holder of voting trust certificates for shares of a corporation, the corporation shall mail to such shareholder or holder of voting trust certificates its most recent financial statements showing in reasonable detail its assets and liabilities and the results of its operations. [271 B. 16-200]

State Tax Information

Kentucky Revenue Cabinet, Frankfort
502-564-4581
http://revenue.state.ky.us

Kentucky imposes a graduated corporate income tax, with rates that depend on corporate taxable income. Kentucky also imposes a license tax on capital employed in the business, with a minimum yearly license tax of $30.

Corporation Law Online

The Kentucky Business Corporation Act is contained in Title XXIII (Private Corporations and Associations), Chapter 271B, of the Kentucky Revised Statutes, starting with Section 271B.1-010. To find the Act, visit the legal research area of Nolo's website at www.nolo.com/statute/state.cfm. Click on "Kentucky." Choose "Access KRS through Title & Chapter" to begin browsing Title XXIII, Chapter 271B.

State Securities Information

Kentucky Department of Financial Institutions
Division of Securities
1025 Capital Center Drive, Suite 200
Frankfort, KY 40601
800-223-2579
www.dfi.state.ky.us/

The Division of Securities posts the Kentucky Securities Act (Chapter 292 of the Kentucky Statutes) and associated regulations on its site. The law and regulations contain exemptions from registration, including an exemption in Section 292.410(I) for the private sale of stock worth $500,000 or less to 35 or fewer people (15 within Kentucky) who qualify as accredited investors under Rule 501 of Federal Regulation D. Other requirements apply. Check the Division website and call the Division for further information.

Creating Your Own Articles Form

You must create your own articles following the Articles Instructions above.

LOUISIANA

Corporate Filing Office

Louisiana Secretary of State
Corporations Division
P.O. Box 94125
Baton Rouge, LA 70804-9125
225-925-4704
www.sec.state.la.us/comm/corp/corp-index.htm

State Corporate Forms

Louisiana provides Articles of Incorporation-Business Corporation (Form 399) with instructions, as well as a Transmittal Form (Form 984) and an "Initial Report" (Form 341) that you must file with your Articles. The report states basic corporate information such as its address, the names of initial directors, and the name and address of the corporation's registered agent.

Internet Forms: You can download Articles of Incorporation (Form 399), a Transmittal Form (984), and an Initial Report (Form 341), plus other statutory forms such as a Reservation of Corporate Name, from the state corporate filing office website.

Articles Instructions

Article 1: The name of a Louisiana corporation must contain the words "Corporation," "Incorporated," or "Limited," or the abbreviation of any of those words, or may contain instead the word "Company" or the abbreviation "Co." if the latter word or abbreviation is not immediately preceded by the word "and" or the symbol "&." No corporate name shall contain the phrase "doing business as" or the abbreviation "d/b/a." The corporate name shall not imply that the corporation is an administrative agency of any parish or of the state of Louisiana or of the United States.

You can check name availability online or by calling the state filing office website. An available corporate name may be reserved for 60 days for $25. Two 30-day reservation extensions are available on request.

Article 2: Most incorporators check the first box, which allows your corporation to engage in any lawful activity. Do not check the second box unless you wish to state a more limited purpose for your corporation.

Article 3: Most incorporators insert "perpetual" to give the corporation an unlimited legal life. If you wish to limit the legal life of your corporation, insert the date on which your corporation will automatically dissolve.

Article 4: Insert the total number of shares you wish to authorize. The number should be at least sufficient to cover your initial stock issuance, but you can authorize as many shares as you wish, because your filing fee is not based upon the number of authorized shares.

Article 5: You can authorize shares with a stated par value or without par value; modern practice is to issue shares without par value. Indicate "0" or "no par value" in the par value blank if you wish to authorize shares without a stated par value. If you wish to authorize par value shares instead, insert the actual par value amount—for example, "$1.00."

Most incorporators authorize one class of common shares with equal voting, dividend, and liquidation rights and no special restrictions, and the state form is set up to do this. If you want to authorize special classes of stock, you must retype your articles and include your own stock authorization language instead of Articles 4 and 5. If you do so, you must state the designation of each class of stock, the number of shares in each class, and the rights and restrictions associated with each class.

Article 6: You need list only one incorporator, who may be anyone you choose. Include a street address (not a P.O. Box).

Article 7: You may leave this article blank.

Article 8: Insert your corporation's federal employer identification number (even a one-person corporation must get one from the IRS). If you do not yet have one, simply respond "applied for" in this blank. Use IRS Form SS-4 to apply for your employer ID. (You can download Form SS-4 from the IRS website at www.irs.ustreas.gov, or call 800-TAX-FORM to have a copy mailed to you.). Note: You can obtain an EIN immediately online at the IRS site at www.irs.gov/businesses/small/article/0,,id=102767,00.html

The incorporator listed in Article 6 must sign the articles in the presence of a notary public, and must also sign the Initial Report. In addition, the corporation's registered agent named in the Initial Report must sign the report form in the presence of a notary.

Note: If you file your articles within five working days of the date of notarization of the Initial Report, your corporation's legal existence begins on the date of notarization—that is, prior to the date the articles are filed. If you file later, your corporation's legal existence begins on the date your articles are filed.

Filing Fee: $60, payable to the "Secretary of State."

Mail your completed and notarized Initial Report, plus the completed Transmittal Information page (prepared as the first page of your Articles) together with your check for the filing fee to the corporate filing office. You can request expedited (one-day) filing service for an additional $20 fee. You will receive a certified copy of your Articles and Initial Report. Use copies of these returned documents to make the parish filing, explained below.

Within 30 days after filing your articles with the Secretary of State, you must file a copy of the certified articles and Initial Report with the office of the recorder of mortgages in the parish where the corporation's initial agent is located. For an alphabetical list of parish clerk of court offices where you can make this filing, go to www.sec.state.la.us/comm/ucc-clerks.htm.

Director and Officer Rules

Subject to the provisions of the articles, the bylaws, or this chapter, all the corporate powers shall be vested in, and the business and affairs of the corporation shall be managed by, a board of directors of not less than one natural person. If not fixed in the articles or bylaws, the number of directors shall be the number named in the initial report or supplemental report, or, if the directors are not so named, the number elected from time to time by the shareholders. No amendment to the bylaws reducing the number of directors shall have the effect of shortening the term of any incumbent director. Unless the articles or bylaws provide otherwise, the directors of the corporation shall hold office for one year and until their successors are chosen and have qualified. No director shall be elected for a longer single term than five years.

Except as provided in subsection C(3) of this section, directors, other than the first directors named in the initial report filed with the articles, or in a supplemental report filed prior to issuance of any voting shares, shall be elected by the shareholders. [12:81]

The board of directors shall elect a president, a secretary, and a treasurer, and may elect one or more vice presidents. Unless otherwise provided in the articles, none of the officers need be a director, and any two of these offices may be combined in one person, provided that no person holding more than one office may sign, in more than one capacity, any certificate or other instrument required by law to be signed by two officers.

Except as otherwise provided in the articles or bylaws, or by resolution of the board of directors, the president, vice president, or director of any corporation or any foreign corporation doing business in this state shall have power in the name and behalf of the corporation to authorize the institution, prosecution, or defense of any suit and other legal proceedings, and no exception of want of authority shall lie on the part of any other party. Such persons shall have authority in the corporation's name

and behalf to direct the issuance of conservatory writs and to bond property in custodia legis, to execute bonds in connection with any legal proceedings, and to make any affidavit required by law or the rules of the court. Such acts shall have the same force and effect as the act of the corporation itself, and be binding on it. [12:82]

Share Issuance Rules

Par value shares may be issued initially for such consideration expressed in dollars, not less than the par value thereof, as shall be fixed by the board of directors. Shares without par value may be issued from time to time for such consideration expressed in dollars as may be fixed by the board of directors or by the shareholders by a vote of a majority of the voting power present, if the articles reserve to the shareholders the right to fix the consideration, provided, however, the consideration for such shares may be initially fixed by the incorporators. Treasury shares may be disposed of by the corporation for such consideration as may be fixed from time to time by the board of directors. All fully paid shares shall be non-assessable.

The consideration for shares issued otherwise than as stated in subsection B of this section [which covers stock dividends and other special cases], shall be paid in cash or in corporeal or incorporeal property, or services actually rendered to the corporation, the fair value of which is not less than the dollar amount of the consideration fixed for the shares, before the shares are issued. On payment of the consideration fixed therefor, such shares shall be considered as fully paid. Cash consideration for shares may not be paid by the purchaser's note, secured or unsecured, or uncertified check; and in case of delivery of such a note or check in payment for shares, the shares shall not be issued until the note or check has been paid in full. [12:52]

Every shareholder shall be entitled to a certificate of stock signed by the president and secretary, or by such other officer or officers of the corporation as the articles or bylaws may provide. When the certificate is countersigned by a transfer agent or by a registrar, other than the corporation itself or an employee of the corporation, the signatures of the president and secretary or other officers may be facsimile. No certificate shall be invalid by reason of the fact that any officer whose real or facsimile signature appears thereon, ceased to be an officer of the corporation before the certificate was issued.

Every certificate of stock shall state: (1) the name of the corporation; (2) that the corporation is incorporated under the laws of this state; (3) the name of the registered holder of the shares represented thereby; (4) the number and class, and designation of series, if any, of shares represented thereby; and (5) the par value of the shares represented thereby, or a statement that such shares have no par value.

A certificate for shares having no par value shall not state any par value, nor any value thereof in money, except as to liquidation preference or redemption price, nor any rate of dividend to which such shares shall be entitled in terms of a percentage of any par or other value. [12: 57]

On initial issuance of par value shares, the par value thereof, plus any part of any consideration received therefor in excess of the par value as the board of directors or the shareholders may fix, shall be allocated to stated capital, and the remainder of any consideration shall be allocated to capital surplus. On initial issuance of shares without par value, the board of directors shall state an amount to be allocated to stated capital, and the remainder of any consideration therefor shall be allocated to capital surplus. If such shares without par value have a preferential right to participate in the corporation's assets in event of liquidation, only the excess of the consideration over the aggregate amount payable to the holders thereof on liquidation may be allocated to capital surplus.

The board of directors may at any time transfer any amount from earned surplus or capital surplus to stated capital in respect of any issued shares or otherwise.

The board may at any time transfer from stated capital to capital surplus any amount of net assets in excess of (1) the aggregate par value of the issued shares having no preferential right to participate in the corporation's assets in event of liquidation, plus (2) the greater of the aggregate par value of, or the aggregate amount payable in liquidation on, any issued shares which have a preferential right to participate in the assets in event of liquidation, provided that only the shareholders may transfer from stated capital any amount allocated by them to stated capital.

On cancellation of shares, stated capital shall be reduced by an amount equal to (1) the aggregate par value of such shares having par value, and the aggregate allocated value of such shares without par value, plus (2) to the extent of the price paid on purchase or redemption of such par value shares in excess of the par value thereof, any excess of the allocated value over the par value thereof.

Stated capital, capital surplus, and earned surplus shall respectively be reduced by amounts applied therefrom to dividends or purchase or redemption of shares, and by amounts transferred therefrom in connection with stock dividends, reclassifications of stock, or otherwise.

Notwithstanding the provisions of Subsection (A) of this section, any excess over the consideration allocated to stated capital on issuance of shares in a merger, consolidation, or acquisition of all or substantially all of the outstanding shares or of the assets of a business, nonprofit or foreign corporation, may, to the extent of the earned surpluses of the business corporations, nonprofit corporations, and foreign corporations which do not survive the merger or consolidation or the shares or assets of which are acquired, be allocated to earned surplus. [12:61]

Director Meeting Rules

The meetings of the board of directors may be held at such place, whether in Louisiana or elsewhere, as a majority of the directors may from time to time appoint, or as may be fixed in the call of the meeting.

Such notice of meetings of the board shall be given as provided in the articles or bylaws. If not so provided: (i) regular meetings of the board may be held without notice of the date, time, place, or purpose of the meeting, provided that the date, time, and place are fixed by the board or are determinable pursuant to the articles or bylaws; (ii) special meetings of the board shall be preceded by at least two days' notice of the date, time, and place of the meeting; (iii) the notice of a special meeting of the board shall describe the purpose of the special meeting.

Meetings of the board may be called by the chairman, by the president, or by a majority of the directors then in office, unless otherwise provided in the articles or the bylaws.

A majority of the board of directors shall be necessary to constitute a quorum for the transaction of business, and the acts of a majority of the directors present at a meeting at which a quorum is present shall be the acts of the board of directors. [12:81]

Shareholder Meeting Rules

Unless otherwise provided in the articles or bylaws, shareholders' meetings may be held anywhere in or outside of the state of Louisiana. At least one meeting of the shareholders shall be held in each calendar year for election of directors, if any are to be elected, but failure to hold the annual meeting shall not affect or vitiate the corporate existence. If no annual shareholders' meeting is held for a period of 18 months, any shareholder may call such meeting to be held at the registered office.

Special meetings of shareholders may be called at any time by the president or the board of directors, or in any manner provided for in the articles or bylaws. At any time, on written request of any shareholder or shareholders holding in the aggregate one-fifth (or such lesser or greater proportion as may be fixed in the articles or in a bylaw adopted by the shareholders) of the total voting power, the secretary shall call a special meeting of shareholders to be held at the registered office at such time as the secretary may fix, not less than 15 nor more than 60 days after the receipt of said request, and if the secretary shall neglect or refuse to fix such time or to give notice of the meeting, the shareholder or shareholders making the request may do so.

Unless otherwise provided in the articles or bylaws, and except as otherwise provided in the Louisiana Business Law, the authorized person or persons calling a shareholders' meeting shall cause written notice of the time, place, and purpose of the meeting to be given to all shareholders entitled to vote at such meeting, at least ten days and not more than 60 days prior to the day fixed for the meeting. Notice of the annual meeting need not state the purpose thereof, except as otherwise provided in the Louisiana Business Law if a specified action is to be taken at the meeting. If such written notice is placed in the United States mail, postage prepaid, and addressed to a shareholder at his last known address, notice shall be deemed to have been given him. Notice of any shareholders' meeting may be waived in writing by any shareholder at any time; the written waiver need not specify the purpose of or the business to be transacted at the meeting; and such notice shall be deemed to have been given to, or waived by, all shareholders present or represented at any such meeting except any shareholder who, at the beginning of the meeting, objects to the transaction of any business because the meeting is not lawfully called or convened. Notice need not be given to any shareholder with whom communication is made unlawful by any law of the United States of America, or by any rule, regulation, proclamation, or executive order issued under any such law; and any action or meeting taken or held without notice to any such shareholder shall have the same force and effect as if notice had been given to him as otherwise required. [12:73]

A shareholders' meeting properly called on due notice, if notice is required, may be organized for the transaction of business whenever a quorum is present.

Except as otherwise provided in the Louisiana Business Law or in the articles or bylaws ... the presence, in person or by proxy, of the holders of a majority of the total voting power shall constitute a quorum, except that in no event shall a quorum consist of less than one-fourth of the total voting power. [12:74]

Except as provided in Sections 12:136 and 12:140.12 [covering special voting rules related to corporate acqui-

sitions], and except as otherwise provided in the articles, each shareholder of record shall have the right, at every shareholders' meeting, to one vote for each share standing in his name on the books of the corporation, provided that on and after the date on which written notice of redemption of redeemable shares has been mailed to the holders thereof and a sum sufficient to redeem such shares has been deposited with a bank or trust company with irrevocable instruction and authority to pay the redemption price to the holders thereof on surrender of certificates therefor, such shares shall not be entitled to vote on any matter and shall not be deemed to be outstanding shares.

The articles may provide that in the election of directors, each shareholder of record shall have the right to multiply the number of votes to which he may be entitled under Subsection A of this section [previous paragraph], by the number of directors to be elected, and to cast all such votes for one candidate, or distribute them among any two or more candidates.

Except as otherwise provided in the articles or bylaws or in other provisions of the Louisiana Business Law, a majority of votes actually cast shall decide any matter properly brought before a shareholders' meeting organized for the transaction of business, except that directors shall be elected by plurality vote. [12:75]

Financial Disclosure Rules

Every corporation, and every foreign corporation doing business in the state of Louisiana, shall once in every calendar year, on the written request of any shareholder of record, deliver to the shareholder, or send to him by mail addressed to his last known address, a report signed by the president or vice president and secretary or assistant secretary, containing the information herein above required to be contained in the last annual report of the corporation preceding said request [to see the type of basic corporate information stated in an annual report (corporate and registered agent addresses, number of issued shares, names and addresses of directors and officers, and the like), see the annual report form available online from the state filing office website], together with a condensed balance sheet (showing among other things and separately the amounts of its stated capital, capital surplus, and earned surplus) as of the last day of, and a combined statement of income and earned surplus for, the last preceding fiscal year ended more than four months before receipt of such request. [12:102]

State Tax Information

Department of Revenue & Taxation, Baton Rouge
225-922-0447
www.rev.state.la.us

Louisiana imposes a graduated corporate income tax, with rates that depend on corporate taxable income. Louisiana also imposes a corporate franchise tax based on the corporation's capital stock, surplus, and profits. The minimum annual franchise tax is $10.

Corporation Law Online

The Louisiana Business Law is contained in Title XII (Corporations and Associations), Chapter 1, of the Louisiana Revised Statutes, starting with Section 1. To find the Law, visit the legal research area of Nolo's website at www.nolo.com/statute/state.cfm. Click on "Louisiana." Then type "12" in the "Title" box, and "1" in the "Section" box to begin browsing the laws. But note that there are gaps in the numbering of the statutes. The bulk of the relevant laws are contained in Sections 1 through 100. (For easier browsing of the law, order a copy of the Louisiana Corporation Laws for $10 from www.sec.state.la.us/notary-pub/pub-idx.htm.)

State Securities Information

Office of Financial Institutions
Securities Division
8660 United Plaza Boulevard
Second Floor
Baton Rouge, LA 70809-7024
225-925-4660
www.ofi.state.la.us

Currently, the Securities Division website provides only contact information. The Louisiana Securities Law is contained in Title 51, Chapter 2, of the Louisiana Statutes, beginning with Section 701. To find it, follow the instructions in "Corporation Law Online," above. Enter "51" in the "Title" box and "701" in the Section box. Section 51:709(15) of the Law authorizes the Commissioner to provide a private offering exemption compatible with similar federal exemptions. Contact the securities office for additional information on private placement and other available exemptions. Start by asking for the "Louisiana Register," a pamphlet that explains the requirements of the private offering rules.

Creating Your Own Articles Form

You can create your own articles form.

MAINE

Corporate Filing Office

Secretary of State
Corporate Examining Section
101 State House Station
Augusta, ME 04333-0101
ATTN: Corporate Examining Section
207-624-7740
www.state.me.us/sos/cec/cec.htm

State Corporate Forms

Maine provides fill-in-the-blanks forms for most corporate statutory filings, including Articles of Incorporation (Form MBCA-6).

Internet Forms: The latest Maine Articles of Incorporation with instructions, plus other Maine corporate forms (Application for Reservation of Corporate Name and others), can be downloaded from the state's website.

Articles Instructions

Note: Maine adopted a new Business Corporation Act, called the "Model Business Corporation Act in Maine," effective July 1, 2003. The new law simplifies the articles form, eliminates the concept of par value in Maine, changes the shareholder preemptive rights provision (see below), allows corporations to issue shares in return for future services and promissory notes, allows corporations to have just one director regardless of the number of shareholders, and makes other changes. For additional information summarizing the Maine BCA 7/1/2003 changes, see the BCA information posted on the Maine corporate filing office website.

Top of Articles: We assume you are not forming a professional corporation (to practice law, accounting, medicine, or another special licensed profession), and that you will not check the box at the top of the articles that applies only to professional corporations. If you are forming a corporation to engage in a specially licensed profession such as a law, accountancy, or medical corporation, or one that must be formed as a professional corporation under Maine law (check with your state licensing board if you are unsure), check this box, and fill in the type of professional services your corporation will provide in the blanks under this box. Note the instructions at the bottom of the second page of the articles that explain that special corporate name requirements that apply to a Maine professional corporation.

First Article: The name of a Maine corporation is not required to include a corporate designator, such as "Incor-

porated," "Corporation," "Inc.," or "Corp.," but you will probably want to include one of these words at the end of your name, anyway, just to let others know that your business is incorporated.

You can search for available corporate names at the state filing office website. An available corporate name can be reserved for 120 days for $25.

Second Article: Insert the name of the corporation's clerk (the person whom you designate to receive legal papers on behalf of your corporation—also called a registered agent) and the registered office address of your corporation, which should be the same as the business address of your clerk. Typically, the name of an initial director or shareholder and the address of the corporation are shown here. Note: The clerk named in this article must sign the Acceptance of Appointment of Agent section of the articles at the end of the second page. The registered office must be in Maine, and your clerk must be a Maine resident. Note that you may insert a mailing address for the clerk on the last line of this article if it is different from the street address of the registered office listed on the second line.

Third Article: Maine law no longer uses the concept of par value for shares, so you only need to specify the number of shares you wish to authorize for later issuance to your shareholders. The filing fee is not based on your authorized shares, so you can authorize as many as you wish. We assume you will wish to authorize one class of common stock with equal dividend, voting, and liquidation rights and no special restrictions. This is usually sufficient for new corporations. To accomplish this, check the first box, insert the number of authorized shares in the blank after the first box, and insert "Common" as the name of the class of shares in the second blank. If you wish to authorize one or more special classes or series of shares, you must check the second box instead of the first box and attach an exhibit to your articles that lists the name of each class or series, the number of shares in each, and the rights and restrictions associated with each class or series.

Fourth Article: Check the first box to show that you will have a board of directors, and leave the second box unchecked. The second box is used only by those corporations that wish to organize a special type of nontraditional corporation that operates under the terms of s shareholders' agreement that puts the shareholders in charge of managing the corporation.

Fifth Article: Most incorporators will not check the first box nor fill in the blanks in this paragraph. This means that your shareholders are allowed to vote to decrease or increase the number of authorized directors of the corporation. If you wish to prevent your shareholders from changing the number of directors within minimum and maximum limits, you can check this box then fill in the minimum and maximum number beyond which your board size can not be decreased or increased by the shareholders.

We assume most incorporators will check the second and third boxes to provide the special statutory liability protection for directors and to require maximum statutory indemnification by the corporation to corporate directors and officers (go to the index for the Maine BCA online—see the instructions in see "Corporation Law Online," below—if you wish to read the specific language of these special liability and indemnification provisions).

Sixth Article: If you leave this box unchecked, this means your shareholders will not have special rights to acquire new shares before the new shares can be offered to new shareholders. If you are interested in providing such preemptive rights to your shareholders, see Section 641 of the Maine BCA. If you do wish to provide preemptive rights for your shareholders under Section 641, check this box.

Seventh Article: Typically, an initial director is named as incorporator.

Eighth Article: You do not need to add other provisions to your articles unless you wish to do so. If you do, insert the letter or numerical designation of the exhibit you attach to your articles that contains these additional provisions.

Incorporator's Signature: Have the incorporator listed in the seventh article sign on the signature line to the right of the date line.

Acceptance of Appointment of Clerk: Have your initial clerk (registered agent) listed in the second article accept the position by signing on the signature line to the left just below the date line.

Submit your original articles for filing. The state filing office will mail you a file-stamped copy of the articles.

Filing Fee: $145, payable to the "Maine Secretary of State."

Director and Officer Rules

A corporation's board of directors must consist of one or more individuals. The corporation's Articles of Incorporation or bylaws may fix the number of directors or otherwise regulate the size of the board.

Unless the corporation's Articles of Incorporation or bylaws provide otherwise, the number of directors may be increased or decreased from time to time by resolution of the shareholders or the directors. A decrease in the number of directors may not have the effect of shortening the term of any incumbent director.

Directors are elected at the first annual shareholders' meeting and at each annual meeting thereafter unless their terms are staggered under Section 806. [803.]

A corporation must have the officers described in its bylaws or appointed by the corporation's board of directors in accordance with the bylaws.

A duly appointed officer may appoint one or more officers or assistant officers if authorized by the bylaws or the corporation's board of directors.

The bylaws or the corporation's board of directors shall delegate to one of the officers responsibility for preparing minutes of the directors' and shareholders' meetings and for authenticating records of the corporation.

The same individual may simultaneously hold more than one office in a corporation. [841]

Share Issuance Rules

The board of directors of a corporation may authorize shares to be issued for consideration consisting of any tangible or intangible property or benefit to the corporation, including cash, promissory notes, services performed, contracts for services to be performed, or other securities of the corporation.

The corporation may place in escrow shares issued for a contract for future services or benefits or for a promissory note or may make other arrangements to restrict the transfer of the shares and may credit distributions in respect of the shares against their purchase price until the services are performed, the note is paid, or the benefits received. If the services are not performed, the note is not paid, or the benefits are not received, the shares escrowed or restricted and the distributions credited may be cancelled in whole or part. [622.]

Shares may but need not be represented by certificates. Unless this Act or another law expressly provides otherwise, whether the shares are represented by certificates or not does not affect the rights and obligations of shareholders.

At a minimum each share certificate must state on its face: A. the name of the issuing corporation and that the corporation is organized under the laws of this State; B. the name of the person to whom issued, and C. the number and class of shares and the designation of the series, if any, the certificate represents.

If the issuing corporation is authorized to issue different classes of shares or different series within a class, the designations, relative rights, preferences, and limitations applicable to each class and the variations in rights, preferences, and limitations determined for each series and the authority of its board of directors to determine variations for future series must be summarized on the front or back of each certificate. Alternatively, each certificate may state conspicuously on its front or back that the corporation will furnish the shareholder this information on request in writing and without charge.

Each share certificate must be signed, either manually or in facsimile, by: A. two officers designated in the bylaws; B. the clerk and an officer designated in the bylaws; or C. the corporation's board of directors. [626]

Director Meeting Rules

The corporation's board of directors may hold regular or special meetings in or out of this State.

Unless the corporation's Articles of Incorporation or bylaws provide otherwise, the corporation's board of directors may permit any or all directors to participate in a regular or special meeting by, or conduct the meeting through the use of, any means of communication by which all directors participating may simultaneously hear each other during the meeting. A director participating in a meeting by this means is deemed to be present in person at the meeting. [821]

Unless the corporation's Articles of Incorporation or bylaws provide otherwise, regular meetings of the corporation's board of directors may be held without notice of the date, time, place, or purpose of the meeting.

Unless the corporation's Articles of Incorporation or bylaws provide for a longer or shorter period, special meetings of the corporation's board of directors must be preceded by at least two days' notice of the date, time, and place of the meeting. The notice need not describe the purpose of the special meeting unless required by the corporation's Articles of Incorporation or bylaws.

Unless the corporation's Articles of Incorporation or bylaws otherwise provide, special meetings of the corporation's board of directors may be called by the chair of the board, by the president or, if the president is absent or is unable to act, by any vice president, by any two directors, or by any other person or persons authorized by the bylaws.

At the written request of any person permitted to call a special meeting of the corporation's board of directors pursuant to Subsection 3 [previous paragraph], the secretary or clerk shall send notices of the meeting to all the

directors, or the person calling the meeting may send such notices. The person calling the special meeting shall set the time of the meeting and, unless the place of meetings is specified in the bylaws or by prior resolution of the directors, the place of the meeting. [823]

Unless the corporation's Articles of Incorporation or bylaws require a greater number or unless otherwise specifically provided in this Act, a quorum of a corporation's board of directors consists of: A. a majority of the fixed number of directors if the corporation has a fixed board size; or B. a majority of the number of directors prescribed, or if no number is prescribed, the number in office immediately before the meeting begins, if the corporation has a variable-range size board.

The corporation's Articles of Incorporation or bylaws may authorize a quorum of a corporation's board of directors to consist of no fewer than 1/3 of the fixed or prescribed number of directors determined under Subsection 1 [previous paragraph]

If a quorum is present when a vote is taken, the affirmative vote of a majority of directors present is the act of the corporation's board of directors unless the corporation's Articles of Incorporation or bylaws require the vote of a greater number of directors. [825]

Shareholder Meeting Rules

A corporation shall hold a meeting of shareholders annually at a time stated in or fixed in accordance with its bylaws. [701]

A corporation shall hold a special meeting of its shareholders: A. on call of the board of directors or the person or persons authorized to do so by its Articles of Incorporation or bylaws; B. if the holders of at least 10% of all the votes entitled to be cast on an issue proposed to be considered at the proposed special meeting sign, date, and deliver to the corporation one or more written demands for the meeting describing the purpose or purposes for which it is to be held, except that the Articles of Incorporation may fix a lower percentage or a higher percentage not exceeding 25% of all the votes entitled to be cast on any issue proposed to be considered. Unless otherwise provided in the Articles of Incorporation, a written demand for a special meeting may be revoked by a writing to that effect received by the corporation prior to the receipt by the corporation of demands sufficient in number to require the holding of a special meeting.

Only business within the purpose or purposes described in the meeting notice required by Section 705, Subsection 3 [see below] may be conducted at a special meeting. [702]

A corporation shall notify shareholders of the date, time, and place of each annual or special shareholders' meeting no fewer than 10 days, or three days for close corporations, nor more than 60 days before the meeting date. Unless this Act or the corporation's Articles of Incorporation require otherwise, the corporation is required only to give notice to shareholders entitled to vote at the meeting.

Unless this Act or a corporation's Articles of Incorporation require otherwise, notice of an annual meeting need not include a description of the purpose or purposes for which the meeting is called.

Notice of a special meeting must include a description of the purpose or purposes for which the meeting is called. [705]

At each meeting of a corporation's shareholders under this chapter, a chair shall preside. The chair must be appointed as provided in the bylaws or, in the absence of such provision, by the board of directors.

The chair, unless the corporation's Articles of Incorporation or bylaws provide otherwise, shall determine the order of business and has the authority to establish rules for the conduct of a meeting held pursuant to this chapter.

Rules adopted for the meeting and the conduct of a meeting held pursuant to this chapter must be fair to shareholders.

The chair of a meeting held pursuant to this chapter shall announce at the meeting when the polls close for each matter voted on. If no announcement is made, the polls are deemed to have closed on the final adjournment of the meeting. After the polls close, no ballots, proxies, or votes nor any revocations or changes thereto may be accepted. [708]

Shares entitled to vote as a separate voting group may take action on a matter at a meeting only if a quorum of those shares exists with respect to that matter. Unless the corporation's Articles of Incorporation or this Act provides otherwise, a majority of the votes entitled to be cast on the matter by the voting group constitutes a quorum of that voting group for action on that matter.

If a quorum exists, action on a matter, other than the election of directors, by a voting group is approved if the votes cast within the voting group favoring the action exceed the votes cast opposing the action unless the corporation's Articles of Incorporation or this Act requires a greater number of affirmative votes.

The election of directors is governed by section 730 [see Section 730 provisions below]. [727]

Unless otherwise provided in a corporation's Articles of Incorporation, directors are elected by a plurality of the votes cast by the shares entitled to vote in the election at a meeting at which a quorum is present.

Shareholders do not have a right to cumulate their votes for directors unless a corporation's Articles of Incorporation so provide.

A statement included in a corporation's Articles of Incorporation that "all or a designated voting group of shareholders are entitled to cumulate their votes for directors," or containing words of similar import, means that the shareholders designated are entitled to multiply the number of votes they are entitled to cast by the number of directors for whom they are entitled to vote and cast the product for a single candidate or distribute the product among two or more candidates.

Shares otherwise entitled to vote cumulatively may not be voted cumulatively at a particular meeting unless: A. the meeting notice or proxy statement accompanying the notice states conspicuously that cumulative voting is authorized; or B. a shareholder who has the right to cumulate votes gives notice to the corporation not less than 48 hours before the time set for the meeting of the shareholder's intent to cumulate that shareholder's votes during the meeting, and if one shareholder gives this notice all other shareholders in the same voting group participating in the election are entitled to cumulate their votes without giving further notice. [730]

Financial Disclosure Rules

No later than five months after the close of each fiscal year, each corporation that is not a close corporation shall prepare annual financial statements, which may be consolidated or combined statements of the corporation and one or more of its subsidiaries, as appropriate, that include a balance sheet as of the end of the fiscal year, an income statement for that year, and a statement of changes in shareholders' equity for the year unless that information appears elsewhere in the financial statements. If financial statements are prepared for the corporation on the basis of generally accepted accounting principles, the annual financial statements must also be prepared on that basis.

On written demand of any shareholder of a corporation, the corporation shall mail to that shareholder a copy of the most recent annual financial statement prepared in accordance with Subsection 1 [previous paragraph]. If the annual financial statement is reported on by a public accountant, the accountant's report must accompany it. If the annual financial statement is not reported on by a public accountant, the statement must be accompanied by a statement of the president or the person responsible for the corporation's accounting records: A. stating the reporter's reasonable belief whether the statement was prepared on the basis of generally accepted accounting principles and, if not, describing the basis of preparation; and B. describing any respects in which the statement was not prepared on a basis of accounting consistent with the statement prepared for the preceding year.

The Articles of Incorporation or bylaws of a corporation may impose reasonable restrictions regarding the disclosure of financial information as a condition to delivery of an annual financial statement to a shareholder in accordance with this section. [1620]

State Tax Information

Maine Revenue Services, Augusta
207-287-2076
www.state.me.us/revenue

Maine imposes a graduated corporate income tax.

Corporation Law Online

The Maine Business Corporation Act is contained in Title 13-C (Maine Business Corporation Act), Chapters 1 through 17 of the Maine Statutes, starting with section 101. You can browse it from the Web page listed below. Note: Maine also posts Chapter 13-A, its prior Business Corporation Act, that was effective until 6/30/2003, when it was repealed and replaced by the new Maine BCA contained in Chapter 13-C, which became effective 7/1/2003. To view the Act, go to the URL below, then click "Title 13-C":

http://janus.state.me.us/legis/statutes

State Securities Information

Department of Professional and Financial Regulation
Securities Division
121 State House Station
Augusta, Maine 04333
207-624-8551
www.state.me.us/pfr/sec/sec_index.htm

The Maine Securities Act is contained in Title 32, Chapter 105, of the Maine Statutes. It can be browsed from a link provided on the Securities Division website. Section 10502(2)(P) of the Act provides an exemption for offers and sales of securities if the number of security holders, at the time of sale or in consequence of the sale, does not exceed ten, and if the securities have not been offered by general solicitation or advertisement. In addition, Section 10502(2)(Q) provides an exemption for offers and sales of securities if the number of security holders, at the time of sale or in consequence of the sale, does not exceed 25, and if the securities have not been offered by general solicitation or advertisement. This exemption differs from the first-mentioned exemption because you must file a formal notice form with the Securities Division to qualify. A more general exemption is provided under Section 10502(2)(R) for transactions by an issuer not involving any public offering within the meaning of the United States Securities Act of 1933, Section 4(2), and associated rules. This exemption carries both a notification and filing fee requirement. For further information on Maine security exemptions, procedures, and forms, see both the Securities Division and Small Business Center websites. (The Securities Division website provides a link to the Small Business Center.)

Creating Your Own Articles Form

You can create your own articles form. Leave space in the upper right corner of the first page for a file stamp.

MARYLAND

Corporate Filing Office

Maryland Department of Assessments & Taxation
Corporate Charter Division
8th Flfoor
301 West Preston Street, Room 809
Baltimore, MD 21201
410-767-1340
Outside the Baltimore Metro Area: 888-246-5941
www.dat.state.md.us/sdatweb/charter.html

State Corporate Forms

Maryland provides fill-in-the-blanks Articles of Incorporation, with instructions.

Internet Forms: The latest Maryland Articles of Incorporation and guidelines for preparing the form can be downloaded from the state filing office website. (In the general information posted on the filing office website and in the Maryland statutes, this form is referred to as the "Corporate Charter," but the official name of the form is "Articles of Incorporation.")

Articles Instructions

The articles, including information in the blanks, must be computer printed or typed, not handwritten.

First Article: In the first blank, insert the name of your incorporator, who may be any person over 18 years of age. In the second blank, insert the incorporator's mailing address. The incorporator must sign at the bottom of the articles.

Second Article: The name of a Maryland corporation must contain the word "Corporation," "Incorporated," "Limited," "Company," or the abbreviation "Inc.," "Corp.," "Ltd.," or "Co." If "Company" or "Co." is used, it cannot preceded by the word "and" or a symbol for the word "and."

You can check to see whether your proposed name is already in use by searching the corporate database, which is linked to the state filing office website, or by calling the state filing office. It costs $7 to reserve an available name for 30 days. There is no official name reservation form. Simply send a name reservation request letter to the filing office with a check for the reservation fee.

Third Article: A short general purpose clause is sufficient—for example, "to engage in any lawful act or other activity."

Fourth Article: Insert the street address of the corporation's principal office in Maryland. Do not use a P.O. box.

Fifth Article: Any individual who is a resident of the state may act as your resident agent. Typically, an initial director or officer is named, and the address of the corporation is given as the agent's address. MAKE SURE TO HAVE THE AGENT SIGN ON THE REGISTERED AGENT SIGNATURE LINE AT THE BOTTOM RIGHT OF THE ARTICLES FORM.

Sixth Article: Fill in Article 6 to show the total number of authorized shares and the par value of each share. You can authorize shares with a stated par value or without par value; modern practice is to issue shares without par value. Insert "$0" in the par value blank if you wish to authorize shares without a par value. As explained in the filing fee instructions below, Maryland imposes a stock fee that depends on the number of shares you authorize in your articles. You can authorize up to 5,000 shares without par value or a number of par value shares whose total par value equals $100,000 for the minimum filing fee of $120 ($100 recording fee plus a $20 minimum stock fee). Authorizing 100,000 shares with a stated par value of $1 or 1,000,000 shares with a stated par value of $.10 both result in an aggregate par value of $100,000 and therefore qualify for the minimum $120 filing fee. Most incorporators authorize one class of common shares with equal voting, dividend, and liquidation rights and no special restrictions. The state articles form is set up to do this.

If you wish to authorize special classes of stock, you must retype your articles and insert your own stock authorization language. It must specify the name, number of shares, par value or lack of par value, and rights and restrictions associated with each class of shares.

Seventh Article: Insert the number of directors and the names of the initial board members. You must have at least three directors if you will have three or more shareholders. You may have just two directors if you will have just two shareholders, and you may have just one director if you will have just one shareholder.

The incorporator named in Article 1 and the resident agent named in Article 5 must sign on the lines provided at the bottom of the form. Submit the signed original for filing. In the "Return to" section, you can type the name and address of your incorporator. After approving your articles, the state filing office will send a copy to this address.

Filing Fee: $120 minimum, payable to "SDAT" (this is the acronym for the State Department of Assessments & Taxation). The $120 minimum fee includes a $20 recording fee plus a minimum stock fee of $100. If you ask for a certified copy, it costs $20 plus $1 per extra page.

Note that the $20 stock fee portion of the filing fee increases if the aggregate par value—that is, the number of authorized shares specified in the articles multiplied by their par value—exceeds $100,000, or if you authorize more than 5,000 shares of stock without par value. Specifically, the stock fee is $20 for the first $100,000 of par value authorized in the articles, plus $1 for each additional $5,000 or fractional part of $5,000 in par value. Shares without par value are considered to have a par value of $20 per share for purposes of computing the stock fee. Here are some examples.

Examples:

If your articles authorize 200,000 shares with a par value of $1 each, the stock fee is $20 for the first $100,000 of par value plus $20 more for the additional $100,000 of par value ($100,000/$5,000 = 20 x $1) for a total stock fee of $40. The total filing fee is $140 ($100 recording fee plus $40 stock fee).

If your articles authorize 15,000 shares without par value, the stock fee is $20 for the first 5,000 shares (5,000 x $20 = $100,000 assumed par value), plus $40 more for the additional 10,000 no-par shares (10,000 x $20 = an assumed additional par value of $200,000; $200,000/$5,000 = 40 x $1 = $40). The total stock fee is $60. The total filing fee, therefore, is $160 ($100 recording fee plus $60 stock fee).

You will have to pay additional stock fees based on a different fee schedule if you authorize more than $1 million of par value stock or more than 50,000 shares of stock without par value. Call the state filing office to determine the increased filing fee if you are over these thresholds, or if you need help computing your stock fee and total filing fee.

Director and Officer Rules

Each corporation shall have at least three directors at all times, provided that: (1) if there is no stock outstanding the number of directors may be less than three but not less than one; and (2) if there is stock outstanding and so long as there are less than three stockholders, the number of directors may be less than three but not less than the number of stockholders.

Subject to the provisions of subsection (a) of this section [above], the bylaws may: (1) alter the number of directors set by the charter; and (2) authorize a majority of the entire board of directors to alter within specified limits the number of directors set by the charter or the bylaws, but the action may not affect the tenure of office of any director. [2-402]

Each Maryland corporation shall have the following officers: (1) a president, (2) a secretary, and (3) a treasurer. [2-412]

Unless the bylaws provide otherwise, an officer serves for one year and until his successor is elected and qualifies. [2-413]

If permitted by the bylaws, a person may hold more than one office in a corporation but may not serve concurrently as both president and vice president of the same corporation.

A person who holds more than one office in a corporation may not act in more than one capacity to execute, acknowledge, or verify an instrument required by law to be executed, acknowledged, or verified by more than one officer. [2-415]

Share Issuance Rules

The consideration for the issuance of stock, convertible securities, warrants, or options may consist in whole or in part of: (1) money, (2) tangible or intangible property, (3) labor or services actually performed for the corporation; (4) a promissory note or other obligation for future payment in money, or (5) contracts for labor or services to be performed.

The corporation may place in escrow shares issued for a contract for future labor or services or a promissory note or other obligation for future payment in money, or make other arrangements to restrict the transfer of the shares, and may credit distributions in respect of the shares against their purchase price, until the labor or services are performed or the note or other obligation for future payment in money is paid. If the labor or services are not performed or the note or other obligation for future payment in money is not paid, the shares escrowed or restricted and the distributions credited may be canceled in whole or in part. [2-206]

Each stock certificate shall include on its face: (1) the name of the corporation that issues it, (2) the name of the stockholder or other person to whom it is issued, and (3) the class of stock and number of shares it represents. [2-211]

Each stock certificate shall be signed by the president, a vice president, or the chairman of the board and countersigned by the secretary, an assistant secretary, the treasurer, or an assistant treasurer.

Each certificate which represents any stock, bond, note, guaranty, obligation, or other corporate security: (1) may be sealed with the actual corporate seal or a facsimile of it or in any other form, and (2) the signatures may be either manual or facsimile signatures. [2-212]

The entire consideration received by a corporation for issuing stock with par value constitutes stated capital to the extent of the aggregate par value of the stock.

Any consideration received in excess of the aggregate par value constitutes capital surplus.

Except as permitted by paragraph (2) of this subsection [below], the entire consideration received by a corporation for issuing stock without par value constitutes stated capital.

Before issuing stock without par value, the board of directors may allocate any portion of the consideration to capital surplus. However, if the stock has a preference in the assets of the corporation in the event of involuntary liquidation, the board may allocate to capital surplus only a portion which does not exceed the amount by which the consideration exceeds the aggregate amount of the preference. [2-303]

By resolution of its board of directors, a corporation may apply any part of its capital surplus for: (1) the reduction or elimination of a corporate deficit arising from a loss, however incurred, or from diminution in the value of its assets, but only after earned surplus is exhausted; or (2) any other proper corporate purpose.

An application of capital surplus under subsection (a) of this section [above] shall be disclosed to the stockholders of the corporation in its next annual report. [2-304]

Director Meeting Rules

Unless the Maryland Business Law or the Charter or by-laws of the corporation require a greater proportion, the action of a majority of the directors present at a meeting at which a quorum is present is the action of the board of directors.

Unless the bylaws of the corporation provide otherwise, a majority of the entire board of directors constitutes a quorum for the transaction of business.

The bylaws may provide that less than a majority, but not less than one-third of the entire board of directors, may constitute a quorum unless: (i) there are only two or three directors, in which case not less than two may constitute a quorum; or (ii) there is only one director, in which case that one will constitute a quorum. [2-408]

Notice of each meeting of the board of directors shall be given as provided in the bylaws.

Unless the bylaws provide otherwise, the notice: (i) shall be in writing, and (ii) need not state the business to be transacted at or the purpose of any regular or special meeting of the board of directors. [2-409]

Shareholder Meeting Rules

Each corporation shall hold an annual meeting of its stockholders to elect directors and transact any other business within its powers.

Except as the Maryland Business Law provides otherwise, any business may be considered at an annual meeting without the purpose of the meeting having been specified in the notice. [2-501]

Except as provided in paragraph (2) of this Subsection [next paragraph], at each annual meeting of stockholders, the stockholders shall elect directors to hold office until the earlier of: (i) the next annual meeting of stockholders and until their successors are elected and qualify, or (ii) the time provided in the terms of any class or series of stock pursuant to which such directors are elected.

If the directors are divided into classes, the term of office may be provided in the bylaws, except that: (i) the term of office of a director may not be longer than five years or, except in the case of an initial or substitute director, shorter than the period between annual meetings; and (ii) the term of office of at least one class shall expire each year.

Each share of stock may be voted for as many individuals as there are directors to be elected and for whose election the share is entitled to be voted.

Unless the Charter or bylaws of a corporation provide otherwise, a plurality of all the votes cast at a meeting at which a quorum is present is sufficient to elect a director. [2-404]

A special meeting of the stockholders of a corporation may be called by: (1) the president, (2) the board of directors, or (3) any other person specified in the Charter or the bylaws.

Except as provided in Subsections (c) and (d) of this section [below], the secretary of a corporation shall call a special meeting of the stock holders on the written request of stock holders entitled to cast at least 25 percent of all the votes entitled to be cast at the meeting.

A request for a special meeting shall state the purpose of the meeting and the matters proposed to be acted on at it.

The secretary shall: (i) inform the stock holders who make the request of the reasonably estimated cost of preparing and mailing a notice of the meeting; and (ii) on payment of these costs to the corporation, notify each stock holder entitled to notice of the meeting.

Unless requested by stock holders entitled to cast a majority of all the votes entitled to be cast at the meeting, a special meeting need not be called to consider any matter which is substantially the same as a matter voted on at any special meeting of the stockholders held during the preceding 12 months.

Subject to paragraph (2) of this subsection [above], a corporation may include in its Charter or bylaws a provision that requires the written request of stockholders entitled to cast a greater or lesser percentage of all votes entitled to be cast at the meeting than that required by Subsection (b)(1) of this section [above] in order to call a special meeting of the stock holders.

The percentage provided for in the Charter or bylaws may not be greater than a majority of all the votes entitled to be cast at the meeting. [2-502]

Not less than ten nor more than 90 days before each stock holders' meeting, the secretary of the corporation shall give written notice of the meeting to: (1) each stock holder entitled to vote at the meeting, and (2) each other stock holder entitled to notice of the meeting.

The notice shall state: (1) the time and place of the meeting, and (2) the purpose of the meeting, if: (i) the meeting is a special meeting, or (ii) notice of the purpose is required by any other provision of the Maryland Business Law. [2-504]

Unless the Maryland Business Law or the Charter of a corporation provides otherwise, at a meeting of stock holders: (1) the presence in person or by proxy of stock holders entitled to cast a majority of all the votes entitled to be cast at the meeting constitutes a quorum; and (2) a majority of all the votes cast at a meeting at which a quorum is present is sufficient to approve any matter which properly comes before the meeting. [2-506]

Financial Disclosure Rules

The president or, if provided in the bylaws, some other executive officer of each corporation shall prepare annually a full and correct statement of the affairs of the corporation, to include a balance sheet and a financial statement of operations for the preceding fiscal year.

Except as provided below, the statement of affairs shall be submitted at the annual meeting of stock holders and, within 20 days after the meeting, placed on file at the corporation's principal office.

If a corporation is not required to hold an annual meeting of stock holders under a Charter or bylaw provision adopted in accordance with Section 2-501 of this title [allows investment companies to dispense with annual shareholders' meetings], the statement of affairs shall be placed on file at the corporation's principal office within 120 days after the end of the fiscal year. [2-313]

State Tax Information

Comptroller of Maryland, Revenue Administration Division, Annapolis
410-260-7980
www.comp.state.md.us/default.asp

Maryland imposes a graduated corporate income tax, based on federal taxable income after state modifications.

Also note: An annual report fee for business corporations of $300 must also be paid each year and is payable with the corporation's annual property return filed with the corporate filing office. The Legal Entity Annual Report/Personal Property Return (Form 1) is available from the filing office website.

Corporation Law Online

The Maryland General Corporation Law is contained in the Corporations and Associations heading of the Maryland Statutes, Titles 1 through 3, starting with Section 1-101. You can browse it from the following Web page (click "Maryland," then "Maryland Code," then 'Corporations and Associations," then select "Title 1" to begin browsing the law): www.michie.com/resources1.html

State Securities Information

The Office of the Attorney General
Securities Division
200 St. Paul Place
Baltimore, MD 21202
410-576-7050
www.oag.state.md.us/Securities/index.htm

The Maryland Securities Act is contained in the Corporations and Associations heading of the Maryland Statutes, Title 11, starting with Section 11-101. You can browse it from the Web page noted in "Corporation Law Online," above. (Enter the appropriate section number in the search box—for example "11-101." Select the "Corporations and Associations" statute listed on the search results page.) You can also order a complete copy of the Securities Act from the Securities Division for a small fee.

The Securities Division website does not currently provide information on specific exemptions available under the Maryland Securities Act. You can visit the website to obtain a list of forms and fees, but the division requests that you call to learn about exemptions and exemption procedures.

Exempt security transactions are contained in Section 11-602 of the Act. Section 11-602(9) contains an exemption for the offer and sale of securities to not more than 35 persons in Maryland during any period of 12 consecutive months if the seller reasonably believes that all the purchasers are purchasing for investment, and if the securities have not been offered to the general public by advertisement or general solicitation. Other requirements apply. Contact the Securities Division for more information about this and other available exemptions.

Creating Your Own Articles Form

You may create your own form following the Articles Instructions set out above.

MASSACHUSETTS

Corporate Filing Office

Commonwealth of Massachusetts
Corporations Division
One Ashburton Place, 17th Floor
Boston, MA 02108
617-727-9640
www.state.ma.us/sec/cor

State Corporate Forms

Massachusetts provides a fill-in-the-blanks Articles of Organization form, plus line-by-line instructions.

Internet Forms: You can download Articles of Organization and instructions from the state filing office website. You can also find sample language you can use if you wish to add restrictions on the transfer of stock to your articles in Article V of the state-provided form.

Massachusetts provides an online Articles of Organization preparation and filing service. If you wish to use this service rather than preparing and paper articles, go to the state corporate filing office website, then click "Online Corporate Filings" on the main corporate filing office website to go to the link to the online corporate articles preparation and filing page.

Articles Instructions

Article I: The name of a Massachusetts corporation must include the words "corporation," "incorporated," "company," "limited," or the abbreviation "corp.," "inc.," or "ltd." The Corporations Division will not allow symbols as part of a corporate name—for example, the name $ensible $ales would not be allowed. The Corporations Division also discourages the use of initials, numbers, hyphens, apostrophes, and commas in corporate names. If you do include punctuation in the name, it must be included on all filings with the office.

To check the availability of your proposed corporate name, search the corporate database (for names in use by existing corporations) and the name reservation database (for names currently on reserve) online at the state filing office website. You may reserve an available corporate name for 60 days for $30.

Article II: Your corporation can engage in any lawful business. Do not include a specific purpose for your corporation unless you wish to limit the purposes of your corporation to a specific purpose.

Article III: The Massachusetts Business Corporation law no longer contains the concept of par value, so you do not need to specify one (modern practice is to issue

shares without par value). If you do not wish to specify a par value, simply insert the total number of shares you wish to authorize in the WITHOUT PAR VALUE portion (left side) of the table. If, like most incorporators, you wish to authorize common shares only (shares with equal dividend, voting, and liquidation rights), insert "Common" as the type of shares authorized. As explained in "Filing Fees," below, you can authorize up to 275,000 shares and pay the minimum $275 filing fee, so most incorporators will authorize 275,00 shares.

Article IV: If you authorize special classes of stock in Article III (classes other than common shares), you must state the name of each class, and the rights and restrictions associated with each.

Article V: If you wish to impose restrictions on the transfer of shares, you may do so in this article. However, most incorporators who adopt transfer restrictions include them in their bylaws, not in the articles. This is because bylaws are easier to adopt and change; in contrast, any future changes to articles must be filed with the state. If you don't wish to include restrictions on the transfer of shares here, simply insert "None."

If you wish to limit future transfers of shares by your shareholders (perhaps with the help of a business lawyer), see Massachusetts Business Corporations Law, Section 627, for information on the types of permissible transfer restrictions and requirements on noting these restrictions on your stock certificates.

Article VI: You may leave this area blank or insert "None."

Article VIII: In Sections (a) and (b), insert the street address of the corporation's registered office (which also is the registered agent's business address) and the name of the registered agent. Most incorporators specify a director or shareholder as the registered agent and specify the corporation's principal office in Massachusetts as the registered office. In Section (c), insert the name and address of the corporation's president, treasurer, and secretary. Massachusetts law requires you to fill each of these officer positions. One person may hold one or more officer positions. Next, list the names and addresses of the corporation's initial directors, who will serve on the board until the election or reelection of the board at the first annual meeting of shareholders. Your corporation must have at least three directors unless it has fewer than three stockholders. If there are two stockholders, you can name just two directors; if you have one shareholder, you can name one director.

In Section (d), insert the name of the month when your fiscal (tax) year will end. (Your tax adviser can help you decide the best month to end your corporate fiscal year.) To ensure the first fiscal year is a full year, some incorporators choose the last day of the month prior to the month when the Articles of Organization are filed as the ending date of the corporate fiscal year.In Section (e), insert the type or character of your corporation's business. Note that this is incidental information and is not legally binding. Your corporation can engage in any lawful business as long as Article II does not limit your business purposes.

Insert the street address (not a post office box) of the principal office of your corporation in Section (f). We assume you will specify a location within Massachusetts that will also serve as the location where corporate records are kept (the corporate records office must be within Massachusetts), Also insert this address in Section (g), then check the "principal office" box to show that item (g) is your corporation's principal office address.

Insert the date and have someone who is at least 18 years old sign the articles as your incorporator. You need only one incorporator. Print the incorporator's name and address under the signature. Typically, one of the initial directors, officers, or shareholders acts as incorporator, but this is not required, and anyone may sign and submit your articles for filing.

Contact Information on Last Page: The state corporate filing office fills in he first section of the last page (which starts with "I hereby certify that, upon examination of these Articles of Organization, duly submitted to me, it appears that the provisions ..."). In the Contact Information section, insert the incorporator's name, address, and telephone number. You can also supply an email address for the incorporator at the end of the contact information, if you wish.

Submit an original and one copy of your Articles of Organization. The office will file-stamp and return a copy of the articles to you

Filing Fees: $275 minimum fee, payable to the "Commonwealth of Massachusetts."

The filing fee is based on the total number of shares authorized in the articles, computed as follows: The fee is .001 multiplied by the authorized number of shares.

Examples:

If your articles authorize 275,000 shares, you pay the minimum filing fee of $275 (275,000 x $1 x .001 = $275). This is the maximum number of shares you can authorize for the minimum filing fee.

If your articles authorize 300,000 shares, you pay a filing fee of $300 (300,000 x $1 x .001 = $300).

Director and Officer Rules

A board of directors shall consist of one or more individuals, with the number specified in or fixed in accordance with the Articles of Organization or bylaws, but, unless otherwise provided in the articles of organization, if the corporation has more than one shareholder, the number of directors shall not be less than three, except that whenever there shall be only two shareholders, the number of directors shall not be less than two.

Directors shall be elected at the first annual shareholders' meeting and at each annual meeting thereafter unless their terms are staggered under section 8.06. [8.03]

The terms of all directors shall expire at the next annual shareholders' meeting following their election, unless their terms are staggered under section 8.06. [8.05]

A corporation shall have a president, a treasurer, and a secretary and such other officers described in its bylaws or appointed by the board of directors in accordance with the bylaws.

The same individual may simultaneously hold more than one office in a corporation. [8.40]

Share Issuance Rules

The board of directors may authorize shares to be issued for consideration consisting of any tangible or intangible property or benefit to the corporation, including cash, promissory notes, services performed, contracts for services to be performed, or other securities of the corporation.

The corporation may place in escrow shares issued for a contract for future services or benefits or a promissory note, or make other arrangements to restrict the transfer of the shares, and may credit distributions in respect of the shares against their purchase price, until the services are performed, the note is paid, or the benefits received. If the services are not performed, the note is not paid when due, or the benefits are not received, the shares escrowed or restricted and the distributions credited may be canceled in whole or part. [6.21]

At a minimum, each share certificate shall state on its face: (1) the name of the issuing corporation and that it is organized under the laws of the commonwealth; (2) the name of the person to whom issued; and (3) the number and class of shares and the designation of the series, if any, that the certificate represents.

Each share certificate shall be signed either manually or in facsimile by two officers designated in the bylaws or by the board of directors and may bear the corporate seal or its facsimile. [6.25]

Director Meeting Rules

The board of directors may hold regular or special meetings within or without the commonwealth. [8.20]

Unless the articles of organization or bylaws provide otherwise, regular meetings of the board of directors may be held without notice of the date, time, place, or purpose of the meeting.

Unless the articles of organization or bylaws otherwise provide, special meetings of the board of directors must be preceded by at least two days' notice of the date, time, and place of the meeting. The notice need not describe the purpose of the special meeting unless required by the articles of organization or bylaws. [8.22]

(a) Subject to subsection (b) [see below], unless the articles of organization or bylaws otherwise provide or unless otherwise specifically provided in this chapter, a quorum of a board of directors consists of: (1) a majority of the fixed number of directors if the corporation has a fixed board size; or (2) a majority of the number of directors prescribed, or if no number is prescribed, the number in office immediately before the meeting begins, if the corporation has a variable-range size board.

(b) The articles of organization or bylaws may authorize a quorum of a board of directors to consist of no fewer than: (1) one-third of the fixed or prescribed number of directors determined under subsection (a); or (2) a majority of the directors then in office, without regard to the number of directors determined under subsection (a) of this section.

(c) If a quorum is present when a vote is taken, the affirmative vote of a majority of directors present is the act of the board of directors unless the articles of organization or bylaws require the vote of a greater number of directors. [8.24]

Shareholder Meeting Rules

A corporation shall hold a meeting of shareholders annually at a time stated in or fixed in accordance with the bylaws.

Unless otherwise provided in the articles of organization, an annual meeting shall be held for the purpose of electing directors and such other purposes as are specified in the notice of the meeting, and only business within such purposes may be conducted at the meeting. [7.01]

A corporation shall hold a special meeting of shareholders: (1) on call of its board of directors or the person authorized to do so by the articles of organization or bylaws; or (2) in the case of a corporation other than a public corporation, if the holders of at least 10%, or such lesser percentage as the articles of organization permit, of all the votes entitled to be cast on any issue to be considered at the proposed special meeting sign, date, and deliver to the corporation's secretary one or more written demands for the meeting describing the purpose for which it is to be held.

Only business within the purpose or purposes described in the meeting notice required by subsection (a) of section 7.05 may be conducted at a special shareholders' meeting. [7.02]

A written notice of the date, time, and place of each annual and special shareholders' meeting describing the purposes of the meeting shall be given to shareholders no fewer than 7 nor more than 60 days before the meeting date. Unless this chapter or the articles of organization require otherwise, the corporation is required to give notice only to shareholders entitled to vote at the meeting. [7.05]

Shares entitled to vote as a separate voting group may take action on a matter at a meeting only if a quorum of those shares exists with respect to that matter. Unless otherwise provided in this Act, or in the articles of organization, the bylaws, or a resolution of the board of directors, as permitted by subsection (a) of section 7.27, a majority of the votes entitled to be cast on the matter by the voting group constitutes a quorum of that voting group for action on that matter.

If a quorum of a voting group exists, favorable action on a matter, other than the election of directors, is taken by a voting group if the votes cast within the group favoring the action exceed the votes cast opposing the action, unless either this chapter, or the articles of organization, the bylaws, or a resolution of the board of directors, as permitted by subsection (a) of section 7.27, requires a greater number of affirmative votes.

The election of directors is governed by section 7.28. [7.25]

Unless otherwise provided in the articles of organization or bylaws, directors are elected by a plurality of the votes cast by the shares entitled to vote in the election at a meeting at which a quorum is present.

Shareholders do not have a right to cumulate their votes for directors unless the articles of organization so provide.

A statement included in the articles of organization that "a designated voting group of shareholders are entitled to cumulate their votes for directors," or words of similar import, means that the shareholders designated are entitled to multiply the number of votes they are entitled to cast by the number of directors for whom they are entitled to vote and cast the product for a single candidate or distribute the product among two or more candidates. [7.28]

Financial Disclosure Rules

A corporation shall furnish to its shareholders upon request annual financial statements, which may be consolidated or combined statements of the corporation and one or more of its subsidiaries, as appropriate, that include a balance sheet as at the end of the fiscal year, an income statement for that year, and, if available, a statement of changes in shareholder equity for that year unless that information appears elsewhere in the financial statements. If prepared by the corporation, the corporation shall also furnish a statement of cash flows for that year. If financial statements are prepared by the corporation on the basis of generally accepted accounting principles, the annual financial statements must also be prepared on that basis. For purposes of this subsection, financial statements may consist of copies of federal tax returns or other comparable information that is reasonable under the circumstances in the case where the corporation does not prepare financial statements as described above.

If the annual financial statements are reported upon by a public accountant, his or her report shall accompany those statements. If not, those statements shall be accompanied by a certificate of the president or the person responsible for the corporation's accounting records: (1) stating his or her reasonable belief whether the statements were prepared in accordance with generally accepted accounting principles or, if not, describing the basis of preparation; and (2) describing any respects in which the statements were not prepared on a basis of accounting consistent with the statements prepared for the preceding year.

A corporation shall deliver the annual financial statements, or a written notice of their availability, to each shareholder before the earlier to occur of the annual meeting of shareholders or 120 days after the close of the fiscal year. Thereafter, the corporation shall deliver its most recent financial statements upon the written request of any shareholder to whom the statements were not delivered.

A corporation shall not be required to furnish its annual financial statements to a shareholder if it can demonstrate a proper corporate purpose for withholding information contained in those statements from that shareholder. [16.20]

State Tax Information

Department of Revenue, Boston
800-392-6089
www.dor.state.ma.us/Dorpg.htm

Massachusetts imposes a corporate excise tax, calculated by adding two different measures of tax: a net income measure and either a property measure or a net worth measure, depending on whether the corporation is a tangible or intangible property corporation. A corporation's total excise tax is the combination of the property/net worth and net income measures, or the minimum corporate excise tax of $456, whichever is greater.

Corporation Law Online

The Massachusetts Business Corporation Act is contained in Title XXII (Corporations), Chapter 156D, of the Massachusetts General Laws, starting with Section 1. You can browse it from the following Web page (note that Chapter 156D, effective July 1, 2004, replaces the old Massachusetts Business Corporation Act, which is located in Chapter 156B):

www.mass.gov/legis/laws/mgl/gl-156d-toc.htm

State Securities Information

Secretary of the Commonwealth
Securities Division
One Ashburton Place, Room 1701
Boston, MA 02108
617-727-3548 (Toll Free in Massachusetts: 800-269-5428)
www.magnet.state.ma.us/sec/sct

The Securities Division website does not currently provide exemption information or forms. The Uniform Securities Act is contained in Chapter 110A of the Massachusetts General Laws. To find the Act, go to the legal research area of Nolo's website at www.nolo.com. Click on "State Laws" and then on "Massachusetts." Click on Part I and then choose the link to Chapter 110A to browse the Act.

Exemptions from registration of securities under the Act are contained in Section 402. These include a securities transaction exemption under Section 402(b)(9) of the Act for offers to more than 25 people during any period of 12 consecutive months if the corporation reasonably believes that all the buyers in the commonwealth are purchasing for investment, and other conditions are met. You may need to file a notice form to qualify for this exemption. For information on this and other available exemptions, call the Securities Division.

Creating Your Own Articles Form

The state filing office prefers that you use its own form for articles, but it will accept a form you create if you follow certain rules. You must type or computer-print your articles on 8.5" x 11" white, 25% cotton bond paper in black ink only. To meet all other requirements, we recommend that you submit pages printed on one side only, with at least 1" margins on each page.

MICHIGAN

Corporate Filing Office

Michigan Department of Labor & Economic Growth
Bureau of Commercial Services
Corporation Division
P.O. Box 30054
Lansing, MI 48909
Telephone: 517-241-6470
www.michigan.gov/cis

State Corporate Forms

Michigan provides an Articles of Incorporation form with instructions. Articles can be filed by fax after filling out an application for a filer number. To obtain a filer number, download and complete Form BCS/CD-90 (MICH-ELF application) from the state corporate filing office website.

Internet Forms: You can find a fill-in-the-blanks Articles of Incorporation (Form BCS/CD-500) with instructions on the state corporate filing office website.

Articles Instructions

Top of Form: Insert the name and address of your incorporator as the contact person. The state will return a copy of the articles to this person at this address.

Article I: The name of a Michigan corporation must contain the word "corporation," "company," "incorporated," or "limited," or the abbreviation "corp.," "co.," inc.," or "ltd." You can check name availability online at the state corporate filing office website or by calling the office. It costs $10 to reserve an available corporate name for six months.

Article II: You do not need to state a specific purpose for your corporation. The basic text that is already included in the state form is sufficient.

Article III: Michigan law does not use the concept of par value. Most incorporators authorize one class of common shares with equal voting, dividend, and liquidation rights and no special restrictions. To do this, insert the total number of common shares you wish to authorize in the "Common Shares" blank. You can authorize up to 60,000 shares and still qualify for the minimum filing fee. (See the filing fee information, below.) To create additional classes of shares you must fill in the "Preferred Shares" blank or add your own line that specifies the classes you wish to add. You must specify the rights and restrictions associated with each additional class of shares in the second part of Article III. If you authorize only common shares, leave the second portion (Article III, part 2) blank.

Article V: Specify an incorporator, who need not be a director, officer, or shareholder. Your incorporator must be at least 18 years of age.

Article VI: Most incorporators delete this wordy article. (You can simply cross it out.) The article applies to complicated corporate reorganization plans. You will undoubtedly see a lawyer if you later want to update your corporate paperwork to handle this sort of restructuring.

Article VII: This article allows shareholders to take action by written consent without holding a meeting. In a small corporation, the ability to take action without a meeting is a helpful convenience. Most incorporators adopt this article by leaving it in the form. (Note that you are required to notify nonconsenting shareholders of any action taken by written consent.)

Bottom of Page 2: The incorporator named in Article V must date and sign the form at the bottom.

Top of Page 3: Insert the name of the incorporator as the person "remitting fees" (signing the check for fees), and also insert the incorporator's name and telephone number in the preparer information at the right. MAKE SURE TO INCLUDE PAGE THREE, WHICH ALSO INCLUDES THE OFFICIAL STATE INSTRUCTIONS TO THE FORM, WITH YOUR ARTICLES DOCUMENT.

Submit your original articles to the state filing office. This document will be returned to you after it is copied and stored in the state's database. It will be sent to the registered agent at the registered office address shown in the articles unless you specify a different name and address in the boxes above Article 1. Note that you can file your articles by fax if you apply for a filer number. To get a fax filer number, download and complete Form BCS/CD-90 (MICH-ELF application) from the state corporate filing office website.

Filing Fee: $60 minimum fee, payable to the "State of Michigan." This fee includes a $10 nonrefundable fee, plus a $50 organization tax for the first 60,000 shares authorized in your articles. If you authorize additional shares, the organization portion of the fee increases as follows: For each additional 20,000 shares or portion thereof, add $30 to your organization tax. The maximum organization tax for the first 10 million shares is $5,000. The fee schedule changes if you authorize more than 10 million shares; see the state corporate filing office website for more information. Most incorporators simply authorize 60,000 shares and pay the minimum filing fee.

Director and Officer Rules

The board shall consist of one or more members [although no statutory reference could be found, the state filing office website says that directors must be at least 18 years of age].

The first board of directors shall hold office until the first annual meeting of shareholders. At the first annual meeting of shareholders and at each annual meeting thereafter, the shareholders shall elect directors to hold office until the succeeding annual meeting, except in case of the classification of directors as permitted by this act. A director shall hold office for the term for which he or she is elected and until his or her successor is elected and qualified, or until his or her resignation or removal.

The shareholders or board may designate one or more directors as an independent director. Any director so designated shall be entitled to reasonable compensation in addition to compensation paid to directors generally, as determined by the board or shareholders, and reimbursement for expenses reasonably related to service as an independent director. An independent director may communicate with shareholders at the corporation's expense, as part of a communication or report sent by the corporation to shareholders. An independent director shall not have any greater duties or liabilities than any other director. [505]

The officers of a corporation shall consist of a president, secretary, treasurer, and, if desired, a chairman of the board, one or more vice presidents, and such other officers as may be prescribed by the bylaws or determined by the board.

Two or more offices may be held by the same person but an officer shall not execute, acknowledge, or verify an instrument in more than one capacity if the instrument is required by law or the articles or bylaws to be executed, acknowledged, or verified by two or more officers. [531]

Share Issuance Rules

The board may authorize shares to be issued for consideration consisting of any tangible or intangible property or benefit to the corporation, including but not limited to cash, promissory notes, services performed, contracts for services to be performed, or other securities of the corporation. [314]

Except as provided in section 336, the shares of a corporation shall be represented by certificates which shall be signed by the chairperson of the board, vice chairperson of the board, president, or a vice president and which also may be signed by another officer of the corporation. The certificate may be sealed with the seal of the corporation or a facsimile of the seal. [331]

A certificate representing shares shall state on its face all of the following: (a) that the corporation is formed under the laws of this state; (b) the name of the person to whom issued; (c) the number and class of shares, and the designation of the series, if any, which the certificate represents. [332]

Director Meeting Rules

Regular or special meetings of a board may be held either in or outside the state of Michigan.

A regular meeting may be held with or without notice as prescribed in the bylaws. A special meeting shall be held on notice as prescribed in the bylaws. A director's attendance at or participation in a meeting waives any required notice to him or her of the meeting unless he or she at the beginning of the meeting, or on his or her arrival, objects to the meeting or the transacting of business at the meeting and does not thereafter vote for or assent to any action taken at the meeting. Unless required by the bylaws, neither the business to be transacted at, nor the purpose of, a regular or special meeting need be specified in the notice or waiver of notice of the meeting. [521]

A majority of the members of the board then in office, or of the members of a committee of the board, constitutes a quorum for transaction of business, unless the Articles of Incorporation or bylaws, or, in the case of a committee, the board resolution establishing the committee, provide for a larger or smaller number. The vote of the majority of members present at a meeting at which a quorum is present constitutes the action of the board or of the committee, unless the vote of a larger number is required by the Business Corporation Act, the articles, or the bylaws, or, in the case of a committee, the board resolution establishing the committee. [523]

Shareholder Meeting Rules

An annual meeting of shareholders for election of directors and for such other business as may come before the meeting shall be held at a time as provided in the bylaws, unless such action is taken by written consent as provided in Section 407 [allows shareholders to take action without a meeting by written consent]. [450.1402]

A special meeting of shareholders may be called by the board, or by officers, directors, or shareholders as provided in the bylaws. Notwithstanding any such provision, on application of the holders of not less than 10% of all the shares entitled to vote at a meeting, the circuit court of the county in which the principal place of business or registered office is located, for good cause shown, may order a special meeting of shareholders to be called and held at such time and place, on such notice, and for the transaction of such business as may be designated in the order. At any such meeting ordered to be called by the court, the shareholders present in person or by proxy and having voting powers constitute a quorum for transaction of the business designated in the order. [403]

Except as otherwise provided in the Business Corporation Act, written notice of the time, place, and purposes of a meeting of shareholders shall be given not less than ten nor more than 60 days before the date of the meeting, either personally or by mail, to each shareholder of record entitled to vote at the meeting.

Unless the corporation has securities registered under Section 12 of the Securities Exchange Act of 1934, chapter 404, 48 Stat. 892, 15 U.S.C. 78 l, notice of the purposes of a meeting shall include notice of shareholder proposals that are proper subjects for shareholder action and are intended to be presented by shareholders who have notified the corporation in writing of their intention to present the proposals at the meeting. The bylaws may establish reasonable procedures for the submission of proposals to the corporation in advance of the meeting. [404]

At each meeting of shareholders, a chairperson shall preside. The chairperson shall be appointed as provided in the bylaws or, in the absence of a provision in the bylaws, by the board of directors.

The chairperson, unless the Articles of Incorporation or bylaws provide otherwise, shall determine the order of business and shall have the authority to establish rules for the conduct of the meeting. Any rules adopted for, and the conduct of, the meeting shall be fair to shareholders.

The chairperson of the meeting shall announce at the meeting when the polls close for each matter voted on. If no announcement is made, the polls shall close on the final adjournment of the meeting. After the polls close, no ballots, proxies, or votes nor any revocations or changes to ballots, proxies, or votes may be accepted. [406]

Unless a greater or lesser quorum is provided in the Articles of Incorporation, in a bylaw adopted by the shareholders or incorporators, or in the Business Corporation Act, shares entitled to cast a majority of the votes at a meeting constitute a quorum at the meeting. [415]

Except as provided in Sections 794 and 798 [covering special voting rules for the approval of corporate mergers and acquisitions], each outstanding share is entitled to one vote on each matter submitted to a vote, unless otherwise provided in the Articles of Incorporation. A vote may be cast either orally or in writing, unless otherwise provided in the bylaws.

If an action, other than the election of directors, is to be taken by vote of the shareholders, it shall be authorized by a majority of the votes cast by the holders of shares

entitled to vote on the action, unless a greater vote is required by the articles or another section of the Business Corporation Act. Except as otherwise provided by the articles, directors shall be elected by a plurality of the votes cast at an election. [441]

The Articles of Incorporation may provide that a shareholder entitled to vote at an election for directors may vote, in person or by proxy, the number of shares owned by him for as many persons as there are directors to be elected and for whose election he has a right to vote, or to cumulate his votes by giving one candidate as many votes as the number of such directors multiplied by the number of his shares, or by distributing his votes on the same principle among any number of the candidates. [451]

Financial Disclosure Rules

Each domestic corporation at least once in each year shall cause a financial report of the corporation for the preceding fiscal year to be made and distributed to each shareholder thereof within four months after the end of the fiscal year. The report shall include the corporation's statement of income; its year-end balance sheet; and, if prepared by the corporation, its statement of source and application of funds and such other information as may be required by the Business Corporation Act. [901]

On written request of a shareholder, a corporation shall mail to the shareholder its balance sheet as at the end of the preceding fiscal year; its statement of income for the fiscal year; and, if prepared by the corporation, its statement of source and application of funds for the fiscal year. [487]

State Tax Information

Michigan Department of Treasury, Lansing
800-487-7000
www.michigan.gov/treasury

Michigan imposes a single business tax on both corporate and noncorporate business income.

Corporation Law Online

The Michigan Business Corporation Act is contained in Chapter 450 (Corporations) of the Michigan Compiled Laws, starting with Section 450.1101. To find the Act, visit the legal research area of Nolo's website at www.nolo.com/statute/state.cfm. Click on "Michigan." Then select "Chapter Index" and "Chapter 450." Scroll down until you see the link for the Business Corporation Act. Click on that link to browse the laws. (Note that the section numbers are preceded by "450.1." For example, to view Section 404, click on "450.1404" in the table of contents.)

State Securities Information

Office of Financial and Insurance Services
Division of Securities
P.O. Box 30701
Lansing, MI 48909-8201
517-241-6350 (Toll Free: 877-999-6442)
www.michigan.gov/cis/0,1607,7-154-10555—,00.html

The Michigan Uniform Securities Act is contained in Chapter 451 of the Michigan Statutes. You can browse the Act and related regulations from the Division of Securities website. You can also download the "Business Guide to Selling Securities in Michigan." This guide explains the basic requirements of the various securities exemptions available to you when issuing the initial shares of your corporation. For example, Section 402(b)(10) of the Securities Act contains an exemption for the issuance of shares of a new corporation to up to ten subscribers. Section 402(b)(9) contains five additional exemptions, each with its own requirements. Read the guide for further information, and call the Division of Securities if you have questions.

Creating Your Own Articles Form

You can create your own articles form.

MINNESOTA

Corporate Filing Office

Minnesota Secretary of State
Business Services Division
180 State Office Building
100 Rev. Dr. Martin Luther King Boulevard
St. Paul, MN 55155-1299
651-296-2803 (Toll Free: 877-551-6767)
www.sos.state.mn.us/business/index.html

State Corporate Forms

Minnesota provides fill-in-the-blanks Articles of Incorporation, which cover both profit and nonprofit corporations.

Internet Forms: You can download a fill-in-the-blanks Articles of Incorporation form (Business and Nonprofit Corporations) and other statutory forms from the state corporate filing office website.

Note: The state filing office website offers Express (one-day) filing of Articles for an additional $10 fee—this service consists of sending your incorporation information in an email to the filing office rather than preparing and mailing an Articles form. Note, however, that this service is only available to subscribers to the state's direct access account, which costs $75 annually.

Articles Instructions

Articles must be printed in black ink only.

Top of Form: Check the box that shows you are forming a for-profit business corporation.

Article I: The name of a Minnesota corporation must contain the words "corporation," "incorporated," "company," or "limited," or must contain an abbreviation of one or more of these words. If the name includes the word "company" or its abbreviation, that word or abbreviation may not be immediately preceded by the word "and" or the character "&."

You can perform a corporate name availability search online for free from the state filing office website. You can also browse the name availability guidelines used by the corporate filing office online. It costs $35 to reserve an available corporate name for 12 months.

Article III: In Minnesota, you do not need to state a par value for your shares. The filing fee is not based on your authorized shares, so you can authorize as many as you wish. Most incorporators authorize one class of common shares with equal voting, dividend, and liquidation rights and no special restrictions. To do this, simply indicate the total number of authorized shares in the designated

blank. If you want to authorize special classes of shares, you must retype your articles to list the designation of each class, the authorized number of shares in each class, and the rights and restrictions associated with each class.

Only one incorporator is required to sign your articles. Your incorporator can be anyone who is 18 years of age or older. Insert the name and telephone number of your incorporator in the contact information blanks at the bottom of the articles form.

Submit the original articles for filing. The office will mail you a filing receipt after it approves your articles.

Filing Fee: $135, payable to "Minnesota Secretary of State."

Director and Officer Rules

The board shall consist of one or more directors. [302A.203]

Unless fixed terms are provided for in the articles or bylaws, a director serves for an indefinite term that expires at the next regular meeting of the shareholders. A fixed term of a director shall not exceed five years. A director holds office for the term for which the director was elected and until a successor is elected and has qualified, or until the earlier death, resignation, removal, or disqualification of the director. [302A.207]

The holders of the shares entitled to vote for directors of the corporation may, by unanimous affirmative vote, take any action that this chapter [the Business Corporation Act] requires or permits the board to take. [302A.201 (2)]

A corporation shall have one or more natural persons exercising the functions of the offices, however designated, of chief executive officer and chief financial officer. [302A.301]

Unless the articles, the bylaws, or a resolution adopted by the board and not inconsistent with the articles or bylaws, provide otherwise, the chief executive officer and chief financial officer have the duties specified in this section.

The chief executive officer shall: (a) have general active management of the business of the corporation; (b) when present, preside at all meetings of the board and of the shareholders; (c) see that all orders and resolutions of the board are carried into effect; (d) sign and deliver in the name of the corporation any deeds, mortgages, bonds, contracts, or other instruments pertaining to the business of the corporation, except in cases in which the authority to sign and deliver is required by law to be exercised by another person or is expressly delegated by the articles or bylaws or by the board to some other officer or agent of the corporation; (e) maintain records of and, whenever necessary, certify all proceedings of the board and the shareholders; and (f) perform other duties prescribed by the board.

The chief financial officer shall: (a) keep accurate financial records for the corporation; (b) deposit all money, drafts, and checks in the name of and to the credit of the corporation in the banks and depositories designated by the board; (c) endorse for deposit all notes, checks, and drafts received by the corporation as ordered by the board, making proper vouchers therefor; (d) disburse corporate funds and issue checks and drafts in the name of the corporation, as ordered by the board; (e) render to the chief executive officer and the board, whenever requested, an account of all transactions by the chief financial officer and of the financial condition of the corporation; and (f) perform other duties prescribed by the board or by the chief executive officer. [302A.305]

Any number of offices or functions of those offices may be held or exercised by the same person. If a document must be signed by persons holding different offices or functions and a person holds or exercises more than one of those offices or functions, that person may sign the document in more than one capacity, but only if the document indicates each capacity in which the person signs. [302A.315]

Share Issuance Rules

Subject to any restrictions in the articles, a corporation may issue securities and rights to purchase securities only when authorized by the board.

All the shares of a corporation: (a) shall be of one class and one series, unless the articles establish, or authorize the board to establish, more than one class or series; (b) shall be common shares entitled to vote and shall have equal rights and preferences in all matters not otherwise provided for by the board, unless and to the extent that the articles have fixed the relative rights and preferences of different classes and series; and (c) shall have, unless a different par value is specified in the articles, a par value of one cent per share, solely for the purpose of a statute or rule imposing a tax or fee based on the capitalization of a corporation, and a par value fixed by the board for the purpose of a statute or rule requiring the shares of the corporation to have a par value. [302A.401]

Subject to any restrictions in the articles: (a) shares may be issued for any consideration, including, without limitation, money or other tangible or intangible property received by the corporation or to be received by the corporation under a written agreement, or services rendered to the corporation or to be rendered to the corporation, as authorized by resolution approved by the affirmative vote of the directors required by section 302A.237, or, if provided for in the articles, approved by the affirmative vote of the shareholders required by section 302A.437, establishing a price in money or other consideration, or a minimum price, or a general formula or method by which the price will be determined. [302A.405]

Unless denied or limited in the articles or by the board pursuant to section 302A.401, subdivision 2, clause (b), a shareholder of a corporation has the preemptive rights provided in this section.

A preemptive right is the right of a shareholder to acquire a certain fraction of the unissued securities or rights to purchase securities of a corporation before the corporation may offer them to other persons. [302A.413]

The shares of a corporation shall be either certificated shares or uncertificated shares. Each holder of certificated shares issued in accordance with section 302A.405, subdivision 3, paragraph (a) is entitled to a certificate of shares.

Certificates shall be signed by an agent or officer authorized in the articles or bylaws to sign share certificates or, in the absence of an authorization, by an officer.

A certificate representing shares of a corporation shall contain on its face: (a) the name of the corporation; (b) a statement that the corporation is incorporated under the laws of this state; (c) the name of the person to whom it is issued; and (d) the number and class of shares, and the designation of the series, if any, that the certificate represents. [302A.417]

Director Meeting Rules

Meetings of the board may be held from time to time as provided in the articles or bylaws at any place within or without the state that the board may select or by any means described in Subdivision 2 [allows the board to use electronic means, such as a telephone conference call, to hold meetings].

Unless the articles or bylaws provide for a different time period, a director may call a board meeting by giving at least ten days' notice or, in the case of organizational meetings pursuant to Section 302A.171, Subdivision 2 [covers meetings held by incorporators to elect initial directors], at least three days' notice, to all directors of the date, time, and place of the meeting. The notice need not state the purpose of the meeting unless the articles or bylaws require it. [302A.231]

A majority, or a larger or smaller proportion or number provided in the articles or bylaws, of the directors currently holding office is a quorum for the transaction of business. [302A.235]

The board shall take action by the affirmative vote of the greater of (1) a majority of directors present at a duly held meeting at the time the action is taken, or (2) a majority of the minimum proportion or number of directors that would constitute a quorum for the transaction of business at the meeting, except where the Business Corporation Act or the articles require the affirmative vote of a larger proportion or number. If the articles require a larger proportion or number than is required by the Business Corporation Act for a particular action, the articles shall control. [302A.237]

Shareholder Meeting Rules

Regular meetings of shareholders may be held on an annual or other less frequent periodic basis, but need not be held unless required by the articles or bylaws or by Subdivision 2 [allows a shareholder to demand the holding of a shareholders' meeting if one has not been held during the previous 15-month period]. [302A.431]

At each regular meeting of shareholders there shall be an election of qualified successors for directors who serve for an indefinite term or whose terms have expired or are due to expire within six months after the date of the meeting. No other particular business is required to be transacted at a regular meeting. Any business appropriate for action by the shareholders may be transacted at a regular meeting. [302A.431]

Unless the articles provide that there shall be no cumulative voting, and except as provided in Section 302A.223, Subdivision 5 [covers special voting rules to elect replacements to the board after one or more directors have been removed], each shareholder entitled to vote for directors has the right to cumulate those votes in the election of directors by giving written notice of intent to cumulate those votes to any officer of the corporation before the meeting, or to the presiding officer at the meeting at which the election is to occur at any time before the election of directors at the meeting, in which case: (a) the presiding officer at the meeting shall announce, before the election of directors, that shareholders shall cumulate their votes; and (b) each shareholder shall cumulate those votes either by casting for one candidate the number of votes equal to the number of directors to be elected multiplied by the number of votes represented by the shares, or by distributing all of those votes on the same principle among any number of candidates. [302A.215]

Special meetings of the shareholders may be called for any purpose or purposes at any time, by: (a) the chief executive officer, (b) the chief financial officer, (c) two or more directors, (d) a person authorized in the Articles or bylaws to call special meetings, or (e) a shareholder or shareholders holding 10% or more of the voting power of all shares entitled to vote, except that a special meeting for the purpose of considering any action to directly or indirectly facilitate or effect a business combination, including any action to change or otherwise affect the composition of the board of directors for that purpose, must be called by 25% or more of the voting power of all shares entitled to vote.

The business transacted at a special meeting is limited to the purposes stated in the notice of the meeting. Any business transacted at a special meeting that is not included in those stated purposes is voidable by or on behalf of the corporation, unless all of the shareholders have waived notice of the meeting in accordance with Section 302A.435, Subdivision 4 [allows approval of decisions by the written consent of shareholders]. [302A.433]

Except as otherwise provided in the Business Corporation Act, notice of all meetings of shareholders shall be given to every holder of shares entitled to vote. [Section 302A.435, which also lists various exceptions to this rule.]

In all instances where a specific minimum notice period has not otherwise been fixed by law, the notice shall be given at least ten days before the date of the meeting, or a shorter time provided in the articles or bylaws, and not more than 60 days before the date of the meeting.

The notice shall contain the date, time, and place of the meeting, the information with respect to dissenters' rights [see Section 302A.473, Subdivision 2, of the Business Corporation Act], if applicable, and any other information required by the Business Corporation Act. In the case of a special meeting, the notice shall contain a statement of the purposes of the meeting. [302A.435]

The holders of a majority of the voting power of the shares entitled to vote at a meeting are a quorum for the transaction of business, unless a larger or smaller proportion or number is provided in the articles or bylaws.

The shareholders shall take action by the affirmative vote of the holders of the greater of (1) a majority of the voting power of the shares present and entitled to vote on that item of business, or (2) a majority of the voting power of the minimum number of the shares entitled to vote that would constitute a quorum for the transaction of business at the meeting, except where the Business Corporation Act or the articles require a larger proportion or number. If the articles require a larger proportion or number than is required by the Business Corporation Act for a particular action, the articles control. [302A.437]

Financial Disclosure Rules

A corporation shall prepare annual financial statements within 180 days after the close of the corporation's fiscal year. The financial statement shall include at least a balance sheet as of the end of each fiscal year and a statement of income for the fiscal year, which shall be prepared on the basis of accounting methods reasonable in the circumstances and may be consolidated statements of the corporation and one or more of its subsidiaries. In the case of statements audited by a public accountant, each copy shall be accompanied by a report setting forth the opinion of the accountant on the statements; in other cases, each copy shall be accompanied by a statement of the chief financial officer or other person in charge of the corporation's financial records stating the reasonable belief of the person that the financial statements were prepared in accordance with accounting methods reasonable in the circumstances, describing the basis of presentation, and describing any respects in which the financial statements were not prepared on a basis consistent with those prepared for the previous year.

On written request by a shareholder, a corporation shall furnish its most recent annual financial statements as required above no later than ten business days after receipt of a shareholder's written request. "Furnish" for purposes of this paragraph means that the corporation shall deliver or mail, postage prepaid, the financial statements to the address specified by the requesting shareholder. [302A.463]

State Tax Information

Department of Revenue, St. Paul
800-297-5309
www.taxes.state.mn.us

Minnesota imposes an annual corporate franchise tax.

Corporation Law Online

The Minnesota Business Corporation Act is contained in Chapter 302A of the Minnesota Statutes, starting with Section 322B.01. To find the Act, visit the legal research area of Nolo's website at www.nolo.com/statute/state.cfm. Click on "Minnesota." From there, choose "Table of Contents" and scroll down to click on the link "Chapters 300 thru 319B." Finally, click on "Chapter 302A" to begin browsing the Act.

State Securities Information

Minnesota Department of Commerce
Securities Division
133 East Seventh Street
St. Paul, MN 55101
651-296-4520
www.state.mn.us/cgi-bin/portal/mn/jsp/home.do?agency=Commerce

The Securities Division provides links to the Minnesota Securities Act, contained in Chapter 80A of the Minnesota Statutes, and provides basic information on applying for an exemption from registration of securities under the Act. For example, Section 80A.15, Subdivision 2(a), provides an exemption for certain private offerings of stock to ten or fewer persons in a 12-month period. (Sales to an additional 25 people are allowed if you meet other requirements and file a notice form with the Division.) An additional exemption is provided under Section 80A.15, Subdivision 2(h), which parallels and works in conjunction with a Federal Regulation D securities offering. For additional information, see the Division website and call the Division office.

Creating Your Own Articles Form

You can create your own articles form.

MISSISSIPPI

Corporate Filing Office

Mississippi Secretary of State
Corporate Division
P.O. Box 136
Jackson, MS 39205-0136
601-359-1633 (Toll Free: 800-256-3494)
www.sos.state.ms.us

State Corporate Forms

The Mississippi Secretary of State provides an Articles of Incorporation form for Mississippi profit and nonprofit corporations.

Internet Forms: You can download the Mississippi Articles of Incorporation form (Form F0001) with instructions, as well as other statutory corporate forms, from the state corporate filing office website.

Articles Instructions

If you use the Word version of the form, rather than completing the pdf version, make sure a bar code appears in the upper-left corner of pages one and two. The barcode font that produces this barcode is named "3of9.TTF." You should install this font in your system fonts folder prior to printing out the form. (The font file and instructions for installing it on your Windows computer are provided online.)

Article 1: Put an "X" in the "Profit" box at the top of the form.

Article 2: The name of a Mississippi corporation must contain the word "corporation," "incorporated," "company," or "limited," or the abbreviation "corp.," "inc.," "co.," or "ltd."

To see if your proposed name is already being used by another corporation, click the "Search for Business Entity" link on the state corporate filing website. You can also check name availability by calling the state filing office. You can reserve an available corporate name for 180 days for $25.

Article 3: Leave this box blank unless you want the effective date of filing to be later than the date on which your articles are received by the state filing office. If you wish, you can request a delayed effective date that is up to 90 days later than the date on which your articles are received.

NOTE: Any date specified must be in MM/DD/YYYY format (4 digits for the year), for example, 5/1/2007 or 05/01/2007.

Article 4: Ignore the duration box. It applies only to non-profit corporations.

Article 5: : Mississippi law does not use the concept of par value, so you need to specify only the number of shares you wish to authorize for later issuance to your shareholders. The filing fee is not based on your authorized shares, so you can authorize as many as you wish. Most incorporators authorize one class of common shares with equal voting, dividend, and liquidation rights and no special restrictions. To do this, simply insert the word "common" in the "Class" box, and the number of shares authorized in the "# of Shares Authorized" box, leaving the other boxes empty. If you do wish to authorize special classes of shares, insert the name of each class in the "Classes" boxes, then the number of shares in each class in the corresponding "# of Shares Authorized" box. In the large box at the right, either insert the rights and restrictions for each class or refer to an attachment page that lists these rights and restrictions. (Undoubtedly, you'll need an attachment page if you authorize special classes; there's very little space in this box.)

NOTE: The number of authorized share should be specified as numerals without commas.

Article 6: Typically, an initial director or shareholder is named as initial registered agent (the person authorized to receive legal documents on behalf of the corporation). Most incorporators use the street address of the corporation as the registered office address (which must be the same as the business address of the registered agent). The registered agent must be a Minnesota resident and the registered office must be in Minnesota.

NOTE: Make sure the registered agent and registered office information is formatted according to the state requirements. Specifically, the registered agent's name must not be more than 40 characters. The street address cannot be more than 45 characters. The city cannot be more than 20 characters. Make sure the five-digit portion of the zip code appears in the left zip code box, and the last four digits of a nine-digit zip, if you use one, appear in the right zip code box. You also can add a P.O. Box (mailing address) for your agent in the "P.O. Box" field. If you do, just insert a number (it is assumed to be a P.O. Box).

Article 7: Insert the name and address of your incorporator, who must sign your articles in the box provided under 9. The requirements for the format of the incorporator name and address are the same as the name and address requirements given above for Article 6.

Filing Fee: $50, payable to the "Secretary of State."

Director and Officer Rules

A board of directors must consist of one or more individuals, with the number specified in or fixed in accordance with the Articles of Incorporation or bylaws.

If a board of directors has power to fix or change the number of directors, the board may increase or decrease by thirty percent (30%) or less the number of directors last approved by the shareholders, but only the shareholders may increase or decrease by more than thirty percent (30%) the number of directors last approved by the shareholders.

Directors are elected at the first annual shareholders' meeting and at each annual meeting thereafter unless their terms are staggered under Section 79-4-8.06. [79-4-8.03]

The terms of the initial directors of a corporation expire at the first shareholders' meeting at which directors are elected.

The terms of all other directors expire at the next annual shareholders' meeting following their election unless their terms are staggered under Section 79-4-8.06. [79-4-8.05]

A corporation has the officers described in its bylaws or appointed by the board of directors in accordance with the bylaws.

The bylaws or the board of directors shall delegate to one (1) of the officers responsibility for preparing minutes of the directors' and shareholders' meetings and for authenticating records of the corporation.

The same individual may simultaneously hold more than one (1) office in a corporation. [79-4-8.40]

Share Issuance Rules

The board of directors may authorize shares to be issued for consideration consisting of any tangible or intangible property or benefit to the corporation, including cash, promissory notes, services performed, contracts for services to be performed, or other securities of the corporation.

The corporation may place in escrow shares issued for a contract for future services or benefits or a promissory note, or make other arrangements to restrict the transfer of the shares, and may credit distributions in respect of the shares against their purchase price, until the services are performed, the note is paid, or the benefits received. If the services are not performed, the note is not paid, or the benefits are not received, the shares escrowed or re-

stricted and the distributions credited may be cancelled in whole or part. [79-4-6.21]

The shareholders of a corporation do not have a preemptive right to acquire the corporation's unissued shares except to the extent the Articles of Incorporation so provide.

A statement included in the Articles of Incorporation that "the corporation elects to have preemptive rights" (or words of similar import) means that the following principles apply except to the extent the Articles of Incorporation expressly provide otherwise: [see this code section for more info]. [79-4-6.30]

At a minimum each share certificate must state on its face: (1) the name of the issuing corporation and that it is organized under the law of this state; (2) the name of the person to whom issued; and (3) the number and class of shares and the designation of the series, if any, the certificate represents.

Each share certificate (1) must be signed (either manually or in facsimile) by two (2) officers designated in the bylaws or by the board of directors, and (2) may bear the corporate seal or its facsimile. [79-4-6.25]

Director Meeting Rules

Unless the Articles of Incorporation or bylaws provide otherwise, regular meetings of the board of directors may be held without notice of the date, time, place, or purpose of the meeting.

Unless the Articles of Incorporation or bylaws provide for a longer or shorter period, special meetings of the board of directors must be preceded by at least two days' notice of the date, time, and place of the meeting. The notice need not describe the purpose of the special meeting unless required by the Articles of Incorporation or bylaws. [79-4-8.22]

Unless the Articles of Incorporation or bylaws require a greater number or unless otherwise specifically provided in the Business Corporation Act, a quorum of a board of directors consists of: (1) a majority of the fixed number of directors if the corporation has a fixed board size; or (2) a majority of the number of directors prescribed, or if no number is prescribed, the number in office immediately before the meeting begins, if the corporation has a variable-range size board.

The Articles of Incorporation or bylaws may authorize a quorum of a board of directors to consist of no fewer than 1/3 of the fixed or prescribed number of directors determined under Subsection (a) [previous paragraph].

If a quorum is present when a vote is taken, the affirmative vote of a majority of directors present is the act of the board of directors unless the Articles of Incorporation or bylaws require the vote of a greater number of directors. [79-4-8.24]

Shareholder Meeting Rules

A corporation shall hold annually at a time stated in or fixed in accordance with the bylaws a meeting of shareholders. [79-4-7.01]

A corporation shall hold a special meeting of shareholders: (1) on call of its board of directors or the person or persons authorized to do so by the Articles of Incorporation or bylaws; or (2) unless the Articles of Incorporation provide otherwise, if shareholders having at least 10% of all the votes entitled to be cast on an issue proposed to be considered at the proposed special meeting sign, date, and deliver to the corporation one or more written demands for the meeting describing the purpose or purposes for which it is to be held. Unless otherwise provided in the Articles of Incorporation, a written demand for a special meeting may be revoked by a writing to that effect received by the corporation prior to the receipt by the corporation of demands sufficient in number to require the holding of a special meeting.

A corporation shall notify shareholders of the date, time, and place of each annual and special shareholders' meeting no fewer than ten nor more than 60 days before the meeting date. Unless the Business Corporation Act or the Articles of Incorporation require otherwise, the corporation is required to give notice only to shareholders entitled to vote at the meeting.

Unless the Business Corporation Act or the Articles of Incorporation require otherwise, notice of an annual meeting need not include a description of the purpose or purposes for which the meeting is called.

Notice of a special meeting must include a description of the purpose or purposes for which the meeting is called. [79-4-7.05] Only business within the purpose or purposes described in the meeting notice may be conducted at a special shareholders' meeting. [79-4-7.02]

Shares entitled to vote as a separate voting group may take action on a matter at a meeting only if a quorum of those shares exists with respect to that matter. Unless the Articles of Incorporation or the Business Corporation Act provides otherwise, a majority of the votes entitled to be

cast on the matter by the voting group constitutes a quorum of that voting group for action on that matter.

If a quorum exists, action on a matter (other than the election of directors) by a voting group is approved if the votes cast within the voting group favoring the action exceed the votes cast opposing the action, unless the Articles of Incorporation or the Business Corporation Act requires a greater number of affirmative votes.

The election of directors is governed by Section 79-4-7.28. [79-4-7.25]

Unless otherwise provided in the Articles of Incorporation, directors are elected by a plurality of the votes cast by the shares entitled to vote in the election at a meeting at which a quorum is present.

Shareholders shall have a right to cumulate their votes for directors unless the Articles of Incorporation provide otherwise.

A statement included in the Articles of Incorporation that "a designated voting group of shareholders is entitled to cumulate their votes for directors," or words of similar import, means that the shareholders designated are entitled to multiply the number of votes they are entitled to cast by the number of directors for whom they are entitled to vote and cast the product for a single candidate or distribute the product among two or more candidates. [79-4-7.28]

Financial Disclosure Rules

A corporation shall furnish its shareholders annual financial statements, which may be consolidated or combined statements of the corporation and one or more of its subsidiaries, as appropriate, that include a balance sheet as of the end of the fiscal year, an income statement for that year, and a statement of changes in shareholders' equity for the year unless that information appears elsewhere in the financial statements. If financial statements are prepared for the corporation on the basis of generally accepted accounting principles, the annual financial statements must also be prepared on that basis.

If the annual financial statements are reported on by a public accountant, his report must accompany them. If not, the statements must be accompanied by a statement of the president or the person responsible for the corporation's accounting records: (1) stating his reasonable belief whether the statements were prepared on the basis of generally accepted accounting principles and, if not, describing the basis of preparation; and (2) describing any respects in which the statements were not prepared on a basis of accounting consistent with the statements prepared for the preceding year.

A corporation shall mail the annual financial statements to each shareholder within 120 days after the close of each fiscal year. Thereafter, on written request from a shareholder who was not mailed the statements, the corporation shall mail him the latest financial statements. [79-4-16.20]

State Tax Information

Mississippi State Tax Commission, Jackson
601-923-7099
www.mstc.state.ms.us

Mississippi imposes an annual corporate franchise tax, currently set at $2.50 per $1,000 of corporate capital, surplus, and profits, plus a corporate income tax. There is a minimum annual franchise payment of $25. You must file a combined corporate franchise and income tax return each year.

Corporation Law Online

The Mississippi Business Corporation Act is contained in Title 79 (Corporations, Associations, and Partnerships) of the Mississippi Code, Chapter 4, starting with Section 79-4-1.01. You can browse the act from the following website. Click on the Mississippi Code folder in the left pane, then scroll down to open the Title 79 folder, then select Chapter 4.

www.michie.com/resources1.html

State Securities Information

Mississippi Secretary of State
Business Services
Securities Enforcement and Regulation
202 N. Congress Street, Suite 601
Jackson, MS 39201
601-359-2894 (Toll Free: 800-804-6364)
www.sos.state.ms.us/regenf/securities/securities.asp

The Mississippi Securities Act is contained in Title 75, Chapter 71, of the Mississippi Code. You can browse the Act from www.michie.com/resources1.html. (Use the instructions in "Corporation Law Online," above, but select the Title 75 folder and choose Chapter 71.) Exemptions from the registration of securities are listed in Section 75-71-203 of the Act. The easiest exemption to use is provided in Subsection (9). It exempts private sales of stock and other securities to ten or fewer persons during a 12-month period. No commissions may be paid, and the purchasers must buy the stock for investment purposes only (not resale). Another exemption is the Uniform Limited Offering exemption, which is used in conjunction with the Federal Regulation D exemption. It is provided under State Securities Rule 703 (these rules implement the Securities Act). A third exemption is provided under State Securities Rule 705. It provides an exemption for sales to no more than 35 persons within a 12-month period. Other restrictions apply to each of the exemptions listed here. The Securities Home Page offers the necessary forms and instructions for each of these as well as other available exemptions.

Creating Your Own Articles Form

You are permitted to create a typed or computer-printed articles form that contains the same information as the state form. If you do so, however, you must pay an extra $25 processing fee and filing takes longer.

MISSOURI

Corporate Filing Office

Secretary of State
Corporation Division
P.O. Box 778
Jefferson City, MO 65102
Telephone: 573-751-4153
Toll-free:1-866-223-6535
www.sos.mo.gov/business/corporations/Default.asp

State Corporate Forms

Missouri provides fill-in-the-blanks Articles of Incorporation (Form 41) with instructions.

Internet Forms: Missouri Articles of Incorporation and other corporate forms are available for downloading from the state filing office website.

Articles Instructions

Article One: The name of a Missouri corporation must contain the words "corporation," "company," "incorporated," or "limited," or end with an abbreviation of one of these words. You can check the names of existing corporations by clicking on the "Business Entity Database" link at the state filing office website. You can also check name availability by calling the state filing office. An available corporate name can be reserved for 60 days for $25.

Article Three: You can authorize shares with a stated par value or without par value; modern practice is to issue shares without par value. Most incorporators authorize one class of common shares with equal voting, dividend, and liquidation rights and no special restrictions. As explained below, to pay the minimum $58 incorporation fee, most incorporators authorize either 30,000 shares without par value or par value shares worth a total of $30,000 or less. Simply insert the class, number of shares, and par value, if any, in this article. Examples: "30,000 common shares without par value" or "30,000 common shares with a par value of $1 (One Dollar) each." Also, if you authorize either 30,000 shares or less without par value, or par value shares worth a total of $30,000 or less, make sure to check the box that appears at the end of paragraph 1. Note: If you authorize more than 30,000 shares without par value or more than $30,000 worth of par value shares, don't check the box after paragraph 1, and supply the information requested after paragraph 2. This additional information includes the number of authorized shares without par value (for no-par shares) or the total par value of your authorized

shares (if you authorize par value shares). Also, if you authorize additional classes of shares, you must state the name of each class, and the rights and restrictions associated with each class in the second part of this article, after paragraph 2. If you authorize only common shares, you do not need to supply this additional information about each class of shares.

Article Four: You must list at least one incorporator, who must be 18 years of age or older.

Article Five: Most incorporators insert "perpetual" in this blank to give their corporation an unlimited legal life. However, if you wish to limit the life of your corporation, you may insert an automatic dissolution date in this blank.

Article Six: Insert the specific purpose of your corporation, such as "retail sales of computer systems." You can add a general overall purpose, as well—for example "retail sales of computer systems and all other legal acts permitted general and business corporations." Your corporation can engage in any lawful purpose or business regardless of the exact language you use here, unless you specifically say that your corporation's business is limited to a specific purpose or purposes.

Article Seven: This item is optional, and you can leave it blank.

Signature: Have your incorporator (who was named in Article Four) sign the Articles.

Submit an original and one copy of your Articles for filing, together with your check for fees.

Fees: The filing fee is $3 plus a minimum authorized stock fee of at least $55, so the minimum incorporation fee is $58. The stock portion of the fee is based on the authorized capital stated in the articles. Authorized capital is computed as follows: (1) for shares without par value, multiply $1 by the number of no-par shares authorized; (2) for shares with a stated par value, multiply the par value amount of each share by the number of par value shares authorized. You can authorize up to $30,000 of capital for the minimum $55 stock fee. For each additional $10,000 of authorized capital, add $5 to the stock portion of the fee.

Examples:

If your articles authorize 30,000 shares without par value, you pay the minimum incorporation fee of $58 (30,000 X $1 = $30,000 authorized capital for a minimum stock fee of $55 plus the $3 filing fee).

If your articles authorize 30,000 shares with a par value of $1, you pay the minimum filing fee of $58 (30,000 X

$1 par value per share = $30,000 authorized capital for a minimum stock fee of $55 plus the $3 filing fee).

If your articles authorize 300,000 shares with a par value of 10 cents per share, you pay the minimum filing fee of $58 (30,000 X $.10 par value per share = $30,000 authorized capital for a minimum stock fee of $55 plus the $3 filing fee).

Director and Officer Rules

A corporation shall have three or more directors, except that a corporation may have one or two directors provided the number of directors to constitute the board of directors is stated in the Articles of Incorporation. Any corporation may elect its directors for one or more years, not to exceed three years, the time of service and mode of classification to be provided for by the Articles of Incorporation or the bylaws of the corporation; but, there shall be an annual election for such number or proportion of directors as may be found on dividing the entire number of directors by the number of years composing a term. At the first annual meeting of shareholders and at each annual meeting thereafter the shareholders entitled to vote shall elect directors to hold office until the next succeeding annual meeting, except as herein provided. Each director shall hold office for the term for which he is elected or until his successor shall have been elected and qualified.

The corporation shall give written notice to the secretary of state of the number of directors of the corporation as fixed by any method. The notice shall be given within thirty days of the date when the number of directors is fixed, and similar notice shall be given whenever the number of directors is changed. [351.315]

Every corporation organized under this chapter shall have a president and a secretary, who shall be chosen by the directors, and such other officers and agents as shall be prescribed by the bylaws of the corporation. Unless the Articles of Incorporation or bylaws otherwise provide, any two or more offices may be held by the same person.

Any act required or permitted by any of the provisions of this chapter [the Missouri Business Corporation Act] to be done by the president of the corporation may be done instead by the chairman of the board of directors, if any, of the corporation if the chairman of the board has previously been designated by the board of directors or in the bylaws to be the chief executive officer of the corporation, or to have the powers of the chief executive officer coextensively with the president, and such designation has been filed in writing with the secretary of state and such notice attested to by the secretary of the corporation. [351.360]

Share Issuance Rules

Every corporation may issue one or more classes of stock or one or more series of stock within any class thereof, any or all of which classes may be of stock with par value or stock without par value and which classes or series may have such voting powers, full or limited, or no voting powers; and such designations, preferences, and relative, participating, optional, or other special rights, and qualifications, limitations, or restrictions thereof, as shall be stated and expressed in the Articles of Incorporation or any amendment thereto, or in the resolution or resolutions providing for the issue of such stock adopted by the board of directors pursuant to authority expressly vested in it by the provisions of its Articles of Incorporation. [351.180]

Shares having a par value shall be issued for such consideration not less than the par value thereof as shall be fixed from time to time by the board of directors. Shares without par value may be issued for such consideration as may be fixed from time to time by the board of directors unless the Articles of Incorporation reserve to the shareholders the right to fix the consideration. [351.185]

No corporation shall issue shares, or bonds or other obligations for the payment of money, except for money paid, labor done, or property actually received; and all fictitious issues or increases of shares or indebtedness shall be void provided that no such issue or increase made for valid bona fide antecedent debts shall be deemed fictitious or void.

Bonded indebtedness of a corporation shall be incurred or increased only on prior approval by the board of directors. Unless the Articles of Incorporation otherwise provide, no vote or consent of shareholders shall be necessary to authorize or approve the incurrence of or an increase in bonded indebtedness. [351.160]

No note or obligation given by any shareholder, whether secured by deed of trust, mortgage, or otherwise, shall be considered as payment of any part of any original issue share or shares, and no loan of money for the purpose of such payment shall be made by the corporation to any shareholder therein; and if such loan shall be made to a shareholder, the officers making it, or who shall assent thereto, shall be jointly and severally liable to the corporation for the repayment of such loan and interest. [351.165]

A corporation may determine that only a part of the consideration for which its shares may be issued, from time to time, shall be stated capital; provided, that in the event of any such determination: (1) if the shares issued shall consist wholly of shares having a par value, then the stated capital represented by such shares shall be the aggregate par value of the shares so issued; (2) if the shares issued shall consist wholly of shares without par value, all of which have a preferential right in the assets of the corporation in the event of its involuntary liquidation, then the stated capital represented by such shares shall not be less than the aggregate preferential amount payable on such shares in the event of involuntary liquidation; (3) if the shares issued consist wholly of shares without par value, and none of such shares has a preferential right in the assets of the corporation in the event of its involuntary liquidation, then the stated capital represented by such shares shall be the total consideration received therefor less such part thereof as may be allocated to paid-in surplus; (4) if the shares issued shall consist of several or all of the classes of shares enumerated in subdivisions (1), (2), and (3) of this subsection, then the stated capital represented by such shares shall not be less than the aggregate par value of any shares so issued having a par value and the aggregate preferential amount payable on any shares so issued without par value having a preferential right in the event of involuntary liquidation.

In order to determine that only a part of the consideration for which shares without par value may be issued from time to time shall be stated capital, the board of directors shall adopt a resolution setting forth the part of such consideration allocated to stated capital and the part otherwise allocated, and expressing such allocation in dollars. If the board of directors shall not have determined at the time of the issuance of any shares issued for cash, or within sixty days after the issuance of any shares issued for labor or services actually performed for the corporation or issued for property other than cash, that only a part of the consideration for shares so issued shall be stated capital, then the stated capital of the corporation represented by such shares shall be an amount equal to the aggregate par value of all such shares having a par value, plus the consideration received from all such shares without par value.

The stated capital of the corporation may be increased from time to time by resolution of the board of directors directing that all or a part of the surplus of the corporation be transferred to stated capital. The board of directors may direct that the amount of the surplus so transferred shall be deemed to be stated capital in respect of any designated class of shares. [351.190]

Except as otherwise provided in the Articles of Incorporation or bylaws, the shares of a corporation shall be represented by certificates signed by the president or a vice president and by the secretary or an assistant secretary or the treasurer or an assistant treasurer of such corporation and sealed with the seal of the corporation.

Every certificate for shares without par value shall have plainly stated on its face the number of shares which it represents, and no certificate shall express any par value for such shares or a rate of dividend to which such shares shall be entitled in terms of percentage of any par or other value. [351.295]

Director Meeting Rules

Regular meetings of the board of directors may be held with or without notice as the bylaws may prescribe. Special meetings of the board of directors shall be held on such notice as the bylaws may prescribe. Attendance of a director at any meeting shall constitute a waiver of notice of the meeting except where a director attends a meeting for the express purpose of objecting to the transaction of any business because the meeting is not lawfully called or convened. Neither the business to be transacted at, nor the purpose of, any regular meeting of the board of directors need be specified in the notice or waiver of notice of the meeting. [351.340]

A majority of the full board of directors shall constitute a quorum for the transaction of business unless a greater number is required by the Articles of Incorporation or the bylaws. The act of the majority of the directors present at a meeting at which a quorum is present shall be the act of the board of directors, unless the act of a greater number is required by the Articles of Incorporation or the bylaws. [351.325]

Shareholder Meeting Rules

An annual meeting of shareholders for the election of directors shall be held on a day which each corporation shall fix by its bylaws; and if no day be so provided, then on the second Monday in the month of January. Failure to hold the annual meeting at the designated time shall not work a forfeiture or dissolution of the corporation.

Special meetings of the shareholders may be called by the board of directors or by such other person or persons as may be authorized by the Articles of Incorporation or the bylaws. [351.225]

Written or printed notice of each meeting of shareholders stating the place, day, and hour of the meeting and, in case of a special meeting, the purpose or purposes for which the meeting is called, shall be given not less than ten or more than 70 days before the date of the meeting, by or at the direction of the president, or the secretary, or the officer or persons calling the meeting, to each shareholder of record entitled to vote at such meeting. Written notice shall include, but not be limited to, notice by electronic transmission, which means any process of communication not directly involving the physical transfer of paper that is suitable for the retention, retrieval, and reproduction of information by the recipient. [351.230]

Every meeting, for whatever object, of the shareholders in any corporation shall be convened by its president, secretary, or other officer or any of the persons calling the meeting by a notice given as herein provided. If the object of such meeting be to elect directors or to take a vote of the shareholders on any proposition, then, if the bylaws of the corporation require, but not otherwise, the president or other person presiding at such meeting shall appoint not less than two persons, who are not directors, inspectors to receive and canvass the votes given at such meeting and certify the result to him. In all cases where the right to vote any share or shares in any corporation shall be questioned, it shall be the duty of the inspectors, if any, or the persons conducting the vote to require the transfer books of such corporation as evidence of shares held in such corporation, and all shares that may appear standing thereon in the name of any person or persons shall be voted on by such person or persons, directly by themselves or by proxy. [351.235]

Unless otherwise provided in the Articles of Incorporation, each outstanding share entitled to vote under the provisions of the Articles of Incorporation shall be entitled to one vote on each matter submitted to a vote at a meeting of shareholders. If the Articles of Incorporation provide for more or less than one vote for any share on any matter, every reference in the Business Corporation Act to a vote by a majority or other proportion of stock shall refer to such majority or other proportion of the votes of such stock.

Unless the Articles of Incorporation or bylaws provide otherwise, each shareholder in electing directors shall have the right to cast as many votes in the aggregate as shall equal the number of votes held by the shareholder in the corporation, multiplied by the number of directors to be elected at the election, and each shareholder may cast the whole number of votes, either in person or by proxy, for one candidate, or distribute them among two or more candidates. [351.245]

Unless otherwise provided in the Articles of Incorporation or bylaws, a majority of the outstanding shares entitled to vote at any meeting, represented in person or by proxy, shall constitute a quorum at a meeting of shareholders, provided that in no event shall a quorum consist of less than a majority of the outstanding shares entitled to vote, but less than such quorum shall have the right successively to adjourn the meeting as provided in Section 351.268.

In all matters, every decision of a majority of shares entitled to vote on the subject matter and represented in person or by proxy at a meeting at which a quorum is present shall be valid as an act of the shareholders, unless a larger vote is required by the Business Corporation Act, the bylaws, or the Articles of Incorporation, provided that in the case of cumulative voting in the election of directors pursuant to Subsection 3 of Section 351.245 [above], directors shall be elected by a plurality of the votes of the shares entitled to vote on the election of the directors and represented in person or by proxy at a meeting at which a quorum is present. [351.265]

Financial Disclosure Rules

If any officer of a corporation having charge of the books of the corporation shall, on the demand of a shareholder, refuse or neglect to exhibit and submit them to examination, the officer shall, for each offense, forfeit the sum of $250. [351.215]

State Tax Information

Department of Revenue, Jefferson City
573-751-4541
http://dor.state.mo.us/tax

Missouri imposes a corporate income tax.

Corporation Law Online

The General and Business Corporation Law of Missouri is contained in the Title XXIII (Corporations, Associations, and Partnerships) of the Missouri Statutes, Chapter 351, starting with Section 351.010. To find the Act, visit the legal research area of Nolo's website at www.nolo.com/statute/state/cfm. Click on "Missouri." Click on "View Missouri Revised Statutes," then scroll down and choose Title XXIII to begin browsing the Act.

State Securities Information

Missouri Secretary of State
Division of Securities
P.O. Box 1276
Jefferson City, MO 65102
573-751-4136
www.sos.mo.gov/securities/Default.asp

The Missouri Uniform Securities Act is contained in Title XXVI (Trade and Commerce), Chapter 409, of the Missouri Statutes. To browse the Act, follow the instructions in "Corporation Law Online," above. After you reach the statutes, choose Title XXVI and then click on Chapter 409.

The Division of Securities website provides information on exemptions from security registration and on registering an offering under the Small Corporation Offering Registration (SCOR) procedures. (See Chapter 2, Section 11.) Exemptions from registration include an exemption for sales to 25 or fewer stock holders under Section 409.402(b)(9) of the Securities Act. The sales issuance may not include advertising or the payment of commissions. This exemption does not require a filing with the Commissioner of Securities. For information on this and other exemptions see "Raising Capital in Missouri," a guide posted on the Division website. From the home page, click on "Publications From the Securities Division," then choose the guide.

Creating Your Own Articles Form

You can create your own articles form.

MONTANA

Corporate Filing Office

Montana Secretary of State
Corporation Bureau
P.O. Box 202801
Helena, MT 59620-2801
406-444-3665
http://sos.state.mt.us

State Corporate Forms

Montana provides a fill-in-the-blanks form called "Articles of Incorporation for Domestic Profit Corporation" (Form DP-1).

Internet Forms: You can download Montana's Articles of Incorporation and other corporate forms from the state filing office website.

Articles Instructions

First Article: The name of a Montana corporation must contain the word "corporation," "incorporated," "company," or "limited," or the abbreviation "corp.," "inc.," "co.," or "ltd."

You can check available corporate names by calling the state filing office or by doing a business entity search from the link provided on the state corporate filing office website. You can reserve an available corporate name for 120 days $10. Ignore the line with close corporation boxes. This is a special type of small corporation that operates under customized rules spelled out in a shareholders' agreement. Most incorporators will want to operate under and rely on standard corporate rules and procedures.

Second Article: Most small corporations appoint an initial director or officer as the corporation's registered agent. Make sure your agent signs in the blank provided in this article.

Third Article: Montana does not use the concept of par value, so you do not need to state a par value for your shares. Most incorporators authorize one class of common shares with equal voting, dividend, and liquidation rights and no special restrictions. To do this, insert the total number of common shares you wish to authorize in the blank—for example, "100,000 Common Shares." Your filing fee is not based on the number of authorized shares, so you can authorize as many shares as you wish.

If you want to authorize more than one class of shares, you must retype your articles to list the designation of each class, the authorized number of shares in each class, and the rights and restrictions associated with each class.

Fourth Article: You must designate one incorporator, who need not be a director or officer. The incorporator must sign and date the articles on the blank line at the bottom of the form.

Mail the original signed articles. After the state filing office approves your articles, it will send you a letter of acknowledgment.

Fees: $70, payable to the "Montana Secretary of State."

Director and Officer Rules

A board of directors consists of one or more individuals, with the number specified in or fixed in accordance with the articles of incorporation or bylaws.

If a board of directors has power to fix or change the number of directors, the board may increase or decrease by 30% or less the number of directors last approved by the shareholders, but only the shareholders may increase or decrease by more than 30% the number of directors last approved by the shareholders.

Directors are elected at the first annual shareholders' meeting and at each annual meeting thereafter unless their terms are staggered under 35-1-422. [35-1-419]

The terms of the initial directors of a corporation expire at the first shareholders' meeting at which directors are elected.

The terms of all other directors expire at the next annual shareholders' meeting following their election unless their terms are staggered under 35-1-422. [35-1-421]

A corporation has the officers described in its bylaws or appointed by the board of directors in accordance with the bylaws.

The bylaws or the board of directors shall delegate to one of the officers responsibility for preparing minutes of the directors' and shareholders' meetings and for authenticating records of the corporation.

The same individual may simultaneously hold more than one office in a corporation. [35-1-441]

Share Issuance Rules

The board of directors may authorize shares to be issued for consideration consisting of any tangible or intangible property or benefit to the corporation, including cash, promissory notes, services performed, contracts for services to be performed, or other securities of the corporation.

The corporation may place in escrow shares issued for a contract for future services or benefits or a promissory note, or the corporation may also make other arrangements to restrict the transfer of the shares and may credit distributions in respect of the shares against their purchase price until the services are performed, the note is paid, or the benefits received. If the services are not performed, the note is not paid, or the benefits are not received, the shares escrowed or restricted and the distributions credited may be canceled in whole or in part. [35-1-623]

If a corporation issues or authorizes the issuance of shares for promissory notes or for promises to render services in the future, the corporation shall report in writing to the shareholders the number of shares authorized or issued and the consideration received by the corporation with or before the notice of the next shareholders' meeting. [35-1-1111]

At a minimum, each share certificate must state on its face: (a) the name of the issuing corporation and that it is organized under the law of this state; (b) the name of the person to whom issued; and (c) the number and class of shares and the designation of the series, if any, that the certificate represents.

Each share certificate must be signed, either manually or in facsimile, by two officers designated in the bylaws or by the board of directors and may bear the corporate seal or its facsimile. [35-1-626]

Director Meeting Rules

Unless the Articles of Incorporation or bylaws provide otherwise, regular meetings of the board of directors may be held without notice of the date, time, place, or purpose of the meeting.

Unless the Articles of Incorporation or bylaws provide for a longer or shorter period, special meetings of the board of directors must be preceded by at least two days' notice of the date, time, and place of the meeting. The notice is not required to describe the purpose of the special meeting unless required by the Articles of Incorporation or bylaws. [35-1-433]

Unless the Articles of Incorporation or bylaws require a greater number, a quorum of a board of directors consists of: (a) a majority of the fixed number of directors if the corporation has a fixed board size; or (b) a majority of the number of directors prescribed or, if no number is prescribed, the number in office immediately before the meeting begins, if the corporation has a variable-range size board.

The Articles of Incorporation or bylaws may authorize a quorum of a board of directors to consist of no fewer than one-third of the fixed or prescribed number of directors.

If a quorum is present when a vote is taken, the affirmative vote of a majority of directors present is the act of the board of directors unless the Articles of Incorporation or bylaws require the vote of a greater number of directors. [35-1-435]

If requested by a director, minutes of any regular or special meeting [of directors] must be prepared and be distributed to each director. [35-1-431]

Shareholder Meeting Rules

A corporation shall hold an annual meeting of shareholders at a time stated in or fixed in accordance with the bylaws.

If the corporation has 50 or fewer shareholders and if permitted by the bylaws, shareholders may participate in an annual meeting of the shareholders through a conference telephone or similar communication equipment by means of which all persons participating in the meeting can hear each other at the same time. Participation in this manner constitutes presence in person at a meeting. [35-1-516]

A corporation shall hold a special meeting of shareholders: (a) on the call of its board of directors or the person authorized to do so by the Articles of Incorporation or bylaws; or (b) if the holders of at least 10% of all the votes entitled to be cast on any issue proposed to be considered at the proposed special meeting sign, date, and deliver to the corporation's secretary one or more written demands for the meeting that describe the purpose for which it is to be held.

If the corporation has 50 or fewer shareholders and if permitted by the bylaws, shareholders may participate in a special meeting of the shareholders by means of a conference telephone or similar communication equipment through which all persons participating in the meeting can hear each other at the same time. Participation in this manner constitutes presence in person at a meeting. [35-1-517]

A corporation shall notify shareholders of the date, time, and place of each annual and special shareholders' meeting not less than ten nor more than 60 days before the meeting date. Unless the Business Corporation Act or the Articles of Incorporation require otherwise, the corporation is required to give notice only to shareholders entitled to vote at the meeting.

Unless the Business Corporation Act or the Articles of Incorporation require otherwise, notice of an annual meeting need not include a description of the purpose for which the meeting is called.

Notice of a special meeting must include a description of the purpose or purposes for which the meeting is called. [35-1-520] Only business within the purpose described in the meeting notice may be conducted at a special share-holders' meeting. [35-1-517]

Shares entitled to vote as a separate voting group may take action on a matter at a meeting only if a quorum of those shares exists with respect to that matter. Unless the Articles of Incorporation or the Business Corporation Act provides otherwise, a majority of the votes entitled to be cast on the matter by the voting group constitutes a quorum of that voting group for action on that matter.

If a quorum exists, action on a matter other than the election of directors by a voting group is approved if the votes cast within the voting group favoring the action exceed the votes cast opposing the action, unless the Articles of Incorporation or the Business Corporation Act requires a greater number of affirmative votes.

The election of directors is governed by 35-1-531. [35-1-528]

Unless otherwise provided in the Articles of Incorporation, directors are elected by a plurality of the votes cast by the shares entitled to vote in the election at a meeting at which a quorum is present.

Except as limited by Subsection (3) [next paragraph], at each election for directors each shareholder entitled to vote at the election has the right: (a) to vote, in person or by proxy, the number of shares owned by the shareholder for as many persons as there are directors to be elected and for whose election the shareholder has a right to vote; or (b) to cumulate the shareholder's votes: (i) by giving one candidate as many votes as the number of directors to be elected multiplied by the number of shareholders' shares, or (ii) by distributing the votes on the same principle among any number of the candidates.

The right of all shareholders to cumulate their shares provided by Subsection (2) [previous paragraph] may be denied by a statement to that effect included in the Articles of Incorporation, but only if: (a) the statement is included in the Articles of Incorporation at the time the initial Articles of Incorporation are filed; or (b) the statement is included in an amendment to the Articles of Incorporation unless the number of votes sufficient to elect one director, if voted on a cumulative basis, was voted against the amendment. [35-1-531]

Financial Disclosure Rules

On the written request of any shareholder of a corporation, the corporation shall mail to the shareholder its most recent financial statements showing in reasonable detail its assets and liabilities and the results of its operations. [35-1-1110]

State Tax Information

Department of Revenue, Helena

406-444-6900

www.discoveringmontana.com/revenue/default.asp

Montana imposes an annual corporation license tax. The minimum payment is $50.

Corporation Law Online

The Montana Business Corporation Act is contained in Title 35 (Corporations, Partnerships, and Associations) of the Montana Code, Chapter 1, starting with Section 35-1-112. To find the Act, visit the legal research area of Nolo's website at www.nolo.com. Click on "State Laws" and then on "Montana." From the statute's table of contents, expand the file for Title 35 and then click on the link for Chapter 1 to start browsing the laws.

State Securities Information

State Auditor's Office
Securities Division
P.O. Box 4009
Helena, MT 59604
406-444-2040 (Toll Free: 800-332-6148)
www.discoveringmontana.com/sao

The Securities Division website offers only very basic information on the Montana Securities Act and exemptions. The Act itself is contained in Title 30, Chapter 10, of the Montana Statutes. You can browse the Act by following the instructions in "Corporation Law Online," above, except that once you reach the statute's table of contents you should expand the file for Title 30 and click on the link for Chapter 10.

Exemptions from securities registration are listed in Section 30-10-105 of the Act, and include an exemption under Section 30-10-105(8)(a) for certain offerings made in Montana to not more than ten people, and an exemption under Section 30-10-105(8)(b) for private offers made to not more than 25 people. You must file an application for exemption from registration if you use the 8(b) exemption. (You can download the necessary form from the Securities Division website.) See the statutes and call the Securities Division for further information on these and other available exemptions.

Creating Your Own Articles Form

You can create your own typewritten or computer-printed articles form.

NEBRASKA

Corporate Filing Office

Nebraska Secretary of State
Corporations Division
P.O. Box 94608
Lincoln, NE 68509
402-471-4079
www.sos.state.ne.us/htm/corpmenu.htm

State Corporate Forms

Nebraska does not currently provide Articles of Incorporation.

Internet Forms: You can download an Application for Reservation of Corporate Name from the state filing office website.

Articles Instructions

Because Nebraska does not currently provide an official Articles of Incorporation form, you must type or computer-print your own. Your articles must meet the requirements of Section 21-2018 of the Nebraska Business Corporation Act, as follows:

1. The name of a Nebraska corporation must include one of the following corporate designators: "corporation," "incorporated," "company," or "limited," or the abbreviation "corp.," "inc.," "co.," or "ltd." You can check name availability online only if you subscribe to the Nebraska Business Entity Search Service, linked to the state filing office website. If you do not subscribe, mail or fax a name availability request to the state filing office with a list of names you want to check. You may reserve an available corporate name for 120 days for $30. You can download an Application for Name Reservation for the state filing office website.

2. The number of shares the corporation is authorized to issue and their par value. Nebraska requires that your shares have a stated par value. (See Section 21-2018 of the Nebraska BCA.) Most incorporators make sure that the capital value of their authorized shares (number of shares x par value) is $10,000 or less in order to pay the minimum filing fee (see below).

If you want to authorize more than one class of shares, you must list the designation of each class, the number of shares in each class, a statement of the par value of the shares in each class, and the rights and restrictions associated with each class.

3. The street address of the corporation's initial registered office and the name of its initial registered agent at that office. The registered agent must be a Nebraska resident and the registered office address must be in Nebraska. Use a street address, not a P.O. box. Most incorporators use the street address of the corporation as the registered office address and designate one of the corporation's initial directors or officers as the agent at this registered office address.

4. The name and street address of each incorporator. You need just one incorporator, who must sign your articles. He or she need not be a director, officer, or shareholder.

5. Any provision limiting or eliminating the requirement to hold an annual meeting of the shareholders if the corporation is registered or intends to register as an investment company under the Federal Investment Company Act of 1940. This provision is unlikely to apply to your corporation, so you can ignore it.

Below is a sample articles form you can use to create one class of common shares. The articles must be entirely typewritten or computer-printed.

Articles of Incorporation

Pursuant to the Nebraska Business Corporation Act, the undersigned incorporator submits the following Articles of Incorporation:

1. The name of the corporation is [insert name of corporation].

2. The corporation is authorized to issue one class of common shares, with a par value of $[insert par value amount] per share. The total number of such shares it is authorized to issue is [insert number here].

3. The street address of the corporation's initial registered office is [typically, the address of the corporation is inserted here] and the name of its initial registered agent at this address is [typically the name of an initial director or officer is inserted].

4. The name and street address of the incorporator is [insert name and street address of incorporator, who dates and signs, below].

Date: _____

Signature of Incorporator:

_____

Filing Fee: $5 per page filing fee plus a $60 minimum capital stock fee if your corporation's capital stock does not exceed $10,000, for a minimum filing fee of $65 for one-page articles. Your corporation's capital stock is the number of shares authorized in your articles multiplied by the par value of these shares (in Nebraska, your shares must have a stated par value). The stock fee increases if your corporation's capital stock exceeds $10,000, as follows:

If the capital stock is more than $10,000 but does not exceed $25,000, the capital stock fee is $100.

If the capital stock is more than $25,000 but does not exceed $50,000, the capital stock fee is $150.

If the capital stock is more than $50,000 but does not exceed $75,000, the capital stock fee is $225.

If the capital stock is more than $75,000 but does not exceed $100,000, the capital stock fee is $300.

If the capital stock is more than $100,000, the capital stock fee is $300, plus an additional $3 for each $1,000 in excess of $100,000.

Examples:

If your articles authorize 10,000 shares with a par value of $1 each, your capital stock is $10,000. You must pay the minimum $60 capital stock fee plus $5 per page as a filing fee.

If your articles authorize 100,000 shares with a par value of ten cents each, your capital stock is $10,000. You must pay the minimum $60 capital stock fee plus $5 per page as a filing fee.

If your articles authorize 100,000 shares with a par value of $1 each, your capital stock is $100,000. You must pay a $300 capital stock fee plus $5 per page as a filing fee.

Mail an original and copy of the Articles, together with a check for the filing fee (see below), payable to the "Secretary of State." Add $10 if you wish to request a stamped Certificate of Incorporation from the Secretary of State (add your request for a Certificate of Incorporation to your cover letter if you pay the additional $10).

Post-filing Publication: Section 21-20,189 of the Nebraska Business Corporation Act requires the publication of a notice of incorporation after you incorporate. The notice must be published for three successive weeks in a newspaper located in the county of the corporation's principal office. It must state the name of the corporation, the number of its authorized shares, the address of its registered office, the name of initial registered agent, and the name and address of its incorporator. A proof of publication must be mailed for filing to the state filing office after the publication is made. There is no fee for this filing. Contact a local newspaper to publish this notice for

a small charge. The newspaper should mail you a proof of publication, which you should mail for filing to the state filing office.

Director and Officer Rules

A board of directors shall consist of one or more individuals, with the number specified in or fixed in accordance with the Articles of Incorporation or bylaws.

If a board of directors has power to fix or change the number of directors, the board may increase or decrease by thirty percent or less the number of directors last approved by the shareholders, but only the shareholders may increase or decrease by more than thirty percent the number of directors last approved by the shareholders.

Directors shall be elected at the first annual shareholders' meeting and at each annual meeting thereafter unless their terms are staggered under section 21-2083. [21-2080]

The terms of all other directors shall expire at the next annual shareholders' meeting following their election unless their terms are staggered under section 21-2083.

A corporation shall have the officers described in its bylaws or appointed by the board of directors in accordance with the bylaws.

The bylaws or the board of directors shall delegate to one of the officers the responsibility for preparing minutes of the directors' and shareholders' meetings and for authenticating records of the corporation.

The same individual may simultaneously hold more than one office in a corporation. [21-2097]

Share Issuance Rules

The board of directors may authorize shares to be issued for consideration consisting of any tangible or intangible property or benefit to the corporation, including cash, promissory notes, services performed, contracts for services to be performed, or other securities of the corporation.

The corporation may place in escrow shares issued for a contract for future services or benefits or a promissory note or make other arrangements to restrict the transfer of the shares and may credit distributions in respect of the shares against their purchase price until the services are performed, the note is paid, or the benefits received. If the services are not performed, the note is not paid, or the benefits are not received, the shares escrowed or restricted and the distributions credited may be canceled in whole or in part. [21-2040]

At a minimum, each share certificate shall state on its face: (a) the name of the issuing corporation and that it is organized under the laws of this state; (b) the name of the person to whom issued; and (c) the number and class of shares and the designation of the series, if any, the certificate represents.

Each share certificate (a) shall be signed, either manually or in facsimile, by two officers designated in the bylaws or by the board of directors, and (b) may bear the corporate seal or its facsimile. [21-2044]

The shareholders of a corporation shall not have a pre-emptive right to acquire the corporation's unissued shares except to the extent the Articles of Incorporation so provide. [21-2048]

Director Meeting Rules

Unless the Articles of Incorporation or bylaws provide otherwise, regular meetings of the board of directors may be held without notice of the date, time, place, or purpose of the meeting.

Unless the Articles of Incorporation or bylaws provide for a longer or shorter period, special meetings of the board of directors shall be preceded by at least two days' notice of the date, time, and place of the meeting. The notice shall not be required to describe the purpose of the special meeting unless required by the Articles of Incorporation or bylaws. [21-2091]

Unless the Articles of Incorporation or bylaws require a greater number or unless otherwise specifically provided in the Business Corporation Act, a quorum of a board of directors shall consist of: (a) a majority of the fixed number of directors if the corporation has a fixed board size; or (b) a majority of the number of directors prescribed or, if no number is prescribed, the number in office immediately before the meeting begins if the corporation has a variable-range board size.

The Articles of Incorporation or bylaws may authorize a quorum of a board of directors to consist of no fewer than one-third of the fixed or prescribed number of directors determined under Subsection (1) of this section [previous paragraph].

If a quorum is present when a vote is taken, the affirmative vote of a majority of directors present shall be the act of the board of directors unless the Articles of Incorporation or bylaws require the vote of a greater number of directors. [21-2093]

Shareholder Meeting Rules

A corporation shall hold annually, at a time stated in or fixed in accordance with the bylaws, a meeting of shareholders. [21-2051]

A corporation shall hold a special meeting of shareholders: (a) on call of its board of directors or the person or persons authorized to do so by the Articles of Incorporation or bylaws; or (b) if the holders of at least 10% of all the votes entitled to be cast on any issue proposed to be considered at the proposed special meeting sign, date, and deliver to the corporation's secretary one or more written demands for the meeting describing the purpose or purposes for which it is to be held.

A corporation shall notify shareholders of the date, time, and place of each annual and special shareholders' meeting no fewer than ten nor more than 60 days before the meeting date. Unless the Business Corporation Act or the Articles of Incorporation require otherwise, the corporation shall be required to give notice only to shareholders entitled to vote at the meeting.

Unless the Business Corporation Act or the Articles of Incorporation require otherwise, notice of an annual meeting shall not be required to include a description of the purpose or purposes for which the meeting is called.

Notice of a special meeting shall include a description of the purpose or purposes for which the meeting is called. [21-2055] Only business within the purpose or purposes described in the meeting notice may be conducted at a special shareholders' meeting. [21-2052]

Shares entitled to vote as a separate voting group may take action on a matter at a meeting only if a quorum of those shares exists with respect to that matter. Unless the Articles of Incorporation or the Business Corporation Act provides otherwise, a majority of the votes entitled to be cast on the matter by the voting group shall constitute a quorum of that voting group for action on that matter.

If a quorum exists, action on a matter, other than the election of directors, by a voting group shall be approved if the votes cast within the voting group favoring the Business Corporation Action exceed the votes cast opposing the action unless the Articles of Incorporation or the Business Corporation Act requires a greater number of affirmative votes.

The election of directors shall be governed by Section 21-2066. [21-2063]

Unless otherwise provided in the Articles of Incorporation, directors shall be elected by a plurality of the votes cast by the shares entitled to vote in the election at a meeting at which a quorum is present.

In all elections for directors, every shareholder entitled to vote at such elections shall have the right to vote in person or by proxy for the number of shares owned by him or her, for as many persons as there are directors to be elected, or to cumulate such shares and give one candidate as many votes as the number of directors multiplied by the number of his or her shares shall equal, or to distribute them on the same principle among as many candidates as he or she thinks fit, and such directors shall not be elected in any other manner. [21-2066]

Financial Disclosure Rules

A corporation shall furnish its shareholders annual financial statements which may be consolidated or combined statements of the corporation and one or more of its subsidiaries, as appropriate, that include a balance sheet as of the end of the fiscal year, an income statement for that year, and a statement of changes in shareholders' equity for that year unless such information appears elsewhere in the financial statements. If financial statements are prepared for the corporation on the basis of generally accepted accounting principles, the annual financial statements shall also be prepared on that basis.

If the annual financial statements are reported on by a public accountant, the accountant's report shall accompany the financial statements. If not, the financial statements shall be accompanied by a statement of the president or the person responsible for the corporation's accounting records: (a) stating his or her reasonable belief whether the financial statements were prepared on the basis of generally accepted accounting principles and, if not, describing the basis of preparation; and (b) describing any respects in which the statements were not prepared on a basis of accounting consistent with the statements prepared for the preceding year.

A corporation shall mail the annual financial statements to each shareholder within 120 days after the close of each fiscal year. Thereafter, on written request from a shareholder who was not mailed the statements, the corporation shall mail him or her the latest financial statements. [21-20,186]

State Tax Information

Department of Revenue, Lincoln
800-742-7474
www.revenue.state.ne.us/index.html

Nebraska corporations are subject to an annual corporation income tax.

Corporation Law Online

The Nebraska Business Corporation Act is contained in Sections 21-2001 to 21-20,193 of the Nebraska Statutes. To find the Act, visit the legal research area of Nolo's website at www.nolo.com. Click on "State Laws" and then on "Nebraska." Follow the links until you reach the Nebraska Statutes home page. Once there, expand the Table of Contents on the left side of the screen, then click on "21 Corporations and Other Companies." Scroll down to Section 21-2001 to begin stepping through or browsing the Act.

State Securities Information

Department of Banking and Finance
Securities Bureau
1200 "N" Street
The Atrium, Suite 311
P.O. Box 95006
Lincoln, NE 68509-5006
877-471-3445 (Toll Free)
www.ndbf.org/sec.htm

The Securities Bureau website contains links to the Nebraska Securities Act (Chapter 8, Article 11, of the Nebraska Statutes) as well as the Securities Rules. Section 8-1111 of the Act contains exemptions from registration, including an exemption contained in Section 8-1111(9) for private sales of securities to 15 or fewer people. To take advantage of this exemption, you must meet certain other conditions and file a notice form with the Bureau. Section 8-1111(16) contains a general nonpublic offering exemption as well. You must file a notice and pay a fee. Complete information about complying with these exemptions is contained in the Securities Rules. See the Securities Bureau website and call the Bureau for additional information.

Creating Your Own Articles Form

You must create your own articles form, following the rules in "Articles Instructions," above.

NEVADA

Corporate Filing Office

Secretary of State
New Filings Section
101 N. Carson Street, Suite 3
Carson City, NV 89701-4786
775-684-5708
sos.state.nv.us/comm_rec/index.htm

State Corporate Forms

Nevada provides fill-in-the-blanks Articles of Incorporation.

Internet Forms: You can download a "Domestic Corporations Packet" from the state filing office website. The packet includes articles, instructions, a fee schedule, a form to use if you want to pay your fees by credit card, and a customer order form that you should use as a cover letter when you file your articles.

Articles Instructions

Article 1: If your corporate name appears to contain the name of a real person, it must also include one of the following designators: "Incorporated," "Limited," "Inc.," "Ltd.," "Company," "Co.," "Corporation," or "Corp." However, you will probably want to use one of these designators no matter what kind of corporate name you have, because it tells others that your business is incorporated.

You can check name availability on the state filing office website.

You can reserve an available name online by clicking the link on the home page to Name Reservations. It costs $40 to reserve an available corporate name for 90 days.

Alternatively, you can fill in and mail a paper name-reservation form, available online, for a lesser filing fee of $25.

Article 2: Most incorporators designate an initial director or officer as registered agent for the corporation and insert the street address of the corporation here. Make sure the agent signs and dates the form in Article 8. The registered agent must be a Nevada resident, and the registered agent's address must be in Nevada. You can insert an additional mailing address for your registered agent in the last line of this article, if you wish.

Article 3: You can authorize shares with a stated par value or without par value; modern practice is to issue shares without par value. Most incorporators authorize one class of common shares with equal voting, dividend,

and liquidation rights and no special restrictions. If you authorize shares without par value, simply insert the number of authorized shares in the rightmost blank. If you authorize par value shares, insert the number of authorized shares in the leftmost blank, then insert the par value of each share in the par value blank. In Nevada, your filing fee is based on the number of shares that you authorize. Read the filing fee rules, below, before you settle on a number. Most incorporators will authorize either 75,000 shares without par value or par value shares with a total par value of $75,000 or less, to pay the minimum filing fee.

If you authorize additional classes of shares, you use an attachment page to list the name of each class, the number of shares in each class, and the rights and restrictions associated with each class.

Article 4: Your corporation needs just one director, who must be at least 18 years of age.

Article 5: Unless your corporation will engage in the banking or insurance business, you may leave this article blank.

Article 6: You need only one incorporator, who need not be a director, office,r or shareholder. Make sure the incorporator signs on the line provided in this article.

Article 7: Have the registered agent specified in Article 2 sign and date on designated lines.

File an original and a copy of the articles. The extra copy will be certified (for a $30 fee; see below) and returned to you. Additional certified copies cost $30.00 each.

Note: Although not required, the filing office asks you to submit a customer order instruction page with your Articles. This form is available from the forms page on the state filing office website.

Filing Fee: $105 minimum total filing fee payable to the "Secretary of State." This includes $30 for certifying one copy of your articles (Nevada law requires you to keep a certified copy of your filed articles at the office of your certified agent) and a minimum $75 authorized capital fee (see below). You will also have to file a Statement of Officers form (which the state will send you) for $125 ($125 minimum or more according to the number of shares authorized in your Articles—see the state filing office website for annual list fee information).

The Nevada articles filing fee includes an authorized capital fee based on the number and type of authorized shares specified in your articles as follows: (1) for shares without par value, multiply $1 by the number of no-par shares authorized; (2) for shares with a stated par value, multiply the par value amount of each share by the number of par value shares authorized. If you specify a stated par value less than $.001 (one tenth of one cent), the state filing office will assume a stated par value of $.001 for each par value share. You must pay the minimum authorized capital fee of $75 for up to $75,000 of authorized capital (resulting in a total incorporation fee of $105). For authorized capital above $75,000, increase the filing fee as follows:

Authorized Capital	Filing Fee
up to $75,000:	$75
$75,001 to $200,000:	$175
$200,001 to $500,000:	$275
$500,001 to $1,000,000:	$375
Each additional $500,000 (or fraction thereof):	$275
Maximum Fee: $35,000	

Examples:

If your articles authorize 75,000 shares without a par value, you pay the minimum incorporation fee of $105 (75,000 X $1 = $75,000 authorized capital, for a minimum fee of $75 plus the $30 certified copy fee).

If your articles authorize 75,000 shares with a par value of $1, you pay the minimum incorporation fee of $105 (75,000 X $1 = $75,000 authorized capital, for a minimum fee of $75 plus the $30 certified copy fee).

If your articles authorize 1,000,000 shares with a par value of 10 cents per share, you pay a filing fee of $205 (1,000,000 X $.10 par value per share = $100,000 authorized capital, for a fee of $175 plus the $30 filing fee).

Director and Officer Rules

The business of every corporation must be managed by a board of directors or trustees, all of whom must be natural persons who are at least 18 years of age. A corporation must have at least one director, and may provide in its Articles of Incorporation or in its bylaws for a fixed number of directors or a variable number of directors within a fixed minimum and maximum, and for the manner in which the number of directors may be increased or decreased. Unless otherwise provided in the articles of incorporation, directors need not be stock holders. [78.115]

Every corporation must have a president, a secretary, and a treasurer.

All officers must be natural persons and must be chosen in such manner, hold their offices for such terms, and have such powers and duties as may be prescribed by the bylaws or determined by the board of directors. Any natural person may hold two or more offices. [78.130]

Share Issuance Rules

The board of directors may authorize shares to be issued for consideration consisting of any tangible or intangible property or benefit to the corporation, including, but not limited to, cash, promissory notes, services performed, contracts for services to be performed, or other securities of the corporation.

The corporation may place in escrow shares issued for a contract for future services or benefits or a promissory note, or make any other arrangements to restrict the transfer of the shares. The corporation may credit distributions made for the shares against their purchase price, until the services are performed, the benefits are received, or the promissory note is paid. If the services are not performed, the benefits are not received, or the promissory note is not paid, the shares escrowed or restricted and the distributions credited may be canceled in whole or in part. [78.211]

Except as otherwise provided in subsection 4 [see the statute for more information], every stock holder is entitled to have a certificate, signed by officers or agents designated by the corporation for the purpose, certifying the number of shares owned by him in the corporation. [78.235]

Director Meeting Rules

Meetings of stock holders and directors of any corporation organized under the provisions of this chapter may be held within or without the state of Nevada, in the manner provided by the bylaws of the corporation. [78.310]

Unless the Articles of Incorporation or the bylaws provide for a different proportion, a majority of the board of directors of the corporation then in office, at a meeting duly assembled, is necessary to constitute a quorum for the transaction of business, and the act of directors holding a majority of the voting power of the directors, present at a meeting at which a quorum is present, is the act of the board of directors. [78.315]

Shareholder Meeting Rules

Meetings of stock holders and directors of any corporation organized under the provisions of this chapter may be held within or without the state of Nevada, in the manner provided by the bylaws of the corporation. [78.310]

If, under the provisions of the Business Corporation Act, stock holders are required or authorized to take any action at a meeting, the notice of the meeting must be in writing and signed by the president or a vice president, or the secretary, or an assistant secretary, or by such other natural person or persons as the bylaws may prescribe or permit or the directors may designate.

The notice must state the purpose or purposes for which the meeting is called and the time when, and the place, which may be within or without the state of Nevada, where it is to be held.

A copy of the notice must be delivered personally or mailed postage prepaid to each stock holder of record entitled to vote at the meeting not less than ten nor more than 60 days before the meeting. If mailed, it must be directed to the stock holder at his address as it appears on the records of the corporation, and on the mailing of any such notice the service thereof is complete, and the time of the notice begins to run from the date on which the notice is deposited in the mail for transmission to the stock holder. Personal delivery of any such notice to any officer of a corporation or association, or to any member of a partnership, constitutes delivery of the notice to the corporation, association, or partnership.

The Articles of Incorporation or the bylaws may require that the notice be also published in one or more newspapers. [78.370]

Unless the Business Corporation Act, the Articles of Incorporation, or the bylaws provide for different proportions: (a) a majority of the voting power, which includes the voting power that is present in person or by proxy, regardless of whether the proxy has authority to vote on all matters, constitutes a quorum for the transaction of business; and (b) action by the stock holders on a matter other than the election of directors is approved if the number of votes cast in favor of the action exceeds the number of votes cast in opposition to the action. [78.320]

Unless elected pursuant to NRS 78.320 [by written consent of shareholders], directors of every corporation must be elected at the annual meeting of the stock holders by a plurality of the votes cast at the election. Unless otherwise provided in the bylaws, the board of directors have the authority to set the date, time, and place for the annual meeting of the stock holders. If for any reason directors are not elected pursuant to NRS 78.320 [by written shareholder consent] or at the annual meeting of the stock holders, they may be elected at any special meeting of the stock holders which is called and held for that purpose. [78.330]

The Articles of Incorporation of any corporation may provide that at all elections of directors of the corporation each holder of stock possessing voting power is entitled to as many votes as equal the number of his shares of stock multiplied by the number of directors to be elected, and that he may cast all of his votes for a single director or may distribute them among the number to be voted for or any two or more of them, as he may see fit. To exercise the right of cumulative voting, one or more of the stock holders requesting cumulative voting must give written notice to the president or secretary of the corporation that the stock holder desires that the voting for the election of directors be cumulative.

The notice must be given not less than 48 hours before the time fixed for holding the meeting, if notice of the meeting has been given at least ten days before the date of the meeting, and otherwise not less than 24 hours before the meeting. At the meeting, before the commencement of voting for the election of directors, an announcement of the giving of the notice must be made by the chairman or the secretary of the meeting or by or on behalf of the stock holder giving the notice. Notice to stockholders of the requirement of this subsection must be contained in the notice calling the meeting or in the proxy material accompanying the notice. [78.360]

Financial Disclosure Rules

Any person who has been a stock holder of record of any corporation and owns not less than 15% of all of the issued and outstanding shares of the stock of such corporation or has been authorized in writing by the holders of at least 15% of all its issued and outstanding shares, on at least five days' written demand, is entitled to inspect in person or by agent or attorney, during normal business hours, the books of account and all financial records of the corporation, to make extracts therefrom, and to conduct an audit of such records. Holders of voting trust certificates representing 15% of the issued and outstanding shares of the corporation shall be regarded as stock holders for the purpose of this subsection. The right of stock holders to inspect the corporate records may not be limited in the articles or bylaws of any corporation. [78.257]

State Tax Information

Department of Taxation, Carson City
775-687-4892
http://tax.state.nv.us

Nevada does not have a state individual or corporate income tax. However, any business that has one or more employees in the state must obtain a Nevada business license and pay an annual business tax. Remember: Typically the owners of small corporations also are corporate employees.

Corporation Law Online

The Nevada Business Corporation Act is contained in Chapter 78 of the Nevada Revised Statutes (NRS), starting with Section 78.010. To find the Act, visit the legal research area of Nolo's website at www.nolo.com/statute/state/cfm. Click on "Nevada." Under the latest version of the Nevada Revised Statutes, choose "Table of Contents." Scroll down and click on Chapter 78 to begin browsing the Act.

State Securities Information

State of Nevada
Secretary of State
Securities Division
555 East Washington Street
Suite 5200
Las Vegas, NV 89101
702-486-2440 (In Reno: 775-688-1855)
http://sos.state.nv.us/securities

The Nevada Securities Act is contained in Chapter 90 of the Nevada Revised Statutes. You can browse the Act from the "Statutes and Regulations" link provided at the Securities Division website. General information on state securities registration and information on exemptions from registration are also posted on the site. For example, a limited offering exemption contained in Section 90.530.11 of the Act allows you to avoid registration for the sale of securities to 25 or fewer purchasers in the state of Nevada if you meet certain conditions. See the Securities Division website and contact the Division for further information on this and other available exemptions.

Creating Your Own Articles Form

You can create your own articles form.

NEW HAMPSHIRE

Corporate Filing Office

Corporation Division
Department of State
State House, Room 204
107 North Main Street
Concord, NH 03301-4989

603-271-3246

www.state.nh.us/sos/corporate/index.htm

State Corporate Forms

New Hampshire provides an Articles of Incorporation form with instructions plus an securities Addendum form (Form SRA), which must be filed with the articles.

Internet Forms: You can download a fill-in-the-blanks New Hampshire articles form (Form 11) with instructions, which includes the required Addendum (Form SRA), and other statutory forms from the state corporate filing office website.

Articles Instructions

First Article: The name of a New Hampshire corporation must contain the word "corporation," "incorporated," or "limited," or the abbreviation "corp.," "inc.," or "ltd."

You can check on available names by calling the state filing office or perform a business name lookup search from the state filing office website. An available corporate name may be reserved for 120 days for $15.

Note for Professional Corporations: If you are forming a professional corporation, the statute (RSA 294-A:7) requires that the corporate name end with the term "Professional Corporation," "Professional Association," " Prof. Corp.," "Prof. Ass'n.," "P.C.," or "P.A." Also, the articles of a professional corporation must state that the corporation is being formed under RSA 294-A.

Second Article: In New Hampshire, you do not need to state a par value for your shares. Most incorporators authorize one class of common shares with equal voting, dividend, and liquidation rights and no special restrictions. To do this, simply insert the total number of authorized shares in the blank. If you want to authorize special classes of shares, you must retype your articles to list the designation of each class, the authorized number of shares in each class, and the rights and restrictions associated with each class.

Fourth Article: This standard statement simply means that you plan to offer and sell your shares in compliance with the New Hampshire Securities Act. In other words, you must either register the offer and sale of your initial shares with the New Hampshire Bureau of Securities Regulation or make sure that you qualify for an exemption from registration under the new Hampshire Securities Act. The Addendum form you prepare with your articles (see below) shows the state filing office that you will comply with the New Hampshire Securities Act when you issue your initial shares.

Fifth Article: You do not have to insert the specific business purpose of your corporation at the end of this article, but we recommend that you do You do not have to list a principal business purpose at the end of this article, but we recommend you do. Listing a specific principal purpose can help convince the state filing office to accept your articles if a name similar to your proposed corporate name is already in use. If the specific business purpose stated here is different from the purpose of the other corporation, the state filing office is more likely to allow you to use your similar corporate name. You can state your corporation's principal purpose very briefly—for example, "retail sales of computer equipment."

Sixth Article: You must choose one incorporator, who need not be a director, officer, or shareholder. The incorporator must date and sign the articles in the designated lines at the end of the form. The incorporator must also sign the Addendum form.

Form SRA: This form is included as the last page of the articles form available online from the state corporate filing office website.

Part I: Insert your corporation's name and address. List your incorporator as the contact person. You can insert a separate email address and a separate mailing address for your contact person if you wish.

Part II: Check the appropriate box in this part after you print the form. This section is designed to determine whether you are eligible for the New Hampshire small offering exemption for securities interests (contained in the New Hampshire Uniform Securities Act Section 421-B:17, II(k)). Under this exemption, you do not have to register your stock issuance if you sell shares, without advertising, to no more than 10 people within 60 days after the date when you file your articles (see "State Securities Information," below). Most New Hampshire corporations with ten or fewer shareholders should be eligible. If you will be eligible for this exemption, check box 1 in Part II of the Addendum form. Make sure to sell your initial shares and issue share certificates to your shareholders no later than 60 days after your Articles are filed. If you will not qualify for the small offering exemption, you will need to qualify for another exemption (box 2) or register your securities (box 3). Of course, we assume box 4 does not apply to you—it applies only if you will not sell shares in New Hampshire. If you plan to check box 2 or 3, you will need to fill in the blank associated with each box. Call the New Hampshire Division of Securities Regulation, at 603-271-1463, or ask a small business lawyer for help in completing box 2 or 3 and in obtaining another exemption for or registering your securities.

Part III: Check box 2 to indicate that you are forming a New Hampshire corporation and the Articles indicate that you will be selling shares of stock.

Part IV: Show the name of your incorporator on the first line in the section and insert the date at the bottom of the form. Your incorporator must sign on the blank to the right of his or her printed name.

Submit the original and one copy of the articles, including Form SRA, Addendum to Business Organization, and Registration Forms.

Filing Fee: $100, payable to the "Secretary of State." This fee includes a $50 articles filing fee plus a $50 fee for filing the required Addendum form.

Director and Officer Rules

A board of directors must consist of one or more individuals, with the number specified in or fixed in accordance with the Articles of Incorporation or bylaws.

If a board of directors has power to fix or change the number of directors, the board may increase or decrease by 30 percent or less the number of directors last approved by the shareholders, but only the shareholders may increase or decrease by more than 30 percent the number of directors last approved by the shareholders.

Directors are elected at the first annual shareholders' meeting and at each annual meeting thereafter, unless their terms are staggered under RSA 293-A:8.06. [293-A:8.03]

The terms of all other directors expire at the next annual shareholders' meeting following their election unless their terms are staggered under RSA 293-A:8.06. [293-A:8.05]

A corporation has the officers described in its bylaws or appointed by the board of directors in accordance with the bylaws.

The bylaws or the board of directors shall delegate to one of the officers responsibility for preparing minutes of the directors' and shareholders' meetings and for authenticating records of the corporation.

The same individual may simultaneously hold more than one office in a corporation. [293-A:8.40]

Share Issuance Rules

The board of directors may authorize shares to be issued for consideration consisting of any tangible or intangible property or benefit to the corporation, including cash, promissory notes, services performed, contracts for services to be performed, or other securities of the corporation.

The corporation may place in escrow shares issued for a contract for future services or benefits or a promissory note, or make other arrangements to restrict the transfer of the shares, and may credit distributions in respect of the shares against their purchase price, until the services are performed, the note is paid, or the benefits received. If the services are not performed, the note is not paid, or the benefits are not received, the shares escrowed or restricted and the distributions credited may be cancelled in whole or in part. [293-A:6.21]

At a minimum each share certificate must state on its face: (1) the name of the issuing corporation and that it is organized under the law of this state; (2) the name of the person to whom issued; (3) the number and class of shares and the designation of the series, if any, the certificate represents.

Each share certificate: (1) must be signed, either manually or in facsimile, by two officers designated in the bylaws or by the board of directors; and (2) may bear the corporate seal or its facsimile. [293-A:6.25]

The shareholders of a corporation do not have a preemptive right to acquire the corporation's unissued shares except to the extent the Articles of Incorporation so provide. [293-A:6.30]

Director Meeting Rules

The board of directors may hold regular or special meetings in or out of the state of New Hampshire. [293-A:8.20]

Unless the Articles of Incorporation or bylaws provide otherwise, regular meetings of the board of directors may be held without notice of the date, time, place, or purpose of the meeting.

Unless the Articles of Incorporation or bylaws provide for a longer or shorter period, special meetings of the board of directors shall be preceded by at least two days' notice of the date, time, and place of the meeting. The notice need not describe the purpose of the special meeting unless required by the Articles of Incorporation or bylaws. [293-A:8.22]

Unless the Articles of Incorporation or bylaws require a greater number, a quorum of a board of directors consists of either: (1) a majority of the fixed number of directors if the corporation has a fixed board size; (2) a majority of the number of directors prescribed, o,r if no number is prescribed, the number in office immediately before the meeting begins, if the corporation has a variable-range size board.

The Articles of Incorporation or bylaws may authorize a quorum of a board of directors to consist of no fewer than 1/3 of the fixed or prescribed number of directors determined under Subsection (a) [previous paragraph].

If a quorum is present when a vote is taken, the affirmative vote of a majority of directors present is the act of the board of directors, unless the Articles of Incorporation or bylaws require the vote of a greater number of directors. [293-A:8.24]

Shareholder Meeting Rules

A corporation shall hold a meeting of shareholders annually at a time stated in or fixed in accordance with the bylaws. [293-A:7.01]

A corporation shall hold a special meeting of shareholders: (1) on call of its board of directors or the person or persons authorized to do so by the Articles of Incorporation or bylaws; or (2) if the holders of at least 10% of all the votes entitled to be cast on any issue proposed to be considered at the proposed special meeting sign, date, and deliver to the corporation's secretary one or more written demands for the meeting describing the purpose or purposes for which it is to be held.

A corporation shall notify shareholders of the date, time, and place of each annual and special shareholders' meeting no fewer than ten nor more than 60 days before the meeting date. Unless the Business Corporation Act or the Articles of Incorporation require otherwise, the corporation is required to give notice only to shareholders entitled to vote at the meeting.

Unless the Business Corporation Act or the Articles of Incorporation require otherwise, notice of an annual meeting need not include a description of the purpose or purposes for which the meeting is called.

Notice of a special meeting must include a description of the purpose or purposes for which the meeting is called. [293-A:7.05] Only business within the purpose or purposes described in the meeting notice may be conducted at a special shareholders' meeting. [293-A:7.02]

Shares entitled to vote as a separate voting group may take action on a matter at a meeting only if a quorum of those shares exists with respect to that matter. Unless the Articles of Incorporation or the Business Corporation Act

provides otherwise, a majority of the votes entitled to be cast on the matter by the voting group constitutes a quorum of that voting group for action on that matter.

If a quorum exists, action on a matter, other than the election of directors, by a voting group is approved if the votes cast within the voting group favoring the action exceed the votes cast opposing the action, unless the Articles of Incorporation or the Business Corporation Act requires a greater number of affirmative votes.

The election of directors is governed by RSA 293-A:7.28. [293-A:7.25]

Unless otherwise provided in the Articles of Incorporation, directors are elected by a plurality of the votes cast by the shares entitled to vote in the election at a meeting at which a quorum is present.

Shareholders do not have a right to cumulate their votes for directors unless the Articles of Incorporation so provide.

A statement included in the Articles of Incorporation that "all or a designated voting group of shareholders are entitled to cumulate their votes for directors," or words of similar import, means that the shareholders designated are entitled to multiply the number of votes they are entitled to cast by the number of directors for whom they are entitled to vote and cast the product for a single candidate or distribute the product among two or more candidates.

Shares otherwise entitled to vote cumulatively may not be voted cumulatively at a particular meeting unless: (1) the meeting notice or proxy statement accompanying the notice states conspicuously that cumulative voting is authorized; or (2) a shareholder who has the right to cumulate his votes gives notice to the corporation not less than 48 hours before the time set for the meeting of his intent to cumulate his votes during the meeting, and if one shareholder gives this notice, all other shareholders in the same voting group participating in the election are entitled to cumulate their votes without giving further notice. [293-A:7.28]

Financial Disclosure Rules

A corporation shall furnish its shareholders annual financial statements, which may be consolidated or combined statements of the corporation and one or more of its subsidiaries, as appropriate, that include a balance sheet as of the end of the fiscal year, an income statement for that year, and a statement of changes in shareholders' equity for the year unless that information appears elsewhere in the financial statements. If financial statements are prepared for the corporation on the basis of generally accepted accounting principles, the annual financial statements shall also be prepared on that basis.

If the annual financial statements are reported on by a public accountant, his report shall accompany them. If not, the statements shall be accompanied by a statement of the president or the person responsible for the corporation's accounting records: (1) stating his reasonable belief whether the statements were prepared on the basis of generally accepted accounting principals and, if not, describing the basis of preparation; and (2) describing any respects in which the statements were not prepared on a basis of accounting consistent with the statements prepared for the preceding year.

A corporation shall mail the annual financial statements to each shareholder within 120 days after the close of each fiscal year. Thereafter, on written request from a shareholder who was not mailed the statements, the corporation shall mail him the latest financial statements. [293-A:16.20]

State Tax Information

State of New Hampshire
Department of Revenue Administration, Concord
603-271-6121
http://webster.state.nh.us/revenue/index.htm

New Hampshire corporations are subject to an annual business profits tax. Corporations are also subject to a state business enterprise tax, imposed on the value of the business activity of the enterprise. This includes receipts from the transfer of property and sale of services. See the Department of Revenue Administration website for more information.

Corporation Law Online

The New Hampshire Business Corporation Act is contained in Title 27 (Corporations, Associations, and Proprietors of Common Lands), Chapter 293A, of the New Hampshire Statutes, starting with Section 293-A:1.0. To find the Act, visit the legal research area of Nolo's

website at www.nolo.com/statute/state.cfm. Click on "New Hampshire." Type "Title 27" in the search box, then click Search. This brings you to a page with a link titled "New Hampshire Revised Statutes Annotated — Index Of Titles." Click this link, which takes you to a title list. Scroll down and select the Title 27 heading. Then scroll down and select Chapter 293A to view the BCA.

State Securities Information

Bureau of Securities Regulation
State House Annex, Third Floor
Concord, N.H. 03301
603-271-1463
http://webster.state.nh.us/sos/securities

The New Hampshire Securities Act is contained in Chapter 421B of the New Hampshire Revised Statutes (RSA). Section 421-B:17 (II)(k) contains an exemption from registration for stock and other securities sold by a new business entity, including a new corporation, to ten or fewer investors as long as no advertising is used in connection with the sale and all sales are completed within 60 days of the date your articles are filed. The purchasers must buy shares for investment (not for resale), and commissions may not be paid. The Addendum form you file with your articles helps to show that you qualify for this exemption. If you cannot meet the requirements of this exemption, you may qualify for another exemption or you may need to register your shares.

The Bureau of Securities website provides links to the Securities Act and to the rules that enforce the Act. It also provides basic information on the securities exemption noted above, plus other exemptions you may be able to use if you don't qualify for that exemption. Visit the website, then call the Bureau for additional securities exemption and registration information.

Creating Your Own Articles Form

You can create your own articles form. Your form must be computer-printed or typed using black ink and one-inch margins on the left and right sides.

NEW JERSEY

Corporate Filing Office

New Jersey Department of Treasury
Division of Revenue
Corporate Filing Unit
P.O. Box 308
Trenton, NJ 08625-0308
609-292-9292
www.state.nj.us/njbgs

State Corporate Forms

New Jersey no longer publishes a distinct Certificate of Incorporation form. Instead, New Jersey provides an on-line corporate formation and business registration service (click "Services/Online Services" on the state corporate filing office home page, scroll to the list of Online Services, and select "One-Stop Business Filing and Registration"). If you use the online service, you do not need to file a Certificate of Incorporation to form your corporation or register your corporation for tax and employment purposes by mail.

If you do not have an Internet connection or prefer to file paperwork to form your corporation, you can complete the New Jersey Business Registration Package (Form NJ-REG, provided online, which includes a two-page Public Record Filing for New Business Entity portion that can be used to form a corporation). Simply complete and mail the entire NJ-REG form to the state.

Internet Forms: The New Jersey Business Registration Package (Form NJ-REG) and other corporate forms are available for downloading from the state filing office website.

Articles Instructions

Fill in the online formation questionnaire or prepare the Public Records Filing of the NJ-REG form according to the state-supplied instructions (either the online questionnaire instructions or the NJ-REG instructions) and the following special instructions (our instructions are geared to the Public Record Filing portion of the NJ-REG form, but they also can be used to help you fill in the online corporate formation questionnaire).

Again, if you are not connected to the Internet or simply prefer to form your corporation by mail (instead of using the state's online corporate formation and registration service discussed just above), follow these guidelines to complete the two-page Public Record Filing for New Business Entity portion of the NJ-REG registration package.

Business Name: The name of a New Jersey corporation must include the word "corporation," "company," or "incorporated"; an abbreviation of one of those words; or the abbreviation "Ltd." You can check corporate name availability and reserve a corporate name online (corporate name availability is automatically checked if you use the online corporate formation service). The fee for a separate online name availability check is $15; the fee for a name reservation is $50 (billed to your credit card). You can also check corporate name availability online by comparing your proposed name to names already registered with the state. Click "Browse Business Names for Free." You also can check name availability by calling the state filing office.

Type of Business Entity: Insert DP to indicate you are forming a domestic profit corporation.

Business Purpose: You can leave this line blank. This means your corporation will be able to engage in any activity for which corporations may be organized.

Stock: New Jersey does not use the concept of par value, so you do not need to state a par value for your shares. Most incorporators will wish to authorize one class of common shares with equal voting, dividend, and liquidation rights and no special restrictions. To do this, insert the total number of authorized shares here. If you do wish to authorize special classes of shares, you must add language (on an attachment page to your NJ-REG form, if necessary) that lists the designation of each class, the authorized number of shares in each class, and the rights and restrictions associated with each class. Note: The online formation service provides additional text boxes you can use to specify the names, rights, and restrictions associated with different classes of shares.

Duration: Most incorporators leave this line blank to give the corporation an unlimited (perpetual) legal life.

State and Date of Formation: Leave this line blank (it applies only to out-of-state corporations).

Registered Agent and Office. Typically, an initial director or shareholder is named as initial registered agent (the person authorized to receive legal documents on behalf of the corporation). Most incorporators use the street address of the corporation as the registered office address (which must be the same as the business address of the registered agent). The registered agent must be a New Jersey resident, and the registered office address must be in New Jersey. If the registered office address is the same as the corporation's principal office address, simply insert "same as registered office" in the blank that asks for the principal business address of the corporation.

Management: Show the name(s) and address(es) of your board members. You need only one director, who must be at least 18 years of age. If you need more space to list additional directors, include an attachment page.

Incorporators: You need just one incorporator, who must be 18 years of age or older. The incorporator need not be a director, officer, or shareholder (but typically, an initial director is named as incorporator). List the incorporator's name and address, then have the incorporator date and sign the page at the bottom, showing "Incorporator" as the title.

Additional Entity-Specific Information: You can ignore all the questions here (the entire page). These questions do not apply to a New Jersey business corporation. If you are forming a corporation by mail, mail the uncompleted page with your NJ-REG package.

Filing Fee: Check or money order for $125, payable to "Treasurer, State of New Jersey."

Director and Officer Rules

The business and affairs of a corporation shall be managed by or under the direction of its board, except as in this act or in its Certificate of Incorporation otherwise provided. Directors shall be at least 18 years of age and need not be United States citizens or residents of this State or shareholders of the corporation unless the Certificate of Incorporation or bylaws so require. The Certificate of Incorporation or bylaws may prescribe other qualifications for directors. [14A:6-1]

The board of directors of a corporation shall consist of one or more members. Subject to any provisions contained in the Certificate of Incorporation, the bylaws shall specify the number of directors, or that the number of directors shall not be less than a stated minimum nor more than a stated maximum, with the actual number to be determined in the manner prescribed in the bylaws, except as to the number constituting the first board. [14A:6-2]

The directors named in the Certificate of Incorporation shall hold office until the first annual meeting of shareholders, and until their successors shall have been elected and qualified. At the first annual meeting of shareholders and at each annual meeting thereafter, the shareholders shall elect directors to hold office until the next succeeding annual meeting, except in case of the classification of directors pursuant to subsection 14A:6-4(1) and in the case of directors whose terms expire as provided for in subsection 14A:6-4(2). Each director shall hold office for the term for which he is elected and until his successor shall have been elected and qualified. [14A:6-3]

The officers of a corporation shall consist of a president, a secretary, a treasurer, and, if desired, a chairman of the board; one or more vice presidents; and such other officers as may be prescribed by the bylaws. Unless otherwise provided in the bylaws, the officers shall be elected by the board.

Any two or more offices may be held by the same person but no officer shall execute, acknowledge, or verify any instrument in more than one capacity if such instrument is required by law or by the bylaws to be executed, acknowledged, or verified by two or more officers. [14A:6-15]

Share Issuance Rules

Subject to any restrictions contained in the certificate of incorporation, the consideration for the issuance of shares may be paid, in whole or in part, in: (a) money; (b) real property; (c) tangible or intangible personal property, including stock of another corporation, and obligations of the subscriber or of another person, whether secured or unsecured; (d) labor or services actually performed for the corporation or in its formation; or (e) labor or services to be performed in the future for the corporation. A new employee's termination of employment with a prior employer or the employee's acceptance of employment with the corporation is adequate consideration for the issuance of shares. [14A:7-5]

Unless otherwise provided in the Certificate of Incorporation, all shares shall have no par value and no stated capital shall be required to be maintained. [14A:7-8.1]

The shares of a corporation shall be represented by certificates or, in accordance with subsection 14A:7-11(6), shall be uncertificated shares. Certificates shall be signed by, or in the name of the corporation by, the chairman or vice-chairman of the board, or the president or a vice president, and may be countersigned by the treasurer or an assistant treasurer, or the secretary or an assistant secretary of the corporation, and may be sealed with the seal of the corporation or a facsimile thereof.

Each certificate representing shares shall state on the face thereof (a) that the corporation is organized under the laws of this State; (b) the name of the person to whom issued; and (c) the number and class of shares, and the designation of the series, if any, which such certificate represents.

No certificate shall be issued for any share until such share is fully paid. [14A:7-11]

Director Meeting Rules

Each director shall have one vote at meetings of the board or at meetings of board committees unless the Certificate of Incorporation provides the director is entitled to more than one vote pursuant to a provision in the Certificate of Incorporation consistent with Subsection 14A:6-7.1(2) [allows the corporation to give a director more than one vote when deciding board matters].

The participation of directors with a majority of the votes of the entire board, or of any committee thereof, shall constitute a quorum for the transaction of business, unless the Certificate of Incorporation or the bylaws provide that a greater or lesser proportion shall constitute a quorum, which in no case shall be less than one-third of the votes of the entire board or committee.

Any action approved by a majority of the votes of directors present at a meeting at which a quorum is present shall be the act of the board or of the committee, unless the Business Corporation Act, or the Certificate of Incorporation, or the bylaws require a greater proportion, including a unanimous vote. [14A:6-7.1]

Regular meetings of the board may be held with or without notice as prescribed in the bylaws. Special meetings of the board shall be held on such notice as is prescribed in the bylaws. Notice of any meeting need not be given to any director who signs a waiver of notice, whether before or after the meeting. The attendance of any director at a meeting without protesting prior to the conclusion of the meeting the lack of notice of such meeting shall constitute a waiver of notice by him. Neither the business to be transacted at, nor the purpose of, any meeting of the board need be specified in the notice or waiver of notice of such meeting unless required by the bylaws. [14A:6-10]

Shareholder Meeting Rules

An annual meeting of the shareholders shall be held at such time as may be provided in the bylaws, or as may be fixed by the board pursuant to authority granted in the bylaws, and, in the absence of such a provision, at noon on the first Tuesday of April. Failure to hold the annual meeting at the designated time, or to elect a sufficient number of directors at such meeting or any adjournment thereof, shall not affect otherwise valid corporate acts or work a forfeiture or dissolution of the corporation. If the annual meeting for election of directors is not held on the date designated therefor, the directors shall cause the meeting to be held as soon thereafter as convenient. If there is a failure to hold an annual meeting for a period of 30 days after the date designated therefor, or if no

date has been designated for a period of 13 months after the organization of the corporation or after its last annual meeting, the Superior Court may, on the application of any shareholder, summarily order the meeting or the election, or both, to be held at such time and place, on such notice and for the transaction of such business, as may be designated in such order. At any meeting ordered to be called pursuant to this section, the shareholders present in person or by proxy and having voting powers shall constitute a quorum for the transaction of the business designated in such order. [14A:5-2]

Special meetings of the shareholders may be called by the president or the board, or by such other officers, directors, or shareholders as may be provided in the bylaws. Notwithstanding any such provision, on the application of the holder or holders of not less than 10% of all the shares entitled to vote at a meeting, the Superior Court, in an action in which the court may proceed in a summary manner, for good cause shown, may order a special meeting of the shareholders to be called and held at such time and place, on such notice and for the transaction of such business as may be designated in such order. At any meeting ordered to be called pursuant to this section, the shareholders present in person or by proxy and having voting powers shall constitute a quorum for the transaction of the business designated in such order. [14A:5-3]

Except as otherwise provided in the Business Corporation Act, written notice of the time, place, and purpose or purposes of every meeting of shareholders shall be given not less than ten nor more than 60 days before the date of the meeting, either personally or by mail, to each shareholder of record entitled to vote at the meeting. [14A:5-4]

Except as otherwise provided in the Certificate of Incorporation and subject to the provisions of this subsection [provides special rules for the approval by written consent of corporate mergers], any action required or permitted to be taken at a meeting of shareholders by the Business Corporation Act, the Certificate of Incorporation, or bylaws, other than the annual election of directors, may be taken without a meeting, without prior notice, and without a vote, on the written consent of shareholders who would have been entitled to cast the minimum number of votes which would be necessary to authorize such action at a meeting at which all shareholders entitled to vote thereon were present and voting. [14A:5-6]

Unless otherwise provided in the Certificate of Incorporation or the Business Corporation Act, the holders of shares entitled to cast a majority of the votes at a meeting shall constitute a quorum at such meeting. [14A:5-9]

Whenever any action, other than the election of directors, is to be taken by vote of the shareholders, it shall be authorized by a majority of the votes cast at a meeting of shareholders by the holders of shares entitled to vote thereon, unless a greater plurality is required by the Certificate of Incorporation or another section of the Business Incorporation Act. [14A:5-11]

Elections of directors need not be by ballot unless a shareholder demands election by ballot at the election and before the voting begins. If the bylaws require election by ballot at any shareholders' meeting, such requirement is waived unless compliance therewith is requested by a shareholder entitled to vote at such meeting.

At each election of directors every shareholder entitled to vote at such election shall have the right to vote the number of shares owned by him for as many persons as there are directors to be elected and for whose election he has a right to vote, or, if the Certificate of Incorporation so provides, to cumulate his votes by giving one candidate as many votes as the number of such directors multiplied by the aggregate number of his votes shall equal, or by distributing such votes on the same principle among any number of such candidates.

Except as otherwise provided by the Certificate of Incorporation, directors shall be elected by a plurality of the votes cast at an election. [14A:5-24]

Financial Disclosure Rules

On the written request of any shareholder, the corporation shall mail to such shareholder its balance sheet as at the end of the preceding fiscal year, and its profit and loss and surplus statement for such fiscal year. [14A:5-28]

State Tax Information

Division of Taxation, Trenton
609-292-6400
www.state.nj.us/treasury/taxation

New Jersey corporations are subject to a business tax based on their taxable income. The minimum annual income tax is $200.

Corporation Law Online

The New Jersey Business Corporation Act is contained in Title 14A (Corporations, General) New Jersey Statutes, starting with Section 14A:1-1. To find the Act, visit the legal research area of Nolo's website at www.nolo.com/statute/state.cfm. Click on "New Jersey." Choose "Statutes" and then any link for "New Jersey Statutes." From there, you can click on and browse Title 14A.

State Securities Information

New Jersey Bureau of Securities
153 Halsey Street
P.O. Box 47029
Newark, NJ 07101
973-504-3600
www.state.nj.us/lps/ca/bos.htm

The New Jersey Uniform Securities Law is contained in Title 49, Chapter 3, of the New Jersey Statutes, beginning with Section 49:3-47. To find it, follow the instructions in "Corporation Law Online," above, but scroll down to Title 49. Click on the "+" to expand the table of contents for Title 49, then select Chapter 3-47 to begin browsing the law.

The Bureau of Securities website offers little specific information on the Securities Law or exemptions from securities registration. Section 49:3-50(b) of the Law contains exemptions, including an exemption under 49:3-50(b)(9) for a private sale of stock to not more than ten people (with limited exceptions listed in Subsection (b)(8)) in New Jersey during any period of 12 consecutive months. Buyers must purchase the shares for investment only, no commissions can be paid, and advertising of the shares is not allowed. Another exemption is provided under Section 49:3-50(b)(12) that generally parallels the federal Regulation D exemption requirements for sales to 35 or fewer investors. To qualify, you must file a notice form with the Bureau. For additional information on these and other available exemptions, see the Securities Law and call the Bureau of Securities.

Creating Your Own Articles Form

You can prepare and file your own articles form.

NEW MEXICO

Corporate Filing Office

Public Regulation Commission
Corporations Bureau
Chartered Documents Division
P.O. Box 1269
Santa Fe, NM 87504
Telephone: 505-827-4508 (Toll Free: 1-800-947-4722)
www.nmprc.state.nm.us/corporations/corpshome.htm

State Corporate Forms

New Mexico provides an Articles of Incorporation form (with instructions) and a Statement of Acceptance of Appointment by Designated Initial Registered Agent, which must be filed with the Articles.

Internet Forms: You can download New Mexico Articles of Incorporation (Form DPR) with instructions, which includes a Statement of Acceptance of Appointment, from the state corporate filing office website.

Articles Instructions

Article One: The name of a New Mexico corporation must contain the word "corporation," "company," "incorporated," or "limited," or an abbreviation of one of these words.

You can check corporate name availability online by comparing your proposed name to names already registered with the state. Click "Corporations Information Inquiries" on the state filing office home page, then enter your proposed name in the search box to see if a similar name is already registered. You can also check name availability by calling the state filing office. It costs $25 to reserve an available corporate name for 120 days.

Article Two: Insert "perpetual" to give your corporation an indefinite legal life. Or, if you wish to limit the legal life of your corporation, insert the date on which the corporation will automatically dissolve. (Most incorporators give their corporation a perpetual duration.)

Article Three: You must state at least one specific business purpose for your corporation. You may include a general purpose with your specific purpose. For example, you might insert "to develop and sell real estate and to engage in the transaction of any lawful business for which corporations may be incorporated under the New Mexico Business Corporation Act."

Article Four: In New Mexico, you do not need to state a par value for your shares. Most incorporators authorize one class of common shares with equal voting, dividend, and liquidation rights and no special restrictions. To do this, simply insert the total number of authorized shares in the space provided in this article. Most incorporators simply authorize 100,000 shares (the maximum number you can authorize for the minimum filing fee of $100—see "Filing Fee," below). If you do want to authorize special classes of shares, you list (on an attachment page, if necessary) the designation of each class, the authorized number of shares in each class, and the rights and restrictions associated with each class.

Article Five: Typically, an initial director or shareholder is named as initial registered agent (the person authorized to receive legal documents on behalf of the corporation). Most incorporators use the street address of the corporation as the registered office address (which must be the same as the business address of the registered agent). The registered agent must be a New Mexico resident, and the registered office address must be in New Mexico. Your initial agent must sign the Statement of Acceptance of Appointment by Designated Initial Registered Agent (see below).

Article Six: You may have one or more directors. Insert name and address information.

Article Seven: Name at least one incorporator, who need not be a director, officer, or shareholder. The incorporator must sign and date the form on the lines provided at the bottom of the articles form.

Submit the original and one copy of your articles for filing. You must complete the Statement of Acceptance of Appointment, which is included as the last page of the articles form provided on the state filing office website. Your registered agent (designated in Article Six) must sign the Statement. The registered agent signs on the first signature line at the bottom of the Statement [above the line that reads "Sign on this line if the registered agent named in the articles of incorporation is an individual."].

Filing Fee: $100 minimum filing fee (see below), payable to the "New Mexico Public Regulation Commission" or "NMPRC."

The filing fee is based on the number of shares authorized in your articles. The fee is $1 for each 1,000 shares authorized, subject to a minimum payment of $100. Therefore, you may authorize up to 100,000 shares in your Articles for the minimum $100 filing fee. If you authorize more than 100,000 shares, increase your filing fee by $1 for each additional 1,000 shares. The maximum filing fee is $1,000 (for 1 million or more authorized shares).

Examples:

If you authorize 100,000 shares in your articles, you'll pay the minimum $100 filing fee.

If you authorize 200,000 shares, you'll pay a filing fee of $200 (200,000 divided by 1,000 = 200 x $1 = $200).

Director and Officer Rules

The number of directors of a corporation shall consist of one or more members. The number of directors shall be fixed by, or in the manner provided in, the Articles of Incorporation or the bylaws. The number of directors may be increased or decreased from time to time by amendment to, or in the manner provided in, the Articles of Incorporation or the bylaws, but no decrease shall have the effect of shortening the term of any incumbent director. If the number of directors is not fixed by, or in the manner provided in, the bylaws or the Articles of Incorporation, the number shall be the same as the number of directors constituting the initial board of directors. The names and addresses of the members of the first board of directors shall be stated in the Articles of Incorporation. Such persons shall hold office until the first annual meeting of shareholders and until their successors have been elected and qualified. At the first annual meeting of shareholders and at each annual meeting thereafter, the shareholders shall elect directors to hold office until the next succeeding annual meeting, except in case of the classification of directors as permitted by the Business Corporation Act [Chapter 53, Articles 11 to 18 NMSA 1978]. Each director shall hold office for the term for which the director is elected and until a successor has been elected and qualified. [53-11-36]

Every corporation organized under the Business Corporation Act [53-11-1 to 53-18-12 NMSA 1978] shall have officers, with titles and duties as shall be stated in the bylaws or in a resolution of the board of directors which is not inconsistent with the bylaws, and as many officers as may be necessary to enable the corporation to sign instruments and stock certificates required under the Business Corporation Act. One of the officers shall have the duty to record the proceedings of the meetings of the shareholders and directors in a book to be kept for that purpose. [53-11-48]

Share Issuance Rules

The board of directors may authorize shares to be issued for consideration consisting of tangible or intangible property or benefit to the corporation, including cash, promissory notes, services performed, contracts for ser-vices to be performed, or other securities of the corporation.

The corporation may place in escrow shares issued for a contract for future services or benefits or a promissory note, or make other arrangements to restrict the transfer of the shares, and may credit distributions in respect of the shares against their purchase price, until the services are performed, the note is paid, or the benefits received. If the services are not performed, the note is not paid, or the benefits are not received, the shares escrowed or restricted and the distributions credited may be canceled in whole or part. [53-11-19]

The shares of a corporation shall be represented by certificates or shall be uncertificated shares. Certificates shall be signed by the chairman or vice chairman of the board of directors or the president or a vice president, and by the treasurer or an assistant treasurer, or the secretary or an assistant secretary of the corporation, and may be sealed with the seal of the corporation or a facsimile thereof.

Each certificate representing shares shall state on its face: (1) that the corporation is organized under the laws of this state; (2) the name of the person to whom issued; and (3) the number and class of shares, and the designation of the series, if any, which the certificate represents. [53-11-23]

Director Meeting Rules

Meetings of the board of directors, regular or special, or any committee designated thereby, may be held either within or without the state of New Mexico. Regular meetings of the board of directors or any committee designated thereby may be held with or without notice as prescribed in the bylaws. Special meetings of the board of directors or any committee designated thereby shall be held on the notice prescribed in the bylaws. Attendance of a director at a meeting constitutes a waiver of notice of the meeting, except where a director attends a meeting for the express purpose of objecting to the transaction of any business because the meeting is not lawfully called or convened. Neither the business to be transacted at, nor the purpose of, any regular or special meeting of the board of directors or any committee designated thereby need be specified in the notice or waiver of notice of the meeting unless required by the bylaws. [53-11-42]

A majority of the number of directors as fixed pursuant to Section 53-11-36 NMSA 1978 [above] shall constitute a quorum for the transaction of business unless a greater number is required by the Articles of Incorporation or the bylaws. A quorum, once attained at a meeting, shall be deemed to continue until adjournment notwithstanding the voluntary withdrawal of enough directors to leave less than a quorum. The act of the majority of the directors present at a meeting at which a quorum is present shall be the act of the board of directors, unless the act of a greater number is required by the Articles of Incorporation or the bylaws. [53-11-40]

Shareholder Meeting Rules

An annual meeting of the shareholders shall be held at the time designated in or fixed in accordance with the bylaws. If the annual meeting is not held within any 13-month period, the district court may, on the application of any shareholder, order a meeting to be held.

Special meetings of the shareholders may be called by the board of directors, the holders of not less than one-tenth of all the shares entitled to vote at the meeting, or such other persons as may be authorized in the Articles of Incorporation or the bylaws. [53-11-28]

Written notice stating the place, day, and hour of the meeting and, in case of a special meeting, the purpose or purposes for which the meeting is called, shall be delivered not less than ten nor more than 50 days before the date of the meeting, either personally or by mail, at the direction of the president, the secretary, or the officer or persons calling the meeting, to each shareholder of record entitled to vote at the meeting. [53-11-29]

Unless otherwise provided in the Articles of Incorporation, a majority of the shares entitled to vote, represented in person or by proxy, shall constitute a quorum at a meeting of shareholders, but in no event shall a quorum consist of less than one-third of the shares entitled to vote at the meeting. A quorum, once attained at a meeting, shall be deemed to continue until adjournment notwithstanding the voluntary withdrawal of enough shares to leave less than a quorum. If a quorum is present, the affirmative vote of the majority of the shares represented at the meeting and entitled to vote on the subject matter shall be the act of the shareholders, unless the vote of a greater number or voting by classes is required by the Business Corporation Act or the Articles of Incorporation. [53-11-32]

The Articles of Incorporation may provide that at each election for directors every shareholder entitled to vote at the election has the right to vote, in person or by proxy, the number of shares owned by him for as many persons as there are directors to be elected and for whose election he has a right to vote, or to cumulate his votes by giving one candidate as many votes as the number of such directors multiplied by the number of his shares shall equal, or by distributing such votes on the same principle among any number of the candidates. A statement in the Articles of Incorporation that cumulative voting exists is sufficient to confer such right. [53-11-33]

Financial Disclosure Rules

Each corporation shall provide its shareholders access to at least a balance sheet as of the end of each taxable year and a statement of income for such taxable year, if the corporation prepares such financial statements for such taxable year for any purpose. Such financial statements may be consolidated statements of the corporation and one or more of its subsidiaries, but shall not be required to include the statements' supporting data or information. [53-11-50]

State Tax Information

Taxation and Revenue Department, Santa Fe
505-827-0700
www.state.nm.us/tax

New Mexico corporations are subject to a corporate income tax. They must also pay an annual franchise tax of $50.

Corporation Law Online

The New Mexico Business Corporation Act is contained in Chapter 53 (Corporations), Articles 11 through 18 of the New Mexico Statutes, starting with section 53-11-1. You can browse it from the following Web page (first select "New Mexico Statues" in the left panel, then click the HTML tab at the top of the page; in the left panel select the folder titled "Statutory Chapters in New Mexico Statutes Annotated 1978," then scroll down in the left panel and select the Chapter 53 folder, then use the right panel to scroll down to select Articles 11 through 18 to browse the sections of the Act contained in each Article).

http://legis.state.nm.us

State Securities Information

Securities Division
Regulation and Licensing Department
725 St. Michael's Drive
Santa Fe, NM 87505
505-827-7140 (Toll Free: 800-704-5533)
www.rld.state.nm.us/Securities/index.htm

The New Mexico Security Act is contained in Chapter 58, Article 13B, of the New Mexico Statutes. You can browse the Act from www.michie.com/resources1.html. Follow the instructions in "Corporation Law Online," above, but open the folders for Chapter 58 and Article 13B.

The Securities Division website offers information on various exemptions available under the Act, including what's called the "27K" exemption under Section 58-13B-27(k). The 27K exemption is a private placement exemption; no general solicitation is permitted. It allows an issuer organized as a corporation, limited partnership, or limited liability company to raise an unlimited amount of capital from up to 25 investors. The issuer must disclose all material facts to purchasers in compliance with the antifraud provisions of the Securities Act. (See Chapter 2, Section 11, for a discussion of material disclosure.) Resale of the securities is restricted and the issuer (corporation) must have a reasonable belief that the securities are purchased for investment purposes. If the issuer is formed under the laws of another state or jurisdiction, it must file a notice with the securities Division on Form K. There are no fees for this exemption.

Another exemption is provided under the Security Act, known as the "27U" exemption. This exemption is contained in Section 58-13B-27(u) of the Securities Act, and is a state-level private placement exemption that parallels the federal private placement exemption. You must file a completed Form 27U with the Securities Division no less than five business days before the first sale of securities in New Mexico. The issuer may not sell to more than ten people in New Mexico within any 12-month period. In addition, the issuer must meet one of the following two conditions: (1) the company does not have more than 50 beneficial owners (owners who have a direct or indirect interest in the shares) and has not raised more than $500,000 during any consecutive period; or (2) the seller reasonably believes that all of the purchasers in New Mexico are purchasing for investment. There is no filing fee for this exemption. Other exemptions are available. See the Securities Division website for more information.

Creating Your Own Articles Form

You do not have to use the New Mexico state articles form. If you create your own form, it must be typewritten or legibly printed (as explained in the introduction to the state sheets, we assume you will use a computer, not print the entire form by hand) in black or blue-black ink on 8-1/2" x 11" paper.

NEW YORK

Corporate Filing Office

Department of State
Division of Corporations, State Records, and Uniform
Commercial Code
41 State Street
Albany, NY 12231
518-473-2492
www.dos.state.ny.us/corp/corpwww.html

State Corporate Forms

New York provides a fill-in-the-blanks Certificate of Incorporation (Form DOS-1239). You should also obtain the booklet titled "Forming a Corporation in New York State." It contains specific instructions for completing your Certificate of Incorporation and useful corporate legal and tax information.

Internet Forms: You can download corporate form samples from the Division of Corporations website, including a standard Certificate of Incorporation and the instruction booklet mentioned above.

Articles Instructions

Type or fill in the blanks on the New York Certificate of Incorporation using black ink.

First Article: The name of a New York corporation must contain the word "corporation," "incorporated," or "limited," or an abbreviation of one of these words.

Certain words may not be used in a New York corporate name unless you obtain special permission from the state. These prohibited or restricted words include the following: community renewal, tenant relocation, urban development, urban relocation, acceptance, guaranty, annuity, indemnity, assurance, insurance, investment, benefit, loan, bond, mortgage, casualty, savings, surety, endowment, title, fidelity, trust, finance, and underwriter.

You can check corporate name availability online by comparing your proposed name to names already registered with the state. Click "Search Our Corporation/Business Database" on the Division of Corporations home page, then enter your proposed name in the search box to see if a similar name is already registered. This is an informal search; it does not tell you whether any names you find will be considered legally "distinguishable" from your proposed name. To get a definitive answer, you must mail a written request to the state filing office, together with a check for $5 for each name that you want

to check. You can reserve an available corporate name for 60 days for a $20 fee.

Note: You can also fax name availability and reservation requests to the Division after you submit a Credit Card Authorization Form (available online). The fees for these fax services are charged to your credit card (see the state corporate filing office website for information on fax filings). The Division will return your receipts and other papers by first-class mail, not by fax.

Third Article: Insert the name of the county where the primary corporate office is located.

Fourth Article: Most incorporators authorize one class of common shares with equal voting, dividend, and liquidation rights and no special restrictions. To do this, simply insert the number and type of shares you wish to authorize at the end of this article. You may specify shares either with or without par value. To pay the lowest incorporation fee (see filing fee information, below) and to follow the modern trend of authorizing shares without par value (no-par shares can be sold for any price-per-share amount, while par value shares must be sold for at least their stated par value), most incorporators authorize 200 shares without par value. To do this, insert "200 No Par Value" in the designated blank.

If you wish to authorize par value shares, insert the number and par value amount—for example, "20,000 shares; $1 par value per share." And if you want to authorize special classes of shares, you must type your own certificate, listing the designation of each class; the authorized number of shares in each class, whether the shares of each class do or do not have a par value; and the rights and restrictions associated with each class.

Fifth Article: Insert the mailing address of the corporation. The Secretary of State will forward any legal papers filed against your corporation to this address.

Sixth Article: You do not need to designate a registered agent, so you may leave this article blank.

Seventh Article: If you wish to delay the date when your corporation becomes a legal entity, insert a date in this blank. It may not be more than 90 days after the date you file your certificate. If you leave this item blank, your corporation starts its legal (and tax) life on the date your certificate is filed.

Signature: You need just one incorporator, who must be at least 18 years of age. The incorporator need not be a director, officer, or shareholder. Have the incorporator sign the certificate and fill in the incorporator's name and address. (Use a street address, not a P.O. box.) You must also include the incorporator's name and address in the additional statement included with your certificate (see the following paragraph).

You must include the following statement at the end of your Certificate of Incorporation or on a separate cover page: "Certificate of Incorporation of [your corporate name] Under Section 402 of the Business Corporation Law." This statement should be followed by the name and mailing address of your incorporator. New York's standard Certificate of Incorporation includes this statement at the end of the certificate form. If you prepare your own certificate, you can include this information on a separate cover sheet as follows:

> Certificate of Incorporation of
>
> [your corporate name]
>
> Under Section 402 of the Business Corporation Law
>
> Filed by:
>
> [incorporator's name]
>
> [incorporator's address]

If you have reserved a corporate name, also include your reservation receipt with the certificate.

Mail the original certificate together with the cover sheet and fees. After filing, the state filing office will send you a receipt.

Note: You can file your Certificate by fax to the Division after submitting a Credit Card Authorization Form (available online). The filing fee is charged to your credit card. (See the state corporate filing office website for information on fax filings.) The Division will return your copies by first-class mail (not by fax) or by Federal Express for an extra charge, if you so request.

Filing Fee: $135 minimum, consisting of a $125 filing fee plus a $10 minimum shares tax (described below), payable to the "Department of State." (If you request certified copies of your certificate, add $10 for each.) You must pay your fee by check or money order. Fees over $500 must be paid by certified check.

If you want expedited filing, send a separate check for the following additional fees: $150 for filing within two hours of receipt; $75 for filing on the same business day; $25 for filing within 24 hours of receipt. Print the following note on the envelope: "Attention: Expedited Handling."

Tax on Shares: The minimum tax on shares is $10. This allows you to authorize up to 200 shares without par value or par value shares with a total par value of $20,000 in your Certificate of Incorporation. If you authorize more than 200 no-par shares or par value shares with a total par value in excess of $20,000, the shares tax portion of your fee is computed as follows:

Shares Without Par Value: The shares tax is 5 cents for each share authorized without par value. For example, if your certificate authorizes 500 shares without par value, the shares tax portion of your fee is $25 (500 x $.05 = $25). Your total filing fee is $150 ($125 filing fee plus $25 shares tax).

Shares with Par Value: The shares tax is 1/20 of 1% (.0005) of the stated par value of all par value shares authorized. For example, if your certificate authorizes 50,000 shares with a stated par value of $1, the shares tax is $25 (50,000 x $1 = $50,000 total par value x .0005 = $25). Your total filing fee is $150 ($125 filing fee plus $25 shares tax).

Director and Officer Rules

Subject to any provision in the Certificate of Incorporation authorized by paragraph (b) of Section 620 (Agreements as to voting; provision in Certificate of Incorporation as to control of directors) or by paragraph (b) of Section 715 (Officers), the business of a corporation shall be managed under the direction of its board of directors, each of whom shall be at least eighteen years of age. [701]

The board of directors shall consist of one or more members. The number of directors constituting the board may be fixed by the bylaws, or by action of the shareholders or of the board under the specific provisions of a bylaw adopted by the shareholders. If not otherwise fixed under this paragraph, the number shall be one. [702]

At each annual meeting of shareholders, directors shall be elected to hold office until the next annual meeting except as authorized by Section 704 (Classification of directors). [703]

The board may elect or appoint a president, one or more vice presidents, a secretary, and a treasurer, and such other officers as it may determine, or as may be provided in the bylaws.

Unless otherwise provided in the Certificate of Incorporation or the bylaws, all officers shall be elected or appointed to hold office until the meeting of the board following the next annual meeting of shareholders or, in the case of officers elected by the shareholders, until the next annual meeting of shareholders.

Any two or more offices may be held by the same person. When all of the issued and outstanding stock of the corporation is owned by one person, such person may hold all or any combination of offices. [715]

Share Issuance Rules

Every corporation shall have power to create and issue the number of shares stated in its Certificate of Incorporation. Such shares may be all of one class or may be divided into two or more classes. Each class shall consist of either shares with par value or shares without par value, having such designation and such relative voting, dividend, liquidation, and other rights, preferences, and limitations, consistent with this chapter, as shall be stated in the Certificate of Incorporation. [501]

Consideration for the issue of shares shall consist of money or other property, tangible or intangible; labor or services actually received by or performed for the corporation or for its benefit or in its formation or reorganization; a binding obligation to pay the purchase price or the subscription price in cash or other property; a binding obligation to perform services having an agreed value; or a combination thereof. In the absence of fraud in the transaction, the judgment of the board or shareholders, as the case may be, as to the value of the consideration received for shares shall be conclusive.

Shares with par value may be issued for such consideration, not less than the par value thereof, as is fixed from time to time by the board.

Shares without par value may be issued for such consideration as is fixed from time to time by the board unless the Certificate of Incorporation reserves to the shareholders the right to fix the consideration.

Certificates for shares may not be issued until the amount of the consideration therefor determined to be stated capital pursuant to Section 506 (Determination of stated capital) has been paid in the form of cash, services rendered, personal or real property, or a combination thereof and consideration for the balance (if any) complying with paragraph (a) of this section has been provided, except as provided in paragraphs (e) and (f) of Section 505 (Rights and options to purchase shares; issue of rights and options to directors, officers, and employees). [504]

On issue by a corporation of shares with a par value, the consideration received therefor shall constitute stated capital to the extent of the par value of such shares.

On issue by a corporation of shares without par value, the entire consideration received therefor shall constitute stated capital unless the board within a period of sixty days after issue allocates to surplus a portion, but not all, of the consideration received for such shares. No such allocation shall be made of any portion of the consideration received for shares without par value having a preference in the assets of the corporation on involuntary liq-

uidation except all or part of the amount, if any, of such consideration in excess of such preference, nor shall such allocation be made of any portion of the consideration for the issue of shares without par value which is fixed by the shareholders pursuant to a right reserved in the Certificate of Incorporation, unless such allocation is authorized by vote of the shareholders. [506]

The shares of a corporation shall be represented by certificates or shall be uncertificated shares. Certificates shall be signed by the chairman or a vice chairman of the board, or the president or vice president and the secretary or an assistant secretary, or the treasurer or an assistant treasurer of the corporation, and may be sealed with the seal of the corporation or a facsimile thereof.

Each certificate representing shares shall state on the face thereof: (1) that the corporation is formed under the laws of this state; (2) the name of the person or persons to whom issued; (3) the number and class of shares, and the designation of the series, if any, which such certificate represents. [508]

Director Meeting Rules

Unless otherwise provided by the bylaws, regular meetings of the board may be held without notice if the time and place of such meetings are fixed by the bylaws or the board. Special meetings of the board shall be held on notice to the directors.

The bylaws may prescribe what shall constitute notice of meeting of the board. A notice, or waiver of notice, need not specify the purpose of any regular or special meeting of the board, unless required by the bylaws. [711]

Unless a greater proportion is required by the Certificate of Incorporation, a majority of the entire board shall constitute a quorum for the transaction of business or of any specified item of business, except that the Certificate of Incorporation or the bylaws may fix the quorum at less than a majority of the entire board but not less than one-third thereof. [707]

Except as otherwise provided in the Business Incorporation Act, the vote of a majority of the directors present at the time of the vote, if a quorum is present at such time, shall be the act of the board. [708]

Shareholder Meeting Rules

A meeting of shareholders shall be held annually for the election of directors and the transaction of other business on a date fixed by or under the bylaws.

Special meetings of the shareholders may be called by the board and by such person or persons as may be so authorized by the Certificate of Incorporation or the bylaws. At any such special meeting only such business may be transacted which is related to the purpose or purposes set forth in the notice required by Section 605 [below]. [602]

Whenever under the provisions of the Business Corporation Act shareholders are required or permitted to take any action at a meeting, notice shall be given stating the place, date, and hour of the meeting and, unless it is the annual meeting, indicating that it is being issued by or at the direction of the person or persons calling the meeting. Notice of a special meeting shall also state the purpose or purposes for which the meeting is called. Notice of any meeting of shareholders may be written or electronic. If, at any meeting, action is proposed to be taken which would, if taken, entitle shareholders fulfilling the requirements of Section 623 (Procedure to enforce shareholder's right to receive payment for shares) [covers a special type meeting called to force the corporation to pay certain shareholders for their shares] to receive payment for their shares, the notice of such meeting shall include a statement of that purpose and to that effect and shall be accompanied by a copy of Section 623 or an outline of its material terms. Notice of any meeting shall be given not fewer than ten nor more than 60 days before the date of the meeting, provided, however, that such notice may be given by third-class mail not fewer than 24 nor more than 60 days before the date of the meeting, to each shareholder entitled to vote at such meeting. [605]

The holders of a majority of the votes of shares entitled to vote thereat shall constitute a quorum at a meeting of shareholders for the transaction of any business, provided that when a specified item of business is required to be voted on by a particular class or series of shares, voting as a class, the holders of a majority of the votes of shares of such class or series shall constitute a quorum for the transaction of such specified item of business.

The Certificate of Incorporation or bylaws may provide for any lesser quorum not less than one-third of the votes of shares entitled to vote, and the Certificate of Incorporation may, under Section 616 (Greater requirement as to quorum and vote of shareholders), provide for a greater quorum. [608]

Directors shall, except as otherwise required by the Business Corporation Act or by the Certificate of Incorporation as permitted by the Business Corporation Act, be elected by a plurality of the votes cast at a meeting of shareholders by the holders of shares entitled to vote in the election.

Whenever any corporate action, other than the election of directors, is to be taken under the Business Corpora-

tion Act by vote of the shareholders, it shall, except as otherwise required by the Business Corporation Act or by the Certificate of Incorporation as permitted by the Business Corporation Act or by the specific provisions of a bylaw adopted by the shareholders, be authorized by a majority of the votes cast in favor of or against such action at a meeting of shareholders by the holders of shares entitled to vote thereon. Except as otherwise provided in the Certificate of Incorporation or the specific provision of a bylaw adopted by the shareholders, an abstention shall not constitute a vote cast. [614]

The Certificate of Incorporation of any corporation may provide that in all elections of directors of such corporation each shareholder shall be entitled to as many votes as shall equal the number of votes which, except for such provisions as to cumulative voting, he would be entitled to cast for the election of directors with respect to his shares multiplied by the number of directors to be elected, and that he may cast all of such votes for a single director or may distribute them among the number to be voted for, or any two or more of them, as he may see fit, which right, when exercised, shall be termed cumulative voting. [618]

Financial Disclosure Rules

On the written request of any shareholder, the corporation shall give or mail to such shareholder an annual balance sheet and profit and loss statement for the preceding fiscal year, and, if any interim balance sheet or profit and loss statement has been distributed to its shareholders or otherwise made available to the public, the most recent such interim balance sheet or profit and loss statement. The corporation shall be allowed a reasonable time to prepare such annual balance sheet and profit and loss statement. [624]

State Tax Information

Taxation and Finance Department, Albany
518-438-8581
www.tax.state.ny.us

New York corporations are subject to a corporate franchise tax. This tax is based on four separate computations related to corporate income, capital, and payroll, with a minimum payment of $100. See the Department website for more information on franchise tax rates and computations.

Corporation Law Online

The New York Business Corporation Law is contained in Chapter 4 of the New York State Consolidated Laws, starting with section 101. You can browse it from the following Web page (click "New York State Laws," then "New York State Consolidated Laws," then "Business Corporation").

http://assembly.state.ny.us/ALIS/laws.html

State Securities Information

Bureau of Investor Protection and Securities
Office of the Attorney General, State of New York
120 Broadway
New York, NY 10271
212-416-8200 and 212-416-8222
www.oag.state.ny.us/investors/investors.html

The New York Securities Law is contained in the "Martin Act," Chapter 359 of the New York State Consolidated Laws, Article 23-A. The Act currently is not posted online. Go to the Investor Protection Bureau website to see information on the Martin Act requirements, and call the office to ask for the Bureau's pamphlet that describes the basic Martin Act requirements.

Section 359-e of the Martin Act regulates dealers who sell securities in New York to the public. The term "dealer" includes a corporation that sells its shares to investors in New York. A dealer must file a State Notice form with the Bureau of Investor Protection and Securities before offering or selling securities in New York. You may also have to file a broker-dealer statement, and, if applicable, a salesman's statement. (Fees for filing these statements vary, starting at $200.) In certain cases, you can file for exemption from these dealer registration requirements. Section 359-f(2) allows an exemption for limited offerings of securities to 40 or fewer people. The filing fee for exemption applications is $200.

In addition to the dealer registration requirements, Section 359-ff of the Martin Act requires the registration of intrastate offerings of securities (offerings within New York). This registration is accomplished by filing a prospectus (Form INTRASTATE-1) with the Department of Law, a division of the Bureau. Additional forms may be required. The prospectus asks for detailed information about the corporation and its stock offering, including financial statements. You must give a copy of the prospectus to each prospective purchaser of shares. The fee for filing a prospectus is based on the value of the offering, with a minimum fee of $25 and a maximum of $1,500.

Section 359-ff(3) also allows the Bureau to provide exemptions to these intrastate offering registration requirements. You can find these exemptions in the New York Intrastate Financing Act. You can browse the Act by visiting the Bureau of Investor Protection and Securities website listed above. First, click "Index" on the left side of the page. Next, click "Real Estate Rules and Regulations." Finally, choose "Part 80 Intrastate Financing." Section 80.9 contains an exemption from the prospectus requirements for securities offerings by a corporation to fewer than ten people. This popular exemption can relieve you from the requirement of filing a prospectus for your intrastate offering to your initial shareholders. You do not need to file an application for this exemption. Other exemptions from the prospectus requirements also are contained in Section 80.9 and other sections of the Intrastate Financing Act; if you rely on another exemption you may be required to file an exemption application form.

The best way to comply with New York securities laws is to carefully review the laws above before deciding how you want to proceed. After reading the laws, many incorporators feel comfortable that they are exempt from the 359-ff intrastate offering prospectus requirements. As to the dealer registration requirements, remember that registration is required if you are offering securities to the public. A lawyer may be able to help ensure that you are making a private offering and sale of your initial shares of stock. And if it turns out that you do have to file dealer registration forms and pay associated fees, you may want a lawyer's help preparing and filing the paperwork. Forms are posted on the Bureau website. Call the Bureau if you have questions or need additional assistance.

Creating Your Own Articles Form

You can create your own Certificate of Incorporation form following the guidelines in "Articles Instructions," above. Your certificate must be typed or printed (as explained in the introduction to these state sheets, we assume you will use a computer printer, not print by hand) in black ink.

NORTH CAROLINA

Corporate Filing Office

North Carolina Department of the Secretary of State
Corporations Division
P.O. Box 29622
Raleigh, NC 27626-0622
919-807-2225 (Toll Free 1-888-246-7636)
www.secretary.state.nc.us/corporations

State Corporate Forms

North Carolina provides fill-in-the-blanks Articles of Incorporation (Form B-01).

Internet Forms: Articles of Incorporation with instructions, plus other corporate forms, are available for downloading from the state filing office website. You can also download a guide to incorporating, which includes helpful corporate name, trademark and securities law information plus state business and licensing office listings.

Articles Instructions

Article 1: The name of a North Carolina corporation must contain the word "corporation," "incorporated," "company," or "limited," or the abbreviation "corp.," "inc.," "co.," or "ltd." Note that you cannot use the word "wholesale" in your corporate name unless you submit a letter to the state filing office stating that your corporation will comply with N.C. General Statute 75-29 by engaging principally in wholesale rather than retail business.

You can check corporate name availability online by comparing your proposed name to names already registered with the state. Click "Search by Corporate Name" on the state filing office home page. You can also check name availability by calling the state filing office. An available corporate name may be reserved for 120 days for $30.

Article 2: In North Carolina, you do not need to state a par value for your shares. The filing fee is not based on how many shares you authorize, so you can authorize as many as you wish. Most incorporators authorize one class of common shares with equal voting, dividend, and liquidation rights and no special restrictions. To do this, simply insert the number of shares you wish to authorize in the blank, then check blank "a." If you do wish to authorize special classes of shares, check blank "b," then include an attachment page that lists the name of each class, the number of shares in each class, and the rights and restrictions associated with each class. The total number of shares in all classes should equal the number of shares specified in the first blank in Article 2.

Articles 3, 4, & 5: Typically, an initial director or shareholder is named as initial registered agent (the person authorized to receive legal documents on behalf of the corporation). Most incorporators use the street address of the corporation as the registered office address (which must be the same as the business address of the registered agent). The registered agent must be a North Carolina resident, and the registered office must be in North Carolina. The agent must be at least 18 years old. If you wish to specify a separate mailing address for your registered office, you can insert it in Article 4.

Article 6. Select item "a" if you have decided on the location of your corporation's principal office. Enter the complete street address of the principal office and the county in which it is located. If mail is not delivered to the street address of the principal office or if you prefer to receive mail at a P.O. Box or Drawer, enter the complete mailing address of the principal office. Select item "b" if your corporation does not yet have a principal office.

Article 8: You need just one incorporator, who need not be a director, officer, or shareholder.

Article 9: Normally, your corporation is formed on the date the articles are filed, but you can specify a different effective date (up to 90 days after filing) in the blank.

The incorporator named in Article 8 signs the articles on the SECOND blank line after the date (the first blank line is used in case another entity, such as another corporation, acts as incorporator—you should leave the first signature line blank). Submit the original and one copy of your completed articles form, together with a check for the filing fee. Also prepare and include the state-supplied articles cover letter, Form BE-01, titled "Cover Letter for Corporate Filings." This form is available on the state corporate filing office website.

Filing Fee: $125, payable to "Secretary of State." Same-day filing costs $200 extra; 24-hour filing costs $100 extra. Normal filing time is five business days from the date that the state filing office receives your articles.

Director and Officer Rules

A board of directors must consist of one or more individuals, with the number specified in or fixed in accordance with the Articles of Incorporation or bylaws. [55-8-03]

The terms of the initial directors of a corporation expire at the first shareholders' meeting at which directors are elected.

The terms of all other directors expire at the next annual shareholders' meeting following their election unless their terms are staggered under G.S. 55-8-06. [55-8-05]

A corporation has the officers described in its bylaws or appointed by the board of directors in accordance with the bylaws.

The secretary or any assistant secretary or any one or more other officers designated by the bylaws or the board of directors shall have the responsibility and authority to maintain and authenticate the records of the corporation.

The same individual may simultaneously hold more than one office in a corporation, but no individual may act in more than one capacity where action of two or more officers is required. [55-8-40]

Share Issuance Rules

The board of directors may authorize shares to be issued for consideration consisting of any tangible or intangible property or benefit to the corporation, including cash, promissory notes, services performed, contracts for services to be performed, or other securities of the corporation.

The corporation may place in escrow shares issued for a contract for future services or benefits or for a promissory note, or make other arrangements to restrict the transfer of the shares, and may credit distributions in respect of the shares against their purchase price, until the services are performed, the note is paid, or the benefit received. If the services are not performed, the note is not paid, or the benefits are not received, the shares escrowed or restricted and the distributions credited may be cancelled in whole or part. [55-6-21]

At a minimum each share certificate must state on its face: (1) the name of the issuing corporation and that it is organized under the law of North Carolina; (2) the name of the person to whom issued; and (3) the number and class of shares and the designation of the series, if any, the certificate represents.

Each share certificate (1) must be signed (either manually or in facsimile) by two officers designated in the bylaws or by the board of directors, and (2) may bear the corporate seal or its facsimile. [55-6-25]

Director Meeting Rules

The board of directors may hold regular or special meetings in or out of the state of North Carolina.

Unless the bylaws provide otherwise, special meetings of the board of directors may be called by the president or any two directors. [55-8-20]

Unless the Articles of Incorporation or bylaws provide otherwise, regular meetings of the board of directors may be held without notice of the date, time, place, or purpose of the meeting.

Special meetings of the board of directors shall be held on such notice as is provided in the Articles of Incorporation or bylaws, or in the absence of any such provision, on notice sent by any usual means of communication not less than five days before the meeting. The notice need not describe the purpose of the special meeting unless required by the Business Corporation Act, the Articles of Incorporation, or bylaws. [55-8-22]

Unless the Articles of Incorporation or bylaws require a greater number, a quorum of a board of directors consists of: (1) a majority of the fixed number of directors if the corporation has a fixed board size, or (2) a majority of the number of directors prescribed, or if no number is prescribed the number in office immediately before the meeting begins, if the corporation has a variable-range size board.

The Articles of Incorporation or a bylaw adopted by the shareholders may authorize a quorum of a board of directors to consist of no fewer than one-third of the fixed or prescribed number of directors determined under Subsection (a) [previous paragraph].

If a quorum is present when a vote is taken, the affirmative vote of a majority of directors present is the act of the board of directors unless the Articles of Incorporation or bylaws require the vote of a greater number of directors. [55-8-24]

Shareholder Meeting Rules

A corporation shall hold a meeting of shareholders annually at a time stated in or fixed in accordance with the bylaws.

Any matter relating to the affairs of a corporation that is appropriate for shareholder action is a proper subject for action at an annual meeting of shareholders, and unless required by some provision of the Business Corporation Act, the matter need not be specifically stated in the notice of meeting. [55-7-01]

A corporation shall hold a special meeting of shareholders: (1) on call of its board of directors or the person or persons authorized to do so by the Articles of Incorporation or bylaws; or (2) within 30 days after the holders of at least 10% of all the votes entitled to be cast on any issue proposed to be considered at the proposed special meeting sign, date, and deliver to the corporation's secretary one or more written demands for the meeting describing the purpose or purposes for which it is to be held; except however that, unless otherwise provided in the Articles of Incorporation or bylaws, the call of a special meeting by shareholders is not available to the shareholders of a public corporation.

A corporation shall notify shareholders of the date, time, and place of each annual and special shareholders' meeting no fewer than ten nor more than 60 days before the meeting date. Unless the Business Corporation Act or the Articles of Incorporation require otherwise, the corporation is required to give notice only to shareholders entitled to vote at the meeting.

Unless the Business Corporation Act or the Articles of Incorporation require otherwise, notice of an annual meeting need not include a description of the purpose or purposes for which the meeting is called.

Notice of a special meeting must include a description of the purpose or purposes for which the meeting is called. [55-7-05] Only business within the purpose or purposes described in the meeting notice required may be conducted at a special shareholders' meeting. [55-7-02]

Shares entitled to vote as a separate voting group may take action on a matter at a meeting only if a quorum of that voting group exists with respect to that matter, except that, in the absence of a quorum at the opening of any meeting of shareholders, such meeting may be adjourned from time to time by the vote of a majority of the votes cast on the motion to adjourn. Unless the Articles of Incorporation, a bylaw adopted by the shareholders, or the Business Corporation Act provides otherwise, a majority of the votes entitled to be cast on the matter by the voting group constitutes a quorum of that voting group for action on that matter.

If a quorum exists, action on a matter (other than the election of directors) by a voting group is approved if the votes cast within the voting group favoring the action exceed the votes cast opposing the action, unless the Articles of Incorporation, a bylaw adopted by the shareholders, or the Business Corporation Act requires a greater number of affirmative votes.

The election of directors is governed by G.S. 55-7-28. [55-7-25]

If the Articles of Incorporation, a bylaw adopted by the shareholders, or the Business Corporation Act provides for voting by a single voting group on a matter, action on that matter is taken when voted on by that voting group as provided in G.S. 55-7-25. [55-7-26]

Unless otherwise provided in the Articles of Incorporation or in an agreement valid under G.S. 55-7-31 [allows shareholders to agree to establish their own rules for electing directors], directors are elected by a plurality of the votes cast by the shares entitled to vote in the election at a meeting at which a quorum is present.

Except as provided in Subsection (e) [applies to corporations formed prior to 1990] of this section, shareholders do not have a right to cumulate their votes for directors unless the Articles of Incorporation so provide. [55-7-28]

Financial Disclosure Rules

A corporation shall make available to its shareholders annual financial statements, which may be consolidated or combined statements of the corporation and one or more of its subsidiaries, as appropriate, that include a balance sheet as of the end of the fiscal year, an income statement for that year, and a statement of cash flows for the year unless that information appears elsewhere in the financial statements. If financial statements are prepared for the corporation on the basis of generally accepted accounting principles, the annual financial statements must also be prepared on that basis.

If the annual financial statements are reported on by a public accountant, his report must accompany them. If not, the statements must be accompanied by a statement of the president or the person responsible for the corporation's accounting records: (1) stating his reasonable belief whether the statements were prepared on the basis of generally accepted accounting principles and, if not, describing the basis of preparation; and (2) describing any respects in which the statements were not prepared on a basis of accounting consistent with the statements prepared for the preceding year.

A corporation shall mail the annual financial statements, or a written notice of their availability, to each shareholder within 120 days after the close of each fiscal year, provided that the failure of the corporation to comply with this requirement shall not constitute the basis for any claim of damages by any shareholder unless such failure was in bad faith. Thereafter, on written request from a shareholder who was not mailed the statements, the corporation shall mail him the latest financial statements. [55-16-20]

State Tax Information

Department of Revenue, Raleigh
919-733-3991
www.dor.state.nc.us

North Carolina corporations are subject to a corporate income tax. They must also pay an annual franchise tax. The minimum annual franchise tax is $35.

Corporation Law Online

The North Carolina Business Corporation Act is contained in Chapter 55 of the North Carolina Statutes, starting with Section 55-1-01. To find the Act, visit the legal research area of Nolo's website at www.nolo.com. Click on "State Laws" and then on "North Carolina." From there, scroll down and click on "Chapters 1-57A" under "Browse the NC General Statutes." Select Chapter 55 from the chapter list.

State Securities Information

The Securities Division
Department of the Secretary of State
P.O. Box 29622
Raleigh, NC 27626-0622
919-733-3924 (Toll Free: 800-688-4507)
www.secretary.state.nc.us/sec

The North Carolina Securities Act is contained in Chapter 78A of the North Carolina General Statutes. To find the Act, follow the instructions in "Corporation Law Online," above—but select Chapter 78A from the chapter list. The rules that enforce the Act are contained in various sections of Title 18 of the N.C. Administrative Code, which you can browse from links provided on the Securities Division website. Title 18.06-12 contains many of the exemption rules.

Section 78A-17 of the Securities Act contains exemptions from registration for certain securities transactions. For example, Section 78A-17(9) provides an exemption for qualified offerings to 25 or fewer persons during a 12-month period, if the seller reasonably believes that all the buyers in North Carolina are purchasing for investment only. You must also meet certain other conditions specified in Title 18.06-12, Section .1205, of the Administrative Code. Other limited offering exemptions are available. For further information on qualifying for any exemption under the Act and the securities rules, and for information on providing required notice, paying fees, and coordinating your state exemption with any federal Regulation D filing, call the Securities Division.

Creating Your Own Articles Form

You can prepare and file your own articles form.

NORTH DAKOTA

Corporate Filing Office

North Dakota Secretary of State
Corporations Division
600 East Boulevard Avenue
Bismarck, ND 58505-0500
701-328-4284 (Toll Free: 800-352-0867, ext. 4284)
www.state.nd.us/sec/Business/businessinforegmnu.htm

State Corporate Forms

North Dakota provides fill-in-the-blank Articles of Incorporation for a Business or Farming Corporation, along with a Registered Agent Consent to Serve form that must be filed with the articles.

Internet Forms: You can download Articles of Incorporation for a Business or Farming Corporation with instructions (Form SFN 16812A, which includes the required Registered Agent Consent to Serve form) and other statutory forms from the state filing office website.

Articles Instructions

Top of Form: Check the box titled "North Dakota Business Corporation Act." (If you are forming a farming corporation, you will need to check the second box and follow the special instructions for farm corporations, not covered here. You will also need to complete and attach a special farm corporation initial report form to your articles (you can get this form online or by calling the state filing office). Call the state filing office or visit the website for more information.)

Article 1: The name of a North Dakota corporation must contain the word "corporation," "incorporated," "company," or "limited," or an abbreviation of one of these words.

Check name availability by calling the state filing office or check your proposed name online by using the Business Record Search link on the state filing office website. An available corporate name may be reserved for one year for $10.

Article 2: Most incorporators name an initial director, officer, or shareholder as the corporate agent, and provide the street address of the corporation as the registered agent address. Make sure to insert the agent's Social Security number in blank 2B. As mentioned above, your agent must sign the form called "Registered Agent Consent to Serve," and you must include it with your articles when you file.

Article 3: Most incorporators check the box "when filed with the Secretary of State" to start the legal life of their

corporation on the date the articles are filed. If you want a delayed effective date, check the second box instead, and insert the date when you want your corporation's legal life to begin. This delayed date must be within 90 days of the date you file your articles.

Article 4: You don't have to include a statement of specific corporate purposes. The standard language in this article, which states that your corporation was organized for "general business purposes," is sufficient for most corporations. You cannot form a North Dakota business corporation for the purpose of engaging in the banking, farming, ranching, or insurance business. A business corporation may be an insurance agency that sells or services insurance products but cannot be the insurer that backs claims.

Note: Providing a statement of specific purposes can help the state corporate filing office determine whether you are entitled to use your proposed corporate name if the name is similar to that of another corporation. Even if your name is similar to the name of another corporation, the filing office may allow you to use the name if the specific purpose of your corporation is very different from the other corporation's purpose. If you provide a specific purpose, you should also include a general purpose (for example, "to sell retail merchandise and for any lawful purpose").

Article 5: Most incorporators authorize one class of common shares with equal voting, dividend, and liquidation rights and no special restrictions. To do this, simply insert the number and type of shares you wish to authorize in the blanks. You may specify shares that are either with or without par value. To pay the lowest incorporation fee (see below) and to follow the modern trend of authorizing shares without par value, most incorporators authorize 50,000 shares without par value. If you want to do this, insert "50,000" in the aggregate number of shares blank, then insert "None" in the par value blank. If you wish to authorize par value shares instead, insert the par value amount per share in the par value blank.

If you want to authorize special classes of shares, you must fill in Section C of this article, providing the designation of each class of shares, the number of shares in each class, and the par value (or lack of par value) for each class. Also, you will need to specify the rights and restrictions associated with each class of shares in Article 6 or on a separate attachment page that you refer to in Article 6.

Article 6: You can state "None" if you do not wish to add additional provisions to the standard articles.

Article 7: You need just one incorporator, who must be at least 18 years old. The incorporator need not be a director, officer, or shareholder. The incorporator must sign and date the articles form at the bottom. You may include the incorporator's name and telephone number on the last line of the form as your contact person.

Registered Agent Consent to Serve Form: This form is included as the last page of the state-provided articles. Complete the information, including the agent's social security number in item 5. The agent must sign the form at the bottom.

Mail the original articles and a completed original Registered Agent Consent to Serve form together with a check for fees to the state filing office.

Filing Fee: $90 minimum ($30 for articles and $10 for filing Registered Agent Consent to Serve form, plus a minimum $50 license fee; see below), payable to the "Secretary of State."

The license fee is based on the authorized capital specified in your articles, computed as follows: (1) for shares without par value, multiply the number of no-par shares authorized by $1; (2) for shares with a stated par value, multiply the par value amount of each share by the number of par value shares authorized. The fee is $10 for each $10,000 of capital, or fraction thereof. You must pay a minimum license fee of $50, so you should authorize at least $50,000 of capital.

Examples:

If your articles authorize 50,000 shares without a par value, you pay the minimum incorporation fee of $90 (50,000 X $1 = $50,000 authorized capital for a minimum license fee of $50 plus the $30 filing fee plus the $10 registered agent consent form fee).

If your articles authorize 50,000 shares with a par value of $1, you pay the minimum incorporation fee of $90 (50,000 X $1 = $50,000 authorized capital for a minimum license fee of $50 plus the $30 filing fee plus the $10 registered agent consent form fee).

If your articles authorize 1,000,000 shares with a par value of 10 cents per share, you pay an incorporation fee of $140 (1,000,000 X $.10 par value per share = $100,000 authorized capital for a license fee of $100 ($100,000 divided by $10,000 = 10 x $10 = $100). Your total incorporation fee would be $140.

Director and Officer Rules

The board must consist of one or more directors. [10-19.1-33]

With respect to length of terms: Unless fixed terms are provided for in the articles or bylaws, a director serves for an indefinite term that expires at the next regular meeting of the shareholders. (1) A fixed term of a direc-

tor, other than an ex officio director, may not exceed five years. (2) An ex officio director serves as long as the director holds the office or position designated in the articles or bylaws. [10-19.1-35]

The officers of a corporation must be individuals who are 18 years of age or more and shall consist of a president, a secretary, and a treasurer and may also include one or more vice presidents and any other officers or agents as may be prescribed by the bylaws. Each of the officers must be elected by the board at a time and in a manner as may be provided in the bylaws unless the articles or bylaws provide that the shareholders may elect the officers. [10-19.1-52]

Any number of offices or functions of those offices may be held or exercised by the same individual. If a document must be signed by individuals holding different offices or functions and an individual holds or exercises more than one of those offices or functions, that individual may sign the document in more than one capacity, but only if the document indicates each capacity in which the individual signs. [10-19.1-55]

Share Issuance Rules

Subject to any restrictions in the articles: The consideration for the issuance of shares may be paid, in whole or in part, in money; in other property, tangible or intangible; or in labor or services actually performed for the corporation. When payment of the consideration for which shares are to be issued is received by the corporation, the shares are considered fully paid and nonassessable. Neither promissory notes nor future services constitute payment or part payment for shares of a corporation. [10-19.1-63]

The shares of a corporation must be represented by certificates signed by the president or a vice president, and by the secretary or an assistant secretary of the corporation.

Each certificate representing shares must state on its face: a. The name of the corporation. b. That the corporation is organized under the laws of this state. c. The name of the person to whom issued. d. The number and class of shares and the designation of the series, if any, the certificate represent. e. The par value of any share represented by the certificate or a statement the shares are without par value. [10-19.1-66]

Director Meeting Rules

Unless the articles or bylaws provide for a different time period, a director may call a board meeting by giving at least ten days' notice or, in the case of organizational meetings pursuant to Subsection 2 of Section 10-19.1-30, at least three days' notice, to all directors of the date, time, and place of the meeting. The notice need not state the purpose of the meeting unless the articles or bylaws require it.

If the date, time, and place of a board meeting have been provided in the articles or bylaws, or announced at a previous meeting of the board, no notice is required. Notice of an adjourned meeting need not be given other than by announcement at the meeting at which adjournment is taken. [10-19.1-43]

A majority, or a larger or smaller proportion or number provided in the articles or bylaws, of the directors currently holding office is a quorum for the transaction of business. In the absence of a quorum, a majority of the directors present may adjourn a meeting from time to time until a quorum is present. [10-19.1-45]

The board shall take action by the affirmative vote of the greater of a majority of the directors present at a duly held meeting at the time the action is taken, or a majority of the minimum proportion or number of directors that would constitute a quorum for the transaction of business at the meeting, except where the Business Corporation Act or the articles require the affirmative vote of a larger proportion or number. If the articles require a larger proportion or number than is required by the Business Corporation Act for a particular action, the articles control. [10-19.1-46]

Shareholder Meeting Rules

Regular meetings of shareholders may be held on an annual or other less-frequent periodic basis, but need not be held unless required by the articles or bylaws or by Subsection 2 [next paragraph].

If a regular meeting of shareholders has not been held during the earlier of six months after the fiscal year end of the corporation or 15 months after its last meeting: a. A shareholder or shareholders holding 5% or more of the voting power of all shares entitled to vote may demand a regular meeting of shareholders by written notice of demand given to the president or secretary of the corporation. b. Within 30 days after receipt of the demand by one of those officers, the board shall cause a regular meeting of shareholders to be called and held at the expense of the corporation on notice no later than 90 days after receipt of the demand. c. If the board fails to cause a regular meeting to be called as required by this subsection, the shareholders making the demand may call the meeting by giving notice as required by Section 10-19.1-73 [below].

At each regular meeting of shareholders: a. There must be an election of qualified successors for directors who serve for an indefinite term or whose terms have expired or are due to expire within six months after the date of the meeting. b. No other particular business is required to be transacted. c. Any business appropriate for action by the shareholders may be transacted. [10-19.1-71]

Special meetings of the shareholders may be called for any purpose or purposes at any time, by: a. The president; b. Two or more directors; c. A person authorized in the articles or bylaws to call special meetings; or d. A shareholder or shareholders holding 10% or more of the voting power of all shares entitled to vote, except that a special meeting for the purpose of considering any action to directly or indirectly facilitate or effect a business combination, including any action to change or otherwise affect the composition of the board of directors for that purpose, must be called by 25% or more of the voting power of all shares entitled to vote.

A shareholder or shareholders holding the voting power specified in Subdivision d of Subsection 1 [above] may demand a special meeting of shareholders by written notice of demand given to the president or secretary of the corporation and containing the purposes of the meeting. a. Within 30 days after receipt by one of those officers of the demand, the board shall cause a special meeting of shareholders to be called and held on notice no later than 90 days after receipt of the demand. b. If the board fails to cause a special meeting to be called as required by this subsection, the shareholder or shareholders making the demand may call the special meeting by giving notice as required by Section 10-19.1-73 [below]. c. All necessary expenses of the notice and the meeting shall be paid by the corporation.

The business transacted at a special meeting is limited to the purposes stated in the notice of the meeting. Any business transacted at a special meeting that is not included in those stated purposes is voidable by or on behalf of the corporation, unless all of the shareholders have waived notice of the meeting in accordance with Subsection 4 of Section 10-19.1-73 [allows shareholders to sign a written waiver of notice for a shareholder's meeting]. [10-19.1-72]

Except as otherwise provided in the Business Corporation Act, notice of all meetings of shareholders must be given to every holder of shares entitled to vote unless: a. The meeting is an adjourned meeting to be held not more than 120 days after the date fixed for the original meeting and the date, time, and place of the meeting were announced at the time of the original meeting or any adjournment of the original meeting; [other subsections omitted].

The notice: a. In all instances where a specific minimum notice period has not otherwise been fixed by law, must be given at least ten days before the date of the meeting, or a shorter time provided in the articles or bylaws, and not more than 50 days before the date of the meeting; b. Must contain the date, time, and place of the meeting; c. Must contain the information with respect to dissenters' rights required by Subsection 2 of Section 10-19.1-88, if applicable; d. Must inform shareholders if proxies are permitted at the meeting and, if so, state the procedure for appointing proxies; e. Must contain a statement of the purpose of the meeting, in the case of a special meeting. [10-19.1-73]

Unless otherwise provided in the articles or bylaws, a quorum for a meeting of shareholders is the holders of a majority of the voting power of the shares entitled to vote at the meeting. [10-19.1-76]

Unless the Business Corporation Act or the articles require a greater vote or voting by class, the shareholders shall take action by the affirmative vote of the holders of the greater of: a. A majority of the voting power of the shares present and entitled to vote on that item of business; or b. A majority of the voting power of the minimum number of shares entitled to vote that would constitute a quorum for the transaction of business at the meeting. If the articles require a larger proportion or number than is required by the Business Corporation Act for a particular action, the articles control. [10-19.1-74]

Each shareholder entitled to vote for directors has the right to cumulate those votes in all elections of directors by giving written notice of intent to cumulate those votes to any officer of the corporation before the meeting, or to the presiding officer at the meeting at which the election is to occur at any time before the election of directors at the meeting, in which case: 1. The presiding officer at the meeting shall announce, before the election of directors, that shareholders may cumulate their votes; and 2. Each shareholder shall cumulate those votes either by casting for one candidate the number of votes equal to the number of directors to be elected multiplied by the number of votes represented by the shares entitled to vote, or by distributing all of those votes on the same principle among any number of candidates. [10-19.1-39]

Financial Disclosure Rules

A corporation shall, on the written request of a shareholder, prepare annual financial statements within 180 days after the close of the corporation's fiscal year including at least a balance sheet as of the end of the fiscal year and a statement of income for the fiscal year, prepared on the basis of accounting methods reasonable in the circumstances. The financial statements may be consolidated statements of the corporation and one or more of its subsidiaries.

If the statements are audited by a public accountant, each copy must be accompanied by a report setting forth the opinion of the accountant on the statements. If these statements are not audited by a public accountant, each copy must be accompanied by a statement of the treasurer or other person in charge of the corporation's financial records: (1) stating the reasonable belief of the person that the financial statements were prepared in accordance with accounting methods reasonable in the circumstances; (2) describing the basis of presentation; and (3) describing any respects in which the financial statements were not prepared on a basis consistent with those prepared for the previous year.

On written request by a shareholder, a corporation shall furnish its most recent annual financial statements as required under Subsection 1 no later than ten business days after receipt of a shareholder's written request. "Furnish" for purposes of this Subsection means that the corporation shall deliver or mail, postage prepaid, the financial statements to the address specified by the requesting shareholder. [10-19.1-85]

State Tax Information

Office of State Tax Commission, Bismarck
701-328-2046
www.state.nd.us/taxdpt

North Dakota corporations are subject to a corporate income tax. A deduction for federal income taxes is allowed before calculating North Dakota corporate income taxes.

Corporation Law Online

The North Dakota Business Corporation Act is contained in Title 10 of the North Dakota Century Code, Chapters 19.1 through 23, starting with section 10-19.1-01. You can browse it from the Web page listed below (scroll down the page, select 10-Corporations, then scroll down and select Chapter 10-19.1). Most of the sections relevant to the formation and operation of business corporations are contained in Chapter 19.1.

www.state.nd.us/lr/information/statutes/cent-code.html

State Securities Information

Office of the Securities Commissioner
State Capitol, 5th Floor
600 East Boulevard Avenue
Bismarck, ND 58505-0510
701-328-2910 (Toll Free: 800-297-5124)
www.state.nd.us/securities

The North Dakota Securities Act is contained in Title 10, Chapter 04, of the North Dakota Century Code. You can browse the Act from the "Rules & Regs" link provided on the Securities Commissioner website. In addition to the Act itself, the Securities Commissioner website offers a good deal of information about the Act and exemptions from registration under the Act. You can take advantage of many exemptions without filing a notice. However, there are other exemptions that do require you to file an application and go through an approval process before the offer or sale of the security. The simplest exemption is the Incorporation Stage exemption under Section 10-04-06(17) of the Securities Act. This exemption allows you to issue common stock for the purpose of organizing a corporation (or other entity) provided certain conditions are met, including the following: (1) the number of purchasers or subscribers is limited to ten; (2) the offer or sale of the security is for the sole purpose of organization in North Dakota; (3) the stock may not be resold to others for a period of 12 months; (4) no advertising can be published or circulated; and (5) all sales are completed within ten days after the date of organization (the date of filing articles). You are not required to file a notice or pay a fee to use this exemption. See the Securities Commissioner website and read the Securities Act for additional information on this and other available exemptions.

Creating Your Own Articles Form

You can prepare and file your own articles form.

OHIO

Corporate Filing Office

Ohio Secretary of State
Business Services Division
P.O. Box 670
Columbus, OH 43216
Toll Free: 1-877-SOS-FILE (1-877-767-3453)
www.sos.state.oh.us/sos/busiserv/index.html

State Corporate Forms

Ohio provides fill-in-the-blanks Articles of Incorporation, along with an Original Appointment of Statutory Agent, which must be filed with the articles.

Internet Forms: You can download Initial Articles of Incorporation (Form 532), which includes the Appointment of Agent form, plus instructions for completing the articles and other statutory forms from the state filing office website. The articles also are available in Microsoft Excel 97 format. The Excel form is a fill-in-the-blanks form, which you can complete and print in Microsoft Excel.

Articles Instructions

Top of Form: Check box 1 ("Articles of Incorporation—Profit").

First Article: The name of an Ohio corporation must end with or include the word or abbreviation "company," "co.," "corporation," "corp.," "incorporated," or "inc."

You can check corporate name availability online by comparing your proposed name to those already listed in the corporate filing office name database. You can also check name availability by calling the state filing office or emailing your name availability request to busserv@sos.state.oh.us.

It costs $50 to reserve an available corporate name for 180 days.

Second Article: Location: Make sure the city (or village or township) and county of your corporation's principal office location in Ohio appear in the appropriate blanks.

Effective Date: This is an optional item. Any delayed date must fall after the articles are filed and no more than 90 days after the date of filing.

Optional Provisions. Check this box if you add additional provisions to your articles (on an attachment page).

Third Article: This is an optional article for regular profit corporations, which you can leave blank. If this article is blank, your corporation can engage in any lawful business activity for which a corporation can be formed under the Ohio General Corporation Law (which is what most incorporators will want).

Fourth Article: Most incorporators wish to authorize one class of common shares with equal voting, dividend, and liquidation rights and no special restrictions. To pay the minimum filing fee, most incorporators authorize 1,500 shares (see the filing fee information, below). Also, the modern trend is to authorize shares without a stated par value. For example, to authorize 1,500 no-par common shares, insert "1,500" in the number of shares blank, then state "common" in the type of shares blank, and "no par value" in the par value blank. If you wish, you can specify a par value in the blank—for example, "1,500 shares, common, par value $1.00 each."

If you want to authorize special classes of shares, you must indicate the designation of each class and the number of authorized shares in each class in the blank. Also, you must attach a statement to your articles that specifies the rights and restrictions associated with each class of shares. Refer to any attachment page in this article.

Fifth Article: Initial Directors: You don't have to fill in the names and addresses of your directors and can leave this article blank. If you include this information, note that your Ohio corporation must have three directors, unless it has fewer than three shareholders (a corporation with two shareholders can have only two directors, and a corporation with one shareholder can have only one director).

Authorized Representative: You need only one authorized representative, who will be your incorporator. Typically, an initial director is named as the incorporator, but anyone may serve in this capacity. The incorporator should sign in the authorized representative box just above the incorporator's printed name.

Appointment of Statutory Agent: The incorporator must prepare and sign an Original Appointment of Statutory Agent form, which must be included with your articles when you file. This form is included with the state-provided articles available online at the state corporate filing office. Typically, an initial director or shareholder is named as initial registered agent (the person authorized to receive legal documents on behalf of the corporation), and the street address of the corporation is given as the registered agent's business address (which also constitutes the registered office of the corporation). The registered agent must be an Ohio resident, and the registered agent's business address must be in Ohio. The incorporator (who signed the articles as the authorized representative) must also sign the Appointment form as the authorized representative (in the first authorized representative box on the Appointment form), and the agent must sign on the signature line at the very bottom of the Appointment form.

You need to file original articles only. The standard wait time for filing articles is 8 to 10 weeks. If you wish to have your articles processed more quickly, check the "Yes" box at the top of the first page under the words "Expedite this form." Include an additional $100 with your check, and mail the articles to the special P.O. Box address shown in the "Yes" box. Also, write the word "EXPEDITE" on the mailing envelope. If you do not want expedited service, mail your articles to the standard state corporate filing office mailing address (P.O. Box 670).

Filing Fee: Make your fee check payable to the "Secretary of State." The minimum filing fee is $125, which allows you to authorize up to 1,500 shares. If you authorize more than 1,500 shares, the following fee schedule applies (the state filing office provides a share calculator online to help you compute the filing fee):

Number of shares	Fee amount per share
1 to 1,000	10 cents
1,001 to 10,000	5 cents
10,001 to 50,000	2 cents
50,001 to 100,000	1 cent
100,001 to 500,000	1/2 cent
More than 500,000	1/4 cent

Examples:

If your articles authorize 1,500 shares or less, you pay the minimum $125 fee.

If your articles authorize 5,000 shares, you pay a $300 fee (1,000 x .10 = $100 for the first 1,000 shares, plus 4,000 x .05 = $200 for the next 4,000 shares).

Director and Officer Rules

Note: If an initial stated capital is set forth in its articles [the standard articles do not specify the initial stated capital of the corporation] and a corporation commences business before there has been paid in the amount of that initial stated capital, no corporate transaction shall be invalidated thereby, but incorporators participating in such transaction before the election of directors, and directors participating therein, shall be jointly and severally liable for the debts of the corporation up to an amount not exceeding in the aggregate the amount by which the stated capital paid in at the time the corporation commenced business fails to equal the initial stated capital set forth in the articles, until the amount set forth in the articles has been paid in. [1701.12]

Except as provided in division (B) of this section and section 1701.911 of the Revised Code, the number of directors as fixed by the articles or the regulations shall be not less than three or, if not so fixed, shall be three, provided that where all shares of a corporation are owned of record by one or two shareholders, the number of directors may be less than three but not less than the number of shareholders. [1701.56]

Unless the articles or the regulations provide for a different term (which may not exceed three years from the date of his election and until his successor is elected), each director shall hold office until the next annual meeting of the shareholders and until his successor is elected, or until his earlier resignation, removal from office, or death. [1701.57]

The officers of a corporation shall consist of a president, a secretary, a treasurer, and, if desired, a chairman of the board, one or more vice presidents, and such other officers and assistant officers as may be deemed necessary. The officers shall be elected by the directors. The chairman of the board shall be a director. Unless the articles or the regulations otherwise provide, none of the other officers need be a director. Any two or more offices may be held by the same person, but no officer shall execute, acknowledge, or verify any instrument in more than one capacity if such instrument is required by law or by the articles, the regulations, or the bylaws to be executed, acknowledged, or verified by two or more officers. Unless the articles or the regulations otherwise provide, all officers shall be elected annually. [1701.64]

Share Issuance Rules

Payment for shares shall be made with money or other property of any description, or any interest in property, actually transferred to the corporation, or labor or services actually rendered to the corporation.

In the case of shares with par value, other than treasury shares, the consideration shall be not less than the par value of the shares, provided that the shares may be sold and paid for at such a discount from the par value of the shares that would amount to or not exceed reasonable compensation for the sale, underwriting, or purchase of the shares, and, regardless of the discount, the shares shall be deemed to be fully paid.

Promissory notes, drafts, or other obligations of a subscriber or purchaser do not constitute payment for shares.

An agreement by a person to perform services as the consideration for shares does not, of itself, constitute the person a shareholder and does not, of itself, constitute payment for such shares prior to the performance of the services.

Except in the case of convertible shares or obligations, shares with par value shall not be issued or disposed of on change of shares, share dividends or distributions, reorganization, merger, consolidation, exchange of shares for other shares or securities, or otherwise, if as a result the aggregate liabilities of the corporation plus its stated capital would exceed its aggregate assets or any existing excess would be increased. [1701.18]

Every corporation shall have and shall carry on its books a stated capital for each class of outstanding shares with par value and for each class of outstanding shares having preference in the event of the involuntary liquidation of the corporation. Every corporation may have and, if it does have, shall carry on its books a stated capital for any other class of outstanding shares. The stated capital of each outstanding share with par value shall be not less than its par value. The stated capital of the corporation shall be the aggregate stated capital of all classes of outstanding shares. If a particular class has stated capital, the stated capital of every share of that class outstanding at a particular time shall be identical.

Subject to division (A) of this section [above]: (1) the stated capital of shares with stated capital that are issued or disposed of otherwise than on conversion, change, exchange, merger, consolidation, or reorganization is the amount of consideration for such shares, unless prior to the execution and delivery of the certificates for such shares, the incorporators, directors, or shareholders, as the case may be, who fix the consideration or otherwise determine the value of any consideration for such shares, specify, in a manner not inconsistent with this section, the portion of the consideration that constitutes stated capital, whereon any excess over such portion (except to the extent entered on the books of a transferee corporation as earned surplus in the manner provided in division (H)(3) of section 1701.32 of the Revised Code on a combination) is capital surplus; except that in the case of shares having preference in the event of involuntary liquidation of the corporation, the portion of the consideration that constitutes stated capital shall be not less than the lesser of the entire consideration for such shares or the amount of such preference. [1701.30]

Each holder of shares is entitled to one or more certificates, signed by the chairperson of the board or the president or a vice president; and by the secretary, an assistant secretary, the treasurer, or an assistant treasurer of the corporation; which shall certify the number and class of shares held by the holder in the corporation, but no certificate for shares shall be executed or delivered until such shares are fully paid. [1701.24]

Each certificate for shares of a corporation shall state: (1) that the corporation is organized under the laws of this state; (2) the name of the person to whom the shares represented by the certificate are issued; (3) the number of shares represented by the certificate; (4) if the shares of the corporation are classified, the designation of the class, and the series, if any, of the shares represented by the certificate. [1701.25]

Director Meeting Rules

Unless otherwise provided in the articles, the regulations, or the bylaws, and subject to the exceptions, applicable during an emergency as that term is defined in Section 1701.01 of the Revised Code, for which provision is made in Division (F) of Section 1701.11 of the Revised Code: (A) meetings of the directors may be called by the chairman of the board, the president, any vice president, or any two directors; [other subsections omitted].

Written notice of the time and place of each meeting of the directors shall be given to each director either by personal delivery or by mail, telegram, or cablegram at least two days before the meeting, which notice need not specify the purposes of the meeting. [1701.61]

Unless the articles or the regulations otherwise provide, and subject to the exceptions, applicable during an emergency, as that term is defined in Section 1701.01 of the Revised Code, for which provision is made in division (F) of Section 1701.11 of the Revised Code, a majority of the whole authorized number of directors is necessary to constitute a quorum for a meeting of the directors, except that a majority of the directors in office constitutes a quorum for filling a vacancy in the board. The act of a majority of the directors present at a meeting at which a quorum is present is the act of the board, unless the act of a greater number is required by the articles, the regulations, or the bylaws. [1701.62]

Shareholder Meeting Rules

An annual meeting of shareholders for the election of directors and the consideration of reports to be laid before such meeting shall be held on a date designated by, or in the manner provided for in, the articles or in the regulations. In the absence of such designation, the annual meeting shall be held on the first Monday of the fourth month following the close of each fiscal year of the corporation. When the annual meeting is not held or directors are not elected thereat, they may be elected at a special meeting called for that purpose. [1701.39]

Meetings of shareholders may be called by any of the following: (1) the chairman of the board, the president, or, in case of the president's absence, death, or disability, the vice president authorized to exercise the authority of the president; (2) the directors by action at a meeting, or a majority of the directors acting without a meeting; (3) persons who hold 25% of all shares outstanding and entitled to vote thereat, unless the articles or the regulations specify for such purpose a smaller or larger proportion, but not in excess of 50%; (4) such other officers or persons as the articles or the regulations authorize to call such meetings. [1701.40]

Written notice stating the time, place, and purposes of a meeting of the shareholders shall be given either by personal delivery or by mail not less than seven nor more than 60 days before the date of the meeting unless the articles or the regulations specify a longer period: (1) to each shareholder of record entitled to notice of the meeting; (2) by or at the direction of the president or the secretary or any other person required or permitted by the regulations to give such notice. If mailed, such notice shall be addressed to the shareholder at his address as it appears on the records of the corporation. Notice of adjournment of a meeting need not be given if the time and place to which it is adjourned are fixed and announced at such meeting.

On request in writing delivered either in person or by registered mail to the president or the secretary by any persons entitled to call a meeting of shareholders, such officer shall forthwith cause to be given to the shareholders entitled thereto notice of a meeting to be held on a date not less than seven nor more than 60 days after the receipt of such request, as such officer may fix, unless the articles or the regulations specify a longer period for such purpose. If such notice is not given within 15 days after the delivery or mailing of such request, or such shorter or longer period as the articles or the regulations specify for such purpose, the persons calling the meeting may fix the time of meeting and give notice thereon as provided in Division (A) of this section [previous paragraph], or cause such notice to be given by any designated representative. [1701.41]

Except to the extent that the voting rights of the shares of any class are increased, limited, or denied by the express terms of such shares, and except as provided in scrip issued in lieu of a certificate for a fraction of a share, each outstanding share regardless of class shall entitle the holder thereof to one vote on each matter properly submitted to the shareholders for their vote, consent, waiver, release, or other action, subject to the provisions with respect to cumulative voting in Section 1701.55 of the Revised Code. [1701.44]

Unless the articles or the regulations otherwise provide: (A) The shareholders present in person or by proxy at any meeting of shareholders shall constitute a quorum for such meeting, but no action required by law, the articles, or the regulations to be authorized or taken by the holders of a designated proportion of the shares of any particular class or of each class, may be authorized or taken

by a lesser proportion; [other subsections omitted]. [1701.51]

Notwithstanding any provision in Sections 1701.01 to 1701.98, inclusive, of the Revised Code requiring for any purpose the vote, consent, waiver, or release of the holders of a designated proportion (but less than all) of the shares of any particular class or of each class, the Articles may provide that for such purpose the vote, consent, waiver, or release of the holders of a greater or lesser proportion of the shares of such particular class or of each class shall be required, but unless otherwise expressly permitted by such sections such proportion shall be not less than a majority. [1701.52]

At a meeting of shareholders at which directors are to be elected, only persons nominated as candidates shall be eligible for election as directors.

At all elections of directors, the candidates receiving the greatest number of votes shall be elected.

Unless the articles are amended as permitted by Division (B)(10) of Section 1701.69 of the Revised Code to provide that no shareholder of a corporation may cumulate his voting power, each shareholder has the right to vote cumulatively if notice in writing is given by any shareholder to the president, a vice president, or the secretary of a corporation, not less than 48 hours before the time fixed for holding a meeting of the shareholders for the purpose of electing directors if notice of the meeting has been given at least ten days before the meeting, and, if the ten days' notice has not been given, not less than 24 hours before such meeting time, that he desires that the voting at such election shall be cumulative, provided that an announcement of the giving of such notice is made on the convening of the meeting by the chairman or secretary or by or on behalf of the shareholder giving such notice.

Unless the articles are amended as permitted by Division (B)(10) of Section 1701.69 of the Revised Code to provide that no shareholder of a corporation may cumulate his voting power, each shareholder has the right, subject to the notice requirements contained in Division (C) of this section [previous paragraph], to cumulate the voting power he possesses and to give one candidate as many votes as the number of directors to be elected multiplied by the number of his votes equals, or to distribute his votes on the same principle among two or more candidates, as he sees fit. [1701.55]

Financial Disclosure Rules

At the annual meeting of shareholders, or the meeting held in lieu of it, every corporation, except a banking corporation, shall lay before the shareholders financial statements, which may be consolidated, consisting of: (1)

a balance sheet containing a summary of the assets, liabilities, stated capital, if any, and surplus (showing separately any capital surplus arising from unrealized appreciation of assets, other capital surplus, and earned surplus) as of the end of the corporation's most recent fiscal year, except that, if consolidated financial statements are laid before the shareholders, the consolidated balance sheet shall show separately or disclose by a note the amount of consolidated surplus that does not constitute under the Revised Code earned surplus of the corporation or any of its subsidiaries and that is not classified as stated capital or capital surplus on the consolidated balance sheet; (2) a statement of profit and loss and surplus, including a summary of profits, dividends or distributions paid, and other changes in the surplus accounts, for the period commencing with the date marking the end of the period for which the last preceding statement of profit and loss required under this section was made and ending with the date of the balance sheet or, in the case of the first statement of profit and loss, for the period commencing with the date of incorporation of the corporation and ending with the date of the balance sheet.

The financial statements shall have appended to them an opinion signed by the president or a vice president or the treasurer or an assistant treasurer of the corporation or by a public accountant or firm of public accountants to the effect that the financial statement presents fairly the financial position of the corporation and the results of its operations in conformity with generally accepted accounting principles applied on a basis consistent with that of the preceding period, or to the effect that the financial statements have been prepared on the basis of accounting practices and principles that are reasonable in the circumstances.

On the written request of any shareholder made prior to the date of the meeting described in Division (A) of this section [first paragraph under this heading], the corporation shall mail a copy of the financial statements laid or to be laid before the shareholders at the meeting to the shareholder on or before the later of the following: (1) the fifth day after the receipt of the written request; (2) the earlier of the following: (a) the fifth day before the date of the meeting; (b) the fifth day after the expiration of four months from the date of the balance sheet described in Division (A)(1) of this section [first paragraph under this heading]. [1701.38]

State Tax Information

Department of Taxation, Columbus
888-405-4039
www.state.oh.us/tax

Ohio corporations are subject to a franchise tax based on the value of their outstanding shares of stock. This value is determined by corporate net income or corporate net worth.

Corporation Law Online

The Ohio General Corporation Law is contained in Title 17 (Corporations-Partnerships), Chapter 1701, of the Ohio Revised Code, starting with Section 1701.1. To find the Law, visit the legal research area of Nolo's website at www.nolo.com/statute/state/cfm. Click on "Ohio." From there, click on "Title 17" on the left side of the page, then on "Chapter 1701." From there, you can select the section of the Act that you wish to browse.

State Securities Information

Ohio Division of Securities
77 South High Street, 22nd Floor
Columbus, OH 43215
614-466-3440
www.securities.state.oh.us

The Ohio Securities Act is contained in Title 17 (Corporations-Partnerships), Chapter 1707, of the Ohio Revised Code. You can browse the Act and associated rules from links on the Division of Securities website. (Click "Laws, Rules & Guidelines" at the bottom of the home page). The Division of Securities website has valuable information on exemptions available under the Ohio Securities Act. For example, one FAQ states: "Most frequently, newly formed corporations intend on having fewer than 10 shareholders for the first year. If there is no advertising or general solicitation to obtain those shareholders, and they are purchasing for investment and not a subsequent distribution, you may have an exemption under Section 1707.03(O) of the Revised Code. Additionally, if there is a broker or dealer involved in the sale, commissions and other remuneration may not exceed 10 percent. The broker/dealer and any salesperson receiving commissions must be licensed in Ohio." This exemption is "self-executing," meaning that no filing is required. For more information on the exemption discussed here and other available exemptions, see the Division website and browse the Act and Securities Rules from the links provided on the site. Call the Division for further information.

Creating Your Own Articles Form

You can create your own articles form. Your form must be printed or typed on 8-1/2" x 11" paper, and each article must be numbered. You must submit a typed Appointment of Statutory Agent form with your articles.

OKLAHOMA

Corporate Filing Office

Oklahoma Secretary of State
Business Filing Department
2300 N. Lincoln Boulevard, Room 101
Oklahoma City, OK 73105-4897
405-521-3912
www.sos.state.ok.us/business/business_filing.htm

State Corporate Forms

Oklahoma provides a fill-in-the-blanks Certificate of Incorporation with instructions.

Internet Forms: You can download a Certificate of Incorporation, separate instructions for completing the certificate, and other statutory forms from the state filing office website. Oklahoma is also implementing an online service called "SoonerAccess," which will allow users to prepare and file the certificate online. To find out whether this new service is up and running, visit the state filing office website.

Note: The state corporate filing office no longer allows walk-in, while-you-wait service. You must file your certificate by mail or online (once the online SoonerAccess filing service is enabled).

Articles Instructions

Article 1: The name of an Oklahoma corporation must contain the word "association," "company," "corporation," "club," "foundation," "fund," "incorporated," "institute," "society," "union," "syndicate," or "limited," or the abbreviations "co.," "corp.," "inc.," or "ltd."

Call the state filing office to check name availability, or use the online name availability search service on the state corporate filing office website. It costs $10 to reserve an available corporate name for 60 days.

Article 2: Typically, an initial director or shareholder is named as initial registered agent (the person authorized to receive legal documents on behalf of the corporation). Most incorporators use the street address of the corporation as the registered office address (which must be the same as the business address of the registered agent). The registered agent must be an Oklahoma resident, and the registered office must be in Oklahoma.

Make sure the name of the county is the LAST item in the street address information for the registered office.

Article 3: State "perpetual" to give your corporation an unlimited legal life. Or you can limit your corporation's life by inserting a date on which it will automatically dissolve (few incorporators will wish to do this).

Article 4: You may simply state "to engage in any lawful act or activity for which corporations may be organized under the General Corporation Law of Oklahoma."

Article 5: Most incorporators authorize one class of common shares with equal voting, dividend, and liquidation rights and no special restrictions. Although the modern trend is to authorize shares without a stated par value, the minimum filing fee of $50 allows you to authorize only one share of stock without par value, so most incorporators authorize par value shares. If you wish to pay the minimum $50 filing fee for your par value shares, the total par value of the shares—that is, the number of shares authorized multiplied by the par value of each share—should equal $50,000 or less. (See below for more filing fee information.)

To authorize common shares with a par value, insert the number of shares you wish to authorize in the "Common" blank, ignore the "Series" column, and insert the par value amount per share in the "Par Value per Share" blank. If you want to authorize special classes of shares, you must indicate the designation of each class, the number of authorized shares in each class, and their par value (or a statement that the shares are without par value). You can use the "Common" and "Preferred" rows to do this if you are authorizing just these two classes of shares. To authorize additional classes, you must retype the certificate and insert your own statement of the designations of each class or series of shares. In all cases, when authorizing special classes or series of shares, you must also state or summarize the rights and restrictions associated with each class of shares in this article or elsewhere in your certificate.

Article 6: This is an optional article where you can list the names and addresses of your initial directors (one or more) if you wish.

Article 7: You need just one incorporator, who is not required to be a director, officer, or shareholder. Have the incorporator date and sign the form on the lines provided at the bottom of the form.

Send one signed original plus one copy for filing (each copy should contain an original signature of the incorporator).

Filing Fee: $50 minimum fee (see below), payable to the "Oklahoma Secretary of State."

The filing fee is based on the authorized capital specified in your certificate, calculated as follows: (1) for shares without par value, multiply the number of authorized no-par shares by $50 (in other words, the minimum $50 filing fee allows you to authorize just one share without par value); (2) for shares with a stated par value, multiply the par value amount of each share by the number of par value shares authorized. The filing fee for par value shares is $1 for each $1,000 of capital or fraction thereof. The minimum $50 filing fee allows you to authorize $50,000 of capital (for example, 50,000 shares with a par value of $1 each or 500,000 shares with a par value of ten cents). Most incorporators authorize par value shares with a total par value of $50,000 in order to authorize an adequate number of shares for the minimum filing fee.

Preapproval of Your Certificate of Incorporation: If you form a business for the purpose of breeding, raising, farming, or ranching, the certificate must be approved by the Oklahoma Agriculture Department prior to filing with the Oklahoma Secretary of State. (Go to the Department of Agriculture website at www.state.ok.us/~okag/main/main.html for more information.) If the corporation will engage in the practice of a licensed profession (lawyers, doctors, architects, engineers, land surveyors, and the like), the certificate must be preapproved by the state regulatory agency that oversees the profession.

Director and Officer Rules

The board of directors of a corporation shall consist of one or more members. The number of directors shall be fixed by or in the manner provided for in the bylaws, unless the Certificate of Incorporation fixes the number of directors, in which case a change in the number of directors shall be made only by amendment of the certificate. Directors need not be shareholders unless so required by the Certificate of Incorporation or the bylaws. The Certificate of Incorporation or bylaws may prescribe other qualifications for directors. Each director shall hold office until a successor is elected and qualified or until his or her earlier resignation or removal. [1027]

Every corporation organized in accordance with the provisions of the Oklahoma General Corporation Act shall have such officers with such titles and duties as shall be stated in the bylaws or in a resolution of the board of directors which is not inconsistent with the bylaws and as may be necessary to enable it to sign instruments and stock certificates which comply with the provisions of paragraph 2 of subsection A of Section 7 and Section 39 of this act. One of the officers shall have the duty to record the proceedings of the meetings of the shareholders and directors in a book to be kept for that purpose. Any number of offices may be held by the same person unless the Certificate of Incorporation or bylaws provide otherwise. [1028]

Share Issuance Rules

Every corporation may issue one or more classes of stock or one or more series of stock within any class thereof, any or all of which classes may be of stock with par value or stock without par value and which classes or series may have voting powers, full or limited, or no voting powers; and designations, preferences, and relative, participating, optional, or other special rights, and qualifications, limitations, or restrictions thereof; as shall be stated and expressed in the Certificate of Incorporation or of any amendment thereto, or in the resolution or resolutions providing for the issue of the stock adopted by the board of directors pursuant to authority expressly vested in it by the provisions of its Certificate of Incorporation. [1032]

The consideration, as determined pursuant to the provisions of subsections A and B of Section 34 of this act [Section 1034], for subscriptions to, or the purchase of, the capital stock to be issued by a corporation shall be paid in such form and in such manner as the board of directors shall determine. In the absence of actual fraud in the transaction, the judgment of the directors as to the value of such consideration shall be conclusive. The capital stock so issued shall be deemed to be fully paid and nonassessable stock, if: 1. the entire amount of such consideration has been received by the corporation in the form of cash, services rendered, personal property, real property, leases of real property, or a combination thereof; or 2. not less than the amount of the consideration determined to be capital pursuant to the provisions of Section 35 of this act [Section 1035] has been received by the corporation in such form and the corporation has received a binding obligation of the subscriber or purchaser to pay the balance of the subscription or purchase price. [1033]

Shares of stock with par value may be issued for such consideration, having a value not less than the par value thereof, as is determined from time to time by the board of directors, or by the shareholders if the Certificate of Incorporation so provides.

Shares of stock without par value may be issued for such consideration as is determined from time to time by the board of directors, or by the shareholders if the Certificate of Incorporation so provides. [1034]

Any corporation, by resolution of its board of directors, may determine that only a part of the consideration which shall be received by the corporation for any of the shares of its capital stock which it shall issue from time to time shall be capital; but, in case any of the shares issued shall be shares having a par value, the amount of the part of such consideration so determined to be capital shall be in excess of the aggregate par value of the shares issued for such consideration having a par value, unless all the shares issued shall be shares having a par value, in which case the amount of the part of such consideration so determined to be capital need be only equal to the aggregate par value of such shares. In each such case the board of directors shall specify in dollars the part of such consideration which shall be capital. If the board of directors shall not have determined, at the time of issue of any shares of the capital stock of the corporation issued for cash or within sixty (60) days after the issue of any shares of the capital stock of the corporation issued for property other than cash, what part of the consideration for such shares shall be capital, the capital of the corporation in respect of such shares shall be an amount equal to the aggregate par value of such shares having a par value, plus the amount of the consideration for such shares without par value. The amount of the consideration so determined to be capital in respect of any shares without par value shall be the stated capital of such shares. The capital of the corporation may be increased from time to time by resolution of the board of directors directing that a portion of the net assets of the corporation in excess of the amount so determined to be capital be transferred to the capital account. The board of directors may direct that the portion of such net assets so transferred shall be treated as capital in respect of any shares of the corporation of any designated class or classes. The excess, if any, at any given time, of the net assets of the corporation over the amount so determined to be capital shall be surplus. "Net assets" means the amount by which total assets exceed total liabilities. Capital and surplus are not liabilities for this purpose. [1035]

Every holder of stock in a corporation shall be entitled to have a certificate signed by, or in the name of, the corporation by the chairman or vice chairman of the board of directors, or the president or vice president, and by the treasurer or an assistant treasurer or the secretary or an assistant secretary of such corporation certifying and representing the number of shares owned by him in such corporation. [1039]

Director Meeting Rules

A majority of the total number of directors shall constitute a quorum for the transaction of business unless the Certificate of Incorporation or the bylaws require a greater number. Except as provided in Subsection G of this section [applies to nonprofit corporations], neither the Certificate of Incorporation nor the bylaws may provide that a quorum may be less than one-third of the total number of directors. The vote of the majority of the directors present at a meeting at which a quorum is present shall be the act of the board of directors unless the Certificate of Incorporation or the bylaws shall require a vote of a greater number. [1027]

Shareholder Meeting Rules

Unless directors are elected by written consent in lieu of an annual meeting as permitted by this subsection, an annual meeting of shareholders shall be held for the election of directors on a date and at a time designated by or in the manner provided for in the bylaws. Shareholders may, unless the Certificate of Incorporation otherwise provides, act by written consent to elect directors; provided however, that if the consent is less than unanimous, the action by written consent may be in lieu of holding an annual meeting only if all of the directorships to which directors could be elected at an annual meeting held at the effective time of the action are vacant and are filled by the action.

Any other proper business may be transacted at the annual meeting. Special meetings of the shareholders may be called by the board of directors or by the person or persons as may be authorized by the Certificate of Incorporation or by the bylaws.

All elections of directors shall be by written ballot, unless otherwise provided for in the Certificate of Incorporation. [1056]

The Certificate of Incorporation of any corporation may provide that at all elections of directors of the corporation, or at elections held under specified circumstances, each holder of stock or of any class or classes or of a series or series thereof shall be entitled to as many votes as shall equal the number of votes which, except for such provision as to cumulative voting, he would be entitled to cast for the election of directors with respect to his shares of stock multiplied by the number of directors to be elected by him, and that he may cast all of such votes for a single director or may distribute them among the number to be voted for, or for any two or more of them as he may see fit. [1059]

Subject to the provisions of the Oklahoma General Corporation Act, in respect of the vote that shall be required for a specified action, the Certificate of Incorporation or bylaws of any corporation authorized to issue stock may specify the number of shares and/or the amount of other securities having voting power the holders of which shall be present or represented by proxy at any meeting in order to constitute a quorum for, and the votes that shall be necessary for, the transaction of any business, but in no event shall a quorum consist of less than one-third of the shares entitled to vote at the meeting, except that, where a separate vote by a class or series or classes or series is required, a quorum shall consist of no less than one-third of the shares of that class or series or classes or series. In the absence of such specification in the Certificate of Incorporation or bylaws of the corporation: (1) a majority of the shares entitled to vote, present in person or represented by proxy, shall constitute a quorum at a meeting of shareholders; (2) in all matters other than the election of directors, the affirmative vote of the majority of shares present in person or represented by proxy at the meeting and entitled to vote on the subject matter shall be the act of the shareholders; (3) directors shall be elected by a plurality of the votes of the shares present in person or represented by proxy at the meeting and entitled to vote on the election of directors; and (4) where a separate vote by a class or series or classes or series is required, a majority of the outstanding shares of such class series or classes or series, present in person or represented by proxy, shall constitute a quorum entitled to take action with respect to that vote on that matter and the affirmative vote of the majority of shares of such class or series or classes or series present in person or represented by proxy at the meeting shall be the act of such class or series or classes or series.

Whenever shareholders are required or permitted to take any action at a meeting, a written notice of the meeting shall be given which shall state the place, date, and hour of the meeting, and, in the case of a special meeting, the purpose or purposes for which the meeting is called.

Unless otherwise provided for in the Oklahoma General Corporation Act, the written notice of any meeting shall be given not less than ten nor more than 60 days before the date of the meeting to each shareholder entitled to vote at such meeting. If mailed, notice is given when deposited in the United States mail, postage prepaid, directed to the shareholder at his address as it appears on the records of the corporation. An affidavit of the secretary or an assistant secretary or of the transfer agent of the corporation that the notice has been given, in the absence of fraud, shall be prima facie evidence of the facts stated therein. [1067]

Financial Disclosure Rules

Any shareholder, in person or by attorney or other agent, on written demand under oath stating the purpose thereof, shall have the right during the usual hours for business to inspect for any proper purpose the corporation's stock ledger, a list of its shareholders, and its other books and records, and to make copies or extracts therefrom. A proper purpose shall mean a purpose reasonably related to such person's interest as a share-

holder. In every instance where an attorney or other agent shall be the person who seeks the right to inspection, the demand under oath shall be accompanied by a power of attorney or such other writing which authorizes the attorney or other agent to so act on behalf of the shareholder. The demand under oath shall be directed to the corporation at its registered office in the state of Oklahoma or at its principal place of business.

If the corporation or an officer or agent thereof refuses to permit an inspection sought by a shareholder or attorney or other agent acting for the shareholder pursuant to the provisions of Subsection B of this section [previous paragraph] or does not reply to the demand within five business days after the demand has been made, the shareholder may apply to the district court for an order to compel an inspection. The court may summarily order the corporation to permit the shareholder to inspect the corporation's stock ledger, an existing list of shareholders, and its other books and records, and to make copies or extracts therefrom; or the court may order the corporation to furnish to the shareholder a list of its shareholders as of a specific date on condition that the shareholder first pay to the corporation the reasonable cost of obtaining and furnishing the list and on other conditions as the court deems appropriate. [1065]

State Tax Information

Tax Commission, Oklahoma City
405-521-2035
www.oktax.state.ok.us

Oklahoma corporations are subject to a corporate income tax. Oklahoma corporations also pay an annual franchise tax, currently set at a rate of $1.25 for each $1,000 of capital invested or used in Oklahoma. Corporations can pay the franchise tax annually when they file their Oklahoma corporate income tax returns.

Corporation Law Online

The Oklahoma General Corporation Act is contained in Title 18 (Corporations) Oklahoma Statutes, Chapter 22, starting with section 1001. You can browse it from links provided on the Secretary of State homepage listed below. It includes provisions that apply to both profit and nonprofit corporations. First, click "Links to Statutes" in the left margin. Then click the "Expand" link for "Title 18, Corporations." Finally, scroll down the chapter index to Chapter 21 and click on section 1001, which marks the beginning of Chapter 22 and the Oklahoma GCA.

www.sos.state.ok.us/exec_legis/exec_leg_home.htm

State Securities Information

Oklahoma Department of Securities
Suite 860, First National Center
120 N. Robinson
Oklahoma City, OK 73102
405-280-7700
www.securities.state.ok.us

The Department of Securities website provides a link to the Oklahoma Securities Act (contained in Title 71 of the Oklahoma Statutes) and to the related Securities Rules. Section 401(b) of the Act contains various exemptions for securities transactions. For example, Section 401(b)(10)(a) contains an exemption for the sale of securities to not more than 25 purchasers during any period of 12 consecutive months. To qualify for this exemption: (1) you must reasonably believe that all purchasers, other than institutional investors or licensed broker-dealers, are purchasing for investment; (2) you must not provide any commission (directly or indirectly) in exchange for the solicitation or sale; and (3) you may not use public advertising or solicitation in connection with the solicitation or sale. For further information on the requirements for this and other exemptions available under the Securities Act and Rules, see the Department of Securities website and call the Department.

Creating Your Own Articles Form

You can prepare your own articles form.

OREGON

Corporate Filing Office

Oregon Secretary of State
Corporation Division
Business Registry Section
Public Service Building
255 Capitol Street NE
Salem, OR 97310-1327
503-986-2200
www.filinginoregon.com

State Corporate Forms

Oregon provides fill-in-the-blanks Articles of Incorporation with instructions.

Internet Forms: You can find a fill-in-the-blanks Articles with Incorporation form (Form 111) plus other statutory forms on the state filing office website. You can also browse and download the Oregon Business Guide and Checklist, which contain helpful information on forming an Oregon corporation.

Articles Instructions

Type or print your Articles with black ink.

Top of Form: Check the "Business Corporation" box. (If you are forming a professional service corporation to practice a licensed profession such as law, accounting, or medicine, check the second box instead. See the state filing office website for special instructions and rules that apply to forming a professional service corporation.)

Leave the Registry Number line blank; the state filing office will assign a number and insert it in this blank.

Article 1: The name of an Oregon corporation must contain the word "corporation," "incorporated," "company," or "limited," or an abbreviation of one or more of these words. A business corporation name cannot contain the word "cooperative."

To check name availability, call the state filing office or use the business name search service available on the state corporate filing office website. It costs $50 to reserve an available corporate name for 120 days.

Articles 2 and 3: Typically, an initial director or shareholder is named as initial registered agent (the person authorized to receive legal documents on behalf of the corporation). Most incorporators use the street address of the corporation as the registered office address (which must be the same as the business address of the registered agent). The registered agent must be an Oregon resident, and the registered office must be in Oregon.

Article 4: Insert the address where the state can mail notices to your corporation. Most incorporators use the street or mailing address (P.O. Box address) of the corporation.

Article 6: In Oregon, you do not need to state a par value for your shares. Your filing fee is not based on how many shares you authorize in your articles, so you can authorize as many shares as you wish. Most incorporators authorize one class of common shares with equal voting, dividend, and liquidation rights and no special restrictions. To do this, simply insert the total number of authorized shares in the designated blank. If you want to authorize special classes of shares, you must include an attachment page (indicated in Article 5) listing the designation of each class, the authorized number of shares in each class, and the rights and restrictions associated with each class.

Article 7: Ignore this article unless you are forming a professional corporation.

Article 8: You need just one incorporator, who must be at least 18 years of age. The incorporator need not be a director, officer, or shareholder.

Article 9: Print the incorporator's name (the person listed in Article 8) and have the incorporator sign on the line provided.

Article 10: Typically, the name of the incorporator listed in Article 8 is included as the contact name, along with the incorporator's daytime phone number.

Mail the signed original with a check for fees to the state filing office.

Note: You can file your articles by fax (see the fax filing instructions on the state corporate filing office website). You can pay for fax and regular mail filings by credit card. If you use this method, make sure to include your credit card information on a separate page attached to your articles (the state provides an online credit card filing sheet that you can use for this purpose).

Filing Fee: $50, payable to the "Corporation Division."

Director and Officer Rules

A board of directors must consist of one or more individuals, with the number specified in or fixed in accordance with the Articles of Incorporation or bylaws. Directors are elected at the first annual shareholders' meeting and at each annual meeting thereafter unless their terms are staggered under ORS 60.317. [60.307]

The terms of the initial directors of a corporation expire at the first shareholders' meeting at which directors are elected.

The terms of all other directors expire at the next annual shareholders' meeting following their election unless their terms are staggered under ORS 60.317. [60.314]

A corporation has the officers described in its bylaws or appointed by the board of directors in accordance with the bylaws which shall include a president and a secretary.

The secretary shall have the responsibility for preparing minutes of the directors' and shareholders' meetings and for authenticating records of the corporation.

The same individual may simultaneously hold more than one office in a corporation. [60.371]

Share Issuance Rules

The board of directors may authorize shares to be issued for consideration consisting of any tangible or intangible property or benefit to the corporation, including cash, promissory notes, services performed, contracts for services to be performed, or other securities of the corporation.

The corporation may place in escrow shares issued for a contract for future services or benefits or a promissory note or make other arrangements to restrict the transfer of shares, and may credit distributions in respect of the shares against their purchase price, until the services are performed, the note is paid, or the benefits received. If the services are not performed, the note is not paid, or the benefits are not received, the shares placed in escrow or restricted and the distributions credited may be canceled in whole or in part. [60.147]

At a minimum, each share certificate shall state on its face: (a) the name of the issuing corporation and that it is organized under the law of this state; (b) the name of the person to whom the share is issued; (c) the number and class of shares and the designation of the series, if any, the certificate represents.

Each share certificate must be signed, either manually or in facsimile, by two officers designated in the bylaws or by the board of directors. [60.161]

Director Meeting Rules

The board of directors may hold regular or special meetings in or out of the state of Oregon. [60.337]

Unless the Articles of Incorporation or bylaws provide otherwise, regular meetings of the board of directors may be held without notice of the date, time, place, or purpose of the meeting.

Unless the Articles of Incorporation or bylaws provide for a longer or shorter period, special meetings of the board of directors must be preceded by at least two days' notice of the date, time, and place of the meeting. The notice need not describe the purpose of the special meeting unless required by the Articles of Incorporation or bylaws. [60.344]

Unless the Articles of Incorporation or bylaws require a greater number or a lesser number as authorized under Subsection (2) of this section [quoted, in part, in the next paragraph], a quorum of a board of directors consists of: (a) if the corporation has a fixed board size, a majority of the fixed number of directors; or (b) if the corporation has a variable-range size board, a majority of the number of directors prescribed, or, if no number is prescribed, a majority of the number in office immediately before the meeting begins.

The Articles of Incorporation or bylaws may authorize a quorum of a board of directors to consist of no fewer than one-third of the fixed or prescribed number of directors determined under Subsection (1) of this section [previous paragraph].

If a quorum is present when a vote is taken, the affirmative vote of a majority of directors present is the act of the board of directors unless the Articles of Incorporation or bylaws require the vote of a greater number of directors. [60.351]

Shareholder Meeting Rules

Except as provided in Subsection (4) of this section [applies to Investment Companies], a corporation shall hold an annual meeting of the shareholders at a time stated in or fixed in accordance with the bylaws. [60.201]

A corporation shall hold a special meeting of shareholders: (a) on call of its board of directors or the person or persons authorized to do so by the Articles of Incorporation or bylaws; or (b) if the holders of at least 10% of all votes entitled to be cast on any issue proposed to be considered at the proposed special meeting sign, date, and deliver to the corporation's secretary one or more written demands for the meeting describing the purpose or purposes for which it is to be held.

A corporation shall notify shareholders of the date, time, and place of each annual and special shareholders' meeting not earlier than 60 days nor less than ten days before the meeting date. Unless the Business Corporation Act or the Articles of Incorporation require otherwise, the corporation is required to give notice only to shareholders entitled to vote at the meeting.

Unless required by the Business Corporation Act or the Articles of Incorporation, notice of an annual meeting need not include a description of the purpose or purposes for which the meeting is called.

Notice of a special meeting must include a description of the purpose or purposes for which the meeting is called. [60.214] Only business within the purpose or purposes described in the meeting notice may be conducted at a special shareholders' meeting. [60.204]

Shares entitled to vote as a separate voting group may take action on a matter at a meeting only if a quorum of those shares exists with respect to that matter. Unless the Articles of Incorporation or the Business Corporation Act provide for a lesser or greater number in accordance with ORS 60.247 [quoted, in part, below], a majority of the votes entitled to be cast on the matter by the voting group constitutes a quorum of that voting group for action on that matter.

If a quorum exists, action on a matter, other than the election of directors, by a voting group is approved if the votes cast within the voting group favoring the action exceed the votes cast opposing the action, unless the Articles of Incorporation or the Business Corporation Act requires a greater number of affirmative votes.

The election of directors is governed by ORS 60.251. [60.241]

If the Articles of Incorporation or the Business Corporation Act provides for voting by a single group on a matter, action on that matter is taken when voted on by that voting group as provided in ORS 60.241 [previous paragraph]. [60.244]

The Articles of Incorporation may provide for a lesser or greater quorum requirement for shareholders, or voting groups of shareholders, than is provided for by the Business Corporation Act, but in no event shall a quorum for shareholders, or any voting group of shareholders, consist of less than one-third of the votes entitled to be cast on any matter by the shareholders, or voting group of shareholders. [60.247]

Unless otherwise provided in the Articles of Incorporation, directors are elected by a plurality of the votes cast by the shares entitled to vote in the election at a meeting at which a quorum is present.

Shareholders do not have a right to cumulate their votes for directors unless the Articles of Incorporation so provide.

A statement included in the Articles of Incorporation that "all shareholders are entitled to cumulate their votes for directors," "a designated voting group of shareholders are entitled to cumulate their votes for director," or words of similar import means that the shareholders designated are entitled to multiply the number of votes they are entitled to cast by the number of directors for whom they are entitled to vote and cast the product for a single can-

didate or distribute the product among two or more candidates. [60.251]

Financial Disclosure Rules

Subject to ORS 60.777 (3) [allows the corporation to charge shareholders a copying fee for making copies of records], a shareholder of a corporation is entitled to inspect and copy, during regular business hours at the corporation's principal office, any of the records of the corporation described in ORS 60.771 (5) [lists standard corporate documents, including articles, bylaws, and minutes of meetings] if the shareholder gives the corporation written notice of the shareholder's demand at least five business days before the date on which the shareholder wishes to inspect and copy.

A shareholder of a corporation is entitled to inspect and copy, during regular business hours at a reasonable location specified by the corporation, any of the following records of the corporation if the shareholder meets the requirements of Subsection (3) of this section [requires the shareholder to submit a request for specific corporate records for a reason related to the person's stock ownership in the corporation] and gives the corporation written notice of the shareholder's demand at least five business days before the date on which the shareholder wishes to inspect and copy: (a) excerpts from minutes of any meeting of the board of directors, records of any action of a committee of the board of directors while acting in place of the board of directors on behalf of the corporation, minutes of any meeting of the shareholders and records of action taken by the shareholders or board of directors without a meeting, to the extent not subject to inspection under Subsection (1) of this section [previous paragraph]; (b) accounting records of the corporation, including tax returns; and (c) the record of shareholders. [60.774]

State Tax Information

Department of Revenue, Salem
503-945-8738
www.dor.state.or.us

Oregon corporations are subject to a corporate excise tax. The minimum annual excise tax is $10.

Corporation Law Online

The Oregon Business Corporation Act is contained in Chapter 60 of the Oregon Statutes, starting with Section 60.001. To find the Act, visit the legal research area of Nolo's website at www.nolo.com/statute/state/cfm. Click on "Oregon." From there, click on "ORS Chapters 59-113" and then choose "Chapter 60" to begin browsing the Act.

State Securities Information

Department of Consumer and Business Services
Corporate Securities Section
350 Winter Street NE, Room 410
Salem, OR 97310
503-378-4140
www.cbs.state.or.us/external/dfcs

The Oregon Securities Act is contained in Chapter 59 of the Oregon Statutes. The Corporate Securities Section website provides links to the Act and to related securities rules. The Act permits various exemptions from securities registration. For example, Section 59.035(12) contains an exemption for sales of securities to ten or fewer people in Oregon within 12 months. To qualify, you must meet certain requirements—for instance, you may not provide commission or other compensation (directly or indirectly) in connection with the offer or sale, you may not use public advertising or general solicitation in connection with any transaction under the exemption, and, at the time of any transaction under the exemption, you may not have on file an application for registration or an effective registration of securities under the Oregon Securities Law which are part of the same offering. Filing fees are required for some exemptions. Browse the Corporate Securities Section website and call the Corporate Securities Section for more information on the Securities Act and rules, and to discuss exemptions that may be available to you.

Creating Your Own Articles Form

You can prepare and file your own form, following the guidelines set out in "Articles Instructions," above.

PENNSYLVANIA

Corporate Filing Office

Commonwealth of Pennsylvania
Department of State
Corporation Bureau
P.O. Box 8722
Harrisburg, PA 17105-8722
717-787-1057
www.dos.state.pa.us/corps/site/default.asp

State Corporate Forms

Pennsylvania provides fill-in-the-blanks Articles of Incorporation with instructions, as well as a Docketing Statement, which you must submit with your Articles.

Internet Forms: Articles of Incorporation and the Docketing Statement are available for downloading from the state filing office website.

Articles Instructions

Fill out the Articles in black or blue-black ink.

Top of Form: Check the first box, "Business-stock'" corporation. Leave the Entity Number box blank. Insert your incorporator's name and address information in the blanks. A copy of the filed articles will be mailed to this person at this address.

Heading and Article 1: The name of a Pennsylvania corporation must contain the word or abbreviation "Corporation," "Corp.," "Company," "Co.," "Incorporated," "Inc.," "Limited," "Ltd.," "Association," "Fund," or "Syndicate." The words ''Company'' or ''Co.'' may be immediately preceded by ''and'' or ''&.''

You can check proposed names against those in the state business entity database online or call the state corporate filing office to check name availability. It costs $70 to reserve an available name for 120 days. The state filing office does not provide a form for name reservation on its website. Prepare a Name Reservation Letter included with this book and mail it, together with a check for the reservation fee, to the state corporate filing office.

Article 2: In 2(a), most incorporators list the street address and county of the corporation or one of its directors or shareholders as the registered office address. Leave 2(b) blank unless you decide to pay another firm to serve as your registered agent (there is no need for you to hire such a firm).

Article 4: In Pennsylvania, you do not need to state a par value for your shares. Most incorporators authorize one class of common shares with equal voting, dividend, and liquidation rights and no special restrictions. To do this, simply insert the total number of authorized shares in the space provided in this article. Your filing fee is not based on the number of shares authorized in your articles, so you can authorize as many shares as you wish. Even if you do wish to authorize special classes of shares, it is not necessary to set forth in the Articles of Incorporation the designations of the classes of shares of the corporation, or the maximum number of shares of each class that may be issued. Instead, your bylaws should list the designation of each class, the authorized number of shares in each class, and the rights and restrictions associated with each class.

Article 5: You need specify just one incorporator, who does not have to be a corporate director, officer, or shareholder. The incorporator must be at least 18 years old.

Article 6: You can leave the specified effective date blank. This means your corporation is formed on the date that you file your articles. You can insert a specific formation date if you wish to have the legal existence of your corporation begin on a different date and time. (Pennsylvania imposes no restrictions on this date, except that it must be later than the date your articles are received by the state filing office.)

Article 8: Most incorporators cross out this statement. It applies only if you wish to set up a "close" corporation—a corporation organized and operated under special rules that forbid a public offering of shares and that may also limit the number of shareholders.

Article 9: Cross out this article. It applies to special member-owned cooperatives.

Docketing Statement: Fill in the required information in a New Entity Docketing Statement (available online at the state corporate filing office website). Most responses are obvious or repeat information you supplied in your articles. In the top left column titled "Pennsylvania Entities," check "business-stock." In item 4, state "date of filing of articles" or the date you specified in Article 6. In item 5, insert "applied for" if you have applied (or will soon be applying) for a new federal Employer Identification Number for your corporation. Note: You can apply for and obtain a federal EIN immediately by going to the IRS website at: www.irs.gov/businesses/small/article/0,,id=102767,00.html.

Have the incorporator named in Article 5 date and sign the articles at the bottom. Submit the original Certificate of Organization form and original Docketing Statement for filing. If you wish to obtain a file-stamped copy of your articles from the state filing office, enclose an additional copy of the articles with a self-addressed, stamped envelope.

Filing Fee: $125, payable to the "PA Department of State."

Post-filing Publication: The incorporator must publish either his or her intention to file or the actual filing of the Articles of Incorporation once in two local newspapers. The incorporator can make this publication before or after the articles are filed. One of the two newspapers should be in general circulation and the other a designated legal newspaper in the county of the corporation's registered office (specified in Article 2). If there is no designated legal newspaper, the publication can be made in two newspapers of general circulation in the county.

Note: For a list of legal newspapers, go to the state corporate filing office main Web page, click "Additional Resources" in the left panel, then click "List of Legal Newspapers."

At a minimum, the notices must contain the following information: (1) the name of the proposed corporation, and (2) a statement that the corporation is to be or has been organized under the Pennsylvania Business Corporation Law. Most newspapers will handle this simple filing for a nominal fee. You do not need to file proof of publication with the state. Just place a copy of the proofs of publication that you receive from the newspapers in your corporate records.

Director and Officer Rules

The board of directors of a business corporation shall consist of one or more members. The number of directors shall be fixed by, or in the manner provided in, the bylaws. If not so fixed, the number of directors shall be the same as that stated in the articles or three if no number is so stated. [1723]

Each director of a business corporation shall hold office until the expiration of the term for which he was selected and until his successor has been selected and qualified or until his earlier death, resignation, or removal. Any director may resign at any time on written notice to the corporation. The resignation shall be effective on receipt thereof by the corporation or at such subsequent time as shall be specified in the notice of resignation. Each director shall be selected for the term of office provided in the bylaws, which shall be one year and until his successor has been selected and qualified or until his earlier death, resignation, or removal, unless the board is classified as provided by Subsection (b). [1724]

Every business corporation shall have a president, a secretary, and a treasurer, or persons who shall act as such,

regardless of the name or title by which they may be designated, elected, or appointed; and may have such other officers and assistant officers as it may authorize from time to time. The bylaws may prescribe special qualifications for the officers. The president and secretary shall be natural persons of full [18 years of] age. The treasurer may be a corporation but, if a natural person, shall be of full age. Unless otherwise restricted in the bylaws, it shall not be necessary for the officers to be directors. Any number of offices may be held by the same person. The officers and assistant officers shall be elected or appointed at such time, in such manner, and for such terms as may be fixed by or pursuant to the bylaws. Unless otherwise provided by or pursuant to the bylaws, each officer shall hold office for a term of one year and until his successor has been selected and qualified or until his earlier death, resignation, or removal. Any officer may resign at any time on written notice to the corporation. The resignation shall be effective on receipt thereof by the corporation or at such subsequent time as may be specified in the notice of resignation. The corporation may secure the fidelity of any or all of the officers by bond or otherwise.

Unless otherwise provided in the bylaws, all officers of the corporation. as between themselves and the corporation. shall have such authority and perform such duties in the management of the corporation as may be provided by or pursuant to the bylaws or, in the absence of controlling provisions in the bylaws, as may be determined by or pursuant to resolutions or orders of the board of directors. [1732]

Share Issuance Rules

Consideration for shares, unless otherwise restricted in the bylaws: (1) may consist of money, obligations (including an obligation of a shareholder), services performed whether or not contracted for, contracts for services to be performed, shares or other securities or obligations of the issuing business corporation, or any other tangible or intangible property or benefit to the corporation; if shares are issued for other than money, the value of the consideration shall be determined by or in the manner provided by the board of directors; (2) shall be provided or paid to or as ordered by the corporation. [1524]

Share certificates shall state: (1) that the corporation is incorporated under the laws of this Commonwealth; (2) the name of the person to whom issued; (3) the number and class of shares and the designation of the series, if any, that the certificate represents.

Every share certificate shall be executed, by facsimile or otherwise, by or on behalf of the corporation issuing the shares in such manner as it may determine. [1528]

Director Meeting Rules

Meetings of the board of directors may be held at such place within or without this Commonwealth as the board of directors may from time to time appoint or as may be designated in the notice of the meeting.

Regular meetings of the board of directors may be held on such notice, if any, as the bylaws may prescribe. Unless otherwise provided in the bylaws, written notice of every special meeting of the board of directors shall be given to each director at least five days before the day named for the meeting. Neither the business to be transacted at, nor the purpose of, any regular or special meeting of the board need be specified in the notice of the meeting. [1703]

Unless otherwise provided in the bylaws, a majority of the directors in office of a business corporation shall be necessary to constitute a quorum for the transaction of business, and the acts of a majority of the directors present and voting at a meeting at which a quorum is present shall be the acts of the board of directors. [1727]

Shareholder Meeting Rules

The bylaws of a business corporation may provide for the number and the time of meetings of shareholders. Except as otherwise provided in the articles, at least one meeting of the shareholders shall be held in each calendar year for the election of directors at such time as shall be provided in or fixed pursuant to authority granted by the bylaws. Failure to hold the annual or other regular meeting at the designated time shall not work a dissolution of the corporation or affect otherwise valid corporate acts. If the annual or other regular meeting is not called and held within six months after the designated time, any shareholder may call the meeting at any time thereafter.

Special meetings of the shareholders may be called at any time: (1) by the board of directors; (2) unless otherwise provided in the articles, by shareholders entitled to cast at least 20% of the votes that all shareholders are entitled to cast at the particular meeting; or (3) by such officers or other persons as may be provided in the bylaws. At any time, on written request of any person who has called a special meeting, it shall be the duty of the secretary to fix the time of the meeting which, if the meeting is called pursuant to a statutory right, shall be held not more than 60 days after the receipt of the request. If the secretary neglects or refuses to fix the time of the meeting, the person or persons calling the meeting may do so. [1755]

Written notice of every meeting of the shareholders shall be given by, or at the direction of, the secretary or other authorized person to each shareholder of record entitled to vote at the meeting at least: (1) ten days prior to the day named for a meeting that will consider a fundamental change under Chapter 19 [of the Business Corporation Law, which applies to corporate mergers] (relating to fundamental changes); or (2) five days prior to the day named for the meeting in any other case. If the secretary or other authorized person neglects or refuses to give notice of a meeting, the person or persons calling the meeting may do so.

In the case of a special meeting of shareholders, the notice shall specify the general nature of the business to be transacted, and in all cases the notice shall comply with the express requirements of this subpart. The corporation shall not have a duty to augment the notice. [1704]

A meeting of shareholders of a business corporation duly called shall not be organized for the transaction of business unless a quorum is present. Unless otherwise provided in a bylaw adopted by the shareholders: (1) the presence of shareholders entitled to cast at least a majority of the votes that all shareholders are entitled to cast on a particular matter to be acted on at the meeting shall constitute a quorum for the purposes of consideration and action on the matter; [Second subsection omitted.] [1756]

Except as otherwise provided in the Business Corporation Law or in a bylaw adopted by the shareholders, whenever any corporate action is to be taken by vote of the shareholders of a business corporation, it shall be authorized on receiving the affirmative vote of a majority of the votes cast by all shareholders entitled to vote thereon and, if any shareholders are entitled to vote thereon as a class, on receiving the affirmative vote of a majority of the votes cast by the shareholders entitled to vote as a class. [1757]

Except as otherwise provided in Paragraph (2) [applies to special types of corporations, not regular business corporations] or in the articles, in each election of directors every shareholder entitled to vote shall have the right to multiply the number of votes to which he may be entitled by the total number of directors to be elected in the same election by the holders of the class or classes of shares of which his shares are a part, and he may cast the whole number of his votes for one candidate or he may distribute them among any two or more candidates. [1758]

Financial Disclosure Rules

Except as otherwise provided in Subsection (d) [applies to a corporation required by law to file financial statements annually with any state office] or unless otherwise agreed between a business corporation and a shareholder, every corporation shall furnish to its shareholders annual financial statements, including at least a balance sheet as of the end of each fiscal year and a statement of income and expenses for the fiscal year. The financial statements shall be prepared on the basis of generally accepted accounting principles, if the corporation prepares financial statements for the fiscal year on that basis for any purpose, and may be consolidated statements of the corporation and one or more of its subsidiaries.

The financial statements shall be mailed by the corporation to each of its shareholders entitled thereto within 120 days after the close of each fiscal year and, after the mailing and on written request, shall be mailed by the corporation to any shareholder or beneficial owner entitled thereto to whom a copy of the most recent annual financial statements has not previously been mailed. Statements that are audited or reviewed by a public accountant shall be accompanied by the report of the accountant; in other cases, each copy shall be accompanied by a statement of the person in charge of the financial records of the corporation: (1) stating his reasonable belief as to whether or not the financial statements were prepared in accordance with generally accepted accounting principles and, if not, describing the basis of presentation; (2) describing any material respects in which the financial statements were not prepared on a basis consistent with those prepared for the previous year.

Subsection (a) [above] shall not apply to a corporation that is required by law to file financial statements at least once a year in a public office. [1554]

State Tax Information

Department of Revenue, Harrisburg
717-783-3682
www.revenue.state.pa.us

Pennsylvania corporations are subject to a corporate net income tax and corporate loans tax (based on corporate indebtedness). In addition, Pennsylvania corporations must pay capital stock tax based on their net worth, with a current minimum annual payment of $200.

Corporation Law Online

The Pennsylvania Business Corporation Law is contained in Title 15 of the Pennsylvania Consolidated Statutes. The statutes currently are not posted online, but rules that explain the statutory requirements can be found in Title 17 (Corporations and Business Associations), Chapter 23 of

the Pennsylvania Code, starting with Section 23.1. You can browse them from the URL listed below—select "Corporations and Business Associations" in the headings list, then select "Chapter 23"). Note: To obtain a copy of the Pennsylvania Business Corporation Law, call the Pennsylvania State Bookstore in Harrisburg (under state of Pennsylvania listings in directory assistance) and ask for a one-item purchase of the Associations Code. It contains Title 15 (the BCL) plus other statutes, and currently sells for about $15 including shipping and sales tax.

www.pacode.com/secure/browse.asp

State Securities Information

Pennsylvania Securities Commission
Harrisburg Office
Eastgate Office Building, 2nd Floor
1010 North Seventh Street
Harrisburg, PA 17102-1410
717-787-5401 (Toll Free: 800-600-0007)
www.psc.state.pa.us

The Pennsylvania Securities Act is contained in Title 70 of the Pennsylvania Statutes. You can browse the Act and associated rules from the Securities Commission website. (Click "Statutes, Rules, and Regulations.") The Commission website contains a topic, "Raising Small-Business Capital," that explains the basic requirements of the Pennsylvania Securities Law. There are a number of exemptions available under the Act and rules. For example, Rule 203.184 allows a corporation to issue shares to principals of the corporation, including the chairperson, president, chief executive officer, general manager, chief operating officer, chief financial officer, vice president or other officer in charge of a principal business function (such as sales, administration, finance, marketing, research, and credit), secretary, treasurer, and controller. Rule 203.187 contains an exemption for the issuance of shares to ten or fewer people without advertising or commissions. Other requirements apply to each of these exemptions. Browse the website and call the Securities Commission to find out the best available exemption for your corporation, and to learn how to comply with all necessary requirements.

Creating Your Own Articles Form

You can prepare and file your own articles form, following the guidelines in "Articles Instructions," above.

RHODE ISLAND

Corporate Filing Office

Rhode Island Secretary of State
Corporations Division
100 North Main Street, 1st Floor
Providence, RI 02903-1335
401-222-3040
http://155.212.254.78/corporations.htm

State Corporate Forms

Rhode Island provides Articles of Incorporation (Form 100) with instructions.

Internet Forms: You can fill in your Articles of Incorporation at the state filing office website. After completing them, you must print them out and mail them to the state filing office. Other corporate forms also are available online.

Articles Instructions

Article 1: The name of a Rhode Island corporation must contain the word "corporation," "company," "incorporated," or "limited," or an abbreviation of one of these words.

You can find out whether your proposed name is available by calling the state filing office or by searching the online corporation database at the state filing office website. It costs $50 to reserve an available name for 120 days.

Note: We assume you will want to cross the sentence below the name line that begins with "This is a close corporation pursuant to § 7-1.1-51 of the General Laws ..." This statement only applies if you wish to form a "close" corporation—one that is managed by its shareholder pursuant to a special shareholders' agreement. Few incorporators will wish to form this nontraditional type of business corporation; see a lawyer if you are interested in forming one.

Article 2: Most incorporators insert "perpetual" to give their corporation an unlimited legal life. If you want to limit the term of existence of your corporation, insert the termination date instead.

Article 3: Insert a brief statement that describes the specific business purpose of your corporation. If you like, you may also include a general business statement along with your specific purpose—for example, "to operate an automotive repair facility and the transaction of any or all lawful business for which corporations may be incorporated under the Rhode Island Business Corporation Act."

Even if you do not include this general purpose statement, your corporation can transact any lawful business, not just the specific purpose that you indicate in this article.

Article 4: Most incorporators authorize one class of common shares with equal voting, dividend, and liquidation rights and no special restrictions. Also, the modern trend is to authorize shares without a stated par value. To authorize no-par common shares, simply insert the number of shares you wish to authorize in the first blank in Section (a).). Incorporators will make sure to authorize less than 75,000,000 shares in their articles to pay the minimum filing fee as explained below (see "Filing Fee," below). Then insert "without par value" in the second blank in Section (a). If you wish to authorize par value shares instead, state the par value in the second blank in Section (a)—for example, "par value $1.00 each."

If you want to authorize special classes of shares, fill out Section (b) instead of (a). You must indicate the total number of shares in all classes in the blank, then insert a statement that specifies the designation of each class, the number of authorized shares in each class, whether the shares are par value or without par value, and the rights and restrictions associated with each class of shares. There's not much room to do all this in the lines provided in Section (b), so you will probably need to include an attachment page with this additional information.

Article 5: This is an optional item that many incorporators will wish to leave blank (or type "N/A" in the blank). Most incorporators do not deal with preemptive rights when forming their corporations. Preemptive rights give existing shareholders the right to buy future shares before new shareholders can buy. Section 7-1.1-24 of the Pennsylvania Business Corporation Act gives shareholders basic preemptive rights to buy future shares, subject to certain limitations, unless these rights are limited or denied in the articles. You probably don't care about this now, and you can leave this article blank. If you wish to deal with this issue now, insert the special preemptive rights language that you have prepared (probably with the help of a lawyer) following the requirements of section 7-1.1-24.

Article 6: If you have prepared any special language for operating your corporation, insert it here. If not, simply insert "N/A." Most incorporators will insert "N/A."

Article 7. Typically, an initial director or shareholder is named as initial registered agent (the person authorized to receive legal documents on behalf of the corporation), and the street address of the corporation is given as the registered office address (which must be the business office of the registered agent). The registered agent must be a Rhode Island resident, and the registered office address must be in Rhode Island.

Article 8: Indicate the number of directors. You must have at least one, unless you did not strike out the close corporation language as explained to the instructions to Article 1, above. (A close corporation is a special type of corporation that most incorporators will not want to form. It limits the number of shareholders and has the ability to operate informally without a board of directors. If you do form a close corporation without a board of directors, insert the number of officers instead.) On the lines provided, insert the title ("director") and name and address of each director.

Article 9: You need just one incorporator, who need not be a director, officer, or shareholder.

Article 10: Most incorporators will insert "N/A" to have the legal existence of their corporation begin when the articles are filed. If you wish to delay the start date of your corporation, insert a specific date instead. This delayed start date cannot be more than 30 days after the date that you file your Articles.

Have the incorporator designated in Article 9 date and sign the articles at the bottom in the presence of a notary public. File two original, signed articles forms. After approving your articles, the state filing office will send you a Certificate of Incorporation together with a file-stamped duplicate original of the articles.

Filing Fee: The minimum filing fee is $230, payable to the "Rhode Island Secretary of State." This fee includes a minimum $160 license fee plus a $70 filing fee. Rhode Island has a very unusual license fee scheme, at least according to the official instructions to its articles form and its Corporations Division website. Specifically, the site and form says that you may authorize up but not including 75,000,000 shares in your articles for the minimum $160 license fee. However (and here is where it gets tricky), if you authorize 75,000,00 or more shares, the fee jumps to an incredibly high amount. Specifically, if you authorize 75,000,000 shares or more, the fee is computed at the rate of one-fifth cent ($.002) per share for each authorized share. This means if you authorize 74,999,999 shares in your articles, according to the official information we found, you pay the minimum license fee of $160 (plus the $70 filing fee). But if you authorize one additional share so that you authorize 75,000,000 shares in your articles, the license portion of your fee jumps from the minimum $160 dollar amount to an incredible $150,000! (75,000,000 times $.002 = $150,000). We're sure you will want to stay below the 75-million share limit for this reason. We recommend you go online to the state corporate filing office website to confirm this unusual fee schedule information prior to deciding on the number of authorized shares to specify in your articles.

Examples:

If you authorize 74,999,999 shares in your articles, you pay the minimum $160 license fee plus the $70 filing fee for a minimum total fee of $230.

If you authorize 75,000,000 shares in your articles, the license fee is $150,000 ($.002), and the total filing fee is $150,070 (again, we're sure you will not let this happen, and will make sure to authorize less than 75,000,000 shares in your articles).

Director and Officer Rules

The board of directors of a corporation consists of one or more members. The number of directors are fixed by, or in the manner provided in, the Articles of Incorporation or the bylaws except as to the number constituting the initial board of directors, which number is fixed by the Articles of Incorporation. The number of directors may be increased or decreased from time to time by amendment to, or in the manner provided in, the Articles of Incorporation or the bylaws, but no decrease has the effect of shortening the term of any incumbent director. If the Articles of Incorporation provide for the election of directors in the manner specified in Subsection (d) of § 7-1.1-31, the number of directors may not be decreased unless approved by the stock holders with less than the number of shares previously entitled to elect one director voting against the decrease. In the absence of a bylaw fixing the number of directors, the number is the same as that provided for in the Articles of Incorporation. The names and addresses of the members of the first board of directors shall be stated in the Articles of Incorporation. Those persons hold office until the first annual meeting of shareholders, and until their successors have been elected and qualified. At the first annual meeting of shareholders and at each subsequent annual meeting, the shareholders shall elect directors to hold office until the next succeeding annual meeting, except in the case of the classification of directors as permitted by this chapter. Each director holds office for the term for which he or she is elected and until his or her successor has been elected and qualified. [7-1.1-34]

The officers of a corporation consist of a chairperson of the board of directors, if prescribed by the bylaws, a president; one or more vice presidents, if prescribed by the bylaws; a secretary; and a treasurer, each of whom is elected by the board of directors or by the stock holders at a time and in a manner as prescribed by the bylaws. Any other officers and assistant officers and agents as that are necessary may be elected or appointed by the board of directors or by the stock holders or chosen in another manner prescribed by the bylaws. Any two (2) or more offices may be held by the same person. A failure to elect officers does not dissolve or otherwise affect the corporation. [7-1.1-44]

Share Issuance Rules

Shares having a par value may be issued for the consideration expressed in dollars, not less than the par value of the shares, as is fixed from time to time by the board of directors.

Shares without par value may be issued for the consideration expressed in dollars that is fixed from time to time by the board of directors unless the Articles of Incorporation reserve to the shareholders the right to fix the consideration. In the event that the right is reserved as to any shares, the shareholders shall, prior to the issuance of the shares, fix the consideration to be received for the shares, by a vote of the holders of a majority of all shares entitled to vote on the consideration. [7-1.1-17]

The consideration for the issuance of shares may be paid, in whole or in part, in money; in other property, tangible or intangible; or in labor or services actually performed for the corporation. When payment of the consideration for which shares are to be issued has been received by the corporation, the shares are deemed to be fully paid and nonassessable.

Neither promissory notes nor future services constitute payment or part payment, for the issuance of shares of a corporation. [7-1.1-18]

In the case of the issuance by a corporation of shares having a par value, the consideration received for the shares constitutes stated capital to the extent of the par value of the shares, or, if the shares have a preference in the assets of the corporation in the event of involuntary liquidation which is greater than the par value, then to the extent of the preference, and the excess, if any, of the consideration constitutes capital surplus.

In the case of the issuance by a corporation of shares without par value, the entire consideration received for the shares constitutes stated capital unless the corporation determines as provided in this section that only a part of the shares is stated capital. Within a period of sixty (60) days after the issuance of any shares without par value, the board of directors may allocate to capital surplus any portion of the consideration received for the issuance of the shares. No allocation shall be made of any portion of the consideration received for shares without par value having a preference in the assets of the corporation in the event of involuntary liquidation except the amount, if any, of the consideration in excess of the preference. [7-1.1-19]

Notwithstanding the adoption of the resolution by the board of directors, every holder of stock represented by certificates and on request every holder of uncertificated shares is entitled to have a certificate signed by the officer or officers designated for the purpose by the bylaws of the corporation, and in absence of any designation, by the chairperson or the vice chairperson of the board of directors, or the president or a vice president, and by the treasurer or the assistant treasurer, or the secretary or an assistant secretary of the corporation, representing the number of shares registered in certificate form and may be sealed with the seal of the corporation or a facsimile of the seal.

Each certificate representing shares shall state on the face of the certificate: (1) that the corporation is organized under the laws of this state; (2) the name of the person to whom issued; (3) the number and class of shares, and the designation of the series, if any, which the certificate represents; (4) if the shares are without par value, a statement of the fact. [7-1.1-21]

Director Meeting Rules

Regular meetings of the board of directors or any committee designated by the board may be held with or without notice as prescribed in the bylaws. Special meetings of the board of directors or any committee designated by the board shall be held on notice that is prescribed in the bylaws. Attendance of a director at a meeting constitutes a waiver of notice of the meeting, except where a director attends a meeting for the express purpose of objecting to the transaction of any business because the meeting is not lawfully called or convened. Neither the business to be transacted at, nor the purpose of, any regular or special meeting of the board of directors or any committee designated by the board of directors need be specified in the notice or waiver of notice of the meeting unless required by the bylaws. [7-1.1-39]

A majority of the number of directors fixed by or in the manner provided in the bylaws, or by the stock holders, or in the absence of a bylaw or stock holder action fixing the number of directors, then of the number stated in the Articles of Incorporation, constitutes a quorum for the transaction of business unless a greater number is required by the Articles of Incorporation or the bylaws. The act of the majority of the directors present at a meeting at which a quorum is present is the act of the board of directors, unless the act of a greater number is required by the Articles of Incorporation or the bylaws. [7-1.1-37]

Shareholder Meeting Rules

Meetings of shareholders may be held at any place, either within or without the state of Rhode Island, that may be stated in or fixed in accordance with the bylaws.

Special meetings of the shareholders may be called by the board of directors, or by a person or persons that may be authorized by the Articles of Incorporation or by the bylaws. [7-1.1-26]

Written notice stating the place, day, and hour of the meeting and, in case of a special meeting, the purpose or purposes for which the meeting is called, shall be delivered not less than ten nor more than 60 days before the date of the meeting, either personally or by mail, by or at the direction of the president, the secretary, or the officer or persons calling the meeting, to each shareholder of record entitled to vote at the meeting. [7-1.1-27]

Unless otherwise provided in the Articles of Incorporation or bylaws, a majority of the shares entitled to vote, represented in person or by proxy, constitutes a quorum at a meeting of shareholders, but in no event does a quorum consist of less than one-third of the shares entitled to vote at the meeting. If a quorum is present, the affirmative vote of the majority of the shares represented at the meeting and entitled to vote on the subject matter is the act of the shareholders, unless the vote of a greater number or voting by classes is required by the Business Corporation Act or the Articles of Incorporation or bylaws. [7-1.1-30]

The Articles of Incorporation may provide that at each election of directors, or at elections held under specified circumstances, every shareholder entitled to vote at the election has the right to vote, in person or by proxy, the number of shares owned by him or her for as many persons as there are directors to be elected and for whose election he or she has a right to vote, or to cumulate his or her votes by giving one candidate as many votes as the number of directors multiplied by the number of his or her shares shall equal, or by distributing the votes on the same principle among any number of the candidates. [7-1.1-31]

Financial Disclosure Rules

Any person who has been a shareholder of record or of voting trust certificates for the shares for at least six months immediately preceding his or her demand or is be the holder of record of, or the holder of record of voting trust certificates for, at least 5% of all the outstanding shares of a corporation, on written demand stating the purpose for the demand, shall have the right to examine, in person, or by agent or attorney, at any reasonable time or times, for any proper purpose, its relevant books and records of account, minutes, and record of shareholders and to make extracts from those books and records of account, minutes, and record of shareholders.

On the written request of any shareholder or holder of voting trust certificates for shares of a corporation, the corporation shall mail to the shareholder or holder of voting trust certificates its most recent financial statements showing in reasonable detail its assets and liabilities and the results of its operations. [7-1.1-46]

State Tax Information

Division of Taxation, Providence
401-222-1120
www.tax.state.ri.us

Rhode Island corporations are subject to a corporate income tax, with a minimum annual payment of $250.

Corporation Law Online

The Rhode Island Business Corporation Act is contained in Title 7 (Corporations, Associations, and Partnerships), Chapter 7-1.1, of the Rhode Island General Laws, starting with Section 7-1.1-1. To find the Act, visit the legal research area of Nolo's website at www.nolo.com/statute/state.cfm. Click on "Rhode Island." Choose Title 7 and then Chapter 7-1.1 to begin browsing the laws.

State Securities Information

State of Rhode Island
Department of Business Regulation
Securities Division
Richmond Street
Suite 237
Providence, RI 02903-4237
401-222-3048
www.dbr.state.ri.us

The Rhode Island Uniform Securities Act is contained in Title 7, Chapter 7-11, of the Rhode Island General Laws. You can browse the Act by following the directions in "Corporation Law Online," above and choosing Chapter 7-11 from the chapter list. Section 7-11-402 of the Act contains exemptions from registration for certain securities transactions. For example, the section provides an exemption for offers of securities to no more than 25 purchasers in the state of Rhode Island during any 12 consecutive months if (1) no general solicitation or general advertising is used in connection with the offer, and (2) no commission is paid to a person, other than a properly licensed (or exempt) broker-dealer who solicits prospective purchasers in the state. Other conditions apply. Call the Securities Division for information on the requirements associated with this and other available securities exemptions.

Creating Your Own Articles Form

You can prepare and file your own typewritten or printed form.

SOUTH CAROLINA

Corporate Filing Office

South Carolina Secretary of State
Corporations Department
P.O. Box 11350
Columbia, SC 29211
803-734-2158
www.scsos.com/Corporations.htm

State Corporate Forms

South Carolina provides Articles of Incorporation and Form CL-1, the Initial Annual Report form, you must file with your articles.

Internet Forms: Articles with instructions, Form CL-1, plus other corporate forms, are available for downloading from the state filing office website.

Note: SOUTH CAROLINA, UNLIKE ALL OTHER STATES, REQUIRES YOUR ARTICLES TO BE SIGNED BY A LAWYER LICENSED TO PRACTICE IN THE STATE. The lawyer must make sure your articles contain the required information listed in Section 33-2-102 of the Business Corporation Act. This is a short, simple list, and if you use the state articles form, you should automatically meet the requirements. Look for a cooperative lawyer who will review and sign your articles for a relatively small charge.

Articles Instructions

Article 1: The name of a South Carolina corporation must contain the word "corporation," "incorporated," "company," or "limited," or the abbreviation "corp.," "inc.," "co.," or "ltd."

To find out whether your proposed name is available, call the state filing office or search the online corporation database linked to the state filing office website. You can reserve a corporate name for 120 days by filing two copies of an Application to Reserve Corporate Name along with a $10 fee.

Article 2: The registered office address can be the corporation's street address, and the initial agent may be one of the corporation's initial directors, officers, or shareholders. Make sure to have the registered agent sign on the blank line provided in Article 2.

Article 3: In South Carolina, you do not need to state a par value for your shares. Most incorporators authorize one class of common shares with equal voting, dividend, and liquidation rights and no special restrictions. To do this, simply check Box "a," then insert the total number of authorized shares in the space provided. Your filing fee is not based on the number of shares authorized in your

articles, so you can authorize as many shares as you wish. If you want to authorize special classes of shares, check Box "b" instead. Then insert the name of each class and the number of shares in each class in the corresponding blanks. Also specify the rights and restrictions associated with each class in the bottom portion of the article under the last paragraph in Section "b."

Article 4: Leave this item blank if you want your corporation's life to begin on the date that you file your articles. You can insert a specific formation date if you wish to delay the beginning of your corporation. Your delayed date must fall within 90 days of the date you file your articles.

Article 5: You may leave this article blank. If you want to add optional provisions, insert them here.

Article 6: You may have just one incorporator, who need not be a director, officer, or shareholder. The incorporator must sign on the signature line just under the incorporator's address in Article 6.

Article 7: SOUTH CAROLINA, UNLIKE ALL OTHER STATES, REQUIRES YOUR ARTICLES TO BE SIGNED BY A LAWYER (a lawyer licensed to practice in South Carolina). The lawyer is legally responsible for making sure that your Articles contain the required information listed in Section 33-2-102 of the Business Corporation Act. This is a short and simple list—if you use the state form, you will meet these requirements. You should be able to find a cooperative lawyer who will sign your Articles for a reasonable charge. This is a routine task that will take only a few minutes of a competent lawyer's time. THE LAWYER MUST SIGN, DATE, AND PROVIDE THE ADDITIONAL NAME/ADDRESS/TELEPHONE NUMBER INFORMATION ON THE LINES PROVIDED AT THE END OF THIS ARTICLE.

File two original, signed copies of the articles, together with Form CL-1, the Initial Annual Report form. The Cl-1 form is available on the state corporate filing office website. The CL-1 form repeats much of the information contained in the articles. The rest is basic information.

Filing Fee: $135, payable to the "South Carolina Secretary of State." Because South Carolina requires a lawyer to sign your articles, expect to pay for the lawyer's time—but it should not take more than a few minutes for the lawyer to check your articles if you use the standard form.

CL-1 fee. The standard fee for the Cl-1 form is $25.00. YOU MUST INCLUDE A SEPARATE CHECK FOR THIS AMOUNT PAYABLE TO THE "SC DEPARTMENT OF REVENUE."

Director and Officer Rules

A board of directors consists of one or more individuals with the number specified in or fixed in accordance with the articles of incorporation or bylaws.

Directors are elected at the first annual shareholders' meeting and at each annual meeting thereafter unless their terms are staggered under Section 33-8-106. [33-8-103]

The terms of the initial directors of a corporation expire at the first shareholders' meeting at which directors are elected.

The terms of all other directors expire at the next annual shareholders' meeting following their election unless their terms are staggered under Section 33-8-106. [33-8-105]

A corporation has the officers described in its bylaws or appointed by the board of directors in accordance with the bylaws.

The bylaws or the board of directors shall delegate to one of the officers responsibility for preparing minutes of the directors' and shareholders' meetings and for authenticating records of the corporation.

The same individual may hold more than one office in a corporation simultaneously. [33-8-400]

Share Issuance Rules

The board of directors may authorize shares to be issued for consideration consisting of any tangible or intangible property or benefit to the corporation, including cash, promissory notes, services performed, written contracts for services to be performed, or other securities of the corporation.

Before the corporation issues shares, the board of directors must determine that the consideration received or to be received for shares to be issued is adequate. That determination by the board of directors is conclusive insofar as the adequacy of consideration for the issuance of shares relates to whether the shares are validly issued, fully paid, and nonassessable.

Except as otherwise provided in subsection (f) [next paragraph], the corporation must place in escrow shares issued for a contract for future services or benefits or for a promissory note. Any share dividends in respect of the shares escrowed also must be placed in escrow. Distributions in respect of escrowed shares must be escrowed or credited against their purchase price. The shares and distributions escrowed must remain in escrow until the services are performed, the note is paid, or the benefits are received. If the services are not performed, the note is not paid, or the benefits are not received, the shares es-

crowed and the distributions credited may be canceled in whole or in part and the distributions escrowed may be reclaimed by the corporation.

A corporation subject to the registration requirements of Section 12 of the Securities Exchange Act of 1934 [for example, a publicly traded corporation] may issue shares for a contract for future services without having to place the shares and share dividends and distributions in respect of the shares in escrow and without having to credit distributions against their purchase price if the shares are issued or authorized pursuant to a plan that has been approved by the shareholders of the corporation. [33-6-210]

At a minimum, each share certificate must state on its face: (1) the name of the issuing corporation and that it is organized under the laws of this State; (2) the name of the person to whom issued; and (3) the number and class of shares and the designation of the series, if any, the certificate represents.

Each share certificate (1) must be signed (either manually or in facsimile) by two officers designated in the bylaws or by the board of directors and (2) may bear the corporate seal or its facsimile. [33-6-250]

The shareholders of a corporation have a preemptive right to acquire the corporation's unissued shares except to the extent the Articles of Incorporation otherwise provide. [33-6-300]

Director Meeting Rules

Unless the articles or bylaws provide otherwise, the board of directors may hold regular or special meetings in or out of the state of South Carolina. [33-8-200]

Unless the Articles of Incorporation or bylaws provide otherwise, regular meetings of the board of directors may be held without notice of the date, time, place, or purpose of the meeting.

Unless the Articles of Incorporation or bylaws provide for a longer or shorter period, special meetings of the board of directors must be preceded by at least two days' notice of the date, time, and place of the meeting. The notice need not describe the purpose of the special meeting unless required by the Articles of Incorporation or bylaws. [33-8-220]

Unless the Articles of Incorporation or bylaws require a greater number, a quorum of a board of directors consists of: (1) a majority of directors then in office if the corporation has a fixed board size; or (2) a majority of the number of directors prescribed, or, if no number is prescribed, the number in office immediately before the meeting begins, if the corporation has a variable-range size board.

The Articles of Incorporation or bylaws may authorize a quorum of a board of directors to consist of no fewer than one-third of the fixed or prescribed number of directors determined under Subsection (a) [previous paragraph].

If a quorum is present when a vote is taken, the affirmative vote of a majority of directors present is the act of the board of directors unless the Articles of Incorporation or bylaws require the vote of a greater number of directors. [33-8-240]

Shareholder Meeting Rules

A corporation shall hold a meeting of shareholders annually at a time stated in or fixed in accordance with the bylaws or, in the alternative, may take such action as would be taken at an annual meeting by taking action by unanimous written consent under Section 33-7-104. [33-7-101]

A corporation shall hold a special meeting of shareholders: (1) on call of its board of directors or the person authorized to do so by the Articles of Incorporation or bylaws; or (2) in the case of a corporation which is not a public corporation or of a public corporation which elects in its Articles of Incorporation, if the holders of at least 10% of all the votes entitled to be cast on any issue proposed to be considered at the proposed special meeting sign, date, and deliver to the corporation's secretary one or more written demands for the meeting describing the purpose for which it is to be held.

A corporation shall notify shareholders of the date, time, and place of each annual and special shareholders' meeting no fewer than ten nor more than 60 days before the meeting date. Unless Chapters 1 through 20 of the Business Corporation Act or the Articles of Incorporation require otherwise, the corporation is required to give notice only to shareholders entitled to vote at the meeting.

Unless Chapters 1 through 20 of the Business Corporation Act or the Articles of Incorporation require otherwise, notice of an annual meeting need not include a description of the purpose for which the meeting is called.

Notice of a special meeting must include a description of the purpose for which the meeting is called. [33-7-105] Only business within the purpose described in the meeting notice may be conducted at a special shareholders' meeting. [33-7-102]

Shares entitled to vote as a separate voting group may take action on a matter at a meeting only if a quorum of those shares exists with respect to that matter. Unless the Articles of Incorporation or Chapters 1 through 20 of the Business Corporation Act provides otherwise, a majority of the votes entitled to be cast on the matter by the voting group constitutes a quorum of that voting group for action on that matter.

If a quorum exists, action on a matter (other than the election of directors) by a voting group is approved if the votes cast within the voting group favoring the action exceed the votes cast opposing the action, unless the Articles of Incorporation or Chapters 1 through 20 of the Business Corporation Act requires a greater number of affirmative votes.

The election of directors is governed by Section 33-7-280. [33-7-250]

If the Articles of Incorporation or Chapters 1 through 20 of the Business Corporation Act provides for voting by a single voting group on a matter, action on that matter is taken when voted on by that voting group as provided in Section 33-7-250 [previous three paragraphs]. [33-7-260]

Unless otherwise provided in the Articles of Incorporation, directors are elected by a plurality of the votes cast by the shares entitled to vote in the election at a meeting at which a quorum is present.

Shareholders have a right to cumulate their votes for directors unless the Articles of Incorporation otherwise provide. The right to cumulate votes means that the shareholders are entitled to multiply the number of votes they are entitled to cast by the number of directors for whom they are entitled to vote and cast the product for a single candidate or distribute the product among two or more candidates.

Shares otherwise entitled to vote cumulatively may not be voted cumulatively at a particular meeting unless: (1) the meeting notice or proxy statement accompanying the notice states conspicuously that cumulative voting is authorized; or (2) a shareholder who has the right to cumulate his votes shall either (1) waive written notice of his intention to the president or other officer of the corporation not less than 48 hours before the time fixed for the meeting, which notice must be announced in the meeting before the voting, or (2) announce his intention in the meeting before the voting for directors commences; and all shareholders entitled to vote at the meeting shall without further notice be entitled to cumulate their votes. If cumulative voting is to be used, persons presiding may, or if requested by any shareholder shall, recess the meeting for a reasonable time to allow deliberation by shareholders, not to exceed two hours. [33-7-280]

Financial Disclosure Rules

A corporation shall furnish its shareholders annual financial statements, which may be consolidated or combined statements of the corporation and one or more of its subsidiaries, as appropriate, that include a balance sheet as of the end of the fiscal year, an income statement for that year, and a statement of changes in shareholders' equity for the year unless that information appears elsewhere in the financial statements. If financial statements are prepared for the corporation on the basis of generally accepted accounting principles, the annual financial statements also must be prepared on that basis.

If the annual financial statements are reported on by a public accountant, his report must accompany them. If not, the statements must be accompanied by a statement of the president or the person responsible for the corporation's accounting records: (1) stating his reasonable belief whether the statements were prepared on the basis of generally accepted accounting principles and, if not, describing the basis of preparation; and (2) describing any respects in which the statements were not prepared on a basis of accounting consistent with the statements prepared for the preceding year.

A corporation shall mail the annual financial statements to each shareholder within 120 days after the close of each fiscal year. Thereafter, on written request from a shareholder who was not mailed the statements, the corporation shall mail him the last financial statements. [33-16-200]

State Tax Information

Department of Revenue, Columbia
803-737-9881
www.sctax.org

South Carolina corporations are subject to a corporate income tax and an annual license tax of .001 times their capital stock and paid-in surplus plus $15. The minimum annual license tax is $25.

Corporation Law Online

The South Carolina Business Corporation Act is contained in Title 33 (Corporations, Partnerships, and Associations), Chapters 1 through 20, of the South Carolina Code of Laws, starting with Section 33-1-101. To find the Act, visit the legal research area of Nolo's website at www.nolo.com/statute/state/cfm. Click on "South Carolina." Choose Title 33 from the table of contents, then select the appropriate chapter from the list (chapter numbers are referenced in the right margin).

State Securities Information

Office of the S.C. Attorney General
Securities Division
P.O. Box 11549
Columbia, SC 29211-1549
803-734-9916 (Toll Free: 877-232-5378)
www.scsecurities.org/index.html

The South Carolina Securities Act is contained in Title 35 of the Code of Laws of South Carolina. You can browse the Act from a link provided on the Securities Division website or by following the instructions in "Corporation Law Online," above, and choosing Title 33. The Securities Division website asks individuals who are raising capital for their business to call the Division for help in determining if an exemption is available. We suggest you take advantage of this assistance. Section 35-1-320 of the Securities Act contains various exemptions from registration of securities transactions. For example, Subsection (9) provides a limited offering exemption for offers of securities to not more than 25 people during a 12-month period if the purchasers are buying for investment and no commissions are paid as part of the transaction. Other exemptions are also available. Call the Division for more specific information.

Creating Your Own Articles Form

You can submit your own typewritten or computer-generated form.

SOUTH DAKOTA

Corporate Filing Office

South Dakota Secretary of State
State Capitol
500 East Capitol
Pierre, SD 57501
605-773-4845
www.state.sd.us/sos/corporations

State Corporate Forms

South Dakota provides fill-in-the-blanks Articles of Incorporation with instructions.

Internet Forms: Articles with instructions and other corporate forms are available for downloading from the state filing office website.

Articles Instructions

Article I: The name of a South Dakota corporation must contain the word "corporation," "company," "incorporated," or "limited," or an abbreviation of one of these words.

You can check the availability of your proposed corporate name by calling the state filing office. An available corporate name can be reserved for 120 days for $20.

Article II: Most incorporators insert "perpetual" to give their corporation an unlimited legal life. If you want to specify an automatic termination date for your corporation, insert that date instead.

Article III: State the specific business purpose of your corporation. Your statement should be short and sweet, for example, "to sell retail merchandise." You are not limited to the specific purpose that you specify; your corporation can engage in any lawful business activity (except banking or insurance, which are specially regulated).

IMPORTANT: If your corporation will engage in farming, you must prepare and file a special qualification form with your articles. Also, if your corporation will engage in the practice of a licensed professional service, such as accounting, medicine, or law, you will have to follow special requirements when preparing your articles. See the online "Domestic Business Corporations Booklet" for additional information on these special requirements.

Article IV: Your filing fee is not based upon the number of shares authorized in your Articles, so you can authorize as many shares as you wish. Most incorporators will wish to authorize one class of common shares with equal voting, dividend, and liquidation rights and no special restrictions. Also, the modern trend is to authorize shares

without a stated par value. To authorize common shares, insert the number of authorized shares in the first column. Then, insert "common" in the class column. Leave the series column blank. In the par value column, insert "without par value" if you authorize no-par shares. (If you wish to authorize par value shares instead, insert the par value amount per share—for example, $1, $.10, or $.01.)

If you want to authorize special classes of shares, you must use this article to specify the name of each class, the number of shares in each class, and the par value of each class.

Article V: If you authorized more than one class of common stock in Article IV, you must specify the rights and restrictions associated with each class here. If you authorized only common stock in Article IV, ignore this article.

Article VI: You need not insert anything here. South Dakota law requires your corporation to issue at least $1,000 worth of stock before you begin doing business. This requirement has nothing to do with par value. It simply means that the actual amount your initial shareholders paid for their shares must be at least $1,000 before the corporation commences operations. You may receive payment in the form of money, tangible or intangible property, or labor or services performed for the corporation. When you file your first Annual Report with the state, you must verify that your initial shareholders have paid at least $1,000. This is an old-fashioned requirement that is supposed to help protect creditors doing business with the corporation. The outdated idea is that paid-in capital is kept on the books as a cushion for creditors. However, no creditor these days will choose to do business with a corporation simply because it has $1,000 worth of capital reflected in its capital account. Nevertheless, you must comply with this legal requirement or face possible penalties.(For penalty information, see Section 47-5-19 of the South Dakota Business Corporation Act, quoted in "Director and Officer Rules," below.)

Article VII: Most incorporators list the street address of the corporation as the registered office and show the name of an initial director, officer, or shareholder as the registered agent. Note that the agent named here must date and sign the Consent of Appointment portion of the articles at the bottom of the state articles form.

Article VIII: Insert the number of directors on your board. You need one or more directors. Then, insert the name and address of each director in the lines provided.

Article IX: You need just one incorporator, who is not required to be a director, officer, or shareholder. Your incorporator must be at least 18 years of age.

Article X: You can leave this article blank.

The incorporator named in Article IX must sign the articles in the presence of a notary public.

Submit one signed and notarized original and one exact copy of your articles to the Secretary of State's office for review. After approving and filing your articles, the office will return a file-stamped copy of the articles attached to a Certificate of Incorporation.

Filing Fee: $125 filing fee, payable to the "Secretary of State."

Director and Officer Rules

The board of directors of a corporation shall consist of one or more members. [47-5-4]

In addition to any other liabilities imposed by law on directors, if a corporation shall commence business before it has received at least one thousand dollars as consideration for the issuance of shares, the directors who assent thereto shall be jointly and severally liable to the corporation for such part of one thousand dollars as shall not have been received before commencing business, but such liability shall be terminated when the corporation has actually received one thousand dollars as consideration for the issuance of shares. [47-5-19]

A corporation shall have the officers described in its bylaws or appointed by the board of directors in accordance with the bylaws. Any duly appointed officer may appoint one or more officers or assistant officers if authorized by the bylaws or the board of directors. Either the bylaws or the board of directors shall delegate to one of the officers responsibility for preparing minutes of the directors' and shareholders' meetings and for authenticating records of the corporation. Any individual may simultaneously hold more than one office in a corporation. [47-5-24.1]

Share Issuance Rules

Each corporation shall have power to create and issue the number of shares stated in its Articles of Incorporation. Such shares may be divided into one or more classes, any or all of which classes may consist of shares with par value or shares without par value, with such designations, preferences, limitations, and relative rights as shall be stated in the Articles of Incorporation. [47-3-1]

The consideration for the issuance of shares may be paid, in whole or in part, in money; in other property, tangible or intangible; or in labor or services actually performed for the corporation. [47-3-26]

Neither promissory notes nor future services shall constitute payment or part payment for shares of a corporation. [47-3-28]

Shares having a par value may be issued for such consideration expressed in dollars, not less than the par value thereof, as shall be fixed from time to time by the board of directors. [47-3-31]

In case of the issuance by a corporation of shares having a par value, the consideration received therefor shall constitute stated capital to the extent of the par value of such shares, and the excess, if any, of such consideration shall constitute capital surplus.

In case of the issuance by a corporation of shares without par value, the entire consideration received therefor shall constitute stated capital unless the corporation shall determine as provided in § 47-3-37 or 47-3-38 that only a part thereof shall be stated capital. [47-3-36]

Within a period of sixty days after the issuance of any shares without par value, the board of directors may allocate to capital surplus any portion of the consideration received for the issuance of such shares. No such allocation shall be made of any portion of the consideration received for shares without par value having a preference in the assets of the corporation in the event of involuntary liquidation except the amount, if any, of such consideration in excess of such preference. [47-3-37]

A corporation except corporations not for profit shall not do or engage in any business or incur any indebtedness, except such as shall be incidental to its organization or to obtaining subscriptions to or payment for its shares, until there has been paid in for the issuance of shares consideration of the value of at least one thousand dollars. [47-3-40]

The shareholders of a corporation shall have the preemptive right to acquire unissued or treasury shares of the corporation, or obligations of the corporation convertible into such shares, except to the extent, if any, that such right is limited or denied in the articles of incorporation. [47-3-47]

Except as provided in § 47-3-12.1, the shares of a corporation shall be represented by certificates signed by the president or a vice president and the secretary or an assistant secretary of the corporation, and may be sealed with the seal of the corporation or a facsimile thereof. [47-3-12]

Each certificate representing shares issued by a corporation shall state on the face thereof: (1) that the corporation is organized under the laws of this state; (2) the name of the person to whom issued; (3) the number and class of shares and the designation of the series, if any, which such certificate represents; (4) the par value of each share represented by such certificate, or a statement that the shares are without par value. [47-3-14]

Director Meeting Rules

Regular meetings of the board of directors may be held with or without notice as prescribed in the bylaws. Special meetings of the board of directors shall be held on such notice as is prescribed in the bylaws. Attendance of a director at a meeting shall constitute a waiver of notice of such meeting, except where a director attends a meeting for the express purpose of objecting to the transaction of any business because the meeting is not lawfully called or convened. Neither the business to be transacted at, nor the purpose of, any regular or special meeting of the board of directors need be specified in the notice or waiver of notice of such meeting unless required by the bylaws. [47-5-9]

A majority of the number of directors fixed by the bylaws, or in the absence of a bylaw fixing the number of directors, then of the number stated in the Articles of Incorporation, shall constitute a quorum for the transaction of business unless a greater number is required by the Articles of Incorporation or the bylaws. The act of the majority of the directors present at a meeting at which a quorum is present shall be the act of the board of directors, unless the act of a greater number is required by the Articles of Incorporation or the bylaws. [47-5-12]

Shareholder Meeting Rules

An annual meeting of the shareholders shall be held at such time as may be provided in the bylaws. [47-4-2]

At the first annual meeting of shareholders and at each annual meeting thereafter the shareholders shall elect directors to hold office until the next succeeding annual meeting, except in case of the classification of directors as permitted by the Business Corporation Act. Each director shall hold office for the term for which he is elected and until his successor shall have been elected and qualified. [47-5-2]

Special meetings of the shareholders may be called by the president, the board of directors, the holders of not less than one-tenth of all the shares entitled to vote at the meeting, or such other officers or persons as may be provided in the Articles of Incorporation or the bylaws. [47-4-3]

Except for the increase of stock and indebtedness when 60 days' notice is required by Article XVII, Section 8, of the South Dakota Constitution, written notice stating the place, day, and hour of the meeting and, in case of a special meeting, the purpose or purposes for which the meeting is called, shall be delivered not less than ten nor more than 50 days before the date of the meeting, either personally or by mail, by or at the direction of the president, the secretary, or the officer or persons calling the meeting, to each shareholder of record entitled to vote at such meeting. [47-4-5]

Unless otherwise provided in the Articles of Incorporation, a majority of the shares entitled to vote, represented in person or by proxy, shall constitute a quorum at a meeting of shareholders, but in no event shall a quorum consist of less than one-third of the shares entitled to vote at the meeting. If a quorum is present, the affirmative vote of the majority of the shares represented at the meeting and entitled to vote on the subject matter shall be the act of the shareholders unless the vote of a greater number or voting by classes is required by the Business Incorporation Act, Articles of Incorporation, or bylaws. [47-4-13]

At each election for directors every shareholder entitled to vote at such election shall have the right to vote, in person or by proxy, the number of shares owned by him for as many persons as there are directors to be elected and for whose election he has a right to vote, or to cumulate his votes by giving one candidate as many votes as the number of such directors multiplied by the number of his shares shall equal, or by distributing such votes on the same principle among any number of candidates. [47-4-17]

To render effective the cumulative voting rights provided by Article XVII, Section 5, of the Constitution of South Dakota, and except as hereinafter provided, where several directors are to be elected for terms of the same duration: (1) they shall be chosen by the same ballot or vote, each shareholder entitled to vote to have the right to multiply the number of votes to which he may be entitled under provisions hereof, by the number of directors to be so elected, and cast all of such votes for one candidate, or distribute them among two or more candidates, as he may prefer; (2) where such right of cumulative voting is exercised, there shall be deemed elected the candidates receiving the most votes for the places to be filled by such election, but where such right of cumulative voting is not exercised, an election shall require a majority of the eligible votes represented at such corporate meeting; (3) if there exists a tie vote between candidates, with resulting failure of choice as to any place as director, such choice shall be determined by drawing of lots under such procedure that all rights of the candidates involved in such tie are adequately safeguarded. [47-5-6]

Financial Disclosure Rules

On the written request of any shareholder of a corporation, the corporation shall mail to such shareholder its most recent financial statements showing in reasonable detail its assets and liabilities and the results of its operations. [47-4-29]

State Tax Information

Department of Revenue, Pierre
605-773-3311
www.state.sd.us/revenue/revenue.html

South Dakota does not impose a corporate or personal income tax.

Corporation Law Online

The South Dakota Business Corporation Act is contained in Title 47 (Corporations) of the South Dakota Codified Laws, starting with section 47-1-1. You can browse it from the URL shown below. Click "Title List," then click "47, Corporation" in the index list. Chapters 2 through 7 contain most of the relevant sections.

http://legis.state.sd.us/statutes/index.cfm

State Securities Information

Division of Securities
118 West Capitol Avenue
Pierre, SD 57501
605-773-4823
www.state.sd.us/drr2/securities/index.htm

The South Dakota Uniform Securities Act is found in Chapter 47-31A of the South Dakota Statutes. You can browse the Act from the Division of Securities website or by following the directions in "Corporation Law Online," above, and choosing Chapter 31A from the chapter list. Section 47-31A-402(b) exempts certain securities transactions from registration. For example, Section 47-31A-402(b)(10) exempts offers or sales of securities to up to ten of a South Dakota corporation's original incorporators or subscribers (people who agree to buy shares), provided that (1) the securities are not acquired for the purpose of sale to others; (2) no commission or other compensation has been paid; (3) no advertising has been published or circulated in connection with the sale; and (4) all sales are complete within 30 days after the corporation begins to do business. There are other exemptions, such as the one found in Section 47-31A-402(b)(9) that exempts qualified sales of securities by a South Dakota corporation to not more than five people in the state during a period of 12 consecutive months if (1) you reasonably believe that all the buyers (other than banks, savings institutions, trust companies, insurance companies, and investment companies) are purchasing for investment; (2) no commission or other compensation is paid or given directly or indirectly for soliciting any prospective buyer; and (3) no public advertisement is used in connection with the sale. You may need to file a notice form and pay fees to qualify for an exemption. Call the Division of Securities to obtain complete qualification requirements before issuing your initial shares.

Creating Your Own Articles Form

You can prepare and file your own typewritten or printed form.

TENNESSEE

Corporate Filing Office

Tennessee Department of State
Business Services Division
312 Eighth Avenue North
6th Floor, Snodgrass Tower
Nashville, TN 37243
615-741-2286
www.state.tn.us/sos/bus-svc/corporations.htm

State Corporate Forms

Tennessee provides a fill-in-the-blanks Charter form (Form SS-4417). ("Charter" is the Tennessee name for Articles of Incorporation.)

Internet Forms: You can download a Charter form with instructions, plus other plus other corporate forms, from the state filing office website. The website also provides a downloadable "Filing Guide."

Articles Instructions

Note for Specially Licensed Professionals: The Charter of a professional corporation must state that it is a professional corporation and that its purpose is to render specified professional services (for example, medicine or law). The state-provided articles form does not include this provision. Also, prior to rendering professional services, a professional firm may have to file a certified copy of the Charter with appropriate licensing authorities. See the "Filing Guide" posted on the state corporate filing office website for additional information if you wish to form a professional corporation.

Article 1: The name of a Tennessee corporation must contain the word "corporation," "incorporated," or "company," or the abbreviation "corp.," "inc.," or "co."

You can check to see whether your proposed corporate name is available by calling the state corporate filing office or by using the business name availability search at the filing office's website. You can reserve an available corporate name for four months for $20.

Article 2: In Tennessee, you do not need to state a par value for your shares. Most incorporators authorize one class of common shares with equal voting, dividend, and liquidation rights and no special restrictions. To do this, simply insert the total number of authorized shares in the space provided. Your filing fee is not based on the number of shares authorized in your articles, so you can authorize as many shares as you wish.

If you want to authorize special classes of shares, you must specify the name of each class, the number of shares in each class, and the rights and restrictions associated with each class in your Charter. You can do this by attaching a separate page to your articles, which you can refer to in Article 8 (where you will include any additional provisions with your Charter).

Article 4: You need have only one incorporator, who is not required to be a director, officer, or shareholder.

Article 7: You can leave this item blank. Doing so means that your corporation will be formed on the date you file your Charter. If you wish to have the legal existence of your corporation delayed until after you file your Charter, insert a specific formation date and time. Your delayed date cannot be later than the 90th day after the date the Charter is filed.

Submit the original Charter and one copy for filing. After approving your Charter, the state filing office will return to you a file-stamped copy of the document. You must file a copy of the file-stamped Charter with the Registry of Deeds in the county where the corporation has its principal office.

Filing Fee: $100, payable to the "Tennessee Secretary of State."

Director and Officer Rules

A board of directors must consist of one (1) or more individuals, with the number specified in or fixed in accordance with the Charter or bylaws.

Directors are elected at the first annual shareholders' meeting and at each annual meeting thereafter, unless their terms are staggered under Section 48-18-106 or unless their terms are for more than one (1) year as provided by Section 48-18-105. [48-18-103]

The terms of the initial directors of a corporation expire at the first shareholders' meeting at which directors are elected.

The terms of all other directors expire at the next annual shareholders' meeting following their election unless their terms are staggered under Section 48-18-106, or unless the Charter provides for terms of more than one (1) year but not more than three (3) years. [48-18-105]

A corporation has the officers described in its bylaws or designated by its board of directors in accordance with the bylaws, provided that every corporation shall have a president and a secretary. Unless the Charter or bylaws provide otherwise, officers shall be elected or appointed by the board of directors.

The bylaws or the board of directors shall delegate to one (1) of the officers responsibility for preparing minutes of the directors' and shareholders' meetings and for authenticating records of the corporation.

The same individual may simultaneously hold more than one (1) office in a corporation, except the offices of president and secretary. If the corporation has only one (1) shareholder, such shareholder may hold the offices of president and secretary. [48-18-401]

Share Issuance Rules

The board of directors may authorize shares to be issued for consideration consisting of any tangible or intangible property or benefit to the corporation, including cash, promissory notes, services performed, contracts for services to be performed, or other benefits to be received, or other securities of the corporation.

The corporation may place in escrow shares issued for a contract for future services or benefits or a promissory note, or make other arrangements to restrict the transfer of the shares, and may credit distributions in respect of the shares against their purchase price, until the services are performed, the note is paid, or the benefits received. If the services are not performed, the note is not paid, or the benefits are not received, the shares escrowed or restricted and the distributions credited may be cancelled in whole or in part. [48-16-202]

At a minimum each share certificate must state on its face: (1) the name of the issuing corporation and that it is organized under the laws of this state; (2) the name of the person to whom issued; and (3) the number and class of shares and the designation of the series, if any, the certificate represents.

Each share certificate: (1) shall be signed (either manually or in facsimile) by two (2) officers designated in the bylaws or by the board of directors; and (2) may bear the corporate seal or its facsimile. [48-16-206]

Director Meeting Rules

The board of directors may hold regular or special meetings in or out of the state of Tennessee. Unless the bylaws otherwise provide, special meetings of the board of directors may be called by the chair of the board, the president, or any two directors. [48-18-201]

Unless the Charter or bylaws provide otherwise, regular meetings of the board of directors may be held without notice of the date, time, place, or purpose of the meeting.

Unless the Charter or bylaws provide for a longer or shorter period, special meetings of the board of directors must be preceded by at least two days' notice of the

date, time, and place of the meeting. The notice need not describe the purpose of the special meeting unless required by the Charter or bylaws. [48-18-203]

Unless the Charter or bylaws require a greater number, a quorum of a board of directors consists of: (1) a majority of the fixed number of directors if the corporation has a fixed board size; or (2) a majority of the number of directors prescribed, or, if no number is prescribed, the number in office immediately before the meeting begins, if the corporation has a variable-range size board.

The Charter or bylaws may authorize a quorum of a board of directors to consist of no fewer than one-third of the fixed or prescribed number of directors determined under Subsection (a) [above].

If a quorum is present when a vote is taken, the affirmative vote of a majority of directors present is the act of the board of directors unless the Charter or bylaws require the vote of a greater number of directors. [48-18-205]

Shareholder Meeting Rules

At a time stated in or fixed in accordance with the bylaws, a corporation shall hold annually a meeting of shareholders. [48-17-101]

A corporation shall hold a special meeting of shareholders: (1) on call of its board of directors or the person or persons authorized to do so by the Charter or bylaws; or (2) unless the Charter otherwise provides, if the holders of at least 10% of all the votes entitled to be cast on any issue proposed to be considered at the proposed special meeting sign, date, and deliver to the corporation's secretary one or more written demands for the meeting describing the purpose or purposes for which it is to be held.

A corporation shall notify shareholders of the date, time, and place of each annual and special shareholders' meeting no fewer than ten days nor more than two months before the meeting date. Unless the Business Corporation Act or the Charter requires otherwise, the corporation is required to give notice only to shareholders entitled to vote at the meeting.

Unless the Business Corporation Act or the Charter requires otherwise, notice of an annual meeting need not include a description of the purpose or purposes for which the meeting is called.

Notice of a special meeting must include a description of the purpose or purposes for which the meeting is called. [48-17-105]. Only business within the purpose or purposes described in the meeting notice may be conducted at a special shareholders' meeting. [48-17-102]

Shares entitled to vote as a separate voting group may take action on a matter at a meeting only if a quorum of those shares exists with respect to that matter. Unless the Charter or the Business Corporation Act provides otherwise, a majority of the votes entitled to be cast on the matter by the voting group constitutes a quorum of that voting group for action on that matter.

If a quorum exists, action on a matter (other than the election of directors) by a voting group is approved if the votes cast within the voting group favoring the action exceed the votes cast opposing the action, unless the Charter or the Business Corporation Act requires a greater number of affirmative votes.

The election of directors is governed by Section 48-17-209. [48-17-206]

Unless otherwise provided in the Charter, directors are elected by a plurality of the votes cast by the shares entitled to vote in the election at a meeting at which a quorum is present.

Shareholders do not have a right to cumulate their votes for directors unless the Charter so provides.

A statement included in the Charter that "(all) (a designated voting group of) shareholders are entitled to cumulate their votes for directors" (or words of similar import) means that the shareholders designated are entitled to multiply the number of votes they are entitled to cast by the number of directors for whom they are entitled to vote and cast the product for a single candidate or distribute the product among two or more candidates.

Shares otherwise entitled to vote cumulatively may not be voted cumulatively at a particular meeting unless: (1) the meeting notice or proxy statement accompanying the notice states conspicuously that cumulative voting is authorized; or (2) a shareholder who has the right to cumulate that shareholder's votes gives notice to the corporation no fewer than 48 hours before the time set for the meeting of that shareholder's intent to cumulate that shareholder's votes during the meeting, and if one shareholder gives this notice, all other shareholders in the same voting group participating in the election are entitled to cumulate their votes without giving further notice. [48-17-209]

Financial Disclosure Rules

A corporation shall prepare annual financial statements, which may be consolidated or combined statements of the corporation and one or more of its subsidiaries, as appropriate, that include a balance sheet as of the end of the fiscal year, an income statement for that year, and a statement of changes in shareholders' equity for the year unless that information appears elsewhere in the financial statements. If financial statements are prepared for the corporation on the basis of generally accepted accounting principles, the annual financial statements must also be prepared on that basis. If requested in writing by any shareholder, the corporation shall furnish such statements to the shareholder as set out in Subsection (c) [below].

If the annual financial statements are reported on by a public accountant, the public accountant's report must accompany them. If not, the statements must be accompanied by a statement of the president or the person responsible for the corporation's accounting records: (1) stating the president's or other person's reasonable belief whether the statements were prepared on the basis of generally accepted accounting principles and, if not, describing the basis of preparation; and (2) describing any respects in which the statements were not prepared on a basis of accounting consistent with the statements prepared for the preceding year.

A corporation shall mail the annual financial statements to each requesting shareholder within one month after notice of the request, provided that with respect to the financial statements for the most recently completed fiscal year, the statements shall be mailed to the shareholder within four months after the close of the fiscal year. [48-26-201]

State Tax Information

Department of Revenue, Nashville

615-741-2461

www.state.tn.us/revenue

Tennessee corporations are subject to an annual excise tax and a franchise tax. The minimum annual franchise tax is $100.

Corporation Law Online

The Tennessee Business Corporation Act is contained in Title 48 (Corporations and Associations), Chapter 11 through 35 of the Tennessee Code, starting with Section 48-11-101. You can browse it from the following web page:

www.michie.com/resources1.html

State Securities Information

Department of Commerce and Insurance
Securities Division
Securities Registration Section
500 James Robertson Parkway
Davy Crockett Tower, Suite 680
Nashville, TN 37243-0584
615-741-5911 (Toll Free: 800-863-9117)
www.state.tn.us/commerce/securdiv.html

The Tennessee Securities Act is contained in Title 48, Chapter 2, Part 1, of the Tennessee Code. You can browse it by following the instructions in "Corporation Law Online," above, except that you should open Chapter 2 and Part 1. Section 48-2-103(b)(4) contains an exemption for the sale of securities to 15 or fewer persons within a 12-month period without advertising provided other conditions are met. The Securities Division website currently provides only investor, not issuer, information. See the Act and call the Securities Division for additional information about exemptions.

Creating Your Own Articles Form

Your Charter form must be typewritten or legibly printed in ink, on only one side of letter or legal size paper.

TEXAS

Corporate Filing Office

Texas Secretary of State
Statutory Filings Division
Corporations Section
P.O. Box 13697
Austin, TX 78711
512-463-5583
www.sos.state.tx.us/corp/index.shtml

State Corporate Forms

Texas provides fill-in-the-blanks Articles of Incorporation (Form 201).

Internet Forms: You can find the Articles of Incorporation form (Form 201) and other statutory forms at the state corporate filing office website. You can fill in and file Texas articles online through the state's SOSDirect online form filing service, which is linked to the state corporate filing office website.

Articles Instructions

These instructions are geared to the state-provided articles form, but they apply as well to the SOSDirect questionnaire used to prepare and file articles online.

Article 1: The name of a Texas corporation must contain the word "corporation," "company," or "incorporated," or an abbreviation of one of these words.

You can check name availability online by using the SOSDirect name availability search service, over the phone by calling the state filing office, or by email to corpinfo@sos.state.tx.us. You can reserve an available corporate name for 120 days for $40. If you reserve a name, we recommend that you do it online using the SOSDirect service linked to the corporate filing office website, but you can prepare and mail a name reservation request to the office if you prefer.

Article 2: Check box B, and insert the name of the registered agent and registered office information. The registered agent must be a Texas resident, and the registered office address must be in Texas. You may use a P.O. Box address as the registered office address if the population of the city where the registered office is located is less than 5,000.

Article 3: Insert a name and address for each of your initial directors. Your corporation may have one or more directors.

Article 4: Check box A or B and fill in the blank to show the total number of authorized shares. The filing fee is not based on the number of authorized shares, so you may authorize as many as you wish. The modern trend is to authorize shares without par value. If you authorize no-par shares, check box B; if you authorize par value shares, check box A and also insert the par value amount per share. In either case, insert the total number of authorized shares in the designated blank.

Most incorporators authorize one class of common shares with equal voting, dividend, and liquidation rights and no special restrictions. If you wish to authorize separate classes of shares, specify the name of each class, the par value of each class or the fact that the shares in a class are without par value, the number of shares in each class, and the rights and restrictions associated with each class in the Supplemental Provisions/Information portion of the Articles. Refer to this supplemental information in Article 4, box A or B.

Article 6: The general purpose clause in the standard form works just fine for most incorporators of a regular business corporation. However, if you are incorporating as an insurance agent, you must retype your articles and insert a statement that specifies the specific type or types of insurance agency you are incorporating. Insurance agents can either use this form to incorporate a business corporation, or they may file special articles for a professional corporation. Other licensed professionals should incorporate by using a special Articles of Incorporation for a Professional Corporation posted on the state corporate filing office website. See the state corporate filing office website for additional information when incorporating any type of licensed professional practice to make sure you use the proper articles form.

Incorporator: You need have only one incorporator, who is not required to be a director, officer, or shareholder. Your incorporator must be at least 18 years old. The state filing office will accept just a city and state as the address of your incorporator. Have your incorporator sign the articles at the bottom of the page.

Effective Date of Filing: If you do not wish to specify a delayed effective date for your articles, check the first box. This means that the legal life of your corporation begins when the articles are filed. Alternatively, you can check the second box instead, then insert a delayed effective date in the blank. In this case, the legal life of your corporation begins on the specified delayed effective date. Your delayed date cannot be more than 90 days after the articles are filed by the Secretary of State.

Submit the original and one copy of your Articles of Incorporation. After the state approves and files your articles, the filing office will send you a Certificate of Incorporation and a file-stamped copy of the articles.

Filing Fee: $300, payable to the "Secretary of State."

Publication Requirement for Some Incorporators: The Texas Miscellaneous Corporation Laws Act requires an existing unincorporated business that plans to incorporate without changing its name to publish its intent to incorporate in the local newspaper for four consecutive weeks.

Director and Officer Rules

The board of directors of a corporation shall consist of one or more members.

At the first annual meeting of shareholders and at each annual meeting thereafter, the holders of shares entitled to vote in the election of directors shall elect directors to hold office until the next succeeding annual meeting, except in case of the classification of directors as permitted by this Act. [Art. 2.32]

The officers of a corporation shall consist of a president and a secretary, each of whom shall be elected by the board of directors at such time and in such manner as may be prescribed by the bylaws. Such other officers, including assistant officers and agents as may be deemed necessary, may be elected or appointed by the board of directors or chosen in such other manner as may be prescribed by the bylaws. Any two (2) or more offices may be held by the same person. [Art. 2.42]

Share Issuance Rules

Shares having a par value may be issued for such consideration, not less than the par value thereof, as shall be fixed from time to time by the board of directors or, in the case of shares issued by a converted entity, in the plan of conversion or, in the case of a corporation created by a merger, in the plan of merger.

Shares without par value may be issued for such consideration, as may be fixed: (1) by the board of directors from time to time, unless the Articles of Incorporation reserve to the shareholders the right to fix the consideration, in which case, prior to the issuance of such shares, the shareholders shall fix the consideration to be received for such shares, by a vote of the holders of a majority of all shares entitled to vote thereon; (2) by a plan of conversion, in the case of shares to be issued pursuant to the plan of conversion by a corporation that is a converted entity; or (3) by a plan of merger, in the case of shares to be issued pursuant to the plan of merger by a corporation created pursuant to the plan of merger. [Art. 2.15]

The board of directors or, in the case of shares to be issued pursuant to a plan of conversion by a corporation that is a converted entity, the plan of conversion, or, in the case of shares to be issued pursuant to a plan of merger by a corporation created pursuant to the plan of merger, the plan of merger may authorize shares to be issued for consideration consisting of any tangible or intangible benefit to the corporation or other property of any kind or nature, including cash, promissory notes, services performed, contracts for services to be performed, other securities of the corporation, or securities of any other corporation, domestic or foreign, or other entity. [2.16]

Certificates representing shares shall be signed by such officer or officers as the bylaws of the corporation shall prescribe, and may be sealed with the seal of the corporation or a facsimile thereof.

Each certificate representing shares shall state on the face thereof: (1) that the corporation is organized under the laws of this State; (2) the name of the person to whom issued; (3) the number and class of shares and the designation of the series, if any, which such certificate represents; (4) the par value of each share represented by such certificate, or a statement that the shares are without par value. [Art. 2.19]

Director Meeting Rules

Regular meetings of the board of directors may be held with or without notice as prescribed in the bylaws. Special meetings of the board of directors shall be held on such notice as is prescribed in the bylaws. Attendance of a director at a meeting shall constitute a waiver of notice of such meeting, except where a director attends a meeting for the express purpose of objecting to the transaction of any business on the ground that the meeting is not lawfully called or convened. Neither the business to be transacted at, nor the purpose of, any regular or special meeting of the board of directors need be specified in the notice or waiver of notice of such meeting, unless required by the bylaws. [Art. 2.37]

A majority of the number of directors fixed by, or in the manner provided in, the Articles of Incorporation or the bylaws shall constitute a quorum for the transaction of business unless a different number or portion is required by law or the Articles of Incorporation or the bylaws. In no case may the Articles of Incorporation or bylaws provide that less than one-third of the number of directors so fixed constitute a quorum. The act of the majority of the directors present at a meeting at which a quorum is present shall be the act of the board of directors, unless the act of a greater number is required by law or the Articles of Incorporation or the bylaws. [Art. 2.35]

Shareholder Meeting Rules

An annual meeting of the shareholders shall be held at such time as may be stated in or fixed in accordance with the bylaws.

Special meetings of the shareholders may be called (1) by the president, the board of directors, or such other person or persons as may be authorized in the Articles of Incorporation or the bylaws or (2) by the holders of at least 10% of all the shares entitled to vote at the proposed special meeting, unless the Articles of Incorporation provide for a number of shares greater than or less than 10%, in which event special meetings of the shareholders may be called by the holders of at least the percentage of shares so specified in the Articles of Incorporation, but in no event shall the Articles of Incorporation provide for a number of shares greater than 50%. If not otherwise stated in or fixed in accordance with the bylaws of the corporation, the record date for determining shareholders entitled to call a special meeting is the date the first shareholder signs the notice of that meeting. Only business within the purpose or purposes described in the notice required by Article 2.25 of the Business Corporation Act [below] may be conducted at a special meeting of the shareholders. [Art. 2.24]

Written or printed notice stating the place, day, and hour of the meeting and, in case of a special meeting, the purpose or purposes for which the meeting is called, shall be delivered not less than ten nor more than 60 days before the date of the meeting, either personally or by mail, by or at the direction of the president, the secretary, or the officer or person calling the meeting, to each shareholder entitled to vote at such meeting. [Art. 2.25]

With respect to any meeting of shareholders, a quorum shall be present for any matter to be presented at that meeting if the holders of a majority of the shares entitled to vote at the meeting are represented at the meeting in person or by proxy, unless otherwise provided in the Articles of Incorporation in accordance with this section. The Articles of Incorporation may provide: (1) that a quorum shall be present at a meeting of shareholders only if the holders of a specified greater portion of the shares entitled to vote are represented at the meeting in person or by proxy; or (2) that a quorum shall be present at a meeting of shareholders if the holders of a specified lesser portion, but not less than one-third, of the shares entitled to vote are represented at the meeting in person or by proxy.

With respect to any matter, other than the election of directors or a matter for which the affirmative vote of the holders of a specified portion of the shares entitled to vote is required by the Business Corporation Act, the affir-

mative vote of the holders of a majority of the shares entitled to vote on, and that voted for or against or expressly abstained with respect to, that matter at a meeting of shareholders at which a quorum is present shall be the act of the shareholders, unless otherwise provided in the Articles of Incorporation or the bylaws in accordance with this section. With respect to any matter, other than the election of directors or a matter for which the affirmative vote of the holders of a specified portion of the shares entitled to vote is required by the Business Corporation Act, the Articles of Incorporation or the bylaws may provide: (1) that the act of the shareholders shall be the affirmative vote of the holders of a specified portion, but not less than a majority, of the shares entitled to vote on that matter; (2) that the act of the shareholders shall be the affirmative vote of the holders of a specified portion, but not less than a majority, of the shares entitled to vote on that matter and represented in person or by proxy at a meeting of shareholders at which a quorum is present; (3) that the act of the shareholders shall be the affirmative vote of the holders of a specified portion, but not less than a majority, of the shares entitled to vote on, and voted for or against, that matter at a meeting of shareholders at which a quorum is present; or (4) that the act of the shareholders shall be the affirmative vote of the holders of a specified portion, but not less than a majority, of the shares entitled to vote on, and that voted for or against or expressly abstained with respect to, that matter at a meeting of shareholders at which a quorum is present.

Unless otherwise provided in the Articles of Incorporation or the bylaws in accordance with this section, directors shall be elected by a plurality of the votes cast by the holders of shares entitled to vote in the election of directors at a meeting of shareholders at which a quorum is present. The Articles of Incorporation or the bylaws may provide: (1) that a director shall be elected only if the director receives the vote of the holders of a specified portion, but not less than a majority, of the shares entitled to vote in the election of directors; (2) that a director shall be elected only if the director receives the vote of the holders of a specified portion, but not less than a majority, of the shares entitled to vote in the election of directors and represented in person or by proxy at a meeting of shareholders at which a quorum is present; or (3) that a director shall be elected only if the director receives a specified portion, but not less than a majority, of the votes cast by the holders of shares entitled to vote in the election of directors at a meeting of shareholders at which a quorum is present. [Art. 2.28]

At each election for directors every shareholder entitled to vote at such election shall have the right (a) to vote the number of shares owned by him for as many persons as there are directors to be elected and for whose election he has a right to vote or (b) unless expressly prohibited by the Articles of Incorporation (in general or with respect to a specified class or series of shares or group of classes or series of shares) and subject to Subsection (2) of this Section D [next paragraph], to cumulate his votes by giving one candidate as many votes as the number of such directors multiplied by his shares shall equal, or by distributing such votes on the same principle among any number of such candidates.

Cumulative voting shall not be allowed in an election of directors unless a shareholder who intends to cumulate his votes as herein authorized shall have given written notice of such intention to the secretary of the corporation on or before the day preceding the election at which such shareholder intends to cumulate his votes. All shareholders entitled to vote cumulatively may cumulate their votes if any shareholder gives the written notice provided for herein. [Art. 2.29]

Financial Disclosure Rules

Any person who shall have been a shareholder for at least six months immediately preceding his demand, or shall be the holder of at least 5% of all the outstanding shares of a corporation, on written demand stating the purpose thereof, shall have the right to examine, in person or by agent, accountant, or attorney, at any reasonable time or times, for any proper purpose, its relevant books and records of account, minutes, and share transfer records, and to make extracts therefrom. [Art. 2.44]

State Tax Information

Comptroller of Public Accounts, Austin
800-252-1381
www.window.state.tx.us

Texas corporations are subject to an annual franchise tax.

Corporation Law Online

The Texas Business Corporation Act is contained in Title 32 (Corporations) of Vernon's Texas Revised Statutes, starting with Article 1.01. To find the Act, visit the legal research area of Nolo's website at www.nolo.com/statute/state.cfm. Click on "Texas." Choose "Business Corporation Act" from the top of the list to view the BCA.

State Securities Information

Texas State Securities Board
P.O. Box 13167
Austin, TX 78711-3167
512-305-8300
www.ssb.state.tx.us

The Texas Securities Act is contained in Article 581 of the Texas Revised Statutes. You can browse the Act, along with the Administrative Code and the Rules adopted under it, from the State Securities Board website. Section 5 of the Act contains exemptions for certain securities transactions. For example, Section 5(i) contains a small offering exemption for the nonadvertised sale of securities to 15 or fewer people during a 12-month period. It also exempts nonadvertised sales as long as the total number of all corporate security holders after the sale does not exceed 35. Rule 109.13 of the Administrative Code explains the requirements of the 5(i) exemptions. In addition, Sections (k) and (l) of Rule 109.13 create further limited offering exemptions and list their requirements. And you can find more exemptions in Rule 139.16 and Rule 139.19. For complete information on exemptions, see the Securities Board website and call its office at the telephone number shown above.

Creating Your Own Articles Form

You can prepare and file your own articles form.

UTAH

Corporate Filing Office

Utah Division of Corporations and Commercial Code
160 East 300 South, 2nd Floor
Box 146705
Salt Lake City, UT 84114-6705
801-530-4849 (Toll Free: 877-526-3994)
www.commerce.state.ut.us/corporat/corpcoc.htm

State Corporate Forms

Utah provides a guide called "Preparing Articles of Incorporation," which includes sample Articles of Incorporation.

Internet Forms: You can download "Preparing Articles of Incorporation" from the state filing office website, along with other corporate forms.

Articles Instructions

Use the sample Articles format shown in "Preparing Articles of Incorporation." Copy just the text shown in bold; the rest are instructions and explanations. Ignore all the references to the hypothetical pet-grooming corporation and substitute your own corporate information. Here is how your completed form should look, with additional instructions provided in brackets.

Articles of Incorporation of

[your corporate name]

We, the undersigned persons acting as incorporators under the Utah Revised Business Corporation Act, adopt the following Articles of Incorporation for such Corporation:

Article 1. The name of the corporation is [your corporate name].

[The name of a Utah corporation must contain the word "corporation," "incorporated," or "company," or the abbreviation "corp.," "inc.," or "co." You can check the availability of a corporate name on the state filing office website or by calling the office. An available corporate name can be reserved for 120 days for $22.]

Article 2. The purposes for which the corporation has been formed is to engage in and do any lawful act concerning any and all lawful business for which corporations may be organized under the Utah Business Corporation Act and any amendments thereto."

[The above general purposes clause is sufficient; you do not need to specify the specific business purposes of your corporation.]

Article 3. The corporation shall have authority to issue [number of shares of stock], which stock shall be of one class only, which shall be common voting stock. The common stock shall have unlimited voting rights pursuant to the Utah Revised Business Corporation Act.

[Note that we changed the wording of the sample language provided by the state filing office slightly for clarity. In Utah, you do not have to state a par value for your shares. Most incorporators authorize one class of common shares with equal voting, dividend, and liquidation rights and no special restrictions—as described in the article above. To do this, simply fill in the total number of shares you wish to authorize. Your filing fee is not based on the number of shares authorized in your articles, so you can authorize as many as you wish. If you want to authorize special classes of shares, you must specify the name of each class, the number of shares in each class, and the rights and restrictions associated with each class.]

Article 4. The address of the corporation's initial registered office shall be [registered office street address]. The corporation's initial registered agent at such address shall be [name of initial registered agent].

I hereby acknowledge and accept appointment as the corporation's registered agent. Signature: [have the registered agent sign in this space].

[Most incorporators show the street address of the corporation as the registered office (the registered office must be a Utah street address, not a P.O. Box), and designate one of the initial directors, officers, or shareholders as the initial agent. The agent must be a Utah resident. Make sure to have the person designated as the initial agent sign in the designated space.]

Article 5. The name and address of the incorporator is [insert the name and address of your incorporator].

[You need just one incorporator, who is not required to be a director, officer, or shareholder. Your incorporator must be at least 18 years old.]

In Witness Whereof, I, [name of incorporator as stated in Article 5], have executed these Articles of Incorporation in duplicate this _____ day of _____ __, and say:

That I am the incorporator named herein; that I have read the above and foregoing Articles of Incorporation; know the contents thereof and that the same is true to the best of my knowledge and belief, excepting as to matters herein alleged on information and belief and as to those matters I believe to be true.

[Have your incorporator designated in Article 5 sign here]. The incorporator should also manually sign a copy of the completed articles. Submit signed original and signed copy of the articles for filing.

Filing Fee: $52, payable to "State of Utah."

Director and Officer Rules

Except as provided in Subsection (1)(b) [below], a corporation's board of directors must consist of a minimum of three individuals.

Before any shares are issued, a corporation's board of directors may consist of one or more individuals.

After shares are issued and for as long as a corporation has fewer than three shareholders entitled to vote for the election of directors, its board of directors may consist of a number of individuals equal to or greater than the number of those shareholders.

Directors are elected at each annual meeting of the shareholders except as provided in Section 16-10a-806 [which allows directors to be elected for staggered terms]. [16-10a-803]

Except as provided in Section 16-10a-806, the terms of the initial directors of a corporation expire at the first shareholders' meeting at which directors are elected.

Except as provided in Section 16-10a-806, the terms of all other directors expire at the next annual shareholders' meeting following their election. [16-10a-805]

A corporation shall have the officers designated in its bylaws or by the board of directors in a manner not inconsistent with the bylaws. Any officer shall be a natural person.

The bylaws or the board of directors shall delegate to one of the officers responsibility for the preparation and maintenance of minutes of the directors' and shareholders' meetings and other records and information required to be kept by the corporation under Section 16-10a-1601 and for authenticating records of the corporation.

The same individual may simultaneously hold more than one office in a corporation. [16-10a-830]

Share Issuance Rules

The board of directors may authorize the issuance of shares for consideration consisting of any tangible or intangible property or benefit to the corporation, including cash, promissory notes, services performed, contracts or arrangements for services to be performed, or other securities of the corporation. The terms and conditions of any tangible or intangible property or benefit to be provided in the future to the corporation, including contracts or arrangements for services to be performed, shall be set forth in writing. However, the failure to set forth the terms and conditions in writing does not affect the validity of the issuance of any shares issued for any consideration, or their status as fully paid and nonassessable shares.

The corporation may place in escrow shares issued in consideration for contracts or arrangements for future services or benefits or in consideration for a promissory note, or make other arrangements to restrict the transfer of the shares issued for any such consideration, and may credit distributions in respect of the shares against their purchase price, until the services are performed, the note is paid, or the benefits are received. If specified future services are not performed, the note is not paid, or the benefits are not received, the shares escrowed or restricted and the distributions credited may be cancelled in whole or part. [16-10a-621]

Each share certificate must state on its face: (a) the name of the issuing corporation and that it is organized under the laws of this state; (b) the name of the person to whom the certificate is issued; and (c) the number and class of shares and the designation of the series, if any, the certificate represents.

Each share certificate: (a) must be signed by two officers designated in the bylaws or by the board of directors; (b) may bear the corporate seal or its facsimile. [16-10a-625]

Director Meeting Rules

The board of directors may hold regular or special meetings in or out of the state of Utah. [16-10a-820]

Unless the Articles of Incorporation, bylaws, or Business Corporation Act provide otherwise, regular meetings of the board of directors may be held without notice of the date, time, place, or purposes of the meeting.

Unless the Articles of Incorporation or bylaws provide for a longer or shorter period, special meetings of the board of directors must be preceded by at least two days' notice of the date, time, and place of the meeting. The notice need not describe the purpose of the special meeting unless required by the Articles of Incorporation, bylaws, or Business Corporation Act. [16-10a-822]

Unless the Articles of Incorporation or bylaws require a greater number, or, as permitted in Subsection (2) [next paragraph], a lower number, a quorum of a board of directors consists of: (a) a majority of the fixed number of directors if the corporation has a fixed board size; or (b) a majority of the number of directors prescribed, or if no number is prescribed, of the number in office immediately before the meeting begins, if a range for the size of the board is established pursuant to Subsection 16-10a-803(2) [allows the corporation to set up a variable board size with a minimum and maximum number of directors].

The Articles of Incorporation or bylaws may authorize a quorum of a board of directors to consist of no fewer than 1/3 of the fixed or prescribed number of directors determined under Subsection (1) [previous paragraph].

If a quorum is present when a vote is taken, the affirmative vote of a majority of directors present is the act of the board of directors unless the Articles of Incorporation, bylaws, or Business Corporation Act require the vote of a greater number of directors. [16-10a-824]

Shareholder Meeting Rules

A corporation shall hold a meeting of shareholders annually at a time stated in or fixed in accordance with the bylaws. [16-10a-701]

A corporation shall hold a special meeting of shareholders: (a) on call of its board of directors or the person or persons authorized by the bylaws to call a special meeting; or (b) if the holders of shares representing at least 10% of all the votes entitled to be cast on any issue proposed to be considered at the proposed special meeting sign, date, and deliver to the corporation's secretary one or more written demands for the meeting, stating the purpose or purposes for which it is to be held.

A corporation shall give notice to shareholders of the date, time, and place of each annual and special shareholders' meeting no fewer than ten nor more than 60 days before the meeting date. Unless the Business Corporation Act or the Articles of Incorporation require otherwise, the corporation is required to give notice only to shareholders entitled to vote at the meeting.

Unless the Business Corporation Act or the Articles of Incorporation require otherwise, notice of an annual meeting need not include a description of the purpose or purposes for which the meeting is called.

Notice of a special meeting must include a description of the purpose or purposes for which the meeting is called. [16-10a-705]. Only business within the purpose or purposes described in the meeting notice may be conducted at a special shareholders' meeting, unless notice of the meeting is waived by all shareholders pursuant to Section 16-10a-706. [16-10a-702]

Shares entitled to vote as a separate voting group may take action on a matter at a meeting only if a quorum of those shares exists with respect to that matter. Unless the Articles of Incorporation or the Business Corporation Act provide otherwise, a majority of the votes entitled to be cast on the matter by the voting group constitutes a quorum of that voting group for action on that matter.

If a quorum exists, action on a matter, other than the election of directors, by a voting group is approved if the votes cast within the voting group favoring the action exceed the votes cast within the voting group opposing the action, unless the Articles of Incorporation or the Business Corporation Act requires a greater number of affirmative votes.

The election of directors is governed by Section 16-10a-728. [16-10a-725]

At each election of directors, unless otherwise provided in the Articles of Incorporation or the Business Corporation Act, every shareholder entitled to vote at the election has the right to cast, in person or by proxy, all of the votes to which the shareholder's shares are entitled for as many persons as there are directors to be elected and for whose election the shareholder has the right to vote.

Unless otherwise provided in the Articles of Incorporation or the Business Corporation Act, directors are elected by a plurality of the votes cast by the shares entitled to vote in the election, at a meeting of shareholders at which a quorum is present.

Shareholders do not have a right to cumulate their votes for the election of directors unless the Articles of Incorporation so provide.

A statement included in the Articles of Incorporation to the effect that all or a designated voting group of shareholders are entitled to cumulate their votes for directors, means that the shareholders designated are entitled to multiply the number of votes they are entitled to cast by the number of directors for whom they are entitled to vote and cast the product for a single candidate or distribute the product among two or more candidates.

Shares entitled to vote cumulatively may be voted cumulatively at each election of directors unless the Articles of Incorporation provide alternative procedures for the exercise of the cumulative voting rights. [16-10a-728]

Financial Disclosure Rules

None.

State Tax Information

Utah State Tax Commission, Salt Lake City
801-297-2200 (Toll Free: 800-662-4335)
http://tax.utah.gov

Utah corporations are subject to an annual corporate franchise tax with a minimum annual payment of $100.

Corporation Law Online

The Utah Revised Business Corporation Act is contained in Title 16 (Corporations), Chapter 10a of the Utah Code, starting with Section 16-10a-101. To find the Act, visit the legal research area of Nolo's website at www.nolo.com/statute/state.cfm. Click on "Utah." Select Title 16, then choose Chapter 10a to begin browsing the Act section by section.

State Securities Information

Division of Securities
Utah Department of Commerce
160 East 300 South, Box 146760
Salt Lake City, UT 84114-6760
801-530-6600 (Toll Free: 800-721-7233)
www.securities.state.ut.us

The Utah Uniform Securities Act is contained in Chapter 61 of the Utah Code. You can browse the Act, and associated securities rules, from the Division of Securities website (click "Statutes & Rules" on the home page). The site also provides information on registration and exemptions to registration (there are more than 30), plus downloadable forms. Section 61-1-14(2) of the Securities Act contains various exemptions for security transactions. For example, Section 61-1-14(2)(q) contains an exemption for issuers that meet the following requirements: (1) the transaction must be part of an issue in which there are not more than 15 purchasers in the state of Utah during any 12 consecutive months; (2) you may not use general solicitation or general advertising in connection with the offer or sale; (3) you may not pay a commission or other compensation, directly or indirectly, to a person other than a broker-dealer or agent licensed under the Business Corporation Act for soliciting a prospective purchaser in the state of Utah; (4) you must reasonably believe that all the purchasers in the state of Utah are purchasing for investment; and (5) the transaction must be part of an aggregate offering that does not exceed $500,000 (or a greater amount as prescribed by a Division rule) during any 12 consecutive months. (The last requirement means that the exempted stock sale cannot exceed $500,000 when added with similar stock sales made during the same one-year period.) Section 61-1-14(2)(n) contains another exemption for which you may qualify. It is very general and applies to "transactions not involving a public offering." (This language comes from the general nonpublic offering exemption contained in Section 4(2) of the federal Securities Act.) Additional exemptions are provided under the Rules for limited offerings as well as offerings to accredited investors. You may be required to file a form and pay a fee to qualify for an exemption. In most cases, you can ask for a confirmation of the availability of an exemption for your security transaction by writing to the Division and paying a $60 fee. To learn more, browse the website and pay particular attention to the Table of Exemptions, then call the Division of Securities.

Creating Your Own Articles Form

You must prepare and file your own articles form in Utah, following the "Articles Instructions," above. The state filing office does not provide a ready-to-use form.

VERMONT

Corporate Filing Office

Vermont Secretary of State
Corporations Division
81 River Street
Montpelier, VT 05609-1104
802-828-2386
www.sec.state.vt.us/corps/corpindex.htm

State Corporate Forms

Vermont provides fill-in-the blanks Articles of Incorporation.

Internet Forms: The Vermont Articles of Incorporation form is provided as an HTML page on the state filing office website. You can save the page as a text file from your browser, then edit the form and fill in the blanks with your word processor. No special document formatting is required, though you will probably wish to delete the instructions that appear on the sample form.

Articles Instructions

Corporate Name: The name of a Vermont corporation must contain the word "corporation," "incorporated," "company," or "limited," or the abbreviation "corp.," "inc.," "co.," or "ltd."

You can find out whether the name you want is available by searching the corporate database from the state filing office website, or you can call the filing office. An available corporate name can be reserved for 120 days for a $20 fee.

Note: You can insert a second name in the alternate name blank. Most incorporators will not specify an alternate name. To ensure that their first choice for a corporate name is available, savvy incorporators check name availability and reserve their first choice for a corporate name before preparing and filing articles.

Statutory Reference: Check the "General (T.11A)" box to form a regular business corporation. If you want to form a "close" corporation, operated under the terms of a specially drafted shareholders' agreement (most incorporators will not), or a professional corporation to render specially licensed services such as medicine, law, or accounting, go online to the state corporate filing office website for additional information on completing and filing your Articles form.

Registered Agent and Office: Typically, an initial director or shareholder is named as initial registered agent (the person authorized to receive legal documents on behalf of the corporation), and the street address of the corporation is given as the registered office address (which must be the business office of the registered agent). The registered agent must be a Vermont resident, and the registered office address must be in Vermont.

Fiscal Year: Specify the month when the corporation's fiscal (tax) year ends. If you are not yet sure, make your best guess. Many corporations have a calendar tax year and insert "December." If you leave this item blank, the state will assume that your corporate fiscal year ends in December, and will mail the corporation an annual report form after the end of the calendar year.

Number of Shares: In Vermont, you do not need to specify a par value for your shares. The modern trend is to issue shares without par value. In the first blank, insert the total number of shares you wish to authorize. (Your filing fee is not based on the number of shares, so you can authorize as many as you wish.) There are three additional blanks in this section of the articles, which you should fill in according to the type of shares you wish to issue. Most incorporators authorize one class of common shares with equal voting, dividend, and liquidation rights and no special restrictions. To do this, in the second blank, insert "Common Shares," then repeat the total number of shares you specified in the first blank. For example, if you showed "100,000" as the total number of shares in the first blank, fill in the second blank as follows: "Common Shares: 100,000." You can leave the next two blanks empty. If you want to authorize separate classes of shares, you must show the class name and amount of shares in each class in the second blank, then fill in the third and fourth blanks to show the names of the classes that have unlimited voting rights and are entitled to receive net corporate assets on dissolution, respectively. Again, if you authorize only common shares, you can leave the second and third lines blank—your common shares automatically have unlimited voting rights and are entitled to share in net corporate assets on dissolution.

Professional Corporations: Only professional corporations must fill in these blanks. Generally, a professional corporation is one that is specially licensed by the state and that needs state approval to incorporate—for example, doctors, lawyers, and accountants. See the state filing office website for additional requirements for forming a professional corporation.

Close Corporations: Most incorporators will not wish to set up a close corporation and will leave this section of the articles blank or delete this section from their form. A close corporation is one that has built-in restrictions on the transfer of its shares and is normally run under the terms of a specially prepared shareholders' agreement. For more information on close corporations, see the state filing office website.

Directors: Providing information about your directors is optional, and you can leave these lines blank. Your corporation needs at least three directors unless you have one or two shareholders only. If you have two shareholders, you must have two directors; if you have just one shareholder, you need only one director.

Incorporator: Insert the name and address of your incorporator, and also have the person sign on the line. You need just one incorporator, who need not be a director, officer, or shareholder. The incorporator must be at least 18 years of age.

Delayed Effective Date: Normally, your corporation's legal life starts on the date your articles are filed. However, you can insert a specific effective date in this blank if you wish to have your corporation's existence begin after the articles are filed. The delayed date cannot be more than 90 days after the date of filing.

Filing Fee: $75, payable to "Vermont Secretary of State."

Mail the original signed articles together with a check for fees to the state corporate filing office. After filing, the office will mail a Certificate of Incorporation to your incorporator.

Director and Officer Rules

A board of directors of a corporation which is not a close corporation dispensing with a board of directors pursuant to section 20.13 of this title must consist of three or more individuals, with the number specified in or fixed in accordance with the Articles of Incorporation or bylaws. If the number of shareholders in any corporation is less than three, the number of directors may be as few as the number of shareholders.

Directors are elected at the first annual shareholders' meeting and at each annual meeting thereafter unless their terms are staggered under Section 8.06 of this title. [8.03]

The terms of the initial directors of a corporation expire at the first shareholders' meeting at which directors are elected.

The terms of all other directors expire at the next annual shareholders' meeting following their election unless their terms are staggered under Section 8.06 of this title. [8.05]

A corporation has the officers described in its bylaws or appointed by the board of directors in accordance with

the bylaws, provided that a corporation shall have a president and a secretary. Any two or more offices may be held by the same person, except the offices of president and secretary, unless the corporation is a professional corporation organized under chapter 3 of Title 11.

The bylaws or the board of directors shall delegate to one of the officers responsibility for preparing minutes of the directors' and shareholders' meetings and for authenticating records of the corporation.

The same individual may simultaneously hold more than one office in a corporation.

An individual who holds more than one office may execute, acknowledge, or verify in more than one capacity any document required to be executed, acknowledged, or verified by the holders of two or more officers. [8.40]

Share Issuance Rules

The board of directors may authorize shares to be issued for consideration consisting of any tangible or intangible property or benefit to the corporation, including cash, services performed, or other securities of the corporation. Future services shall not constitute payment or part payment for shares of a corporation. [6.21]

At a minimum each share certificate must state: (1) on its face, the name of the issuing corporation and that it is organized under the law of this state; (2) on its face, the name of the person to whom issued; and (3) on its face, the number and class of shares and the designation of the series, if any, the certificate represents; [6.25]

The shareholders of a corporation do not have a preemptive right to acquire the corporation's unissued shares unless the Articles of Incorporation contain a statement that "the corporation elects to have preemptive rights," or words of similar import. [6.30]

Director Meeting Rules

The board of directors may hold regular or special meetings in or out of the state of Vermont. [8.20]

Unless the Articles of Incorporation or bylaws provide otherwise, regular meetings of the board of directors may be held without notice of the date, time, place, or purpose of the meeting.

Unless the Articles of Incorporation or bylaws provide for a longer or shorter period, special meetings of the board of directors must be preceded by at least two business days' notice of the date, time, and place of the meeting. The notice need not describe the purpose of the special meeting unless required by the Articles of Incorporation or bylaws. [8.22]

Unless the Articles of Incorporation or bylaws require a greater number, a quorum of a board of directors consists of: (1) a majority of the fixed number of directors if the corporation has a fixed board size; or (2) a majority of the number of directors prescribed, or, if no number is prescribed, the number in office immediately before the meeting begins, if the corporation has a variable-range size board.

If a quorum is present when a vote is taken, the affirmative vote of a majority of directors present is the act of the board of directors unless the Articles of Incorporation or bylaws require the vote of a greater number of directors. [8.24]

Shareholder Meeting Rules

A corporation shall hold a meeting of shareholders annually at a time stated in or fixed in accordance with the bylaws. [7.01]

A corporation shall hold a special meeting of shareholders: (1) on call of its board of directors or the person or persons authorized to do so by the Articles of Incorporation or bylaws; or (2) if the holders of at least 10% of all the votes entitled to be cast on any issue proposed to be considered at the proposed special meeting sign, date, and deliver to the corporation's secretary one or more written demands for the meeting describing the purpose or purposes for which it is to be held.

A corporation shall notify shareholders of the date, time, and place of each annual and special shareholders' meeting no fewer than ten nor more than 60 days before the meeting date. Unless the Business Corporation Act or the Articles of Incorporation require otherwise, the corporation is required to give notice only to shareholders entitled to vote at the meeting.

Unless the Business Corporation Act or the Articles of Incorporation require otherwise, notice of an annual meeting need not include a description of the purpose or purposes for which the meeting is called.

Notice of a special meeting must include a description of the purpose or purposes for which the meeting is called. [7.05] Only business within the purpose or purposes described in the meeting notice may be conducted at a special shareholders' meeting. [7.02]

Shares entitled to vote as a separate voting group may take action on a matter at a meeting only if a quorum of those shares exists with respect to that matter. Unless the Articles of Incorporation or the Business Corporation Act provides for a greater quorum, a majority of the votes entitled to be cast on the matter by the voting group constitutes a quorum of that voting group for action on that matter.

If a quorum exists, action on a matter (other than the election of directors) by a voting group is approved if the votes cast within the voting group favoring the action exceed the votes cast opposing the action, unless the Articles of Incorporation or the Business Corporation Act requires a greater number of affirmative votes. [7.25]

The election of directors is governed by Section 7.28 of the Business Corporation Act. [7.25]

If the Articles of Incorporation or the Business Corporation Act provides for voting by a single voting group on a matter, action on that matter is taken when voted on by that voting group as provided in Section 7.25 of the Business Corporation Act [previous paragraph]. [7.26]

Unless otherwise provided in the Articles of Incorporation, directors are elected by a plurality of the votes cast by the shares entitled to vote in the election at a meeting at which a quorum is present.

Shareholders do not have a right to cumulate their votes for directors unless the Articles of Incorporation so provide.

A statement included in the Articles of Incorporation that "(all) (a designated voting group of) shareholders are entitled to cumulate their votes for directors" (or words of similar import) means that the shareholders designated are entitled to multiply the number of votes they are entitled to cast by the number of directors for whom they are entitled to vote and cast the product for a single candidate or distribute the product among two or more candidates.

Shares otherwise entitled to vote cumulatively may not be voted cumulatively at a particular meeting unless: (1) the meeting notice or proxy statement accompanying the notice states conspicuously that cumulative voting is authorized; or (2) a shareholder who has the right to cumulate his or her votes gives notice to the corporation not less than 48 hours before the time set for the meeting of his or her intent to cumulate his or her votes during the meeting, and if one shareholder gives this notice all other shareholders in the same voting group participating in the election are entitled to cumulate their votes without giving further notice. [7.28]

Financial Disclosure Rules

A corporation shall furnish its shareholders annual financial statements, which may be consolidated or combined statements of the corporation and one or more of its subsidiaries, as appropriate, that include a balance sheet as of the end of the fiscal year, an income statement for that year, and a statement of changes in shareholders' equity for the year unless that information appears elsewhere in the financial statements. If financial statements are prepared for the corporation on the basis of generally accepted accounting principles, the annual financial statements must also be prepared on that basis.

If the annual financial statements are reported on by a public accountant, his or her report must accompany them. If not, the statements must be accompanied by a statement of the president or the person responsible for the corporation's accounting records: (1) stating his or her reasonable belief whether the statements were prepared on the basis of generally accepted accounting principles and, if not, describing the basis of preparation; and (2) describing any respect in which the statements were not prepared on a basis of accounting consistent with the statements prepared for the preceding year.

A corporation shall mail the annual financial statements to each shareholder within 120 days after the close of each fiscal year. Thereafter, on written request from a shareholder who was not mailed the statements, the corporation shall mail to the shareholder the latest financial statements. [16.20]

State Tax Information

Vermont Department of Taxes, Montpelier
802-828-2551
www.state.vt.us/tax

Vermont corporations are subject to a corporate income tax, with an annual minimum payment of $250.

Corporation Law Online

The Vermont Business Corporation Act is contained in Title 11A of the Vermont Statutes, starting with Section 1.01. To find the Act, visit the legal research area of Nolo's website at www.nolo.com/statute/state.cfm. Click on "Vermont." Choose "Statutes by Title" from the left margin of the page, then click on Title 11A to begin browsing the Act.

State Securities Information

Banking, Insurance, Securities, and Health Care Administration
Securities Division
80 Main Street, Drawer 20
Montpelier, VT 05620-3101
802-828-3420
www.bishca.state.vt.us/SecuritiesDiv/securindex.htm

The Vermont Securities Act is contained in Title 9 (Commerce and Trade), Chapter 131, of the Vermont Statutes, starting with Section 4201. To browse the Act, follow the directions in "Corporation Law Online," above. Select Title 9 and scroll down to Chapter 131 to read the laws. Section 4204(a) contains registration exemptions for certain securities transactions. For example, Section 4204(a)(9) contains an exemption for the sale of securities to no more than 25 people in the state of Vermont during any period of 12 consecutive months, if: (1) you reasonably believe that all the buyers in the state are purchasing for investment; (2) you do not pay commission or provide other compensation, directly or indirectly, for soliciting any prospective buyer in the state; and (3) you do not publish or circulate general advertising in connection with the sale. The Securities Division website provides general information about another exemption, the Vermont Small Business Offering Exemption (VSBOE). It permits you to raise $500,000 from up to 50 Vermont residents during a 12-month period if you meet the following requirements: (1) any public advertising of the securities is made in restricted format; (2) you provide a disclosure document that includes required information on the nature and risks of the investment; the document must be delivered to investors 24 hours before any sale; (3) you must file a notice with the Securities Division ten days prior to offering your securities and pay a $200 filing fee; (4) you must file a copy of any advertising you intend to circulate five days prior to its publication; and (5) you may not pay commissions to anyone for soliciting investors.

For more information regarding VSBOE and other Vermont Securities Laws, browse the Securities Division website and the Securities Act. Call the Division to obtain complete information on the requirements of available exemptions for the issuance of shares in your corporation.

Creating Your Own Articles Form

You can prepare and file your own aticles form.

VIRGINIA

Corporate Filing Office

Clerk of the State Corporation Commission
P.O. Box 1197
Richmond, VA 23218-1197
804-371-9733
Toll-free:1-866-SCC-CLK1
www.state.va.us/scc/division/clk/index.htm

State Corporate Forms

Virginia provides an Articles of Incorporation-Stock Corporation form (Form SCC619).

Internet Forms: You can download an Articles of Incorporation-Stock Corporation form (Form SCC619), as well as a Business Registration Guide, which contains tax, licensing, and other state information, from the state filing office website.

Note: Incorporators forming a corporation to practice a specially licensed profession such as law, medicine, accounting, engineering, or architecture, should use a special articles form (Form SCC544), which is posted on the state corporate filing office website.

Articles Instructions

Article 1: The name of a Virginia corporation must contain the word "corporation," "incorporated," "company," or "limited," or the abbreviation "corp.," "inc.," "co.," or "ltd."

Check to see whether your proposed name is available by performing a business entity name search on the Clerk's Information System, which is linked to the corporate filing office website. You can also check name availability by calling the state filing office. It costs $10 to reserve an available corporate name for 120 days. Note that corporate names must be distinguishable from names in use by all other types of entities registered with the state, including corporations, limited liability companies, and others. So make sure to check your proposed name against names used by all other entities registered with the state (select "Name Search all Entities" when performing an online name search).

Article 2: In Virginia, you do not need to specify a par value for shares. In the "Number of Shares Authorized" column, insert the total number of shares you wish to authorize. You can authorize up to 25,000 shares for the minimum incorporation fee (see below). Most incorporators authorize one class of common shares with equal voting, dividend, and liquidation rights and no special restrictions. To do this, in the "Class(es)" column, insert "Common Shares." If you want to authorize separate

classes of shares, you must show number of shares in each class in the first column, then the name of each class in the second column. Your articles will also need to specify the rights and restrictions associated with each class in this article; you must retype the articles to include this additional information.

Article 3: Insert the name of your corporation's initial agent, then select the type of agent by checking the appropriate box. Most incorporators choose an initial director who is a Virginia resident as the registered agent and check the first box that states "an initial director of the corporation."

Article 4: The registered office address (which is also the business address of your agent) must include a street address (or a rural route and box number if there is no street address). A post office box is an acceptable address only for towns or cities with a population 2,000 or less, if no street address (or rural route and box number) is associated with the registered office location.

IMPORTANT: Make sure the name of the county where the registered office is located appears in the blank in paragraph B (if you wish to specify the city instead, mark an "X" in the "city" box rather than the "county" box in paragraph B, then insert the name of the city in the blank at the end of paragraph B.

Article 5: Insert the names and addresses of your initial directors. Make sure that at least one director appears on this list, and that the initial director who is designated as your initial registered agent in Article 3 is included on the list. The initial directors hold the first board meeting and serve on the board of directors until directors are elected or reelected at the first annual meeting of shareholders.

Article 6: You need just one incorporator, who is not required to be an initial director, officer, or shareholder. Have the incorporator sign and insert the incorporator's name in the line next to the signature.

Submit the original articles for filing, along with the correct filing fee.

Filing Fee: $75 minimum, payable to "State Corporation Commission." Same- or next-day expedited filing is available for an additional fee, which ranges from $50 to $200.

Note: Virginia corporations also must pay an annual registration fee, which starts at $100 if the corporation authorizes from 1 to 5,000 shares in its Articles. The annual fee is higher for corporations that authorize more than 5,000 shares—see the annual registration fee schedule posted on the state filing office website.

The filing fee consists of a $25 filing fee plus a charter fee based on the number of shares authorized in the articles. The charter fee is $50 for each 25,000 shares or fraction thereof, up to one million shares. If your articles authorize more than a million shares, the charter portion of the incorporation fee is $2,500. The minimum charter fee is $50.

Examples:

If your articles authorize 25,000 shares, the incorporation fee is the minimum $75 ($50 charter fee plus $25 filing fee).

If your articles authorize 50,000 shares, the incorporation fee is $125 ($100 charter fee plus $25 filing fee).

If your articles authorize 60,000 shares, the incorporation fee is $175 ($150 charter fee plus $25 filing fee).

Director and Officer Rules

A board of directors shall consist of one or more individuals, with the number specified in or fixed in accordance with the bylaws, or, if not specified in or fixed in accordance with the bylaws, with the number specified in or fixed in accordance with the Articles of Incorporation.

Directors are elected at the first annual shareholders' meeting and at each annual meeting thereafter unless their terms are staggered under Section 13.1-678. [13.1-675]

The terms of the initial directors of a corporation expire at the first shareholders' meeting at which directors are elected.

The terms of all other directors expire at the next annual shareholders' meeting following their election unless their terms are staggered under Section 13.1-678. [13.1-677]

A corporation shall have such officers with such titles and duties as shall be stated in the bylaws or in a resolution of the board of directors that is not inconsistent with the bylaws and as may be necessary to enable it to execute documents that comply with Subsection F of Section 13.1-604.

The secretary or any other officer as designated in the bylaws or by resolution of the board shall have the responsibility for preparing and maintaining custody of minutes of the directors' and shareholders' meetings and for authenticating records of the corporation.

The same individual may simultaneously hold more than one office in a corporation. [13.1-693]

Share Issuance Rules

Any issuance of shares must be authorized by the board of directors. Shares may be issued for consideration consisting of any tangible or intangible property or benefit to the corporation, including cash, promissory notes, services performed, contracts for services to be performed, or other securities of the corporation.

The corporation may place in escrow shares issued for a contract for future services or benefits or a promissory note, or make other arrangements to restrict the transfer of the shares, and may credit distributions in respect of the shares against their purchase price, until the services are performed, the benefits are received, or the note is paid. If the services are not performed, the benefits are not received, or the note is not paid, the shares escrowed or restricted and the distributions credited may be canceled in whole or part. [13.1-643]

At a minimum each share certificate shall state on its face: 1. the name of the issuing corporation and that it is organized under the law of this Commonwealth; 2. the name of the person to whom issued; and 3. the number and class of shares and the designation of the series, if any, the certificate represents.

Each share certificate (i) shall be signed by two officers designated in the bylaws or by the board of directors and (ii) may bear the corporate seal or its facsimile. [13.1-647]

Unless limited or denied in the Articles of Incorporation and subject to the limitation in Subsection C of this section, the shareholders of a corporation have a preemptive right, granted on uniform terms and conditions prescribed by the board of directors to provide a fair and reasonable opportunity to exercise the right, to acquire proportional amounts of the corporation's unissued shares on the decision of the board of directors to issue them. [13.1-651]

Director Meeting Rules

The board of directors may hold regular or special meetings in or out of the Commonwealth of Virginia. [13.1-684]

Unless the Articles of Incorporation or bylaws provide otherwise, regular meetings of the board of directors may be held without notice of the date, time, place, or purpose of the meeting.

Special meetings of the board of directors shall be held on such notice as is prescribed in the Articles of Incorporation or bylaws, or when not inconsistent with the Articles of Incorporation or bylaws, by resolution of the board of directors. The notice need not describe the purpose of the special meeting unless required by the Articles of Incorporation or bylaws. [13.1-686]

Unless the Articles of Incorporation or bylaws require a greater number for the transaction of all business or any particular business, a quorum of a board of directors consists of: (1) a majority of the fixed number of directors if the corporation has a fixed board size; or (2) a majority of the number of directors prescribed, or if no number is prescribed the number in office immediately before the meeting begins, if the corporation has a variable-range size board.

The Articles of Incorporation or bylaws may authorize a quorum of a board of directors to consist of no fewer than one-third of the fixed or prescribed number of directors determined under Subsection A of this section.

If a quorum is present when a vote is taken, the affirmative vote of a majority of directors present is the act of the board of directors unless the Articles of Incorporation or bylaws require the vote of a greater number of directors. [13.1-688]

Shareholder Meeting Rules

A corporation shall hold annually at a time stated in or fixed in accordance with the bylaws a meeting of shareholders, except that if the Articles of Incorporation or bylaws of a corporation registered under the Investment Company Act of 1940 so provide, the corporation is not required to hold an annual meeting in any year in which the election of directors is not required to be held under the Investment Company Act of 1940. [13.1-654]

A corporation shall hold a special meeting of shareholders: (1) on call of the chairman of the board of directors, the president, the board of directors, or the person or persons authorized to do so by the Articles of Incorporation or bylaws; or (2) in the case of corporations having 35 or fewer shareholders of record, if the holders of at least 20% of all votes entitled to be cast on any issue proposed to be considered at the special meeting sign, date, and deliver to the corporation's secretary one or more written demands for the meeting describing the purpose or purposes for which it is to be held.

A corporation shall notify shareholders of the date, time, and place of each annual and special shareholders' meeting. Such notice shall be given no less than ten nor more than 60 days before the meeting date except that notice of a shareholders' meeting to act on an amendment of the Articles of Incorporation, a plan of merger or share exchange, a proposed sale of assets pursuant to Section 13.1-724, or the dissolution of the corporation shall be given not less than 25 nor more than 60 days before the meeting date. Unless the Stock Corporation Act or the Articles of Incorporation require otherwise, the corporation is required to give notice only to shareholders entitled to vote at the meeting.

Unless the Stock Corporation Act or the Articles of Incorporation require otherwise, notice of an annual meeting need not state the purpose or purposes for which the meeting is called.

Notice of a special meeting shall state the purpose or purposes for which the meeting is called. [13.1-658] Only business within the purpose or purposes described in the meeting notice may be conducted at a special shareholders' meeting. [13.1-655]

Shares entitled to vote as a separate voting group may take action on a matter at a meeting only if a quorum of those shares exists with respect to that matter. Unless the Articles of Incorporation or the Stock Corporation Act provides otherwise, a majority of the votes entitled to be cast on the matter by the voting group constitutes a quorum of that voting group for action on that matter.

If a quorum exists, action on a matter, other than the election of directors, by a voting group is approved if the votes cast within the voting group favoring the action exceed the votes cast opposing the action, unless the Articles of Incorporation or the Stock Corporation Act requires a greater number of affirmative votes.

The election of directors is governed by Section 13.1-669. [13.1-666]

If the Articles of Incorporation or the Stock Corporation Act provides for voting by a single voting group on a matter, action on that matter is taken when voted on by that voting group as provided in Section 13.1-665. [Note: This is a mistake in the Act; the reference should be to Section 13.1-666, quoted above.] [13.1-667]

The Articles of Incorporation may provide for (i) a lesser or greater quorum requirement for shareholders, but not less than one-third of the shares eligible to vote, or voting groups of shareholders; or (ii) a greater voting requirement for shareholders, or voting groups of shareholders, than is provided by the Stock Corporation Act. [13.1-668]

Unless otherwise provided in the Articles of Incorporation, directors are elected by a plurality of the votes cast by the shares entitled to vote in the election at a meeting at which a quorum is present.

Shareholders do not have a right to cumulate their votes for directors unless the Articles of Incorporation so provide.

A statement included in the Articles of Incorporation that "all of a designated voting group of shareholders are entitled to cumulate their votes for directors" or words of similar import means that the shareholders designated are entitled to multiply the number of votes they are entitled to cast by the number of directors for whom they are entitled to vote and cast the product for a single candidate or distribute the product among two or more candidates.

Shares otherwise entitled to vote cumulatively may not be voted cumulatively at a particular meeting unless: (1) the meeting notice or proxy statement accompanying the notice states conspicuously that cumulative voting is authorized; or (2) a shareholder who has the right to cumulate his votes gives notice to the secretary of the corporation not less than 48 hours before the time set for the meeting of his intent to cumulate his votes during the meeting. If one shareholder gives his notice all other shareholders in the same voting group participating in the election are entitled to cumulate their votes without giving further notice. [13.1-669]

Financial Disclosure Rules

If requested in writing by any shareholder, a corporation shall furnish the shareholder with the financial statements for the most recent fiscal year, which may be consolidated or combined statements of the corporation and one or more of its subsidiaries, as appropriate, that include a balance sheet as of the end of the fiscal year, an income statement for that year, and a statement of changes in shareholders' equity for the year unless that information appears elsewhere in the financial statements. If financial statements are prepared for the corporation on the basis of generally accepted accounting principles, the annual financial statements must also be prepared on that basis.

If the annual financial statements are reported on by a public accountant, his report must accompany them. If the annual financial statements are not reported on by a public accountant, the president or the person responsible for the corporation's accounting records shall provide the shareholder with a statement of the basis of accounting used in preparation of the annual financial statements and a description of any respects in which the statements were not prepared on a basis of accounting consistent with the statements prepared for the preceding year.

If a corporation does not comply with a shareholder's request for financial statements within 30 days of delivery of such request to the corporation, the circuit court in the city or county where the corporation's principal office is located, or, if none in this Commonwealth, where its registered office is located may, on application of the shareholder, summarily order the corporation to furnish such financial statements. [13.1-774]

State Tax Information

Virginia Department of Taxation, Richmond
804-367-8037
www.tax.virginia.gov

Virginia corporations are subject to a corporate income tax.

Corporation Law Online

The Virginia Stock Corporation Act is contained in Title 13.1 (Corporations) of the Virginia Code, Chapter 9, starting with Section 13.1-601. To find the Act, visit the legal research area of Nolo's website at www.nolo.com/statute/state.cfm. Click on "Virginia." Select "Table of Contents" and choose Title 13.1. Then select Chapter 9 to begin browsing the Act.

State Securities Information

State Corporation Commission
Securities and Retail Franchising Division
P.O. Box 1197
Richmond, VA 23218
804-371-9051
www.state.va.us/scc/division/srf/webpages/homepagejavab.htm

The Virginia Securities Act is contained in Title 13.1 (Corporations) of the Virginia Code, Chapter 5, starting with Section 13.1-501. You can browse the Act by following the directions in "Corporation Law Online," above (choosing Chapter 5 instead of Chapter 9) or by visiting the Securities and Retail Franchising Division website. From the Division website, you can also browse the associate rules that enforce the Securities Act. Section 13.1-514(B) of the Act contains exemptions from registration for certain security transaction. For example, Section 13.1-514(B)(7)(a) contains an exemption for sales of securities if, after the sale, the issuer has no more than 35 security holders (both within and outside Virginia), and if the securities have not been offered to the general public by advertisement or solicitation. Section 13.1-514(B)(7)(b) allows the Division to provide an exemption for other sales to 35 or fewer investors during a one-year period. The Division has done so in Section 100 of Chapter 40 of the Securities Rules, which lists the requirements of this limited transaction exemption. Section 13.1-514(B)(10) of the Act provides an exemption for the issuance of up to three shares of common stock to one or more incorporators. Other exemptions are available under the Act and the Securities Rules. See the Division website, browse the Act and Rules, and call the Division for complete information and requirements.

Creating Your Own Articles Form

You can prepare and file your own articles form. Use white, opaque 8-1/2" x 11" paper. Print on only one side of the page. Use a minimum 1" margin at the left, top, and bottom, and a minimum 1/2" right margin. Your form must be typewritten or printed with black ink.

WASHINGTON

Corporate Filing Office

Washington Secretary of State
Corporations Division
P.O. Box 40234
Olympia, WA 98504-0234
360-753-7115
www.secstate.wa.gov/corps

State Corporate Forms

Washington provides an Articles of Incorporation form.

Internet Forms: Washington provides an online Articles of Incorporation preparation and filing service on its state filing office website. Just click on the "Online Application to Form a Profit Corporation" link on the main page of the website, then fill in the screens as you follow the online instructions. You can also download a Washington Articles of Incorporation form (Application to Form a Profit Corporation) from the state corporate filing office website.

Articles Instructions

Top of Form: In the box at the top of the form, insert information about the person the state filing office can contact with any questions about your Articles. You'll probably want to give the name and telephone number of your incorporator—the person who signs your Articles.

Name of Corporation: The name of a Washington corporation must contain the word "corporation," "incorporated," "company," or "limited," or the abbreviation "corp.," "inc.," "co.," or "ltd."

You can check to see whether your proposed corporate name is available online by clicking the "Online Corporations Lookup" link from the state filing office website. You can also check name availability by calling the filing office. It costs $30 to reserve an available corporate name for 180 days.

Note: If you choose to file your Articles online, you'll automatically search for name availability as you step through the screens to prepare your application to form a corporation online.

Share Information: In Washington, you do not need to state a par value for your shares. In the "Number of Shares Authorized" box, insert the total number of shares you wish to authorize. Your filing fee is not based on the number of authorized shares, so you may authorize as many shares as you wish. Most incorporators authorize one class of common shares with equal voting, dividend,

and liquidation rights and no special restrictions. To do this, check "Common" in the "Class of Shares" box. If you want to authorize a separate class of preferred shares, you also must check the "Preferred" box. Your articles must specify the rights and restrictions associated with each class of shares other than common shares. (You will need to retype the articles to include this additional information.)

Effective Date of Incorporation: Most incorporators check "Upon filing by the Secretary of State." This means your corporation's legal existence starts on the date that you file your articles. If you want to start your corporation's legal life on a later date, check the "Specific Date" box and insert the date when you want your corporation to begin. This delayed date may not be later than 90 days after the state filing office receives your articles.

Registered Agent: Insert the name and street address in Washington of the initial registered agent of your corporation. Your agent must be a Washington resident. Most incorporators give the name of an initial director, shareholder, or officer. You may also show a separate mailing address in Washington. Make sure to have the initial agent sign and date on the line provided at the end of the article.

Incorporator: You need have just one incorporator, who is not required to be a director, shareholder, or officer.

Signature: Have the incorporator sign and date on the line provided at the bottom of the form. Mail two copies of the completed form to the state corporate filing office (at least one of the copies must contain the original signature of the incorporator—for simplicity, have your incorporator manually sign each copy).

Filing Fee: $175, payable to "Secretary of State."

Director and Officer Rules

A board of directors must consist of one or more individuals, with the number specified in or fixed in accordance with the articles of incorporation or bylaws.

Directors are elected at the first annual shareholders' meeting and at each annual meeting thereafter unless (a) their terms are staggered under RCW 23B.08.060, or (b) their terms are otherwise governed by RCW 23B.05.050. [23B.08.030]

The terms of the initial directors of a corporation expire at the first shareholders' meeting at which directors are elected.

The terms of all other directors expire at the next annual shareholders' meeting following their election unless (a) their terms are staggered under RCW 23B.08.060, or (b) their terms are otherwise governed by RCW 23B.05.050. [23B.08.050]

A corporation has the officers described in its bylaws or appointed by the board of directors in accordance with the bylaws.

The bylaws or the board of directors shall delegate to one of the officers responsibility for preparing minutes of the directors' and shareholders' meetings and for authenticating records of the corporation.

The same individual may simultaneously hold more than one office in a corporation. [23B.08.400]

Share Issuance Rules

Shares may be issued for consideration consisting of any tangible or intangible property or benefit to the corporation, including cash, promissory notes, services performed, contracts for services to be performed, or other securities of the corporation.

The corporation may place in escrow shares issued for a contract for future services or benefits or a promissory note, or make other arrangements to restrict the transfer of the shares, and may credit distributions in respect to the shares against their purchase price, until the services are performed, the benefits are received, or the note is paid. If the services are not performed, the benefits are not received, or the note is not paid, the shares escrowed or restricted and the distributions credited may be canceled in whole or part. [23B.06.210]

At a minimum each share certificate must state on its face: (a) the name of the issuing corporation and that it is organized under the laws of this state; (b) the name of the person to whom issued; and (c) the number and class of shares and the designation of the series, if any, the certificate represents.

Each share certificate (a) must be signed, either manually or in facsimile, by two officers designated in the bylaws or by the board of directors, and (b) may bear the corporate seal or its facsimile. [23B.06.250]

Unless the Articles of Incorporation provide otherwise, and subject to the limitations in subsections (3) and (4) of this section, the shareholders of a corporation have a preemptive right, granted on uniform terms and conditions prescribed by the board of directors to provide a fair and reasonable opportunity to exercise the right, to acquire proportional amounts of the corporation's unissued shares on the decision of the board of directors to issue them. [23B.06.300]

Director Meeting Rules

The board of directors may hold regular or special meetings in or out of the state of Washington. [23B.08.200]

Unless the Articles of Incorporation or bylaws provide otherwise, regular meetings of the board of directors may be held without notice of the date, time, place, or purpose of the meeting.

Unless the Articles of Incorporation or bylaws provide for a longer or shorter period, special meetings of the board of directors must be preceded by at least two days' notice of the date, time, and place of the meeting. The notice need not describe the purpose of the special meeting unless required by the Articles of Incorporation or bylaws. [23B.08.220]

Unless the Articles of Incorporation or bylaws require a greater or lesser number, a quorum of a board of directors consists of a majority of the number of directors specified in or fixed in accordance with the Articles of Incorporation or bylaws.

Notwithstanding Subsection (1) of this section [above], a quorum of a board of directors may in no event be less than one-third of the number of directors specified in or fixed in accordance with the Articles of Incorporation or bylaws.

If a quorum is present when a vote is taken, the affirmative vote of a majority of directors present is the act of the board of directors unless the Articles of Incorporation or bylaws require the vote of a greater number of directors. [23B.08.240]

Shareholder Meeting Rules

Except as provided in Subsection (2) of this section [which applies to investment companies], a corporation shall hold a meeting of shareholders annually at a time stated in or fixed in accordance with the bylaws. [23B.07.010]

A corporation shall hold a special meeting of shareholders: (a) on call of its board of directors or the person or persons authorized to do so by the Articles of Incorporation or bylaws; or (b) except as set forth in Subsections (2) and (3) of this section [apply to publicly held companies and to privately held corporation that specify rules in their articles or bylaws], if the holders of at least 10% of all the votes entitled to be cast on any issue proposed to be considered at the proposed special meeting sign, date, and deliver to the corporation's secretary one or more written demands for the meeting describing the purpose or purposes for which it is to be held.

A corporation shall notify shareholders of the date, time, and place of each annual and special shareholders' meeting. Such notice shall be given no fewer than ten nor more than 60 days before the meeting date, except that notice of a shareholders' meeting to act on an amendment to the Articles of Incorporation, a plan of merger or share exchange, a proposed sale of assets pursuant to RCW 23B.12.020, or the dissolution of the corporation shall be given no fewer than 20 nor more than 60 days before the meeting date. Unless the Business Corporation Act or the Articles of Incorporation require otherwise, the corporation is required to give notice only to shareholders entitled to vote at the meeting.

Unless the Business Corporation Act or the Articles of Incorporation require otherwise, notice of an annual meeting need not include a description of the purpose or purposes for which the meeting is called.

Notice of a special meeting must include a description of the purpose or purposes for which the meeting is called. [23B.07.050] Only business within the purpose or purposes described in the meeting notice may be conducted at a special shareholders' meeting. [23B.07.020]

Shares entitled to vote as a separate voting group may take action on a matter at a meeting only if a quorum of those shares exists with respect to that matter. Unless the Articles of Incorporation or the Business Corporation Act provides otherwise, a majority of the votes entitled to be cast on the matter by the voting group constitutes a quorum of that voting group for action on that matter.

If a quorum exists, action on a matter, other than the election of directors, is approved by a voting group if the votes cast within the voting group favoring the action exceed the votes cast within the voting group opposing the action, unless the Articles of Incorporation or the Business Corporation Act requires a greater number of affirmative votes.

The election of directors is governed by RCW 23B.07.280. [23B.07.250]

If the Articles of Incorporation or the Business Corporation Act provides for voting by a single voting group on a matter, action on that matter is taken when voted on by that voting group as provided in RCW 23B.07.250. [23B.07.260]

The Articles of Incorporation may provide for a greater or lesser quorum, but not less than one-third of the votes entitled to be cast, for shareholders, or voting groups of shareholders, than is provided for by the Business Corporation Act.

Under RCW 23B.10.030, 23B.11.030, 23B.12.020, and 23B.14.020, the Articles of Incorporation may pro-

vide for a lesser vote than is otherwise prescribed in those sections or for a lesser vote by separate voting groups, so long as the vote provided for each voting group entitled to vote separately on the plan or transaction is not less than a majority of all the votes entitled to be cast on the plan or transaction by that voting group. [23B.07.270]

Unless otherwise provided in the Articles of Incorporation, shareholders entitled to vote at any election of directors are entitled to cumulate votes by multiplying the number of votes they are entitled to cast by the number of directors for whom they are entitled to vote and to cast the product for a single candidate or distribute the product among two or more candidates.

Unless otherwise provided in the Articles of Incorporation, in any election of directors the candidates elected are those receiving the largest numbers of votes cast by the shares entitled to vote in the election, up to the number of directors to be elected by such shares. [23B.07.280]

Financial Disclosure Rules

Not later than four months after the close of each fiscal year, and in any event prior to the annual meeting of shareholders, each corporation shall prepare (a) a balance sheet showing in reasonable detail the financial condition of the corporation as of the close of its fiscal year, and (b) an income statement showing the results of its operation during its fiscal year. Such statements may be consolidated or combined statements of the corporation and one or more of its subsidiaries, as appropriate. If financial statements are prepared by the corporation for any purpose on the basis of generally accepted accounting principles, the annual statements must also be prepared, and disclose that they are prepared, on that basis. If financial statements are prepared only on a basis other than generally accepted accounting principles, they must be prepared, and disclose that they are prepared, on the same basis as other reports and statements prepared by the corporation for the use of others.

On written request, the corporation shall promptly mail to any shareholder a copy of the most recent balance sheet and income statement. If prepared for other purposes, the corporation shall also furnish on written request a statement of sources and applications of funds, and a statement of changes in shareholders' equity, for the most recent fiscal year.

If the annual financial statements are reported on by a public accountant, the accountant's report must accompany them. If not, the statements must be accompanied by a statement of the president or the person responsible for the corporation's accounting records: (a) stating the person's reasonable belief whether the statements were prepared on the basis of generally accepted accounting principles and, if not, describing the basis of preparation; and (b) describing any respects in which the statements were not prepared on a basis of accounting consistent with the basis used for statements prepared for the preceding year.

For purposes of this section, "shareholder" includes a beneficial owner whose shares are held in a voting trust or by a nominee on the beneficial owner's behalf. [23B.16.200]

State Tax Information

Department of Revenue, Olympia
800-647-7706
http://dor.wa.gov

Washington corporations are subject to Business and Occupation Tax (B & O tax), based on gross income received from activities in the state. Tax rates vary depending on the type of business activity. The state does not have an income tax, as such.

Corporation Law Online

The Washington Business Corporation Act is contained in Title 23B of the Revised Code of Washington, starting with Section 23B.01. To find the Act, visit the legal research area of Nolo's website at www.nolo.com/statute/state.cfm. Click on "Washington." From there, click "Search the Revised Code of Washington," and then choose the link that says "Click here to search the RCW." Finally, open the table of contents on the left side of the page that says "Revised Code of Washington" and scroll down to Title 23B. When you click on "Title 23B," you will be able to browse the BCA section by section.

State Securities Information

Department of Financial Institutions
Securities Division
P.O. Box 9033
Olympia, WA 98507-9033
360-902-8760
www.dfi.wa.gov/sd/default.htm

The Washington Securities Act is contained in Title 21.20 of the Revised Code of Washington. The related Securities Rules are contained in Chapter 460-10A of the Washington Administrative Code. You can browse the Act and Rules from links provided on the Securities Division website. (Click on "Statutes and Rules," then on "RCWs," then on "Securities Act 21.20" to view sections of the Act. Click on "WACs" to view the Rules.) The Division provides an online guide called "Options for Small Business in the Securities Market," which explains the various exemptions available to smaller corporations when issuing stock. Of particular interest is the Small Offering Exemption under Section 460-44A-504 of the Washington State Administrative Code (WAC). It allows offerings of up to $1 million in securities to 20 or fewer nonaccredited investors in Washington and an unlimited number of accredited investors. (The statutes and rules define these terms. "Accredited investor" is defined in WAC 460-44A-501, and generally corresponds to the federal definition of an accredited investor under the federal Regulation D exemption rules.) You must file a Notification of Claim of Exemption form (or a copy of a federal Form D you are filing Form D with the SEC) and pay a $50 filing fee. Advertising and commissions are prohibited. For specific information on this and other available exemptions, see the Division website. Also, the Division office has a Small Business Section that is ready to answer your questions on complying with the Washington Securities Act and exemption requirements. We suggest you call the Section to find out the best and most efficient way to issue the initial shares of your corporation's stock.

Creating Your Own Articles Form

You can prepare and file your own articles form.

WEST VIRGINIA

Corporate Filing Office

West Virginia Secretary of State
Corporations Division
Bldg. 1, Suite 157-K
1900 Kanawha Boulevard East
Charleston, WV 25305-0770
304-558-8000
www.wvsos.com

State Corporate Forms

West Virginia provides fill-in-the-blanks Articles of Incorporation (Form CD-1).

Internet Forms: Articles of Incorporation, plus other statutory forms such as an application to reserve a corporate name, are available for downloading from the state filing office website.

Articles Instructions

Article 1: The name of a West Virginia corporation must contain the word "corporation," "company," "incorporated," or "limited," or an abbreviation of one of these words.

You can check name availability online using the Business Organizations Data System at the state filing office website. Then, follow up by calling the state corporate filing office to confirm availability. You can check the availability of up to three proposed corporate names per phone call by calling the state filing office. It costs $15 to reserve an available corporate name for 120 days.

Articles 2 and 3: The street address of the principal office shown in Article 2, and the street address of the principal place of business in West Virginia will normally be the same address.

Article 4: Insert the name of the registered agent of your corporation. This person should be a West Virginia resident, and normally will be an initial director, officer, or shareholder.

Article 5: Check the "For-Profit" box.

Article 6: In the first blank of this article, insert the dollar amount of the total value of your corporation's authorized capital stock. (The license fee portion of your filing fee is based on this amount, as explained under "Filing Fee," below.) If you authorize par value shares, this dollar value is the number of shares authorized multiplied by the par value amount of each share. For example, if you authorize 5,000 shares with a par value of $1 each, the total value of your authorized capital stock is $5,000.

(This is the amount of authorized capital that results in the lowest filing fee.) If you authorize shares without par value (this is the modern trend), they are assumed to have a par value of $25 per share for purposes of calculating your total authorized capital. Thus, if you authorize 200 shares of stock without par value, you would insert $5,000 in the blank (200 x $25 = $5,000). (This is the largest number of shares without par value you can authorize for the minimum filing fee.)

In the second blank, insert the number of shares and the par value of each share. If you authorize shares without par value, insert "0" in the par value blank. Do not insert the assumed par value amount of $25. Most incorporators authorize only one class of common shares with equal voting, dividend, and liquidation rights and no special restrictions. If you want to authorize special classes of stock, attach a statement to your articles that specifies the name of each class of shares, the number and par value (or lack of par value) of shares in each class, and the rights and restrictions associated with each class of shares.

Article 7: Insert the specific purpose of your corporation. We recommend that you add a general purpose phrase to the end of your statement to make it clear that your corporation can engage in any lawful business. For example, "sale of retail merchandise and the transaction of any and all lawful business for which corporations may be incorporated in West Virginia."

Article 8: You can ignore this article (it applies to nonprofit corporations only).

Articles 9 & 10: You need only one incorporator, who does not have to be a corporate director, officer, or shareholder (typically, an initial director is designated as incorporator). Also insert the incorporator's name (and telephone number) as the contact person in the blank in Article 10, and repeat the incorporator's name in the blank in Article 10 that shows the name of the person who signed your articles. You can add an optional email address on line c in Article 10 if you wish to be contacted by email. Make sure that your incorporator sings the articles at the bottom of the form.

Submit two originally-signed articles to the state corporate filing office plus a check for fees (see below). The state filing office will mail you a file-stamped copy after filing your articles.

Filing Fee: Make check payable to the "Secretary of State." The incorporation fee has three components: 1) a registration fee of $50; 2) an attorney-in-fact fee (the amount depends on the month when the state filing office receives your articles); and 3) a license fee (the amount depends on the value of the shares you authorize in your articles and the month when your articles are received for filing).

To determine how much you will have to pay for the attorney-in-fact and license components of your incorporation fee, please refer to the fee chart included in the instructions provided with the pdf articles form posted online. Here's a quick tip: To pay the smallest license fee, keep the authorized capital of your corporation at or below $5,000. For par value shares, authorized capital simply means the number of shares authorized in your articles multiplied times the par value amount of each share. Shares without par value are assumed to have a par value of $25 per share for purposes of this calculation.

Examples:

If your articles authorize 5,000 shares with a par value of $1 each, your authorized capital is $5,000 and you will pay the lowest possible license fee (remember that the actual amount of the license fee depends on the month when your articles are received by the state—see the fee chart provided online).

If your articles authorize 500,000 shares with a par value of 1¢ each, your authorized capital also is $5,000 and your license fee will be the smallest possible.

If your articles authorize 200 shares without par value, your authorized capital is $5,000 (200 x assumed par value of $25 per share = $5,000). Your license fee will be the smallest possible.

Director and Officer Rules

A board of directors must consist of one or more individuals, with the number specified in or fixed in accordance with the Articles of Incorporation or bylaws.

If a board of directors has power to fix or change the number of directors, the board may increase or decrease by thirty percent or less the number of directors last approved by the shareholders, but only the shareholders may increase or decrease by more than thirty percent the number of directors last approved by the shareholders.

The Articles of Incorporation or bylaws may establish a variable range for the size of the board of directors by fixing a minimum and maximum number of directors. If a variable range is established, the number of directors may be fixed or changed, from time to time, within the minimum and maximum, by the shareholders or the board of directors. After shares are issued, only the shareholders may change the range for the size of the board or change from a fixed- to a variable-range size board or change from a variable- to a fixed-range size board.

Directors are elected at the first annual shareholders' meeting and at each annual meeting thereafter unless their terms are staggered under section eight hundred six of this article. [31D-8-803]

A corporation has the officers described in its bylaws or appointed by the board of directors in accordance with the bylaws.

A duly appointed officer may appoint one or more officers or assistant officers if authorized by the bylaws or the board of directors.

The bylaws or the board of directors must delegate to one of the officers responsibility for preparing minutes of the directors' and shareholders' meetings and for authenticating records of the corporation.

The same individual may simultaneously hold more than one office in a corporation. [31D-8-840]

Share Issuance Rules

The Articles of Incorporation must prescribe the classes of shares and the number of shares of each class that the corporation is authorized to issue. If more than one class of shares is authorized, the Articles of Incorporation must prescribe a distinguishing designation for each class and, prior to the issuance of shares of a class, the preferences, limitations, and relative rights of that class must be described in the Articles of Incorporation. All shares of a class must have preferences, limitations, and relative rights identical with those of other shares of the same class except to the extent otherwise permitted by section six hundred two of this article.

The Articles of Incorporation must authorize: (1) one or more classes of shares that together have unlimited voting rights; and (2) one or more classes of shares which may be the same class or classes as those with voting rights that together are entitled to receive the net assets of the corporation on dissolution. [31D-6-601]

The board of directors may authorize shares to be issued for consideration consisting of any tangible or intangible property or benefit to the corporation, including cash, promissory notes, services performed, contracts for services to be performed, or other securities of the corporation.

The corporation may place in escrow shares issued for a contract for future services or benefits or a promissory note, or make other arrangements to restrict the transfer of the shares, and may credit distributions in respect of the shares against their purchase price until the services are performed, the note is paid, or the benefits received. If the services are not performed, the note is not paid, or the benefits are not received, the shares escrowed or restricted and the distributions credited may be canceled in whole or in part. [31D-6-621]

At a minimum each share certificate must state on its face: (1) the name of the issuing corporation and that it is organized under the law of this state; (2) the name of the person to whom issued; and (3) the number and class of shares and the designation of the series, if any, the certificate represents.

Each share certificate: (1) must be signed, either manually or in facsimile, by two officers designated in the bylaws or by the board of directors; and (2) may bear the corporate seal or its facsimile. [31D-6-625]

The shareholders of a corporation do not have a preemptive right to acquire the corporation's unissued shares except to the extent the Articles of Incorporation provide. [31D-6-630]

Director Meeting Rules

The board of directors may hold regular or special meetings in or out of this state. [31D-8-820]

Unless the Articles of Incorporation or bylaws provide otherwise, regular meetings of the board of directors may be held without notice of the date, time, place or purpose of the meeting.

Unless the Articles of Incorporation or bylaws provide for a longer or shorter period, special meetings of the board of directors must be preceded by at least two days' notice of the date, time, and place of the meeting. The notice need not describe the purpose of the special meeting unless required by the Articles of Incorporation or bylaws. [31D-8-822]

Unless the Articles of Incorporation or bylaws require a greater number or unless otherwise specifically provided in this chapter, a quorum of a board of directors consists of: (1) a majority of the fixed number of directors if the corporation has a fixed-board size; or (2) a majority of the number of directors prescribed, or, if no number is prescribed, the number in office immediately before the meeting begins if the corporation has a variable-range size board.

The Articles of Incorporation or bylaws may authorize a quorum of a board of directors to consist of no fewer than one-third of the fixed or prescribed number of directors determined under subsection (a) of this section.

If a quorum is present when a vote is taken, the affirmative vote of a majority of directors present is the act of the board of directors unless the Articles of Incorporation or bylaws require the vote of a greater number of directors. [31D-8-824]

Shareholder Meeting Rules

A corporation must hold a meeting of shareholders annually at a time stated in or fixed in accordance with the bylaws. [31D-7-701]

A corporation must hold a special meeting of shareholders: (1) on call of its board of directors or the person or persons authorized by the Articles of Incorporation or bylaws; or (2) if the holders of at least ten percent of all the votes entitled to be cast on an issue proposed to be considered at the proposed special meeting sign, date, and deliver to the corporation one or more written demands for the meeting describing the purpose or purposes for which it is to be held, provided that the Articles of Incorporation may fix a lower percentage or a higher percentage not exceeding twenty-five percent of all the votes entitled to be cast on any issue proposed to be considered. Unless otherwise provided in the Articles of Incorporation, a written demand for a special meeting may be revoked by a writing to that effect received by the corporation prior to the receipt by the corporation of demands sufficient in number to require the holding of a special meeting. [31D-7-702]

A corporation is to notify shareholders of the date, time, and place of each annual and special shareholders' meeting no fewer than ten nor more than sixty days before the meeting date. Unless this chapter [the WV BCA] or the Articles of Incorporation requires otherwise, the corporation is required to give notice only to shareholders entitled to vote at the meeting.

Unless this chapter [the WV BCA], the Articles of Incorporation, or the bylaws require otherwise, notice of an annual meeting need not include a description of the purpose or purposes for which the meeting is called.

Notice of a special meeting must include a description of the purpose or purposes for which the meeting is called. [31D-7-705]

At each meeting of shareholders, a chair shall preside. The chair is to be appointed as provided in the bylaws or, in the absence of a provision in the bylaws, by the board of directors.

The chair, unless the Articles of Incorporation or bylaws provide otherwise, shall determine the order of business and has the authority to establish rules for the conduct of the meeting.

Any rules adopted for, and the conduct of, the meeting are to be fair to shareholders.

The chair of the meeting shall announce at the meeting when the polls close for each matter voted on. If no announcement is made, the polls are to be deemed to have closed on the final adjournment of the meeting. After the polls close, no ballots, proxies, or votes nor any revocations or changes to a ballot, proxy, or vote may be accepted.

If the Articles of Incorporation or bylaws authorize the use of electronic communication for shareholders' meetings, any or all of the shareholders may participate in a regular or special meeting by, or conduct the meeting through the use of, any means of communication by which all shareholders may simultaneously hear each other during the meeting. [31D-7-708]

Shares entitled to vote as a separate voting group may take action on a matter at a meeting only if a quorum of those shares exists with respect to that matter. Unless the Articles of Incorporation or this chapter provide otherwise, a majority of the votes entitled to be cast on the matter by the voting group constitutes a quorum of that voting group for action on that matter.

If a quorum exists, action on a matter, other than the election of directors, by a voting group is approved if the votes cast within the voting group favoring the action exceed the votes cast opposing the action unless the Articles of Incorporation or this chapter require a greater number of affirmative votes. [31D-7-725]

Unless otherwise provided in the Articles of Incorporation, directors are elected by a plurality of the votes cast by the shares entitled to vote in the election at a meeting at which a quorum is present.

Each shareholder or designated voting group of shareholders holding shares having the right to vote for directors has a right to cumulate his or her votes for directors.

A statement included in the Articles of Incorporation that "all or a designated voting group of shareholders are entitled to cumulate their votes for directors," or words of similar import, means that the shareholders designated are entitled to multiply the number of votes they are entitled to cast by the number of directors for whom they are entitled to vote and cast the product for a single candidate or distribute the product among two or more candidates.

Shares otherwise entitled to vote cumulatively may not be voted cumulatively at a particular meeting unless: (1) the meeting notice or proxy statement accompanying the notice states conspicuously that cumulative voting is authorized; or (2) a shareholder who has the right to cumulate his or her votes gives notice to the corporation not less than forty-eight hours before the time set for the meeting of his or her intent to cumulate his or her votes during the meeting and if one shareholder gives this notice all other shareholders in the same voting group participating in the election are entitled to cumulate their votes without giving further notice. [31D-7-728]

Financial Disclosure Rules

Unless unanimously waived by the shareholders, a corporation shall furnish its shareholders annual financial statements, which may be consolidated or combined statements of the corporation and one or more of its subsidiaries, as appropriate, that include a balance sheet as of the end of the fiscal year, an income statement for that year, and a statement of changes in shareholders' equity for the year unless that information appears elsewhere in the financial statements. If financial statements are prepared for the corporation on the basis of generally accepted accounting principles, the annual financial statements must also be prepared on that basis.

If the annual financial statements are reported on by a public accountant, his or her report must accompany them. If not, the statements must be accompanied by a statement of the president or the person responsible for the corporation's accounting records: (1) stating his or her reasonable belief whether the statements were prepared on the basis of generally accepted accounting principles and, if not, describing the basis of preparation; and (2) describing any respects in which the statements were not prepared on a basis of accounting consistent with the statements prepared for the preceding year.

A corporation shall mail the annual financial statements to each shareholder within one hundred twenty days after the close of each fiscal year. On written request from a shareholder who was not mailed the statements, the corporation shall mail him or her the latest financial statements. [31D-16-1620]

State Tax Information

Department of Tax and Revenue, Charleston
304-558-3333 (Toll Free: 800-982-8297)
www.state.wv.us/taxdiv

West Virginia corporations are subject to a corporation net income tax and a business franchise tax.

Corporation Law Online

The latest West Virginia Business Corporation Act, which took effect on October 1, 2002, is contained in Chapter 31D of the West Virginia Code, starting with Section 31D-1-101. You can browse it from the corporate filing office Web page listed below (the corporate filing office currently also has a link to the old law—Chapter 31— that you should ignore; Chapter 31D contains the current WV Business Corporation Act):

www.wvsos.com/business/code/wvcdomcorp.htm

State Securities Information

West Virginia State Auditor's Office
Division of Securities
State Capitol Bldg. 1, Room W-100
Charleston, WV 25305
304-558-2257
www.wvauditor.com

The Securities Division website contains links to the West Virginia Uniform Securities Act, contained in Chapter 32 of the West Virginia Code, and related securities regulations. Section 32-4-402(b) of the Act contains exemptions for certain securities transactions. For example, Section 32-4-402(b)(9) contains an exemption for offers of securities to ten or fewer persons during a 12-month period if: (A) the corporation reasonably believes that all the buyers in this state are purchasing for investment; and (B) no commissions are paid in connection with the stock offering. Section 15.06 of the Regulations says that even if you take advantage of this exemption, you must meet the registration requirements that apply to broker-dealers under the Act—that is, you still must find an exemption under the Act or Regulations from registration as a seller of securities. Also note that this Section 15.06 creates a limited offering exemption for the sale of securities under federal Regulation D, provided certain conditions are met. For complete information on available security registration exemptions and requirements, and to determine whether your corporation's sale of stock is exempt from the broker-dealer registration requirements, see the Division website and call the Division office.

Creating Your Own Articles Form

You can prepare and file your own articles form.

WISCONSIN

Corporate Filing Office

Department of Financial Institutions
Division of Corporate and Consumer Services
Corporations Section, 3rd Floor
P.O. Box 7846
Madison, WI 53707-7846
608-261-7577
www.wdfi.org/corporations

State Corporate Forms

Wisconsin provides Articles of Incorporation—Stock For-Profit Corporation (Form 2).

Internet Forms: Wisconsin corporate forms, including Articles of Incorporation, are available for downloading from the state website.

Articles Instructions

Article 1: The name of a Wisconsin corporation must contain the word "corporation," "incorporated," "company," or "limited," or the abbreviation "corp.," "inc.," "co.," or "ltd."

You can check available corporate names online from the state filing office website by clicking the CRIS (Corporate Registration Information System) link or by calling the state filing office. You can reserve an available corporate name for 120 days. If you reserve by telephone, it will cost $30 to reserve a name; reserving by mail costs $15. You can insert your second choice for a corporate name in the optional "second choice corporate name" blank at the bottom of the articles form. Most incorporators will not specify an alternate name. Instead, savvy incorporators will check name availability and reserve their first choice for a corporate name prior to preparing and filing articles.

Article 3: In Wisconsin, you do not need to specify a par value for your shares. Most incorporators authorize one class of common shares with equal voting, dividend, and liquidation rights and no special restrictions. To do this, insert the total number of shares you wish to authorize in the blank. Your filing fee is not based on how many shares you authorize, so you may authorize as many shares as you wish. If you want to authorize different classes of shares, you must specify the name of each class, the number of shares in each class and the rights and restrictions associated with each class. (You can provide this additional information in Article 6.)

Articles 4 and 5: Typically, an initial director or shareholder is named as initial registered agent (the person authorized to receive legal documents on behalf of the corporation), and the street address of the corporation is given as the registered office address (which must be the business office of the registered agent). The registered agent must be a Wisconsin resident, and the registered office address must be in Wisconsin.

Article 6: If you have special provisions to add to your articles, insert them here. For example, you can ask that your Articles of Incorporation become effective on a date after the date you file your articles. To do this, add the following statement in this article: "This document has a delayed effective date of [insert date]." The delayed date may not be more than 90 days after the filing office receives your articles.

Article 7: You need just one incorporator, who is not required to be a director, officer, or shareholder. Have the incorporator sign on the line provided in this article. Also, complete the statement that says, "This document was drafted by [insert incorporator's name]." Insert the incorporator's name, mailing address, and daytime telephone number at the bottom of the form.

Send one signed original of the articles plus one copy for filing. The state filing office will return a file-stamped copy to your incorporator.

Filing Fee: $100, payable to the "Department of Financial Institutions."

Director and Officer Rules

A board of directors shall consist of one or more natural persons, with the number specified in or fixed in accordance with the Articles of Incorporation or bylaws.

Directors shall be elected at the first annual shareholders' meeting and at each annual meeting thereafter unless their terms are staggered under Section 180.0806. [180.0803]

The terms of the directors of a corporation, including the initial directors, expire at the next annual shareholders' meeting unless their terms are staggered under Section 180.0806. [180.0805]

A corporation shall have the officers described in its bylaws or appointed by its board of directors by resolution not inconsistent with the bylaws.

The same natural person may simultaneously hold more than one office in a corporation. [180.0840]

Share Issuance Rules

The board of directors may authorize shares to be issued for consideration consisting of any tangible or intangible property or benefit to the corporation, including cash, promissory notes, services performed, contracts for services to be performed, or other securities of the corporation.

The corporation may place in escrow shares issued for a contract for future services or benefits or a promissory note, or make other arrangements to restrict the transfer of the shares, and may credit distributions in respect of the shares against their purchase price, until the services are performed, the benefits are received, or the note is paid. If the services are not performed, the benefits are not received, or the note is not paid, the corporation may cancel, in whole or in part, the shares escrowed or restricted and the distributions credited. [180.0621]

Except as provided in Subsection (7), the shareholders or holders of other securities of a corporation do not have a preemptive right to acquire the corporation's unissued shares or other securities except to the extent provided in the articles of incorporation. If the Articles of Incorporation state that "the corporation elects to have preemptive rights," or words of similar meaning, Subsections (3) to (6) govern the preemptive rights, except to the extent that the Articles of Incorporation expressly provide otherwise. [180.0630]

At a minimum, a share certificate shall state on its face all of the following: (a) the name of the issuing corporation and that it is organized under the laws of this state; (b) the name of the person to whom issued; (c) the number and class of shares and the designation of the series, if any, that the certificate represents.

Each share certificate shall be signed either manually or in facsimile, by the officer or officers designated in the bylaws, or by the board of directors. [180.0625]

Director Meeting Rules

The board of directors may hold regular or special meetings in or outside the state of Wisconsin.

If requested by a director, minutes of any regular or special meeting shall be prepared and distributed to each director. [180.0820]

Unless the Articles of Incorporation or bylaws provide otherwise, regular meetings of the board of directors may be held without notice of the date, time, place, or purpose of the meeting.

Except as provided in Section 180.0303(3) [says that notice need only be given to directors whom it is practical to reach], and unless the Articles of Incorporation or bylaws provide for a longer or shorter period, special meetings of the board of directors shall be preceded by at least 48 hours' notice of the date, time, and place of the meeting. The notice shall comply with Section

180.0141 [allows oral, written, and electronic forms of notice]. The notice need not describe the purpose of the special meeting unless required by the Articles of Incorporation or bylaws. [180.0822]

Unless the Articles of Incorporation or bylaws require a greater or, under Subsection (2) [next paragraph], a lesser number, and except as provided in Sections 180.0303(3) (b) [allows officers present at a directors' meeting to be counted as directors for purposes of meeting director quorum requirements] and 180.0831(4) [contains special quorum rules for director approval of transactions that financially benefit one or more directors], a quorum of a board of directors shall consist of a majority of the number of directors specified in or fixed in accordance with the Articles of Incorporation or bylaws.

The Articles of Incorporation or bylaws may authorize a quorum of a board of directors to consist of no fewer than one-third of the number of directors specified in or fixed in accordance with the Articles of Incorporation or bylaws.

Except as provided in Sections 180.0825(2) and (3) [special director-voting rules for the establishment of committees of the board], 180.0831(4) [special voting rules for director approval of transactions that financially benefit one or more directors], and 180.0855(1) and (2) [special voting rules for director approval of indemnification of corporate directors and officers], if a quorum is present when a vote is taken, the affirmative vote of a majority of directors present is the act of the board of directors or a committee of the board of directors created under Section 180.0825 [allows the full board to set up committees], unless the Articles of Incorporation or bylaws require the vote of a greater number of directors. [180.0824]

Shareholder Meeting Rules

Except as provided in Subsection (4) [which relates to investment companies], a corporation shall hold a meeting of shareholders annually at a time stated in or fixed in accordance with the bylaws. [180.0701]

A corporation shall hold a special meeting of shareholders if any of the following occurs: (a) a special meeting is called by the board of directors or any person authorized by the Articles of Incorporation or bylaws to call a special meeting; (b) the holders of at least 10% of all the votes entitled to be cast on any issue proposed to be considered at the proposed special meeting sign, date, and deliver to the corporation one or more written demands for the meeting describing one or more purposes for which it is to be held.

A corporation shall notify shareholders of the date, time, and place of each annual and special shareholders' meeting not less than ten days nor more than 60 days before the meeting date, unless a different time is provided by the Business Corporation Law, the Articles of Incorporation, or the bylaws. The notice shall comply with Section 180.0141. Unless the Business Corporation Law or the Articles of Incorporation require otherwise, the corporation is required to give notice only to shareholders entitled to vote at the meeting.

Unless the Business Corporation Law or the Articles of Incorporation require otherwise, notice of an annual meeting need not include a description of the purpose for which the meeting is called.

Notice of a special meeting shall include a description of each purpose for which the meeting is called. [180.0705] Only business within the purpose described in the meeting notice may be conducted at a special shareholders' meeting. [180.0702]

Shares entitled to vote as a separate voting group may take action on a matter at a meeting only if a quorum of those shares exists with respect to that matter. Unless the Articles of Incorporation, bylaws adopted under authority granted in the Articles of Incorporation, or the Business Corporation Law provides otherwise, a majority of the votes entitled to be cast on the matter by the voting group constitutes a quorum of that voting group for action on that matter.

If a quorum exists, action on a matter, other than the election of directors under Section 180.0728, by a voting group is approved if the votes cast within the voting group favoring the action exceed the votes cast opposing the action, unless the Articles of Incorporation, bylaws adopted under authority granted in the Articles of Incorporation, or the Business Corporation Law requires a greater number of affirmative votes. [180.0725]

If the Articles of Incorporation or the Business Corporation Law provides for voting by a single voting group on a matter, action on that matter is taken when voted on by the voting group as provided in Section 180.0725 [previous paragraph]. [180.0726]

Unless otherwise provided in the Articles of Incorporation, directors are elected by a plurality of the votes cast by the shares entitled to vote in the election at a meeting at which a quorum is present. In this subsection, "plurality" means that the individuals with the largest number of votes are elected as directors up to the maximum number of directors to be chosen at the election.

Shareholders do not have a right to cumulate their votes for directors unless the Articles of Incorporation provide for cumulative voting. If the Articles of Incorporation contain a statement indicating that all or a designated voting group of shareholders are entitled to cumulate their votes for directors, the shareholders so designated are entitled to multiply the number of votes that they are entitled to cast by the number of directors for whom they are entitled to vote and cast the product for a single candidate or distribute the product among two or more candidates.

Except as provided in Paragraph (c) [applies to close corporations], shares entitled under Subsection (2) [above] to vote cumulatively may not be voted cumulatively at a particular meeting unless any of the following notice requirements are satisfied: 1. the meeting notice or proxy statement accompanying the notice states conspicuously that cumulative voting is authorized; 2. a shareholder who has the right to cumulate his or her votes gives notice that complies with Section 180.0141 to the corporation not less than 48 hours before the time set for the meeting of his or her intent to cumulate his or her votes during the meeting.

If one shareholder gives notice under Paragraph (a) 2 [above], all other shareholders in the same voting group participating in the election are entitled to cumulate their votes without giving further notice.

For purposes of this section, votes against a candidate are not given legal effect and are not counted as votes cast in an election of directors. [180.0728]

Financial Disclosure Rules

Within 120 days after the close of each fiscal year, a corporation shall prepare annual financial statements, which may be consolidated or combined statements of the corporation and one or more of its subsidiaries, as appropriate, that include a balance sheet as of the end of the fiscal year, an income statement for that year, and a statement of changes in shareholders' equity for the year unless that information appears elsewhere in the financial statements. If financial statements are prepared for the corporation on the basis of generally accepted accounting principles, the annual financial statements must also be prepared on that basis.

On written request from any shareholder, the corporation shall mail him or her the latest financial statements. [180.1620]

State Tax Information

Department of Revenue, Madison
608-266-1143
www.dor.state.wi.us

Wisconsin corporations are subject to a corporation franchise tax.

Corporation Law Online

The Wisconsin Business Corporation Law is contained in Chapter 180 of the Wisconsin Statutes, starting with Section 180.0101. To find it, visit the legal research area of Nolo's website at www.nolo.com/statute/state.cfm. Click on "Wisconsin." Click on "Statutes" and then choose "Statutes Table of Contents." Scroll down and select "Chapter 180" to begin browsing the laws.

State Securities Information

Department of Financial Institutions
Division of Securities
P.O. Box 1768
Madison, WI 53701-1768
608-266-1064
www.wdfi.org/fi/securities/default.htm

The Wisconsin Uniform Securities Law is contained in Chapters 551 through 553 of the Wisconsin Statutes. You can browse the Securities Law and associated Administrative Code Rules from links provided on the Division of Securities website. In addition, the Division of Securities provides a downloadable guide called "Raising Capital." The guide provides overviews of the exemptions available when selling corporate stock or other securities. For example, it describes an exemption available under Sections 551.22(10) and 551.23(18) of the Securities Law for sales to officers, directors, and employees. This exemption is self-executing and requires no filing with the Division. Sales to employees must meet additional requirements.

The guide also outlines an exemption under Section 551.23(10) that applies if, after the sale of securities, there are 15 or fewer holders of all the corporation's securities, not counting certain "institutional investors" such as banks, insurance companies, mutual funds, and principal officers and directors of the business. You don't have to file a form or pay a fee to take advantage of the exemption, but you must meet the following conditions: (1) you may not pay commissions, finders' fees or other forms of compensation for soliciting investors in Wisconsin, except to securities broker-dealers or agents who are licensed in the state; and (2) you may not publish advertising in connection with the sale unless the advertising is filed with and permitted by the Division. Consult Section 551.23(8) of the Securities Act and Sections DFI-Sec 2.02(4), (5)(a) and (b) of the Administrative Code Rules to learn who should be counted as a holder of the issuer's securities under this exemption.

Another exemption discussed in the guide is contained in Section 551.23(11) of the Securities Law. It is available if you make offers and sales to not more than ten people in Wisconsin in any consecutive 12-month period, not counting certain "institutional investors," as described in the paragraph above. Sales of securities made under this exemption may result only from the ten or fewer offers. (In other words, you don't qualify for the exemption if you make offers to 11 people, even if you ultimately sell shares to only ten of them.) Other requirements apply, including the following: (1) you must reasonably believe that all investors are purchasing for investment purposes rather than for resale; (2) you may not pay commissions, finders' fees, or other forms of compensation to any person for soliciting investors in Wisconsin, other than reasonable commissions to securities broker-dealers or agents who are licensed in the state; and (3) If the securities represent limited partnership interests in oil, gas or mining activities; investment contracts; or certificates of interest or participation in oil, gas, or mining leases or titles, a notice (no specific form required) and filing fee of $200 may be required by the Division at least ten days prior to offering the securities to any person in Wisconsin under circumstances described in Section DFI-Sec 2.02 (5)(d)1 of the Wisconsin Administrative Code. Certain issuers are not permitted to use this exemption. See Section DFI-Sec 2.02(5)(d)2 or the Wisconsin Administrative Code for complete information.

Note that officers, directors, employees, or other people representing an issuer in the sale of its securities must be licensed as securities agents if they receive compensation related to the sale of those securities. Compensation, whether cash or not, may be in the form of commission, bonus, or even salary, if the compensation is based, in whole or in part, on the person's sales activity.

The Small Business Information Center, a part of the Division of Securities, can help you understand and comply with the Wisconsin Uniform Securities Law. For additional information on these and other available exemptions and their requirements, see the Division website and call the Small Business Information Center at the telephone number listed above.

Creating Your Own Articles Form

You can prepare and file your own articles form.

WYOMING

Corporate Filing Office

Secretary of State's Office
Corporations Division
The Capitol Building, Room 110
Cheyenne, WY 82002-0020
307-777-7311
http://soswy.state.wy.us/corporat/corporat.htm

State Corporate Forms

Wyoming provides Articles of Incorporation, including instructions. The state also provides a Consent to Appointment by Registered Agent, which you must file with your articles.

Internet Forms: You can download all required corporate forms from the state filing office website.

Articles Instructions

Article 1: You are not required to use a corporate designator in your corporate name, although most incorporators do include the word "corporation," "company," "incorporated," or an abbreviation of one of these words.

You can check name availability online by clicking the Corporation Database link from the state filing office website or by calling the state filing office. The fee to reserve an available corporate name for 120 days is $50.

Articles 2 and 3: Most incorporators designate an initial director, officer, or shareholder as agent, and give the street address of the corporation as the agent's address. Your agent must be a Wyoming resident. Make sure the agent completes and signs the Consent to Appointment included with the Articles form.

Article 4: In Wyoming, you do not need to specify a par value for your shares. Your filing fee is not based on the number of shares you authorize, so you can authorize as many as you wish. Most incorporators authorize one class of common shares with equal voting, dividend, and liquidation rights and no special restrictions. To do this, on the first line insert the total number of authorized shares followed by the designation "Common Shares"—for example, "100,000 Common Shares." (Note that Wyoming allows you to state an unlimited number here, so you do not have to amend your articles later to increase the authorized number of shares. If you wish to create an unrestricted number of shares, simply state "Unlimited Common Shares.") On the second line, which asks for the number and class of shares that are entitled to receive the net assets of the corporation on dissolution,

insert "Same as Above" (shares of common stock participate equally in net assets on corporate dissolution).

If you want to authorize separate classes of shares, you must include the class name and the number of shares in each class in the first blank of the article, then show the number and class of shares that are eligible to share in net assets on dissolution. If you specify additional classes of stock, you must also list the rights and restrictions of each class in your articles. (You can do this on an attachment page or by retyping your articles.)

Article 5: Most incorporators show the corporate address as the place where the state filing office should send annual report forms.

Article 6: You need have just one incorporator, who is not required to be a director, officer or shareholder. The agent should be a Wyoming resident.

Article 7: Have the incorporator named in Article 6 sign and date on the lines provided.

Article 8: The name and phone number of the incorporator is typically given for contact information.

Consent to Appointment: Have the agent named in Article 2 sign and date the form. Check the appropriate box on the consent form to show the type of registered agent named in your articles—usually, it will be an individual who resides in the state.

Submit an original plus one copy of your articles for filing, along with a signed copy of the Consent to Appointment form.

Filing Fee: $100, payable to the "Secretary of State."

Director and Officer Rules

A board of directors shall consist of one (1) or more individuals, with the number specified in or fixed in accordance with the Articles of Incorporation or bylaws.

Directors are elected at the first annual shareholders' meeting and at each annual meeting thereafter unless their terms are staggered under W.S. 17-16-806. [17-16-803]

The terms of the initial directors of a corporation expire at the first shareholders' meeting at which directors are elected.

The terms of all other directors expire at the next annual shareholders' meeting following their election unless their terms are staggered under W.S. 17-16-806. [17-16-805]

A corporation has the officers described in its bylaws or appointed by the board of directors in accordance with the bylaws.

The bylaws or the board of directors shall delegate to one (1) of the officers responsibility for preparing minutes of the directors' and shareholders' meetings and for authenticating records of the corporation.

The same individual may simultaneously hold more than one (1) office in a corporation. [17-16-840]

Share Issuance Rules

The board of directors may authorize shares to be issued for consideration consisting of any tangible or intangible property or benefit to the corporation, including cash, promissory notes, services performed, contracts for services to be performed, or other securities of the corporation.

The corporation may place in escrow shares issued for a contract for future services or benefits or a promissory note, or make other arrangements to restrict the transfer of the shares, and may credit distributions in respect of the shares against their purchase price, until the services are performed, the note is paid, or the benefits are received. If the services are not performed, the note is not paid, or the benefits are not received, the shares escrowed or restricted and the distributions credited may be cancelled in whole or part. [17-16-621]

At a minimum each share certificate shall state on its face: (i) the name of the issuing corporation and that it is organized under the law of this state; (ii) the name of the person to whom issued; and (iii) the number and class of shares and the designation of the series, if any, the certificate represents.

Each share certificate: (i) shall be signed, either manually or in facsimile, by two (2) officers designated in the bylaws or by the board of directors; and (ii) May bear the corporate seal or its facsimile. [17-16-625]

The shareholders of a corporation do not have a preemptive right to acquire the corporation's unissued shares except to the extent the Articles of Incorporation so provide. [17-16-630]

Director Meeting Rules

The board of directors may hold regular or special meetings within or outside of the state of Wyoming. [17-16-820]

Unless the Articles of Incorporation or bylaws provide otherwise, regular meetings of the board of directors may be held without notice of the date, time, place, or purpose of the meeting.

Unless the Articles of Incorporation or bylaws provide for a longer or shorter period, special meetings of the board of directors shall be preceded by at least two days' notice of the date, time, and place of the meeting. The notice need not describe the purpose of the special meeting unless required by the Articles of Incorporation or bylaws. [17-16-822]

Unless the Articles of Incorporation or bylaws require a greater number or unless otherwise specifically provided in the Business Corporation Act, a quorum of a board of directors consists of: (i) a majority of the fixed number of directors if the corporation has a fixed board size; or (ii) a majority of the number of directors prescribed, or, if no number is prescribed, the number in office immediately before the meeting begins, if the corporation has a variable-range size board.

The Articles of Incorporation or bylaws may authorize a quorum of a board of directors to consist of no fewer than one-third of the fixed or prescribed number of directors determined under Subsection (a) of this section [previous paragraph].

If a quorum is present when a vote is taken, the affirmative vote of a majority of directors present is the act of the board of directors unless the Articles of Incorporation or bylaws require the vote of a greater number of directors. [17-16-824]

Shareholder Meeting Rules

A corporation shall hold a meeting of shareholders annually at a time stated in or fixed in accordance with the bylaws. [17-16-701]

A corporation shall hold a special meeting of shareholders: (i) on call of its board of directors or the person or persons authorized to do so by the Articles of Incorporation or bylaws; or (ii) if the holders of at least 10% of all the votes entitled to be cast on any issue proposed to be considered at the proposed special meeting sign, either manually or in facsimile, date, and deliver to the corporation one or more written demands for the meeting describing the purpose or purposes for which it is to be held, provided that the Articles of Incorporation may fix a lower percentage or a higher percentage not exceeding 25% of all the votes entitled to be cast on any issue proposed to be considered.

A corporation shall notify shareholders of the date, time, and place of each annual and special shareholders' meeting no fewer than ten nor more than 60 days before the meeting date. Unless the Business Corporation Act or the Articles of Incorporation require otherwise, the corporation is required to give notice only to shareholders entitled to vote at the meeting.

Unless the Business Corporation Act or the Articles of Incorporation require otherwise, notice of an annual meeting need not include a description of the purpose or purposes for which the meeting is called.

Notice of a special meeting shall include a description of the purpose or purposes for which the meeting is called. [17-16-705] Only business within the purpose or purposes described in the meeting notice may be conducted at a special shareholders' meeting. [17-16-702]

Shares entitled to vote as a separate voting group may take action on a matter at a meeting only if a quorum of those shares exists with respect to that matter. Unless the Articles of Incorporation or the Business Corporation Act provides otherwise, a majority of the votes entitled to be cast on the matter by the voting group constitutes a quorum of that voting group for action on that matter.

If a quorum exists, action on a matter other than the election of directors by a voting group is approved if the votes cast within the voting group favoring the action exceed the votes cast opposing the action, unless the Articles of Incorporation or the Business Corporation Act requires a greater number of affirmative votes.

The election of directors is governed by W.S. 17-16-728. [17-16-725]

If the Articles of Incorporation or the Business Corporation Act provides for voting by a single voting group on a matter, action on that matter is taken when voted on by that voting group as provided in W.S. 17-16-725 [above]. [17-16-726]

Unless otherwise provided in the Articles of Incorporation, directors are elected by a plurality of the votes cast by the shares entitled to vote in the election at a meeting at which a quorum is present.

Shareholders do not have a right to cumulate their votes for directors unless the Articles of Incorporation so provide.

A statement included in the Articles of Incorporation that "(all) (a designated voting group of) shareholders are entitled to cumulate their votes for directors," or words of similar import, means that the shareholders designated are entitled to multiply the number of votes they are entitled to cast by the number of directors for whom they are entitled to vote and cast the product for a single candidate or distribute the product among two or more candidates.

Shares otherwise entitled to vote cumulatively may not be voted cumulatively at a particular meeting unless: (i) the meeting notice or proxy statement accompanying the notice states conspicuously that cumulative voting is authorized; or (ii) a shareholder who has the right to cumulate his votes gives notice to the corporation not less than 48 hours before the time set for the meeting of his intent to

cumulate his votes during the meeting. If one shareholder gives this notice, all other shareholders in the same voting group participating in the election are entitled to cumulate their votes without giving further notice. [17-16-728]

Financial Disclosure Rules

A corporation shall furnish, on request, to its shareholders annual financial statements, which may be consolidated or combined statements of the corporation and one or more of its subsidiaries, as appropriate, that include a balance sheet as of the end of the fiscal year, an income statement for that year, and a statement of changes in shareholders' equity for the year unless that information appears elsewhere in the financial statements. If financial statements are prepared for the corporation on the basis of generally accepted accounting principles, the annual financial statements shall also be prepared on that basis. If detailed financial statements are not prepared for the corporation on an annual basis, then a copy of its federal income tax return will satisfy the requirements of this section.

If the annual financial statements are reported on by a public accountant, his report shall accompany them. If not, the statements shall be accompanied by a statement of the president or the person responsible for the corporation's accounting records: (i) stating his reasonable belief whether the statements were prepared on the basis of generally accepted accounting principles and, if not, describing the basis of preparation; and (ii) describing any respects in which the statements were not prepared on a basis of accounting consistent with the statements prepared for the preceding year.

A corporation shall mail, on request, the annual financial statements to each shareholder within 120 days after the close of each fiscal year. Thereafter, on written request from a shareholder who was not mailed the statements, the corporation shall mail him the latest financial statements. [17-16-1620]

State Tax Information

Department of Revenue, Cheyenne
307-777-5242
http://revenue.state.wy.us

Wyoming does not have a corporate income tax (or an individual income tax). However, corporations and other entities must pay an annual license tax when they file their annual report with the Secretary of State. This tax is based on all assets located and used in Wyoming. An entity with $250,000 or less in assets pays a minimum annual license tax of $50.

Corporation Law Online

The Wyoming Business Corporation Act is contained in Title 17 of the Wyoming Statutes, Chapter 16, starting with Section 17-16-101. To find the Act, visit the legal research area of Nolo's website at www.nolo.com/statute/state.cfm. Click on "Wyoming." Choose "Wyoming Statutes" and then scroll down to Title 17. Click on the link to begin browsing the Act.

State Securities Information

Securities Division
Secretary of State's Office
The Capitol
Cheyenne, WY 82002-0020
307-777-7370
http://soswy.state.wy.us/securiti/securiti.htm

Wyoming's Uniform Securities Act is contained in Title 17, Chapter 4, of the Wyoming Statutes. You can find links to the Act and to the related securities rules on the Securities Division website. The website also provides information on exemptions from the registration of securities under the Securities Act. Among these exemptions is a private offering exemption under Section 17-4-114(b)(ix). It allows you to make offers to not more than 15 people in the state of Wyoming during any 12-month period if you believe that all buyers are purchasing for investment. You may not pay commissions or use advertising in connection with the offers. You do not have to file a form to qualify for this exemption. However, for a fee of $200, you can ask the Division to rule that you are eligible for the exemption or ask for variances from its statutory requirements. For additional information, see the Securities Division website, browse the Act and rules, and call the Division office.

Creating Your Own Articles Form

You can prepare and file your own articles form.

Federal Tax Act Updates

Every business owner's life is complicated by laws and regulations. While many laws stay the same from year to year, federal tax laws change at least a little bit every year, and have changed significantly in the past decade. Sometimes savvy business owners can turn new tax rules to their advantage. This is especially true of the 2003 federal tax act, known as the Jobs and Growth Tax Relief Reconciliation Act of 2003 (JGTRRA, pronounced "jigtra"), which we cover in this section. We take a look at another recent federal tax law, the American Jobs Creation Act, in Section 2 of this appendix.

Part I: The Jobs and Growth Tax Relief Reconciliation Act

What JGTRRA Gives, It May Also Take Away

The tax breaks that JGTRRA gives business owners and others don't uniformly begin as of a certain date—nor are they perpetual.

- When can you begin using JGTRRA? Some provisions begin in 2003, but others won't kick in until later—as late as 2006, for example.
- How long do the tax breaks in JGTRRA last? The JGTRRA provisions lapse, or "sunset," at various times, but even the longest-lived will lapse at the end of 2010. For example, some will lapse as early as the end of 2004. While these sunset times are firm now, they're subject to change if Congress passes another tax bill to extend or change them (which it undoubtedly will). Keep in mind that you are reading about a shifting tax landscape.

Some of JGTRRA's provisions benefit all small businesses, no matter whether you're a sole proprietorship, partnership, LLC, or corporation. For example, you can now deduct up to $100,000 in one year for tangible personal property used in your business, up from $25,000. (Tangible personal property includes computers and off-the-shelf software.) This increased expensing provision applies through 2006, and will be a major incentive to upgrade or invest in new equipment.

Another generally applicable provision concerns "bonus" depreciation (the depreciation you can take against brand-new business property). It's increased from 30% to 50%, as long as you bought the property after May 5, 2003 and before January 1, 2005. This bonus depreciation will last through 2005.

Many of JGTRRA's provisions apply when a business takes a particular step, such as paying its owners who also work for the company or declaring a dividend. The rest of this appendix gives you a thumbnail sketch of JGTRRA's benefits for:

- sole proprietors, partners, or limited liability company owners (members) who pay taxes on business profits via their personal income tax returns (Section A)
- corporate owners (shareholders) who are salaried employees in their company (Section B)
- corporations who choose to keep earnings in the company (Section C)
- shareholders receiving dividends (whether from their own corporation or another corporation) (Section D)
- shareholders selling stock (lower capital gains) (Section E)
- "small" corporations selling stock (Section F), and
- married couples and parents (Section G).

 Consult an accountant, tax planner, or tax lawyer before implementing new tax strategies in your business.
This appendix doesn't go into the details you'll need to consider before implementing a tax strategy based on JGTRRA—before taking that step, you'll need to consult an expert. It's also a good idea to meet with your tax planner before the end of your business's tax year to find out how tax laws will affect your business planning for the coming year.

A. Benefits for Sole Proprietors, Partners, and LLC Owners

If you own a small business organized as a sole proprietorship, a partnership, or an LLC, you know that business profits are taxed on your personal tax return. That's why sole proprietorships, partnerships, and LLCs are known as "pass-through" business entities (their profits and expenses "pass through" the business to their owners). Thanks to JGTTRA, starting in 2003 you'll pay less tax on your income—the top tax rates are lower and a little more income is taxed at the lowest rate. The table below, "2005 Federal Individual Tax Rates," reflects these adjustments (updated to show the latest 2005 post-JGTTRA figures).

Lower rates for high income earners. The highest individual rate is lowered to 35% (down from 38.6%). Other upper brackets have also been lowered by a couple of percentage points (35% to 33%, 30% to 28%, and 27% to 25%). This change sunsets at the end of 2010.

More income applies to low brackets. The 10% bracket now applies to more income than it did in the past (up from $6,000 to $7,000-plus for single returns, and from $12,000 to $14,000-plus for married filing jointly). This may help you pay less income tax if you are starting a business, don't expect much profit at first, and have no other income. This change sunsets in 2006, then comes back in 2007 under the terms of a prior tax bill.

2005 Federal Individual Tax Rates							
Single				**Head of Household**			
Taxable Income Over	But Not Over	The Tax Is	of the Amount Over	Taxable Income Over	But Not Over	The Tax Is	of the Amount Over
$0	$7,300	10%	$0	$0	$10,450	10%	$0
$7,300	$29,700	$730 + 15%	$7,300	$10,450	$39,800	$1,045 + 15%	$10,450
$29,700	$71,950	$4,090 + 25%	$29,700	$39,800	$102,8000	$5,447.50 + 25%	$39,800
$71,950	$150,150	$14,652 + 28%	$71,950	$102,800	$166,450	$21,197.50 + 28%	$102,800
$150,150	$326,450	$36,548.50 + 33%	$150,150	$166,450	$326,450	$39,019.50 + 33%	$166,450
$326,450	∞	$94,727.50 + 35%	$326,450	$326,450	∞	$91,819.50+ 35%	$326,450
Married Filing Jointly				**Married Filing Separately**			
Taxable Income Over	But Not Over	The Tax Is	of the Amount Over	Taxable Income Over	But Not Over	The Tax Is	of the Amount Over
$0	$14,600	10%	$0	$0	$7,300	10%	$0
$14,600	$59,400	$1,460 + 15%	$14,600	$7,300	$29,700	$730 + 15%	$7,300
$59,400	$119,950	$8,180 + 25%	$59,400	$29,700	$59,975	$4,090 + 25%	$29,700
$119,950	$182,800	$23,317.50 + 28%	$119,950	$59,975	$91,400	$11,658.75 + 28%	$59,975
$182,800	$326,450	$40,915.50 + 33%	$182,800	$91,400	$163,225	$20,457.75 + 33%	$91,400
$326,450	∞	$88,320s + 35%	$326,450	$163,225	∞	$44,160 + 35%	$163,225

B. Benefits for Salaried Corporate Owners

JGTTRA significantly affects the taxes owed by corporate owners who also work for and are paid by the company. It changes some of the calculations for determining the optimal amount of salaries and bonuses for tax purposes. Dividends are also more attractive—this is covered in Section D, below.

1. Income Splitting Opportunities

The owners of a small corporation, who typically also work for the corporation as officers, pay individual income taxes on their salaries and bonuses, while the corporation pays corporate income taxes on the profits retained in the corporation (after it deducts the salaries and bonuses). A basic benefit of incorporating your business is your ability to determine, through your decisions to distribute or retain corporate profits, whether you want to pay taxes on your corporate profits at corporate rates or at individual rates. This tax strategy is called corporate "tax splitting" or "income splitting."

Let's take a closer look at income splitting. The goal of income splitting is to take advantage of any difference between individual and corporate tax brackets at the same level of taxable income. If you make distributions to yourselves as owners, you effectively split corporate profits between the corporation's taxable income and your taxable income. The result of spreading your income among both corporate and individual income tax brackets is that you can avoid having all business profits pile up into higher brackets on either the corporate or the individual side. Even better, you get to choose whether you or the corporation pay taxes on the

next piece of corporate income, based on which of you will be taxed at a lower rate on those dollars.

In effect, the real value of having a corporation with separate tax brackets is that you have two additional tax brackets—the lowest 15% and 25% corporate income tax brackets—into which you can pour business income. If these extra corporate tax rates are lower than the top individual rate that you'd pay if more business income were paid out to you, you'll save tax dollars by keeping the income in the corporation rather than paying it out to yourself at a higher "marginal" (top) rate.

Now let's return to the effect of JGTRRA on income splitting. As explained in Section A, JGTTRA lowered the individual tax rate, though corporate income tax rates have not changed. Consequently, you may decide to keep less profit in your corporation (and take out more as salaries or bonuses), and pay less tax on those payouts. JGTTRA doesn't change the basic benefit of income splitting. It just changes the calculations.

2. Using Income Splitting After JGTRRA

The table below, "2005 Income Tax Payments and Brackets," lists corporate and individual rates and tax payments side by side. Use the table to compare individual and corporate taxes on a set amount of taxable income. Each time a tax bracket changes, a new row starts, which calculates the total amount of tax paid by an individual or corporation up to that point. (An extra row has been added at the $30,000 income level for purposes of the discussion that follows the table.) For simplicity, the chart compares corporate tax rates with the rates of only two individual tax-filing categories: single and married filing jointly.

2005 Income Tax Payments and Brackets						
Taxable Income	Individual (Single)		Individual (Married Filing Jointly)		Corporate	
More Than	Tax Payment So Far	Bracket Rate	Tax Payment So Far	Bracket Rate	Tax Payment So Far	Bracket Rate
$0	$0	10%	$0	10%	$0	15%
$7,300	$730 +	15%	$700	15%	$1,050	15%
$14,000	$1,825	15%	$1,460	15%	$2,190	15%
$29,700	$4,090	25%	$3,725	15%	$4,445	15%
$30,000	$4,165	25%	$3,770	15%	$4,500	15%
$50,000	$9,165	25%	$6,770	15%	$7,500	25%
$59,400	$11,515	25%	$8,180	25%	$9,850	25%
$71,950	$14,652.50	28%	$11,317.50	25%	$12,987.50	25%
$75,000	$15,506	28%	$12,080	25%	$13,750	34%
$100,000	$22,506.50	28%	$18,330	25%	$22,250	39%
$119,950	$28,092.50	28%	$23,317.50	28%	$21,530.50	39%
$150,150	$36,548.50	33%	$31,773.50	28%	$33,308.50	39%
$182,800	$47,323	33%	$40,915.50	33%	$46,042	39%
$326,450	$94,727.50	35%	$88,320	35%	$102.065.50	39%
$335,000	$97,720	35%	$91,312.50	35%	$113,900	34%
$400,000	$120,470	35%	$114,062.50	35%	$136,000	34%
$500,000	$155,470	35%	$149,062.50	35%	$170,000	34%
$1,000,000	$330,470	35%	$324,062.50	35%	$340,000	34%

Let's look closely at how this table works, and what it tells you about how to handle corporate profits. To compare tax rates and taxes owed on $100,000 of taxable income, for example, find the $100,000 row in the table. The three columns in this row show that on this amount of taxable income:

- single individual taxpayers pay $22,506.50
- married taxpayers filing jointly pay $18,330, and
- corporations pay $22,250.

The row also shows the tax bracket that applies to each taxpayer on taxable incomes above $100,000. A single taxpayer will pay a tax rate of 28%, married filing jointly taxpayers 25%, and corporate taxpayers 39% on taxable income above $100,000 (up to the next tax bracket).

If you use this table to compare tax brackets and payments for corporations and single taxpayers, you'll notice that a corporation pays less income tax than an individual on the same income between roughly $30,000 and $100,000. Above and below these thresholds, a single taxpayer pays less income tax than a corporation on the same income.

Now, let's compare the *married* and corporate tax payments and rates on the same levels of taxable income. You can see that married taxpayers filing jointly always pay less income tax than a corporation on the same levels of income. However, at $100,000, taxes paid by corporations and married taxpayers filing jointly are very close. So, keep in mind that you don't always get a tax advantage by paying out corporate profit as salaries instead of keeping the earnings in the corporation.

What do these tax payment and bracket comparisons mean for the owner-employees of a small corporation? Can you conclude that single-owner corporations that earn between $30,000 to $100,000 will save taxes if they keep the profits in the corporation? Or, is it true that if corporate owners are married, the owners should always make sure to pay out all profits to themselves as deductible salaries so that they only pay individual income taxes on the profits? Or perhaps, should married business owners never incorporate their business?

Actually, none of the above conclusions is valid. In fact, the traditional one-to-one comparisons of individual versus corporate tax payments and brackets really miss the whole point of corporate income and tax splitting. Remember, the real value of having a corporation with separate tax brackets is that you have two additional corporate 15% and 25% tax brackets (or buckets) into which you can pour business income. If these extra corporate tax brackets are lower than the marginal (top) rate that would apply if a given amount of business income is paid out to you (which is often true for many single and married business owners), you will save tax dollars by keeping the income in the corporation rather than paying it out to yourself at a higher marginal rate.

> **Example:** After taking your normal salary from your corporation, you expect to have $50,000 net income left in your corporation. If you keep the retained earnings in your corporation, it will pay a 15% corporate income rate on the $50,000. If you paid this extra $50,000 out to yourself as a salary increase or a bonus, it would be deducted from corporate income (the corporation would not pay income taxes on the $50,000). Instead, the extra $50,000 would be added to your regular salary on your individual income tax return and be taxed to you. If your regular salary puts you in an individual income tax bracket greater than 15%, you will pay more individual income taxes on the extra $50,000 than the amount of taxes your corporation would pay on it if the $50,000 were retained in the corporation. So, regardless of your marital

status and despite the strict bracket-to-bracket comparison that seems to favor individuals, the lower corporate tax brackets let you shelter business income at rates that often are lower than the rates individuals pay on business income.

For a further discussion of corporate income splitting, see Nolo's *Save Taxes With Corporate Income Splitting* eFormKit, available at www.nolo.com.

C. Benefits for Corporations With Retained Earnings

The Internal Revenue Code lets most corporations accumulate earnings and profits of up to $250,000, no questions asked. Owners can keep amounts above this ceiling if they establish a valid business purpose for the extra accumulations (for example, to pay off debt or establish a corporate reserve for expected expenses). Corporations that hold onto excessive income without a valid business purpose are subject to an "accumulated earnings" penalty tax. This penalty used to be tied to the top individual tax rate (38.6%) before JGTTRA. The good news after JGTTRA is that these penalty rates are now tied to the top tax rate that shareholders pay on dividends: 15%.

As the example above in Section B shows, you may want to keep corporate profits in the corporation for income tax reasons. But don't neglect to consider the accumulated earnings penalty—after all, though reduced, it's not zero.

There are additional potential tax reasons to retain profits in the corporation. Retained corporate earnings can eventually be "pulled out" of your corporation when you later sell your shares, at capital gains rates (which can be lower than individual tax rates; see Section E, below). Or they can be passed to your heirs after your death. Because your heirs will receive the shares with a basis "stepped up" to market value, they'll pay capital gains tax only on the appreciation in value that happens between the time they inherit and the time they sell the shares.

D. Benefits for Shareholders Receiving Dividends

JGTTRA reduces the taxes individuals pay on dividends, whether these dividends come from a corporation they own or not. Dividends are now a more desirable way to distribute corporate profits than they used to be, because:

- Individual recipients pay less tax (Subsection 1).
- Corporations are less tempted to structure payouts in ways that raise IRS suspicions (subsection 2).
- Owners who are salaried employees pay no FICA taxes on dividends, which saves them money (Subsection 3).

1. Lower Taxes on Dividends

A corporation can deduct salaries and bonuses, as we learned in discussing tax splitting in Section B, above, but it can't deduct the dividends it pays. This means the company must pay income tax on profits used as the source of dividend payments to shareholders, so both the corporation and the shareholders end up paying income taxes on dividends. Until 2003, dividends were taxed to shareholders at the top income tax rate of the shareholder, just like earned income (the top individual tax rate before JGTRRA was 38.6%). Understandably, owners were hesitant to declare dividends since they paid both corporate income and marginal (top-bracket) individual income taxes on the dividend payout, and also because it required a board meeting and the help of an accountant or lawyer to answer the financial and legal questions preliminary to declaring a dividend.

JGTRRA gives corporate owners a reason to reconsider this traditional reluctance. The 2003 tax law lowers the tax rate on dividends paid by most individuals to 15% (very low income taxpayers pay only 5%). In other words, dividends are taxed separately from other individual income, not added to your other income to be taxed at your top individual tax rate. This change will sunset in 2008.

2. Fewer Fights With the IRS

Lowering the tax rate on dividends will probably have a salutary effect on shareholder-IRS relations, too. Because dividends were taxed at the recipient's top individual rate, corporations were tempted to devise creative methods of paying money out to shareholders—without calling these payouts dividends (these methods included excessive salary payments, buy-backs of a portion of an owner's stock, and the like). The IRS frequently challenged these actions. Now that the dividend tax rate is so attractive, there's less need for creative maneuvers to avoid dividend treatment.

3. Save Money on FICA Taxes

FICA taxes support the Social Security and Medicare systems. Employees, whether salaried or wage earners, pay half the tax from their earnings; the employer pays the other half. If you're incorporated and work in your business, you're an employee and will ordinarily get a salary—and, just like any other employee, you'll pay FICA taxes on your salary (the corporation pays the other half). But think of what happens when you own the corporation—in effect, you pay both the corporate and the individual portion. The total FICA tax is 15.3%, or $13,770, on the first $90,000 (the 2005 FICA wage-base amount, which is subject to change), and 2.9% tax on any salary over $90,000.

FICA applies only to earned income, and *dividends are not considered earned income*. Consequently, you don't pay FICA taxes on dividends, which means that dividends have a built-in potential 15.3% tax savings when they replace a portion of the owner's corporate salary. In other words, it can make sense for a small corporation to pay out some money to its owners as dividends rather than salaries. This little-recognized strategy can save some tax dollars in some situations, but understand that it makes sense only if the corporation's income tax on that money, plus the 15% individual tax on dividends, is less than the individual income tax and FICA taxes that would be paid on the same money if it were paid as additional salary (remember, the corporation deducts salaries paid out to employees, so the corporation does not pay corporate income tax on salaries).

Shareholders That Are Corporations

Corporations that own shares in other corporations have a dividend tax rate break under pre-JGTRRA tax law that stays in effect. They can exclude from 70% to 100% of dividend income from the corporate shareholder's taxable income. A corporation that pays a maximum 35% income tax on only 30% of its dividend income pays an effective corporate dividend tax rate of 10.5%, at most.

The rationale for this corporate tax break is that dividends should be taxed twice, not three times. The corporate shareholder may distribute its dividend income to its own shareholders, who will themselves pay income tax on it. And the corporation that distributed the original dividend already paid tax on that money as income.

⚠ **Make sure your tax adviser does the math before you decide on a dividend.**
The tax savings achieved by owners paying out a dividend on a small corporation's earnings may not be worth the hassle of calling a board meeting and making the necessary analysis before declaring the dividend. You'll also experience a long-term disadvantage if you underfund your Social Security and Medicare account.

Example: Camilus and Patrick form a specialized flight instruction school for air-show acrobatic pilots, Blue Sky Barnstorming. They incorporate to limit their personal exposure to lawsuits and claims that might be made against their high-risk venture. The corporation earns $100,000 in net profits and pays out the entire amount as salary to the owners. Each owner is single, and each has no additional (noncorporate) taxable income to report for the year.

Here are the tax costs:

Corporate tax	$ 0
Patrick's individual income tax on $50,000 salary payout	$9,165
Camilus's individual income tax on $50,000 salary payout	$9,165
Total Social Security cost on salaries ($50,000 x .153 x 2)	$15,300
Total income and FICA taxes	$33,630

After talking to their tax adviser, they learn that they can save a few dollars by declaring and paying a dividend instead of paying the total $50,000 out to each owner as a salary. They decide to pay each owner a salary of $29,700 (the point at which the single individual tax bracket changes from 15% to 25%) and the balance of the payout ($50,000 - $29,700 = $20,300) as a dividend. This means the corporation will retain $40,600 to pay out as a dividend to both owners ($20,300 x 2 = $40,600).

Here are the recomputed tax costs:

Corporate tax on retained $40,600	$6,090
Patrick's individual income tax on $29,700 salary payout	$4,090
Camilus's individual income tax on $29,700 salary payout	$4,090
Patrick's and Camilus's income tax on the dividend ($20,300 dividend x .15 individual dividend tax rate x 2)	$6,090
Total social security cost on salaries ($29,700 x 15.3 x 2)	$9,089
Total income and FICA taxes	$29,449

This is a tax savings of $4,181 ($33,630 - 29,449) compared to the previous scenario. While not a mammoth tax cut, the $4,000+ may come in handy when, as here, the owners are only able to pull modest amounts of profits from their corporation.

Choosing an Exchange Over a Dividend

When JGTRRA lowered the corporate dividend tax rate to 15%, it became the same as the reduced long-term capital gains tax rate. This new twist makes much traditional corporate tax maneuvering less necessary.

Tax advisers pre-JGTRRA tried to avoid having corporate distributions treated as dividends, because they were taxed to shareholders at their highest individual tax rates. The goal was to pay out corporate earnings that were taxed to the corporate business owner at lower long-term capital gains rates, often by having the corporation "redeem" (buy back) stock from shareholders in a transaction called a "stock redemption." But the IRS wanted to prevent shareholders from selling shares back to the corporation simply to get some money out at a lower tax cost, unless such a sale resulted in a meaningful change in their stock ownership percentages.

Example 1: If two shareholders each own half of a corporation, and they both sell back the same portion of their shares to their corporation, they're still 50/50 shareholders after the sale. They really haven't reduced their percentages of stock ownership—they've simply pulled earnings and profits out of their corporation in the guise of a stock sale. In the pre-JGTRRA days, the IRS was likely to recharacterize the transaction as a payout of a corporate dividend and make the shareholders pay ordinary (not capital gains) tax rates on the "stock sale" proceeds.

Since the dividends and capital gains tax rates are now the same, it doesn't matter as much to a shareholder or the IRS whether a payout to a shareholder is structured as a redemption of shares or as a dividend—either way, the tax rate (long-term capital gain or dividend) paid by the shareholder is the same.

Example 2: Mandrake is the majority shareholder and director of a small corporation, and he wants some cash in his pocket instead of shares of stock. He doesn't want to approve a dividend, which would mean paying out profits to all shareholders. However, he knows he can vote at a board meeting to have the corporation approve a buy-back of some of his shares at their fair market value. In 2002, prior to JGTRRA, Mandrake's accountant Fenton advised against the

proposed sale, because the buy-back would be treated as a dividend and taxed at Mandrake's highest individual tax rate of over 30%. It wouldn't qualify as a more tax-favorable capital gains rate "exchange" under Internal Revenue Code Section 302, because Mandrake was not selling enough stock to effectively reduce his stock ownerships. (Mandrake essentially would need to become a minority shareholder in his corporation, which he wasn't willing to do.)

After reading about JGTRRA, Fenton called back and told Mandrake that the new dividend tax rate is only 15%. Mandrake was thrilled and got going on the stock sale.

There is still a post-JGTRRA advantage to qualifying a stock redemption as an exchange, because with an exchange the shareholder pays income tax only on the amount of sales proceeds that exceed the shareholder's "basis" in the shares. (Basis is determined by the amount a shareholder paid to buy his shares plus adjustments that may occur while the shareholder held the shares.) This is called a "recovery of basis," and it's potentially a huge tax advantage.

Example 3: Mandrake originally paid $10,000 for his shares of stock in his corporation, and their fair market value at the time of the stock redemption is $100,000. Mandrake's initial cost basis in his stock is $10,000, and we'll assume there have been no adjustments to the basis since then. If the redemption does not qualify for exchange treatment, Mandrake pays a 15% dividends tax on the entire $100,000, which amounts to $15,000 in tax.

However, if the buy-back qualifies as an exchange, the first $10,000 of the sales proceeds reduces his basis in his stock to zero. Only the remaining $90,000 will be taxed at the 15% capital gains tax rates ($13,500 in taxes). This $1,500 tax savings might not make much difference to Mandrake. But if he had a $50,000 basis, and the sale qualified as an exchange, the first $50,000 of the proceeds reduces his basis to zero, and only the remaining $50,000 is subject to a 15% tax ($7,500 in taxes). That tax savings could influence Mandrake's choice of transaction.

E. Benefits for Shareholders Selling Stock: Lower Capital Gains

Individuals pay long-term capital gains tax on the sale of stock, certain real estate, and other types of property held for more than one year. JGTTRA lowered the long-term capital gains rate from 20% to 15%. (For very low income taxpayers, the new rate is 5% or 0%, depending on the year of sale of the property.)

There are a number of exceptions to the new rule, and lots of higher capital gains rates that apply to different sorts of transactions. The new lower JGTRRA capital gains rates are valid through 2008.

F. Benefits for "Small Corporation" Stock Sales

JGTRRA keeps in place a couple of capital gains and loss incentives for small corporation owners. Under Section 1244 of the Internal Revenue Code, a married couple can deduct against ordinary income up to $100,000 of capital losses ($50,000 for single taxpayers) caused by the sale or worthlessness of qualified small business corporation stock. This is a big tax break, because normally capital losses can offset only up to $3,000 of ordinary income in a year.

Section 1202 of the Code lets the owners of qualified small business stock exclude from capital gains taxes 50% of the gains from the sale of the stock. This cuts in half the capital gains tax on profits from the sale. Note that there is a special Section 1202 capital gains tax rate of 28% that is applied to the half of the Section 1202 stock that is taxed. This means that the effective 1202 capital gains tax on a sale of qualified stock is 14%, which is 1% less than the standard post-JGTRRA long-term capital gains tax rate.

G. Tax Breaks for Families

JGTTRA gives some additional tax breaks to people who are married or have children.

1. Reduced Marriage Penalty

Before 2003, a two-income married couple filing jointly paid more tax than if each had filed separately. This was called the "marriage penalty." Under JGTTRA, the 15% bracket has been widened for couples filing jointly. It's now twice as wide as the 15% bracket for single taxpayers. (See Section A, above, for the individual tax rate table.) This change in the 15% bracket eliminates the marriage penalty on the first $114,650 of a married couple's taxable income if they file jointly.

This provision is good in 2003 and 2004, but it's temporary. In 2005 the 15% bracket for married filing jointly will contract again and then increase gradually until 2009. The old pre-JGTRRA rules come back in full force in 2011, unless Congress passes another tax bill in the meantime.

2. Increased Child Care Credit

JGTRRA gives an increased child credit in 2003 and 2004, but it's reduced again in 2005 and gradually rises through 2010. The lower pre-JGTRRA credit comes back in 2011, unless a future tax bill revives the increased credit.

Part II: The American Jobs Creation Act

The American Jobs Creation Act of 2004 (AJCA) became effective January 1, 2005 (except for some provisions that will take effect later). This section highlights a few of the provisions that will impact small corporations. This is preliminary and partial information, however. To get the latest and most complete information, you will want to do your own research, by going to the IRS website at www.irs.gov and checking with your tax adviser.

A. Tax Deductions for Manufacturing Companies

AJCA allows corporations (including S corporations), LLCs, partnerships, and sole proprietorships to deduct from their taxable income 3% of business income derived from or related to U.S. manufacturing. Under this rule, a small corporation that earns $30,000 of qualified manufacturing income in 2005 can deduct $900 from its taxable corporate income ($30,000 x .03 = $900). The deductible percentage will increase from 3% to 9% by the year 2010. The definition of manufacturing activities is not obvious—according to the Committee Report, for example, selling roasted coffee beans can qualify, but making sausages for a restaurant will not.

The deduction is limited to 50% of wages paid to employees during the year. Because of this limitation, S corporations, LLCs, partnerships, and sole proprietorships may not be able to take advantage of the deduction, because their owners are not considered " employees." Under the tax code, owners who share in profits are not considered to be employees unless they are guaranteed a salary or a set payment regardless of actual profits earned in the business. Small C corporations, on the other hand, stand a better chance of being able to do so because their owners typically work as salaried officers of the corporation, and thus they do qualify as "employees" under the tax code.

B. Extension of Added Deduction for Business Property

As noted in Part I of this Appendix, JGTRRA boosted the deduction for tangible personal property placed in service in a business to $100,000. AJCA extends this deduction until the end of 2007.

C. S Corporation Reform and Simplification

AJCA simplified and liberalized some of the federal S corporation tax rules. Most smaller business owners who want limited liability protection and pass-through taxation now choose to form LLCs rather than S corporations because LLCs enjoy greater legal and tax flexibility (as explained in Chapter 1, Section A4a of this book). The new rules make life easier for S corporations by:

- allowing all members of a family (as defined in AJCA), not just spouses, to be counted as one S corporation shareholder
- increasing the number of permitted S corporation shareholders from 75 to 100, and
- relaxing the technical S corporation requirements that apply to banks that are set up as S corporations.

D. Deduction and Amortization of Organizational Expenses

Up to $5,000 of corporate organizational expenses, plus up to $5,000 of start-up expenses, can be deducted in the first tax year of the corporation. In addition, the corporation can elect to amortize and deduct any additional organization and start-up expenses over the next 15 years. Note that the first-year deduction amount is reduced dollar for dollar to the extent organizational or start-up expenses exceed $50,000.

Under current law, you can elect to amortize start-up and organizational expenses over a shorter 60-month period, but there is no automatically allowed amount of organizational or start-up costs that corporations can deduct in their first tax year. (See Chapter 4, Step 6, special instruction 14 in this book.) ∎

How to Use the CD-ROM

The tear-out forms in Appendix D are included on a CD-ROM in the back of the book. This CD-ROM, which can be used with Windows computers, installs files that can be opened, printed, and edited using a word processor or other software. It is *not* a standalone software program. Please read this appendix and the README.TXT file included on the CD-ROM for instructions on using the Forms CD.

Note to Mac users: This CD-ROM and its files should also work on Macintosh computers. Please note, however, that Nolo cannot provide technical support for non-Windows users.

Two different kinds of forms are contained on the CD-ROM:

- Word processing (RTF) forms that you can open, complete, print, and save with your word processing program (see Section B, below), and
- Forms (PDF) that can be viewed only with Adobe Acrobat Reader 4.0 or higher (see Section C, below. These forms are designed to be printed out and filled in by hand or with a typewriter.

See Appendix D for a list of forms, their file names, and their file formats.

How to View the README File

If you do not know how to view the file README.TXT, insert the Forms CD-ROM into your computer's CD-ROM drive and follow these instructions:

- Windows 9x, 2000, Me, and XP: (1) On your PC's desktop, double click the My Computer icon; (2) double click the icon for the CD-ROM drive into which the Forms CD-ROM was inserted; (3) double click the file README.TXT.
- Macintosh: (1) On your Mac desktop, double click the icon for the CD-ROM that you inserted; (2) double click on the file README.TXT.

While the README file is open, print it out by using the Print command in the File menu.

A. Installing the Form Files Onto Your Computer

Before you can do anything with the files on the CD-ROM, you need to install them onto your hard disk. In accordance with U.S. copyright laws, remember that copies of the CD-ROM and its files are for your personal use only.

Insert the Forms CD and do the following.

1. Windows 9x, 2000, Me, and XP Users

Follow the instructions that appear on the screen. (If nothing happens when you insert the Forms CD-ROM, then (1) double click the My Computer icon; (2) double click the icon for the CD-ROM drive into which the Forms CD-ROM was inserted; and (3) double click the file WELCOME.EXE.)

By default, all the files are installed to the \Incorporation Forms folder in the \Program Files folder of your computer. A folder called "Incorporation Forms" is added to the "Programs" folder of the Start menu.

2. Macintosh Users

Step 1: If the "Incorporation Forms CD" window is not open, open it by double clicking the "Incorporation Forms CD" icon.

Step 2: Select the "Incorporation Forms" folder icon.

Step 3: Drag and drop the folder icon onto the icon of your hard disk.

B. Using the Word Processing Files to Create Documents

This section concerns the files for forms that can be opened and edited with your word processing program.

All word processing forms come in rich text format. These files have the extension ".RTF." For example, the form for the Request for Reservation of Corporate Name discussed in Chapter 4 is on the file NAMERES.RTF. All forms, their file names, and their file formats are listed in Appendix D.

RTF files can be read by most recent word processing programs including all versions of MS Word for Windows and Macintosh, WordPad for Windows, and recent versions of WordPerfect for Windows and Macintosh.

To use a form from the CD to create your documents, you must (1) open a file in your word processor or text editor; (2) edit the form by filling in the required information; (3) print it out; (4) rename and save your revised file.

The following are general instructions. However, each word processor uses different commands to open, format, save, and print documents. Please read your word processor's manual for specific instructions on performing these tasks.

Do not call Nolo's technical support if you have questions on how to use your word processor.

Step 1: Opening a File

There are three ways to open the word processing files included on the CD-ROM after you have installed them onto your computer:

- Windows users can open a file by selecting its "shortcut" as follows: (1) Click the Windows "Start" button; (2) open the "Programs" folder; (3) open the "Incorporation Forms" subfolder; and (4) click on the shortcut to the form you want to work with.

- Both Windows and Macintosh users can open a file directly by double clicking on it. Use My Computer or Windows Explorer (Windows 9x, 2000, Me, or XP) or the Finder (Macintosh) to go to the folder you installed or copied the CD-ROM's files to. Then, double click on the specific file you want to open.

- You can also open a file from within your word processor. To do this, you must first start your word processor. Then, go to the File menu and choose the Open command. This opens a dialog box where you will tell the program (1) the type of file you want to open (*.RTF); and (2) the location and name of the file (you will need to navigate through the directory tree to get to the folder on your hard disk where the CD's files have been installed). If these directions are unclear, you will need to look through the manual for your word processing program—Nolo's technical support department will *not* be able to help you with the use of your word processing program.

Where Are the Files Installed?

Windows Users
- RTF files are installed by default to a folder named \Incorporation Forms in the \Program Files folder of your computer.

Macintosh Users
- RTF files are located in the "Incorporation Forms" folder.

Step 2: Editing Your Document

Fill in the appropriate information according to the instructions and sample agreements in the book. Underlines are used to indicate where you need to enter your information, frequently followed by instructions in brackets. Be sure to delete the underlines and instructions from your edited document. You will also want to make sure that any signature lines in your completed documents appear on a page with at least some text from the document itself. If you do not know how to use your word processor to edit a document, you will need to look through the manual for your word processing program—Nolo's technical support department will *not* be able to help you with the use of your word processing program.

Editing Forms That Have Optional or Alternative Text

Some of the forms have optional or alternate text:
- With optional text, you choose whether to include or exclude the given text.
- With alternative text, you select one alternative to include and exclude the other alternatives.

When editing these forms, we suggest you do the following.

Optional text

If you **don't want** to include optional text, just delete it from your document.

If you **do want** to include optional text, just leave it in your document.

In either case, delete the italicized instructions.

Alternative text

First delete all the alternatives that you do not want to include, then delete the italicized instructions.

Step 3: Printing Out the Document

Use your word processor's or text editor's "Print" command to print out your document. If you do not know how to use your word processor to print a document, you will need to look through the manual for your word processing program—Nolo's technical support department will *not* be able to help you with the use of your word processing program.

Step 4: Saving Your Document

After filling in the form, use the "Save As" command to save and rename the file. Because all the files are "read-only," you will not be able to use the "Save" command. This is for your protection. *If you save the file without renaming it, the underlines that indicate where you need to enter your information will be lost and you will not be able to create a new document with this file without recopying the original file from the CD-ROM.*

If you do not know how to use your word processor to save a document, you will need to look through the manual for your word processing program—Nolo's technical support department will *not* be able to help you with the the use of your word processing program.

C. Using PDF Files to Print Out Forms

An electronic copy of a Stock Certificate is included on the CD-ROM in Adobe Acrobat PDF format. You must have the Adobe Acrobat Reader installed on your computer (see below) to use this form. All forms, their file names, and their file formats are listed in Appendix D.

This form cannot be filled out using your computer. To create your document using this file, you must (1) open the file; (2) print it out; and (3) complete it by hand or typewriter.

Step 1: Opening PDF Files

PDF files, like the word processing files, can be opened one of three ways:

- Windows users can open a file by selecting its "shortcut" as follows: (1) Click the Windows "Start" button; (2) open the "Programs" folder; (3) open the "Incorporation Forms" subfolder; and (4) click on the shortcut to the form you want to work with.
- Both Windows and Macintosh users can open a file directly by double clicking on it. Use My Computer or Windows Explorer (Windows 9x, 2000, Me, or XP) or the Finder (Macintosh) to go to the folder you created and copied the CD-ROM's files to. Then, double click on the specific file you want to open.
- You can also open a PDF file from within Acrobat Reader. To do this, you must first start Reader. Then, go to the File menu and choose the Open command. This opens a dialog box where you will tell the program the location and name of the file (you will need to navigate through the directory tree to get to the folder on your hard disk where the CD's files have been installed). If these directions are unclear, you will need to look through Acrobat Reader's help—Nolo's technical support department will *not* be able to help you with the use of Acrobat Reader.

Where Are the PDF Files Installed?

- Windows Users: PDF files are installed by default to a folder named \Incorporation Forms in the \Program Files folder of your computer.
- Macintosh Users: PDF files are located in the "Incorporation Forms" folder.

Step 2: Printing PDF files

Choose Print from the Acrobat Reader File menu. This will open the Print dialog box. In the "Print Range" section of the Print dialog box, select the appropriate print range, then click OK.

Step 3: Filling in PDF files

The PDF files cannot be filled out using your computer. To create your document using one of these files, you must first print it out (see Step 2, above), and then complete it by hand or typewriter. ■

Tear-Out Forms

Name of Form	Disk File Name	Chapter in Book
1. Request for Reservation of Corporate Name	(NAMERES)	Chapter 4, Step 1, Section F
2. Iowa Articles of Incorporation	(IAARTS)	Chapter 4, Step 2, Section B Iowa State Sheet, Appendix A
3. Nebraska Articles of Incorporation	(NEARTS)	Chapter 4, Step 2, Section B Nebraska State Sheet, Appendix A
4. Cover Letter for Filing Articles	(COVERLET)	Chapter 4, Step 2, Section C
5. Bylaws	(BYLAWS)	Chapter 4, Step 4, Section B
6. Incorporator's Statement	(INCORPST)	Chapter 4, Step 5
7. Minutes of First Meeting of Board of Directors	(MINUTES)	Chapter 4, Step 6, Section A
8. Stock Certificates	(CERTIF)	Chapter 4, Step 7
9. Bill of Sale for Assets of a Business	(BILLSALE)	Chapter 4, Step 7, Section B1
10. Receipt for Cash Payment	(RECEIPTS)	Chapter 4, Step 7, Section B2a
11. Bill of Sale for Items of Property	(RECEIPTS)	Chapter 4, Step 7, Section B2b
12. Receipt for Services Rendered	(RECEIPTS)	Chapter 4, Step 7, Section B2c

Request for Reservation of Corporate Name

_____

_____

_____

_____

_____

_____

Re: Request for Reservation of Corporate Name

Corporate Filing Office:

Please reserve the first available corporate name from the list below for my use.
My proposed corporate names, listed in order of preference, are as follows:

_____

_____

_____

I enclose a check for the required reservation fee.
Sincerely,

_____

_____

Iowa Articles of Incorporation

Pursuant to the _____ Business Corporation Act, the undersigned incorporator submits the following Articles of Incorporation:

1. The name of the corporation is _____.

2. The corporation is authorized to issue one class of common shares. The total number of such shares it is authorized to issue is _____.

3. The street address of the corporation's initial registered office is _____ , and the name of its initial registered agent at this address is _____ .

4. The name and address of the incorporator is _____.

Date: _____

Signature of Incorporator: _____

Nebraska Articles of Incorporation

Pursuant to the _____ Business Corporation Act, the undersigned incorporator submits the following Articles of Incorporation:

1. The name of the corporation is _____.

2. The corporation is authorized to issue one class of common shares. The total number of such shares it is authorized to issue is _____.

3. The street address of the corporation's initial registered office is _____, and the name of its initial registered agent at this address is _____ .

4. The name and address of the incorporator is _____.

Date: _____

Signature of Incorporator: _____

Cover Letter for Filing Articles

_____

_____

_____

_____

_____

Corporate Filing Office:

I enclose an original and _____ copy/copies of the _____,

_____ of _____ . Please file

the original document and return any file-stamped copies to me, at the above address.

This corporate name was reserved by the undersigned incorporator on _____,

_____.

I enclose payment of required filing fees.

Sincerely,

_____

 [Incorporator's typed name]

Bylaws of

_____

ARTICLE 1. OFFICES

SECTION 1. PRINCIPAL OFFICE

The location of the principal office of the corporation shall be within the state of _____ at an address fixed by the board of directors. The secretary of this corporation shall keep a copy of the corporation's Articles of Incorporation (or similar incorporating document), these bylaws, minutes of directors' and shareholders' meetings, stock certificates and stubs, a register of the names and interests of the corporation's shareholders, and other corporate records and documents at the principal office.

SECTION 2. OTHER OFFICES

The corporation may have offices at other locations as decided by its board of directors or as its business may require.

ARTICLE 2. SHAREHOLDERS' MEETINGS

SECTION 1. PLACE OF MEETINGS

Meetings of shareholders shall be held at the principal office of the corporation or at other locations as may be decided by the board of directors.

SECTION 2. ANNUAL MEETINGS

The annual meeting of the shareholders shall be held each year on and at the following date and time: _____. At the annual shareholders' meeting, shareholders shall elect a board of directors and transact any other proper business. If this date falls on a legal holiday, then the meeting shall be held on the following business day at the same time.

SECTION 3. SPECIAL MEETINGS

Special meetings of the shareholders may be called by the individuals authorized to do so under the state's corporation statutes.

SECTION 4. NOTICES OF MEETINGS

Notices of meetings, annual or special, shall be given in writing to shareholders entitled to vote at the meeting by the secretary or an assistant secretary or, if there be no such officer, by any director or shareholder.

Notices of shareholders' meetings shall be given either personally or by first-class mail or other means of written communication, addressed to the shareholder at the address of the shareholder appearing on the stock register of the corporation or given by the shareholder to the corporation for the purpose of notice. Notice of a shareholders' meeting shall be given to each shareholder no less than 30 days prior to the meeting.

Such notice shall state the place, date, and hour of the meeting and the general nature of the business to be transacted. The notice of an annual meeting and any special meeting at which directors are to be elected shall include the names of the nominees that, at the time of the notice, the board of directors intends to present for election.

SECTION 5. WAIVER OF NOTICE

The transactions of any meeting of shareholders, however called and noticed, and wherever held, are as valid as though undertaken at a meeting duly held after regular call and notice, if a quorum is present, whether in person or by proxy, and if, either before or after the meeting, each of the persons entitled to vote, not present in person or by proxy, signs a written waiver of notice or a consent to the holding of the meeting or an approval of the minutes thereof. If the waiver does not include an approval of the minutes of the meeting, it shall state the general nature of the business of the meeting. All such waivers, consents, and approvals shall be filed with the corporate records or made a part of the minutes of the meeting.

SECTION 6. LIST OF SHAREHOLDERS

Prior to any meeting of shareholders, the secretary of the corporation shall prepare an alphabetical list of shareholders entitled to vote at the meeting that shows the address of each shareholder and number of shares entitled to vote at the meeting. This list shall be available for inspection at the principal office of the corporation by any shareholder within a reasonable period prior to each meeting and be made available for inspection at the meeting upon request of any shareholder at the meeting.

SECTION 7. QUORUM AND VOTING

Every shareholder entitled to vote shall be entitled to one vote for each share held, except as otherwise provided by law. A shareholder entitled to vote may vote part of his or her shares in favor of a proposal and refrain from voting the remaining shares or vote them against the proposal. If a shareholder fails to specify the number of shares he or she is affirmatively voting, it will be conclusively presumed that the shareholder's approving vote is with respect to all shares the shareholder is entitled to vote.

A majority of the shares entitled to vote, represented in person or by proxy, shall constitute a quorum at a meeting of shareholders. If a quorum is present, the affirmative vote of the majority of shareholders represented at the meeting and entitled to vote on any matter shall be the act of the shareholders, unless the vote of a greater number is required by law.

The shareholders present at a duly called or held meeting at which a quorum is present may continue to transact business until adjournment notwithstanding the withdrawal of enough shareholders to leave less than a quorum, if any action is approved by at least a majority of the shares required to constitute a quorum.

Notwithstanding other provisions of this section of the bylaws, if permitted by law and not prohibited by provision of the corporation's Articles of Incorporation (or similar incorporating document), shareholders may cumulate votes for the election of directors as provided in this paragraph. If permitted to cumulate votes in such election, a shareholder must state his or her intention to cumulate votes after the candidates' names have been placed in nomination at the meeting and before the commencement of voting for the election of directors. Once a shareholder has so stated his or her intention to cumulate votes, all shareholders entitled to vote must cumulate their votes in the election for directors. A shareholder cumulates votes by giving one candidate a number of votes equal to the number of directors to be elected multiplied by the number of his or her shares or by distributing such votes on the same principle among any number of candidates as he or she decides. The candidates receiving the highest number of votes, up to the number of directors to be elected, shall be elected. Votes cast against a candidate or which are withheld shall have no effect in the cumulative voting results.

In any election for directors at a shareholders' meeting, upon the request of any shareholder made before the voting begins, the election of directors shall be by ballot rather than by voice vote.

SECTION 8. PROXIES

Every person entitled to vote shares may authorize another person or persons to act by proxy with respect to such shares by filing a proxy with the secretary of the corporation. For purposes of these bylaws, a "proxy" is a written authorization signed by a shareholder or the shareholder's attorney-in-fact giving another person or persons power to vote with respect to the shares of the shareholder. Every proxy shall continue in full force and effect until the expiration of any period specified in the proxy or until revoked by the person executing it, except as otherwise provided by law.

SECTION 9. ACTION WITHOUT MEETING

Any action that may be taken at any annual or special meeting of shareholders, except for the election of directors, may be taken without a meeting and without prior notice if a consent, in writing, setting forth the action so taken, is signed by all the holders of outstanding shares entitled to vote on the action.

ARTICLE 3. DIRECTORS

SECTION 1. POWERS

The business and affairs of the corporation shall be managed by, or under the direction of, its board of directors.

SECTION 2. NUMBER

The authorized number of directors shall be _____.

SECTION 3. ELECTION AND TENURE OF OFFICE

The directors shall be elected at the annual meeting of the shareholders and hold office until the next annual meeting and until their successors have been elected and qualified.

SECTION 4. RESIGNATION AND VACANCIES

Any director may resign effective upon giving written notice to the chairperson of the board of directors, the president, the secretary, or the board of directors, unless the notice specifies a later time for the effectiveness of the resignation. If the resignation is effective at a later time, a successor may be elected to take office when the resignation becomes effective.

A vacancy on the board of directors shall exist in the case of death, resignation, or removal of any director or in case the authorized number of directors is increased, or in case the shareholders fail to elect the full authorized number of directors at any annual or special meeting of the shareholders at which directors are elected. The board of directors may declare vacant the office of a director who has been declared of unsound mind by an order of court or who has been convicted of a felony.

Vacancies on the board may be filled by the remaining board members unless a vacancy is required by law to be filled by approval of the shareholders. Each director approved to fill a vacancy on the board shall hold such office until the next annual meeting of the shareholders and until his or her successor has been elected and qualified.

SECTION 5. PLACE OF MEETINGS

Meetings of the board of directors shall be held at any place, within or without the state, that has been designated in the notice of the meeting or, if not stated in the notice or if there is no notice, at the principal office of the corporation or as may be designated from time to time by resolution of the board of directors. Meetings of the board may be held through use of conference telephone, computer, electronic video screen communication, or other communications equipment, as long as all of the following apply:

(a) Each member participating in the meeting can communicate with all members concurrently.

(b) Each member is provided the means of participating in all matters before the board, including the capacity to propose, or to interpose, an objection to a specific action to be taken by the corporation.

(c) The corporation adopts and implements some means of verifying both of the following:

(1) A person communicating by telephone, computer, electronic video screen, or other communications equpment is a director entitled to participate in the board meeting.

(2) All statements, questions, actions, or votes were made by that director and not by another person.

SECTION 6. ANNUAL AND REGULAR MEETINGS

An annual meeting of the board of directors shall be held immediately after and at the same place as the annual meeting of the shareholders.

Other regular meetings of the board of directors shall be held at such times and places as may be fixed from time to time by the board of directors.

SECTION 7. SPECIAL MEETINGS

Special meetings of the directors may be called by the individuals authorized to do so under the state's corporation statutes.

SECTION 8. NOTICES OF MEETINGS

Notices of directors' meetings, whether annual, regular, or special, shall be given in writing to directors by the secretary or an assistant secretary or, if there be no such officer, by any director.

Notices of directors' meetings shall be given either personally or by first-class mail or other means of written communication, addressed to the director at the address of the director appearing on the records of the corporation or given by the director to the corporation for the purpose of notice. Notice of a directors' meeting shall be given to each director at least two weeks prior to the meeting, unless a greater period is required under the state corporation statutes for giving notice of a meeting.

Such notice shall state the place, date, and hour of the meeting and the general nature of the business to be transacted.

SECTION 9. WAIVER OF NOTICE

The transactions of any meeting of the board, however called and noticed or wherever held, are as valid as though undertaken at a meeting duly held after regular call and notice if a quorum is present and if, either before or after the meeting, each of the directors not present signs a written waiver of notice, a consent to holding the meeting, or an approval of the minutes thereof. If the waiver does not include an approval of the minutes of the meeting, it shall state the general nature of the business of the meeting. All such waivers, consents, and approvals shall be filed with the corporate records or made a part of the minutes of the meeting.

SECTION 10. QUORUM AND VOTING

A quorum for all meetings of the board of directors shall consist of a majority of the authorized number of directors.

Except as otherwise required under state corporate statutes, every act or decision done or made by a majority of the directors present at a meeting duly held at which a quorum is present is the act of the board.

SECTION 11. ACTION WITHOUT MEETING

Any action required or permitted to be taken by the board may be taken without a meeting, if all members of the board individually or collectively consent in writing to such action. Such written consent or consents shall be filed with the minutes of the proceedings of the board. Such action by written consent shall have the same force and effect as a unanimous vote of the directors.

SECTION 12. COMPENSATION

No salary shall be paid directors, as such, for their services but, by resolution, the board of directors may allow a reasonable fixed sum and expenses to be paid for attendance at regular or special meetings. Nothing contained herein shall prevent a director from serving the corporation in any other capacity and receiving compensation therefor. Members of special or standing committees may be allowed like compensation for attendance at meetings.

ARTICLE 4. OFFICERS

SECTION 1. OFFICERS

The officers of the corporation shall include a president, a secretary, and a treasurer, or officers with different titles that perform the duties of these offices as described in Sections 2 though 4 of this Article. Except as otherwise provided under state corporate statutes, any number of these offices may be held by the same person. The corporation may also appoint other officers with such titles and duties as shall be determined by the board of directors.

SECTION 2. PRESIDENT

The president (or chief executive officer or alternately titled chief corporate officer designated by the board of directors) shall, subject to the direction and control of the board of directors, have general supervision, direction, and control of the day-to-day business and affairs of the corporation. He or she shall preside at all meetings of the shareholders and directors and be an ex officio member of all the standing committees, including any executive committee of the board, and shall have the general powers and duties of management usually vested in the office of president or chief executive officer of a corporation and shall have such other powers and duties as may from time to time be prescribed by the board of directors or these bylaws.

SECTION 3. SECRETARY

The corporate secretary (or other corporate officer designated by the board of directors to maintain and keep corporate records) shall keep, or cause to be kept, at the principal office of the corporation, a book of minutes of all meetings of directors and shareholders. The minutes shall state the time and place of holding of all meetings; whether regular or special, if special, how called or authorized; the notice thereof given or the waivers of notice received; the names of those present at directors' meetings; the number of shares present or represented at shareholders' meetings; and an account of the proceedings thereof.

He or she shall keep, or cause to be kept, at the principal office of the corporation, or at the office of the corporation's transfer agent, a share register, showing the names of the shareholders and their addresses, the number and classes of shares held by each, the number and date of certificates issued for shares, and the number and date of cancellation of every certificate surrendered for cancellation.

He or she shall keep, or cause to be kept, at the principal office of the corporation, the original or a copy of the bylaws of the corporation, as amended or otherwise altered to date, certified by him or her.

He or she shall give, or cause to be given, notice of all meetings of shareholders and directors required to be given by law or by the provisions of these bylaws. He or she shall prepare, or cause to be prepared, an alphabetical listing of shareholders for inspection prior to and at meetings of shareholders as required by Article 2, Section 6, of these bylaws.

He or she shall have charge of the seal of the corporation and have such other powers and perform such other duties as may from time to time be prescribed by the board or these bylaws.

SECTION 4. TREASURER

The treasurer (or other officer designated by the board of directors to serve as chief financial officer of the corporation) shall keep and maintain, or cause to be kept and maintained, adequate and correct books and records of accounts of the properties and business transactions of the corporation.

He or she shall deposit monies and other valuables in the name and to the credit of the corporation with such depositories as may be designated by the board of directors. He or she shall disburse the funds of the corporation in payment of the just demands against the corporation; shall render to the president and directors, whenever they request it, an account of all his or her transactions as chief financial officer and of the financial condition of the corporation; and shall have such other powers and perform such other duties as may from time to time be prescribed by the board of directors.

SECTION 5. APPOINTMENT, REMOVAL AND RESIGNATION

All officers of the corporation shall be approved by, and serve at the pleasure of, the board of directors. An officer may be removed at any time, either with or without cause, by written notification of removal by the board. An officer may resign at any time upon written notice to the corporation given to the board, the president, or the secretary of the corporation. Any such resignation shall take effect at the date of receipt of such notice or at any other time specified therein. The removal or resignation of an officer shall be without prejudice to the rights, if any, of the officer or the corporation under any contract of employment to which the officer is a party.

ARTICLE 5. EXECUTIVE COMMITTEES

SECTION 1. REGULAR AND EXECUTIVE COMMITTEES OF THE BOARD

The board may designate one or more regular committees to report to the board on any area of corporate operation and performance.

To the extent allowed under state corporate statutes, the board also may designate and delegate specific decision-making authority to one or more executive committees, each consisting of two or more directors, that shall have the authority of the board to approve corporate decisions in the specific areas designated by the board.

ARTICLE 6. CORPORATE RECORDS AND REPORTS

SECTION 1. INSPECTION BY SHAREHOLDERS AND DIRECTORS

The corporate secretary shall make available within a reasonable period after a request for inspection or copying made by a director or shareholder or a director's or shareholder's legal representative the Articles of Incorporation (or similar organizing document) as amended to date; these bylaws as amended to date; minutes of proceedings of the shareholders and the board and committees of the board; the share register of the corporation, its accounting books, and records; and any other corporate records and reports. The requested records shall be made available for inspection and copying at the principal office of the corporation within business hours. Any copying costs incurred by the

corporation necessary to comply with a request for copies of records may be collected by the secretary from a requesting shareholder; the corporation shall assume the cost of copies made for a requesting director.

SECTION 2. ANNUAL REPORTS TO SHAREHOLDERS

The secretary shall mail a copy of any annual financial or other report to shareholders on the secretary's own initiative or upon request made by one or more shareholders as may be required by state corporate statutes.

ARTICLE 7. INDEMNIFICATION AND INSURANCE OF DIRECTORS AND OFFICERS

SECTION 1. INDEMNIFICATION

The directors and officers of the corporation shall be indemnified by the corporation to the fullest extent permitted under law.

SECTION 2. INSURANCE

The corporation shall have the power to purchase and maintain insurance on behalf of any director or officer against any liability asserted against or incurred by the agent in such capacity or arising out of the agent's status as such, whether or not the corporation has the power to indemnify the agent against such liability under law.

ARTICLE 8. SHARES

SECTION 1. CERTIFICATES

The corporation shall issue certificates for its shares when fully paid. Certificates of stock shall be issued in numerical order, and shall state the name of the record holder of the shares represented by each certificate; the number, designation, if any, and class or series of shares represented by the certificate; and other information, including any statement or summary required by any applicable provision of state corporate statutes. Each certificate shall be signed by the corporate officers empowered under state law to sign the certificates and may be sealed with the seal of the corporation.

SECTION 2. TRANSFER OF SHARES

Upon surrender to the secretary or transfer agent of the corporation of a certificate for shares duly endorsed or accompanied by proper evidence of succession, assignment, or authority to transfer, it shall be the duty of the secretary of the corporation to issue a new certificate to the person entitled thereto, to cancel the old certificate, and to record the transaction upon the share register of the corporation.

SECTION 3. RECORD DATE

The board of directors may fix a time in the future as a record date for the determination of the shareholders entitled to notice of and to vote at any meeting of shareholders or entitled to receive payment of any dividend or distribution, or any allotment of rights, or to exercise rights with respect to any other lawful action. The record date so fixed shall conform to the requirements of state law. When a record date is so fixed, only shareholders of record on that date are entitled to notice of and to vote at the meeting or to receive the dividend, distribution, or allotment of rights, or to exercise the rights as the case may be, notwithstanding any transfer of any shares on the books of the corporation after the record date.

ARTICLE 9. AMENDMENT OF BYLAWS

SECTION 1. BY SHAREHOLDERS

Except as otherwise provided by law, these bylaws may be adopted, amended, or repealed by the affirmative vote at a meeting of holders of a majority of the outstanding shares of the corporation entitled to vote.

SECTION 2. BY DIRECTORS

Except as otherwise provided by law, the directors may adopt, amend, or repeal these bylaws.

CERTIFICATE

This is to certify that the foregoing is a true and correct copy of the bylaws of the corporation named in the title thereto and that such bylaws were duly adopted by the board of directors of the corporation on the date set forth below.

Dated: _____

Signature:_____, Secretary

Incorporator's Statement

The undersigned, the incorporator of _____, who signed and filed its Articles of Incorporation or similar organizing document with the state, appoints the following individuals to serve as the initial directors of the corporation, who shall serve as directors until the first meeting of shareholders for the election of directors and until their successors are elected and agree to serve on the board:

_____

_____

_____

_____

_____

Date: _____

Signature: _____, Incorporator

Minutes of First Meeting
of Board of Directors

Waiver of Notice and Consent to Holding
of First Meeting of Board of Directors

We, the undersigned, being all the directors of _____, hereby waive

notice of the first meeting of the board of directors of the corporation and consent to the holding of the

meeting at _____ on _____;

_____ at _____ and consent to the

transaction of any and all business at the meeting including, without limitation, the adoption of bylaws, the

election of officers, the selection of the corporation's accounting period, the designation of the location of

the principal office of the corporation, the selection of the place where the corporation's bank accounts

will be maintained, and the authorization of the sale and issuance of the initial shares of stock of the

corporation.

Date: _____

Signatures:

_____ , Director

_____ , Director

_____ , Director

_____ , Director

_____ , Director

Minutes of First Meeting of the Board of Directors

The board of directors of _____ held its first meeting at
_____ on _____, at _____.

The following directors, marked as present next to their names, were in attendance at the meeting and constituted a quorum of the board:

_____ [ ] Present [ ] Absent

_____ [ ] Present [ ] Absent

_____ [ ] Present [ ] Absent

_____ [ ] Present [ ] Absent

_____ [ ] Present [ ] Absent

On motion and by unanimous vote, _____ was appointed chairperson and then presided over the meeting. _____ was elected secretary of the meeting.

The meeting was held pursuant to written waiver of notice and consent to holding of the meeting signed by each of the directors. Upon a motion duly made, seconded, and unanimously carried, it was resolved that the written waiver of notice and consent to holding of the meeting be made a part of and constitute the first page of the minutes of this meeting.

ARTICLES OF INCORPORATION

The chairperson announced that the Articles of Incorporation or similar organizing document of the corporation were filed with the state corporate filing office on _____
_____
_____. The corporate secretary was asked to place a file-stamped copy of the articles or filing receipt showing such filing in the corporation's records book.

BYLAWS

A proposed set of bylaws of the corporation was presented for adoption. Upon motion duly made and seconded, it was unanimously

RESOLVED, that the bylaws presented to this meeting are adopted as the bylaws of this corporation;

RESOLVED FURTHER, that the secretary of this corporation is asked to execute a Certificate of Adoption of the bylaws, and to place the bylaws as so certified with the corporation's records at its principal office.

PRINCIPAL EXECUTIVE OFFICE

Upon motion duly made and seconded, it was

RESOLVED, that the principal office of this corporation shall be located at _____
_____.

APPOINTMENT OF OFFICERS

Upon motion, the following persons were unanimously appointed to the following offices:

President (CEO): _____

Treasurer (CFO): _____

Secretary: _____

NOLO
www.nolo.com
Minutes of First Meeting of Board of Directors
3 of 8

CORPORATE SEAL

Upon motion duly made and seconded, it was

RESOLVED, that the corporate seal impressed directly below this resolution is adopted as the corporate seal of this corporation. The secretary of the corporation is directed to place the seal with the corporate records at the principal office of the corporation, and to use the seal on corporate stock certificates and other appropriate corporate documents as the secretary sees fit.

STOCK CERTIFICATE

Upon motion duly made and seconded, it was

RESOLVED, that the form of stock certificate attached to these minutes is adopted for use by this corporation for the issuance of its initial shares.

CORPORATE BANK ACCOUNTS

Upon motion duly made and seconded, it was

RESOLVED, that the funds of this corporation shall be deposited with the following bank at the following branch office: _____ , located at _____.

RESOLVED FURTHER, that the treasurer of this corporation is authorized and asked to establish one or more accounts with this bank and to deposit the funds of this corporation in these accounts.

RESOLVED FURTHER, that any officer, employee, or agent of this corporation is authorized to endorse checks, drafts, or other evidences of indebtedness made payable to this corporation, but only for the purpose of deposit.

RESOLVED FURTHER, that all checks, drafts, and other instruments obligating this corporation to pay money shall be signed on behalf of this corporation by any _____ of the following:

_____

_____

_____

RESOLVED FURTHER, that the bank is hereby authorized to honor and pay any and all checks and drafts of this corporation signed as provided herein.

RESOLVED FURTHER, that the authority hereby conferred shall remain in force until revoked by the board of directors of this corporation and until written notice of such revocation shall have been received by the bank.

RESOLVED FURTHER, that the secretary of this corporation is authorized to certify as to the continuing authority of these resolutions and to complete on behalf of the corporation the bank's standard form of resolution, provided that the form does not vary materially from the terms of the foregoing resolutions.

ACCOUNTING PERIOD

After discussion and upon motion duly made and seconded, it was

RESOLVED, that the accounting period of this corporation shall end on _____ of each year.

PAYMENT, DEDUCTION, AND AMORTIZATION OF START-UP AND ORGANIZATIONAL EXPENSES

Upon motion duly made, seconded, and unanimously approved, it was

RESOLVED, that the treasurer of this corporation is authorized and empowered to pay all reasonable and proper expenses incurred in connection with the start-up and organization of the corporation, including, among others, expenses prior to the start of business necessary to investigate and create the business as well as organization costs necessary to form the corporation, and to reimburse any persons making any such disbursements for the corporation, and it was

FURTHER RESOLVED, that the treasurer is authorized to elect to deduct and amortize appropriate start-up and organization expenditures pursuant to and as permitted under Sections 195 and 248 of the Internal Revenue Code and as permitted under similar state tax provisions.

AUTHORIZATION OF ISSUANCE OF SHARES

Upon motion duly made and seconded, it was unanimously

RESOLVED, that the corporation sell and issue the following number of its authorized common shares to the following persons, in the amounts and for the consideration set forth next to their names, below. The board also determined that the fair value to the corporation of any consideration for such shares issued other than for money is as stated below:

Name	Number of Shares	Consideration

RESOLVED FURTHER, that the amount of consideration received by the corporation for each and any of the above shares issued without par value that is to be allocated to capital surplus is $_____.

RESOLVED FURTHER, that the appropriate officers of this corporation are hereby authorized and directed to take such actions and execute such documents as they deem necessary or appropriate to effectuate the sale and issuance of such shares for the consideration listed above.

Since there was no further business to come before the meeting, upon motion duly made and seconded, the meeting was adjourned.

_____, Secretary

Stub (left portion)

Certificate Number _____

for _____ Shares

Issued to: _____

Dated _____ , 20 ____

From Whom Transferred

Dated _____ , 20 ____

No. Original Shares	No. Original Certificate	No. of Shares Transferred

Received Certificate Number _____

for _____ Shares

This ____ Day of _____ , 20 ____

_____
SIGNATURE

Certificate

Number _____   Shares _____

Incorporated Under the Laws of _____

This Certifies that _____ is the owner of _____

_____ of the above Corporation transferable only on the books of the Corporation by the holder in person or by duly authorized attorney on surrender of this Certificate, properly endorsed.

In witness whereof, the Corporation has caused this certificate to be signed by its duly authorized officers and to be sealed with the Seal of the Corporation.

Dated: _____

_____ , _____ ,

Number _____

Shares _____

Incorporated Under the Laws of _____

This Certifies that _____ is the owner of _____ fully paid and assessable _____ of the above Corporation transferable only on the books of the Corporation by the holder in person or by duly authorized attorney on surrender of this Certificate, properly endorsed.

In witness whereof, the Corporation has caused this certificate to be signed by its duly authorized officers and to be sealed with the Seal of the Corporation.

Dated: _____

Number ____

Shares ____

Incorporated Under the Laws of ____

This Certifies that ____ is the owner of ____ fully paid and assessable ____ of the above Corporation transferable only on the books of the Corporation by the holder in person or by duly authorized attorney on surrender of this Certificate, properly endorsed.

In witness whereof, the Corporation has caused this certificate to be signed by its duly authorized officers and to be sealed with the Seal of the Corporation.

Dated: ____

Certificate Number _____

for _____ Shares

Issued to:

_____

Dated _____, 20 ___

From Whom Transferred

Dated _____, 20 ___

No. Original Shares	No. Original Certificate	No. of Shares Transferred
_____	_____	_____

Received Certificate Number _____

for _____ Shares

This _____ Day of _____, 20 ___

_____
SIGNATURE

Number _____

Shares _____

Incorporated Under the Laws of _____

This Certifies that _____ is the owner of

_____ of the above Corporation transferable only on the books of the Corporation by

the holder in person or by duly authorized attorney on surrender of this Certificate, properly endorsed.

In witness whereof, the Corporation has caused this certificate to be signed by its duly authorized officers and to

be sealed with the Seal of the Corporation.

Dated: _____

_____, _____

Certificate Number _____

for _____ Shares

Issued to:

Dated _____, 20 _____

From Whom Transferred

Dated _____, 20 _____

No. Original Shares	No. Original Certificate	No. of Shares Transferred

---

Received Certificate Number _____

for _____

This _____ Day of _____, 20 _____

SIGNATURE _____ Shares

Number _____

Shares _____

Incorporated Under the Laws of _____

This Certifies that _____ is the owner of _____ fully paid and assessable

_____ of the above Corporation transferable only on the books of the Corporation by the holder in person or by duly authorized attorney on surrender of this Certificate, properly endorsed.

In witness whereof, the Corporation has caused this certificate to be signed by its duly authorized officers and to be sealed with the Seal of the Corporation.

Dated: _____

_____ / _____

Certificate Number _____

for _____ Shares

Issued to:

Dated _____, 20 _____

From Whom Transferred

Dated _____, 20 _____

No. Original Shares	No. Original Certificate	No. of Shares Transferred

---

Received Certificate Number _____

for _____ Shares

This _____ Day of _____, 20 _____

SIGNATURE

Number _____   Shares _____

Incorporated Under the Laws of _____

This Certifies that _____ is the owner of _____

_____ fully paid and assessable

of the above Corporation transferable only on the books of the Corporation by

the holder in person or by duly authorized attorney on surrender of this Certificate, properly endorsed.

In witness whereof, the Corporation has caused this certificate to be signed by its duly authorized officers and to

be sealed with the Seal of the Corporation.

Dated: _____

_____ / _____

_____ / _____

Number _____

Shares _____

Incorporated Under the Laws of _____

This Certifies that _____ is the owner of _____

_____ fully paid and assessable

of the above Corporation transferable only on the books of the Corporation by the holder in person or by duly authorized attorney on surrender of this Certificate, properly endorsed.

In witness whereof, the Corporation has caused this certificate to be signed by its duly authorized officers and to be sealed with the Seal of the Corporation.

Dated: _____

_____, _____

Left stub (rotated)

Certificate Number _____

for _____ Shares

Issued to: _____

Dated _____, 20 _____

From Whom Transferred

Dated _____, 20 _____

No. Original Shares	No. Original Certificate	No. of Shares Transferred

Received Certificate Number _____

for _____ Shares

This _____ Day of _____, 20 _____

SIGNATURE

Certificate

Number _____

Shares _____

Incorporated Under the Laws of _____

This Certifies that _____ is the owner of _____ fully paid and assessable _____ of the above Corporation transferable only on the books of the Corporation by the holder in person or by duly authorized attorney on surrender of this Certificate, properly endorsed.

In witness whereof, the Corporation has caused this certificate to be signed by its duly authorized officers and to be sealed with the Seal of the Corporation.

Dated: _____

_____ , _____

Left stub (transfer record)

Certificate Number _____

for _____ Shares

Issued to: _____

Dated _____, 20 _____

From Whom Transferred _____

Dated _____, 20 _____

No. Original Shares	No. Original Certificate	No. of Shares Transferred
_____	_____	_____

Received Certificate Number _____

for _____ Shares

This _____ Day of _____, 20 _____

_____
SIGNATURE

Certificate

Number _____

_____ Shares

Incorporated Under the Laws of _____

This Certifies that _____ is the owner of _____ fully paid and assessable _____ of the above Corporation transferable only on the books of the Corporation by the holder in person or by duly authorized attorney on surrender of this Certificate, properly endorsed.

In witness whereof, the Corporation has caused this certificate to be signed by its duly authorized officers and to be sealed with the Seal of the Corporation.

Dated: _____

_____ , _____

Certificate Number _____

for _____ Shares

Issued to:

Dated _____, 20 ___

From Whom Transferred

Dated _____, 20 ___

No. Original Shares	No. Original Certificate	No. of Shares Transferred

---

Received Certificate Number _____

for _____ Shares

This _____ Day of _____, 20 ___

Number _____

Shares _____

Incorporated Under the Laws of _____

This Certifies that _____ is the owner of _____

_____ fully paid and assessable

of the above Corporation transferable only on the books of the Corporation by the holder in person or by duly authorized attorney on surrender of this Certificate, properly endorsed.

In witness whereof, the Corporation has caused this certificate to be signed by its duly authorized officers and to be sealed with the Seal of the Corporation.

Dated: _____

Bill of Sale for Assets of a Business

This is an agreement between:

_____

_____

_____ ,

herein called "transferor(s)," and _____ , a corporation, herein called "the corporation."

In return for the issuance of _____ shares of stock of the corporation, transferor(s) hereby sell(s), assign(s), and transfer(s) to the corporation all right, title, and interest in the following property:

All the tangible assets listed on the balance sheet attached to this Bill of Sale and all stock in trade, goodwill, leasehold interests, trade names, and other intangible assets [except _____ of _____ , located at _____].

In return for the transfer of the above property to it, the corporation hereby agrees to assume, pay, and discharge all debts, duties, and obligations listed on the balance sheet attached to this Bill of Sale [except _____]. The corporation agrees to indemnify and hold the transferor(s) of this business and their property free from any liability for any such debt, duty, or obligation and from any suits, actions, or legal proceedings brought to enforce or collect any such debt, duty, or obligation.

The transferor(s) hereby appoint(s) the corporation as representative to demand, receive, and collect for itself any and all debts and obligations now owing to the business. The transferor(s) further authorize(s) the corporation to do all things allowed by law to recover and collect any such debts and obligations and to use the transferor's(s') name(s) in such manner as it considers necessary for the collection and recovery of such debts and obligations, provided, however, without cost, expense, or damage to the transferor(s).

Date:_____

_____ , Transferor

_____ , Transferor

_____ , Transferor

Date: _____

_____ , Corporation

By:

_____ , President

_____ , Treasurer

Receipt for Cash Payment

Receipt of $_____ from _____ representing payment

in full for _____ shares of the stock of this corporation is hereby acknowledged.

Dated: _____

Name of Corporation:_____

By: _____, Treasurer

Bill of Sale for Items of Property

In consideration of the issuance of _____ shares of stock in and by _____,

_____ hereby sells, assigns, conveys, transfers, and delivers to the corporation

all right, title, and interest in and to the following property: _____.

Date: _____

Receipt for Services Rendered

In consideration of the performance of the following services actually rendered to _____,

_____, the provider of such services, hereby acknowledges the receipt of

_____ shares of stock in _____ as payment in full for these services,

described as follows:

_____

_____

_____

_____

Date: _____

_____

Contract for Future Services

In return for the issuance of _____ shares of _____,

_____ hereby agrees to furnish the following services to the corporation:

_____

_____

_____

_____

_____

_____

It is understood that the corporation may place the shares in escrow or make other arrangements to restrict the transfer of shares until such time as the above services are performed in accordance with the above schedule.

Date: _____

Signed: _____

Name of Corporation: _____

By: _____, Treasurer

Promissory Note

In consideration of the issuance of shares of _____, _____ promises to pay to said corporation the principal amount of $ _____ together with interest at a rate of _____ rate per annum. Payments are to be made in _____ equal monthly installments of $_____, each payable on the _____ day of each month, with the first installment due on _____.

Date: _____

Signature: _____

Cancellation of Debt

The receipt of _____ shares of this corporation to _____

for the cancellation by _____ of a current loan outstanding to this corporation,

dated _____, with a remaining unpaid principal amount and unpaid accrued

interest, if any, totaling $ _____, is hereby acknowledged.

Date: _____

Signature of shareholder: _____

Notice of Incorporation Letter

_____

_____

Re: Incorporation of _____

Dear _____ :

I'm writing to let you know that our unincorporated business, _____, was

incorporated in _____ on _____ as

_____. This is a formal change that will help the business pursue its mission

and the attainment of its goals with increased structure and efficiency.

We have enjoyed doing business with you in the past and look forward to continuing to do so in the future.

Please call me at the telephone number shown below if you need additional information to update your

records or accounts.

Sincerely,

_____ , _____

_____

_____

General Minutes of Meeting

Minutes of _____ **Meeting**
of
_____

A _____ meeting of the corporation was held on _____ for the purpose(s) of _____.

_____ acted as chairperson, and _____ _____ acted as secretary of the meeting.

The chairperson called the meeting to order.

The secretary announced that the meeting was called by _____ _____.

The secretary announced that the meeting was held pursuant to notice as required under the bylaws of this corporation.

The secretary announced that the following _____ were present at the meeting, representing a quorum: _____.

The secretary announced that the next item of business was the consideration of one or more formal resolutions for approval by the board. After introduction and discussion, and on motion duly made and carried by the affirmative vote of _____ _____ of _____ at the meeting, the following resolutions were adopted by directors entitled to vote at the meeting: _____ _____.

There being no further business to come before the meeting, it was adjourned on motion duly made and carried.

_____, Secretary

Index

A

Remember:

Little publishers have big ears.
We really listen to you.

Take 2 Minutes
& Give Us
Your 2 cents

Your comments make a big difference in the development and revision of Nolo books and software. Please take a few minutes and register your Nolo product—and your comments—with us. Not only will your input make a difference, you'll receive special offers available only to registered owners of Nolo products on our newest books and software. Register now by:

PHONE
1-800-728-3555

FAX
1-800-645-0895

EMAIL
cs@nolo.com

or **MAIL** us
this registration card

fold here

Registration Card

NAME _____ DATE _____

ADDRESS _____

_____

CITY _____ STATE _____ ZIP _____

PHONE _____ E-MAIL _____

WHERE DID YOU HEAR ABOUT THIS PRODUCT? _____

WHERE DID YOU PURCHASE THIS PRODUCT? _____

DID YOU CONSULT A LAWYER? (PLEASE CIRCLE ONE)   YES   NO   NOT APPLICABLE

DID YOU FIND THIS BOOK HELPFUL?   (VERY)   5   4   3   2   1   (NOT AT ALL)

COMMENTS _____

_____

_____

WAS IT EASY TO USE?   (VERY EASY)   5   4   3   2   1   (VERY DIFFICULT)

We occasionally make our mailing list available to carefully selected companies whose products may be of interest to you.

❑   If you do not wish to receive mailings from these companies, please check this box.

❑   You can quote me in future Nolo promotional materials.
Daytime phone number _____.

NIBS 3.0